IET COMPUTING SERIES 25

Big Data-Enabled Internet of Things

IET Book Series on Big Data – Call for Authors

Editor-in-Chief: Professor Albert Y. Zomaya, University of Sydney, Australia

The topic of Big Data has emerged as a revolutionary theme that cuts across many technologies and application domains. This new book series brings together topics within the myriad research activities in many areas that analyze, compute, store, manage, and transport massive amounts of data, such as algorithm design, data mining and search, processor architectures, databases, infrastructure development, service and data discovery, networking and mobile computing, cloud computing, high-performance computing, privacy and security, storage, and visualization.

Topics considered include (but not restricted to) IoT and Internet computing; cloud computing; peer-to-peer computing; autonomic computing; data center computing; multicore and many core computing; parallel, distributed and high-performance computing; scalable databases; mobile computing and sensor networking; green computing; service computing; networking infrastructures; cyberinfrastructures; e-science; smart cities; analytics and data mining; big data applications, and more.

Proposals for coherently integrated International coedited or coauthored handbooks and research monographs will be considered for this book series. Each proposal will be reviewed by the Editor-in-chief and some board members, with additional external reviews from independent reviewers. Please email your book proposal for the IET book series on Big Data to Professor Albert Y. Zomaya at albert.zomaya@sydney.edu.au or to the IET at author_support@theiet.org.

Big Data-Enabled Internet of Things

Edited by
Muhammad Usman Shahid Khan, Samee U. Khan and
Albert Y. Zomaya

The Institution of Engineering and Technology

Published by The Institution of Engineering and Technology, London, United Kingdom

The Institution of Engineering and Technology is registered as a Charity in England & Wales (no. 211014) and Scotland (no. SC038698).

The Institution of Engineering and Technology
Michael Faraday House
Six Hills Way, Stevenage
Herts, SG1 2AY, United Kingdom

www.theiet.org

British Library Cataloguing in Publication Data
A catalogue record for this product is available from the British Library

ISBN 978-1-78561-636-5 (hardback)
ISBN 978-1-78561-637-2 (PDF)

Typeset in India by MPS Limited
Printed in the UK by CPI Group (UK) Ltd, Croydon

Contents

11 A survey on outlier detection in Internet of Things big data 223
Abdullah A. Al-khatib, Mohammed Balfaqih and Abdelmajid Khelil

12 Supporting Big Data at the vehicular edge 273
Lloyd Decker and Stephan Olariu

To our families, for their support and encouragement

Foreword

The convergence of Big Data and the Internet of Things (IoT) was inevitable since both fields have been experiencing massive growth. The IoT growth is in response to the need for connecting physical objects that are getting increasingly smarter and their need to connect to the Internet or connect to one another. Also, the range of the physical objects that needs connectivity is very rich, ranging from simple sensors to mobile devices, vehicles, and buildings. On the other hand, research in Big Data has many challenges including capture, storage, analysis, data curation, search, sharing, transfer, visualization, querying, updating, and privacy. Also, the manipulation of data requires the use of analytics and methods that extract value. Since both of IoT and Big Data have a lot of overlap, it is an ideal time to present the recent advances which are taking place at the intersections of both these fields to identify future trends.

The book covers the important aspects of Big Data-enabled IoT. The main focus of the book is on the analytical techniques for handling the huge amount of data generated by the IoT. The book is oriented toward those professionals and researchers interested in both of these booming fields. The topics covered in the book will be of interest to computing researchers, practitioners, engineers, and Information Technology professionals working in the highly dynamic field of Big Data-enabled IoT. The book can be viewed as an introduction to the area, as it cover the most important issues, presenting applied research works. The book identifies and shows the research challenges that are yet to be solved. Thus, it can also be used by researchers starting their work in the area.

Albert Y. Zomaya
Series Editor

About the editors

Muhammad Usman Shahid Khan is an Assistant Professor at COMSATS University of Islamabad, Abbottabad Campus, Pakistan. He completed a Ph.D. in electrical and computer engineering at North Dakota State University, USA in 2015, on a COMSATS scholarship. Previously, he received a Master degree in Information Security from National University of Science and Technology (NUST), Pakistan in 2008 and a bachelor degree in computer science from Bahauddin Zakariya University, Pakistan in 2005. He is an IEEE Member. His research interests include Data Mining, Social Network Analysis, Recommendation Systems, Computer Security, and Big Data.

Samee U. Khan received a PhD in 2007 from the University of Texas. Currently, he is the Cluster Lead for the Computer Systems Research at the National Science Foundation, and a Full Professor at the North Dakota State University. His research interests include optimization, robustness, and security of computer systems. His work has appeared in over 400 publications. He is on the editorial boards of leading journals, such as Journal of Parallel and Distributed Computing, ACM Computing Surveys, and IEEE IT Pro. He is an ACM Distinguished Speaker and an IEEE Distinguished Lecturer.

Albert Y. Zomaya is currently the Chair Professor of High Performance Computing & Networking in the School of Computer Science, University of Sydney. He is also the Director of the Centre for Distributed and High Performance Computing which was established in late 2009. Professor Zomaya was an Australian Research Council Professorial Fellow during 2010–2014 and held the CISCO Systems Chair Professor of Internetworking during the period 2002–2007 and also was Head of school for 2006–2007 in the same school.

Chapter 1

Introduction to big data-enabled Internet of Things

Muhammad U.S. Khan[1], Samee U. Khan[2]
and Albert Y. Zomaya[3]

In the last couple of years, Internet of Things (IoT) has seen tremendous advancement and growth. The huge number of devices and sensors connected through IoT generates huge amount of data, also known as big data, on a daily basis. This poses new challenges of data handling and information retrieval that not only requires expertise of IoT but also of big data analytics. In this chapter, we review the various facets of big data-enabled IoT, application areas, and challenges.

1.1 Introduction

The past few years have seen tremendous growth in the broadband services that result in increase of smart devices connecting to the internet. From smart phones, coffee makers, wearable devices, and many other smart devices are being connected. It is expected that the total number of devices connected to the internet will exceed 26 billion until 2020 [1].

The smart connected devices are generating huge amount of data. The expected amount of data to be generated per month will exceed 24.3 EB until 2019 [2]. Big data is a term for very large and complex data sets that traditional data processing application software are inadequate to deal with. The big data generated through IoT devices are creating challenges that include capture, storage, analysis, data curation, search, sharing, transfer, visualization, querying, updating, and information privacy. Although both the technologies evolved independently, they are now getting interconnected for the success of the IoT applications.

1.1.1 Internet of Things

The IoT is the inter-networking of physical devices ("connected devices" and "smart devices"), buildings, vehicles and other items which are embedded with electronics,

[1]Department of Computer Science, COMSATS University of Islamabad, Abbottabad, Pakistan
[2]Department of Electrical and Computer Engineering, North Dakota State University, Fargo, ND, USA
[3]School of Computer Science, University of Sydney, Sydney, Australia

software, sensors, actuators, and network connectivity that enable these objects to collect and exchange data. The thing in the IoT can refer to any device that is assigned an IP address. A "thing" generates, collects, or shares data with other devices without any manual intervention using integrated decision-making systems built within the devices.

1.1.2   Big data-enabled IoT

In big data-enabled IoT, the big data analytics are used to understand and analyze the complex, fuzzy, and large data generated from IoT devices. Big data refers to the extremely large volume of structured, unstructured, or semi-structured data that are inadequate to deal with the traditional data-processing software and hardware. International Data Corporation (IDC) defines the term big data in one of their study "The Digital Universe" [3] as

> IDC defines Big Data technologies as a new generation of technologies and architectures, designed to economically extract value from very large volumes of a wide variety of data by enabling high-velocity capture, discovery, and/or analysis. There are three main characteristics of Big Data: the data itself, the analytics of the data, and the presentation of the results of the analytics. Then there are the products and services that can be wrapped around one or all of these Big Data elements.

The big data analytics in the IoT can help in determining future trends and detecting frauds. Big data can make transactions within the IoT applications transparent and make them more useful to the organizations. Big data technologies also help in improving the efficiency of the IoT applications by providing better insight into the data. The taxonomy of the big data-enabled IoT is presented in Figure 1.1.

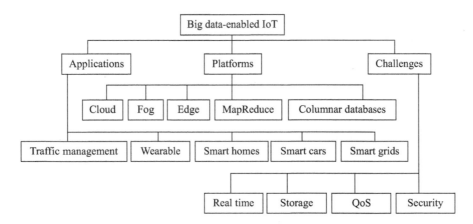

Figure 1.1   Taxonomy of big data-enabled IoT

1.2 Platforms for big data-enabled IoT

The benefits of the big data-enabled IoT are dependent on the platforms for analysis of the IoT data. These platforms are selected based on the time requirement of the results in the big data-enabled IoT applications. Different platforms are discussed in this section.

1.2.1 Cloud computing

Cloud computing is the most popular platform for big data-enabled IoT. The cloud platforms support the Internet-based function, such as analytics, data storage, and security measures. Ease of scalability in these platforms make them an ideal choice for developing big data-enabled smart IoT applications. Several cloud platforms, such as SmartThings [4], AWS [5], Nest [6] provide availability, scalability, interoperability, and security for IoT applications. The cloud platforms also provide device SDKs to help IP addressable devices connect to the cloud.

1.2.2 Fog computing

For latency-sensitive applications, such as in health-care solutions and emergency response systems, managing big data-enabled IoT applications in the cloud is not efficient. Therefore, the fog-computing paradigm has started to replace as platforms for big data-enabled IoT applications. The fog-computing platforms allow the applications to perform analytics and processing of data on fog devices (computing devices with energy and computing resources more than IoT devices) that are installed in-between cloud and the IoT devices. These fog devices are located in the close proximity to the IoT devices for faster response time, and most of the analytics are performed on these devices that release the dependence of IoT devices on cloud.

1.2.3 Edge computing

Edge computing is similar to fog computing with the difference that most of the computation in edge computing is performed on the smart IoT device themselves rather than performing on separate processing devices near to the IoT devices. Although edge computing helps in providing fast response time, providing sufficient computing power for handling big data is still an open challenge for the IoT devices manufacturers. Big data-enabled IoT applications have to merge edge computing and cloud computing to get the most advantages of the big data.

1.2.4 MapReduce platforms

Utilizing a parallel computing infrastructure to efficiently process the data are the critical goals of the big data. MapReduce is a software platform for processing the big data in IoT in parallel across different nodes [7]. Hadoop MapReduce is an open-source framework that is mostly deployed in IoT frameworks. The Cloudera data hub and Hortonworks, frameworks for IoT data processing are also based on Hadoop MapReduce. The MapReduce frameworks in the IoT targets the processing of data on networks of edge devices rather than transferring the data to the cloud. The tasks and data are distributed among edge devices such that each node operate independently and aggregate results at the end. Similarly, supporting tools, such as MapR helps in improvement in performance of MapReduce-based frameworks in data analysis.

1.2.5   Columnar database

Storage of big data is a challenge for IoT frameworks. Column-oriented databases are considered faster than the traditional row-oriented databases and are being deployed in IoT frameworks. 1010data, SAP-Hana, and HP-HAVEn are the examples of the columnar databases for handling big data in IoT frameworks.

1.3   Applications of big data-enabled IoT

1.3.1   Traffic applications

The merger of big data analytics and IoT devices can create new generation of smart traffic applications. The smart traffic applications help users in obtaining real-time traffic situation on roads and help in making traveling plans or in evacuation in life-threatening situations [8].

1.3.2   Wearable IoT applications in health care

IoT has helped in creating numerous applications with wearable devices [9]. These applications are mostly used in health monitoring. Sensors in the wearable devices acquire the physical measurements and communicate the data to the cloud where machine-learning algorithms monitor and predict the health condition of the people wearing the devices. However, these systems depend upon the sensors configurations. The merger of big data and IoT can help in making these applications self-adapting for automatic configuration to make these applications more useful for the people.

1.3.3   Smart homes

The big data analytics is necessary to make applications for smart homes. Connected devices and appliances in the smart home collects a huge amount of data about consumers. The big data analytics aid in personalization of the applications for the consumers for the benefits of the users. It is estimated that 5.5 million new smart home devices are being connected on an average each day.

1.3.4   Smart cars

The self-driving smart car is the fastest growing application of big data-enabled IoT. It is estimated that 10 million self-driving cars will be on the road by 2020. Man-ufacturers need to perfect the self-driving car technology, and big data analytics is taking an important part in their efforts. These big data-enabled IoT connected cars will cut down the traffic accidents and collisions by communicating among each other and predicting any upcoming collision scenarios. Combined with the sensors in the parking areas, the big data-enabled IoT connected cars will also cut down on fuel usage and spacing problems in the cities. A lot of research work is still required to convert this dream into a reality.

1.3.5   Smart grids

The smart grids differ from normal power grids as they depend upon IoT architecture for communication of information among different sections. Moreover, the smart grid also deploy various smart devices for controlling and predicting the states of the smart grids. Using big data analytics, the smart grid predicts the power outages and prepare in advance to minimize the damages. Similarly, big data-enabled IoT-aided smart grids help in reducing the operational cost of the power grids [10].

1.4   Challenges

1.4.1   Real-time analysis

One of the most important challenge in the big data-enabled IoT is the requirement of real-time analysis and communication. In near real-time, decisions have to be taken and data has to be communicated and stored in the operational databases. The delay in either data analysis or in communication can prove to be too costly on IoT applications.

1.4.2   Storage

The number of smart devices is increasing at a tremendous rate. The huge volume of data generated by these devices creates the problem of storing the huge volume of data for the IoT applications. Most IoT services are based on communication protocols that increase the requirement of storing the stream of data. The big data-enabled IoT applications store the data in the cloud, fog, or edge computing platforms and mostly in columnar databases.

1.4.3   Quality of service

The quality of service (QoS) provided by the big data-enabled IoT must be reliable. To ensure the reliability of the QoS support in the big data-enabled IoT, many new technologies must be introduced for an improved, easy, smooth, and fast transfer of data among the IoT devices.

1.4.4   Security challenges

Most of the devices in the IoT have a very limited amount of energy to operate. These devices range from wearable devices to sensors in coffee machines, and these devices transfer their data to a separate data-processing unit, such as cloud. Due to the data transfer, a lot of new challenges including security-related challenges are generate for these devices. One of the biggest challenges is the authentication of the devices. Without proper authentication mechanism, the devices can be abused that can lead serious security risks. The big data algorithms are required to analyze the data traffic between the devices and predict any compromise in the authentication of these devices.

The security of the devices is related to the confidentiality of the data transferred in the IoT. The increase in volume of the data increases the risk of the data getting analyzed by third party. There is a need for a separate big data algorithm that can analyze the data traffic and predict any compromise in the security of the devices. The big data-enabled IoT is expected to be more secured as compared to IoT operating without the use of big data algorithms installed for its security.

1.5   Recent studies in the field of big data-enabled IoT

Recently, big data-enabled IoT is getting attention in the researcher communities. In this section, we have listed a few recent studies in the field of big data-enabled IoT.

Majority of recent studies have examined the roles of big data and IoT in industries. A framework for analysis of industrial IoT big data is presented in [11]. Wang *et al.* [12] studied the challenges of big data-enabled IoT in the maritime industry. Similarly, the adoption of big data-enabled IoT in manufacturing industry is analyzed in [13].

Apart from research on implementation of big data-enabled IoT in industries, smart cities and smart homes using big data analytics on IoT data have remained important research areas. In [14], a big data-enabled IoT framework is proposed to cater the challenges of big data in IoT-aided smart buildings. The framework is implemented in Hadoop MapReduce. The strength and weaknesses of a big data-enabled IoT application in road-traffic-management systems is studied in [15]. In [16], a smart city-management system using big data-enabled IoT is proposed. The proposed system is also built on Hadoop MapReduce in real environment. Similarly, the benefits of a big data-enabled IoT-aided smart city are discussed in [17] for improving the lives of the citizens. The role of big data-enabled IoT in the health care is examined in [18]. In smart cities, the behavior of human is analyzed by Ahmad *et al.* [19,20]. Moreover, the cost of collecting data generated by smart devices in smart city environment is examined in [21].

Development of IoT frameworks for different platforms has also got the attention of the researchers. Big data processing in a collaborated edge environment is analyzed by Zhang *et al.* [22]. Parallel frameworks for big data-enabled IoT are examined in [23,24]. The aggregation of big data, IoT, semantic web is studied by Sezer *et al.* [25]. The authors have also proposed an augmented framework using the combination of three technologies. The framework that performs the analytics of IoT big data at the combination of edge nodes and the cloud is designed by Cheng *et al.* [26]. Hosting IoT workloads in the cloud is examined in [27]. Crowdsensing applications for big data-enabled IoT on fog architecture are studied in [28]. A MapReduce-based Internet of Underwater Things is introduced in [29].

Recent trend in the field of big data-enabled IoT is toward providing the solutions for the challenges faced by the field. The solution to big data-enabled IoT storage problem is proposed in [30]. The clustering mechanism for databases in big data-enabled IoT is proposed in [31]. The service discovery in the big data-enabled IoT applications is investigated in [32]. The applicability of different data mining algorithms for big data-enabled IoT are studied in [33]. The classification of network-enabled devices in the big data-enabled IoT is performed in [34]. The security of big data-enabled IoT deployed in cloud is studied in [35]. Location privacy in IoT is explored using big data in [36].

1.6   Conclusions

In this chapter, we have provided the brief introduction of the big data-enabled IoT. We have discussed various platforms for data processing, storage, and analysis for big data in IoT applications. We discuss the various applications of the big data-enabled IoT that can benefit the society. Moreover, we also present a few important open-research challenges of the big data-enabled IoT in this chapter. With the ever increasing importance of the combination of two fields, big data and IoT, we conclude that research in the field of big data-enabled IoT will continue to propose novel solutions for the challenges posed by the merger of the two fields.

References

[1]   Morgan J. A Simple Explanation of 'The Internet of Things'; 2014. Available from: https://www.forbes.com/sites/jacobmorgan/2014/05/13/simple-explanation-internet-things-that-anyone-can-understand/#572153f71d09.

[2]   Index CVN. Cisco visual networking index: Global mobile data traffic forecast update, 2014–2019. Tech Rep.; 2015.

[3]   Gantz J, and Reinsel D. The digital universe in 2020: Big data, bigger digital shadows, and biggest growth in the far east. IDC iView: IDC Analyze the Future. 2012;2007(2012):1–16.

[4]   SmartThings. SmartThings Developer Documentation. Available from: http://docs.smartthings.com/en/latest/index.html, accessed on December 2018.

[5]   Services AW. AWS IoT. Available from: https://aws.amazon.com/ documentation/iot, accessed on December 2018.

[6]   Labs N. Nest Weave. Available from: https://nest.com/weave/, accessed on December 2018.

[7]   Satoh I. MapReduce-based data processing on IoT. In: 2014 IEEE International Conference on Internet of Things (iThings), and IEEE Green Computing and Communications (GreenCom) and IEEE Cyber, Physical and Social Computing (CPSCom). IEEE; 2014. pp. 161–168.

[8]   Khan MUS, Khalid O, Huang Y, *et al.* MacroServ: A route recommendation service for large-scale evacuations. IEEE Transactions on Services Computing. 2017;10(4):589–602.

[9]   Khan MUS, Abbas A, Ali M, *et al.* On the correlation of sensor location and human activity recognition in body area networks (BANs). IEEE Systems Journal. 2018;12(1):82–91.

[10]   Ali SM, Jawad M, Khan MUS, *et al.* An ancillary services model for data centers and power systems. IEEE Transactions on Cloud Computing. 2017;(1):1. DOI: 10.1109/TCC.2017.2700838.

[11]   Lee C, Yeung C, Cheng M. Research on IoT based cyber physical system for industrial big data analytics. In: Industrial Engineering and Engineering Management (IEEM), 2015 IEEE International Conference on. IEEE; 2015. pp. 1855–1859.

[12]   Wang H, Osen OL, Li G, *et al.* Big data and industrial internet of things for the maritime industry in Northwestern Norway. In: TENCON 2015 – 2015 IEEE Region 10 Conference. IEEE; 2015. pp. 1–5.

[13]   Mourtzis D, Vlachou E, Milas N. Industrial Big Data as a result of IoT adoption in manufacturing. Procedia CIRP. 2016;55:290–295.

[14]   Bashir MR, Gill AQ. Towards an IoT big data analytics framework: Smart buildings systems. In: High Performance Computing and Communications; IEEE 14th International Conference on Smart City; IEEE 2nd International Conference on Data Science and Systems (HPCC/SmartCity/DSS), 2016 IEEE 18th International Conference on. IEEE; 2016. pp. 1325–1332.

[15]   Rizwan P, Suresh K, Babu MR. Real-time smart traffic management system for smart cities by using Internet of Things and big data. In: Emerging Technological Trends (ICETT), International Conference on. IEEE; 2016. pp. 1–7.

[16]   Rathore MM, Ahmad A, Paul A. IoT-based smart city development using big data analytical approach. In: Automatica (ICA-ACCA), IEEE International Conference on. IEEE; 2016. pp. 1–8.

[17]   Ahlgren B, Hidell M, Ngai ECH. Internet of things for smart cities: Interoperability and open data. IEEE Internet Computing. 2016;20(6):52–56.

[18]   Vuppalapati C, Ilapakurti A, Kedari S. The role of big data in creating sense EHR, an integrated approach to create next generation mobile sensor and wearable data driven electronic health record (EHR). In: Big Data Computing Service and Applications (BigDataService), 2016 IEEE Second International Conference on. IEEE; 2016. pp. 293–296.

[19]   Ahmad A, Rathore MM, Paul A, *et al.* Defining human behaviors using big data analytics in social internet of things. In: Advanced Information Networking and Applications (AINA), 2016 IEEE 30th International Conference on. IEEE; 2016. pp. 1101–1107.

[20]   Ahmed E, Rehmani MH. Introduction to the special section on social collaborative internet of things. Computers and Electrical Engineering. 2017;58: 382–384.

[21]   Rathore MM, Ahmad A, Paul A, *et al.* Urban planning and building smart cities based on the internet of things using big data analytics. Computer Networks. 2016;101:63–80.

[22] Zhang Q, Zhang X, Zhang Q, *et al.* Firework: Big data sharing and processing in collaborative edge environment. In: 2016 Fourth IEEE Workshop on Hot Topics in Web Systems and Technologies (HotWeb). IEEE; 2016. pp. 20–25.

[23] Mukherjee A, Paul HS, Dey S, *et al.* Angels for distributed analytics in IoT. In: Internet of Things (WF-IoT), 2014 IEEE World Forum on. IEEE; 2014. pp. 565–570.

[24] Mukherjee A, Dey S, Paul HS, *et al.* Utilising condor for data parallel analytics in an IoT context—An experience report. In: Wireless and Mobile Computing, Networking and Communications (WiMob), 2013 IEEE 9th International Conference on. IEEE; 2013. pp. 325–331.

[25] Sezer OB, Dogdu E, Ozbayoglu M, *et al.* An extended IoT framework with semantics, big data, and analytics. In: Big Data (Big Data), 2016 IEEE International Conference on. IEEE; 2016. pp. 1849–1856.

[26] Cheng B, Papageorgiou A, Cirillo F, *et al.* Geelytics: Geo-distributed edge analytics for large scale IoT systems based on dynamic topology. In: Internet of Things (WF-IoT), 2015 IEEE 2nd World Forum on. IEEE; 2015. pp. 565–570.

[27] Pérez JL, Carrera D. Performance characterization of the servioticy API: An IoT-as-a-service data management platform. In: 2015 IEEE First International Conference on Big Data Computing Service and Applications (BigDataService). IEEE; 2015. pp. 62–71.

[28] Arkian HR, Diyanat A, Pourkhalili A. MIST: Fog-based data analytics scheme with cost-efficient resource provisioning for IoT crowdsensing applications. Journal of Network and Computer Applications. 2017;82:152–165.

[29] Berlian MH, Sahputra TER, Ardi BJW, *et al.* Design and implementation of smart environment monitoring and analytics in real-time system framework based on internet of underwater things and big data. In: Electronics Symposium (IES), 2016 International. IEEE; 2016. p. 403–408.

[30] Villari M, Celesti A, Fazio M, *et al.* AllJoyn Lambda: An architecture for the management of smart environments in IoT. In: Smart Computing Workshops (SMARTCOMP Workshops), 2014 International Conference on. IEEE; 2014. pp. 9–14.

[31] Ding Z, Gao X, Xu J, *et al.* IOT-StatisticDB: A general statistical database cluster mechanism for big data analysis in the internet of things. In: Green Computing and Communications (GreenCom), 2013 IEEE and Internet of Things (iThings/CPSCom), IEEE International Conference on and IEEE Cyber, Physical and Social Computing. IEEE; 2013. pp. 535–543.

[32] Yen IL, Zhou G, Zhu W, *et al.* A smart physical world based on service technologies, big data, and game-based crowd sourcing. In: Web Services (ICWS), 2015 IEEE International Conference on. IEEE; 2015. pp. 765–772.

[33] Alam F, Mehmood R, Katib I, *et al.* Analysis of eight data mining algorithms for smarter Internet of Things (IoT). Procedia Computer Science. 2016;98: 437–442.

[34] Arora D, Li KF, Loffler A. Big data analytics for classification of network enabled devices. In: Advanced Information Networking and Applications

Workshops (WAINA), 2016 30th International Conference on. IEEE; 2016. pp. 708–713.

[35]   Jara AJ, Genoud D, Bocchi Y. Big data for cyber physical systems: An analysis of challenges, solutions and opportunities. In: Innovative Mobile and Internet Services in Ubiquitous Computing (IMIS), 2014 Eighth International Conference on. IEEE; 2014. pp. 376–380.

[36]   Minch RP. Location Privacy in the Era of the Internet of Things and Big Data Analytics; 2015.

Chapter 2

Smarter big data analytics for traffic applications in developing countries

Tran Vu Pham[1], Quang Tran Minh[1],
Hong-Linh Truong[2] and Hoa Dam[3]

Internet of Things (IoT) generates a huge amount of data in real-time. Utilization of such data requires appropriate data storage, analytics, and computation techniques so that valuable information can be extracted and immediate actions could be taken place. In this chapter, we present real-time traffic applications, typical IoT-enabled big data applications in smart city context, but for unreliable and fragmented infrastructures in developing countries. We analyze a case study to show challenges that we need to address when implementing big IoT data applications in such infrastructures. Based on that we outline our key design principles and techniques. We present several examples to particularly discuss how we achieve our designs and lesson learned.

2.1 Introduction

Real-time traffic-monitoring systems use data generated from IoT devices equipped with global positioning systems (GPS) mounted in vehicles moving on city road networks to extract the current states of the traffic, i.e., traffic flows of roads. The data is then analyzed and traffic information is disseminated to the public on a web portal and mobile applications. Users can obtain up-to-date information about the traffic and make proper traveling plans to avoid areas having bad traffic conditions. Such systems are well studied and deployed in many cities. These systems often have common characteristics w.r.t. communications, large-scale data storage, and high-performance computing systems to support traffic analytics. However, most systems are developed and deployed in well infrastructures or in the context of developed countries.

 Our experiences in developing such systems are different: we are building such systems in the context of Vietnam, specifically, and in developing countries, generally.

[1]Faculty of Computer Science and Engineering, Ho Chi Minh City University of Technology, VNU-HCM, Ho Chi Minh City, Vietnam
[2]Department of Computer Science, School of Science, Aalto University, Finland
[3]School of Computing and Information Technology, University of Wollongong, Wollongong, Australia

In our context, we have faced several different issues w.r.t. fragmented Information and Communication Technology (ICT) infrastructures, weak and unstable networks, highly diverse quality of GPS sensors attached to vehicles, mixed types of vehicles, to name just a few, for a very hybrid multimodal traffics of motorbikes, cars, and buses. Even in a not well-connected network whose coverage is limited in Vietnam, currently, our system receives data from around 10,000 vehicles at peak time. The amount of GPS data the system needs to process per day is roughly 4.5 GB, on average 600 data records per second. Due to the fragmented network and computational infrastructures as well as diverse types of devices with different quality, in our case, we face several challenges that need novel solutions.

2.1.1   Research challenges

We will discuss challenges and requirement analysis centered on the following points:

- *Real-time processing of data*: Even under limited capabilities of networks and computational resources, the data still needs to be processed in a real-time manner so that decisions can be made immediately to respond to the current traffic conditions. Because of this requirement, the proper solutions need to be balanced between processing time and the accuracy of results.
- *Noises in data*: The system receives a huge amount of data, but only a fraction of data is with expected accuracy and currency, due to quality of devices, noises, and network delay/reliability. This problem is severe due to the quality of IoT devices and networks in developing environments. For example, the data may come from many vehicles that are stationary, not participating in the traffic. Late arrival of data due to network problems and low quality of GPS-enabled devices are also major sources of noises. The challenge here is how to separate the noise in data in real-time before any calculation can take place.
- *Heterogeneity of data sources*: Given the heterogeneity and diversity of IoT devices, GPS signals are generated from different GPS-enabled devices equipped on various means of transportation such as buses, trucks, taxis, and mobile users on cars or motorcycles. Each means of transportation has different traveling behaviors, rate of noises, and quality of data. Therefore, each of these sources of data needs to be processed differently.
- *Large amount of data*: The size of data causes challenges in processing and storing. A proper storage system needs to be used so that the data can be stored and retrieved for processing at minimal delay.

2.1.2   Contributions and paper structure

In order to address the above challenges, we have developed a system framework for real-time traffic applications, the key solutions of which are

- a modular and scalable IoT application framework that support various traffic applications in smart city domain,

- a scalable key-value (KV) remote direct memory access (RDMA)-based storage system for caching data during processing,
- real-time classification of data and noise reduction using multithreading, and
- simple but fast analytic techniques for GPS signals.

In this chapter, we will present some examples to illustrate our work. We describe details of the traffic-monitoring system for demonstration purpose.

The chapter will include five main parts: Section 2.2 presents scenarios and requirements. Section 2.3 describes our analytics framework. We present our big data applications and challenges in Section 2.4. We discuss related work in Section 2.5 and conclude the chapter in Section 2.6.

2.2   Scenario and requirements

We analyzed the case of traffic management in Ho Chi Minh City (HCMC), the most populous city in Vietnam, to illustrate applications of IoT and big data to solve critical problems in urban areas. Currently, there are more than 10 million people living in the city. HCMC is pushing toward a smart city program, which aims at utilizing modern technologies, such as IoT, machine learning, and high-performance computing, to improve the living conditions of the city's residences. The challenges that HCMC is facing, as a mega city in Asia, are city management, transportation (e.g., traffic jams), air pollution, urban flooding, to name just a few. In the scope of this chapter, we focus on transportation issues.

Per regulations, public-service vehicles, such as buses, taxis, trucks, and coaches, have to install GPS-enabled devices, and frequently send GPS signals in real-time to a government office for monitoring their locations and driving behaviors. Typically, the GPS signal consists of *ID of the vehicle ID, longitude, latitude, velocity*, and *timestamp*. The GPS data may contain other optional information, such as *petrol level and engine status*. The city Transportation Department expects to receive monitoring data from about 67,000 vehicles regularly. Our demonstrating system involves a smaller number of vehicles, about 10,000 at peak time. In addition to the GPS signals from vehicles, we also developed mobile applications for end users (especially motorbikes), enabling them to contribute some limited amount of GPS data to our system.

The real-time GPS data is valuable for a number of applications in scope of the HCMC smart city program. It can be used for extracting the current state of the traffic in the city to detect traffic jams, one of the most crucial problems, and it is the most well-known function of our demonstrating applications. A screenshot of the application is shown in Figure 2.1. In addition, the data can also be used for other types of applications for city residences, such as

- predicting arrival times of buses at bus stops,
- predicting arrival times and routing for taxis,
- navigating commuters to avoid traffic jams,
- predicting traffic jams, and
- predicting traveling directions of mobile users and alerting them with real-time traffic conditions.

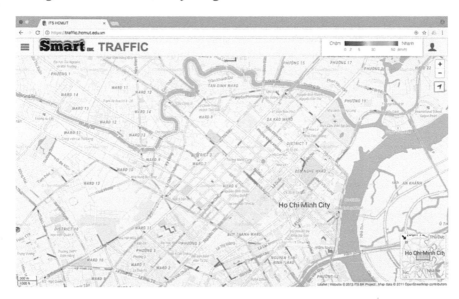

Figure 2.1   Screenshot of Traffic Information System for monitoring traffic conditions of Ho Chi Minh City in real-time. The color labels show the traffic flow velocities of the roads

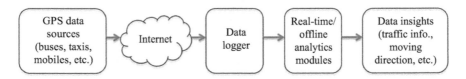

Figure 2.2   GPS signal processing flow for traffic applications

The common characteristic of these applications is that they all need to analyze real-time GPS signals to get insights (knowledge) from the data and then provide recommendations to the users in real-time. The general processing flow for applications is illustrated in Figure 2.2. However, for each application, real-time GPS data is analyzed differently. For example, for extracting traffic conditions, the analysis is focused on estimating traffic flow velocity and density using velocity information in the signals. For predicting bus-arrival times, the analysis module needs to track individual buses' movement, combining with the traffic flow velocity to make the estimation. Therefore, efficient control of the flow of real-time GPS data in the system is very important to the applications.

The GPS data from different sources are very different in terms of quality, quantity, and other characteristics. In terms of quality, devices from different manufacturers have different in quality, and hence, leading to the variety of the data accuracy. The quality of the data is also affected by the quality of communication networks used.

Currently, most GPS devices on vehicles use General Packet Radio Service (GPRS) services from mobile networks. GPS signals from mobile devices, via mostly on at 3G networks, often give best accuracy. However, mobile devices often have problem with batteries. Therefore, their online time is very intermittent. Another issue is that the quality of mobile networks is changing, even within a small area, causing many issues for data delivery. In terms of quantity, the frequency at which signals are sent to the servers is supposed to be a signal per 15 s for each device. However, in reality, the frequency for each device may be different due to network condition, quality of devices, and physical setting (thus we allow, for mobile devices, the frequency to be set by the users). The characteristic of GPS data is also very different. As buses run mostly on major roads of the city at regular intervals, they reflect well the traffic conditions of these roads. However, if we rely only on bus data, we lack information for smaller roads. The coverage of taxis and trucks are larger, but their traveling pattern is irregular. Coaches move mostly in outer city roads for destinations at long distances, and therefore, data from coaches is not very useful for inner city applications. Mobile (motorbike) users can be anywhere, such as on roads, in houses, offices, or coffee bars. Hence, deciding whether a mobile user is on roads or not is also a challenging issue. Most of the time the vehicles are in idle states but still sending real-time signals to servers. To know whether a vehicle is stuck in a traffic jam or in idle state is also a hard problem.

In summary, the abovementioned issues make the development of applications related to traffic very challenging. Many constraints and techniques need to be developed for specific developing countries that are very different from developed environments.

2.3 Analytics system framework for traffic applications

2.3.1 Design objectives

To address issues described in Section 2.2, we have designed a system framework for utilizing GPS data provided by different sources from the city that tackles the following requirements:

- Able to process large volume of GPS data in real-time to give timely responses to end users.
- Efficiently deal with the heterogeneity of GPS data from various sources, with differences in quality, quantity, and characteristics.
- Allow different analytic modules, both real-time and offline, to be plugged-in the system to support different kinds of applications.

In the following, we will discuss the framework and our unique design features.

2.3.2 Framework overview

Figure 2.3 depicts the overall system framework. Generally, the system takes as inputs different GPS data sources by GPS data logger. The raw data is stored in database

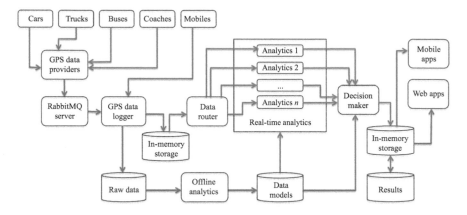

Figure 2.3   Analytics system framework for GPS data

for offline analytics and archiving. A copy of raw data is also kept in in-memory storage for real-time analytics. Because different sources of GPS data have different characteristics, and each application requires to process the data differently, the raw data is classified and fed in different analytics modules by data router. As the volume of data is large, real-time analytics must be done in parallel. The raw data can also be processed by offline analytics modules to build data models for different purposes (e.g., prediction traffic conditions and user movement). The data model extracted by offline analytics modules can be utilized to improve the quality of real-time analytics. When all the analytics are done with the data, the decision maker finalizes the results and stores them in databases for later use by web applications or mobile applications. For quick responses to user requests, copies of the results are also cached in in-memory storage.

2.3.3   GPS data providers

The GPS data comes to the system from many different sources, such as cars, buses, taxis, trucks, coaches, and mobile devices. Except for mobiles, GPS signals from other sources do not come directly to our servers. Instead, the signals from devices on cars, buses, etc., are collected by their device providers, named as GPS data providers, via GPRS/3G networks. The providers then send the collected data to our RabbitMQ server in real-time via the Internet. The data received by RabbitMQ server is forwarded to GPS data logger for archiving and further processing. Because the data has to be processed at multiple steps before coming to our server, the delays of data packages when arriving at the system from different providers may be varied.

For mobile devices, as we build our own applications for collecting GPS data from mobile users, the GPS signals are sent directly to data logger using network connections built atop the User Datagram Protocol (UDP). Even though the UDP protocol is not reliable, the use of UDP helps the system maintenance become easier. As connections of mobile devices to the Internet are intermittent, with UDP we do not need to continuously monitor and reset up the connections when there are network interruptions.

2.3.4   Offline analytics

The framework is designed to allow the system to work with different offline analytics modules. Recall that our infrastructures are fragmented: this offline analytics is not just due to different types of postmortem or predictive traffic analytics but also due to the need to prioritize and balance computation demands. Depending on the kinds of application, different offline analytics methods can be applied. The results of offline analytics processes, usually data models, are used to improve the quality of real-time analytics and final decisions. For example, for traffic-notification applications, machine-learning techniques can be used to extract users' traveling patterns. The patterns can then be used to predict the user movements on roads in real-time so that the right notifications about traffic conditions can be sent to the users. For the bus-arrival-time prediction, machine-learning techniques can also be applied to raw bus data from the past to extract bus behaviors. The knowledge is used by real-time analytics modules to improve the quality of predictions.

2.3.5   Data router and real-time analytics

Real-time analytics is the core of the systems. As any IoT system, the incoming data stream needs to be constantly processed to extract immediate insights so that timely decisions can be made to respond to changes in the real environments. In the transportation domain, real-time GPS data are useful to many different applications. For this reason, the framework is designed in a way that different real-time analytics modules can be used the real-time GPS data stream. Depending on the need of applications, the data router classifies the data packages in the real-time data stream and forks main data streams into substreams and feeds them to the right analytics modules.

The data router splits the main data stream into substreams for different purposes:

- For applications that require to process large amount of data, such as monitoring traffic conditions (i.e., traffic flow velocity and density), it is not possible for one machine to process the data of the whole city, the data router splits the main data stream into smaller ones so that they can be analyzed in parallel to speed up the processing.
- Each data source may also have different characteristics, as analyzed in Section 2.2, and requires different analysis techniques. In this case, the data with similar characteristics is grouped together in substreams for further processing.
- Each application may require a different set of input data. For example, for bus-arrival-time prediction, GPS signals from buses may only be needed. The data router may split the data stream depending on the need of applications.

2.3.6   Decision maker

Based on the intermediate results of real-time and offline analytics, the decision maker concludes the results, which are stored for use by end users applications. For different types of application, different decision mechanisms can be applied. For example, to estimate the velocity of traffic flow of a particular road segment, the decision can be simply an average calculation of all the velocity attributes carried by the GPS signals having coordinates falling on the road segment in a particular period of time. However, to predict a user trajectory on roads in the city, a much more complex decision model needs to be used.

2.3.7   Mobile and web applications

Mobile and web applications provide interfaces for users to interact with the system. We use RESTful services so that application front ends can be easily integrated with backend systems. The system can also be extensible with service-oriented architecture.

2.4   Big data applications and challenges

2.4.1   In-memory storage

One of the challenging problems when handling real-time GPS data for traffic applications is that the data comes from many different sources and needs to be processed in real-time. Traditional relational databases are not suitable. The available NoSQL databases such as MongoDB* are usable, but their performance, especially for read operations, does not meet the need of the applications. The reason is that MongoDB is KV operation orientated. It does not take into account the time and spatio-characteristics of the data. For real-time traffic applications, a database needs to be able to handle large amount of real-time data, particularly the following:

- Able to store and scale with constantly increasing amount of data.
- Support many read operations with low latency, as many different applications need to read data from the data stream in real-time.

In order to reduce latency of read operations, the storage system is separated into two layers: in-memory (cache) and persistent storages on disks, as shown in Figure 2.4. Initially, we have tried Memcached† for in-memory storage. Its performance did not meet our requirements. Memcached does not scale well when the amount of data increases. By exploiting the time-spatial characteristics of GPS data, we have designed a new in-memory storage system for traffic applications. Design of the system has been improved over time and published in [1–4]. Because GPS data also shares common time-spatial characteristics with other classes of IoT datasets, we

---

*https://www.mongodb.com.
†http://memcached.org.

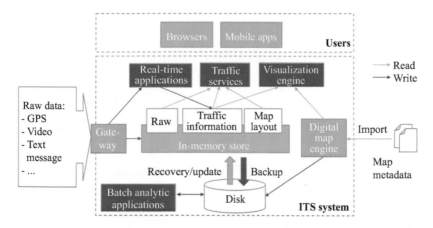

Figure 2.4   In-memory storage system for traffic applications

believe that our in-memory system can be used efficiently for other classes of IoT applications.

Figure 2.5 shows the geographical distribution of GPS data on an overlay of HCMC map in four continuous days. The distribution is almost static. This is explainable because the traveling patterns of city residences are repeated day by day. Based on this distribution, we have designed a scalable mechanism for distributing GPS data into data nodes. Any new indexing and querying mechanisms were also developed for the storage system. Experiment results showed that this new indexing and querying mechanisms could improve the system performance significantly in comparison with traditional methods [3].

In order to reduce read latency, we developed a key-value links (KVL) data model, by utilizing RDMA for our in-memory storage. From design perspective, KVL model is an extension of the common KV data model. Each pair of KV is added with an additional link, similar to pointer, to a related data item. To fetch the related data item, the link is chased via RDMA read operation. Because RDMA reads can bypass kernel operations, they can help to reduce the latency significantly. This in-memory storage system architecture is described in detail in [4].

2.4.2   Filtering unusable data for real-time analytics

GPS data sources continuously generate many signals, but not all the signals are usable for real-time applications. The reasons that make the data unusable are

- inaccuracy of the data signals, due to quality of devices,
- noises in data,
- errors in map data (coordinates of roads shown on map different from their real physical locations),

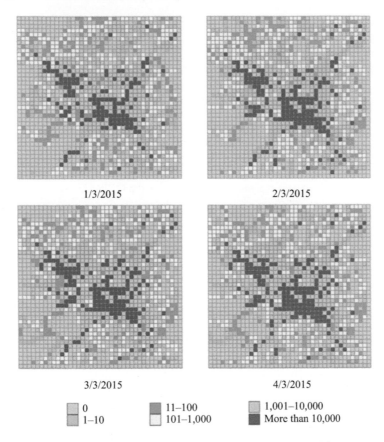

Figure 2.5   Distribution of GPS data over geographical locations

- errors in timing: unsynchronized clocks (timestamp of signal is earlier/later than the actual time), network delays/interruptions (late arrival of data packets), and
- data from stationary vehicles (not participating in traffic).

Therefore, the received data needs to be cleaned or corrected before use. This step is necessary for all traffic applications. In other words, we need to know which signals are from vehicles that are participating in the traffic to further process. The rest of the signals will be filtered out. By analyzing the data manually, we discovered the following information:

- About 35% of the data could not be mapped onto any road segments. This could be because of noises in data, inaccurate GPS signals, or errors in map data.
- About 8% of the data arrives at our server having packet timestamps either earlier or later than expected. For real-time processing, we need to have data arrive within a time window, around the current time. However, due to network delays, network interruptions, unsynchronized clocks, or some other reasons, the timestamps

(recorded by the devices) of the signals are outside the current time window, hence, not usable.

- About 38 data signals have zero speed values. These data signals come from stationary vehicles, not participating in traffic. This is because the GPS devices keep generating signals and send them to the servers 24/7, independently from the operations of the vehicles.

When filtering out the above data signals, only about 17% of the raw data is used for further processing in real-time. Bringing more data into the calculation will significantly improve the quality of the results. However, correcting errors in data to improve its utilization is a challenging problem.

We have taken a couple of methods to improve the utilization of the data:

- For signals from buses, as buses always travel on fixed routes, we can decide the buses' routes based on offline analytics, then, errors caused by incorrect map data or inaccurate GPS signals can be reduced by shifting the coordinates of the signals to the road segments belonging to expected routes.
- For signals from devices physically attached to vehicles, as the vehicles also traveling on roads, we can extend the margins of road segments to include more signals to the calculation when mapping the signals to road segments.
- It is a little more complicated for signals from mobile devices, as the connections of mobile devices to the Internet are intermittent, and the devices can be anywhere (e.g., on roads, coffee bars, offices, etc.). To deal with intermittent Internet connection, when the connection is dropped, the device will temporarily store in the device's buffer. The buffered data will be uploaded to the server when the device is back online. Some of the data may be unsynchronized, hence not be used for real-time calculation, but still valuable for offline analytics. To detect whether a device participates in traffic or not, we have built an offline model based on neural networks to learn the moving characteristics of mobile users. The model can then be applied to detect the traveling status of mobile users.

The above actions could help to improve slightly the utilization of the data, but the challenge we are still facing is how to integrate the models resulted from offline analytics to real-time calculations. If too much calculation and complicated models are required for real-time processing, it will cause more delay in delivering final results. We need to consider the trade-off between accuracy of computation and delivering time.

2.4.3   Traffic monitoring and prediction

Providing real-time traffic information is currently the main functions of our demonstrating system. It is currently running live at http://traffic.hcmut.edu.vn (as only a demonstrating application, the real-time GPS data fed in the system is varied from time to time). Figure 2.1 shows a screenshot of the system. The overall system architecture is depicted in Figure 2.4, which is a specific implementation of the analytics system framework described in Section 2.3.

The main objective of the system is to extract the current traffic conditions (in terms of traffic flow velocity) of city road segments and show the results in the city map. In order to get the traffic flow velocity of a particular road segment (limited by two continuous intersections), we gather all the GPS signals having the coordinates fallen in the segment in the observation time window (currently, it is period of 15 min from the current time back). The flow velocity is the average of all the speed values carried by the GPS signals. As the number of road segments in the city is quite large, the calculations are done in parallel.

The advantage of the current method is that it is very simple, with minimal amount of calculations in real-time, but gives acceptable results. However, to further improve the accuracy of the results, a number of issues need to be addressed:

- What is the best time window for a particular segment? If the time window is small, there will be less GPS signals fallen in the segment, then the estimated results will not be reliable. However, if the time window is large, it will not reflect well the current state of the traffic. Furthermore, GPS signals are not distributed equally on city road segments. Using the same time window may be good for some segments but not appropriate for other segments.
- How GPS data from heterogeneous sources, with different level of accuracy, contribute to the final estimation? Currently, because the number of GPS signals fallen within a segment is relatively small, a simple averaging is acceptable. However, when there is a mix of signals from different sources, a more appropriate method may be required.
- How historical data can help to improve the accuracy of real-time calculation? Furthermore, how the current and past data can help to predict the traffic in near future? This issue leads to traffic-prediction problem.
- How to inform city residences about the current state of city traffic? Broadcasting traffic information to all city commuters is not a good option, because people tend to travel in a particular area of the city interested in some particular types of information. Receiving too much information that is not relevant to user context will result negative impression. To send proper information to users, we need to learn user habit (traveling patterns and interests). This issue needs to be addressed.

Predicting future events in traffic (e.g., arrival times and routing for taxis, traffic jams, or traveling directions) is highly challenging due to the inherent uncertainty, temporal and spatial dependencies, and the dynamic nature of traffic. The analytics component of our framework therefore plays an important part in learning from potentially large datasets and automatically forming a deep understanding of traffic patterns and dependencies. Such an understanding along with relevant memory of experience will be helpful in making predictions and relevant interventions.

A number of challenges exist in building an effective traffic model. First, we need to capture various dimensions of dependencies, including *spatial and temporal dependencies* (e.g., time and location of vehicles). Second, handling *long-term dependencies*: future traffic events may depend on previous events and interventions. For example, a car accident occurred on a road may result in a traffic jam on that road a few minutes later. Third, accurate traffic prediction requires a sufficiently *rich representation of traffic events*. The challenge here is how features representing a traffic event can be *automatically* learned from GPS data. Fourth, we need to model the *episodic and irregular timing* in traffic. Traffic can be seen as a series of episodes and time between traffic events are largely random. We thus need to address the episodic and irregular timing of events of interests when building traffic-prediction models. Finally, modeling *confounding interactions between traffic events and interventions*. For example, directing traffic from a congested road to other roads (as an intervention) may result in congestion elsewhere.

The recent advances of deep learning techniques in machine learning offer a powerful solution to address the above challenges. Deep-learning techniques are capable of dealing with dimensionality issues and modeling deep complex nonlinear dependencies with distributed and hierarchical feature representation. One of the most widely used deep learning models is long short-term memory (LSTM), a special kind of recurrent neural network that is highly effective in learning long-term dependencies in sequential data such as time series in traffic data. Currently, we focus on developing an end-to-end traffic prediction model, which does not require manual feature engineering, i.e., features are automatically learned from GPS data. Our model will be based on LSTM and thus will be capable of reading historical traffic data, memorizing a long history of experience, inferring the current state of traffic, predicting future events and risks, and finally recommending actionable interventions.

We have implemented a deep-learning model for predicting traffic conditions of road segments based on LSTM. The inputs to the model are traffic conditions of the predicted segments from the past. Experimental results showed that the current model is good for extracting regular traffic patterns from past data and using the patterns for the prediction. However, accuracy of the prediction is limited when there are ad hoc traffic incidents. The model needs to be revised in order to improve the quality of prediction.

2.4.4 Trip planning in city bus networks

With large amount of GPS data received from city buses, we also use the data to improve bus services. We have developed solutions to help people plan their trips when traveling with city buses. The two challenges that we need to address are (i) predicting arrival times of buses on a particular bus route and (ii) planning optimal traveling routes from a user current location to desired destination. These problems are even more challenging because of the current conditions of HCMC city bus network. The city is suffering from regular traffic jams; therefore, it is almost impossible to have an on-time bus timetable. The arrival time of the current bus is relative to the last one on the same route. Hence, when planning for a trip, the current state of the bus network, including the locations and traffic conditions, needs to be taken into account.

In order to deal with the above issues, we model the bus network as a stochastic schedule-based transit network. A number of solutions that utilize both real-time and offline analytics using GPS signals from the city have been developed:

- Planning traveling path on city bus network with least expected travel time and minimum number of transfers: the solution is based on correct-labeling algorithm and Bellman's principle of optimality. Experimental results show that running time of the algorithm is suitable for real-time applications [5].

- Finding reliable path with earliest arrival time: Due to stochastic nature of the transit network, the success of a planned route, involved a number transfers, depends on the probability of on-time arrivals of buses at transfers. The solution takes into account this issue to find a path with the reliability above certain threshold [6].
- Finding alternative traveling paths on bus network: The commuters may have personal preferences on bus routes. Therefore, we developed a path-finding algorithm that returns multiple similar cost paths so that they can choose a path to travel based on their preferences [7].

We have developed, experimented, and published technical details of these solutions. However, due to the lack of human resources, we have not yet implemented the solutions in our live-demonstrating system.

2.5 Related work

Recent work related to this chapter from two closely related domains: smart traffic (or intelligent transportation systems—ITS) and, broadly, Smart City. There have been many systems for traffic management as well as the use of big data techniques for such management systems is known [8–10]. In this chapter, we focus more on specific characteristics and techniques that are designed for solving issues related to developing countries.

In smart traffic domain, one of the earliest proposals for ITS system architecture for developing countries could be from the World Bank [11]. However, this proposal only focuses on the functional and service aspects of ITS; such features are common in various architecture. Technical solutions, such as how data should be stored and processed in fragmented environments, are not mentioned. Also in smart traffic domain, there are other suggested system architectures for building analytics applications [12–14]. In general, we have seen the widely use of big data storage, streaming processing, and services in the cloud for ITS, but there is a lack of discussions w.r.t. how to deal the lack of resources, unreliable networks, and bad data quality.

In Smart City, different system architecture has also been introduced [15–17]. Similarly, proposed architecture for traffic applications is very generic [15], very specific to parallel data processing [16], or utilization of network technologies [17], whereas, in our work, we aim at supporting different analytics methods and applications.

In ubiquitous computing and sensor networks, we have seen many works discussed techniques to deal with data quality [18–21] and smart city network connectivity issues [22]. However, such works have not been integrated into the big data pipelines, which bring real-time data from Things to the analytics algorithms through various phases. In our work, we particularly focus on developing suitable solutions that are well integrated with the big data pipelines, and deployed and tested with traffic in developing countries.

2.6 Conclusions

In this chapter, we have introduced a scalable, IoT-based system framework for traffic applications in HCMC, Vietnam. This system utilizes the GPS data generated by buses, taxis, trucks, coaches, etc., and mobile devices for real-time traffic application such as traffic monitoring, traffic predictions, and bus trip planning. The key advantages of the framework are (i) supporting a variety of real-time applications that utilize the same set of real-time data, (ii) allowing the integration of real-time and offline analytics to improve the quality of results, and (iii) providing mechanism for splitting/duplicating real-time data stream into substreams for further analysis by specific applications and/or speeding up the calculation by parallel processing. The chapter also reports a number of demonstrating applications we have developed and discusses their current status and how big data analytics techniques could be employed to improve quality of results. As learned from developing these applications, with real-time analytics system, there should always be a combination of real-time and offline analytics, and for particular applications, the trade-off between the cost of real-time computation and quality of results need to be considered.

References

[1] Tran Vu Pham, Duc Hai Nguyen, and Khue Doan, "S4STRD: A Scalable in Memory Storage System for Spatio-Temporal Real-Time Data," in *IEEE International Conference on Smart City/SocialCom/SustainCom (SmartCity 2015)*, Chengdu, China, 2015, pp. 896–901.

[2] Minh Duc Le, Duc Hieu Nguyen, Tien Hai Ho, Duc Hai Nguyen, and Tran Vu Pham, "KELI: A Key-Value-With-Links In-Memory Store for Realtime Applications," in *The Seventh Symposium on Information and Communication Technology*, Ho Chi Minh City, Vietnam, 2016, pp. 195–201.

[3] Duc Hai Nguyen, Khue Doan, and Tran Vu Pham, "SIDI: A Scalable In-Memory Density-Based Index for Spatial Databases," in *the ACM International Workshop on Data-Intensive Distributed Computing*, Kyoto, Japan, 2016, pp. 45–52.

[4] Hai Duc Nguyen, Duc Hieu Nguyen, Minh Duc Le, Tien Hai Ho, and Tran Vu Pham, "Key-value-links: a new data model for developing efficient RDMA-based in-memory stores," *Informatica*, vol. 41, no. 2, pp. 183–192, 2017.

[5] Dang Khoa Vo, Tran Vu Pham, Nguyen Huynh Tuong, and Van Hoai Tran, "Least expected time paths in stochastic schedule-based transit networks," *Mathematical Problems in Engineering*, vol. 2016, 13 pp., 2016.

[6] Dang Khoa Vo, Hai Vu Le, Tran Vu Pham, Nguyen Huynh Tuong, and Hoai Van Tran, "The Alpha-Reliable Earliest Arrival Paths in Stochastic Public Transit

Networks," in *the 95th Transportation Research Board (TRB) Annual Meeting*, Washington, DC, 2016.

[7]   Dang Khoa Vo, Tran Vu Pham, Tuong Nguyen Huynh, Nghia Nguyen, and Van Hoai Tran, "Finding Alternative Paths in City Bus Networks," in *International Conference on Computer, Control, Informatics and its Applications (IC3INA)*, 2015, pp. 34–39.

[8]   Constantinos Costa, Georgios Chatzimilioudis, Demetrios Zeinalipour-Yazti, and Mohamed F. Mokbel, "Towards Real-Time Road Traffic Analytics Using Telco Big Data," in *The International Workshop on Real-Time Business Intelligence and Analytics (BIRTE '17)*, New York, 2017.

[9]   Sudha Ram, Yun Wang, Faiz Currim, Fan Dong, Ezequiel Dantas, and Luiz Alberto Sabíia, "SMARTBUS: A Web Application for Smart Urban Mobility and Transportation," in *The 25th International Conference Companion on World Wide Web (WWW '16 Companion)*, Republic and Canton of Geneva, Switzerland, 2016, pp. 363–368.

[10] Chao-Tung Yang, Shuo-Tsung Chen, and Yin-Zhen Yan, "The implementation of a cloud city traffic state assessment system using a novel big data architecture," *Cluster Computing*, vol. 20, no. 2, pp. 1101–1121, 2017.

[11] Toshiyuki Yokota and Richard J. Weiland, "ITS System Architectures For Developing Countries," Transport and Urban Development Department, World Bank, Technical Note 2004.

[12] Sasan Amini, Ilias Gerostathopoulos, and Christian Prehofer, "Big Data Analytics Architecture for Real-Time Traffic Control," in *5th IEEE International Conference on Models and Technologies for Intelligent Transportation Systems (MT-ITS)*, Naples, Italy, 2017.

[13] Hamzeh Khazaei, Saeed Zareian, Rodrigo Veleda, and Marin Litoiu, "Sipresk: A Big Data Analytic Platform for Smart Transportation," in *EAI International Conference on Big Data and Analytics for Smart Cities*, Toronto, Canada, 2015.

[14] Harkiran Kaur and Jyoteesh Malhotra, "An IoT based smart architecture for traffic management system," *IOSR Journal of Computer Engineering (IOSR – JCE)*, vol. 19, no. 4, pp. 60–63, 2017.

[15] Narmeen Zakaria Bawany and Jawwad A. Shamsi, "Smart city architecture: vision and challenges," *International Journal of Advanced Computer Science and Applications*, vol. 6, no. 11, pp. 246–255, 2015.

[16] Bhagya Nathali Silva, Murad Khan, and Kijun Han, "Big data analytics embedded smart city architecture for performance enhancement through real-time data processing and decision-making," *Wireless Communications and Mobile Computing*, vol. 2017, 12 pp., 2017.

[17] Aditya Gaura, Bryan Scotneya, Gerard Parra, and Sally McClean, "Smart city architecture and its applications based on IoT," *Procedia Computer Science*, vol. 52, pp. 1089–1094, 2015.

[18] Anja Klein and Wolfgang Lehner, "Representing data quality in sensor data streaming environments," *Journal of Data and Information Quality*, vol. 1, no. 2, 28 pp., 2009.

[19]   Aimad Karkouch, Hajar Mousannif, Hassan Al Moatassime, and Thomas Noel, "Data quality in internet of things," *Journal of Network and Computer Applications*, vol. 73, no. C, pp. 57–81, 2016.

[20]   Tiago Brasileiro Araújo, Cinzia Cappiello, Nádia P. Kozievitch, Demetrio Gomes Mestre, Carlos Eduardo S. Pires, Monica Vitali, "Towards Reliable Data Analyses for Smart Cities," in *The 21st International Database Engineering & Applications Symposium (IDEAS 2017)*, New York, NY, USA, pp. 304–308, 2017.

[21]   Payam Barnaghi, Maria Bermudez-Edo, and Ralf Tönjes, "Challenges for quality of data in smart cities," *Journal of Data and Information Quality*, vol. 6, no. 2–3, 3 pp., 2015.

[22]   Ibrar Yaqoob, Ibrahim Abaker Targio Hashem, Yasir Mehmood, Abdullah Gani, Salimah Mokhtar, and Sghaier Guizani, "Enabling communication technologies for smart cities," *IEEE Communications Magazine*, vol. 55, no. 1, pp. 112–120, 2017.

Chapter 3

Using IoT-based big data generated inside school buildings

*Ioannis Chatzigiannakis¹, Georgios Mylonas²,
Irene Mavrommati³ and Dimitrios Amaxilatis⁴*

The utilization of Internet of Things (IoT) in the educational domain so far has trailed other more commercial application domains. In this chapter, we study a number of aspects that are based on big data produced by a large-scale infrastructure deployed inside a fleet of educational buildings in Europe. We discuss how this infrastructure essentially enables a set of different applications, complemented by a detailed discussion regarding both performance aspects of the implementation of this IoT platform as well as results that provide insights to its actual application in real life, both from educational and business standpoints.

3.1 Introduction

Wireless sensor networks have been the starting point for a tremendous development that has gradually led to the realization of the IoT. Today, there is a large variety of hardware and software to choose from that is easy to set up and use in an increasing set of real-world application domains [1]. One such important domain is education: the deployment of a variety of sensors (e.g., for monitoring electricity consumption, environmental conditions, be them indoor or outdoor) across school buildings can produce real-world data that could be directly used in educational activities or provide input to business processes, making financial sense in terms of cost savings.

Another thing to consider is climate change and our response as a society through the transfer of green technologies inside schools. In the last few years, an emphasis has been given on environmental awareness via education. In many cases, this is achieved by employing lab activities based on off-the-shelf IoT sensors, planned specifically for students as part of science classes. Such hardware is in many aspects identical to what much of the IoT research community is currently using; thus, the potential in

¹Department of Computer, Control and Management Engineering (DIAG), Sapienza University of Rome, Rome, Italy
²Research Unit 1, Computer Technology Institute and Press (CTI), Rio, Greece
³School of Applied Arts, Hellenic Open University, Patras, Greece
⁴Department of Computer Engineering and Informatics, University of Patras, Patras, Greece

combining recent results coming from the research community, with the educational activities already in the curricula of many schools, is promising.

In this context, this chapter deals with energy and environmental awareness as a part of school educational activities. This is handled in two ways: (a) by addressing energy footprint and energy consumption, via individual and group class activities, by using IoT sensors and gamification elements using real sensor data from familiar environments and recording changes in behavior that affect directly the energy consumption; and (b) to raise environmental awareness of the systemic nature of changes (affecting sustainability of ecosystems, climate, etc.), via a quest for inquiry and knowledge using data from sensors distributed across the European continent.

Several studies document the ability of students to influence choices made by their families related to environmental issues [2]. The research interviews conducted in [3] made clear that energy conservation insights learned in school can be applied at home by students and their families. Since about 27% of EU households include at least one child under the age of 18 [4], targeted efforts of reaching families of children and young people will scale further to reach a large portion of the EU population and multiply the benefits toward sustainability of the planet.

Having the above in mind, the aim is to provide a system for monitoring a fleet of educational buildings, enabling a number of different application and implementation aspects. In short, our system aims at the following properties:

- *Openness*, supporting a number of different IoT ecosystems,
- *Versatility*, supporting different application domains, e.g., energy efficiency and educational scenarios,
- *Scalability*, supporting a very large number of buildings and IoT sensing endpoints,
- *Up-to-date support of modern practices* in the design of the system, i.e., cloud-based solutions and easy deployment.

It is currently being used in 18 educational buildings in Europe in different countries, in the context of an EU-funded research project, called Green Awareness In Action (GAIA [5]).The system utilizes a number of different IoT technologies as infrastructure installed inside these school buildings (utilizing up to 850 sensors), while it follows an open, cloud-based approach for its implementation, which enables the development of applications on top of it. In its current setup, this deployment produces daily close to 400 MB of real-world sensor data, resulting in a yearly data volume of approximately 140 GB. Depending on the actual application domain in which such data are used, there is a lot of variance on the actual requirements for data granularity, i.e., sampling rate for generating data. For obtaining near real-time information on the building status, it is necessary to have a small sampling period, even in the scale of milliseconds, e.g., in the case of energy disaggregation. Similarly, usually an averaging scheme is used so that data storage and processing requirements are kept at low level, since more data-intensive aggregation methodologies increase the requirements for processing resources.

In this context, such a large-scale IoT infrastructure deployed at a large number of public and private buildings for a long period of time will generate, handle, transfer and store a tremendous amount of data, which cannot be processed in an efficient manner using current platforms and techniques. Since the community is gradually moving from vertical single-purpose solutions to multipurpose collaborative applications interacting across industry verticals, organizations and people, a cloud-based approach is utilized. The necessity for data collection, storage and availability across large areas, the demand for uninterrupted services even with intermittent cloud connectivity and resource constrained devices, along with the necessity of sometimes near-real-time data processing in an optimal manner, create a set of challenges where only holistic solutions apply.

The remaining chapter is structured as follows: in Section 3.2 previous and related work is presented briefly. The benefits of using data collected from IoT deployments in education are presented in Section 3.3. In Section 3.4, the high-level design of an IoT platform targeting educational activities is presented addressing the end-user requirements. Having in mind the design goals and end-user needs, in Section 3.5, the **GAIA** platform is presented, one among the very few IoT systems that have been developed with a focus on education. Specific implementation decisions are presented in detail, and indicators on the performance of the IoT platform are provided. Section 3.6 provides an analysis of the data collected from the **GAIA** platform in terms of the performance of the educational buildings. We conclude in Section 3.7.

3.2   Related work

The approach of promoting sustainable behavioral change through activities targeting the public building sector falls within the scope of several research projects. Recent examples like [6,7] focus on a variety of public buildings utilizing an IoT infrastructure over which applications like gamified experiences or blockchain-based transactions promote behavioral change among the occupants of such buildings. More focused on school buildings were the VERYSchool [8] and ZEMedS [9] projects, producing recommendation and optimization software components, or methodologies and tools. Reference [10] produced several guidelines and results regarding good energy saving practices in an educational setting. There is however a general lack of works focusing exclusively on the application of the IoT paradigm in an educational realm, in combination with large-scale real-world data. This exact aspect is examined in our work, aiming to combine energy savings and educational goals at the same time.

Overall, the proliferation of relatively cheap IoT hardware has led several parties to establish large-scale building infrastructures, leading to large data sets created and the inevitable exploration of a number of potential utilization of such data inside applications. Miller and Meggers [11] discuss an attempt to create a big data set for building data with respect to energy, while [12] presents an approach toward systems built over the use of big data from buildings. References [13,14] are two recent examples describing ways to utilize big data generated inside buildings in order to implement applications toward better thermal comfort and energy savings, respectively.

Certain aspects of the system, discussed here, place users in the monitoring loop as a first step toward raising awareness. This aspect, categorized as crowdsensing or participatory sensing [15] in which users collect relevant data for applications such as urban planning, public health and creative expression, aims at emphasizing the personalization factor of such systems, among other aspects. This approach has been employed by the Cornell Laboratory of Ornithology [16] in a science educational project on bird biology, while in [17], the authors describe trials for air quality, water quality and plant disease monitoring. Similarly to our context, [18] presents a solution combining a deployed and participatory sensing system for environmental monitoring. In [19], the authors discuss the value of participating to project like these for students, concluding that "Students are gaining deep domain-specific knowledge through their citizen science campaign, as well as broad general STEM knowledge through data-collection best practices, data analysis, scientific methods, and other areas specific to their project."

In the past, several approaches have been proposed in order to address the potentially huge number of sensor data arriving from the IoT domain, each one of them applied in different parts of the network architecture [20–23]. Starting from the low-end devices, the approach of in-network aggregation and data management has been proposed where sensor devices follow local coordination schemes in order to combine data coming from different sources and/or within the same time period based on similarities identified using data analysis. Usually, these techniques operate in combination with network-level routing protocols and/or lower level medium access control protocols [24]. For an overview of different techniques and existing protocols, see [25]. Since this approach relies on spatial and temporal correlation without taking into consideration semantic correlation of the data, very few theoretical algorithms are used in real-world deployment since they significantly limit the concurrent support of different high-level applications.

Information on the design aspects of the **GAIA** IoT platform presented in this chapter are available in [26]. Technical details for efficient stream processing of IoT data collected from school buildings utilizing edge resources are provided in [27]. The design of open-source hardware end devices for monitoring energy consumption and environmental conditions inside schools are presented in [28]. The use of IoT data generated inside school buildings for addressing behavioral change toward energy efficiency is discussed in [29]. The use of the open IoT platform for the development of a building management application is presented in [30].

3.3   IoT and real-world data in education

One approach for addressing the climate change problem is through the development and transfer of green technologies. In the context of reducing the energy spent in residential buildings, new technologies have been introduced improving the energy efficiency of buildings. In fact, till now the dominant approach was to use energy efficient infrastructure and materials to reduce energy consumption of buildings. However, the rates of construction of new buildings as well as the rates of renovation of existing buildings are both generally very low [31] to expect a significant effect on the total amount of energy spent in our everyday life at a global level. Similarly, the approach for reducing the energy consumption in transportation focuses on improving the energy efficiency of motor engines. Also here, given the rate of change of existing fleets with energy efficient one, it is very challenging to save energy in this sector through this approach [32].

An alternative approach, that has recently gathered attention, is the promotion of energy-consumption awareness and behavioral change on people. The main concept is that to address global climate change, people should be informed regarding mitigation actions and sustainable behaviors. In other words, it requires a change in citizens' behavior and practices [33]. Reports indicate that citizens making efficient use of energy in their everyday life can lead to large energy and financial savings, as well as potentially to a substantially positive environmental impact [33].

Raising awareness among young people and changing their behavior and habits concerning energy usage is the key to achieve sustained energy reductions. At EU level, people aged under 30 represent about a third of the total population [34]. Thus, by targeting this group of citizens, a larger part of the population is also affected. Additionally, young people are very sensitive to the protection of the environment, so raising awareness among children is much easier than other groups of citizens (e.g., attempts made to achieve behavioral change and establish new environment-friendly habits to children regarding recycling have had high success rates).

We argue that it is essential to operate an IoT platform that will on the one hand facilitate monitoring and profiling energy use of users and buildings and on the other hand will provide guidelines and recommendations for better energy management by users. Such a platform will increase the self-awareness of users regarding their energy use profile and by proper and continual recommendations will stimulate their behavior change toward more energy economical activities and habits.

3.3.1 End-user requirements

The main objective of environmental sustainability education and energy efficiency awareness is to make students aware that energy consumption is largely influenced by the sum of individual behaviors (at home, school, etc.) and that simple behavior changes and interventions in the building (e.g., replacing old lamps with energy efficient ones) can have a great impact on achieving energy savings. IoT technologies can support these initiatives by mediating people's interaction with the environment in order to provide immediate feedback and actually measure the impact of human actions while automating the implementation of energy savings policy and at the same time maintaining the comfort level perceived by people.

From the end-user point of view, the system aims to support different end-user groups. Within school buildings, there are several such groups: students, educators, building administrators. There is thus a need for the system's interface to provide services and information in a way that suits all of these different end users. In some cases, unifying different school buildings into a single view is necessary to make interaction simpler, make data visualization more natural and create an environment that conveys valuable insights and clear actions related to general as well as specific aspects of the participating building ecosystem. In other cases, the educational scenario requires differentiating each building or room within the building to stress the unique features and emphasize on the needs of each individual involved.

Teachers could potentially use collected data and analytics during class to explain to pupils basic phenomena related to the parameters monitored and organize student projects, where each student monitors specific environmental parameters at their home. In addition, collected IoT data could feed applications informing building managers about the energy profile performance of the building and specific equipment. Similarly, the IoT data collected in schools can be made available to the scientific community, so that studies can be performed on a common data set and results can be more easily compared. Monitoring school buildings situated in different countries can help, e.g., to identify usage or energy-consumption patterns. This, in turn, can be utilized to make comparisons or realize competitions through social networking and game applications (e.g., students of school A compete with students of school B in answering energy-awareness questions). The availability of actual measurements of environmental parameters, such as energy consumption, indoor and outdoor luminosity, temperature, noise and so on, also enables the realization of a number of diverse education-related applications and scenarios. For example, student engagement could be fostered via projects where students monitor environmental parameters at their class or home, or programming software using the data provided by the platform utilizing the available APIs.

3.3.2   IoT platform design aspects

In this section, the most fundamental goals of an IoT-based platform for real-time monitoring and management of public school buildings are presented.

The system's first goal is to build upon an IoT infrastructure that (a) spans throughout a big number of buildings and (b) spreads through several rooms, incorporating various kinds of sensors. Providing a uniform set of hardware devices for such a large number of building is very difficult, if not impossible. We expect the necessary IoT infrastructure to be deployed in phases—in each phase, the IoT infrastructure will be extended to cover additional buildings or introduce new sensors. It is therefore crucial to follow an open-standards approach throughout such a system; use open-source software, protocols *and* hardware components, in order to maximize the adaptability and reusability of the system.

Another important goal of a system deployed at such a scale and operating in real time is the need for quickly handling, storing and analyzing vast quantities of data collected from the IoT nodes. Providing an efficient software platform for data management will enable direct comparisons of energy efficiency between different buildings and cities, taking into account the environmental parameters as well, e.g., rain or low temperatures, helping users quantify their actions in terms of the respective impact to the environment.

Lastly, the system should be expandable and easy to interface with other systems or components. As examples, implementing a basic quiz-based approach to support school classes on sustainability or a serious game-based approach to learning are the ideas that can be augmented by using real-time data from our system. In terms of administration of an institutional infrastructure, interfacing with commercial products and new cloud-based services coming out of the research labs is absolutely necessary to make sure that the IoT infrastructure will not become obsolete.

3.4   Design aspects of an IoT platform targeting education activities

An IoT platform targeting educational activities should be based on the principle that continuous monitoring of the progress of students positively contributes toward reducing the energy consumption and successful behavior change. Since the IoT deployment is multisite and multicountry the data collected can be analyzed, for example, to identify energy consumption patterns in different countries and across different climate zones. This can be used to make comparisons or competitions; for instance, students of school A compete with students of school B in efficiency. This could also help understanding cultural differences with respect to energy efficiency awareness and sustainability.

Such an IoT platform needs to be designed to enable the easy and fast implementation of applications that utilize an IoT infrastructure. It should offer high scalability both in terms of users, number of connected devices and volume of data processed. The platform accommodates real-time processing of information collected from mobile sensors and smartphones and offers fast analytic services. The platform architecture is organized in three layers:

End-device level: It consists of IoT metering devices (electricity, heating, environment) deployed in educational buildings to feed the system information relating to their energy consumption and the indoor/outdoor environmental conditions.

IT service ecosystem level: It comprises the overall system with the capacity to store, manage, analyze and visualize data regarding the behavior of users, the ambient conditions of the buildings and the energy consumption. This level consists of a set of services, exposed through a specially designed set of APIs for data acquiring, storage and diffusion, user and building modeling/profiling, data visualization and user recommendation. On top of these services, GAIA offers end-user applications to engage users.

User involvement level: It consists of end-user applications for providing data analytics and recommendations to the targeted user groups, social networking applications and an educational game for students.

3.4.1   End-device level

A diverse set of deployed devices constitute the end-device level organized in four main categories: (a) classroom environmental comfort sensors (devices within classrooms), (b) atmospheric sensors (devices positioned outdoors), (c) weather stations (devices positioned on rooftops) and (d) power consumption meters (devices attached to the main breakout box of the buildings, measuring energy consumption). For a graphical representation of the different sensing types used throughout the end-device level, see Figure 3.1.

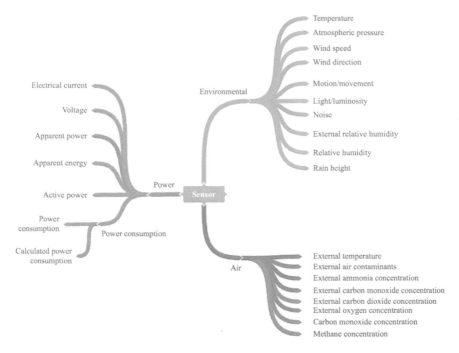

Figure 3.1   The sensing capabilities of an IoT platform targeting school buildings

The end devices that are deployed indoors form wireless networks (802.15.4 or Wi-Fi) and communicate with their respective edge devices by establishing ad hoc multihop bidirectional trees, setup in the time of the deployment and maintained throughout the network lifetime. The end devices deployed outdoors are connected either via power over Ethernet cables to transfer both electricity and maintain communication over a single cable, or they have a Wi-Fi network connection and are supplied with batteries and solar panels to harvest energy from the sun.

3.4.2   IT service ecosystem level

A key principle is to foster education and experimentation activities leveraging the availability of actual measurements of environmental parameters, such as energy consumption, indoor and outdoor luminosity, temperature and noise. The IT service ecosystem allows to feed end-user applications with such monitoring data in order to enhance educational processes with data from real-life scenarios. The system hides the heterogeneity of sensors deployment to end-user applications by managing the communication with the sensor infrastructures through dedicated software modules, handling and storing data according to a uniform model and offering such data to applications through uniform interfaces. When a new school is added to the system, existing applications can easily access sensors' data with only some minor reconfiguration. Moreover, measurements provided by sensors may need some processing to become meaningful and usable by end-user applications. Therefore, filtering, reduction and formatting operations are performed on raw data flows acquired by networks of sensors to transform them in information that is suitable for storage and higher level processing.

3.4.3   User involvement level

Including the users in the loop of monitoring, their daily energy consumption is a first step toward raising awareness. In an educational environment, this step can be further enhanced and capitalized in the framework of educational activities with the support of the application offered at the user-involvement level. In essence, the application set complements an educational approach that encourages customization to the specific requirements of each school, where each school can "fine-tune" which tools are used, when and for how long, during a school year. Overall, the educational activities in each school are based on the data produced within the respective buildings, while the effects of changing certain behaviors can be detected and quantified.

Educational-building-management system is a multi-school BMS developed using the API exposed by the IT service ecosystem. Building managers are able to inspect real-time energy usage, see results from a comparison with similar buildings or within the same building during different time periods (e.g., previous years), and receive energy efficiency recommendations.

Participatory sensing application offers a way to complement the existing IoT infrastructure (end-device level) and provide additional data from the school buildings monitored by the system. Smartphones and tablets are used to provide additional readings from inside the school building, e.g., luminosity or noise levels, while participants can also manually enter data such as electricity meter readings. The teacher can initiate participatory sensing sessions during the courses from the main portal of the project, and then students can use phones and tablets to gather data in real time and then review them in class.

In-class activities and gamification applications with an educational focus have been implemented to support educational content based on the data produced by the IoT infrastructure inside the monitored school buildings. These are based on the fact that students are more driven to engage in class activities regarding sustainability and energy efficiency when the data utilized originates from their environment and are near real time. The activities are built around a sensor kit that the students use to build a small interactive installation that visualizes environmental and energy consumption data from school classrooms.

3.5   The **GAIA** IoT platform

The **GAIA** real-world IoT deployment is spread in three countries (Greece, Italy, Sweden), monitoring in real-time 18 school buildings in terms of electricity consumption and indoor and outdoor environmental conditions. Given the diverse building characteristics and usage requirements, the deployments vary from school to school (e.g., in number of sensors, hardware manufacturer, networking technology and communication protocols for delivering sensor data). The IoT devices used are either open-design IoT nodes (based on the Arduino popular electronics prototyping platform, see [28]) or off-the-shelf products acquired from IoT device manufacturers. The data collected is used as part of series of educational scenarios whose goal is to educate, influence and attempt to transform the behavior of elementary school students through a series of trials conducted in the educational environment and in homes. Feedback mechanisms notify the students on current energy consumption at school and in this way assist toward raising awareness regarding environmental effects of energy spending and promote energy literacy by educating the users.

The cloud services offer real-time processing and analysis of unlimited IoT data streams with minimal delay and processing costs. Storage services use state-of-the-art solutions like NoSQL and time series databases to ensure maximum scalability and minimal response times. In more detail, the cloud services deliver a set of services that are critical for all IoT installations:

Continuous computation engine provides real-time, fast and reliable processing of data collected from IoT devices, smartphones and web services. The computation engine is capable of processing a large amount of data collected from sensor nodes within just seconds.

Online analytics engine operates on the data produced by the continuous processing engine. The post-processing of the data is done to support business intelligence. The online analytics engine allows to organize large volumes of data and visualize them from different points of view.

End-to-end security is established across the components of the architecture. All supported services are compliant with the current standards for Internet security. Communication throughout the service infrastructure is encrypted using data encryption standards like Advanced Encryption Standard (AES) and Transport Layer Security (TLS)/Secure Sockets Layer (SSL) technologies.

Access management and authorization is managed in real-time down to specific user, device or time of day.

Data storage and replay services are responsible for the persistence of all data entering the system in their original format and associated with the output of the continuous processing engine and online analytics engine. Data streams can be forwarded at a later time to different components. Off-line processing of data is facilitated for archiving services or for bench-marking different versions of components.

The services described above can be accessed via a well-defined set of APIs. The data API comprises real-time data API and historical data API. Historical data API allows retrieval of historical data registered into the platform by any device and also aggregated summaries (maximum values, minimum values, average values). Real-time data API is a streaming API which gives low latency access to new data registered to the platform. Directory API and AA (authentication/authorization) API describe how to create and manage devices, users and authorization roles.

3.5.1   Continuous computation engine

The continuous computation engine is a central part of the system architecture and is responsible for the timely processing of the streaming data arriving from the sensors

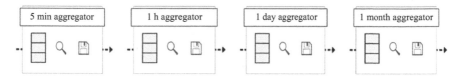

Figure 3.2   Analytics process chain

deployed across all the buildings. It is composed by a *message bus* receiving all the messages arriving from the sensors, the *process engine* which provides the analytics and the *storage system* which is used for storing those results. The process engine receives events from multiple sensors and executes aggregate operations on these events. The output of the engine is stored at the *storage system*.

Sensors and actuators produce (periodically or asynchronously) events that are sent to the *continuous computation engine* via a message bus. Those events are usually tuples of pairs: value and timestamp. All data received are collected and forwarded to a specific queue where they get processed in real time by the *process engine*. The *process engine* supports a number of processing topologies based on the data type of the sensor. Each processing topology is responsible for a unique type of sensor such as general measurement sensors (temperature, wind speed, etc.), actuators and power-measurement sensors. The produced analytics are outputted into *summaries*, stored permanently within the *data storage* service.

The *process engine* is composed by processing topologies for every type of sensor. Each topology has the ability to be easily modified in order to accommodate aggregation operations. The processing topology comprises *Aggregator* steps that are responsible for the analysis of the data based on specific time intervals. Each processing topology aggregates data for specific time intervals (see Figure 3.2). An *aggregator* stores all the events of the time interval, and for each new incoming event, it processes (using functions such as min/max/mean) all the stored values of this interval. After this process, it updates the existing interval value which is used by the next process level.

Events which enter the continuous computation engine are processed consecutively. First, the processing topology performs aggregation operations on the streaming data, i.e., for a temperature sensor, the engine will calculate the average values of the 5 min interval (see Figure 3.3) and it will store it to memory and disk for further process (when the processing topology receives more than one events for the same 5 min interval, it calculates the average of those events). Every consecutive 5 min interval aggregate is kept in memory (topology keeps 48 interval values k for 5 min, hour, day, month intervals for each device)/stored by the *data storage* service. Next step is to update the hour intervals. The processing topology updates the 5 min intervals inside the buffer of the hour processor and stores the average of those 5 min intervals.

The process is similar for the daily processor, but the topology also stores the max/min of the day (based on hour intervals). Same for monthly and yearly processors. For power-consumption sensors, the scheme (topologies inside Storm) is the same with the difference that the topology calculates and stores power consumption. Aggregators are used to perform aggregation operations on input streaming data. The topologies use aggregation for *power-consumption calculation* (calculate the power

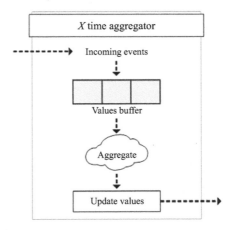

Figure 3.3 Aggregator module

consumption of the stream values), *sum calculation* (summarize the streaming values), *average calculation* (calculate the average of the streaming values).

An important characteristic for evaluating the performance for the system is the load of data the system is able process at any given time. Having in mind the current setup, the fleet of buildings in the system produces an average of 25 measurements per second. The current data-processing topology runs on a single core virtual machine (on an Intel i5-3340 host) with 4 GB of RAM. With this configuration and setup, the system is capable of processing up to 500 measurements per second. To sustain a potential increase in the number of measurements, our system can support two different options:

- Increase the computing power of the virtual machine, by assigning it to a more powerful host or giving access to more resources from the host machine.
- Deploy a second instance of the processing topology that is capable to consume the same number of measurements to reach the required data-processing rates.

Based on the nature of sensor deployed in our system input data require three different types of aggregation: (a) averaging for sensors like temperature or relative humidity, (b) total for sensors like rain height levels and (c) power consumption estimating based on the electrical current values received from the installation. Each type of processing requires a different type of aggregation processing and as a result has a different average execution latency, presented in Table 3.1.

3.5.2 Data access and acquisition

The platform provides a unified API for retrieving data from multiple sites and multiple hardware platforms transparently. Each hardware device integrated to our platform is mapped to a *resource*. Resources are self-described entities and are also software/hardware agnostic. The data API acts as a wrapper function and hides much of the lower level plumbing of hardware specific API calls for querying and retrieving

Table 3.1 *Execution latency statistics for the three different aggregation types used in our system*

Aggregation type	Execution latency (ms)	Measurements (%)
Average	0.608	86.4
Total	0.799	0.9
Power consumption	0.329	12.7

data and provides a common API for retrieving historical or real-time data from resources in a transparent manner.

To facilitate integration between the existing hardware and software technologies, the exchange of the information occurs through *API mappers*. The API mapper acts as a translation proxy for data acquisition, and it is responsible for polling the devices infrastructure through proprietary APIs and translating the received measurements in a ready to process form for the platform. In general, the API mapper transforms data to and from the API. The data input type can be based on each device capabilities, poll based and/or push-based. In more details, the API mapper is capable to receive data from the IoT devices but also to send messages/commands to the devices. Furthermore, according to the system design, the API mappers introduce scalability and modularity in the platform. The solution offers two separate types of API mappers for integrating with external services and to retrieve IoT sensor data: (a) polling API mapper and (b) message bus API mapper. Both solutions will be used in order to integrate with data originating from IoT installation.

The first solution (polling API mapper) is based on polling. A usage example is the following: weather stations are installed in a subset of available school buildings. Data produced by such stations are accessible through the SynField application that provides historical information through a RESTful API provided by the SynField back-end. In order to integrate them in our platform, a SynField API Mapper was implemented for the SynField API based on the polling API mapper. The SynField API is polled every 5 min for updated data. When new data are found, they are formatted to the internal format of the platform and forwarded to the processing/analytics engine for processing and analysis using the AMQP protocol. The data are then processed and can be accessed from the data API. Similar implementations based on the polling API mapper can be used to integrate IoT devices provided by third parties and existing BMSs in school buildings.

The second solution is used when a pub/sub solution exists in the external service to be integrated. In this case, the external service is capable of publishing the IoT data (generated or gathered) to an MQTT endpoint. The API mapper is then able to receive new measurements asynchronously and format them to the internal format of our platform. The data are then forwarded to the **GAIA** processing/analytics engine for processing and analysis using the AMQP protocol. The data are then processed and can be accessed from the **GAIA** data API. Messages inside the MQTT broker can

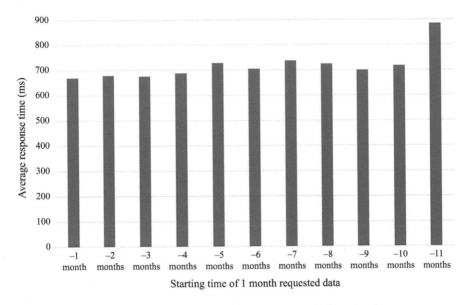

*Figure 3.4   Average response time for accessing 1 month data for the past year
(daily aggregated values)*

be transferred in multiple formats ranging from plain text to any open or proprietary protocol. In our case, messages are transmitted in plain text following a simple format: the topic of the message refers to the device and sensor that generated the message, while the actual payload represents the value generated. For example, if a sensor with a hardware (MAC) address `124B00061ED466` publishes a temperature value of 20 degrees, the topic is `124B00061ED466/temperature` and the message `20`. All sensors forward their measurements periodically (every 30 s) or on events (i.e., when motion is detected) and the API mapper receives them and forwards to the processing engine.

Accessing historical data is crucial for building monitoring applications. Users tend to search for and compare historical data from different time spans and areas of the buildings. In such use cases, it is important that an IoT service is capable of providing these data without delays independently of the targeted time interval. As discussed in [35], application response times larger than 10 s tend to make users lose their attention in the given task, while a 1 s response time is considered the limit for users that are freely navigating an application without waiting for the application's response. In that context, when presenting power-consumption statistics, for example, over the past year, it is important to be able to retrieve and present the stored values in under 1 s independently of the requested interval (latest values versus older values). In Figures 3.4 and 3.5, we present average retrieve times for accessing historical data of 1 month duration for the past 12 months, observing minimal differences in the access times independent of the period requested.

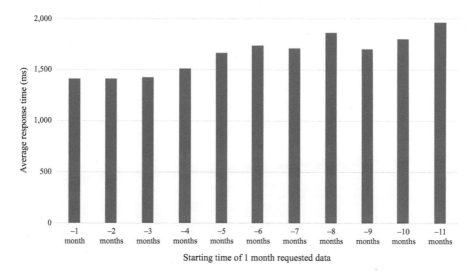

Figure 3.5   Average response time for accessing 1 month data for the past year (hourly aggregated values)

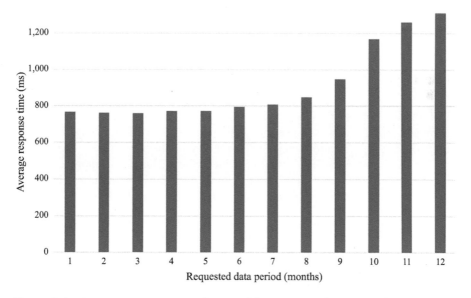

Figure 3.6   Average response time for variable time periods ranging from 1 to 12 months

Note that the data available from the graphs that the response time of our service is independent of the actual time interval, while it is actually dependent on the amount of data requested. This is more clear in Figure 3.6 where it is observed that response times tend to increase as the response times increase when we reach time periods of more than 9 months of data.

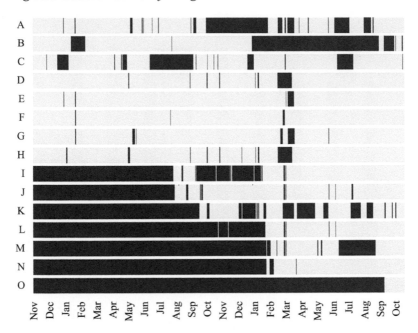

Figure 3.7   Data availability per school building

3.6   Using IoT-generated big data in educational buildings

Ensuring the energy efficiency and sustainable operation of school buildings is an extremely complex process since each building has vastly different characteristics in terms of size, age, location, construction, thermal behavior and user communities. IoT platforms can provide quantitative evidence to evaluate and improve organizational and managerial measures. Some aspects of the business value and benefits of analyzing the data collected from the IoT platform are presented in this section.

3.6.1   High-level IoT data analysis

The IoT deployment of the **GAIA** platform is continuously expanding to include additional school buildings. The collected data was analyzed to determine the variety of the sensors supported and their points of sensing (POS), the velocity of data arriving at the cloud infrastructure as well as the variability of the data collected.

During this initial high-level analysis, it became apparent that the data collected from the IoT devices was not always delivered properly to the cloud. As a first step toward understanding the availability of measurements, Figure 3.7 is included that depicts the availability of measurements on a daily basis, organized based on the site of deployment. A single dark point signifies missing data for the specific on a specific day, while a white part signifies complete availability (i.e., according to the sensing rate of the specific sensor). This visualization shows the stability of the

Table 3.2 Data availability per school building

Site	POS	Sensors	Start time	Outages (%)	Outliers (%)
A	8	43	2015-Oct	17.78	2.67
B	9	56	2015-Oct	28.26	2.84
C	6	32	2015-Oct	13.63	2.82
D	9	50	2015-Oct	2.33	1.45
E	7	43	2015-Oct	1.19	1.63
F	11	54	2015-Oct	0.96	3.36
G	7	45	2015-Oct	1.69	1.33
H	6	27	2015-Oct	6.01	1.31
I	7	36	2016-Sep	12.23	1.68
J	34	103	2016-Apr	3.97	3.19
K	5	26	2016-Sep	15.87	1.7
L	5	109	2016-Oct	36.43	1.22
M	5	24	2017-Feb	23.09	2.67
N	12	55	2017-Feb	1.31	5.09
O	4	22	2017-Sep	0	13.22

IoT deployment. In almost all deployments, there are values missing almost on a daily level. Essentially, these measurements are missing either because they were never reported to the cloud infrastructure or due to a failure occurring while they were processed and stored by the cloud services. In the first case, network failures occur either due to a packet transmission error at the wireless network level (i.e., IEEE 802.15.4 or Wi-Fi) or due to a transmission error while an intermediate gateway transmitted the data to the cloud infrastructure over the Internet. Since the access to the measurements is done through the **GAIA** platform API, the reason for the missing information is completely unknown. However, as it will become evident in the following sections, specific data-mining techniques can be used to overcome the problem of missing values.

A second step for the high-level analysis is to examine the actual values received from the IoT devices. It is very common in the relevant literature to deploy relatively low-cost devices that produce low-quality measurements or are not properly calibrated. For this reason, we examined the values to identify possible outliers, that is, observation points that are distant from the historic values. Such observations may be due to transient errors occurring on the sensing equipment and should be excluded from the data set. The identification of outliers is based on the *interquartile range (IQR)* using the upper and lower quartiles Q_3 (75th percentile) and Q_1 (25th percentile). The lower boundary is set to $Q_1 - 3 \times IQR$ and the upper bounder is set to $Q_3 + 3 \times IQR$ where $IQR = Q_3 - Q_1$. The values are examined per sensor/site basis using a timed-window of size W. If the a value is outside the boundaries $[Q_1 - 3 \times IQR, Q_3 + 3 \times IQR]$, it is flagged as an outlier. In the following sections, we replace it with the minimum or the maximum value observed during the time window W. After examining the values characterized as outliers, two distinct cases

Table 3.3   Data availability per sensor type

Name	POS	Sensors	Inactive (%)	Outlier (%)
Environmental	101	505	14.62	7.76
Atmospheric	7	56	19.56	6.29
Weather	7	28	20.25	0.95
Power	20	56	12.55	4.17

were identified: (a) 0 values which were clearly sensor error rather than natural events (e.g., humidity of 0%, temperature dropping from $\sim$20 to 0) and (b) drastic changes of power consumption (i.e., spikes or fast drops) that could not be justified by the daily school activities.

In Table 3.2, the different school sites are summarized indicating the time when they were incorporated in the GAIA platform. For each school building, the number of POS are listed along with the total number of sensors deployed. The table reports the percentage of outages recorded for the particular site (reflecting the periods during which no measurements were received from it, as a percentage of the period from when it was first incorporated to the platform), the total number of measurements received from this site, along with the percentage of values that have been identified as outliers. In order to avoid issues related to the confidentiality of data, the names of the school buildings have been omitted.

The analysis reveals that certain buildings experience data outages very often. At a second level, the same analysis of data is repeated based on the type of sensor. For each device category, the percentage of outages and the percentage of outliers observed are reported in Table 3.3. In Figure 3.8, the availability of data is depicted on a daily basis for each sensor separately organized by sensor category. Based on this, one observes that all sensors experience periodic loss of data. This may be justified by the wireless networking technology used to interconnect the sensors located in the classrooms, as reported in [26]. Apparently, the low-power, lossy nature of the networking technologies used results to a significant data loss.

To overcome the fact that the IoT deployment (a) experiences outages on a regular basis, and (b) at a significantly lower rate, sensors report values characterized as outliers, a moving window average technique is used. The moving window (a) smooths out short-term fluctuations for the case of outliers and (b) fills-in missing values using a simple local algorithm that introduces historic values to fill in the missing data for the specific time period. The moving window average also helps to highlight longer term trends on the sensor values. Figure 3.9 depicts an example of the analysis conducted over a specific temperature sensor located in a classroom.

3.6.2   Thermal comfort of classrooms

Examining the classrooms' temperature is a measure of understanding the conditions under which students and teachers operate. Hot, stuffy rooms—and cold, drafty

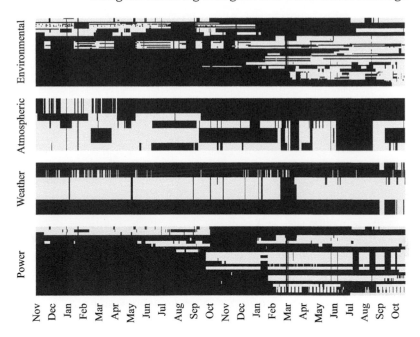

Figure 3.8   Data availability per sensor type

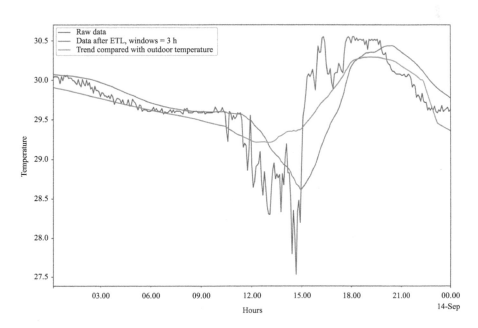

Figure 3.9   Temperature sensor time series processing

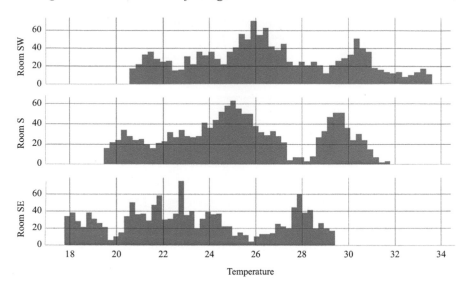

*Figure 3.10   Indoor temperature histogram for 3 classrooms during 2017-Sep to
2017-Oct*

ones—reduce attention span and limit productivity. In Figure 3.10, a histogram is provided for the indoor temperature of three classrooms (facing south, south-west and
south-east) examined during a period of 2 months. Lower temperatures are observed
in the room facing South-East, in contrast to the other two. Evaluating the indoor
conditions requires considering also other factors related to the environment, such as
humidity (e.g., excessively high humidity levels contribute to mold and mildew), as
well as what students are wearing (depending on the period of the year).

A common approach to examine the indoor conditions of the classrooms is in
terms of the *thermal comfort*. The ANSI/ASHRAE Standard 55, Thermal Environmental Conditions for Human Occupancy [36] is defined to specify the combinations
of indoor thermal environmental factors and personal factors that will produce thermal environmental conditions acceptable to the majority of the occupants of an area.
Thermal comfort is primarily a function of the temperature and relative humidity in
a room, but many other factors affect it, such as the airspeed and the temperature
of the surrounding surfaces. Furthermore, thermal comfort is strongly influenced by
how a specific room is designed (e.g., amount of heat the walls and roof gain or lose,
amount of sunlight the windows let in, whether the windows can be opened or not)
and the effectiveness of the HVAC system.

The analysis presented here is done based only on the quantitative information
provided by the IoT deployment of the **GAIA** project, we applied a simple approach
that is able to provide an estimate under the lack of all the necessary data. For this
reason, the CBE Thermal Comfort Tool for ASHRAE-55 [37] was used to evaluate
the thermal comfort of classrooms. Under the *adaptive method* provided, thermal
comfort is computed as a function of the indoor temperature, the outdoor temperature

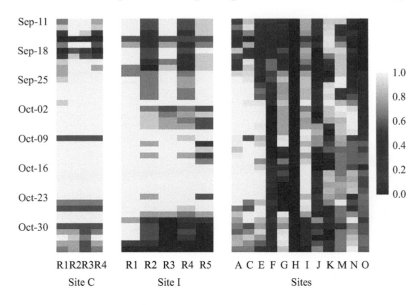

Figure 3.11 Site thermal comfort during 2017-Sep to 2017-Oct

along with the outside air wind speed. The outside conditions (temperature, airspeed) were acquired by the *WeatherMap* service that also provides historical data. For each different classroom, the thermal comfort is computed for each different hour during the operation of the school (from 08.30 to 16.30). In the sequel, the individual values are averaged over each different day. A classroom with a daily comfort of 1.0 signifies that during all hours, the conditions where within the comfort zone defined by this particular formula, while a daily comfort of 0.0 signifies that during all hours, the conditions were outside the comfort zone.

On the right side of Figure 3.11, a summary of all the sites participating in the **GAIA** platform is provided for a period of 2 months (from 2017-Sep to 2017-Oct). On the left side, the individual thermal comfort of the classrooms of site C is compared with those of site I. Site C achieved the highest comfort in contrast to site I that achieved the lowest. One reason for the difference is the actual location of the school, site C being the school located on the southern point in contrast to site I which is one of the northern points. Apart from the external weather conditions, other reasons affect thermal comfort, e.g., such as the construction materials. In the following section, data-mining techniques are applied in order to identify in more detail classrooms with poor performance or user-related activities that may also affect thermal comfort.

3.6.3 Classroom thermal performance

Several factors affect the internal classroom temperature ranging from the local weather conditions to the orientation of the room, the construction materials used (e.g., the insulation, windows) and also the position of the radiators within the classrooms.

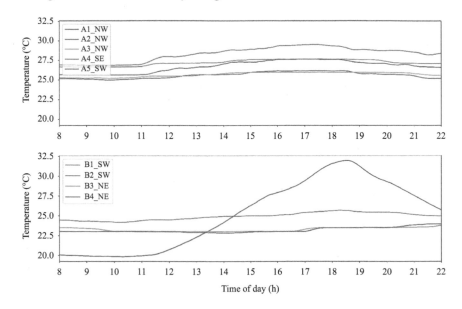

Figure 3.12   Classroom temperature during 30-Sep (Saturday)

The **GAIA** platform includes school buildings located in different climatic zones, constructed in different years ranging from 1950 to 2000, using diverse materials and with different heating and ventilation systems. Unfortunately, such information is not available in an open format so that they can be incorporated via data-integration techniques. In this section, data-mining techniques are used to derive information regarding the thermal efficiency of the classrooms using the quantitative data collected from the IoT deployment.

The goal of the analysis is to identify classrooms with poor thermal performance. One of the leading factors affecting temperature in classrooms is orientation. During a sunny day, at mid-day, the classrooms experience the highest temperatures. We can also see (Figure 3.10) that classrooms facing toward the south-west are exposed to the sun for longer periods, thus maintaining higher temperatures for longer than classrooms with a different orientation. In order to factor in the potential contribution of the sun, the time-series of the temperature sensors are examined in correlation with the external temperature, the cloud coverage, as well as the orientation of the classrooms.

A second important factor that affects the internal temperature of classrooms is the daily activities of the students and teachers. Opening and closing the door, the windows and the window blinds have an immediate effect on the temperature. For example, when a window is open, there is a temperature drop of about 2°C. In order to overcome these effects, the performance of the classrooms is examined only during weekends when there are no school activities.

Given the above considerations, we examine temperature in each room to identify poorly performing classrooms. In Figure 3.12, two specific performance issues

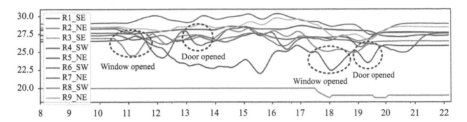

Figure 3.13   Activity in classrooms and effect on temperature

regarding two schools located in the same city are depicted. The first issue is related to the bottom figure, where room R1 achieves very poor performance with temperature starting very low at 20°C and increases up to 32°C within 8 h. The second issue is related with the top figure, where the south-west facing classroom (R5) and the south-east facing classroom (R4) have an increase of 2 degrees during the day, while all the other rooms are not affected. Even the south-west facing room R2 of the bottom figure does not have such an increase during the day. After contacting the school-building managers, it was reported that (a) room R1 (bottom school) is located outside the main building, within a prefab room with poor insulation, and (b) rooms of top school have no window blinds installed, in contrast to the bottom school where window blinds are installed in all rooms. These are just examples of the results of the analysis conducted. We expect that such an analysis can provide strong evidence on how to improve the performance of schools.

A second goal of the analysis is to understand how certain user activities affect the indoor quality of classrooms. The performance of the rooms during weekends when there is no user activity is compared with days of similar external conditions (temperature, cloud coverage) when students are present. In Figure 3.13, the temperature of the classrooms of a specific school is shown. The figure includes annotations for four instances demonstrating the impact of opening/closing the classroom door and windows. It is evident that these four specific events have an immediate impact on the temperature, with the window-related events having a greater impact. Automatic identification of such events in real time may be important for teachers to understand when to open the windows and doors for fresh air to circulate in the classroom. Automatic notifications can be sent when the thermal comfort of a classroom is outside a certain range in order to reduce the temperature (e.g., by opening door/windows).

3.7   Conclusions

In this chapter, the use of IoT sensors in educational environments was discussed. An education-focused real-world IoT deployment in schools in Europe can help promote sustainability and energy awareness. The chapter presents how installing IoT sensors inside school environments and making them available to students and other stakeholders of the educational community can aid in pursuing goals with respect to environmental education and science curricula alike. Large data sets, in particular, are being acquired from classrooms inside school buildings, subject to subsequent data analysis. Results of such analysis has, in turn, prompted human actions onto the actual environment, in order to achieve a more comfortable environment (i.e., indoor comfort levels) in a more energy-efficient manner. By using this infrastructure and the data it produces, we can build tools that better reflect the everyday reality inside school buildings, providing a more meaningful feedback. An interesting future research direction for the IoT infrastructure is to cater for monitoring additional environmental parameters apart from energy consumption, for example, in order to collect data to further promote sustainability awareness and behavioral change, and such big data sets be utilized in educational scenario.

Acknowledgments

This work has been supported by the European Commission and EASME, under H2020 and contract number 696029. This document reflects only the authors' view and the EC and EASME are not responsible for any use that may be made of the information it contains.

References

[1] Chatzigiannakis I, Mylonas G, and Vitaletti A. Urban Pervasive Applications: Challenges, Scenarios and Case Studies. Computer Science Review. 2011; 5(1):103–118.

[2] Schelly C, Cross JE, Franzen WS, *et al.* How to Go Green: Creating a Conservation Culture in a Public High School through Education, Modeling, and Communication. Journal of Environmental Education. 2012;43(3):143–161.

[3] Crosby K, and Metzger AB. Powering Down: A Toolkit for Behavior-Based Energy Conservation in K-12 Schools. Washington DC, USA: U.S. Green Building Council (USGBC); 2012.

[4] Statistical Office of the European Union (Eurostat). Household Structure in the EU. Statistical Office of the European Union (Eurostat); 2010. ISBN: 978-92-79-16760-7.

[5] GAIA (Green Awareness In Action): EU-funded H2020 project, H2020-EE-2015-2-RIA call and contract no 696029, (accessed on February 1, 2018). http://gaia-project.eu.

[6] Papaioannou TG, Dimitriou N, Vasilakis K, *et al.* An IoT-Based Gamified Approach for Reducing Occupants Energy Wastage in Public Buildings. Sensors. 2018;18(2), 537; https://doi.org/10.3390/s18020537.

[7] Fotopoulou E, Zafeiropoulos A, Terroso-Senz F, *et al.* Providing Personalized Energy Management and Awareness Services for Energy Efficiency in Smart Buildings. Sensors. 2017;17(9), 2054; Available from: https://doi.org/10.3390/s17092054.

[8]   Brogan M, and Galata A. The VERYSchool Project: Valuable EneRgY for a Smart School – Intelligent ISO 50001 Energy Management Decision Making in School Buildings. In: Proceedings of the Special Tracks and Workshops at the 11th International Conference on Artificial Intelligence Applications and Innovations (AIAI 2015), Bayonne, France; 2015. pp. 46–58.

[9]   Gaitani N, Cases L, Mastrapostoli E, *et al.* Paving the Way to Nearly Zero Energy Schools in Mediterranean Region – ZEMedS Project. Energy Procedia. 2015;78:3348–3353. 6th International Building Physics Conference, IBPC 2015.

[10] School of the Future: EU-funded FP7 project, (accessed on February 1, 2018). http://www.school-of-the-future.eu/.

[11] Miller C, and Meggers F. The Building Data Genome Project: An Open, Public Data Set From Non-Residential Building Electrical Meters. Energy Procedia. 2017;122C:439–444.

[12] Linder L, Vionnet D, Bacher JP, *et al.* Big Building Data – A Big Data Platform for Smart Buildings. Energy Procedia. 2017;122:589–594.

[13] Peng Y, Rysanek A, Nagy Z, *et al.* Using Machine Learning Techniques for Occupancy-Prediction-Based Cooling Control in Office Buildings. Applied Energy. 1 February 2018;211:1343–1358.

[14] Batra N, Singh A, and Whitehouse K. If You Measure It, Can You Improve It? Exploring The Value of Energy Disaggregation. In: Proceedings of the 2nd ACM International Conference on Embedded Systems for Energy-Efficient Built Environments. BuildSys '15. New York, NY, USA: ACM; 2015.

[15] Burke J, Estrin D, Hansen M, *et al.* Participatory Sensing. In: Workshop on World-Sensor-Web (WSW06): Mobile Device Centric Sensor Networks and Applications; 2006. pp. 117–134.

[16] Brossard D, Lewenstein B, and Bonney R. Scientific Knowledge and Attitude Change: The Impact of a Citizen Science Project. International Journal of Science Education. 2005;27(9):1099–1121.

[17] Kotovirta V, Toivanen T, Tergujeff R, *et al.* Participatory Sensing in Environmental Monitoring – Experiences. In: 2012 6th International Conference on Innovative Mobile and Internet Services in Ubiquitous Computing; 2012.

[18] Sun W, Li Q, and Tham CK. Wireless Deployed and Participatory Sensing System for Environmental Monitoring. In: 2014 11th Annual IEEE International Conference on Sensing, Communication, and Networking (SECON); 2014.

[19] Heggen S. Participatory Sensing: Repurposing a Scientific Tool for STEM Education. Interactions. 2013;20(1):18–21.

[20] Chatzigiannakis I, Mylonas G, and Nikoletseas SE. 50 Ways to Build Your Application: A Survey of Middleware and Systems for Wireless Sensor Networks. In: IEEE International Conference on Emerging Technologies and Factory Automation ETFA. IEEE; 2007. pp. 466–473.

[21] Chatzigiannakis I, Mylonas G, and Nikoletseas SE. jWebDust: A Java-Based Generic Application Environment for Wireless Sensor Networks. In: IEEE International Conference on Distributed Computing in Sensor Systems

DCOSS. vol. 3560 of Lecture Notes in Computer Science. Springer; 2005. pp. 376–386.

[22] Chatzigiannakis I, Hasemann H, Karnstedt M, *et al.* True Self-Configuration for the IoT. In: 3rd IEEE International Conference on the Internet of Things, IOT 2012, Wuxi, Jiangsu Province, China, October 24–26, 2012. IEEE; 2012. pp. 9–15.

[23] Akribopoulos O, Chatzigiannakis I, Koninis C, *et al.* A Web Services-Oriented Architecture for Integrating Small Programmable Objects in the Web of Things. In: 2010 Developments in E-Systems Engineering; 2010. pp. 70–75.

[24] Chatzigiannakis I, Kinalis A, and Nikoletseas SE. Power Conservation Schemes for Energy Efficient Data Propagation in Heterogeneous Wireless Sensor Networks. In: Proceedings 38th Annual Simulation Symposium (ANSS-38 2005), 4–6 April 2005, San Diego, CA, USA; 2005. pp. 60–71.

[25] Fasolo E, Rossi M, Widmer J, *et al.* In-Network Aggregation Techniques for Wireless Sensor Networks: A Survey. Wireless Communications. 2007; 14(2):70–87. Available from: http://dx.doi.org/10.1109/MWC.2007.358967.

[26] Amaxilatis D, Akrivopoulos O, Mylonas G, *et al.* An IoT-Based Solution for Monitoring a Fleet of Educational Buildings Focusing on Energy Efficiency. Sensors. 2017;17(10). Available from: http://www.mdpi.com/1424-8220/17/10/2296.

[27] Akrivopoulos O, Amaxilatis D, Chatzigiannakis I, *et al.* Enabling Stream Processing for People-Centric IoT Based on the Fog Computing Paradigm. In: 2017 IEEE 22nd International Conference on Emerging Technologies and Factory Automation (ETFA); 2017. pp. 1–8.

[28] Pocero L, Amaxilatis D, Mylonas G, *et al.* Open Source IoT Meter Devices for Smart and Energy-Efficient School Buildings. HardwareX. 2017. Available from: http://www.sciencedirect.com/science/article/pii/S2468067216300293.

[29] Mylonas G, Amaxilatis D, Helen L, *et al.* Addressing Behavioral Change towards Energy Efficiency in European Educational Buildings. In: Global Internet of Things Summit (GIoTS), 2017; 2017.

[30] Zacharioudakis E, Leligou HC, and Papadopoulou A. Energy Efficiency Tools for Residential Users. In: 21st Int. Conf. on Circuits, Systems, Communications and Computers, Crete Island, Greece; 2017.

[31] Economidou M, Atanasiu B, Despret C, *et al.* Europe's Buildings Under the Microscope: A Country-By-Country Review of the Energy Performance of Buildings. Buildings Performance Institute Europe (BPIE); 2011.

[32] Capros P, Mantzos L, Papandreou V, *et al.* European Energy and Transport Trends to 2030. In: Office for Official Publications of the European Communities: Institute of Communication and Computer Systems of the National Technical University of Athens (ICCS-NTUA), E3M-Lab, Greece Prepared for the Directorate-General for Energy and Transport; 2008.

[33] Achieving Energy Efficiency Through Behaviour Change: What Does it Take? In: European Environment Agency (EEA); 2013. ISSN 1725-2237. Available from: https://www.eea.europa.eu/publications/achieving-energy-efficiency-through-behaviour/file.

[34]   Key Data on Education in Europe 2012. Education, Audiovisual and Culture Executive Agency (EACEA P9 Eurydice, EUROSTAT); 2012. ISBN 978-92-9201-242-7.

[35]   Card SK, Robertson GG, and Mackinlay JD. The Information Visualizer, An Information Workspace. In: CHI '91 Proceedings of the SIGCHI Conference on Human Factors in Computing Systems. Pages 181–186. New Orleans, Louisiana, USA – April 27 – May 02, 1991.

[36]   ASHRAE. Standard 55 – Thermal Environmental Conditions for Human Occupancy. [Online]. https://www.ashrae.org/resources--publications/bookstore/standard-55-and-user-s-manual.

[37]   Hoyt T, Schiavon S, Piccioli A, *et al.* CBE Thermal Comfort Tool. Center for the Built Environment, University of California Berkeley; 2013. http://cbe.berkeley.edu/comforttool/ .

Chapter 4

Autonomous collaborative learning in wearable IoT applications

*Seyed Ali Rokni[1], Ramin Fallahzadeh[2]
and Hassan Ghasemzadeh[1]*

Internet of Things (IoT) has emerged as a promising paradigm for a large number of application domains such as environmental and medical monitoring, transportation, manufacturing, and home automation [1–3]. Many of these applications involve cooperation of humans and things [4]. At the heart of such systems and applications is human monitoring where wearable sensors are utilized for sensing, processing, and transmission of physiological and behavioral readings. Characteristically, sensors acquire physical measurements, perform local data processing (using computational models such as machine-learning and signal-processing algorithms), and communicate the resulting information to the cloud.

The computational algorithms allow for continuous and real-time extraction of the useful and desired information from raw wearable sensor readings. These algorithms, however, need to be reconfigured (i.e., retrained) upon a slight change in configuration of the system. These changes (or uncertainties) include addition/removal of a sensor to/from the network, displacement/misplacement/misorientation of the sensors, replacement/upgrade of a sensor, adoption of the system by a new user, or changes in physical/behavioral status of user. Without reconfiguration, such uncertainties will cause drastic performance decline of the computational algorithms [5]. The reason for such undesired performance degradation is that the underlying machine-learning algorithms are developed based on a set of training data that is collected in a controlled environment. The outcome of such algorithms, however, decreases significantly, when utilized in real-world settings with the presence of one or more uncertainties.

Retraining the machine-learning algorithms that are robust against uncertainty requires recollecting a sufficiently large amount of labeled training data, per uncertainty type. Collecting such a dataset, if practical, is a time-consuming, labor-intensive, and an expensive process. Therefore, developing self-adaptive algorithms becomes imperative as wearable IoT sensors are periodically subject to alteration in end-user settings. Our vision for future wearables is that their underlying

[1]Washington State University, School of Electrical Engineering and Computer Science, Pullman, WA
[2]Stanford University, School of Medicine, Stanford, CA

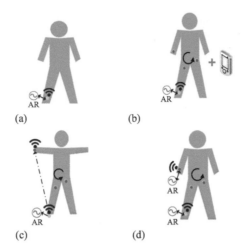

Figure 4.1   *(a) Initial setting, (b) dynamic sensor addition, (c) autonomous learning, and (d) collaborative recognition*

computational algorithms autonomously reconfigure without the need for collecting new labeled training data.

This chapter briefly overviews robust machine-learning solutions for wearable IoT applications. Furthermore, it presents one of the earliest attempts in presenting an autonomous learning framework for wearables. The focus, in particular, is on cases where a new sensor is added to the system and the new (untrained) sensor is worn/used on various body locations. Figure 4.1 shows the evolution of a wearable network when a new dynamic sensor is added to the system with a previously trained machine-learning model (e.g., an activity recognition classifier). The process of autonomous learning automatically leads to a new collaborative decision-making algorithm. Addressing the problem of expanding pattern-recognition capabilities from a single setting algorithm with a predefined configuration to a dynamic setting where sensors can be added, displaced, and used unobtrusively is challenging. In such cases, successful knowledge transfer is needed to improve the learning performance by avoiding expensive data collection and labeling efforts. In this chapter, a novel and generic approach to transfer learning capabilities of an existing static sensor to a newly added dynamic sensor is described.

4.1   Transfer learning in wearable IoT

The idea of having self-configurable systems is based on the concept of transfer learning. Transfer learning applies knowledge learned from one problem domain, the source (e.g., existing sensors in this case), to a new but related problem, the target (e.g., a new sensor). Transfer learning approaches can be classified into instance transfer, feature representation transfer, parameter transfer, and relational knowledge transfer [6]. The approach described in this chapter (developing autonomous learning solutions for sensor additions in synchronous views) falls within the category of *instance transfer.*

In smart home applications, previous research has shown that it is possible to avoid data collection phase by transferring classifier models of activity recognition in one home to another with similar activity-recognition systems [7]. Teacher/learner (TL) transfer learning has being used when there is no direct access to training data. Instead, source-trained classifier operates simultaneously with the target learner and provides labels of newly observed data points to gather enough training data. Although noticeably less studies have focused on using TL approaches, such approaches have shown promising outcomes in increasing the transfer learning performance.

Several studies applied the TL model to develop an opportunistic system capable of performing reliable activity recognition in a dynamic sensor environment [8–10]. These approaches require two sensors to be worn for a long time until a sufficient amount of different activities are performed by the user. Furthermore, it needs constant rate of data transmission between existing sensor and new sensor. One of the main problems of this approach and many other TL approaches is that the accuracy of the learner's training is bounded by the accuracy of the teacher. In addition, it needs a very reliable source classifier because the only source of gathering ground truth labels is the source sensor. Therefore, the learner is completely reliant upon labels provided by the teacher.

The next section, introduces a method for transferring and refining labels while placement of the target sensor changes in real time. It uses a graph propagation method to refine the transferred labels. A similar approach is used in semi-supervised learning when the dataset contains few labeled and many unlabeled instances [11]. Leveraging graph-based semi-supervised learning have shown promising result in Natural Language Processing such as part-of-speech tagging [12] and machine translation [13]. In contrast to semi-supervised learning, this approach utilizes a set of uncertain labeled data with different levels of accuracy. Then, label-propagation methods are employed to refine low-accurate labels to obtain labels of higher accuracy. It is referred to as synchronous dynamic view learning (SDVL).

4.2 Synchronous dynamic view learning

Figure 4.1 shows the evolution of a wearable network when a new dynamic sensor is added to the system with a previously trained machine-learning model (i.e., activity recognition classifier), the process of autonomous learning, and the new activity recognition algorithm in action.

Initially, the network consists of a fixed number of sensors (e.g., one sensor worn on "ankle") with trained machine-learning models for activity recognition. The collection of the existing sensors is referred to as "static view." A new untrained sensor (e.g., a smartphone) is added to the system. The new sensor can be naturally used on different body locations (e.g., "wrist," "waist," and "pocket"). This newly added dynamic sensor is referred to as "dynamic view." The SDVL framework captures sensor data in both views simultaneously, labels instances captured by "dynamic" based on the collective knowledge of "static" and "dynamic," and constructs a new classification algorithm for activity recognition. During the data-collection phase, dynamic sensor can be placed on different body locations, and data gathering continues.

As soon as a new classification algorithm is constructed using the SDVL approach, the system can be used to detect physical activities with higher accuracy in a collaborative fashion. Additionally, it is possible to remove the static node from the network and continue only with the newly added sensor. This is consistent with real scenarios where dynamic wearable sensors are exposed to robust but temporarily available static sensors. For example, a wearable sensor can learn from sensors placed in a home or office (e.g., Kinect, cameras, smart home sensors). The knowledge transferred from these statics sensors can be used to train dynamically changing wearable sensors for the purpose of activity recognition.

4.2.1   Problem definition

An observation X_i made by a wearable sensor at time t_i can be represented as a D-dimensional feature vector, $X_i = \{f_{i1}, f_{i2}, \ldots, f_{iD}\}$. Each feature is computed from a given time window and a marginal probability distribution over all possible feature values. The activity recognition task is composed of a label space $\mathscr{A} = \{a_1, a_2, \ldots, a_m\}$ consisting of the set of labels for activities of interest, and a conditional probability distribution $\mathscr{P}(\mathscr{A}|X_i)$ which is the probability of assigning a label $a_j \in A$ given an observed instance X_i.

Although a sensor with a trained classifier can detect some activities, its observations are limited to the body segment on which the sensor is worn. Therefore, some activities are not recognizable in one sensor's view point. For example, a sensor worn on "ankle," although expert in detecting lower body activities such as "walking," cannot easily detect activities such as "eating" that mainly involves upper body motions. To increase accuracy of activity recognition, it is desirable to add more sensors to the network to cover a larger set of physical activities. We note that advances in embedded sensor design and wearable electronics allow end users to utilize new wearable sensors. In such a realistic scenario, the newly added sensor has not been trained to collaborate with existing sensors in detecting physical activities. The general goal of SDVL is to develop an autonomous learning algorithm for newly added sensor to detect activities that are not recognizable by existing sensors. Without loss of generality, one can assume that the static view consists of a single sensor, in the formulation of SDVL problem. In the case of multiple static sensors, an ensemble classifier on all static sensors can be used as an integrated static view.

Problem 4.1 (SDVL). *Let $P = \{p_1, \ldots, p_k\}$ be a set of k possible sensor placements. Let $P_s \subset P$ be a set of placement of existing sensors with an integrated trained classification model. Furthermore, let $P_t \subset P$ be a set of possible placements of the newly added sensor. Moreover, let $\mathscr{A} = \{a_1, a_2, \ldots, a_m\}$ be a set of m activities/labels that the system aims to recognize, and $\mathscr{X} = \{X_1, X_2, \ldots, X_N\}$ a set of N observations* *made by the dynamic sensor when placed in anybody's locations $l \in P_t$. The SDVL problem is to accurately label observations made by the dynamic sensor such that the mislabeling error is minimized. Once these instances are labeled, it is straightforward to develop a new activity-recognition classifier using the labeled data.*

In Figure 4.1, P_s = {"ankle"} as illustrated in Figure 4.1(a). As shown in Figure 4.1(b), P_t = {"wrist," "waist," "pocket"} denoting that the dynamic sensor may be worn on three different locations on the body. During autonomous learning (i.e., in Figure 4.1(c)), as the user performs physical activities in $\mathscr{A}$, instances in $\mathscr{X}$ are observed by the dynamic sensor.

4.2.2   Problem formulation

The SDVL problem described in Problem 4.1 can be formulated as follows:

$$\text{Minimize} \quad \sum_{i=1}^{N}\sum_{j=1}^{m} x_{ij}\varepsilon_{ij} \tag{4.1}$$

$$\text{Subject to} \quad \sum_{i=1}^{N} x_{ij} \leq \Delta_i, \quad \forall j \in \{1,\ldots,m\} \tag{4.2}$$

$$\sum_{j=1}^{m} x_{ij} = 1, \quad \forall i \in \{1,\ldots,N\} \tag{4.3}$$

$$x_{ij} \in \{0,1\}, \quad \forall i,j \tag{4.4}$$

where x_{ij} is a binary variable indicating whether or not instance $X_i \in \mathscr{X}$ is assigned activity label a_j, and ε_{ij} denotes error due to such labeling. The constraint in (4.2) guarantees that a_j is assigned to at most Δ_i instances, where Δ_i is the upper bound on the number of instances with a_j as their possible labels. Since each instance must be assigned to exactly one actual activity label, the constraint in (4.3) guarantees that each instance X_i receives one and only one activity label. If ε_{ij} and Δ_i are known, this problem can be assumed as a generalized assignment problem [14]. The main challenge in solving the SDVL problem is that the ground truth labels are not available in the dynamic view, and therefore ε_{ij} are unknown a priori. In this chapter, we estimate ε_{ij} using a combination of confusion matrix of the static view and disagreement among hypothetically similar instances in the dynamic view.

Static sensor has a limited ability in detecting activities depending on the physical placement of the sensor on the body. In order to quantify the capability of the static sensor for activity recognition, "ambiguity relation" is defined as follows:

Definition 4.1 (Ambiguity relation). *Let s_p refer to a static sensor placed on body-location p. An ambiguity relation AR_p for sensor s_p is defined as a mapping $P \times \mathscr{A} \rightarrow \mathscr{A}$ such that for each sensor location $p \in P$ and activity pair $a_1, a_2 \in \mathscr{A}$, $((p, a_1), a_2) \in AR_p$ if and only if there exists a sensor s_p placed on body joint p using which a_1 and a_2*

are unrecognizable. In other word, there exists an observation instance with predicted label a_1 made by s_p which corresponds to the actual activity a_2.

The ambiguity relation represents confusion in detecting a particular activity given an instance of the sensor data. The concept of ambiguity relation is used to determine deficiency of a sensor in detecting particular activities given a collection of training instances in the static view. To quantify this deficiency of the static view with a given location p and each $((p, a_i), a_j) \in AR_p$, $L_p(a_i, a_j)$ is defined as likelihood deficiency of sensor s_p in confusing action a_i with activity a_j.

Definition 4.2 (Likelihood deficiency). *Given a sensor s_p and a pair of activity $a_i, a_j \in \mathscr{A}$, where $((p, a_i), a_j) \in AR_p$. Let $n_p(a_i, a_j)$ denote the number of instances of activity a_j predicted by s_p as a_i. The likelihood deficiency $L_p(a_i, a_j)$ is given by:*

$$L_p(a_i, a_j) = \frac{n_p(a_i, a_j)}{\sum_{a_k \in \mathscr{A}} n_p(a_i, a_k)} \tag{4.5}$$

Note that $((p, a_i), a_j) \notin AR_p$ implies $L_p(a_i, a_j) = 0$. As soon as likelihood deficiencies are computed, the static view, instead of sending the predicted label, will transmit its predicted label combined with the likelihood of actual label. This complex label is called a semi-label generated by the static view and will be transmitted to the dynamic view for the purpose of autonomous learning.

Definition 4.3 (Semi-label). *A semi-label SL_i $]r$ s_p is a two-tuple (a_i, W) where $|W| = |\mathscr{A}|$ and $W_j = L_p(a_i, a_j)$. In other word, W is a likelihood vector of all possible actual labels when predicted label is a_i.*

Confusion matrix of the classification algorithm is used in the static view to retrieve values of the likelihood deficiency function. Then, by combining information of multiple sensors through minimum disagreement labeling (MDL) process (described in Section 4.3), recognition deficiency is resolved.

4.2.3 Overview of autonomous learning

In this approach, the set of static sensors acts as a "teacher" and sends a semi-label of the current activity to the dynamic view in real time. The dynamic view, also called "learner," learns from the information provided by "teacher" and boosts the labeling accuracy by combining its local observations with the received semi-labels. Thus, the challenging task is how to convert semi-labels to exact labels such that the overall labeling error is minimized.

Algorithm 4.1 shows the heuristic approach for solving the optimization problem described in Problem 4.1. It assumes that the sensors within the two views are worn on the body at the same time while the user performs physical activities. Because the static and dynamic sensors may have different clocks, the dynamic sensor needs to know to which observation each semi-label corresponds. The problem of different clocks can be resolved by first synchronizing static and dynamic sensors. At time t, the static sensor detects an instance of the current activity, a_t; it extracts corresponding semi-label SL_t and transmits (SL_t, t) at the size of $|A|$ to the dynamic sensor via a

---

Algorithm 4.1: Synchronous dynamic view learning algorithm

---

while (more sensor data are required) **do**

    Static performs activity recognition on its observation at time t.

    Static detects activity a_t.

    Static computes semi-label SL_t for activity a_t.

    Static sends SL_t to the sensors in Dynamic view.

    Dynamic receives semi-label SL_t.

    Dynamic assigns SL_t to its observation X_t at time t.

    if *Dynamic sensor needs displacement* **then**

        change the location of Dynamic sensor

Use Minimum Disagreement Labeling (MDL) to compute the best distribution for each semi-label

---

wireless link. Usually $|A|$ is very small, and we can buffer semi-label values and send them as a batch. When the dynamic sensor receives (SL_t, t), it assigns SL_t to its observation of time t. When sufficient instances of each activity are gathered, the MDL is applied on the gathered data to label all instances in the dynamic view to calibrate transferred labels.

4.3   Minimum disagreement labeling

The intuition behind MDL is that instances of the same location and activity are similar and close in the feature space.

Problem 4.2 (Minimum disagreement). *Let $X = \{X_1, X_2, \ldots, X_N\}$, a set of N observations representing N instances in feature space $\mathbb{R}^D$. Furthermore, let $SL = \{SL_1, SL_2, \ldots, SL_N\}$ be the semi-labels associated with the N observations in X. MDL is the problem of refining each SL_i such that the amount of disagreement among similar instances is minimized.*

The problem of minimum disagreement is solved in two phases. First, a similarity graph is constructed. Then, labels are refined through neighboring nodes in the similarity graph.

Definition 4.4 (Similarity graph). *A similarity graph $G(V, E)$ is a weighted graph where each node in V represents an instance in X (i.e., $X = V$). Each node in the graph maintains a vector of its own feature values and the probability distribution of its labels (i.e., semi-label). Each edge $e_{ij} \in E$ represents the amount of similarity between instances X_i and X_j.*

Gaussian kernel [15] is used to quantify the amount of similarity between X_i and X_j. This similarity measure is denoted by $\eta(X_i, X_j)$ and computed as follows:

$$\eta(i,j) = e^{-\left(\|X_i - X_j\|^2 / 2\sigma^2\right)} \tag{4.6}$$

Because instances of different activities do not contribute to the label of each other, similarity graph is built using k-nearest neighbor (kNN) schema which is one of the most popular approaches in similarity graph construction [16]. Therefore, edge weights in the similarity graph are measured using the following equation:

$$e_{ij} = \begin{cases} \eta(i,j) & \text{if } i \in \kappa(j) \text{ or } j \in \kappa(i) \\ 0 & \text{otherwise} \end{cases} \tag{4.7}$$

where $\kappa(i)$ is the set of kNNs of node X_i based on the defined similarity function.

With the introduced similarity graph and label refinement, now the error ε_{ij} in (4.1) can be measured by amount of disagreement between similar instances. This also converts the SDVL problem into the problem of minimizing the energy function (disagreement) E given by

$$E(\mathbf{F}_i) = \frac{1}{2} \sum_{j \in \kappa(i)} \|\mathbf{F}(i) - \mathbf{F}(j)\|^2 \tag{4.8}$$

where $\mathbf{F}_i$, a vector of size $\mathbf{SL}_i$, denotes the classification function that assigns the probability distribution of label on point X_i. Eventually, the label for X_i is given by $\operatorname{argmax}_{v \leq |A|} F_{iv}$.

4.3.1   Label refinement

The idea of label refinement is similar to label propagation, a well-known approach in the area of semi-supervised learning when the dataset contains both labeled and unlabeled instances [11]. The intuition behind this idea is that similar instances should have same labels. This method tries to connect similar instances first. It then transfers labels of known neighbors to those unlabeled instances. SDVL framework utilizes this idea to refine the semi-labels provided by the static sensor. In contrast to semi-supervised learning, which deals with a set of labeled data and a set of unlabeled data, here we have a set of uncertain labeled data with different levels of accuracy. The label propagation method is used to refine less accurate labels and obtain higher accurate labels. In other words, the activity recognition capability of the static sensor, due to its placement, is limited because the static view cannot reliably distinguish among some activities. Therefore, there is no guarantee that labels predicted by the source view are perfect. Additionally, the dynamic sensor, because it is carried on different body locations, may have some discriminating features which can separate instances of different activities that were overlapped in the static feature space.

To better grasp the label-refinement process, parts of the graph shown in Figure 4.2(a) have been magnified and highlighted in Figure 4.2(b) where different colors correspond to different label distributions. The label/color of each node is determined according to maximum probability. There are three orange nodes, one green node, and one blue node, forming the five closest neighbors of the center node

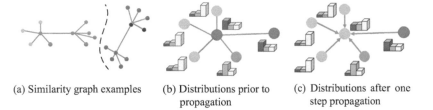

(a) Similarity graph examples   (b) Distributions prior to   (c) Distributions after one
                                       propagation   step propagation

*Figure 4.2   Similarity graph and propagation process: (a) similarity graph
construction: each instance is connected to k (e.g., k = 5) closest
neighbors; (b) prior to label propagation center node has an incorrect
label; (c) as a result of label propagation, similar nodes have similar
label distributions*

with initial distributions similar to its blue neighbor. After performing one update
iteration, as shown in Figure 4.2(c), label distribution of the center node changes and
its color is converted to orange.

The distribution of the labels is refined for one node through its neighbors. A
larger edge weight allows for more contribution to the neighbor's label. First, the
adjacency matrix is normalized for G by defining a contribution matrix C such that:

$$C_{ij} = \frac{e_{ij}}{\sum_{k \in V} e_{ik}} \tag{4.9}$$

C specifies that:

$$\sum_j C_{ij} = 1 \quad C_{ij} \geq 0 \tag{4.10}$$

During each iteration of label propagation, each node takes a fraction of label
information from its neighborhood and maintains some part of its initial distribution.
Consequently, for an instance x_i at time $t + 1$, we have:

$$\mathbf{F}_i^{t+1} = \alpha \sum_j C_{ij} \mathbf{F}_j^t + (1 - \alpha) \mathbf{SL}_i^t \tag{4.11}$$

where $0 \leq \alpha \leq 1$ is a mixing coefficient which specifies the fractional contribution
of the neighbors.

The algorithm starts with initial semi-labels, that is, $\mathbf{F}_i^0 = \mathbf{SL}_i$. Let $\mathbf{F}^t = \{\mathbf{F}_1^t,$
$\mathbf{F}_2^t, \ldots, \mathbf{F}_n^t\}$ be the classification function for n observations. The batch update can
be formulated as follows:

$$\mathbf{F}^{t+1} = \alpha \mathbf{C} \mathbf{F}^t + (1 - \alpha) \mathbf{SL} \tag{4.12}$$

The updating process will continue until it converges to a value such that
$\mathbf{F}^{t+1} = \mathbf{F}^t$.

4.4   Experimental analysis

In this section, the effectiveness of SDVL framework is shown using the data collected in several experiments involving human subjects performing various daily physical activities while wearing motion sensor nodes. Refer to [17] for details on the datasets and experiments presented in this section.

4.4.1   Evaluation methodology

In this section, comparison of SDVL framework with prior research in transfer learning for mobile wearable devices is carried out.

Research in the area of transfer learning for wearables is relatively new. Currently, there exist only three of such algorithms, namely, Naive and System-Supervised suggested in [8], and Plug-n-learn presented in [18], all of which are applicable to the synchronous TL transfer learning studied in this chapter. The SDVL framework is compared with these three algorithms as well as the experimental upper bound obtained using ground truth labels gathered during data collection.

- **Naive**: This method reuses classifier of the "teacher" in "learner" view. This method works well when the "teacher" and "learner" share identical context (e.g., sensors are colocated on the body and are homogeneous). In this approach, static sensor sends its trained classifier to the dynamic sensor. For example, for the case of support vector machine (SVM) as the classification algorithm, static sensor sends the support vectors. As stated before, the limitation of this approach is that the two views are colocated.
- **System-supervised**: This method refers to the case where "learner" labels its observations based on labels predicted by "teacher." In other words, both the teacher and learner sensors should be synchronized in advance. Upon any new observation, the classifier trained for "teacher" predicts label of the current activity and sends its prediction to the "learner" for the purpose of activity recognition. However, the accuracy of this method is limited by accuracy of the teacher sensor.
- **Plug-n-learn**: This approach is designed to address the limitation of the system-supervised method that the accuracy of the learner sensor was limited by that of the teacher sensor. It creates a combinatorial view by incorporating both teacher and learner feature spaces to partition current observations. It then retrieves more accurate labels by solving an assignment problem. However, the underlying assumption in this approach is that the on-body location of the learner sensor is always fixed.
- **Experimental upper bound**: The experimental upper bound can be achieved when the dynamic sensor has access to the classifier trained based on ground truth labels for different body locations.

The analysis presented in this section compares the accuracy of provided labels in "dynamic" using SDVL with that of each of the competing methods. For experimental setting, one sensor node is picked as static sensor and assumed that the dynamic sensor can move from one body location to another for all remaining on-body locations. The sequence of observations are divided into three parts for (1) training the static classifier; (2) transfer learning phase to train the dynamic sensor; and (3) for measuring accuracy of SDVL framework. After training an activity recognition model for the static sensor, the experiment assumes that the dynamic sensor is added to the system moved over all other locations except location of the static senor.

The classifier of dynamic sensor, built upon the computed labels, is compared with all the competing algorithms based on the following metrics:

$$Accuracy = \frac{TP + TN}{TP + TN + FP + FN} \tag{4.13}$$

$$Precision = \frac{TP}{TP + FP} \tag{4.14}$$

$$Recall = \frac{TP}{TP + FN} \tag{4.15}$$

$$F1 = \frac{2 \times Precision \times Recall}{Precision + Recall} \tag{4.16}$$

where *TP*, *TN*, *FP*, and *FN* stand for true-positive, true-negative, false-positive, and false-negative, respectively. Each metric captures different aspect of classifier performance. Specifically, the goal is to increase recall without sacrificing precision.

4.4.2   Accuracy of transferred labels

The investigation of training label accuracy is essential because these labels are being used as training data, and their accuracy significantly contributes to the accuracy of the final classifier trained in the dynamic view.

Figure 4.3 shows average accuracy of training labels over all subjects. According to Figure 4.3(a), on IRH dataset, the accuracy of calibrated labels using SDVL ranged from 69.9% to 72.7% which shows 15.9% and 29.6% improvement from system-supervised and plug-n-learn methods, respectively. Looking at Figure 4.3(b), we observe 87.5% accuracy using SDVL resulting in 21.1% and 42.2% enhancement compared with system-supervised and plug-n-learn in OPP dataset. Similar results can be observed on SDA dataset as shown in Figure 4.3(c).

4.4.3   Accuracy of activity recognition

In Section 4.4.2, the accuracy of training labels of different methods is compared. To create an activity recognition model, an SVM classifier is developed on the labeled data using each algorithm under comparison. According to Figure 4.4(a), the average accuracy of SDVL is 70.2% on the IRH dataset. This shows 15.4% improvement over system-supervised, 30.7% compared to plug-n-learn and 51.8% considering the

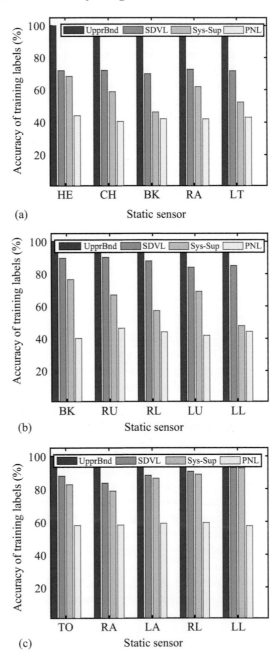

Figure 4.3   Accuracy using labels of different algorithms. The results are presented for IRH dataset (a), OPP dataset (b), and SDA dataset (c).

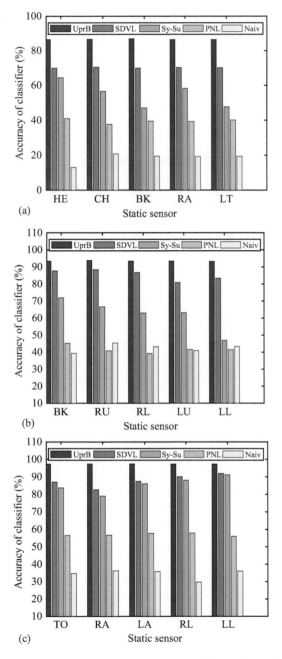

Figure 4.4 Accuracy of activity recognition using different algorithms. The results are presented for IRH dataset (a), OPP dataset (b), and SDA dataset (c).

Table 4.1   Precision and recall of IRH dataset

Static node	Precision					Recall				
	Naive	PNL	Sy-Su	SDVL	Upper bound	Naive	PNL	Sy-Su	SDVL	Upper bound
Head	21.77	40.5	56.54	63.45	86.79	13.05	41	64.39	69.94	86.45
Chest	22.42	35.29	50.6	63.17	86.95	20.74	37.62	56.51	70.48	86.58
Back	21.84	38.47	43.21	64.39	87.26	19.38	39.5	47.07	69.91	86.94
Right arm	26.29	37.14	53.52	65.32	86.69	19.28	39.3	58.23	70.3	86.43
Left thigh	21.48	38.82	45.83	64.15	86.68	19.44	40.12	47.64	70.18	86.41
Average	22.76	38.04	49.94	64.1	86.87	18.38	39.51	54.77	70.16	86.56

Naive approach. Note that the accuracy is about 15% less than the experimental upper bound.

The effect of enhancing the accuracy of labeling is more considerable in Figure 4.3(b). SDVL boosts the accuracy of the training labels by more than 23% and 42% over system-supervised and plug-n-learn, respectively. This suggests that SDVL could be more effectively compared to other approaches in distinguishing loco-motion activities. However, plug-n-learn works better on average over all different scenarios, according to Figure 4.3(b), although there are several cases where it works worse than the Naive approach. One explanation for this observation is that all pairs of node locations are in close proximity and may capture similar patterns in the OPP dataset (i.e., left/right and upper/lower arms). In situations where static and dynamic nodes are close to each other, the decision made using a static classifier on dynamic feature space could be more accurate.

In addition to IRH and OPP datasets, similar experiments on SDA dataset were conducted. As Figure 4.3(c) shows, activity recognition using SDVL achieves an average accuracy of 88% which is 2.6% and 31% higher than system-supervised and plug-n-learn, respectively, and approximately 11% less than experimental upper bound. Here, the Naive achieves the lowest performance with 34.5% accuracy on average.

4.4.4   Precision, recall, and F1-measure

In Table 4.1, precision and recall are compared for different approaches in IRH dataset. For both measures, Naive method achieves lowest performance with an average precision of 23% and recall of 18% while the upper bound precision and recall are approximately 87% on average. Both precision and recall improved using SDVL in comparison with system-supervised and plug-n-play approaches. However, the recall improvement is more considerable than precision enhancement. One explanation is as follows: in system-supervised, if the static sensor makes a wrong decision, it will never be recovered by the dynamic sensor. In SDVL, however, a wrong decision by static node could be revised based on the similarity graph on the observation of dynamic node.

Table 4.2 Precision and recall of OPP dataset

Static node	Precision					Recall				
	Naive	PNL	Sy-Su	SDVL	Upper bound	Naive	PNL	Sy-Su	SDVL	Upper bound
Head	65.79	24.08	88.89	80.18	92.93	45.25	39.3	71.98	87.67	93.42
Right upper arm	59.74	31.94	62.38	85.28	92.66	40.76	45.28	66.63	88.48	93.84
Right lower arm	43.31	31.85	61.68	79.38	93.03	39.16	43.09	63	86.78	93.5
Left upper arm	60.1	31.77	60.58	75.59	93.01	41.57	40.9	63.18	80.93	93.5
Left lower arm	59.16	32.22	36.58	74.1	92.77	41.43	43.34	46.94	83.35	93.25
Average	57.62	30.37	62.02	78.91	92.88	41.63	42.38	62.35	85.44	93.50

Table 4.3 Precision and recall of SDA dataset

Static node	Precision					Recall				
	Naive	PNL	Sy-Su	SDVL	Upper bound	Naive	PNL	Sy-Su	SDVL	Upper bound
Torso	45.22	53.43	83.76	85.86	97.41	34.69	56.5	83.78	87.02	97.33
Right arm	45.79	53.03	80.35	78.04	97.46	36.25	56.67	79.06	82.68	97.38
Left arm	46.24	53.65	86.57	84.92	97.49	35.82	57.69	86.11	87.42	97.41
Right leg	41.7	54.03	86.67	88.08	97.38	29.8	57.87	88	90.11	97.29
Left leg	46.55	52.85	93.02	93.82	97.36	36.05	56.01	91.14	91.96	97.29
Average	45.1	53.4	86.07	86.14	97.42	34.52	56.94	85.61	87.83	97.34

In Table 4.2, a similar case can be observed where the recall improvement is more than that of precision in OPP dataset. However, the average accuracy of plug-n-learn is less. Similar to the explanation of classifier accuracy, in this dataset, some pairs of static and dynamic have similar locations which cause the Naive approach to work better. For SDA dataset, system-supervised and SDVL produce comparable results because the accuracy of the static sensor was high and contributed to the accuracy of the system-supervised method (Table 4.3).

F1-measure combines precision and recalls and provides a powerful metric for comparing the effectiveness of two classifiers. Figure 4.5(a) compares F1-measure of five different methods on the IRH dataset. On average, SDVL improves this metric by 15.7% and 28.6% from system-supervised and plug-n-learn methods, respectively. As expected, F1 of the Naive approach is quite low with an average of 17.6%. Similarly, in OPP and SDA datasets, SDVL successfully boosts the F1-measure by 23.5% and 2.4%, respectively.

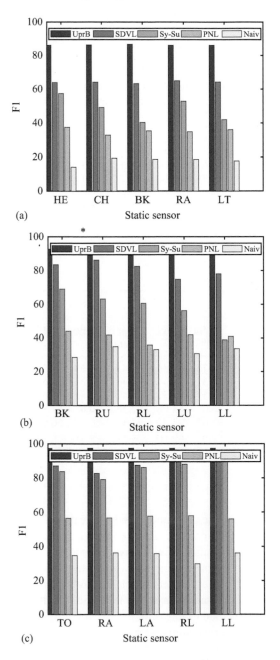

Figure 4.5   F1 measure of classifier using different algorithms. The results are presented for IRH dataset (a), OPP dataset (b), and SDA dataset (c).

4.5 Summary

As wearable sensors are becoming more prevalent, their function becomes more complex, and they operate in highly dynamic environments. Machine-learning algorithms for these sensors cannot be designed only for one specific setting. To address the dynamic nature of wearable sensors, a dynamic-view learning framework is described which uses knowledge of the existing sensors to autonomously learn activity recognition in newly added sensors. Dynamic-view learning approach learns computational algorithms in new dynamically changing settings without any need for labeled training data in the dynamic view. The experiments presented in this chapter show that it is possible to combine knowledge of existing system with the observation of a new sensor to boost accuracy of the predicted labels without ground truth labels in dynamic views. The experimental analysis demonstrates promising results compared to the state-of-the-art solutions with an overall accuracy improvement of 13.8% using three real-world datasets.

References

[1] Ramin Fallahzadeh, Samaneh Aminikhanghahi, Ashley Nichole Gibson, and Diane J Cook. Toward personalized and context-aware prompting for smartphone-based intervention. In *Engineering in Medicine and Biology Society (EMBC), 2016 IEEE 38th Annual International Conference of the*, pages 6010–6013. IEEE, 2016.

[2] Kyle D Feuz and Diane J Cook. Transfer learning across feature-rich heterogeneous feature spaces via feature-space remapping (FSR). *ACM Transactions on Intelligent Systems and Technology (TIST)*, 6(1):3, 2015.

[3] Rokni, S. A., Ghasemzadeh, H., and Hezarjaribi, N. (2017). Smart Medication Management, Current Technologies, and Future Directions. In N. Wickramasinghe (Ed.), *Handbook of Research on Healthcare Administration and Management* (pp. 188–204). Hershey, PA: IGI Global. doi:10.4018/978-1-5225-0920-2.ch012. Available from https://www.igi-global.com/chapter/smart-medication-management-current-technologies-and-future-directions/163830.

[4] John A. Stankovic. Research directions for the internet of things. *IEEE Internet of Things Journal*, 1(1):3–9, 2014.

[5] Ramyar Saeedi, Janet Purath, Krishna Venkatasubramanian, and Hassan Ghasemzadeh. Toward seamless wearable sensing: Automatic on-body sensor localization for physical activity monitoring. In *The 36th Annual International Conference of the IEEE Engineering in Medicine and Biology Society (EMBC)*, 2014.

[6] Sinno Jialin Pan and Qiang Yang. A survey on transfer learning. *IEEE Transactions on Knowledge and Data Engineering*, 22(10):1345–1359, 2010.

[7] Tim L. M. van Kasteren, Gwenn Englebienne, and Ben JA Kröse. Transferring knowledge of activity recognition across sensor networks. In *Pervasive Computing*, pages 283–300. Springer, Berlin, Heidelberg, 2010.

[8]   Alberto Calatroni, Daniel Roggen, and Gerhard Tröster. Automatic transfer of activity recognition capabilities between body-worn motion sensors: Training newcomers to recognize locomotion. In *Eighth International Conference on Networked Sensing Systems (INSS'11)*, Penghu, Taiwan, page 6, 2011.

[9]   Marc Kurz, Gerold Holzl, Alois Ferscha, *et al.* The opportunity framework and data processing ecosystem for opportunistic activity and context recognition. *International Journal of Sensors Wireless Communications and Control*, 1(2):102–125, 2011.

[10]   Daniel Roggen, Kilian Förster, Alberto Calatroni, and Gerhard Tröster. The adAEC pattern analysis architecture for adaptive human activity recognition systems. *Journal of Ambient Intelligence and Humanized Computing*, 4(2):169–186, 2013.

[11]   Xiaojin Zhu, Zoubin Ghahramani, John Lafferty, *et al.* Semi-supervised learning using Gaussian fields and harmonic functions. In *ICML*, volume 3, pages 912–919, 2003.

[12]   Amarnag Subramanya, Slav Petrov, and Fernando Pereira. Efficient graph-based semi-supervised learning of structured tagging models. In *Proceedings of the 2010 Conference on Empirical Methods in Natural Language Processing*, pages 167–176. Association for Computational Linguistics, 2010.

[13]   Atefeh Zafarian, Ali Rokni, Shahram Khadivi, and Sonia Ghiasifard. Semi-supervised learning for named entity recognition using weakly labeled training data. In *Artificial Intelligence and Signal Processing (AISP), 2015 International Symposium on*, pages 129–135. IEEE, 2015.

[14]   Dirk G Cattrysse and Luk N Van Wassenhove. A survey of algorithms for the generalized assignment problem. *European Journal of Operational Research*, 60(3):260–272, 1992.

[15]   Christopher M Bishop. *Pattern Recognition and Machine Learning*, volume 4. Springer, New York, 2006.

[16]   Markus Maier, Matthias Hein, and Ulrike Von Luxburg. Cluster identification in nearest-neighbor graphs. In *Algorithmic Learning Theory*, pages 196–210. Springer, Berlin, Heidelberg, 2007.

[17]   Seyed Ali Rokni and Hassan Ghasemzadeh. Synchronous dynamic view learning: A framework for autonomous training of activity recognition models using wearable sensors. In *Information Processing in Sensor Networks (IPSN), 2017 16th ACM/IEEE International Conference on*, pages 79–90. IEEE, 2017.

[18]   Seyed Ali Rokni and Hassan Ghasemzadeh. Plug-n-learn: Automatic learning of computational algorithms in human-centered internet-of-things applications. In *Proceedings of the 53rd Annual Design Automation Conference*, page 139. ACM, 2016.

Chapter 5

A distributed approach to energy-efficient data confidentiality in the Internet of Things

Andrea G. Forte[1,2,3], Simone Cirani[4] and Gianluigi Ferrari[1]

In the Internet of Things (IoT) everything will be connected, from refrigerators to coffee machines, to shoes. Many such "things" will have a very limited amount of energy to operate, often harvested from their own environment. Providing data confidentiality for such energy-constrained devices has proven to be a hard problem. In this article, we discuss existing approaches to data confidentiality for energy-constrained devices and propose a novel approach to drastically reduce a node's energy consumption during encryption and decryption. In particular, we propose to distribute encryption and decryption computations among a set of *trusted* nodes. We validate the proposed approach through both simulations and experiments. Initial results show that the proposed approach leads to energy savings (from a single node's perspective) of up to 73% and up to 81% of the energy normally spent to encrypt and decrypt, respectively. With such great savings, our approach holds the promise to enable data confidentiality also for those devices, with extremely limited energy, which will become commonplace in the IoT.

5.1 Introduction

The IoT will introduce a drastic change in our society as many common things that we use in our everyday life will stop being just objects and will start interacting with each other, with us, and with the environment. As all of these things talk to each other and to us, they will collect and share a very large amount of sensitive information. For example, car engines will collect and share data about the driver's driving habits; people's whereabouts will be shared and used to automatically provide new services; and what we eat and drink could be shared with insurance companies to monitor our eating habits and lifestyle. Similarly, people's vital signs (e.g., heart rate and blood pressure) may be collected and shared in a completely automated way, with

[1]Internet of Things (IoT) Lab, Department of Engineering and Architecture, University of Parma, Parma, Italy
[2]AT&T, New York, USA
[3]Bitsian, New York, NY 10271, USA
[4]Caligoo srl, Taneto di Gattatico (Reggio Emilia), Italy

privacy implications that are still not very clear. Given the capillarity of the IoT, its pervasiveness in our lives, and given the sensitive nature of the information it will handle, security in the IoT—and, specifically, *data confidentiality*—has become of utmost importance.

The goal of data confidentiality is to prevent disclosure of information to unauthorized parties. When sharing sensitive data, confidentiality is usually enabled by encryption.* Over the years, much work has focused on improving both computational and energy efficiencies of encryption and decryption algorithms in block ciphers (such as AES). Alternatively, new lightweight block ciphers have been proposed trying to address encryption in energy-constrained networks (e.g., wireless sensor networks). While all of these approaches have their merits, often they are not sufficient to provide the energy savings that would allow them to be implemented in many devices in the IoT and, specifically, in energy-harvesting devices.

In this chapter, we propose to distribute block cipher encryption and decryption operations between a set of *trusted* energy-constrained devices. This will be shown to bring significant energy savings to a device. The advantage of such an approach is 2-fold: on one hand, traditional block ciphers can now be used in energy-constrained devices; on the other hand, the energy consumption of "lightweight" block ciphers can further be reduced, thus increasing a node's battery lifetime.

This chapter is structured as follows: in Section 5.2, we start discussing the main challenges in providing data confidentiality in the IoT. In Section 5.3, we show how the energy consumption brought by encryption and decryption operations can be drastically reduced by distributing their computation among a trusted set of energy-constrained nodes. Our approach is validated through energy measurements performed both on an Arduino-based testbed (Section 5.4) and on simulated Zolertia Z1 motes (Section 5.5), showing promising energy savings of our distributed approach. Finally, concluding remarks are presented in Section 5.6.

5.2   Data confidentiality in the IoT

Data confidentiality in the Internet is usually enabled by encryption. Traditional encryption algorithms, however, are too slow and energy-demanding to be applied to the IoT. In particular, the amount of energy spent in encryption and decryption is a critical factor as we move toward wearables, energy-harvesting wireless nodes, and the IoT.

Efforts in reducing block ciphers energy consumption can be divided into three main categories: hardware optimizations, software optimizations, and new "lightweight" algorithms. Let us look at each one of these.

Hardware optimizations [1–3] mainly focus on reducing the number of logic gates necessary to implement a block cipher.† A smaller circuit consumes less energy than a larger one: therefore, by reducing the circuit size, the block cipher consumes

---

*Other means include the use of file permissions and access control lists.
†Another important metric is the number of cycles required to process one block.

less energy. These approaches usually require the use of very specialized hardware, making their feasibility quite difficult if not for very peculiar applications.

Software optimizations [4,5] aim at reducing both the memory footprint and the computational power of block ciphers. Using a smaller amount of computer memory and fewer CPU cycles translates to a lower energy consumption. These approaches achieve some energy savings which, unfortunately, are not sufficiently significant to satisfy the strict energy requirements that some IoT nodes will likely have. Because of this, over the years, new lightweight block ciphers have been proposed [6–9] trying to address the energy requirements typical of wireless sensor networks and the IoT. The basic idea behind these block ciphers is to consume little energy while providing lower throughput and a moderate level of security. In particular, the implicit assumptions behind this idea are the facts that in a constrained environment, the amount of data to encrypt will be small and an attacker will have limited computing capabilities, so that a moderate level of security is appropriate. The key length for such lightweight block ciphers is not too long, typically between 80 and 128 bits, and they usually operate on a smaller 64-bit block size of input data. Their low energy consumption makes them suitable for many resource-constrained devices at the price, however, of limited protection. On the other hand, the reduced level of protection due to the use of smaller encryption keys can be increased by introducing periodic key-changing mechanisms (whose rate strictly depends on the amount of security targeted) in order to make it more difficult to perform brute force attacks on these ciphers [10].

Distributing block ciphers computations further improves on lightweight block ciphers as constrained nodes can now compute a subset of the lightweight block cipher rounds, thus increasing the energy savings even more. Also, such greater energy savings would allow to use block ciphers in energy-harvesting devices, i.e., devices with the most stringent energy requirements. Last, a distributed computation can drastically increase, from a node's perspective, the energy savings for "traditional" block ciphers such as AES, thus enabling the use of AES in constrained environments without the use of any specialized hardware.

5.3   A distributed computation approach

A large number of devices in the IoT will be energy-constrained and will often have to operate using just a few micro-joules of energy [11]. Because of their limited energy, such devices (i.e., nodes) typically form multi-hop networks. In other words, instead of sending packets directly to a far-away gateway, which would require higher transmission power, they relay each others' packets all the way to the gateway by using appropriate routing protocols [12]. In doing so, less energy is consumed in transmission as neighboring nodes are typically much closer than the gateway.

As mentioned in Section 5.1, we propose to distribute block cipher operations among a set of trusted nodes. In particular, this approach is motivated by two consider-ations. The first one is the multi-hop nature of communication for energy-constrained nodes: as such nodes relay each other's packets, they can thus easily apply incremen-tal computations on them. The second one is the iterative structure of block ciphers,

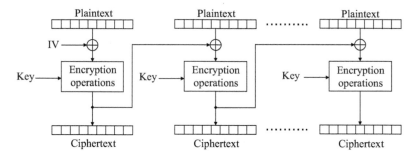

Figure 5.1   Example of block cipher iterative structure in cipher block chaining (CBC) mode

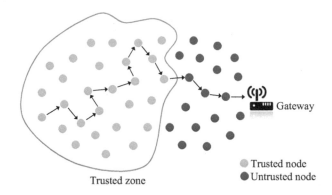

Figure 5.2   Multi-hop network: distributing block-ciphers computations among the trusted nodes

usually either a Feistel network or a substitution–permutation network: an illustrative representation is shown in Figure 5.1. For both block cipher structures, the same operations are repeated multiple times in different stages or rounds. Because of this iterative computation and because of the multi-hop nature of the communication protocol between nodes, it is natural to think to distribute the rounds of encryption of a given block cipher (e.g., ten rounds in AES128) among a selected set of nodes in the multi-hop network.

The nodes participating in the distributed computation need to be *trusted*. More precisely, they must be positioned in such a way that (i) their communication cannot be eavesdropped and (ii) they cannot be hijacked or tampered with. In Figure 5.2, an illustrative representation of such a scenario is shown. For as long as all the required rounds of encryption are completed within the trusted zone, everything is fine. If, however, a packet reaches the boundary of the trusted zone before all rounds of encryption have been performed, then the content of the packet, as well as the secret key used by the block cipher, may be compromised.

A multi-hop network with a trusted set of nodes, as the one just described, could be any network of smart objects deployed in hard-to-reach places, such as undersea or underground networks. Saving energy and prolonging battery lifetime in such networks is very important, given the difficulty in replacing the batteries, if at all possible. For example, a critical infrastructure in the city of New York is the underground network of steam pipes which runs all throughout the city and is meant to keep water pipes temperatures high during winter so as to prevent them from freezing and bursting. In an IoT scenario, one can imagine having sensors and actuators attached to these underground steam pipes. The sensors would monitor the temperature level of the water pipes and communicate with nodes above ground. Such "external" nodes would monitor weather conditions and pipes temperatures in order to "tell" the actuators how much steam to push into the underground system: this would allow efficient management of the pipes and, therefore, economic savings. Clearly, the sensors monitoring the underground water pipes and the actuators cover a very vast area and collect sensitive information—in fact, misuse of such information may cause severe damage. It is, therefore, important that their communication to the external nodes is kept confidential (i.e., encrypted) while, at the same time, using the least amount of energy. In such a scenario, sensors and actuators can distribute block ciphers computations making sure that, by the time packets are sent to nodes above ground, encryption has correctly completed. Nodes operating underground fit our definition of "trusted."

Clearly, the way packets are routed through the multi-hop network is very critical. As part of future work, one attractive research direction is the design of a routing protocol, operating in the trusted zone of the multi-hop network, able to maximize the lifetime of the set of trusted nodes while making sure that packets have been fully encrypted by the time they leave the trusted zone. This opens interesting research questions about possible cooperation strategies among trusted nodes.

5.4 Arduino-based experimental analysis

5.4.1 Testbed setup

In order to measure a node's energy savings when distributing encryption and decryption computations, we use the Arduino testbed shown in Figure 5.3. This testbed includes two Arduino UNO R3 boards equipped with an Atmel ATMEGA-328p microcontroller and an Adafruit INA219 board. In particular, encryption and decryption are performed by one of the Arduino UNO boards (indicated as, namely, the Arduino UNO (2) in Figure 5.3). This board was powered by a 9 V battery. Voltage and current used by the board were measured by the Adafruit INA219. The Adafruit INA219 was powered and driven by another Arduino board (indicated as, namely, the Arduino UNO (1) in Figure 5.3) which would also collect all the measurements received from the Adafruit INA219 and would then send them to a laptop via USB. On the laptop, the measurement readings would be cleaned up and further processed using some Python scripts in order to compute the actual energy consumed by the Arduino board.

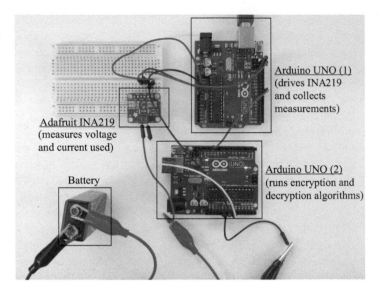

Figure 5.3   Arduino testbed used for the experiments

From a software standpoint, we modified Davy Landman's AESLib library [13] in order to let the Arduino node perform a custom number of rounds of encryption and decryption per packet sent or received.

5.4.2   *Experimental measurements*

We measure the energy consumption and savings of the AES block cipher as it is widely used in the Internet (e.g., Transport Layer Security protocol [14]). AES is a block cipher that operates on 128-bit blocks of plaintext and outputs 128-bit blocks of ciphertext. The key length in AES can be 128, 196, and 256 bits, which correspond to 10, 12, and 14 rounds, respectively. We focus on AES with a key length of 128 bits and, thus, 10 rounds. Furthermore, there are several modes of operation for AES. Throughout our experiments we consider the cipher block chaining (CBC) mode, as it is one of the most used. In CBC mode, an initialization vector must be used in order to make each message unique. Furthermore, as we can see from Figure 5.1, at each round, a block of plaintext is first XORed with the previous block of ciphertext and then encrypted.

5.4.2.1   Energy measurements

Our first objective is to measure how much energy a node would save when using distributed block cipher computations. In order to do this, we measure the energy consumed by a node running AES128-CBC and compare it with the energy spent by the same node running one single round of AES128-CBC. As shown in [15], the encryption operations in our testbed use, on average, 1.24 mW of power, while decryption operations use, on average, 1.79 mW of power. In order to measure the

Table 5.1   Average time and energy spent for encryption and decryption of 1,024 bytes for a different number of rounds of AES128-CBC. The average savings of a node performing a distributed computation of AES128-CBC are also shown.

No. of rounds	Encryption			Decryption		
	Duration (ms)	Energy (μJ)	Savings (%)	Duration (ms)	Energy (μJ)	Savings (%)
1	3.25	4.05	73	2.66	4.77	81
2	4.22	5.26	65	3.92	7.02	72
3	5.19	6.47	56	5.17	9.27	63
4	6.16	7.68	48	6.43	11.52	54
5	7.13	8.89	40	7.68	13.77	45
6	8.1	10.1	32	8.94	16.02	36
7	9.07	11.31	24	10.19	18.27	27
8	10.04	12.52	16	11.43	20.48	18
9	11.01	13.73	8	12.70	22.77	9
10	11.98	14.93	0	13.96	25.02	0

energy consumed, knowing the used power, one needs to measure how long encryption and decryption operations take.

Table 5.1 shows, among various performance metrics, the duration of encryption and decryption operations for different numbers of rounds for a 1,024-byte packet size. One can first observe that while for both one-round and two-round computations, encryption takes longer than decryption, the opposite is true for a number of rounds larger than two. In particular, for full AES128 (i.e., ten rounds), encryption takes, on average, 11.98 ms, while decryption takes, on average, 13.96 ms. On the other hand, for a single round of AES128, encryption takes, on average, 3.25 ms, while decryption takes, on average, 2.66 ms. Interestingly, for both encryption and decryption, the time required to run full AES128 (i.e., ten rounds) is considerably shorter than ten times the time required to run one round of AES128. Consequently, the overall energy spent by running the non-distributed version of AES128 is much lower than the overall energy spent by running one round of AES128 ten times. As we confirmed in our extended measurements [15], this difference is due to the initial overhead of AES128 caused by initialization operations such as key expansion. In particular, this initial overhead is responsible for an additional average consumption of 2.84 μJ for encryption and of 2.53 μJ for decryption. In the Arduino AES library used in our testbed, such overhead is present at each round of the distributed version of AES128, whereas it is present only in the first round of the non-distributed version of AES128. This difference in the initial cost is the reason why running one round of AES128 ten times (i.e., distributed AES128) is much more costly, in terms of energy, than running the non-distributed version of AES128. This clearly shows that one of the optimizations required in distributing block cipher computations is to make sure that any initialization cost incurs only once, at the first round, and does not get propagated to subsequent rounds

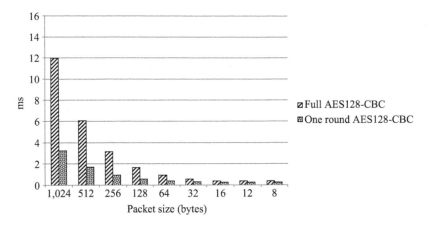

Figure 5.4   Encryption time as a function of the packet size

of computation. By taking this into account, the total amount of energy spent by running distributed block cipher computations must match the amount of energy spent when running the non-distributed version of the same block cipher.

As shown in Table 5.1, in our measurements, we have observed that the node running the first round of distributed encryption consumes, on average, 4.05 μJ of energy. However, nodes performing subsequent rounds of encryption spend, on average, 1.21 μJ per round of encryption due to the lack of initialization costs. Similarly, for decryption, the node running the first round of decryption would consume, on average, 4.77 μJ, while nodes running subsequent rounds would consume, on average, 2.24 μJ.

Naturally, energy savings reduce as nodes run an increasing number of rounds of block-cipher computations. In Table 5.1, we also show the energy savings of a node when performing a different number of rounds. As one can see, from energy savings of 73% in encryption and of 81% in decryption, when performing one-round computation, a node reduces its energy savings to 48% in encryption and 54% in decryption when performing four-round computations of the same block cipher. Such savings drop down to 8% in encryption and 9% in decryption when performing nine-round computations. As expected, the larger the number of computed rounds, the lower the energy savings—obviously reaching zero for ten rounds (i.e., full AES128).

We now investigate the impact of the packet size on AES128 power consumption. In Figures 5.4 and 5.5, the encryption and decryption times are shown, respectively, as functions of the packet size. In both cases, full AES128 (i.e., ten rounds) and one single round of AES128 are considered. In particular, we measure the time required by encryption and decryption operations for packet sizes between 8 and 1,024 bytes. It can be observed that the duration of encryption and decryption decreases linearly with the decrease of packet size. However, below 16 bytes (i.e., 128 bits), encryption and decryption times tend to remain constant. This behavior is due to the fact that in AES128-CBC packets, smaller than 16 bytes are padded to the block size of 16 bytes.

In Figure 5.6, the energies consumed by (a) encryption and (b) decryption are shown as functions of the packet size, considering full AES128 and one round of

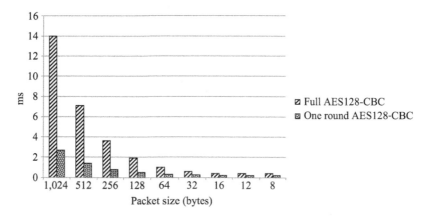

Figure 5.5   Decryption time as a function of the packet size

AES128. In both encryption and decryption, one can see that by using a distributed block cipher, the highest energy savings are obtained with large packet sizes. As the packet size decreases, so do the energy savings, down to a point where performing full AES128 takes almost the same amount of energy as performing a single round of AES128. This result is very surprising, as one would expect the savings to be roughly the same, in relative terms, for any packet size. By comparing Figure 5.6(a) and (b), it can also be concluded that such savings are greater for decryption than for encryption.

Table 5.2 shows the energy savings that a node would have by using a distributed block cipher and computing a single round of AES128 as opposed to running full AES128. As can be seen, for larger packet sizes, one can save up to 73% and up to 81% of the energy usually spent during encryption and decryption, respectively. For decreasing packet sizes, the energy savings decrease as well, although they still remain quite significant. For packet sizes smaller than or equal to 16 bytes, the savings remain constant due to padding.

In many IoT applications, packet sizes tend to be quite small. There is, however, a vast literature on the use of data fusion [16], data aggregation [17,18], and other techniques [19,20], in the IoT, to combine multiple packets together, before sending them to the gateway, in order to save transmission energy. The reason for combining packets together is that while sending a short packet consumes less energy than sending a large one, sending many small packets is less efficient due to the packet headers that, overall, reduce the goodput. Therefore, the following observations hold.

- Just by looking at the packet size, large packets require a higher transmission energy than shorter packets.
- Considering the transmission energy spent per bit of payload (i.e., excluding the headers content), the opposite is true and more energy can be saved by sending a few larger packets.

A data fusion approach thus goes well together with our findings of higher energy savings, in terms of encryption and decryption energy costs, for larger packet sizes. By

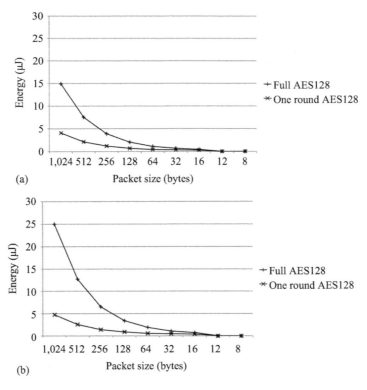

Figure 5.6   Comparison, in terms of consumed energy as a function of packet size, considering full and one-round AES128-CBC: (a) encryption and (b) decryption

Table 5.2   Average energy savings (in both encryption and decryption), for different packet sizes, when using AES128-CBC as a distributed block cipher and performing one round

Size (bytes)	Encryption (%)	Decryption (%)
1,024	73	81
512	72	80
256	69	78
128	65	74
64	59	68
32	49	58
16	36	45
12	36	45
8	36	45

using data fusion together with a distributed block cipher computation, transmission energy costs, as well as encryption and decryption energy costs, can be simultaneously reduced.

5.4.2.2   Lifetime increase: a single node's perspective

As we discussed earlier and shown in Table 5.1, a node performing one round of encryption can save 73% of the energy normally spent in encryption. For an Arduino UNO board powered by a 9 V alkaline battery, this means about 9 min of extra battery lifetime, which roughly corresponds to 3% of the total battery lifetime. While this may seem like a modest energy saving, one needs to keep in mind that we are reducing the energy consumption of encryption and decryption operations which use between 1 and 2 mW of power, while the Arduino UNO board has an *operational power* of hundreds of milliwatts, that is, two orders of magnitude higher than both the encryption and decryption powers. Given this huge difference in power consumption, a 3% battery lifetime increase achieved by reducing only the energy consumption of encryption operations is quite impressive. For energy-harvesting devices, where the power used in cryptographic operations has the same order of magnitude of the operational power, significantly greater savings are expected.

Another cause of significant energy consumption is *transmission power*. In our measurements, a Digi XBee S1 802.15.4 RF module, connected to an Arduino UNO board, used about 71 mW of power to send a 1,024-byte packet at 9.6 kbps. This power is roughly one order of magnitude higher than what is required by encryption and decryption operations. In the IoT, however, a large class of devices will be energy harvesting devices. For such devices, operation and communication costs, in terms of energy, become comparable to computational cost and, as such, to the cost of cryptographic operations. For example, energy-harvesting active networked tags [11] use a few microjoules of energy to transmit a packet. For such devices, great savings in encryption and decryption translate to great savings in overall node energy consumption, as the energy spent in encryption and decryption represents a large part of the node's energy budget.

5.4.2.3   Lifetime increase: a multi-hop network perspective

Up to this point we have discussed energy savings from a single node's point of view, without taking into account network dynamics. When we consider not just one node but the whole multi-hop network of trusted nodes (i.e., trusted zone in Figure 5.2), some important observations can be carried out.

We have seen that a single node performing one round of encryption can save 73% of the energy normally spent in encryption operations. If, however, this node performs multiple rounds of encryption, its energy savings decrease as per Table 5.1. In a multi-hop network, a node can not only generate its own packets but can also relay other nodes' packets. For example, if a node generates one packet and receives nine packets from other trusted nodes, since on each of these ten packets one round of AES128 encryption‡ is performed, it will then consume an amount of energy equal to ten rounds of encryption. This is the same amount of energy the node would have consumed by just encrypting its own packet with "traditional" AES128 (i.e., in a non-distributed manner). Therefore, apparently, there would be no savings in using a distributed computation approach in such a scenario. To make things worse, if the node receives packets from 20 trusted nodes and performs one round of encryption on each one of those, it would spend twice the amount of energy that it would have spent by encrypting only its own packets with "traditional" AES128. More generally, if the trusted zone of the multi-hop network generates and processes a given amount of packets, it will consume, overall, the same amount of energy with or without distributing encryption computations. So, why using a distributed approach for encryption and decryption?

The energy savings obtained by distributing encryption and decryption computations, at a network level, depend on two important factors: battery residual energy distribution among the nodes in the network and network topology. Taking into account those factors, various challenges emerge.

In an IoT application including wireless sensors, for example, nodes will detect events, thus generating traffic, with distributions that are not spatially uniform. Because of this, some nodes will generate a large amount of traffic, while others may not generate any traffic at all but act only as relays. This asymmetry in traffic generation contributes to creating a nonuniform battery residual energy distribution among the nodes in the network—under the implicit assumption that all nodes have the same initial battery energy. Furthermore, if the nodes are energy harvesting, the different rate at which each one can harvest energy will further accentuate the difference between the energies available at the nodes. In such a scenario, a routing protocol, as the one described at the end of Section 5.3, would make it possible to route packets so that nodes with a larger amount of available energy would perform more rounds of encryption while nodes with less energy could save it for routing purposes. In doing so, the overall lifetime of the network would increase as nodes with a small amount of energy would prolong their lifetime by delegating encryption to nodes with a higher energy budget. In other words, a routing protocol using distributed encryption computations would increase the network lifetime by distributing encryption operations in a nonuniform way among nodes, following the nonuniform energy distribution. In multi-hop networks, network topology is very important. In particular, because of various reasons (e.g., physical obstructions, nodes layout), there could be a few nodes that have to relay a large amount of traffic between different parts of the network or between the network and the gateway. This is especially true in network topologies considered in IoT scenarios, such as those created by the use of the IPv6 Routing Protocol for Low-Power and Lossy Networks (RPL) [12]. Such nodes are extremely important since, if they die, large parts of the network, if not the whole network, are likely to remain isolated and packets will not reach the gateway any longer. Therefore, it is important, for such nodes, to live as long as possible regardless of their initial energy budget. In such a scenario, by distributing encryption

---

‡The first, more energy demanding, round for its own packet and a subsequent round for other nodes' packets.

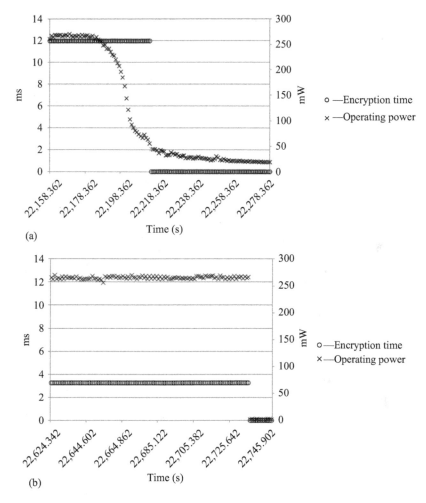

Figure 5.7   Tail of the battery discharging profile: (a) full AES128-CBC encryption and (b) one round AES128-CBC encryption

computations, the routing protocol could take this into account and would not assign any encryption computations to such nodes in order to maximize their lifetime and, thus, the lifetime of the network of trusted nodes.

5.4.2.4   Battery discharging profile

As shown above, nodes participating in a distributed block cipher will be able to encrypt and decrypt packets at a much lower energy level. Because of this, a battery used by such nodes will reach a discharged state with a residual energy lower than that of a node operating the full block cipher.

Figure 5.7 shows the tails of the discharging profiles of (a) a battery powering a node performing full AES128 encryption and (b) a battery powering a node performing one round of distributed AES128 encryption. In both cases, the same battery type was used (i.e., 9 V alkaline battery) and nodes were encrypting a 1,024-byte packet every 10 ms. When the encryption time goes to zero, the node has no longer enough energy to work properly and cannot encrypt or decrypt packets correctly. As can be seen, while discharging for full AES128 is slow and gradual, in the case of one-round AES128, more energy can be "squeezed out" of the battery, which lasts longer but dies abruptly.

5.5 Zolertia-based simulation analysis

5.5.1 *Simulator setup*

While measurements on the Arduino testbed have already proven the very high energy savings our approach can provide, we want to explore what kind of energy savings can be expected when distributing computations of lightweight block ciphers that have been engineered specifically for low-power devices. In particular, in the following simulations, we focus on the energy spent during encryption by the scalable encryption algorithm (SEA) [6] and the tiny encryption algorithm (TEA) [9]. Furthermore, we compare such savings with the ones achieved by AES128-CBC.

Simulations have been conducted on Contiki OS-based constrained devices [21], using the Cooja simulator [22]. Contiki OS is a specialized low-power operating system for constrained devices that provides implementations of the IPv6 stack and RPL routing, as well as several MAC protocols. The version of Contiki OS used is 2.7. The experimental platform is based on Zolertia Z1 nodes, with nominal 92 kB ROM (when compiling with 20-bit architecture support) and an 8 kB RAM. In practice, the compilation with the Z1 nodes has been performed with a 16-bit target architecture, which lowers the amount of available ROM to roughly 52 kB. The energy consumption of the CoAP server has been evaluated using Powertrace, a tool for network-level power profiling of low-power wireless networks. Powertrace determines the energy consumption by estimating the amount of time each operation mode of the device uses. We refer to the current consumption of each component indicated in the Z1 datasheet. In particular, the MSP430f2617 microcontroller consumes 0.515 mA in active mode (CPU) and 0.5 μA in low-power mode (lpm), respectively. Similarly, the CC2420 radio transceiver consumes 17.4 mA in transmitting (TX) mode and 18.8 mA in receiving (RX) mode. In order to obtain the total consumed energy for the node, the following conversion formula has been used:

$$E = \sum_{j \in \mathcal{M}} i_j \cdot v \cdot \Delta t_j \tag{5.1}$$

where $\mathcal{M}$ is the set of all operation modes of the node (active, lpm, TX, and RX); v is the nominal voltage of the node; and Δt_j is the time the node was in the jth operation mode j.

A linear topology has been used to deploy simulated nodes.

Table 5.3   *Average time and energy spent by AES, SEA, and TEA for full encryption*
and one-round encryption of 16-byte, 12-byte, and 8-byte payload
packets, respectively. The average energy savings of a node performing a
distributed computation are also shown

Block cipher	Full encryption		One-round encryption		Energy savings (%)
	Duration (ms)	Energy (μJ)	Duration (ms)	Energy (μJ)	
AES	18.68	28.87	4.9	7.58	73.74
SEA	20.58	31.79	3.1	4.79	84.93
TEA	20.04	30.96	1.9	2.88	90.69

5.5.2   Simulation results

Table 5.3 shows the results of our simulations. As we can see, when doing a full encryption, AES performs much better than SEA and TEA. This is due to the fact that SEA and TEA have been designed to be extremely efficient when implemented using dedicated hardware. In software, however, they do not perform very well and AES represents a better option. On the other hand, by distributing block cipher computations, a single round of SEA and TEA performs better, energy-wise, than a single round of AES. This apparent contradiction is due to the fact that while each round of either SEA or TEA consumes less energy, the total numbers of rounds for SEA and TEA are 51 and 32, respectively: these values are much larger than the 10 rounds of AES. Moreover, in this case, we can see that the energy spent by a block cipher when performing the full encryption is much lower than the product of (i) the energy spent by a single round of encryption and (ii) the number of rounds. This, as discussed for the Arduino measurements, is due to a higher energy cost of the first round of encryption, which takes into account an initialization phase not present in subsequent rounds. As mentioned earlier, when distributing block cipher computations, we have to make sure to incur in this initialization cost only once so that the total amount of energy spent when distributing the computations equals the amount of energy spent in the non-distributed case.

For all three block ciphers, we have very large energy savings. In particular, from a single node's perspective, with TEA, the energy saving for a single node reaches 90.69%, followed by SEA with saving equal to 84.93%, and, lastly, by AES with 73.74%. We remark that, for AES, our simulation results perfectly match, in terms of energy savings, our experimental results. At the network level, however, things are different since the larger number of rounds of SEA and TEA translates into a larger amount of energy spent by the network as a whole. Moreover, routing becomes more challenging given that a larger number of rounds mean that a packet may need to be routed through a larger number of nodes (i.e., longer paths). In such cases, there

Table 5.4   Average energy spent in RX and TX

Block cipher	RX energy (mJ)	TX energy (mJ)
AES	1.12	0.37
SEA	0.94	0.5
TEA	3.24	0.88

are trade-offs between route complexity, nodes energy savings and overall network energy level.

Table 5.4 shows the average energy consumption of AES, SEA, and TEA for packet TX and RX. Given that the packets sent and received by the three block ciphers have different sizes, we cannot compare their TX and RX energy consumptions. However, we can see how, for all three block ciphers, RX energy is higher than TX energy. This is consistent with the observations in [11]. In particular, this is due to the fact that in low-power applications, such as those in the IoT, for packet transmission, the radio needs to stay on only for the duration of the transmission; at the opposite, for packet reception, the radio needs to stay on for a longer amount of time. Since perfect node synchronization consumes much energy and is, therefore, not implemented, the exact arrival time of a packet is, in fact, unknown.

5.6 Conclusions and future work

After a short discussion on the challenges in provisioning data confidentiality in the IoT and after presenting some existing solutions, we have introduced a novel approach to greatly reduce the energy spent by a node during encryption and decryption operations. In particular, given the iterative structure of block ciphers and the multi-hop nature of communication protocols in the IoT, a node can save a large amount of energy by distributing block ciphers computations. We have experimentally measured node's energy savings, for a distributed version of AES128 in CBC mode, of up to 81% and of up to 73% for decryption and encryption, respectively. We have also measured (through simulations) energy savings for lightweight block ciphers (namely, SEA and TEA), showing encryption energy savings up to 84.93% and 90.59% for SEA and TEA, respectively.

Given the sensitive nature of block-cipher computations, such computations should be distributed among a set of *trusted* nodes. One of our current research activities consists of the design of a new routing protocol aimed at maximizing the network lifetime while, at the same time, guaranteeing encryption distribution among the set of *trusted* nodes. Finally, we plan to apply the same distribution principle to the computation of cryptographic hashes.

References

[1] Satoh A, Morioka S, Takano K, *et al.* A compact Rijndael hardware architecture with S-box optimization. In: Springer, editor. Proceedings of the 7th International Conference on the Theory and Application of Cryptology and Information Security (ASIACRYPT) – Advances in Cryptology. Gold Coast, Australia; 2001. pp. 239–254.

[2] Feldhofer M, Wolkerstorfer J, and Rijmen V. AES implementation on a grain of sand. IEE Proceedings – Information Security. 2005;152(1):13–20.

[3] Wolkerstorfer J, Oswald E, and Lamberger M. An ASIC implementation of the AES S-Boxes. In: Springer, editor. Topics in Cryptology (CT-RSA). San Jose, CA, USA; 2002. pp. 67–78.

[4] Tillich S, and Großschädl J. Instruction set extensions for efficient AES implementation on 32-bit processors. In: Springer, editor. Proceedings of the 8th International Workshop on Cryptographic Hardware and Embedded Systems (CHES). Yokohama, Japan; 2006. pp. 270–284.

[5] Oswald E, and Schramm K. An efficient masking scheme for AES software implementations. In: Springer, editor. Information Security Applications; 2006. pp. 292–305.

[6] Standaert FX, Piret G, Gershenfeld N, *et al.* SEA: A scalable encryption algorithm for small embedded applications. In: Springer, editor. International Conference on Smart Card Research and Advanced Applications; 2006. pp. 222–236.

[7] Bogdanov A, Knudsen LR, Leander G, *et al.* PRESENT: An ultra-lightweight block cipher. In: Springer-Verlag, editor. Proceedings of the 9th International Workshop on Cryptographic Hardware and Embedded Systems (CHES). Vienna, Austria; 2007. pp. 450–466.

[8] Wu W, and Zhang L. LBlock: A lightweight block cipher. In: Springer, editor. Proceedings of the 9th International Conference on Applied Cryptography and Network Security (ACNS). Nerja, Spain; 2011. pp. 327–344.

[9] Wheeler DJ, and Needham RM. TEA, a tiny encryption algorithm. In: Springer, editor. Proceedings of the 2nd International Workshop on Fast Software Encryption. Leuven, Belgium; 1995. pp. 363–366.

[10] Veltri L, Cirani S, Busanelli S, *et al.* A novel batch-based group key management protocol applied to the Internet of Things. Ad Hoc Networks. 2013;11(8):2724–2737.

[11] Gorlatova M, Margolies R, Sarik J, *et al.* Prototyping energy harvesting active networked tags (EnHANTs). In: Proceeding of the 32nd IEEE International Conference on Computer Communications (INFOCOM) – Mini Conference. Turin, Italy; 2013. pp. 585–589.

[12] Winter T, Thubert P, Brandt A, *et al.* RPL: IPv6 Routing Protocol for Low-Power and Lossy Networks. IETF; 2012. RFC 6550 (Proposed Standard). Available from: http://www.ietf.org/rfc/rfc6550.txt.

[13] Landman D. Arduino AESLib; 2011–2013. Available from: https://github.com/DavyLandman/AESLib.

[14]   Dierks T, and Rescorla E. IETF, editor. RFC 5246 – The Transport Layer Security (TLS) Protocol Version 1.2; 2008. Available from: http://tools.ietf.org/html/rfc5246.

[15]   Forte AG, and Ferrari G. Towards distributing block ciphers computations. In: Wireless Communications and Networking Conference Workshops (WCNCW), 2015 IEEE. IEEE; 2015. pp. 41–46.

[16]   Alam F, Mehmood R, Katib I, *et al.* Data fusion and IoT for smart ubiquitous environments: A survey. IEEE Access. 2017;5:9533–9554.

[17]   Lu R, Heung K, Lashkari AH, *et al.* A lightweight privacy-preserving data aggregation scheme for fog computing-enhanced IoT. IEEE Access. 2017;5:3302–3312.

[18]   Stojmenovic I. Machine-to-machine communications with in-network data aggregation, processing, and actuation for large-scale cyber-physical systems. IEEE Internet of Things Journal. 2014;1(2):122–128.

[19]   Luong NC, Hoang DT, Wang P, *et al.* Data collection and wireless communication in Internet of Things (IoT) using economic analysis and pricing models: A survey. IEEE Communications Surveys Tutorials. 2016 Fourthquarter;18(4):2546–2590.

[20]   Plageras AP, Psannis KE, Stergiou C, *et al.* Efficient IoT-based sensor big data collection-processing and analysis in smart buildings. Future Generation Computer Systems. 2018;82:349–357.

[21]   The Contiki Operating System. Available from: http://www.contiki-os.org.

[22]   Osterlind F, Dunkels A, Eriksson J, *et al.* Cross-level sensor network simulation with COOJA. In: Proceedings of the 31st IEEE Conference on Local Computer Networks; 2006. pp. 641–648.

Chapter 6

An assessment of the efficiency of smart city facilities in developing countries: the case of Yaoundé, Cameroon

Rhode Ghislaine Nguewo Ngassam[1], Jean Robert Kala Kamdjoug[2] and Samuel Fosso Wamba[3]

This chapter assesses the efficiency of smart city facilities in developing countries to demonstrate how smart solutions are used to address day-to-day problems and to evaluate the efficiency of these solutions in a smart city context. We start by clarifying the smart city concept in terms of characteristics, evolution, dimensions, definitions, applications, and evaluation before studying the city of Yaoundé, its problems, the solutions, and an assessment of its performance in a smart city context.

Yaoundé is the densely populated city in Cameroon with an important economic life which faces daily security, environmental, infrastructural, and administrative challenges. These challenges are addressed by different institutions with solutions using information and communications technologies (ICTs) especially to be reachable.

For the evaluation of smart city facilities in Yaoundé, we use the revised triple helix framework with the actors and components of smart city.

The main result is the fact that Yaoundé is moving to be a smart city, but there are several things that governments and actors in the process may adopt such as the coordination that seems to be the main obstacle at the moment.

6.1 Introduction

The definition given to the term city is very often contextual [1], but it is no less true that, according to the Larousse dictionary, "a city is a densely populated urban area in which there are the majority of human activities of a country." According to the United Nations Population Fund, 2008 marked the year when more than 50% of the world's population, 3.3 billion, lived in urban areas, a figure expected to rise to 70% by 2050 [2]. The expansion of urban areas and the increase of populations in these

[1]Montpellier Management Research Laboratory (MRM), University of Montpellier, France
[2] Management Department, Catholic University of Central Africa, Cameroon
[3]Information, Operations and Management Sciences, Toulouse Business School, France

areas make the management of cities increasingly complex [3]. The importance given to cities is greater than before because economic, environmental, and social issues are involved [4,5].

Traditional neoclassical theories of urban and regional growth are often inadequate in analyzing the urban transformations of the twenty-first century. Theories of regional competitiveness try to fill this gap by focusing not only on the city's endowment of hard infrastructures (physical capital) but also, and increasingly, on the availability and quality of knowledge communication, and social and environmental infrastructures (intellectual, social, and environmental capital) [6]. That is why new strategies to optimize the management of cities are becoming a new interesting topic [7], and the question is often to know how to optimize this management; this issue has been popularized for the past decade using the term "smart city" [5].

Although several studies have been carried out on the topic smart cities, there is still no universally accepted definition of the term; current definitions are based on authors' conceptions and focus [1,8]. The absence of a standard definition causes lack of guidance when it comes to setting up or evaluating smart cities; managers do not give a clear vision of the objectives, and private institutions and actors focus on their specific areas of interest [1].

The importance of smart cities is demonstrated in many developing countries that suffer from urban disorder and dilapidation and that attempt to use information technologies (ITs) to solve problems faced by their cities.

If the "smart city" objectives are to solve problems faced by cities using IT, it is crucial to first identify the problems they face. This chapter aims at describing the problems faced by cities in developing countries and evaluating the solutions implemented or proposed are smart.

The following section presents a background on the concept of "smart city" and its applications. The third section presents the city of Yaoundé, the capital of Cameroon, used as a case study. Section 6.4 presents an evaluation of Yaoundé based on the revised triple helices framework. Section 6.5 presents the conclusion, implications, and future directions.

6.2   Background

This section focuses on the concept of "smart city" regarding the characteristics, evolution, dimensions, definitions, and applications-related thereto.

6.2.1   Smart city concept

Smart city is not a recent concept; researchers have always studied the applications of ICTs in urban life, and with the internet wave and the Web 2.0 technology, this topic has become more interesting [1]. However, there is no universal definition of this concept [1]. This section focuses on the clarification of the concept based on characteristics, dimensions, and definitions found in existing literature.

6.2.1.1   Characteristics and dimensions of smart city

The main focus of smart city is the role of ICT in urban growth [9]. To provide a standard definition of this concept, it is important to look at different characteristics of smart cities evoked by authors.

First of all, smart cities utilize networked infrastructures to improve economic and political efficiency and enable social, cultural, and urban development [10]. This is similar to the concept of "wired city" where infrastructures (business services, housing, leisure and lifestyle services, etc.) are connected to each other with ICTs like mobile and fixed phones, satellite TVs, computer networks, e-commerce, and internet services [9]. This characteristic can be extended to that according to which, in smart cities, high importance is given to high-tech industries because they are an engine of growth [11].

The second group of characteristics is related to social aspects. In smart cities, there is a focus on the inclusion of all dwellers in public services, and a profound attention is given to the role of social and relational capital in urban growth [9]. This point shows that citizens are not forgotten in the process in the sense that they are the users of technology, and they should innovate and adapt.

The last group concerns the environmental aspect of smart cities that focuses on the fact that natural resources used for smart cities must be sustainable and environmentally friendly [9].

These characteristics confirm the fact that a smart city cannot be reduced simply to the application of ICTs to face cities' problems [5]. However, in literature, the meaning given to the term smart cities has evolved over time [5].

The concept of smart city is gone from a purely technical approach in the 1990s [12] to an extension on the social and environmental approach following the criticisms that were made to the first approach by the center of governance and the University of Ottawa [5].

In a study on the definition on smart cities, Dameri [1] concludes that to find a comprehensible definition of this concept, it is important to examine three aspects: (1) components, (2) boundaries, and (3) terminology of smart cities.

1. Components: Talking about smart city components, these elements are generally evoked: land, citizens, technology, and governance [1].
2. Boundaries: Smart city initiatives could have larger or broader boundaries, from the local urban dimension of a single city to a region or a network of cities, toward the national and global dimension [1].
3. Terminology: Regarding the terminology, as smart cities describe the use of high tech to face crucial urban problems, it is observed that several other concepts are used in the same context: wired city, intelligent city, digital city, technocity, etc. [1].
   i. Intelligent city. It is a city that has several competencies, able to produce knowledge and to translate it into unique and distinctive abilities; it is also able to produce synergies between knowledge and competences mixed in an original way, difficult to imitate; this city is smart because it is able to

create intellectual capital and to ground development and well-being of this intellectual capital [13].

ii.   Digital city. It is a wired, digitalized city, using ICT both for data processing and for information sharing, and also to support communication and Web 2.0 democracy [14].

iii. Technocity. It is a city that uses technology to improve the efficiency and effectiveness of its infrastructures and services: it focuses its smart projects on urban space quality, mobility, public transports, and logistic [15].

Despite all the precisions on the concept in terms of characteristics, evolution and dimensions, each author has his own conception.

6.2.1.2   Definitions

The absence of a clear definition of smart city is generally linked to the adopted approach for different projects related to it [1]. The approach can either be a bottom-up or top-down approach.

Bottom-up is the worst approach in terms of clear vision and planning. In this approach, initiatives come from actors to resolve day-to-day problems. There is no strategy and no perspectives, and the risk of failure is very high.

In the top-down approach, governance has a great role to play in terms of long-term vision, planning and definition of projects; all initiatives are complementary and have the same purpose.

Table 6.1 presents how several authors define the smart city concept. These definitions can be clustered in three focus areas: technological, human resources, and governance focus [16].

6.2.2   Smart cities applications

Generally, city management includes several problems related to many clusters: social [32], administrative and environmental aspects. This section focuses on the description of different traditional solutions and modern ones generally classified as smart city solutions.

6.2.2.1   Social aspects

Social problems include road-traffic management, security management, and city crowding [1] to name a few. If it can be assumed that managing this category and the two others increases the welfare of citizens, then the social category must and can be defined as the most important one because the positive results are always to health, security, and the development of people.

Talking about the road traffic, we can define it as all rules and arrangements to avoid an accident, time loss, and disorder [32]. Facilities that can be cited for this purpose are traffic lights, road security agents, and the law. Other authors think it is necessary to model drivers' behavior to study mechanisms that influence it and improve the performance and the utility of road-traffic-management systems [33]. Another group of authors talks about a more automated approach as we can use M2M-based platforms to face situations [34].

Table 6.1 Definitions and focuses of smart city concept

Focus	Definition	Reference
Technological focus	Smart city is a high-tech intensive and advanced city that connects people, information, and city elements using new technologies to create a sustainable, greener city, competitive and innovative commerce, and an increased life quality	[17]
	Smart cities will take advantage of communications and sensor capabilities sewed into the cities' infrastructures to optimize electrical, transportation, and other logistical operations supporting daily life, thereby improving the quality of life for everyone	[18]
	A community of average technology size, interconnected and sustainable, comfortable, attractive, and secure	[19]
	A smart city infuses information into its physical infrastructure to improve conveniences, facilitate mobility, add efficiencies, conserve energy, improve the quality of air and water, identify problems and fix them quickly, recover rapidly from disasters, collect data to make better decisions, deploy resources effectively, and share data to enable collaboration across entities and domains	[20]
Governance focus	Being a smart city means using all available technology and resources in an intelligent and coordinated manner to develop urban centers that are integrated, habitable, and sustainable	[21]
Technological, human resources and governance focus	A city is smart when investments in human and social capital and traditional (transport) and modern (ICT) communication infrastructure fuel sustainable economic growth and a high quality of life, with a wise management of natural resources, through participatory governance	[22]
	Smart community—a community which makes a conscious decision to aggressively deploy technology as a catalyst to solving its social and business needs—will undoubtedly focus on building its high-speed broadband infrastructures, but the real opportunity is in rebuilding and renewing a sense of place, and in the process a sense of civic pride Smart communities are not, at their core, exercises in the deployment and use of technology, but in the promotion of economic development, job growth, and an increased quality of life. In other words, technological propagation of smart communities is not an end, but only a means to reinvent cities for a new economy and society with clear and compelling community benefit	[23]
	A city performing well in a forward-looking way in economy, people, governance, mobility, environment, and living, built on the smart combination of endowments and activities of self-decisive, independent and aware citizens. Smart city generally refers to the search and identification of intelligent solutions which allow modern cities to enhance the quality of the services provided to citizens	[24]

(Continues)

Table 6.1   (Continued)

Focus	Definition	Reference
	A city connecting the physical infrastructure, the IT infrastructure, the social infrastructure, and the business infrastructure to leverage the collective intelligence of the city	[25]
Technological and governance focus	Smart city is a well-defined geographical area, in which high technologies, such as ICT, logistic, and energy production, cooperate to create benefits for citizens in terms of well-being, inclusion, participation, environmental quality, and intelligent development; it is governed by a well-defined pool of subjects, able to state the rules and policy for the city government and development	[1]
	Two main streams of research ideas: (1) smart cities should do everything related to governance and economy using new thinking paradigms and (2) smart cities are all about networks of sensors, smart devices, real-time data, and ICT integration in every aspect of human life	[26]
Human focus	Smart cities are territories with a high capacity for learning and innovation, which is built in the creativity of their population, their institutions of knowledge creation, and their digital infrastructure for communication and knowledge management	[27]
	Smart cities are the result of knowledge-intensive and creative strategies aiming at enhancing the socioeconomic, ecological, logistic, and competitive performance of cities. Such smart cities are based on a promising mix of human capital (e.g., skilled labor force), infrastructural capital (e.g., high-tech communication facilities), social capital (e.g., intense and open network linkages), and entrepreneurial capital (e.g., creative and risk-taking business activities)	[28]
	Smart cities have high productivity as they have a relatively high share of highly educated people, knowledge-intensive jobs, output-oriented planning systems, creative activities and sustainability-oriented initiatives	[29]
	Creative or smart city experiments aimed at nurturing a creative economy through investment in the quality of life which in turn attracts knowledge workers to live and work in smart cities. The nexus of competitive advantage has shifted to those regions that can generate, retain, and attract the best talent	[30]
Technological and human focus	The application of information and communications technology (ICT) with their effects on human capital/education, social and relational capital and environmental issues is often indicated by the notion of smart city	[31]

Another side of social aspects is security management which consists of mastering security threats like crime and violence, insecurity of tenure and forced evictions, natural disasters and terrorism [35]. In a study related to holistic strategy for urban security, [36] presents the limits of simple physical protection and shows the importance of the combination of technology, people, and institutions to construct a robust security system.

6.2.2.2 Environmental aspects

The focus of environmental aspect is pollution monitoring. When defining a smart city, several authors emphasize on the fact that there is no pollution in a smart city or at least a well-monitored one [37,38].

The main targets of the pollution in urban areas are air and water, and the main causes are household and industrial waste, chemicals, and toxic gases mainly emitted by vehicles [39,40].

To avoid or reduce the disasters caused by pollution, there are many techniques developed to monitor and control the main threats.

Ghanem *et al.* [41] present a smart way for cities to monitor and control air pollution by the use of sensor grids. Sensors are also used to monitor and control industrial processes [42].

Sempere-Torres *et al.* [43] present the use of weather radar to monitor and control combined sewer overflows which is a major urban pollution problem.

6.2.2.3 Administrative aspects

As smart cities bring about the need to manage, automate, optimize, and explore all the aspects of a city, it is important to have an integrated management to build a robust architecture to satisfy a minimal number of requirements as part of a vision and a common plan. In a simple way, the different actors must agree to put in place projects with the same purpose and not contradictory projects. This is why, in the different definitions given to smart cities, the authors emphasize on government role, planning, and the harmonization of actions to successfully integrate smart cities [1,21].

Other authors put the government at the center of smart cities as we can see at Amsterdam where there is a unique partnership between businesses, authorities, research institutions and the population with the objective of developing the Amsterdam metropolitan area into a smart city with a focus on the themes living, working, mobility, public facilities, and open data [16].

6.2.3 Evaluation of smart city performance

According to Deakin [44], the real problem in the lack of a universal definition for smart cities is the lack of a real indicator for evaluation. For example, it is often claimed that cities are as smart as the way they use ICTs to develop services [8]. However, to address this lack of objectivity in the evaluation of smart cities, the triple helix model has recently emerged as a reference framework for the analysis of knowledge-based innovation systems [8].

This model evaluates the three main helices: university, government, and industry to which we add "civil society" in the point of view of five components of smart cities: smart governance (related to participation), smart economy (related to competitiveness), smart human (related to people), smart living (related to the quality of life), and smart environment (related to natural resources) [6]. All these components are based on the extension of the smart city concept to the role of human capital/education,

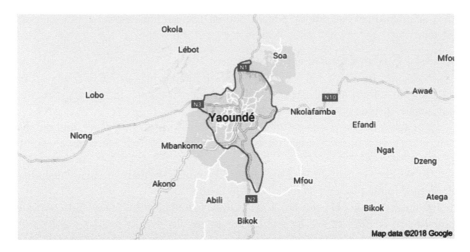

Figure 6.1   Yaoundé map

social and relational capital and environmental issues; they are not limited to ICT infrastructures like it is with the concept of "digital city" or "intelligent city" [45].

With this framework, we can evaluate if a city is smart or if it is moving in the right direction to become smart [6].

6.3   Case study: the city of Yaoundé, Cameroon

6.3.1   *Presentation of the city and its problems*

Yaoundé, a city bound by seven hills, is the political capital of Cameroon. It is in the center region of the country spanning a surface area of 180 square kilometers with about 2.8 million dwellers in 2017 (Figure 6.1).*

This city is headed by a government delegate and is divided into seven districts ranging from Yaoundé 1 to Yaoundé 7, each headed by a mayor.

As a political capital, Yaoundé is home to the highest government institutions such as the presidency, ministries, and the headquarters of national institutions such as the National Social Insurance Fund and the National Hydrocarbons Corporation.

In terms of education, in addition to basic, primary, and secondary schools, Yaoundé is home to many universities and higher education institutions that train young people in several fields: engineering, medicine, management, finance, commerce, agriculture, etc.

Economically, this city includes companies engaged in various activities of the three sectors of the national economy: primary, secondary, and tertiary sectors.

*Source: https://www.populationdata.net statistique de 2017.

The authorities and the actors of the city of Yaoundé face challenges every day that can be grouped into several groups: (1) security, (2) infrastructures, (3) urbanization and environment, (4) natural disaster, (5) administration, etc.[†]

1. Security challenges include crimes, accidents, epidemics, access to health services, management of fires, and abandoned corpses.

    Crimes are all acts committed outside the law by citizens such as murder, theft, road-traffic offenses or in general anything that causes harm to others.

    Regarding epidemics, it is a matter of taking rapid measures to not only prevent the surface of contamination from widening but also to take up all the contaminated.

    Making health services accessible means ensuring that health facilities and health professionals are available for all areas and for all budgets.

    Fire management is to intervene quickly to prevent fire spreading and do more damage to material and human, as for the abandoned corpses, it is those found in the streets or in the houses without the family members or relatives being immediately known. We must take care to preserve them the time to find their origins or to bury them if there is no longer any hope of identifying them.

2. Infrastructural challenges include water and electricity distribution networks, roads, and street lighting.

    The main challenge with the infrastructures is to modernize them and to manage incidents related to them daily. If we take the case of roads, we can mention the case of Yaoundé bad roads or poor road network that does not necessarily leave the choice of routes to users.

    One of the major problems also is the lack of coordination in projects of this type. We can take the case of a road that is built without considering future works such as electrical wiring or water piping.

3. Urbanization challenges include the management of anarchic constructions and traffic lanes; environmental challenges include sanitation and waste management.

    Urbanization considers the infrastructures presented earlier, but on top of that, there is very often the problem of hierarchical constructions which consist of people building where they should not because the state has planned another project. This problem is often at the origin of the destruction of the houses, and the relocation of the citizens and is generally caused by a lack of coordination between the cadastral service and the other services of the government or by the stubbornness of the populations to build without permission.

    Regarding the protection of the environment, the challenges are not only to reduce or avoid water and air pollution but also to manage in a strategic way the industrial and household waste.

4. Natural disasters include mainly flood management in wetlands.

5. Administrative challenges are those related to the coordination of all actions and initiatives implemented in the city.

[†]Interviews with employees of the urban development unit of the Yaoundé urban community.

6.3.2   Solutions and role of ICTs

Among these solutions, some have yielded good results and others have not yet. Though many innovative solutions are increasingly conceived, the lack of finances remains the main obstacle to their implementation (Table 6.2).

Table 6.2   Day-to-day problems and implemented solutions

Problems	Institutions in charge	Solutions	Use of ICTs
Road traffic (traffic jam, accidents)	Road-safety corps	Street lights, camera, road security agents, etc.	Software systems that indicate the most time-effective roads to destinations at any given time
Flood management in wetlands	City council, firefighters	Making wetlands safer, field visit, and evacuation of populations during high-risk periods	
Sanitation and waste management	Urban community, city council, HYSACAM	HYSACAM,[‡] in close collaboration with the urban community and the city council, collects and transfers the waste to a landfill in a remote corner of the city	
Crimes and accidents	Police services, Delegation for National Security, Ministry of Defense	Mainly managed by police corps. To prevent crimes, citizens are identified and agents circulate in high-risk neighborhoods, and police services can be reached by short numbers. When crimes have been committed, investigations are conducted and those responsible are summoned to answer for their actions in the court	Mobile phones are used to reach police services when there is a problem
Epidemics and access to health services	Ministry of Public Health, regional health delegations, hospitals and emergency services, universities	Construction of sanitary maps for the country, screening campaigns and emergency services, training of medical doctors and research on new treatments	

(Continues)

‡Enterprise of hygiene and health in Cameroon.

Table 6.2 (Continued)

Problems	Institutions in charge	Solutions	Use of ICTs
Pollution	Urban community and city council	Installations of low-energy equipment such as energy-saving light bulbs	
Anarchic constructions	Cadastral services, city council	Construction of urbanization plans and issuance of building permits according to these plans	
Administration		Coordination of different institutions with meetings, consultations, and planning by the central institutions	Modern communication tools like mobile and fixed phones, social media, integrated software, email services, etc.

On the other hand, decentralization and lack of coordination of institutions can in some cases be considered as an obstacle in that everyone undertakes important projects from their point of view without questioning the future projects of other services.[§] Indeed, the decentralization in Yaoundé can consist in the fact that each mayor has full power in his constituency, and the lack of coordination very often comes from the fact that the government delegate has projects launched in certain circumscriptions without talking to mayors, or then the cadastral service grants land to a building permit to a person without consulting the projects that are planned for this land.

6.3.3   Smart city project in Yaoundé

For the urban community and city councils of Yaoundé, smart cities are more complex than the simple application of IT in solving everyday problems. It is more of cities with neither pollution, nor hygiene problems, nor traffic congestion, and one with modern facilities and especially a financial autonomy.[¶]

Thus, building a smart city begins with its infrastructure (buildings, roads, water and gas evacuation networks, etc.), and environmental management (low-energy consumption equipment, management of black water and rubbish).[‖]

Apart from one-on-one projects, there will be a question of restructuring the city in a coordinated way.

[§]Interviews with an employee of the City Council of Yaoundé 3.
[¶]Report of the conference on smart cities to the urban community of Yaoundé in December 2017.
[‖]Interview with the head of the development support unit for decentralized cooperation at the Yaoundé III City Council.

6.4   Evaluation of Yaoundé's performance as smart city with the revised triple helix framework

Table 6.3 shows the evaluation of smart city devices in Yaoundé from the revised triple helix model. The data that will be put there are mainly results of statistical surveys or observations.

Most of these statistics concern Cameroon in general because of the scarcity of data especially on each city. Empty cells or simple affirmations are because there are no available statistics concerning those aspects. Thus, many affirmations are made based on direct observations and experiences from the authors who have lived and worked in the city for more than 20 years.

The first comment that can be made in this evaluation is that smart cities are part of an information society context, which does not seem to be the case for Yaoundé now. However, the sector where the evolution and adaptation to the smart city context can be appreciated is the education sector.

We can also mention the fact that most smart city installations are underway in this city, but we maintain the fact that coordination is essential for the success of the great project of smart city in Yaoundé.

6.5   Conclusion, implications, and future directions

Throughout this chapter, we have talked about smart cities in general before zooming in on Cameroon's political capital, Yaoundé, which has a dense population and a varied and intense economic life. This study reveals that Yaoundé is trying to integrate smart city tool snippets in its operation, but much work is needed to meet its smart city goals. Fortunately, the city's administrators are aware of this fact and are already planning to redesign and rebuild the city. Thus, the administrators of Yaoundé could focus on

- the development of e-government services;
- coordination between different intuitions to avoid conflicting strategies and action plans;
- the development and financing of research centers and universities;
- modernize infrastructures (water, light, and gas distribution networks);
- setting equitable access to public services and inclusive management by all inhabitants of the city;
- the establishment of national standards for companies in every public or private sector; and
- the use of energy-saving equipment, and the prohibition of old or high pollution vehicles.

That is why the authors recommend that future studies should focus on describing in detail the process of transformation in each aspect presented earlier.

Table 6.3   Evaluation of Yaoundé

Revised triple helix	Cluster				
	Indicators				
	Smart governance	**Smart economy**	**Smart human**	**Smart living**	**Smart environment**
University	There are approximately 50 highest education institutions (universities, institute, school, etc.) and research centers in the city [46] We have at least four Cameroonian institutions that integrate e-learning [48]	Approximately 3% of the GDP is allocated to education [47]	Approximately 57% of the young population has attained secondary school**		
Government	Government institutions are present online via websites, but only tax payment services for enterprises can be done completely online. However, a project has been launched in this sense [49] Urban communities and city councils are not financially independent‡‡	Twenty-seven percent young people are professionally inactive [50]			There are many green places in Yaoundé, first because there are forests in the city, and other green areas created by the government (reserve, etc.)††

(Continues)

**Source: United Nations Fund, 2016.
††Read in the book related to the presentation of Yaoundé, City Council of Yaoundé III.
‡‡Interviews with the head of the development support unit for decentralized cooperation at the Yaoundé III City Council.

Table 6.3   (Continued)

Revised triple helix	Cluster Indicators				
	Smart governance	Smart economy	Smart human	Smart living	Smart environment
Civil society	Approximately 5% of households have internet access[§§]			The population has the freedom to manage their waste in a profitable way, but HYSACAM keeps the monopoly on the Nkolfoulou landfill, Yaoundé[¶]	
	Only 2.3% of households have a computer[‖‖]			There are customs duty penalties to allow old vehicles to enter the national territory	
	Only businesses use e-government services as they are only for taxes payment				
Industry		Approximately 200 companies in the city[***] among which 20 operate in the ICT sector	The unemployment rate is greater in knowledge-intensive sector [50]		
		None of these companies are registered in the national stock market[†††]		Approximately 720 enterprises in Cameroon are on the way to be certified ISO 14001 [51]	

[§§]This statistic is for the entire country, www.investiraucameroun.com, consulted on January 30, 2018.
[¶]Interviews with the head of the development support unit for decentralized cooperation at the Yaoundé III City Council.
[‖‖]Source survey of households 2014, www.ilo.org consulted on January 30, 2018.
[***]Source: National Institute of Statistics.
[†††]Douala Stock Exchange.

References

[1] Dameri, R.P., *Searching for smart city definition: a comprehensive proposal.* International Journal of Computers & Technology, 2013. **11**(5): pp. 2544–2551.

[2] UN (United Nations), *World Urbanization Prospects: The 2007 Revision Population Database.* 2008.

[3] Ejaz, W., Naeem, M., Shahid, A., Anpalagan, A., and Jo, M., *Efficient energy management for the internet of things in smart cities.* IEEE Communications Magazine, 2017. **55**(1): pp. 84–91.

[4] Mori, K. and Christodoulou, A., *Review of sustainability indices and indicators: towards a new City Sustainability Index (CSI),* 2012. **32**: pp. 94–106.

[5] Albino, V., Berardi, U., and Dangelico, R.M., *Smart cities: definitions, dimensions, performance, and initiatives.* Journal of Urban Technology, 2015. **22**(1): pp. 3–21.

[6] Lombardi, P., Giordano, S., Farouh, H., and Yousef, W., *An analytic network model for Smart cities.* in *Proceedings of the 11th International Symposium on the AHP.* June 2011.

[7] Van Dijk, M.P., *Managing cities in developing countries.* 2006: Edward Elgar Publishing, Cheltenham.

[8] Lombardi, P., *New challenges in the evaluation of smart cities.* Network Industries Quarterly, 2011. **13**(3): pp. 8–10.

[9] Andrea, C. and Del Bo Chiara, N.P., *Smart cities in Europe.* in *3rd Central European Conference in Regional Science-CERS.* 2009.

[10] Hollands, R.G., *Will the real smart city please stand up? Intelligent, progressive or entrepreneurial?* City, 2008. **12**(3): pp. 303–320.

[11] Southampton City Council, *Southampton On-Line.* 2006; Available from: http://www.southampton.gov.uk/thecouncil/thecouncil/you-and-council/smart cities/ Accessed September, 2006. **14**: pp. 2017.

[12] Alawadhi, S., Aldama-Nalda, A., Chourabi, H., *et al., Building understanding of smart city initiatives.* Electronic Government, 2012: Springer, Berlin, pp. 40–53.

[13] Yigitcanlar, T., Velibeyoglu, K., and Martinez-Fernandez, C., *Rising knowledge cities: the role of urban knowledge precincts.* Journal of Knowledge Management, 2008. **12**(5): pp. 8–20.

[14] Ishida, T., *Digital city Kyoto.* Communications of the ACM, 2002. **45**(7): pp. 76–81.

[15] McGuigan, J. and Downey, J. (Eds.), *Technocities.* 1999: London, Sage.

[16] Meijer, A. and M.P.R. Bolívar, *Governing the smart city: a review of the literature on smart urban governance.* International Review of Administrative Sciences, 2016. **82**(2): pp. 392–408.

[17] Bakıcı, T., Almirall, E., and Wareham, J., *A smart city initiative: the case of Barcelona.* Journal of the Knowledge Economy, 2013. **4**(2): pp. 135–148.

[18] Chen, T., *Smart grids, smart cities need better networks [Editor's Note].* IEEE Network, 2010. **24**(2): pp. 2–3.

[19] Lazaroiu, G.C. and Roscia, M., *Definition methodology for the smart cities model.* Energy, 2012. **47**(1): pp. 326–332.

[20]   Nam, T. and Pardo, T.A., *Conceptualizing smart city with dimensions of technology, people, and institutions.* in *Proceedings of the 12th Annual International Digital Government Research Conference: Digital Government Innovation in Challenging Times.* 2011: ACM.

[21]   Barrionuevo, J.M., Berrone, P., and Ricart, J.E., *Smart cities, sustainable progress.* IESE Insight, 2012. **14**: pp. 50–57.

[22]   Caragliu, A., Del Bo, C., and Nijkamp, P., *Smart cities in Europe.* Journal of Urban Technology, 2011. **18**(2): pp. 65–82.

[23]   Eger, J.M., *Smart growth, smart cities, and the crisis at the pump a worldwide phenomenon.* I-WAYS—The Journal of E-Government Policy and Regulation, 2009. **32**(1): pp. 47–53.

[24]   Giffinger, R., Haindlmaier, G., and Kramar, H., *Smart cities. Ranking of European medium-sized cities, final report.* 2007, Centre of Regional Science, Vienna UT.

[25]   Harrison, C., Eckman, B., Hamilton, R., *et al.*, *Foundations for smarter cities.* IBM Journal of Research and Development, 2010. **54**(4): pp. 1–16.

[26]   Cretu, L.-G., *Smart cities design using event-driven paradigm and semantic web.* Informatica Economica, 2012. **16**(4): pp. 57.

[27]   Komninos, N., *Intelligent cities: variable geometries of spatial intelligence.* Intelligent Buildings International, 2011. **3**(3): pp. 172–188.

[28]   Kourtit, K. and Nijkamp, P., *Smart cities in the innovation age.* Innovation: The European Journal of Social Science Research, 2012. **25**(2): pp. 93–95.

[29]   Kourtit, K., Nijkamp, P., and Arribas, D., *Smart cities in perspective – a comparative European study by means of self-organizing maps.* Innovation: The European Journal of Social Science Research, 2012. **25**(2): pp. 229–246.

[30]   Thite, M., *Smart cities: implications of urban planning for human resource development.* Human Resource Development International, 2011. **14**(5): pp. 623–631.

[31]   Lombardi, P., Giordano, S., Farouh, H., and Yousef, W., *Modelling the smart city performance.* Innovation: The European Journal of Social Science Research, 2012. **25**(2): pp. 137–149.

[32]   Vasirani, M. and Ossowski, S., *A market-inspired approach to reservation-based urban road traffic management.* in *Proceedings of The 8th International Conference on Autonomous Agents and Multiagent Systems-Volume 1.* 2009: International Foundation for Autonomous Agents and Multiagent Systems.

[33]   Rossetti, R.J., Bampi, S., Liu, R., Van Vliet, D., and Cybis, H.B.B., *An agent-based framework for the assessment of drivers' decision-making.* in *Intelligent Transportation Systems, 2000. Proceedings. 2000 IEEE.* 2000: IEEE.

[34]   Foschini, L., Taleb, T., Corradi, A., and Bottazzi, D., *M2M-based metropolitan platform for IMS-enabled road traffic management in IoT.* IEEE Communications Magazine, 2011. **49**(11): pp. 50–57.

[35]   Meško, G., Tominc, B., and Sotlar, A., *Urban security management in the capitals of the former Yugoslav republics.* European Journal of Criminology, 2013. **10**(3): pp. 284–296.

[36] Little, R.G., *Holistic strategy for urban security.* Journal of Infrastructure Systems, 2004. **10**(2): pp. 52–59.

[37] Hall, P., *Cities of tomorrow.* 1988: Blackwell Publishers, Oxford.

[38] Jin, J., Gubbi, J., Marusic, S., and Palaniswami, M., *An information framework for creating a smart city through internet of things.* IEEE Internet of Things Journal, 2014. **1**(2): pp. 112–121.

[39] Badami, M.G., *Transport and urban air pollution in India.* Environmental Management, 2005. **36**(2): pp. 195–204.

[40] Goel, P., *Water pollution: causes, effects and control.* 2006: New Age International, New Delhi.

[41] Ghanem, M., Guo, Y., Hassard, J., Osmond, M., and Richards, M., *Sensor grids for air pollution monitoring.* in *Proc. 3rd UK e-Science All Hands Meeting, Nottingham, UK.* 2004.

[42] Fortuna, L., Graziani, S., Rizzo, A., and Xibilia M.G., *Soft sensors for monitoring and control of industrial processes.* 2007: Springer Science & Business Media, New York, NY.

[43] Sempere-Torres, D., Corral, C., Raso, J., and Malgrat, P., *Use of weather radar for combined sewer overflows monitoring and control.* Journal of Environmental Engineering, 1999. **125**(4): pp. 372–380.

[44] Deakin, M., *The IntelCities community of practice: the eGov services model for socially inclusive and participatory urban regeneration programs*, in *Web-Based Learning Solutions for Communities of Practice: Developing Virtual Environments for Social and Pedagogical Advancement.* 2010: IGI Global, Hershey, PA, pp. 263–284.

[45] Lombardi, P., Cooper, I., Paskaleva-Shapira, K., and Deakin, M., *The challenge of designing user-centric e-services: European dimensions.* 2010. IGI Global, Hershey, PA, pp. 259–275.

[46] UUAF, *Liste des universités et instituts du Cameroun.* 2014 [cited 2018 30 January]; Available from: http://www.uuaf.net/liste_des_universites_camerounaises.html.

[47] OCDE, *Regards sur l'éducation 2017.* 2017: OECD Publishing, Paris.

[48] Noubissie, J.-C., *e-Learning: pourquoi les universités camerounaises intègrent davantage la formation à distance?* 2016 [cited 2018 01 February]; Available from: https://cio-mag.com/e-learning-pourquoi-les-universites-camerounaises-integrent-davantage-la-formation-a-distance/.

[49] MINPOSTEL, *Présentation du projet e-government.* 2017; Available from: https://www.minpostel.gov.cm/index.php/fr/les-grands-chantiers/147-presentation-du-projet-e-government.

[50] Moussa, Y.B., *Cameroun: Inactivité: 27% des jeunes sont au chômage.* 2016; Available from: http://camer.be/56983/12:1/cameroun-inactivite-27-de-jeunes-sont-au-chomage-cameroon.html.

[51] Investir au Cameroun, *720 entreprises camerounaises sur le chemin de la certification de leurs produits.* 2015; Available from: http://www.investirau cameroun.com/gestion-publique/0406-6416-720-entreprises-camerounaises-sur-le-chemin-de-la-certification-de-leurs-produits.

Chapter 7

A comparative study of software programming platforms for the Internet of Things

Ming Cai[1], Qian Zhou[2], Fan Ye[2], and Yuanyuan Yang[2]

7.1 Introduction

Internet of Things (IoT) envisages a compelling future where vehicles, machines, buildings, home appliances, and other items embedded with electronics, sensors, actuators, and software are becoming capable of sensing, actuation, communication, computation, and gain insight from collected data as well. In short, IoT brings together devices, cloud, data, and people to make networked connections more relevant and valuable than ever before. A typical cloud-based IoT application scenario is showcased in Figure 7.1.

7.1.1 Device connectivity cloud

However, building IoT applications is expected to face challenges of distributed nature, scalability, reliability, performance, and security. All of these critical factors determine whether applications might be successful or not. The core of establishing applications lies in IoT platforms that offer a set of managed services (e.g., network connectivity, device control and management, data collection and analytics).

In the last few years, considerable industrial efforts have been devoted to offering varieties of IoT software platforms to facilitate the development of applications [1]. As a result, IoT platforms have become an overcrowded space and suffer from severe fragmentation. It is crucial yet quite challenging for developers new to the field to obtain a clear view of the big picture and to determine which platform is right for their applications, what the advantages and disadvantages of each programming models are within a specific application context, and how to trade-off among several critical factors.

There are several published survey papers that cover different aspects of the IoT platform [1–6]. For example, a number of available IoT platforms are evaluated via a gap analysis aiming to highlight the deficiencies of current solutions to improve their integration to IoT ecosystems [1]. The survey by Perera *et al.* [2] examines the

[1]Collage of Computer Science, Zhejiang University, Hangzhou, China
[2]ECE Department, Stony Brook,University, Stony Brook, USA

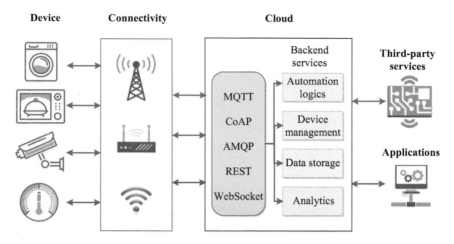

Figure 7.1   A typical cloud-based IoT application scenario

industry-based IoT solutions to identify their applications and the technologies they use, as well as open challenges and opportunities. In [3], the authors summarize the existing IoT middleware platforms as seven categories in terms of their supported functional, nonfunctional, and architectural requirements. Three IoT middleware architectures are analyzed and four challenges in developing an IoT middleware are presented in [4]. The authors in [5] display three categories of IoT platforms and introduce a reference model for IoT middleware. Moreover, Sezer *et al.* [6] review the IoT platforms from perspectives of analytics and learning capability.

As far as we know, no survey has focused on programming models for IoT applications. In general, a programming model defines how an application developer can implement the program. For example, the typical programming models in the domain of end devices can be divided into event-driven and multi-threaded programming [7]. When referring to IoT space, we consider the programming model as an approach, which fits relevant IoT hardware and software physical entities with reasonable protocols, patterns, and methods together to deliver desired IoT applications.

In this chapter, we describe 12 popular and representative IoT software platforms (Table 7.1) provided by industrial communities, both horizontal (e.g., Amazon Web Services (AWS) and Azure IoT) and vertical solutions (e.g., SmartThings and HomeKit), in a systematic way to investigate the features of them based on a detailed analysis around architecture, programming abstractions and patterns, in an effort to explore their underlying programming models so as to give insights into the existing enabling technologies and provide developers with the facts for better designing and programming the IoT applications. It is important to note that we evaluate only a few illustrative IoT platforms that together form a representative sample of the IoT platform landscape for in-depth investigation and demonstration.

The rest of this chapter is organized as follows: Section 7.2 gives an overview of IoT software platforms. Section 7.3 elaborates on the classification and comparison

Table 7.1   An overview of twelve popular IoT platforms

Platform	Provider	Architecture	PHY/MAC	Application protocol
SmartThings	Samsung	Cloud based	Wi-Fi, Z-Wave, 802.15.4	Proprietary, REST
AWS IoT	Amazon	Cloud based	Wi-Fi	MQTT, REST
Watson IoT	IBM	Cloud based	Wi-Fi	MQTT, REST
Azure IoT	Microsoft	Cloud based	Wi-Fi, Bluetooth	MQTT, AMQP, REST
Cloud IoT Core/Android Things	Google	Cloud based	Wi-Fi, Bluetooth, LoWPAN	MQTT, Firebase, XMPP, REST
Nest	Google	Cloud based	Wi-Fi, 802.15.4	Firebase, REST
HomeKit	Apple	Local based	Wi-Fi, Bluetooth	Proprietary
Lab of Things (LoT)	Microsoft	Local based	Wi-Fi, Z-Wave	Proprietary
AllJoyn	Open connectivity foundation	Local based	Wi-Fi, Bluetooth, Powerline	D-Bus, REST
IoTivity	Open connectivity foundation	Local based	Wi-Fi, Bluetooth	CoAP, REST
ZigBee	ZigBee Alliance	Local based	802.15.4	Proprietary
Z-Wave	Z-Wave Alliance	Local based	G.9959	Proprietary

of IoT platforms from an architectural standpoint by describing and differentiating their common and individual features, respectively. Section 7.4 highlights and demonstrates several important mechanisms and implementation details of the programming model for IoT applications on the platforms, including device abstraction, device discovery, communication pattern, and device control. Section 7.5 discusses some key challenges and open issues. Finally, Section 7.6 concludes this chapter and gives future directions of IoT platform.

7.2   Overview of IOT platforms

Each IoT platform focuses on certain requirements and scenarios with different assumptions, which leads to their respective architectures and programming models.

For example, Z-Wave [8] targets monitoring and control functionalities in the home and small commercial facilities. The requirements lie in short-range wireless communication, limited number of appliances, low-power consumption, etc. Therefore, Z-Wave provides a low-power, wireless mesh network that enables device-to-device (D2D) communication either directly or via relays along with a client/server-programming model for device discovery, device control, etc.

As for the Watson IoT [9], the platform aims to build industrial IoT solutions across a large area. So a cloud-based architecture and publish/subscribe programming model is adopted to make the application more agile, as well as namespace isolation and shared subscription mechanism for load-balancing in large-scale computing environment.

In general, we roughly divide these IoT platforms into three levels based on their focus, namely, cloud-level, device-level and radio-level platform, as shown in Figure 7.2. General overview and comparisons of these platforms are summarized in Table 7.2.

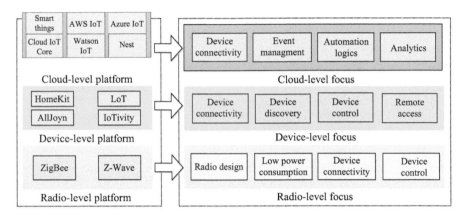

Figure 7.2   Three focuses of IoT platforms

Table 7.2   Comparison of three types of IoT platforms

Function characteristic	Cloud-level platform	Device-level platform	Radio-level platform
Radio support	Multiple radios	Multiple radios	Specific radio
Control entity	Cloud	Local	Local
Role of cloud	Message delivery, event management, data collection and analytics and identity management	Identity management, remote control	No cloud service needed
SDK provided	Multiple SDKs (device, mobile, gateway and cloud)	Multiple SDKs (device, mobile)	Device SDK
API level	High-level API (event, message, web service, REST API)	Medium-level API (event, action, trigger)	Low-level API (frame, packet, timer)
Device discovery	Manual registration, automatic discovery	Automatic discovery	Automatic discovery
Communication pattern	Publish/subscribe, observe/notify	Message passing, observe/notify, RPC	Message passing, observe/notify, RPC

7.3   Comparisons of IoT platforms

7.3.1   Cloud-level platforms

7.3.1.1   Common features of cloud-level platforms

Cloud-based IoT platforms (e.g., SmartThings [10], AWS [11], Nest [12]) are concerned with availability, scalability, interoperability and security when they connect to a large number of devices in an open and heterogeneous environment. They share three key features summarized as follows:

- "Cloud-first" strategy is employed as a key point in these platforms, in which commands are delivered to the cloud first and then passed down to the devices.
- A data-centric architecture with back-end services is commonly used for data management and application-specific analytics. For example, the Nest thermostat can learn personal schedules and energy-saving features from connected sensors through the cloud to create a custom temperature schedule.
- The RESTful application programming interfaces (APIs) and publish/subscribe communication model are widely adopted to facilitate loose coupling between devices and the cloud.

7.3.1.2   Comparisons of cloud-level platforms

Device connectivity

Despite several similarities, device connectivity methods and physical entities involved in platforms are different from one another. Specifically, whether using a hub as a gateway to enable the communication between devices and the cloud makes a significant difference. Three types of device connectivity are listed as follows (Figure 7.3):

- A hub-based solution is utilized in SmartThings for connecting wirelessly with a wide range of smart devices and making them work together. Whether IP is

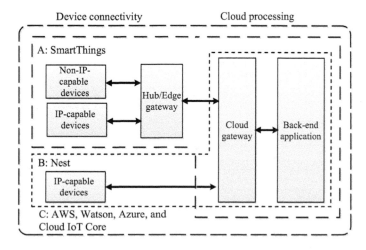

Figure 7.3   Three types of device connectivity in cloud-level platforms

addressable or not, devices must connect to the hub first and then bridge to the cloud. As a home controller, SmartThings hub contains ZigBee [13], Z-Wave and Wi-Fi radios, bridging all the traffic to and from the cloud and enabling control of devices as well. Each device has a paired driver (called device handler) deployed on the cloud for device connectivity.

- Nest does not employ any kinds of hardware hub. All devices should be IP address-able (IP v4 or v6) and connected directly to the cloud using device software development kit (SDKs) that send and receive messages from the platform.
- AWS, Watson, Google Cloud IoT Core [14] and Azure [15] architectures have a mix of previous two communication patterns. On one hand, they offer device SDKs to help IP addressable devices connect to the cloud and on the other hand, they provide gateway SDKs that allow developers to build a device gateway or protocol bridge for accommodating non-IP addressable or low-power device (e.g., ZigBee and Bluetooth).

Device messaging

Another difference lies in device messaging methods. SmartThings hub acts as a protocol gateway that performs protocols translation like ZigBee and Z-Wave and forwards device events and control commands between devices and cloud. All the developmental works for the devices, such as Device Hander and SmartApp, are deployed on the cloud, thereby keeping the maximum compatibility with the com-mercial off-the-shelf home automation products without having to update the original firmware in the devices.

Comparatively, AWS, Watson, Azure, Nest, and Google Cloud IoT Core plat-form adopt messaging protocols, e.g., MQTT [16], AMQP [17], XMPP [18], FCM (Firebase Cloud Messaging) [19], as their communication method over the system. Apart from providing protocol-bridge-like MQTT and HTTP bridge, they also offer a variety of gateway and device SDKs to translate more device's specific protocol (e.g., ZigBee, Z-Wave, and Bluetooth) to messaging protocol (e.g., FCM, AMQP, and XMPP) to send event information from devices to the cloud and accept com-mands from the same. Table 7.3 gives a list of messaging APIs supported by device SDKs. As a matter of fact, these devices need more computing, storage, and power to afford the connection and operation.

Table 7.3   Messaging APIs provided by AWS, Watson, Azure, Nest, and Cloud IoT Core platforms

Messaging API	AWS	Watson	Azure	Nest	Cloud IoT Core
MQTT	✓	✓	✓		✓
AMQP			✓		
XMPP					✓
HTTP/HTTPS	✓	✓	✓	✓	✓
FCM				✓	✓

Device discovery

In terms of device discovery, two methods, namely, auto discovery and registration based, have been presented.

SmartThings is capable of auto-discovery of devices within home area through the hub with built-in ZigBee, Z-Wave, and Wi-Fi radios.

Figure 7.4 indicates how a hub discovers a new device and joins it into the system. The process involves the following two steps:

- In device-discovery process stage, the SmartThings hub is responsible for discovering the new device, assigning the network address to the newcomer and exchanging the device description as well by using of protocol-specific message (e.g., ZigBee and Z-Wave). This process is known as a "join" process where a particular device gets a way to be identified and joined into the SmartThings-hub-hosted network. It should be mentioned that the device description is the key information to be used in the following device-pairing stage.
- After connecting a new device to the SmartThings Hub, a device handler is picked for it based on the signature the device delivered to the Hub as part of its pairing communication. The device handler will have methods defined in it, which support that device. This process is also known as a "fingerprinting" process to setup a driver as the virtual representation for a physical device. Fingerprints are a special form of device description (e.g., device ID, device model, and manufacturer) used for retrieval purposes. All the devices matching the fingerprint are paired with that device handler.

As for other platforms, a registration-based method is employed to connect devices that maybe geographically distributed. Specifically, a new device should first be registered manually to get API key and authentication token from the platform, where

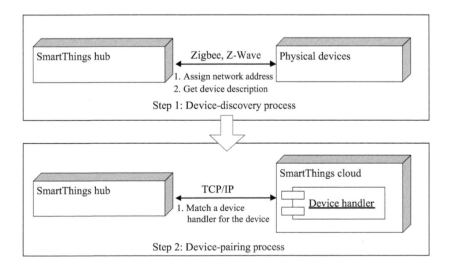

Figure 7.4   Device-discovery process in SmartThings

X.509 [20] or OAuth 2.0 protocol [21] are used for authorization and then attached to an account as its owner.

7.3.2   Device-level platforms

7.3.2.1   Common features of device-level platforms

HomeKit [22], AllJoyn [23], IoTivity [24], and Lab of Things (LoT) [25] are all device-level platforms, whose architectures are device centric. They have several features in common:

- They are basically running on the local area network. The ability of interaction directly with nearby devices and local control of devices differ from those of cloud-level platforms.
- Another major difference lies in device discovery. By using D2D discovery protocols based on either broadcast or multicast, device-level platforms have the ability of fast discovery of neighbor devices, while cloud-level platforms mostly adopt a registration-based method to accommodate devices from different locations.
- The client/server communication model is commonly used in device-level platforms to support D2D interaction, such as status observation, event trigger, and action invocation. On the other hand, publish/subscribe is the dominant communication model in cloud-level platforms.
- Device-level platforms cooperate with cloud service for account management, access control, and remote access. For example, HomeKit stores account and configurations (e.g., home layout, discovered devices, and user permission) in iCloud and synchronizes the data among family members as well as allows the remote access and control of devices via Apple TV or iPad as a gateway.

7.3.2.2   Comparisons of device-level platforms

The distinction among device-level platforms can be summarized into the following three aspects, namely, network topology, device connectivity, and device discovery.

Network topology

Star topology: Star network is a common and low-maintenance network topology that is supported by LoT platform. All devices are centralized and connected to a central hub. In most cases, the hub is a PC that runs HomeOS [26] operating system to communicate with devices and offer their services to other devices and applications.

Point-to-point/Point-to-multipoint topology: Both HomeKit and IoTivity platforms adopt this simple network topology. Compared with start topology, there is no fixed central node or hub in this kind of topology. Device service providers and consumers are bound together dynamically using unicast or broadcast protocols to communicate directly with each other either point-to-point or point-to-multipoint.

Hybrid topology: AllJoyn offers a mesh-of-stars network topology by introducing a router component running on the resource-unconstrained devices that act as an intermediary providing messages relay and routing services. A device can only communicate with other devices by going through a router-deployed device. It is noted that AllJoyn implements a hybrid network at application-level other than radio-level implementation provided by ZigBee and Z-Wave. Although hybrid network is flexible and reliable among the three network topologies, it is much difficult to setup and maintain.

Device connectivity

All of the device-level platforms intend to make devices together seamless, but each is taking a very unique approach. For LoT, it is based on a star network, so D2D communication can occur via the central hub. In this case, every device needs a driver in the hub to support the communication among devices. Therefore, LoT provides SDK for developing drivers at hub side.

HomeKit allows communication between controller (iOS device) and home automation devices by providing a common protocol called HAP (HomeKit Accessory Protocol) and three SDKs (for iOS, tvOS, and watchOS) for configuring and interacting among devices. As for IoTivity, it utilizes Constrained Application Protocol (CoAP) [27] for device connectivity.

In the case of AllJoyn, it uses D-Bus message bus to facilitate communication among devices. Moreover, it provides two SDKs, standard and thin, where the thin is a reduced set of the standard functionality for resource-constrained devices with basic connectivity, discovery, and messaging APIs. On the other hand, for the unconstrained devices, standard SDK provides a router module and higher level functionalities, like multiple devices control, device configuration, and protocol bridge.

Device discovery

Device-level platform is able to undertake discovery of new devices in local area. In terms of discovery procedure, LoT involves two steps: discovering new devices by the hub and then installing drivers to enable interaction between the hub and devices. On the other hand, HomeKit, AllJoyn, and IoTivity have only one step involves without a device installing step. As a result, the handle of newly discovered device will be utilized for communication between devices.

As for discovery protocols, IP-based broadcast or multicast is widely used. Specially, AllJoyn and HomeKit employ the mDNS [28] or DNS-SD [29] based discovery protocol, while IoTivity uses CoAP resource discovery mechanism.

7.3.3 Radio-level platforms

7.3.3.1 Common features of radio-level platforms

ZigBee and Z-Wave provide radio-level development kits (frameworks, libraries, and tools) to embed radio modules into IoT applications. Compared with cloud-level and device-level platforms, they have several features in common:

- Radio-level platforms are dedicated to supporting specific radio standard.
  For example, ZigBee and Z-Wave are based on IEEE802.15.4 [30] and ITU-T G.9959 [31] standard, respectively, offering low-power local-area mesh networking solutions. By contrast, other platforms tend to accommodate multiple radio standards (e.g., Bluetooth, Wi-Fi, and ZigBee), which involve more physical entities (e.g., hub and gateway) for device interoperability.

- Relatively, low-level programming interfaces are provided in radio-level platforms, such as operation of frame, encoding and decoding packets, packet transmission, and control command interfaces. Some parts of the SDK are burned into chips or modules. Therefore, a firmware update is required to bring new features and improvements for devices.
- Event-driven programming is the dominant model to structure a program.
- For example, in Z-Wave, the application is implemented as a state machine, periodically polled from the main loop using Z-Wave library calls to monitor the message from the network [32]. Upon receiving data or commands from other devices, an event-notification callback will be invoked to take actions and synchronize state machine transitions. While in other level platforms, multitasking approaches (preemptive or non-preemptive) are commonly used to establish a device program. Each task runs in its own context and communicates with each other using inter-process communication (IPC) mechanisms. For example, in Android-Things-enabled devices, when a message is received over network, it will be forwarded to the application server (daemon) via the binder IPC and in turn call a handler to process the message.

7.3.3.2   Comparisons of radio-level platforms

ZigBee and Z-Wave have different specifications and applications, which lead to their respective features. Specifically, ZigBee works on IEEE 802.15.4 radio standard that overlaps with Wi-Fi and Bluetooth, while Z-Wave as a novel ITU-T G.9959 standard runs on a different frequency with less interference. Therefore, Z-Wave relies on a simple frequency-shift keying modulation, with lower data-transmission rates (9.6, 40, and 100 kbit/s), while ZigBee uses direct sequence spread spectrum for a more robust modulation. The data rates vary from 20 kbit/s (868 MHz band) to 250 kbit/s (2.4 GHz band).

In terms of usage scenarios, ZigBee aims at versatile applications, such as home automation, health care, telecom, smart energy, whereas Z-Wave concentrates on home automation application. Hence, in order to accommodate multiple applications, ZigBee provides more fine-grained programming abstractions for D2D communication than Z-Wave. A case is the abstraction of device functionality. Z-Wave simply uses a series of commands (SET, GET, and REPORT) to represent ways, in which applications can control or actuate a device. As for ZigBee, two extra abstractions are implemented. An "endpoint" is used to separate different application domains and a "cluster" that defines a related collection of attributes and commands for a unique functionality identifies device control interfaces within an "endpoint." In short, Z-Wave employs a rather lightweight communication protocol and programming model for efficient D2D communication.

7.4   Programming models in practice

Developing an IoT application is based on several key elements, such as smart devices, hyper connectivity, adequate security, and intelligent service. In this section, we mainly focus on programming models related to device abstraction, device discovery, communication pattern, and device control, aiming to demonstrate how IoT hardware and software entities with protocols, patterns, and programming models can be combined to build IoT applications on top of platforms that are capable of discovering, communicating, controlling, and enabling automations around them.

7.4.1   Device abstraction

The purpose of programming abstraction is to hide the complex details of implementation of underlying system so as to preserve essential characteristics and interfaces for programming. For example, a network socket is an abstraction for the local endpoint of a connection across a network, which provides interfaces to access the Internet protocols and helps to create socket-based network programming models.

IoT platforms abstract out the details of physical entity and communication mechanism into two types of abstraction, namely device-functionality abstraction and communication abstraction, providing simple-to-use interfaces for developing applications.

7.4.1.1   Device-functionality abstraction

Device-functionality abstraction provides easy-to-use APIs to access the devices and their functionality regardless of heterogeneous nature of entities and protocols. Overall, IoT platforms present four types of device-functionality abstractions: command/attribute-based, capability-based, content-sensitive-based, and device-shadow-based device abstraction, as shown in Figure 7.5.

Command/attribute-based device abstraction
IoT platforms abstract device functionality into a collection of attributes and commands. Attributes represent states of a device, whereas commands represent ways to control a device. For example, a light bulb has a "status" attribute with values of "on" or "off" to indicate its status. Meanwhile, it has two commands as "on" and "off" for actuation, while some platforms utilize only attributes or commands for device abstraction. For example, Z-Wave uses a series of commands to deliver desired device functionality.

Capability-based device abstraction
The command/attribute-based abstraction works well on the single-function device. When it comes to a multifunctional device like a hue bulb with a "switch" and a "color-control" functionality, it is redundant to redefine all the commands and attributes of the device when the single functionality has been available. Therefore, platforms like ZigBee and SmartThings abstract devices into their underlying capabilities.

A capability represents a unique functionality, such as alarm, lock, and switch. A device can have multiple capabilities, and a capability can have multiple attributes and commands. Consequently, a hue bulb can be defined as a combination of a "switch" and a "color-control" capability instead of reinventing the wheel. In most cases, capabilities are created and maintained by the platform, yet developers can also define custom commands or attributes for additional features.

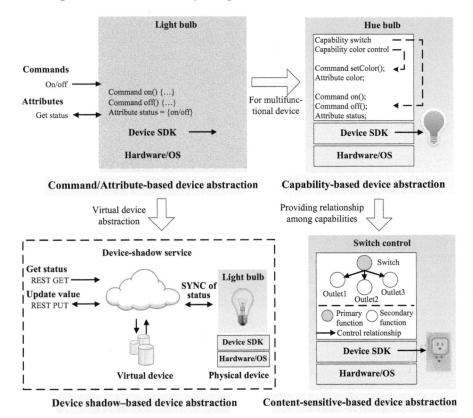

Figure 7.5   Four types of device-functionality abstraction

Content-sensitive-based device abstraction

Though device function can be split into reusable capabilities, the relationships and constraints of the capabilities are not adequately addressed. Considering a device with a switch capability and three outlet capabilities, it is not clear what the switch controls or whether the switch controls one of the outlet or any other combination of these outlets.

Comparing to capability-based approach, HomeKit presents a more meaningful device abstraction that provides context information about capabilities. In the previous example, HomeKit can link the switch to three outlets communicating a logical relationship that the switch controls all the three outlets. Therefore, the state of the outlet can be captured on the basis of the fact whether the switch is powered on or off.

Another case in point is a device with a fan and a light. It is confusing whether this is a light with an exhaust fan or this is a fan which also has a light. HomeKit can mark its primary capability and this is available back to the application. This will be great for setting proper priority to perform accurate actuation in the case of control conflicts.

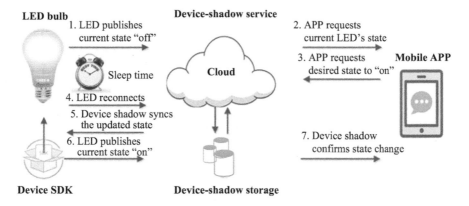

Figure 7.6 An example of toggling a bulb using device-shadow-based service

Device-shadow-based device abstraction

In order to meet the challenge of intermittent Internet connectivity, AWS, Azure, and Nest present a virtual device abstraction called "device shadow" [33] or "device twin" [34] to persist an always-available interface and a point-in-time view of the state-of-the-device.

Instead of staying in a physical device, device shadow is stored in the cloud and maintained by a specific cloud service. On one hand, a physical device is responsible for creating its device shadow and bringing it up-to-date, so that a controller can view the last reported state. On the other hand, the controller can update the device shadow and the physical device will be notified of the change immediately if connected, or at the first reconnect, to perform actions and synchronize the device shadow to the new state.

Figure 7.6 demonstrates how to turn on a sleeping LED bulb using device-shadow service within AWS IoT platform.

7.4.1.2   Device-addressing abstraction

Most of cloud-level platforms employ messaging-oriented communication pattern, so only a cloud entry point is needed to support this kind of device-to-cloud (D2C) communication. While in radio-level and device-level platforms, D2D communications facilitate interaction between devices directly. Therefore, nearly every device needs to expose an entry point for remote-device accessing. Overall, the IoT platforms abstract the device entry point into two kinds of paths, an entity path (endpoint) and a Uniform Resource Identifier (URI) path.

Endpoints are accessible address of functional interfaces exposed by a device. Multiple endpoints can be hosted by a device to implement different functionalities. A connection between two devices can be established by binding a source endpoint of a client device to a server-device endpoint along with a path to reference the unique functionality (e.g., cluster in ZigBee, bus object path in AllJoyn), so that interfaces supported by a device can be reached to get the desired functionalities.

URI path is a string of characters used to identify a service supported by a device over RESTful protocols (HTTP and CoAP). For example, in IoTivity, given a light switch service running on port 5683 in a device at IP address 192.168.1.1, a qualified URI path for accessing this service can be "oc://192.168.1.1:5683/light/1."

In general, URI provides a web-based endpoint and interface for cleaner and easier interaction between an external application and an interior device. It is widely used to make RESTful APIs. The actions for the device should be mapped to standard HTTP methods (e.g., GET, PUT, POST, and DELETE) first, and then to the associated internal handlers for the supported operations.

7.4.2   Device discovery

There are three common methods for integrating new devices into an IoT application, including registration-based device attachment, hub-based device discovery, and D2D discovery.

7.4.2.1   Registration-based device attachment

In order to accommodate numerous devices that likely have wide geographic distribution, most cloud-level platforms (e.g., AWS, Watson, and Azure) employ a registration-based method to connect new devices.

As shown in Figure 7.7, a typical registration process involves classifying the device and providing information to the platform through a user account, which becomes the device owner. Then the platform will generate a certificate (e.g., X.509) and private key for device authentication. Next, appropriate access-control policies or permissions should be created and assigned to the device.

Since the existing devices have no knowledge about the newly registered device, such as location or physical constraint, the publish/subscribe pattern is commonly used to decouple D2D and D2C communication both spatially and temporally.

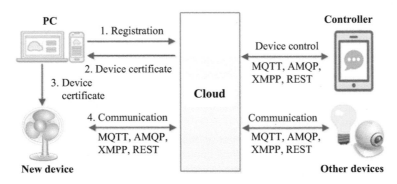

Figure 7.7   Registration-based device attachment

7.4.2.2 Hub-based device discovery

In contrast to registration-based method, SmartThings and LoT rely on a hub-based approach for discovering new devices automatically on the home network through device-discovery protocols.

Figure 7.8 demonstrates a general workflow of hub-based device discovery. Specifically, LoT hub is a PC with a Z-Wave USB stick, running HomeOS. UPnP and Z-Wave protocols are used for device discovery. If an unknown device is found, HomeOS will select a driver for it based on the device type, while SmartThings hub is a specific device equipped with Z-Wave, ZigBee, and Wi-Fi radios, which should be activated first from a controller (e.g., smartphone) with an activation code. When a new device is identified and joins into SmartThings-hub-hosted network, the hub will query it to collect device-description information as a device fingerprinting, such as device descriptor, model, and version. Once the information has been obtained, it will be sent to the cloud for pairing a corresponding driver.

7.4.2.3 Device-to-device discovery

Comparing to hub-based device discovery, IoTivity, HomeKit, and AllJoyn utilize a D2D discovery that supports auto-discovery of devices without depending on any physical entity like a hub.

Another difference between these methods is that D2D discovery holds a service-centric view rather than a device centric method. This means that instead of discovering which device exists on the network, a device can discover a specific service via mDNS/DNS-SD (HomeKit, AllJoyn) or CoAP resource discovery protocol (IoTivity). The process of discovery is modeled as a client device finding the service providers. As a result, each service provider will process the query and respond if the request is satisfied. Moreover, platforms abstract low-level discovery protocols into simple-to-use interfaces. For example, HomeKit defines a "HMAccessoryBrowser" object that can broadcast requests to nearby devices for searching services. In the case of finding a required service, a callback function will be invoked to take actions. Figure 7.9 illustrates a typical workflow for a client device to discover a "light" service provider.

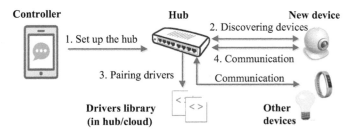

Figure 7.8   Hub-based device discovery

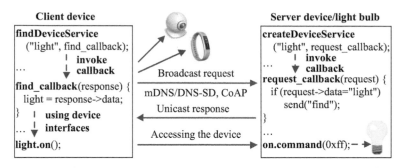

Figure 7.9   *Device-to-device discovery*

Table 7.4   *An overview of four communication patterns*

IoT platform	Message passing	Remote procedure call	Observe/Notify	Publish/Subscribe
ZigBee	✓	✓	✓	
Z-Wave	✓	✓	✓	
HomeKit	✓		✓	
AllJoyn		✓	✓	
IoTivity			✓	
LoT	✓		✓	
Smart Things	✓		✓	✓
AWS			✓	✓
Watson				✓
Azure				✓
Nest			✓	✓
Google Cloud IoT Core	✓		✓	

7.4.3   Communication pattern

Table 7.4 summarizes four widely used communication patterns supported by IoT platforms.

Message passing is a basic communication pattern where participants communicate by sending and receiving messages. For example, Z-Wave applications can periodically poll in the main loop to monitor the message. Upon receiving a command from other device, a callback function will be called to take actions as a response. The participants are coupled both in time and space, because they must both wake up and be active simultaneously and the recipient of a message is known to the sender.

Remote procedure call (RPC) is an extension of local operation calling to a distributed context, which makes remote interactions appear the same way as local ones. RPC is commonly used for establishing client/server-based D2D communication. For example, AllJoyn provides an RPC interface called "BusMethod" to send data synchronously from client to server. The client will be blocked until it receives a reply from the server.

Observe/notify model is based on the observer design pattern, which is composed of an observer and a provider. An observer registers its interested subject (e.g., attributes of a device) to the provider and then it will be notified when the subject undergoes any change of value or at a certain time interval. This model is widely adopted by IoT platforms. For example, ZigBee introduces a command called "attribute reporting" to deliver the values of attributes from a provider to its observer either periodic reporting or any change of attributes, whereas, IoTivity and Nest address observation issues through CoAP resource observing protocol and Firebase network protocol, respectively.

Publish/subscribe is another popular programming model for IoT applications. The model consists of three components, subscriber, publisher, and broker. A subscriber expresses its concerned topics to the broker and will be notified by the same through an event when publishers publish topics that match its interest. By contrast, in observe/notify model, observers register their interest with providers, which manage observations and send notifications, while in publish/subscribe model, with the topic being the focus, publishers and subscribers need not know each other's existence. Therefore, it provides loose coupling among physical entities. Most IoT platforms support this model over MQTT or AMQP protocols.

7.4.4   Device control

7.4.4.1   Device control model

IoT applications require device-control capabilities which involve transfer of command from a controller to an actuator or a group of actuators over designated control paths, as well as managing conflict and consistency. As cloud-based device control is more complex than local control of device, we provide an in-depth analysis of it. Figure 7.10 depicts an example of how to turn on a light bulb using four different device-control models.

Message-passing-based device control
SmartThings uses a message-passing model to actuate a light bulb. When a switch is toggled to "on" state from a controller, an actuation message will get executed to the cloud, then the platform will look up the driver (called device handler) of switch capability and call an on() method, which will in turn send the protocol and device-specific command to the switch through the hub. The actual implementation of on() method varies depending upon the underlying device protocols, which are typically low-level protocol-specific commands to send to the device (like ZigBee or Z-Wave) by means of supporting library.

In SmartThings, message-passing model can team up with event trigger to support automation logics by receiving event or notification to activate the downstream

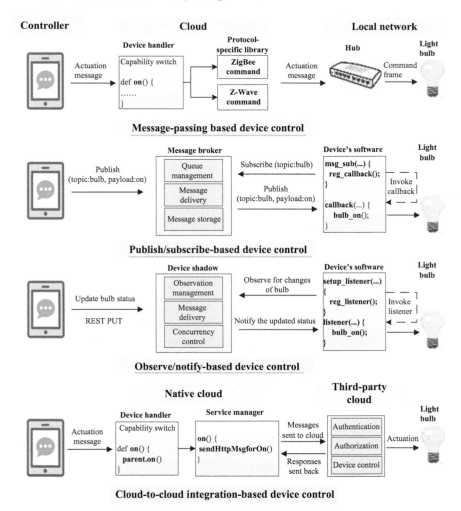

Figure 7.10   Four device-control models in cloud-level IoT platforms

device or group of devices. Figure 7.11 shows how to turn a light switch on when motion is detected, and turn it off when motion stops with an event-handler and two device handlers.

Watson uses a publish/subscribe-based device-control solution. For example, a light bulb is required to subscribe a "bulb/on" topic to receive control message published by controllers to this topic and handle the control command accordingly. Comparing to message-passing model, publish/subscribe-based device control is flexible and scalable due to the decoupling and indirect communication between controllers and devices.

Publish/subscribe model also can be employed to support automation logics. For example, when a motion sensor activates, it turns on the outdoor light. Figure 7.12 illustrates how publish/subscribe model works for this scenario.

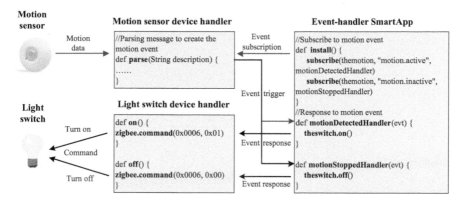

Figure 7.11   An example of automation logic with event trigger and message passing

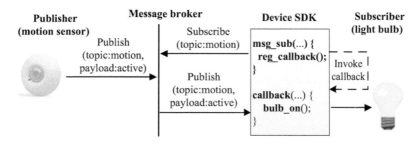

Figure 7.12   An example of automation logic with publish/subscribe model

Observe/notify-based control model

An observe/notify-based control model is presented by AWS with the device-shadow service as an intermediary to maintain a shadow for each device, allowing controllers and actuators to retrieve and update device status. For example, a controller can request to actuate a light bulb by sending an update message to change the desired status of the light bulb shadow to "on." When detecting the difference between the desired and current status of the light bulb shadow, the device-shadow service will send a notification to the light bulb for actuation.

Furthermore, AWS resolves conflict using a version-based optimistic locking [35]. Every update request of device shadow should be supplied with a version. When the current version of device shadow matches the version supplied, the update request is accepted and the version of device shadow is incremented. Therefore, if two persons actuate a device simultaneously, the later request will be rejected due to a version mismatch.

Figure 7.13 is an example that demonstrates the scenario how the AWS addresses control-conflict issue by version tracking when two persons in a home actuate the same light bulb by publishing the desired section to "ON."

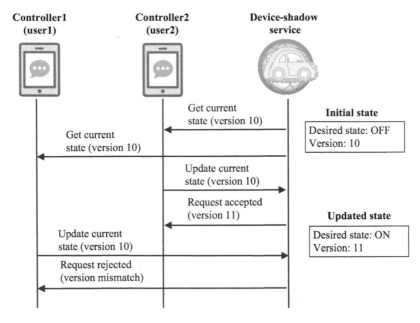

Figure 7.13   An example of version-based optimistic locking strategy for control conflict resolving

Cloud-to-cloud integration-based device control

SmartThings provides a cloud-to-cloud integration mechanism to integrate devices from other ecosystems [36]. An example of such a device is the Ecobee thermostat that pairs with a Wi-Fi router and communicates with its native cloud. A service called Service Manager is introduced to handle authenticating with the Ecobee cloud via OAuth protocol, discovering devices, and communicating with the Ecobee. Combined with device handler, devices operated by the third-party platform can be controlled by SmartThings.

7.4.4.2   Group control method

Besides controlling devices individually, IoT platforms also offer ways to join related devices into a group to make one-to-many or many-to-many control in a concise and efficient way.

In general, there are three kinds of group control methods for different use cases:

- Group is used to express multiple devices receiving the same control commands from a controller. It is useful to include similar devices into one group for convenience sake. For example, all the lights in a living room can be joined into a group to receive the very same switching commands.
- Scene describes the group control in an even more general way than group. Groups tread all devices in a group similarly, while scenes cause a controller to send different commands to different devices in a group. For example, when "I am back!"

scene executes from your smartphone, it can be configured to control several different devices at a time, like unlocking the door, switching the light, and adjusting the thermostat.

- Association depicts an action between a specific sending device and a specific receiving device. An association can be used to establish the relationship between the controller and actuator using an abstraction that makes automation logics in a flexible way. For example, assigning a button on a remote to control a group or scene of lights; when a movement sensor activates, it turns on the outdoor light.

The implementation of group control depends on the underlying mechanism of IoT platforms. For example, ZigBee provides the capability of group addressing in network level, that is, any endpoint on any device may be assigned to one or more groups, each labeled with a 16-bit identifier like a network address. Once a group is established, frames will be delivered to every endpoint assigned to the group address. On the other hand, AllJoyn supports the group control at application level by multipoint session mechanism. A session is a logical connection between devices, which runs over TCP/UDP sockets and allows devices to communicate with each other. Multipoint session provides more than two participants for group communication. As a result, multicast events and commands can be sent to all peers in this session.

7.5   Challenges and future directions

From a real-world perspective, IoT-application programming is still very challenging in many situations. We focus on five key challenges faced by application development.

7.5.1   Challenge 1: Massive scaling

Multiple complaints have been posted on IoT platform communities about occasional (sometimes frequent) glitches, like slow responses, nonexistent, or unreliable responses, when facing the growth of connected devices in a smart home system. The underlying causes may include concurrent transmissions from massive number of devices, message delivery inconsistency, incomplete or out-of-sync device states, and incompatible plugin modules. How to support a large number of devices reliably is a critical issue, as the future of IoT applications will work at scale with hundreds of thousands users, each with various plugin modules hooking up an extremely large number of different devices. Possible approaches may come from efficient MAC protocols, multipath-based reliable transmissions, priority-level-based communication services along with effective management schemes like segregation or coordination mechanism.

7.5.2   Challenge 2: Device connectivity

Current IoT platforms adopt a centralized architecture to afford device connectivity that exclusively relies on a single endpoint (a hub or a broker) to collect, disseminate, and exchange information. However, due to the unpredictable network latency, single point of failure, expensive bandwidth and privacy concerns, and centralized systems will turn into bottlenecks. Therefore, decentralized architectures like edge-centric model [37] are required to move the centralized computing to the edge that carries out direct communication, control, and management among devices. Another decentralized solution involves the use of peer-to-peer communications, where devices identify and authenticate each other directly and exchange information without a broker. This model will introduce several challenges, especially from a security perspective, but these challenges can perhaps be solved with some of the emerging technologies, like Blockchain [38].

7.5.3   Challenge 3: Control conflict

IoT aims to accommodate massive heterogeneous devices in an open environment. As each individual application has its own assumptions, strategies and intentions to execute the actuation without much knowledge of the others. This leads to many interference problems and conflicting situations. For example, an ambient sensor may detect a low temperature and in turn may turn on the thermostat, while a motion detector may decide to turn off the thermostat simultaneously, because no motion is detected. When the system scales up, recognizing and resolving such control collision problems is important for the correctness of applications. No platforms currently offer support for a comprehensive solution to specify, detect, and resolve control conflict across the applications. Consequently, it remains an open problem [39].

7.5.4   Challenge 4: Data consistency

IoT applications often require status or data coordination and synchronization among devices and cloud. For example, HomeKit synchronizes views of the home among owners and guests via iCloud; AWS synchronizes states of a device among the actuator and controllers via the device shadow. According to the CAP Theorem [40], which states that a distributed system can implement only two of the three features (consistency, availability, and partition tolerance) at any one time, most IoT platforms adopt eventual consistency model [41] and its variations for data consistency to maximize availability and performance with a rather weak consistency. Yet, for health care or industrial control applications, information streams from multiple sources should be aligned and synchronized exactly in real-time for control or analytics purposes. Therefore, new consistency models with stronger guarantees are necessary to enable these rich classes of applications.

7.5.5   Challenge 5: Communication model

Observe/notify and publish/subscribe are the two dominant models in current communication-programming domain. Observe/notify model is suitable for fast and efficient delivery of data with less runtime overhead. However, it is coupled both spatially and temporally. Moreover, the burden from management and communication of observation in providers will be heavy as the system grows in size. Publish/subscribe model has the ability to decouple communication between participants. However, it is a data-centric model suitable for device control or event-trigger situations that carry small payload, such as commands or status data. So, it cannot afford much data transfer. For example, the message payload in Watson and AWS is limited to 128 kB. Therefore, new communication models need to be introduced to support full decoupling of the physical entities with a document-centric payload.

7.6 Conclusion

IoT applications have created dramatic business opportunities and improved the quality of our lives [42]. We are currently witnessing an explosion in IoT deployments and solutions around the world. The number of connected devices will continue to grow exponentially and is expected to reach 50 billion by 2020. It is estimated that IoT has a total potential economic impact of $3.9–$11.1 trillion per year in 2025 [43].

IoT platforms are the central backbone for the development of reliable and scalable IoT applications and services that connect the real and virtual worlds among objects, systems, and people. However, as the IoT platform market remains highly fragmented with hundreds of vendors, the landscape is complex and changing very quickly. For a newcomer, it can be difficult to understand the technological elements of these platforms.

On the whole, this chapter reviews 12 popular and representative IoT platforms, a perspective of programming model. The study provides a good foundation for researchers and developers, who are interested to gain an insight into the IoT technologies and protocols to understand the overall architecture and role of the different components that constitute the IoT applications.

We evaluate different IoT stack solutions and group the existing IoT platforms into three levels: cloud, device, and radio-level platforms, in terms of their requirements, architectures, and physical entities. And comparison between the different solutions in each of these platforms is summarized in a systematic way. This, in turn, should provide readers to quick grasp a global view to guide their navigation of this vast field.

Furthermore the chapter highlights four aspects of the programming model for each of these platforms, including device abstraction, device discovery, communication pattern, and device control. We demonstrate individual aspect of the programming model in great detail, so that appropriate application solutions, methods of implementation, and other key choices can be built, made, and evaluated. Finally, we identify the open challenges, opportunities, and trends in the IoT platforms.

Acknowledgment

This work is supported in part by NSF CCF CAREER (grant no. 1652276), NSF CSR (grant no. 1513719), the National Natural Science Foundation of China (grant no. 51775496), and National Defence Foundation of China.

References

[1]   Mineraud J, Mazhelis O, Su X and Tarkoma S. "A gap analysis of Internet-of-Things platforms." Computer Communications, 2016, 89: 5–16.

[2]   Perera C, Liu C H, and Jayawardena S. "The emerging Internet of Things marketplace from an industrial perspective: A survey." IEEE Transactions on Emerging Topics in Computing, 2015, 3(4): 585–598.

[3]   Razzaque M A, Milojevic-Jevric M, Palade A, *et al.* "Middleware for Internet of Things: A survey." IEEE Internet of Things Journal, 2016, 3(1): 70–95.

[4]   Ngu A H, Gutierrez M, Metsis V, *et al.* "IoT middleware: A survey on issues and enabling technologies." IEEE Internet of Things Journal, 2017, 4(1): 1–20.

[5]   da Cruz M A A, Rodrigues J J P C, Al-Muhtadi J, *et al.* "A reference model for Internet of Things middleware." IEEE Internet of Things Journal, 2018, 5(2): 871–883.

[6]   Sezer O B, Dogdu E, and Ozbayoglu A M. "Context-aware computing, learning, and big data in Internet of Things: A survey." IEEE Internet of Things Journal, 2018, 5(1): 1–27.

[7]   Hahm O, Baccelli E, Petersen H, *et al.* "Operating systems for low-end devices in the Internet of Things: A survey." IEEE Internet of Things Journal, 2016, 3(5): 720–734.

[8]   Gomez C and Paradells J. "Wireless home automation networks: A survey of architectures and technologies." IEEE Communications Magazine, 2010, 48(6): 92–101.

[9]   IBM, "Watson IoT Platform," 2018, https://console.bluemix.net/docs/services/IoT/index.html, accessed on January 2018.

[10]   SmartThings, "SmartThings Developer Documentation," 2018, http://docs.smartthings.com/en/latest/index.html, accessed on February 2018.

[11]   Amazon Web Services, "AWS IoT," 2018, https://aws.amazon.com/documentation/iot/, accessed on February 2018.

[12]   Nest Labs, "Nest Weave," 2018, https://nest.com/weave/, accessed on February 2018.

[13]   ZigBee Alliance, "ZigBee PRO Specification," 2018, http://www.zigbee.org/zigbee-for-developers/zigbee-pro/, accessed on February 2018.

[14]   Google, "Cloud IoT Core," 2018, https://cloud.google.com/iot-core/, accessed on February 2018.

[15]   Microsoft, "IoT Suite Documentation," 2018, https://azure.microsoft.com/en-us/documentation/suites/iot-suite/, accessed on February 2018.

[16]   OASIS, "MQTT Version 3.1.1," 2018, http://docs.oasis-open.org/mqtt/mqtt/v3.1.1/os/mqtt-v3.1.1-os.html, accessed on February 2018.

[17]   ISO, "ISO/IEC 19464:2014," 2018, https://www.iso.org/standard/64955.html, accessed on February 2018.

[18]   IETF, "Extensible Messaging and Presence Protocol (XMPP): Core," 2018, https://tools.ietf.org/html/rfc6120, accessed on February 2018.

[19]   Google, "Firebase Cloud Messaging," 2018, https://firebase.google.com/docs/cloud-messaging/, accessed on February 2018.

[20] ITU-T, "Recommendation X.509," 2018, https://www.itu.int/rec/T-REC-X. 509, accessed on February 2018.

[21] IETF, "The OAuth 2.0 Authorization Framework," 2018, https://tools.ietf.org/ html/rfc6749, accessed on February 2018.

[22] Apple, "HomeKit," 2018, https://developer.apple.com/homekit/, accessed on February 2018.

[23] Open Connectivity Foundation, "AllJoyn," 2018, https://openconnectivity.org/ developer/reference-implementation/alljoyn, accessed on February 2018.

[24] Open Connectivity Foundation, "IoTivity," 2018, https://openconnectivity.org/ developer/reference-implementation/iotivity, accessed on February 2018.

[25] Microsoft, "Lab ofThings," 2018, https://archive.codeplex.com/?p=labofthings, accessed on February 2018.

[26] Dixon C, Mahajan R, Agarwal S, *et al.* "An Operating System for the Home." NSDI'12, San Jose, CA, April 2012, pp. 337–352.

[27] IETF, "The Constrained Application Protocol (CoAP)," 2018, https://tools.iet f.org/html/rfc7252, accessed on February 2018.

[28] IETF, "Multicast DNS," 2018, https://tools.ietf.org/html/rfc6762, accessed on February 2018.

[29] IETF, "DNS-Based Service Discovery," 2018, https://tools.ietf.org/html/ rfc6763, accessed on February 2018.

[30] IEEE, "IEEE Std 802.15.4-2015," 2018, https://standards.ieee.org/findstds/sta ndard/802.15.4-2015.html, accessed on February 2018.

[31] ITU-T, "Recommendation G.9959," 2018, http://www.itu.int/rec/T-REC-G.9959, accessed on February 2018.

[32] Galeev MT. "Catching the z-wave." Embedded Systems Design, 2006, 19(10): 28.

[33] Amazon Web Services, "Device Shadow Service for AWS IoT," 2018, https:// docs.aws.amazon.com/iot/latest/developerguide/iot-device-shadows.html, accessed on February 2018.

[34] Microsoft, "Understand and Use Device Twins in IoT Hub," 2018, https://docs. microsoft.com/en-us/azure/iot-hub/iot-hub-devguide-device-twins, accessed on February 2018.

[35] Amazon Web Services, "Device Shadow Service Documents," 2018, https:// docs.aws.amazon.com/iot/latest/developerguide/device-shadow-document. html, accessed on February 2018.

[36] SmartThings, "Cloud-Connected Device Paradigm," 2018, http://docs.smart things.com/en/latest/cloud-and-lan-connected-device-types-developers-guide/ building-cloud-connected-device-types/division-of-labor.html, accessed on February 2018.

[37] Garcia P, Alberto L, Epema M, *et al.* "Edge-centric computing: Vision and chal-lenges." ACM SIGCOMM Computer Communication Review, 2015, 45(5): 37–42.

[38] Tschorsch F and Björn S. "Bitcoin and beyond: A technical survey on decen-tralized digital currencies." IEEE Communications Surveys & Tutorials, 2016, 18(3): 2084–2123.

[39]   Stankovic J A. "Research directions for the Internet of Things." IEEE Internet of Things Journal, 2014, 1(1): 3–9.
[40]   Vogels W. "Eventually consistent." Communications of the ACM, 2009, 52(1): 40–44.
[41]   SmartThings, "Architecture," 2018, http://docs.smartthings.com/en/latest/architecture/, accessed on February 2018.
[42]   Al-Fuqaha A, Guizani M, Mohammadi M, Aledhari M and Ayyash M. "Internet of Things: A survey on enabling technologies, protocols, and applications." IEEE Communications Surveys & Tutorials, 2015, 17(4): 2347–2376.
[43]   Manyika J. "The Internet of Things: Mapping the Value Beyond the Hype." McKinsey Global Institute, 2015.

Chapter 8

Fog computing-based complex event processing for Internet of Things

*Feyza Y. Okay[1], Ibrahim Kok[1], Metehan Guzel[1]
and Suat Ozdemir[1]*

Internet of Things (IoT) is an enormous network consisting of any type of devices (or things) that are able to communicate among themselves via Internet. These IoT devices are connected anytime, anyplace, with anything, and anyone so that they can collect, process, and share context-related information/decisions to their surroundings. Smart homes, electric cars, industry 4.0-based production facilities, telecommunication networks/devices are just a few examples of IoT components. Data collected in such an enormous network that has so many different types of things/devices is expected to have a significant value in many ways. The information extracted from such data can be helpful for enhancing our quality of lives, saving energy, increasing productivity, preventing accidents, etc.

For the last decade, development of IoT is greatly supported by cloud computing and IPv6. While platform as a service cloud service model enables efficient and scalable IoT service delivery, IPv6 solves the addressing need of IoT devices. However, the size of IoT is still growing with a tremendous pace. Many reports and studies predict that the number of IoT devices will be 50 billion by 2020. Along with the size of IoT, the amount of data collected in it increases as well. Hence, processing such big IoT data using a traditional centralized cloud-based architecture results in significant delays and reduces the value of the extracted information. Therefore, in order to process big IoT data, there is a need for a transition from the traditional centralized cloud architecture to a new horizontal distributed architecture.

In this chapter, we address data collection and real-time analysis of massive IoT data using a horizontally distributed computing architecture. By surveying the literature extensively, we first explain how data analysis problem of IoT can be handled in a layered architecture so that information extraction can be achieved in both local and global scales. More specifically, we focus on fog-computing concept that has been shown to be an effective solution for many large-scale problems of several application domains such as handling IoT data, cellular networks, and delay-sensitive and location-aware vehicular ad-hoc networks. We provide a deep investigation of

[1] Computer Engineering Department, Gazi University, Ankara, Turkey

existing fog-computing-based IoT solutions in a categorical manner and discuss the open-research problems. In terms of big data analysis, stream data mining and complex event-processing (CEP) techniques are proven to be quite promising solutions in the literature. Currently, stream data processing tools and techniques are mainly developed for cloud-based systems. However, there is an urgent need for adapting these techniques to horizontally distributed IoT-based data collection and analysis systems. We perform an extensive survey on stream data processing techniques by focusing on their ability to work on fog-computing-based IoT systems. Although there are several studies on CEP applications for IoT data, it is still an unexplored research area. Hence, we document a significant survey of CEP techniques in IoT systems by providing the pros and cons of each scheme. We also provide an example scenario to show that the problem of collection and real-time analysis of massive IoT data can be solved using fog-computation-based distributed architecture and CEP techniques. In this scenario, content curation is realized at the fog layer to extract local valuable information with a minimal latency. Hence, by using distributed fog servers, IoT data requirements such as volume, variety, latency, time and location dependency are satisfied.

8.1   Fog computing

With the rapid growth in the amount of pervasive and ubiquitous IoT data, it has become difficult to deal with huge amount of data through traditional cloud computing models. Although cloud computing offers its services with high computational power and storage capability, collecting, processing and storing all data and requests in a centralized server lead to some undesirable inefficiencies such as high bandwidth consumption, long delays, and poor quality of service (QoS). Fog computing has emerged to compensate these inefficiencies as a complementary system which cooperates with cloud computing to extend network processing and storage capabilities [1].

8.1.1   Architecture of fog computing

Fog devices are located at the edge of the network and integrate end devices and cloud center seamlessly by acting as relay nodes. Placing another layer between cloud and end devices creates a hierarchical structure which generally poses a three-tier structure. Each tier has different responsibilities during the transmission of data from the generation at the IoT end devices to the processing and storage of these data at the cloud center. The components of each tier and their respective duties are as follows:

- Terminal layer: It consists of IoT devices such as sensors, mobile phones, smart vehicles, and small devices. These devices are located in the neighborhood of end users, and each of them produces its data by sensing the physical environment around itself. Then, they send these data to the related fog devices for preprocessing or storage needs of data.
- Fog layer: It consists of fog devices such as routers, switches, base stations, servers, and access points. These devices are widely distributed between terminal

and cloud layer and act as a relay node between them. After collecting data from end devices, they compute and store them temporarily in the fog devices. Then, send these processed data to the cloud center.

- Cloud layer: It consists of multiple cloud servers with high computational power and storage skills for further analysis and permanently storage needs of processed data transmitting from corresponding fog devices.

Fog devices are interconnected to end devices and cloud via different communication technologies. Each end device is connected to one or more fog devices primarily by wireless communication technology such as wireless local area network, Wi-Fi, 3G, 4G, Zigbee, and even fifth generation (5G) in the near future and also by wired communication channels. On the other hand, fog devices are able to connect each other by wired or wireless communication. Lastly, each fog device is connected to cloud server by IP core network.

8.1.2 Related terms

There are some computing paradigms similar to fog computing. Although most of them share same computing, processing, and networking capabilities, they are still different from each other in terms of several aspects as shown in Figure 8.1. We explain each related term as follows:

1. Cloud computing: Over the past decades, cloud-computing technology has been offered as a perfect candidate with its high computation power, storage capability, on-demand access to a virtually shared pool of computing, and storage resources available at the centralized cloud center. However, as the amount of data rises, sending all data to a centralized cloud results in bandwidth bottleneck, high latency, network congestion and QoS degradation [2]. Besides, sometimes it is enough to take some decisions locally, and it is unnecessary to send all data to the cloud which vastly increase the amount of transmission.

2. Cloudlet: It can be a resource-rich computer or cluster of them, considered as a micro-cloud, located closer to the end users so that they can offer its services quickly while maintaining Internet connectivity [3]. However, they generally serve mobile users because mobile users have limited resources, and they can only access cloudlets through Wi-Fi access points. This means, cloudlets have small coverage area and they cannot support ubiquitous computing needs of IoT devices [1]. It can work in both stand-alone mode and with cloud connection.

3. Mobile edge computing: As an edge-centric computing paradigm, it is very close to fog computing concept. Its main difference is that the computation and storage tasks are realized in edge devices, near the things and data sources, while fog computing performs same tasks on network edge devices, one or few hops away from edge devices [4,5]. In addition, its functions mostly work in stand-alone mode. Although edge computing can connect to cloud services, there has not been any work to analyze its interaction with the cloud yet.

4. Mobile cloud computing: It is another trending topic based on a structure where the applications run on handheld devices [6]. Since most of the smart devices have

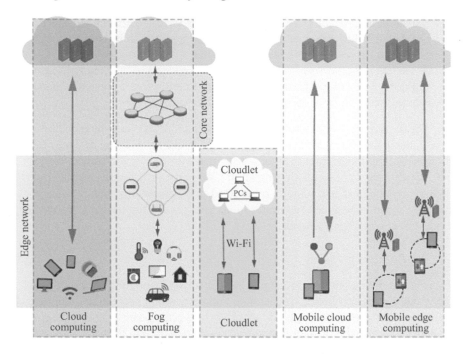

Figure 8.1   Related terms

energy, storage, and computational resource constraints, services are realized in outside the mobile device to make execution feasible for specifically critical scenarios [7].

8.1.3   Characteristics of fog computing

Fog computing is proposed to bridge the gap between cloud servers and IoT devices by taking advantage of the distributed local servers. It presents a highly virtualized platform that extends cloud computing to the edge of the network so that computation, storage, and networking services can be performed locally. Thus, a great number of heterogeneous and ubiquitous IoT devices can connect and interact with each other without intervention of third parties [8]. Fog computing and cloud computing share similar services and attributes. Computing, storing, and networking are the building blocks in both computing systems [9]. Also, they both use virtualized platforms and multi-tenancy property. However, they are not designed to replace each other; on the contrary, they complement each other. Fog computing has the following additional capabilities over cloud-based systems [9–11]:

- Aggregation: Fog servers are capable of aggregating similar or related traffic data coming from end devices instead of routing all data separately. It reduces the network traffic in a massive amount of data applications where many similar and region-based event notifications or monitoring data need to be aggregated [5].

- Locality: Fog computing offers an isolated place as its services run outside the network. Thus, it provides strong protection against intrusion attacks. In addition, fog computing splits data instead of dealing with big and chunky data which makes it easier to manage and control flowing data.
- Proximity: Fog computing is realized closer to end users compared cloud. This attribute gives customers a chance to directly access the source of collected data to simplify the extraction key information, especially when dealing with a huge amount of pervasive data.
- Latency: As a result of proximity property, fog computing significantly reduces both reaction time and congestion probability [12].
- Geo-distribution: Unlike centralized clouds, fog computing shows a highly distributed structure. This feature provides quick extraction and examination of the process of large data. It also provides better support for location-based services.
- Location awareness: Due to their geo-distribution attribute, fog servers are aware of approximate locations of each device connected to fog devices. This location information can be used to provide entire family of business-oriented use cases including location-based services, analytics, location-free billing, and location-free charging [13,14].
- Privacy: Usually data does not need to be stored permanently as they are used to generate timely alarms. Fog servers enable customers to locally store their private data temporarily by ensuring data privacy and low latency [15].
- Mobility: To meet the demand for high-quality mobile services, fog computing serves light-weight cloud like facility to its mobile users by supporting short-fat connection, rather than long-thin connection in cloud computing [16].
- Scalability: As the number of end devices increases, the bandwidth bottleneck becomes a critical problem in computing the cloud. Fog computing handles this issue by aiming at processing incoming data closer to the data source and addresses scalability by dealing with an increased number of end devices.

8.1.4   Service level objectives

Just like cloud computing, fog computing distributes its computational tasks and services under QoS requirements such as latency, energy, resource, reliability, security, and mobility. Most of the service level objectives are management oriented, and in this context, these objectives are studied intensively in the literature.

8.1.4.1   Computation management

Due to the limited capacity of the end devices, they need to off-load their computation tasks to the available fog devices which have more powerful and resourceful computing skills. Fog computing helps improving performance and prolonging battery lifetime. Ye *et al.* [17] present a computational offloading method among fog devices and cloudlets. Because cloudlets are insufficient to do the mobile user's intensive tasks which cause an undesired delay, roadside cloudlets should off-load their workload to the fog server located on the bus in motion, and thus, computing capability of cloudlets is improved to do those tasks. In addition, offloading tasks can be performed among peer fog nodes. Gao *et al.* [18] propose a probabilistic computation offloading mechanism to off-load some tasks to the neighbor fog devices according to computational power, energy level and probability of connection to reduce computational time and save energy.

8.1.4.2 Latency management

Reducing latency is one of the main purposes of fog computing, which is typically designed for latency-sensitive applications such as video streaming or CEP. For example, for augmented reality, slightest latency can cause degradation of performance and therefore user dissatisfaction. Latency minimization can be applied to reduce the required time for computational or communicational tasks. Zeng *et al.* [19] present computational task distribution among end devices and fog devices by aiming to reduce both computation and communication time for the service request. Also, Intharawijitr *et al.* [12] examine the changing of computation and communication times according to workload in fog servers. They propose a fog-computing architecture for 5G cellular networks and evaluate this model through different policies which are random, of lowest latency, and maximum available capacity policies. Results show that the lowest latency policy performs better due to quick access to the resources.

8.1.4.3 Resource management

Even if fog devices have more computational and storage capacity than end devices, they are still not resource-rich when compared with the sources of the cloud servers. These devices, which are often resource-constrained depending on the kind of the fog device (e.g., switch and router as a resource-poor or server as a resource-rich), require different resources according to the area to be deployed or the application to be served. For this reason, fog computing needs a good resource management to share its resources. Aazam *et al.* [20] present a dynamic resource management framework to handle mobile devices and IoT users. They develop a probabilistic resource estimation and pre-allocation mechanism for unpredictable fog service customers according to their user-behavior and their future-use probability. Aazam *et al.* [21], in their another work, present a methodology called MEdia FOg Resource Estimation to provide resource estimation based on service give-up ratio and improved QoS.

8.1.4.4 Energy management

Fog computing has pros and cons in the context of energy efficiency. Since fog computing serves widespread IoT devices in a large area, energy consumption for computation and communication tasks in fog computing is expected to be higher than in cloud computing. However, on the contrary, fog computing avoids back-and-forth traffic between cloud and end devices, which reduces energy consumption significantly [16]. Sarkar *et al.* [22,23] propose a generic fog-computing infrastructure on IoT devices. Basically, they investigate the differences between traditional cloud computing and their generic fog-computing structures. Based on real-time simulation results for 100 cities served by eight data centers, fog computing is more energy efficient than cloud computing. Also, fog computing outperforms in terms of latency and CO_2 emissions. Jalali *et al.* [24] also compare fog computing and cloud computing by addressing energy efficiency. In their work, nano-data servers are assumed as fog device. Result show that fog nano-data centers are more efficient than centralized cloud data centers. However, when network connectivity is ineffective and nano-data centers have high active time, energy consumption can be increased. Also, Deng *et al.* [25] formalize workload allocation problem in the trade-off between delay and energy efficiency. Latency is reduced with a slight increase in energy consumption according to their results.

8.1.4.5   Reliability management

Fog computing deploys its services to large-scale network with the corporation of geographically distributed IoT devices. When considering the reality of such system, it should be considered for failure of system components, failure of whole network, and failure of the service platform. In traditional architecture, reliability can be improved through check-points and rescheduling mechanism to resume tasks. However, these techniques could be not applicable for fog computing because of its dynamic nature and difficulties in adapting to changes. On the other hand, replication can be useful for fog computing to maintain its services provided that multiple fog nodes participation [26].

8.1.4.6   Security and privacy management

Security becomes an important concern for fog-computing environment because fog devices are spread over a large and mostly unsecured area. Therefore, fog devices can be exposed to different kind of security attacks such as man-in-the-middle attack, denial-of-service (DoS) attack and intrusion attacks. In man-in-the-middle attacks, a malicious node can compromise fog devices and act as fog devices. Therefore, they are able to interrupt or eavesdrop packets transmitted between cloud and end device. Besides, it is hardly noticed due to consuming only a small amount of resources in fog devices [27]. Fog devices, which are very resource constrained, are also very vulnerable to DoS attacks. Delivering fog services can take a long time when exposed to these attacks and become a serious problem for latency-sensitive applications. In addition, ubiquitous IoT systems make hard to design a detection system for insider and outsider attacks under limited resource constraints of fog computing [15].

On the other hand, user's concern about the risk of privacy leakage arises, since fog devices collect detailed and essential IoT data with their location information. Especially, for the mission-critical applications, the content of data and its location may be highly critical for network sustainability [28]. Yi *et al.* [29] classify privacy problem as data, usage, and location privacy. Data privacy focuses on preserving the content of the sensitive data, and generally, homomorphic encryption techniques are applied to hide the content of data. Usage pattern privacy is needed for smart grid/city applications where usage frequency of a specific device may reveal important information for the third parties like behavioral profiling and user habits. Lastly, fog devices distribute their services to a specific area. Furthermore, an end device can receive multiple services from multiple fog devices, and in that case, the position of that end device is at risk according to the location of the fog devices where receives services.

8.1.4.7   Mobility management

Nowadays, mobile applications grow rapidly and their demands range from simple computations to complicated computation and data-intensive demands. Although cloud computing offers a lot of innovation on behalf of data processing and storage, it is not always a good choice for latency-sensitive applications. Moreover, storing all information in a public cloud may reveal security and privacy vulnerabilities. Fog computing extends cloud computing by providing high-quality mobile services and accommodating increased mobile traffic [14,16]. In addition to serving mobile devices, fog devices can also be mobile devices. For example, an on-board fog-server (mobile fog device) can be installed on a bus, and during its traveling, it can request available computing resource to be offloaded from roadside static fog servers. Therefore, it is able to perform some tasks that require high computing power [30].

8.1.5   Application areas

Due to its proximity to the users and geographically distributed nature, fog computing is a virtual platform for a number of different critical IoT-enabled application areas such as health-care systems, smart grid environments, vehicular networks, and actuator networks. Figure 8.2 shows that the potential application areas of fog computing structure.

8.1.5.1   Health-care systems

Cloud computing with its unlimited storage capacity has been considered as a viable solution to the health-care systems. However, sending most of data to the remote cloud servers has a negative effect on performance, and it is not suited for the health-care environment, required low solution system for health-care applications. These applications generally need to send real-time notifications to the users; thus, fog computing for health-care systems primarily focuses on reducing latency [31]. In literature, fog-computing services are enabled for specific conditions of health problems like chronic obstructive pulmonary disease, Parkinson, speech disorders, and electrocardiogram (ECG) and electroencephalogram (EEG) feature extraction.

First of all, Liu *et al.* [32] propose a fog-enabled privacy-preserving clinical decision support system called HPCS to monitor patient's health condition in real time. Authors aim to monitor patient's health-care status by preserving privacy against unauthorized parties while balancing real-time and high-accuracy predictions. Rahmani *et al.* [33] propose a fog-assisted system, smart e-Health gateways, to handle and reduce burdens of some remote health-care center challenges such as mobility, energy efficiency, scalability, and reliability. This system is also applied to a medical case study which focuses on monitoring patients with acute illnesses. Farahani *et al.* [34] propose a holistic multi-layer architecture that targets patient-centric health-care systems by enabling seamless connection between hospital, patient, and services. It discusses some example applications by exploiting IoT e-Health architecture and some illustrative fog-driven use cases like smart eyeglass and smart glove to show that how data can be collected and processed in fog layer. Cao *et al.* [35] propose a fog-computing-assisted distributed analytic system, called FAST. In this study,

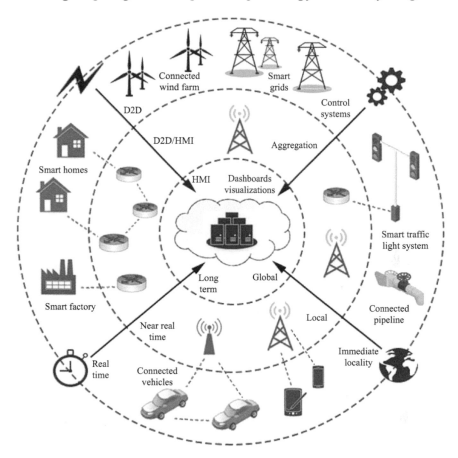

Figure 8.2 Application areas

authors aim to monitor fall for stroke patients. In accordance with this purpose, they implement fall-detection algorithms and design a real-time fog-enabled fall-detection system, which splits the tasks between edge devices and the cloud server. The proposed system ensures high sensitivity and high specificity as well as reduced latency and energy consumption.

Dubey *et al.* [36] propose fog-computing architecture where low-power-embedded computers as fog devices are located into wearable devices and a cloud server to realize data mining and data analytics for telehealth big data applications. The proposed architecture is evaluated with two use case scenarios (for Parkinson and health disease) to show system efficiency by reducing the needs for storage and transmission power at the edge devices.

8.1.5.2 Smart grid/city environment

The smart grid is the only choice to integrate green power resources into the energy distribution system, control power usage, and balance energy load. Smart grids employ smart meters which are responsible for two-way flows of electricity information to monitor and manage the electricity consumption. In a large smart grid, smart meters produce a tremendous amount of data that are hard to process, analyze, and store even with cloud computing. Fog computing is an environment that offers a place for collecting, computing, and storing smart meter data before transmitting them to the cloud [37]. Sarkar *et al.* [23] realize a theoretical modeling of fog computing to support demands of the green computing by collaborating and comparing with cloud computing in terms of latency and energy efficient. Performance evaluations show that fog computing is more efficient and provides a greener computing platform when it is compared to the cloud computing. Similarly, fog computing offers several solutions to the smart-city-involved problems by supporting integration of massive amount smart city component and services. Tang *et al.* [38] analyze fog computing infrastructure for smart cities using a smart pipeline-monitoring system to detect distinct events. A prototype is developed to evaluate the detection performance, and results show that the proposed system is effective and has a potential for the future smart city.

8.1.5.3   Vehicular networks/smart traffic lights

Due to its potential of providing driving safety, traffic efficiency, and comfort to drivers, VANET has gained a lot of attention by industries and researchers. This system manages traffic by providing connections between neighbor vehicles as well as the roadside units (RSU) which can be a smart traffic light, access point, CCTV camera, network camera, etc., and supports various mobile services by exchanging information between components. After VANET integrates with new technologies such as augmented reality or autonomous driving systems, massive and complex data start to need high-level processing and storage capabilities with low latency, and cloud systems fail to meet these requirements. Fog computing is emerged to satisfy these demands with its additional capabilities to control and manage vehicle traffic on the ground [39,40] and drone traffic in the air [41].

The smart traffic light is an important component of VANET to improve traffic efficiency. It organizes traffic flows of traffic by interacting with sensors. Liu *et al.* [32] propose two secure smart traffic light control schemes. The first scheme is a basic scheme used to defend DoSs attacks. To reduce communication and computation overhead, they propose an improved scheme that performs a light-weight operation to secure traffic light control in VANET.

8.1.5.4   Augmented reality

Since augmented reality covers highly latency-sensitive applications, it is influenced by even the slightest delays as it has a negative effect on user feedback. Therefore, fog computing has the capability of deploying its application with less latency to satisfy user experiences.

Zao *et al.* [42] propose a fog-based augmented brain–computer interaction to classify brain state during playing a game by collecting raw data from EEG sensors. Identifying related mental task and classifying them according to user's brain state need to process a huge amount of data, and authors propose fog computing to compensate these needs with real-time responsiveness. Also, Ha *et al.* [43] propose a wearable cognitive assistive system based on Google Glass. It presents a multitier architecture incorporated with Cloudlet due to the demands for low latency for intensive cognitive operations under constraints such as limited battery and processing capability.

8.1.5.5   Pre-caching

Fog computing can be employed as a content delivery system to cache contents by integrating today's technology. Caching techniques can be classified into two subclasses as reactive or proactive cashing. Especially, proactive caching allows the user to obtain the desired information before it is requested to reduce communication bandwidth and latency so that it may require higher network performance in the future. Routing algorithms help content delivery systems accomplish these goals effectively [5].

In the study of Zhu *et al.* [44], a new perspective is presented to improve the web performance by fog computing. Fog servers provide dynamic and customizable web optimization based on client devices and local situations. Because the servers are located closer to the client, both user experiences and client-side network conditions come together to optimize the web page in order to load with an acceptable waiting time. Similarly, caching provides higher bandwidth with less latency by implementing in the fog nodes for content delivery.

In Table 8.1, application areas of fog computing are reviewed in detail by considering the target disease or components, application goals, advantages, and the devices using as an end user, fog, and cloud.

8.1.6   Limitations and challenges

The emergence of fog computing brings cloud computing a number of additional capabilities such as low latency for real-time processing, location awareness, mobility support, scalability, and interoperability. However, distributing the centralized architecture in the cloud-based systems and enabling services closer to the end user, on the other hand, cause some structural, security, and service-oriented challenges [14,45–47]. These challenges are listed and explained below:

- Fog-computing devices are becoming very vulnerable to security attacks because they are spread over a very large area, which is not usually under strict protection and surveillance. Malicious people can compromise fog devices for their own purpose like eavesdropping the network or data hijacking [45].
- The major advantages of fog computing over cloud computing is reducing latency and so, it is more promising for the delay-sensitive applications and services. However, some situations can create an extra delay for fog computing. For example, to complete certain tasks, there can be a delay in provisioning resources since fog nodes are generally resource constrained. Also, fog computing systems need to be resilient against mobility and failure, resulting in extra latency for fog computing [46].
- The collaboration of fog computing with emerging technologies such as software-defined networking (SDN) and network function virtualization facilitates network management but may cause extra latency and low activity [46].

Table 8.1 Fog computing's application areas (H: health-care systems, S: smart grid/city environment, V: vehicular networks/smart traffic lights, A: augmented reality; P: pre-caching)

Application areas					Frameworks	Diseases/components	Goals	End devices	Fog devices	Cloud devices	Advantages
H	S	V	A	P							
✓					HPCS [24]	Patient health status	Monitoring patient's health status	Patients health service provider (HSP)	Fog servers	Cloud servers	Real-time monitoring; High-accuracy prediction of health status; Secure data and prediction model storage
✓					Smart e-health gateway [25]	Patient health status	Monitoring daily life and in-hospitals	Medical sensors Actuator networks	e-Health gateways	Back-end systems	Privacy of patients; Interoperability for heterogeneous platforms; Mobility of patients; Energy efficiency and communication bandwidth
✓					IoT e-health [26]	Health status	Early warning system; Lifetime monitoring; Assisting living	Wearables Smart homes Smart cities	Fog node	Cloud node	Mobility of patients; E-medicine and implants; Cost reduction; Easy to use; Big data processing
✓					FAST [30]	Stroke	Detection fall	Patients	Mobile phones attach to the user	Cloud server	Sensitivity; Specificity; Reduced response time; Less energy consumption
✓					Fog-enabled telehealth [56]	Patient health status	Examination of fog data for health status applications	Smartwatch ECG	Fog computer	Cloud server	Decrease amount of data transmission power saving
		✓			Fog for green computing [51]	Smart grid	Supporting green computing	End devices	Edge gateways	Cloud data centers	Less transmission and processing latency; Less energy consumption
		✓			Fog for smart city [57]	Smart pipeline	Monitoring smart smart pipeline	Optical fibers and sensor	Edge devices	Cloud data centers	Quick response time; High computing performance; Successful hazardous event detection
		✓			Secure intelligent traffic light control [27]	Traffic light	Securing traffic lights control; Privacy protection; Fog device friendliness; Easy deployment	Vehicles	Traffic lights as a specific RSU	Trusted authority	Securing against denial of service attacks; Reducing computational and communication overhead
			✓		Fog-based A-BCI [32]	EEG sensors	Decreasing latency; Ensuring robustness and accuracy	EEG headset Motion sensor Smart phone	On-line data broker/server	Cloud server	Real time response; Ease of use
			✓		Cognitive assistive system [35]	Google glass	Tight end-to-end system	Wearable sensor	Cloudlet	Cloud server	Significant speed improvements
				✓	Improved web performance system [31]	Web pages	Improving web performance	Clients	Edge server	Web server	Dynamic adaptation to the user's condition

- Some policies should be specified among the components of fog cloud infrastructure to distribute computational tasks and services [45].
- Fog devices are not always resource-rich. When they are deployed in large-scale applications, it will be very challenging to maintain services despite its constrained resources.
- Sometimes, bandwidth and latency can degrade the performance of the offloaded task. Fog computing is used for computation offloading for resource-constrained end devices; however, a decision should be made carefully about whether and where to off-load the intensive tasks [14].
- Fog and cloud are complementary systems; fog does not work in stand-alone mode. This integration brings the problem about who will do which tasks. The requirements of the tasks must be clearly defined and sent to appropriate computing layer. For example, tasks which require real-time processing or low computational cost are processed with fog computing. On the other hand, tasks that require massive storage space or high computational cost need to be done with cloud computing [47].

8.1.7 Incorporating fog computing with emerging technologies

Fog computing can take advantage of some emerging technologies in order to provide more adaptable and improved services to its users.

8.1.7.1 Fifth generation

5G cellular network offers enhanced QoS to its user, especially its mobile users, with sub-millisecond latency and 1Gbit/s transmission speed. However, cloud-based systems do not guarantee this QoSs due to a wired connection to the cloud which results in high latency. Fog computing is able to utilize 5G technology and its high-quality services by hosting processing units near to the users [48]. Therefore, it supports a number of time-critical applications such as an autonomous vehicle, healthcare systems, and virtual reality.

8.1.7.2 Software-defined networking

Fog computing deploys cloud services closer to the end users, and local decisions are made in the local distributed fog devices. SDN helps to make flexible and programmable global decisions in situations where fog calculation requires more global decisions such as routing and load balancing [49].

8.1.7.3 Network function virtualization

It offers virtualization of fog devices by decoupling the network functions from proprietary hardware appliances and enables seamless management of fog resources by deploying them fully and flexibly to achieve low latency and high throughput [50].

8.1.7.4 Named data networking

It is an evolutionary technology that changes the semantic of host-centric network architecture (IP) services to a data-centric network architecture by focusing on packet's name rather than its address. Required data is fetched according to given name, and this name can be anything such as endpoint, sensors, routers, and books [51]. Named data networking supports fog computing by enabling its additional features such as scalability, security, efficiency, and robustness.

8.1.7.5   Content delivery network

It is an efficient approach that improves Internet of quality by scattering content from origin to replicate servers located at closer to the users. Content delivery services are now shifting to edge with the emerging of fog computing technology to operate fog devices as content delivery nodes and to serve cache contents. By distributing related content closer to the users, content delivery network helps fog computing with reduced download delays, less bandwidth usage, improved content availability, and reduced cost [52].

8.2   Complex event processing

Due to its unique properties, data storage, distributed processing, real-time data stream analytics, and event processing are all crucial issues for IoT applications. In traditional database-management systems, data is stored and indexed before processing and processed only when requested by users. They are designed to work on persistent data where the need for updating is minimal. These aspects contrast with the requirements of IoT applications where data is usually represented as a series of events in the physical world. In IoT, there are many kinds of things ranging from mobile phones, window sensors, lighting and heating fixtures, washing machines to smart cars, and so on. These things generate a huge amount of potentially unbounded, disordered, continuous, and heterogeneous sequential data items which are called data streams [53,54]. In order to meet IoT's latency requirements, event-processing systems are essential for processing and analyzing such data streams coming from different types of devices.

CEP is a technology that allows us to process and analyze large amounts of heterogeneous data with the aim of detecting complex and important events in real time [55]. The aim of CEP systems is to diagnose events in a fast and effective way when they occur, filter them according to the context, and act for the filtered events. In what follows, we present basic definitions of CEP concept.

8.2.1   Basic definitions

In the literature, there is no standard terminology for event processing. However, some commonly used basic definitions are expressed as follows [56,57]:

- Atomic/primitive event: It is defined as an instantaneous, significant, indivisible occurrence of a happening.
- Complex event: It is defined as a composed or derived event from occurred atomic or other complex event instances. It is the result of applying algebra operators such as disjunction, conjunction, and sequence to atomic events.

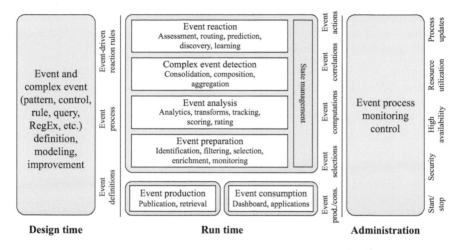

Figure 8.3   Event-processing architecture

- Event pattern/attribute: It describes the essential structure and properties that uniquely identify the occurrence of an event on an abstract level.
- Event instance: It is defined as a concrete instantiation of an event of a particular type.
- Condition/situation: It is defined as a specific sequence of events that initiated or terminated by one or more events.
- Complex action: It is defined as compound action consisting of atomic or other complex action instances.

8.2.2   CEP reference architecture

Event Processing Technical Society reports that the CEP reference architecture consists of three main parts from the functional perspective. These are the design time, run time, and administration shown in Figure 8.3 [58].

8.2.2.1   Design time

At design time, primitive and derived events can be identified along with event patterns. Possible and expected behaviors of event and how they are to be handled in the system are modeled. Processing queries and reaction rules that will detect certain events or patterns are also defined. Design time also offers some improvements for system behaviors such as responses and reactions.

8.2.2.2   Run time

At run time portion of Figure 8.3, there are three partitions that are event production, event-processing functions, and event consumption [59].

Event production: It is the source of events. Events can be published into a communication mechanism or retrieved from an event-detection system.

Event processing: It is a process that is consisted of some functions depicted as event preparation, event analysis, complex-event detection, and event reaction. Within each function, there are manifold sub-functions:

- Preparation: It is the process by which events are defined, filtered, selected, monitored, and enriched, for the further stages of the event processing.
- Analysis: This process is defined as the analyzing of prepared events for getting the significant information. In this process, some computations, such as event analytics, transformation, tracking, scoring, rating, and classification, can be carried out.
- Detection: This process covers deriving or updating different/complex events from individual events. Some of the operations such as event consolidation (combining different events), composition (composing new, complex event from existing events), and aggregation is carried out.
- Reaction: This process identifies the actions to be taken according to the results of event analysis and detection processes. Some of operation processes such as event assessment, routing, discovery, prediction/predictive analytics, and event-based learning can be handled.

Event consumption: It is the process of using event after event publication and processing. In this process, events can be consumed by downstream consumers such as dashboard, applications, and external reaction.

8.2.2.3   Administration

In this part, functions such as starting and stopping the application, managing of highly available and reliable resources, monitoring resource utilization of event-processing components, making updates, and providing and updating security of the system are performed.

It is necessary to consider the characteristics and design requirements in order to design a suitable CEP system for functional architecture. The characteristics of CEP systems can be summarized as follows [60]:

- Input data are a continuous, volatile, and finite stream of the event.
- Input data come from external sources such as sensors and smart devices, and they have strong temporal relationships.
- Input data streams require low latency event detection and real-time processing.
- CEP systems try to combine data from multiple sources and extract useful information from them. Therefore, it must deal with a lot of queries in real time.
- CEP systems use DAHP (database active, human passive) model which does continuous processing and notifies user, while traditional database systems use HADP (human active, database passive) model in which data is stored and users run queries.

There are also some design requirements such as expressiveness, usability, and efficiency in the CEP system design which is suitable for functional architecture [60].

- Effectiveness: CEP system needs event-processing language (EPL) with query expressions that can be applied to different scenarios and powerful operators.

- Usability: Event queries must be expressible in an easy way.
- Efficiency: CEP systems must have strong capabilities of handling thousands of queries at the same time, and must be able to provide low network bandwidth usage and low event-detection latency.

Complex event-detection process is critical in run time part of CEP system architecture. In this part, there are agents that detect events and perform other actions related to the event. Each CEP system uses one or more event detection model and event-handling languages known as EPLs, to detect complex events that need to be identified on the data streams. We have discussed these parts below, respectively.

8.2.3 Event detection models

The presence of different data structures in the detection of complex events offers different capabilities to a CEP system. In this subsection, we review the main type of these models [61].

NFA (nondeterministic finite automata) is one of the most used models in CEP systems. In this model, each state is a full or partial detection of complex events. The transition from one state to another is triggered if a queried event is found in the stream.

Finite state machines are mathematical computation models for software programs and sequential logical programs. The state machines in the CEP are used for the purpose of detecting events and show similar functionality with the NFAs.

Trees have a high potential for adaptivity in the effective query execution. Especially, they can affect the query performance based on transformation and occurrence frequency of events.

Graphs provide an overview of all complex expressions in the system. It is not used in query execution but serves only as a data structure that aims to reveal event dependencies.

Networks (event-processing network) include the processing elements such as producers, consumers, global state components, and event-processing agents. These agents communicate with each other asynchronously through event channels and follow an event-driven logic [59].

8.2.4 Event-processing languages

In CEP systems, it is important to define event patterns in order to detect complex events or situations of interest. These event patterns are defined by using EPLs. Although there are various programming styles and approaches in the literature, it seems that there are no standards for EPLs. In this section, we look at three programming styles, which are termed as the stream-oriented, rule-oriented, and imperative styles [62].

8.2.4.1 Stream-oriented

This programming style is based on data flow programming. In this style, the definition of queries is inspired by structured query language (SQL)-like languages and relational algebra. It includes temporal relationships and data windows. The language and products of this style are STREAM, Aurora, Cayuga Aleri, StreamBase, Esper/Nesper, CQL, Oracle CEP, SPADE [55].

8.2.4.2   Rule-oriented

There are three subtypes within this style. These are event condition action (ECA) rules, inference/production (I/P) rules, and logic programming.

- ECA rules known as active rules. An ECA rule consists of three parts: an event, a condition, and an action. The execution pattern of an ECA rule is: when the event has been occured, evaluate the condition, and if the condition is satisfied, execute the action. Amit, RulePoint, AutoPilot M6, WebSphere Business Events, Reakt, StarRule, and Vantify are some language and product examples of this subtype.
- I/P rules are the type of if-condition-action that trigger action when conditions are satisfied. DROOLS Fusion and TIBCO Business Events are the examples of this subtype.
- Logic programming is based on logical assertions and deductive databases that allow deducing from rules and facts. ELE (ETALIS Language for Events), EP-SPARQL, and Prova are the examples of this subtype.

8.2.4.3   Imperative

In this subtype, rules are directly defined using operators that transform the event streams. MonitorScript and Netcool Impact Policy Language are the examples of this subtype.

8.2.5   *Algorithms used in CEP*

We are living in the age of information; therefore, extraction of knowledge has utmost importance. This situation caused data-mining domain to be a popular research idea. Numerous algorithms and methods are proposed to extract useful information from huge masses of data. These algorithms are implemented on batches of data. However, almost two decades ago, a new type of data emerged. With the advances in hardware technology, data is started to be collected continuously [63]. A huge amount of data is started to flow across IP networks. This concept is named as data streams. Data streams produce huge amounts of data, and huge data means huge knowledge waiting to be extracted. But unique characteristics of data streams made conventional data mining approaches useless in this domain. Emergence of data streams leads to new data-mining challenges.

CEP is more focused on analyzing, identifying, detecting complex event patterns, and extracting information, while stream mining is focused on parallel and large-scale queries on input event streams. Recently, many innovative IoT applications need minimal latency for real-time processing, analyzing the data streams. In this context, combining CEP and stream data mining algorithms provides effective solutions to these type of applications. Therefore, we present following stream data mining algorithms in this subsection.

First, we explain unique properties of data stream mining and how to approach these unique features.

8.2.5.1   Data volume

Data generated from data streams have a very large volume. Acquired data cannot be stored in the memory and are mostly discarded or sent to archives. Either way, retrieval cost of historical stream data is astronomical or even impossible at most cases. Conventional data-mining algorithms require multiple scans over data. Because of retrieval cost, multiple scans over data also cannot be tolerated.

8.2.5.2   Data continuity

Data streams are continuous high-speed flows of data. Proposed methods must cope up with data streams flowing speed and must operate in brief periods of time between data acquisitions. Otherwise, methods cannot process all acquired data and discards them. The amount of discarded data increases as time goes by and at some point may cause a decreasing effect on the success of the method. Therefore, proposed-data mining techniques must be lightweight and operate in near-real-time.

8.2.5.3   Data bound

Data streams are unbounded. Proposed methods must not require a complete set of data to perform knowledge extraction.

8.2.5.4   Data evolution

Data acquired on data streams may/will evolve with time. This phenomenon is named as "concept drifting" in the literature. Data-mining methods in this domain must keep themselves up-to-date, cope up with the recent changes in data, and forget about old, no-longer-relevant data.

After briefly explaining the unique features of data streams and how to confront them, now we deeply investigate the implementations of these confrontations on three popular data-mining domain frequent itemset (pattern) mining, classification, and clustering, respectively. We specifically explain the most important algorithms in each domain that are used to extract a specific type of information from data streams.

Frequent itemset mining

In this domain, the aim is to extract frequent items and k-itemsets/patterns from databases consisting of numerous transactions. Extractions of itemsets are important to uncover correlations, associations, episodes, sequences, and patterns in databases [64,65]. Numerous works have been made to perform frequent itemset mining operations; apriori [64] and FP-growth [66] are two of the most used frequent itemset mining algorithms that are presented in the literature. Apriori is also one of the most used algorithms in data-mining domain [67]. Before diving into vast literature of frequent itemset mining at data streams, we would like to briefly refer to these algorithms.

Apriori algorithm is used to find itemsets that ensure a given minimum support value (frequent). Apriori is based on two ideas; (i) if an itemset ensures a minimum support value, all subsets of the itemset also ensures that support value. (ii) If an item/itemset does not ensure a support value, all itemsets that contain given item/itemset certainly do not ensure that support value. With these ideas in mind, apriori generates longer itemsets (k itemsets) from shorter ones ($k - 1$ itemsets) that are frequent. This reasoning ensures that itemsets that have definitely-not-frequent subsets will be elected and will not be checked. Thus, search space reduces considerably.

Apriori algorithm effectively reduces search space, however multiple database scans are performed in order to do this. Especially, a scan causes a huge amount of work load on big databases. To reduce workload from scans, Han proposes the use of prefix tree [66]. His proposition-reduced database scan count to two and surpassed apriori in the means of performance and scalability. First, the algorithm calculates support values of items. Items that do not ensure a given support value (non-frequent) get removed from all transaction. Frequent ones get prioritized based on a count of occurrence. Each transaction gets ordered based on priorities. Then, the algorithm creates a tree and sets a null node as root. Each transaction gets added to the tree. FP-tree has multiple advantages over previous approaches. First and probably the most important reduces required database scan count to two which boosts the performance of algorithm significantly. It compresses the data, and once the FP-tree is generated, extraction of itemsets takes short time. FP-tree also has advantages, a long time required to build FP-tree, and it requires high memory.

Apriori and FP-tree are outstanding algorithms on static databases. But on stream data, their usability is pretty low because of requirement of multiple database scans. Like we mentioned before, in data stream domain retrieval of stored data is costly and undesirable. Therefore, research on this domain is mostly focused on algorithms that require a single scan of data. Another aspect a stream mining is the challenge to stay up-to-date. Frequencies of items may/will change as time goes by. Therefore, algorithms must be adaptive to changes. Old itemsets must be discarded according to a policy. A window-based approach [68,69] or decaying mechanism [70,71] can be used. To be precise, we would like to refer to some works of scientific literature. Most of them are based on FP-tree, because of its ability to suit these mentioned requirements of stream mining.

Tanbeer *et al.* propose CP-tree, a variation of FP-tree that requires only one data scan [72]. Transactions are first inserted to tree based on a predefined order. This order is stored in a list with frequencies of items, namely, l-list. As transactions arrive, l-list is updated. When changes on l-list reach to a specified degree, tree is restructured. In the paper, three restructuring criteria are proposed:

- $N\%$ technique: Tree restructuring starts after each $N\%$ transactions. N value is determined by the user.
- Top-K technique: Tree restructuring starts after total order change of top K element of l-list is greater than a specified threshold value. K and threshold values are determined by the user.
- N–K technique: This criterion is a combination of previous ones. Starting of restructuring is decided based on top-K technique which is executed after each $N\%$ transactions.

Performance of these criteria is based on parameters (N, K, and I values). Therefore, determination of parameters is an important matter. Highly frequent reconstruction causes an unnecessary overhead but ensures high accuracy. Low-frequency reconstruction decreases overhead but causes to low accuracy. This trade-off must be investigated thoroughly, and parameters must be chosen accordingly.

Tanbeer *et al.* utilize their previous proposed method CP-tree and make it more stream-friendly [68]. By including a window approach, compact pattern stream (CPS) finds a solution to concept drifting problem. The proposal uses panes and windows. Pane is a batch of transactions. Panes have fixed-size and do not overlap with other panes. Windows include multiple numbers of panes and slides over panes. When a new pane arrives, the window removes the oldest one and adds a new pane to itself. Storing of itemsets and tree structure is very similar to Tanbeer's previous work CP-tree [72]. Each window includes a CPS-tree which stores occurrences of itemsets. Every time a pane arrives, transactions of the pane are added to l-list of CPS-tree. Then, the tree is reconstructed. CP-tree and CPS-tree algorithms both require low memory and scan the data single time. Because of these properties, their applicability on stream mining is very high.

Another FP-tree-based method, namely, MWS (Maximal frequent pattern mining with Weight conditions over data Streams) is proposed by Yun *et al.* [73]. MWP method enhances FP-tree method with weighting approach. In real world, items in patterns may have different importances. Therefore, their occurrences may indicate different importance. By calculating support values of itemsets based on not only occurrence count but also predefined item weight, proposed method makes it possible for users to have control over item types and their varying importance. Previously proposed method MWS is carried one step forward with WMFP-SW technique [69]. By adding panes and windows to process, frequent itemsets are kept up-to-date. Window-pane approach and updating of the tree are pretty similar to previously mentioned CPS-tree. The WMFP-SW method enhances CPS-tree by considering item weights.

The estDec method is proposed by Chang *et al.* [70] as an alternative frequent mining algorithm. The proposed method utilizes a monitoring lattice to keep track of itemset that has a minimum support value. Insertion of new itemsets is delayed until their estimation of being frequent surpasses a threshold. When the threshold is surpassed, the itemset is inserted to lattice. In the lattice, itemsets are stored as triplets [cnt, err, MRtid]. cnt stores count of an itemset, err stores the maximum error rate of itemset and MRtid stores the last occurrence of the itemset. Based on this variables frequency of every itemset updated every time a new itemset is received. To keep lattice up-to-date, a decaying mechanism is proposed. Mechanism lowers the weights of an itemset that became less frequent by the time. Mentioned weight is calculated from cnt, MRtid variables from itemset and a given decaying rate. Woo *et al.* propose estMax [71], a method based on previously mentioned estDec. estMax lowers the required computational operations to find MFI's (maximal frequent itemsets) significantly. In order to do that, uses two additional parameters that are not present by estDec method, namely, ML and IS_MAX. ML refers to the maximum lifetime, an itemset has without occurring again. IS_MAX is the Boolean variables that indicate if an itemset is maximal or not. With these two additional variables, estMax extract MFI's at any moment without any need to do additional subset/superset checking.

As seen from Table 8.2, all proposed algorithms focused on knowledge discovery with a single scan of data. In addition, it must be pointed out that prefix-tree and its

Table 8.2   Major frequent itemset mining algorithms for stream data

Algorithm	Based on	Up-to-dateness approach	Database scan
Apriori	Search space reduction	Not present	Multiple
FP-tree	Prefix tree	Not present	Double
CP-tree	FP-tree	Not present	Single
CPS-tree	CP-tree	Window-based approach	Single
MWS	FP-tree	Not present	Single
WMFP-SW	MWS	Window-based approach	Single
EstDec	Prefix tree	Decaying mechanism	Single
EstMax	Prefix tree	Decaying mechanism	Single

variations are the most popular technique of FI mining on stream domain. The reason behind this is robustness of tree-based approaches. But uniformity of data structure selection is not present at the mechanisms of staying up-to-date. Windowing approach, weighting approach, and decaying mechanisms are used to cope up with changing nature of data streams.

Classification
Classification is a process of predicting class labels of items using items' attributes. A classifying model is built from historical data and used for prediction [74]. Mentioned models context may vary according to the used method. k-Nearest-neighbor, support vector machines, decision trees, and Naive-Bayes methods are some of the most used classifying algorithms [67]. For more information, please refer to original articles of algorithms given in the references. In this subsection, we would like to address classification on data streams and investigate its differences from conventional batch-data classification. The most successful classification algorithms mostly rely on multiple scans on data which is not applicable on data-stream mining. Classification algorithms in this domain must learn with a single pass over data [75]. At data streams, data acquisition rate is high. Therefore, proposed methods must be lightweight. If mining speed falls behind of data acquisition rate, some data will not be used and go to waste. And as time goes by, the amount of data that goes to waste will increase [75]. In data streams, data is unbounded; hence, classification methods must be able to perform prediction without full knowledge of data. Moreover, in data streams, the data is continuous and the proposed methods must be incremental. Unlike batch data, data streams evolve in time. Distributions of classes, connections between attributes, and class labels may/will change over time [76,77]. This phenomenon is known as "concept drifting" in the literature. To handle these unique requirements, various methods are proposed. Methods mainly follow two distinct ideas, singular classifier and ensemble classifier methods. We would to briefly explain these ideas and present the important works from literature.

8.2.5.5   Singular classifier approach
In this approach, there is only one classification model. This model gets updated as new observations are acquired. In addition to previously mentioned principles,

singular classifier approach methods also must have a forgetting mechanism. Effects of old observations must be removed from the model. To be more clear, two of most cited singular classifier stream mining approaches from literature—Very Fast Decision Tree (VFDT) [75] and Concept-Adapting Very Fast Decision Tree (CVFDT) [78] are presented below:

Domingos *et al.* [75] propose Hoeffding Tree, a decision tree-based classifier for data streams and VFDT learner method that operates on the proposed tree. Hoeffding tree utilizes Hoeffding Bound method to adapt to work on continuous data. This bounding method can decide the count of observations required for leaves of tree without knowledge of probabilistic distribution at the cost of requiring more observations. Proposed VFDT algorithm uses Gini index to calculate information gains. At conventional decision trees, this costly calculation is performed every time a new observation is added to tree. In contrast, VFDT algorithm calculates Gini index once at every n (a user-defined variable) observations. Therefore reduces computational complexity and processing time significantly. Hulten *et al.* [78] propose CVFDT Learner method, which is an improvement to their previously proposed VFDT method by adding a windowing approach. The method generates a tree same as VFDT. As an addition leaf has count variables. Every time a new observation arrives, corresponding leaves increase the count variable, other leaves decreases counts. As the statistical balance of stream (concept) is stationary, tree does not change. But as concept changes, decision splits corresponding to old concepts start not to be able to pass Hoeffding test. At this point, CVFDT starts a new subtree from the root with the new best attribute. When new tree starts to classify new observations more accurately than the old one, new tree replaces old the one.

8.2.5.6 Ensemble classifier approach

This approach uses multiple classifiers to predict classes. Obtained class predictions are combined to make a final prediction. It is desired for each classifier to shed light on relations between classes and attributes. With this ensemble, classifier can perform prediction on data from multiple perspectives which is a characteristic hard to achieve at singular classifiers. In this approach, classifiers may vary by time periods, classification method [79], train data [80], class label [81], etc.

Street *et al.* propose SEA for large-scale classification on data streams [80]. The method is based on multiple decision tree classifiers. SEA utilizes a fixed-size cluster of classifiers, each trained from a subset of data read sequentially in blocks. Once the cluster is full, new classifiers replace old ones if they can improve the performance of the cluster. Decision mechanism favors classifiers that obtain high success. Wang *et al.* [79] propose AWE (accuracy-weighted ensemble), a method that uses of multiple classifiers for prediction of classes. Method splits incoming stream data into chunks and uses chunks to train different classifiers, respectively, Naive-Bayes, C4.5, and RIPPER. These classifiers are weighted based on their success on latest received data. Later, top K classifiers with highest weight values from a pipeline ordered by weight values. Classification is performed in the pipeline using multiple classifiers in an iterative manner. Iteration process continues until a confident prediction is made. Improved version of AWE, called AUE (accuracy updated ensemble), is proposed by Brzeziński and Stefanowski [82]. AUE improves AWE in three ways. First, AWE method replaces one classifier which has a low success with a more successful classifier and updates weights of classifiers. At the same occasion, AUE performs same operations, as an addition updates base classifiers. The second improvement is a weighting function. AWE's weighting function is cost sensitive; therefore, its predictions cannot adapt to sudden concept drifts. AUE overcomes this drawback by using a simpler weighting function. The final difference is at base classifier updating mechanism. Once a new observation arrives, only "accurate-enough" classifiers are updated. The other classifiers are not changed. With this practice, classifiers that focused on specialized cases are not affected from irrelevant observations. In brief, diversity of ensemble classifier is protected.

Clustering
Clustering data streams is different from conventional clustering in many points. Requirements of stream mining are mentioned before. In addition, data stream clustering has two additional requirements due to unique characteristics of clustering [83]:

- Changing cluster distributions
- Changing individual clusters.

Mentioned characteristics are pretty similar to "concept drifting" problem of classification. As in classification, clusters must dynamically adopt themselves to evolving data streams. In the literature, mostly used techniques to overcome this problem are single-pass algorithms and windowing approach.

8.2.5.7   Single-pass algorithms

As previously explained, in data stream mining domain data retrieval cost is astronomical. Therefore, data must be scanned only once and this has to done at the arrival time. Conventional data mining algorithms require multiple passes on data. Algorithms mentioned in this subsection are basically the ones that are modified to correspond to single-pass requirement.

Domingos and Hulten modify k-means algorithm and propose VFKM [84]. The method utilizes Hoeffding Bound to overcome the effect of a change in the distribution probabilities. Also, the number of observations that form the distribution model are minimized to the point where model's difference from full data expression is not significant. k-Means algorithm is implemented on this approach, and VFKM is obtained. The method results in a success rate very close to the original k-means, but speed is improved significantly. Several variations of k-means algorithm are proposed by Ordonez [85], namely, incremental k-means, scalable k-means, and on-line ACk-means algorithms. All three are modified-to-stream versions of the k-means algorithm and achieve less running time compared to original algorithm by utilizing sparse matrix operations and simplified sufficient statistics.

8.2.5.8   Windowing approaches

In this approach, only a portion of data is used for mining purposes. There are three commonly used window models [82,86].

- Time-window (sliding window) model: This approach only uses latest acquired data to perform operations.
- Damped-window (fading window) model: Like time-window model, this approach uses latest data acquired. But as an addition, data is weighted based on their recentness. The most recent data has the highest weight, and this weight decreases as new data arrive.
- Landmark window model: This approach splits acquired data based on landmark objects that are selected based on a set of conditions predefined by user.

Aggarwal *et al.* propose HPStream framework [87]. HPStream has two important approaches. First one is "fading cluster structure" approach that is used to integrate old and new data based on their recentness. This fading approach helps stream to evolve and catch recent concepts. The second one is "projected clustering," a method that lowers dimension of data based on their effect on clustering. By expelling irrelevant attributes of data, clustering success and clustering speed are increased. Babcock *et al.* [88] implement a sliding-window approach for data stream clustering. The method takes recent N elements to perform the operation. Clustering is performed with the k-median algorithm. Zhou *et al.* [83] propose SWClustering (Sliding Window Clustering) in their work. SWClustering uses EHCF (Exponential Histogram of Cluster Features) structures to keep up with the intra-cluster evolution. The temporal cluster features are employed to reflect the change occurred at cluster distribution. Operations are performed on N recent elements of the stream. In short, their approach separates in-cluster and between-cluster evolutions over a sliding-window.

8.2.6   Application areas

In IoT applications, data streams coming from heterogeneous kinds of sources such as smart devices, sensors, GPS, and RFID readers [89]. The incoming data is a raw form and contains primitive events. Therefore, processing IoT data with CEP systems based on methods, such as machine learning, predictive analytics, deep learning, provide us proactive solutions over the IoT application cases [90]. In this subsection, we discuss CEP-based IoT application examples.

8.2.6.1   Transportation and traffic management

Wang *et al.* [91] propose a proactive CEP architecture and method for controlling traffic congestion intelligently. Proposed model includes network-distributed Markov decision process based on basic CEP and predictive analytics technology. They use some sensors such as RFID, GPS, and induction loop to get the position of vehicles. They also used other sensors (temperature, humidity, wind, etc.) for getting environmental information. Probabilistic event-processing agents are trying to reduce traffic jams based on obtained sensor information. Dunkel *et al.* [92] propose a reference architecture for event-driven traffic-management systems. It uses Esper event stream processing engine and Esper query language which provides its own query language. The system gets sensor information such as road segments, traffic data, and transforms these to events. It processes events as domain data events, problem events, cause events, and action events, respectively. The experiments showed that proposed system architecture is well suited for decision support in sensor-based traffic control systems. Akbar *et al.* [90] propose an architecture based on combining machine learning with CEP for predicting a complex event in IoT application. They also present an adaptive moving window regression algorithm. The author used traffic speed and traffic intensity data in order to compare the performance of prediction results. The proposed proactive architecture has shown that it will help system administrators manage the transportation problems in a better way.

8.2.6.2 Health

Yao *et al.* [93] propose a CEP framework to model critical situations and surgical events. It provides feasible solutions for patient safety and operational efficiency. It uses the raw readings captured by RFID readers, medical sensor data, and information systems data (or database). DROOLS fusion as CEP engine is used in processing all these data. The proposed framework has provided many benefits for hospitals such as increasing patient safety and satisfactory, improving asset tracking and security, and reduced operational costs.

8.2.6.3 Smart building

Chen *et al.* [94] propose a distributed CEP architecture for smart building with building automation system. It takes environmental sensor data such as temperature, humidity, wind speed, rainfall, luminance, radiation, carbon dioxide, carbon monoxide, motion, people counter, and power meter. The proposed architecture realizes real-time processing of heat, lighting, and power consumption for getting active, reactive and proactive actionable insights.

8.2.6.4 Smart grid/smart city

Zhou *et al.* [95] propose a knowledge-infused CEP framework (SCEPter) which processes queries across persistent and real-time event streams. It takes raw event data as input which is collected from 20 airflow sensors in the campus HVAC system. Then raw events are semantically enriched, pipelined through a semantic filter and a CEP engine, and archived onto an RDF database. Authors evaluate the framework within a smart power grid domain. It is envisaged to allow users to easily specify event patterns over diverse knowledge concepts in emerging domains such as IoT, and smart cities. Zu *et al.* [96] propose a data-centric architecture for distributed CEP monitoring applications and the interoperation and integration of CEP and service applications in smart grid. It allows the different application to communicate and share data by domain topic matching. It uses Esper CEP engine and SQL like language over streams. Kok *et al.* [97] propose a deep-learning-based air-quality-prediction model to provide proactive actions on air-quality problems. Authors train the model with pollution data that consists of ozone and nitrogen dioxide gases. They have contributed to the solution of the air-pollution problem in smart cities by estimating future air pollution.

8.2.6.5 Other domains

Vikhorev *et al.* [98] propose an industrial-energy-management framework which continuously obtaining energy-related information from any location of interest at the factory environment and provides system-wide optimization. It takes machine data (machine state, fault type), quality data, admin data (parallel machines, cycle times, number of stations), schedule data as input to provide decision support information for increasing energy efficiency and diagnosing failures at the production process level. The authors have stated that proposed framework will play an important role in companies' real-time, effective strategic, and operational decision-making in the production system.

CEP is also used in IoT sensing system [99], IoT system security [100], business intelligence [101], enterprise information systems [102], cloud-computing platforms [103], and risk-prediction systems [104].

8.2.7 Complex-event-processing challenges

In this subsection, we discuss some challenging topics for application developer in CEP. These topics are grouped as follows.

- In exact event content and uncertain event: Inexactness and uncertainty in events are caused by source malfunctions, malicious and imprecise sources, and temporal anomalies. The operational capability and performance of the CEP systems are adversely affected in the presence of these situations.
- Temporal semantics: Temporal dimensions of events play a major role in event processing. The sequence and the association of events may be important in the perception of another event and its semantics.
- Event occurrence time synchronization: Different event producers (sensors, smart devices, applications) in the application environment include their own internal clocks. They generate events at different times due to production constraints, and this yield faulty results for time order-sensitive event processing.
- Optimization: This task can be highly challenging due to heterogeneous and distributed nature of IoT applications. Each application events differ from another; therefore, good optimization will significantly increase the efficiency and throughput of handling a large number of heterogeneous event streams [105].

8.2.8 Trends and future directions in event processing

In this subsection, we discuss the trends and future research directions on CEP domain. In recent years, with the widespread use of IoT applications, the paradigm shifts from narrow to wide, from monolithic to diversified, from proprietary to standards-based, from stand-alone to embedded, and from reactive to proactive [59]. Each title given above contains some sample cases in itself. We can summarize these briefly as follows:

- Wideness: CEP is spreading and employed a different type of applications such as next-generation navigation, mobile device tracking, detecting unauthorized use of systems, real-time monitoring and management of materials, situation awareness in energy, customer relationship in banking, patient tracking, logistics and scheduling, and autonomous vehicles.

- Diversity: It is also increasing depending on the wideness of application types/fields. This diversity will lead the development of various platforms, EPLs, functions, and QoS requirements.
- Standardization: It is one of the most challenging issues in reaching an agreement on this issue. In the literature, there does not seem to strong coincidence in this matter. In near future, we need standardization on issues such as event structure, domain-specific event metadata, event distribution standards, EPL, and event processing architecture (EPA) component model.
- Embedded: Today, CEP operations are widely carried out on an expert platform. Due to the variety of IoT devices and applications, it is estimated that the CEP process can be placed in a software, layer, or application packages.
- Proactive: Today, CEP is generally used in a reactive manner that reacts when an event occurs. In the future, this situation will evolve proactive manner which will determine the prediction of the event and its mode of action before the event happens. Especially predictive analytic methods will make a major contribution to the CEP [106].

8.3 An example scenario: smart city

In this section, we give a smart city scenario to show that a fog-based CEP can take environmental data and process them with a deep-learning-based prediction model and make proactive decisions for early warning systems. We summarize the basic concept of this fog-based CEP scenario in Figure 8.4.

In smart cities, a huge number of heterogeneous sources generate various type of data such as traffic, weather, pollution, and noise. As explained earlier in this chapter, the amount of data produced by these data sources can be enormous. Besides, the information that lays in this data is mostly location depended. That is, a specific sensor data may be important for its surrounding region but not for the whole city. Therefore, as seen in Figure 8.4, a smart city should be divided into several parts (fog regions). This way, each fog server can be responsible from his region and the collected regional data can be processed by local CEP engines to obtain more meaningful results for the region. In fact, we defined this scenario in our earlier study [97]. In this scenario, city pollutant gas values are read through the sensors and sent to the fog layer. In this layer, future values of gas are predicted from historical gas values by our CEP system that employs a deep-learning-based LSTM prediction model. LSTM is a special kind of recurrent neural network and capable of learning long-term dependencies. It was introduced by Hochreiter and Schmidhuber in order to overcome vanishing gradient problem in 1997 [107].

In each fog server presented in Figure 8.4, the CEP engine analyzes the predicted gas values with the event rules established from international standard air pollution levels. The prediction model used in this scenario is given in Figure 8.5. This model, takes regional sensor values and generates an alarm over the decision table (rule table) taking into account multiple gas values that are predicted from deep learning model. Due to distributed fog architecture, the data of sensors are processed before they are

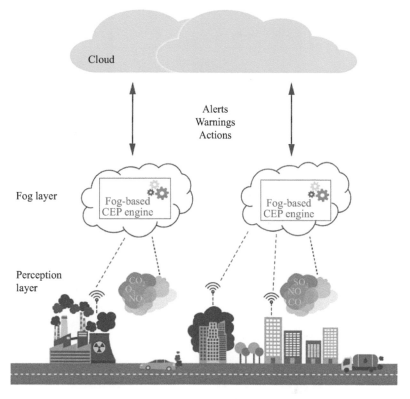

Figure 8.4   Example scenario of fog-based CEP

transmitted to cloud centers which results in generating locality sensitive alarms with less latency and more accuracy compared to traditional cloud-based alarm systems.

8.4   Conclusion

This chapter addresses data collection and real-time analysis of massive IoT data using a horizontally distributed fog-computing architecture. We explain how data-analysis problem of IoT can be handled in a layered fog architecture so that information extraction can be achieved in both local and global scales. We provide a deep investigation of existing fog-computing-based IoT solutions in a categorical manner and discuss the open-research problems. In terms of big data analysis, stream data mining and CEP techniques are proven to be quite promising solutions in the literature. Currently, stream data processing tools and techniques are mainly developed for cloud-based systems. However, there is an urgent need for adapting these techniques to horizontally distribute IoT-based data collection and analysis systems. We perform an extensive survey on stream data processing techniques by focusing on their ability to work on fog-computing-based IoT systems. We document a significant survey of CEP techniques in IoT systems by providing pros and cons of each scheme. We also

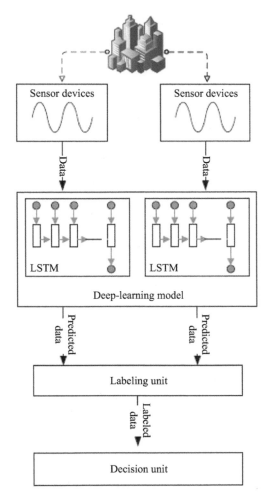

Figure 8.5   Employed prediction model in [97]

provide an example scenario to show that the problem of collection and real-time analysis of massive IoT data can be solved using fog-computation-based distributed architecture and CEP techniques.

References

[1]   Hu P, Dhelim S, Ning H, *et al.* Survey on fog computing: Architecture, key technologies, applications and open issues. Journal of Network and Computer Applications. 2017;98:27–42.

[2]   Cisco. Fog Computing and the Internet of Things: Extend the Cloud to Where the Things are. Cisco White Paper. Available from: https://www.cisco.com/c/dam/en_us/solutions/trends/iot/docs/computing-overview.pdf, Access on March 6, 2019.

[3] Firdhous M, Ghazali O, and Hassan S. Fog computing: Will it be the future of cloud computing? In: The Third International Conference on Informatics & Applications (ICIA2014); 2014.

[4] Ahmed E, and Rehmani MH. Mobile Edge Computing: Opportunities, solutions, and challenges. Future Generation Computer Systems. 2017;70:59–63.

[5] Beck MT, Werner M, Feld S, *et al.* Mobile edge computing: A taxonomy. In: Proc. of the Sixth International Conference on Advances in Future Internet. Citeseer; 2014. pp. 48–55.

[6] Jararweh Y, Doulat A, AlQudah O, *et al.* The future of mobile cloud computing: Integrating cloudlets and mobile edge computing. In: Telecommunications (ICT), 2016 23rd International Conference on. IEEE; 2016. pp. 1–5.

[7] Dinh HT, Lee C, Niyato D, *et al.* A survey of mobile cloud computing: Architecture, applications, and approaches. Wireless Communications and Mobile Computing. 2013;13(18):1587–1611.

[8] Vaquero LM, and Rodero-Merino L. Finding your way in the fog: Towards a comprehensive definition of fog computing. ACM SIGCOMM Computer Communication Review. 2014;44(5):27–32.

[9] Bonomi F. Connected vehicles, the internet of things, and fog computing. In: The Eighth ACM International Workshop on Vehicular Inter-networking (VANET), Las Vegas, USA; 2011. pp. 13–15.

[10] Bonomi F, Milito R, Natarajan P, *et al.* Fog computing: A platform for internet of things and analytics. In: Big data and internet of things: A roadmap for smart environments. Springer; 2014. p. 169–186, Cham.

[11] Khan MA. A survey of security issues for cloud computing. Journal of Network and Computer Applications. 2016;71:11–29.

[12] Intharawijitr K, Iida K, and Koga H. Analysis of fog model considering computing and communication latency in 5G cellular networks. In: Pervasive Computing and Communication Workshops (PerCom Workshops), 2016 IEEE International Conference on. IEEE; 2016. pp. 1–4.

[13] Peng M, Yan S, Zhang K, *et al.* Fog-computing-based radio access networks: Issues and challenges. IEEE Network. 2016;30(4):46–53.

[14] Hassan MA, Xiao M, Wei Q, *et al.* Help your mobile applications with fog computing. In: Sensing, Communication, and Networking-Workshops (SECON Workshops), 2015 12th Annual IEEE International Conference on. IEEE; 2015. p. 1–6.

[15] Alrawais A, Alhothaily A, Hu C, *et al.* Fog computing for the internet of things: Security and privacy issues. IEEE Internet Computing. 2017;21(2): 34–42.

[16] Luan TH, Gao L, Li Z, *et al.* Fog computing: Focusing on mobile users at the edge. arXiv preprint arXiv:150201815. 2015.

[17] Ye D, Wu M, Tang S, *et al.* Scalable fog computing with service offloading in bus networks. In: Cyber Security and Cloud Computing (CSCloud), 2016 IEEE 3rd International Conference on. IEEE; 2016. pp. 247–251.

[18] Gao W. Opportunistic peer-to-peer mobile cloud computing at the tactical edge. In: Military Communications Conference (MILCOM), 2014 IEEE. IEEE; 2014. pp. 1614–1620.

[19]   Zeng D, Gu L, Guo S, *et al.* Joint optimization of task scheduling and image placement in fog computing supported software-defined embedded system. IEEE Transactions on Computers. 2016;65(12):3702–3712.

[20]   Aazam M, and Huh EN. Dynamic resource provisioning through Fog micro datacenter. In: Pervasive Computing and Communication Workshops (PerCom Workshops), 2015 IEEE International Conference on. IEEE; 2015. pp. 105–110.

[21]   Aazam M, St-Hilaire M, Lung CH, *et al.* MeFoRE: QoE based resource estimation at fog to enhance QoS in IoT. In: Telecommunications (ICT), 2016 23rd International Conference on. IEEE; 2016. pp. 1–5.

[22]   Sarkar S, Chatterjee S, and Misra S. Assessment of the Suitability of Fog Computing in the Context of Internet of Things. IEEE Transactions on Cloud Computing. 2015;6(1):46–59.

[23]   Sarkar S, and Misra S. Theoretical modelling of fog computing: A green computing paradigm to support IoT applications. IET Networks. 2016;5(2):23–29.

[24]   Jalali F, Hinton K, Ayre R, *et al.* Fog computing may help to save energy in cloud computing. IEEE Journal on Selected Areas in Communications. 2016;34(5):1728–1739.

[25]   Deng R, Lu R, Lai C, *et al.* Towards power consumption-delay tradeoff by workload allocation in cloud-fog computing. In: Communications (ICC), 2015 IEEE International Conference on. IEEE; 2015. pp. 3909–3914.

[26]   Madsen H, Burtschy B, Albeanu G, *et al.* Reliability in the utility computing era: Towards reliable fog computing. In: Systems, Signals and Image Processing (IWSSIP), 2013 20th International Conference on. IEEE; 2013. pp. 43–46.

[27]   Stojmenovic I, and Wen S. The fog computing paradigm: Scenarios and security issues. In: Computer Science and Information Systems (FedCSIS), 2014 Federated Conference on. IEEE; 2014. pp. 1–8.

[28]   Yi S, Li C, and Li Q. A survey of fog computing: Concepts, applications and issues. In: Proceedings of the 2015 Workshop on Mobile Big Data. ACM; 2015. pp. 37–42.

[29]   Yi S, Qin Z, Li Q. Security and privacy issues of fog computing: A survey. In: International Conference on Wireless Algorithms, Systems, and Applications. Springer; 2015. pp. 685–695.

[30]   Gao L, Luan TH, Yu S, *et al.* FogRoute: DTN-based data dissemination model in fog computing. IEEE Internet of Things Journal. 2017;4(1):225–235.

[31]   Shi Y, Ding G, Wang H, *et al.* The fog computing service for healthcare. In: Future Information and Communication Technologies for Ubiquitous HealthCare (Ubi-HealthTech), 2015 2nd International Symposium on. IEEE; 2015. pp. 1–5.

[32]   Liu J, Li J, Zhang L, *et al.* Secure intelligent traffic light control using fog computing. Future Generation Computer Systems. 2018;78:817–824.

[33]   Rahmani AM, Gia TN, Negash B, *et al.* Exploiting smart e-health gateways at the edge of healthcare internet-of-things: A fog computing approach. Future Generation Computer Systems. 2018;78:641–658.

[34] Farahani B, Firouzi F, Chang V, *et al.* Towards fog-driven IoT eHealth: Promises and challenges of IoT in medicine and healthcare. Future Generation Computer Systems. 2018;78:659–676.

[35] Cao Y, Chen S, Hou P, *et al.* FAST: A fog computing assisted distributed analytics system to monitor fall for stroke mitigation. In: Networking, Architecture and Storage (NAS), 2015 IEEE International Conference on. IEEE; 2015. pp. 2–11.

[36] Dubey H, Yang J, Constant N, *et al.* Fog data: Enhancing telehealth big data through fog computing. In: Proceedings of the ASE BigData & SocialInformatics. ACM; 2015.

[37] Okay FY, and Ozdemir S. A fog computing based smart grid model. In: Networks, Computers and Communications (ISNCC), 2016 International Symposium on. IEEE; 2016. pp. 1–6.

[38] Tang B, Chen Z, Hefferman G, *et al.* A hierarchical distributed fog computing architecture for big data analysis in smart cities. In: Proceedings of the ASE BigData & SocialInformatics 2015. ACM; 2015. p. 28.

[39] Truong NB, Lee GM, and Ghamri-Doudane Y. Software defined networking-based vehicular adhoc network with fog computing. In: Integrated Network Management (IM), 2015 IFIP/IEEE International Symposium on. IEEE; 2015. pp. 1202–1207.

[40] Hou X, Li Y, Chen M, *et al.* Vehicular fog computing: A viewpoint of vehicles as the infrastructures. IEEE Transactions on Vehicular Technology. 2016;65(6):3860–3873.

[41] Loke SW. The internet of flying-things: Opportunities and challenges with airborne fog computing and mobile cloud in the clouds. arXiv preprint arXiv:150704492. 2015.

[42] Zao JK, Gan TT, You CK, *et al.* Augmented brain computer interaction based on fog computing and linked data. In: Intelligent Environments (IE), 2014 International Conference on. IEEE; 2014. pp. 374–377.

[43] Ha K, Chen Z, Hu W, *et al.* Towards wearable cognitive assistance. In: Proceedings of the 12th Annual International Conference on Mobile Systems, Applications, and Services. ACM; 2014. pp. 68–81.

[44] Zhu J, Chan DS, Prabhu MS, *et al.* Improving web sites performance using edge servers in fog computing architecture. In: Service Oriented System Engineering (SOSE), 2013 IEEE 7th International Symposium on. IEEE; 2013. pp. 320–323.

[45] Mahmud R, Kotagiri R, and Buyya R. Fog computing: A taxonomy, survey and future directions. In: Internet of Everything. Springer; 2018. pp. 103–130, Singapore.

[46] Yi S, Hao Z, Qin Z, *et al.* Fog computing: Platform and applications. In: Hot Topics in Web Systems and Technologies (HotWeb), 2015 Third IEEE Workshop on. IEEE; 2015. pp. 73–78.

[47] Chiang M, and Zhang T. Fog and IoT: An overview of research opportunities. IEEE Internet of Things Journal. 2016;3(6):854–864.

[48] Gupta H, Chakraborty S, Ghosh SK, *et al.* Fog computing in 5G networks: An application perspective. IET Digital Library; 2016.

[49]   Xu Y, Mahendran V, and Radhakrishnan S. Towards SDN-based fog computing: MQTT broker virtualization for effective and reliable delivery. In: Communication Systems and Networks (COMSNETS), 2016 8th International Conference on. IEEE; 2016. pp. 1–6.

[50]   Han B, Gopalakrishnan V, Ji L, *et al*. Network function virtualization: Challenges and opportunities for innovations. IEEE Communications Magazine. 2015;53(2):90–97.

[51]   Zhang L, Afanasyev A, Burke J, *et al*. Named data networking. ACM SIGCOMM Computer Communication Review. 2014;44(3):66–73.

[52]   Pallis G, and Vakali A. Insight and perspectives for content delivery networks. Communications of the ACM. 2006;49(1):101–106.

[53]   Chakravarthy S, and Jiang Q. Stream data processing: A quality of service perspective: Modeling, scheduling, load shedding, and complex event processing. vol. 36. Springer Science & Business Media; New York, NY, 2009.

[54]   Qin Y, Sheng QZ, Falkner NJ, *et al*. When things matter: A survey on data-centric internet of things. Journal of Network and Computer Applications. 2016;64:137–153.

[55]   Boubeta-Puig J, Ortiz G, and Medina-Bulo I. ModeL4CEP: Graphical domain-specific modeling languages for CEP domains and event patterns. Expert Systems with Applications. 2015;42(21):8095–8110.

[56]   Fülöp LJ, Tóth G, Rácz R, *et al*. Survey on complex event processing and predictive analytics. In: Proceedings of the Fifth Balkan Conference in Informatics. Citeseer; 2010. pp. 26–31.

[57]   Rizvi S. Complex event processing beyond active databases: Streams and uncertainties. TR EECS-2005–26. 2005.

[58]   Paschke A, Vincent P, Alves A, *et al*. Tutorial on advanced design patterns in event processing. In: Proceedings of the 6th ACM International Conference on Distributed Event-Based Systems. ACM; 2012. pp. 324–334.

[59]   Etzion O, and Niblett P. Event processing in action. Manning Publications, USA; 2011.

[60]   Nagy KA, and Pietzuch P. Distributing complex event detection. Imperial College of Science, Technology and Medicine; 2012.

[61]   Flouris I, Giatrakos N, Deligiannakis A, *et al*. Issues in complex event processing: Status and prospects in the big data era. Journal of Systems and Software. 2017;127:217–236.

[62]   Bry F, Eckert M, Etzion O, *et al*. Event processing language tutorial. In: 3rd ACM Int. Conf. on Distributed Event-Based Systems. ACM; 2009.

[63]   Aggarwal CC. Data streams: Models and algorithms. vol. 31. Springer Science & Business Media; New York, NY, 2007.

[64]   Agrawal R, and Srikant R. Fast algorithms for mining association rules. In: Proc. 20th Int. Conf. Very Large Data Bases, VLDB. vol. 1215; 1994. pp. 487–499.

[65]   Cheng J, Ke Y, and Ng W. A survey on algorithms for mining frequent item-sets over data streams. Knowledge and Information Systems. 2008;16(1): 1–27.

[66] Han J, Pei J, Yin Y, *et al.* Mining frequent patterns without candidate generation: A frequent-pattern tree approach. Data Mining and Knowledge Discovery. 2004;8(1):53–87.

[67] Wu X, Kumar V, Quinlan JR, *et al.* Top 10 algorithms in data mining. Knowledge and Information Systems. 2008;14(1):1–37.

[68] Tanbeer SK, Ahmed CF, Jeong BS, *et al.* Sliding window-based frequent pattern mining over data streams. Information Sciences. 2009;179(22): 3843–3865.

[69] Lee G, Yun U, and Ryu KH. Sliding window based weighted maximal frequent pattern mining over data streams. Expert Systems with Applications. 2014;41(2):694–708.

[70] Chang JH, and Lee WS. Finding recent frequent itemsets adaptively over online data streams. In: Proceedings of the Ninth ACM SIGKDD International Conference on Knowledge Discovery and Data Mining. ACM; 2003. pp. 487–492.

[71] Woo HJ, and Lee WS. EstMax: Tracing maximal frequent item sets instantly over online transactional data streams. IEEE Transactions on Knowledge and Data Engineering. 2009;21(10):1418–1431.

[72] Tanbeer SK, Ahmed CF, Jeong BS, *et al.* Efficient single-pass frequent pattern mining using a prefix-tree. Information Sciences. 2009;179(5):559–583.

[73] Yun U, Lee G, and Ryu KH. Mining maximal frequent patterns by considering weight conditions over data streams. Knowledge-Based Systems. 2014;55:49–65.

[74] Gao J, Ding B, Fan W, *et al.* Classifying data streams with skewed class distributions and concept drifts. IEEE Internet Computing. 2008;12(6).

[75] Domingos P, and Hulten G. Mining high-speed data streams. In: Proceedings of the Sixth ACM SIGKDD International Conference on Knowledge Discovery and Data Mining. ACM; 2000. pp. 71–80.

[76] Kelly MG, Hand DJ, and Adams NM. The impact of changing populations on classifier performance. In: Proceedings of the Fifth ACM SIGKDD International Conference on Knowledge Discovery and Data Mining. ACM; 1999. pp. 367–371.

[77] Kadwe Y, and Suryawanshi V. A review on concept drift. IOSR Journal of Computer Engineering. 2015;17:20–26.

[78] Hulten G, Spencer L, and Domingos P. Mining time-changing data streams. In: Proceedings of the Seventh ACM SIGKDD International Conference on Knowledge Discovery and Data Mining. ACM; 2001. pp. 97–106.

[79] Wang H, Fan W, Yu PS, *et al.* Mining concept-drifting data streams using ensemble classifiers. In: Proceedings of the Ninth ACM SIGKDD International Conference on Knowledge Discovery and Data Mining. ACM; 2003. pp. 226–235.

[80] Street WN, and Kim Y. A streaming ensemble algorithm (SEA) for large-scale classification. In: Proceedings of the Seventh ACM SIGKDD International Conference on Knowledge Discovery and Data Mining. ACM; 2001. pp. 377–382.

[81]   Hashemi S, Yang Y, Mirzamomen Z, *et al.* Adapted one-versus-all decision trees for data stream classification. IEEE Transactions on Knowledge and Data Engineering. 2009;21(5):624–637.

[82]   Brzeziński D, and Stefanowski J. Accuracy updated ensemble for data streams with concept drift. In: International Conference on Hybrid Artificial Intelligence Systems. Springer; 2011. pp. 155–163.

[83]   Zhou A, Cao F, Qian W, *et al.* Tracking clusters in evolving data streams over sliding windows. Knowledge and Information Systems. 2008;15(2):181–214.

[84]   Domingos P, and Hulten G. A general method for scaling up machine learning algorithms and its application to clustering. In: ICML. vol. 1; 2001. pp. 106–113.

[85]   Ordonez C. Clustering binary data streams with K-means. In: Proceedings of the 8th ACM SIGMOD Workshop on Research Issues in Data Mining and Knowledge Discovery. ACM; 2003. pp. 12–19.

[86]   Silva JA, Faria ER, Barros RC, *et al.* Data stream clustering: A survey. ACM Computing Surveys (CSUR). 2013;46(1):13.

[87]   Aggarwal CC, Han J, Wang J, *et al.* A framework for projected clustering of high dimensional data streams. In: Proceedings of the Thirtieth International Conference on Very Large Data Bases-Volume 30. VLDB Endowment; 2004. pp. 852–863.

[88]   Babcock B, Datar M, Motwani R, *et al.* Maintaining variance and k-medians over data stream windows. In: Proceedings of the Twenty-Second ACM SIGMOD-SIGACT-SIGART Symposium on Principles of Database Systems. ACM; 2003. pp. 234–243.

[89]   Wang Y, and Cao K. A proactive complex event processing method for large-scale transportation internet of things. International Journal of Distributed Sensor Networks. 2014;10(3):159052.

[90]   Akbar A, Khan A, Carrez F, *et al.* Predictive Analytics for Complex IoT Data Streams. IEEE Internet of Things Journal. 2017;4(5):1571–1582.

[91]   Wang Y, Geng S, and Li Q. Intelligent Transportation Control based on Proactive Complex Event Processing. In: MATEC Web of Conferences. vol. 77. EDP Sciences; 2016. p. 09004.

[92]   Dunkel J, Fernández A, Ortiz R, *et al.* Event-driven architecture for decision support in traffic management systems. Expert Systems with Applications. 2011;38(6):6530–6539.

[93]   Yao W, Chu CH, and Li Z. Leveraging complex event processing for smart hospitals using RFID. Journal of Network and Computer Applications. 2011;34(3):799–810.

[94]   Chen CY, Fu JH, Sung T, *et al.* Complex event processing for the internet of things and its applications. In: Automation Science and Engineering (CASE), 2014 IEEE International Conference on. IEEE; 2014. pp. 1144–1149.

[95]   Zhou Q, Simmhan Y, and Prasanna V. Knowledge-infused and consistent complex event processing over real-time and persistent streams. Future Generation Computer Systems. 2017;76:391–406.

[96] Zu X, Bai Y, and Yao X. Data-centric publish-subscribe approach for Distributed Complex Event Processing deployment in smart grid Internet of Things. In: Software Engineering and Service Science (ICSESS), 2016 7th IEEE International Conference on. IEEE; 2016. pp. 710–713.

[97] Kok I, Simsek MU, and Ozdemir S. A deep learning model for air quality prediction in smart cities. In: 2017 IEEE International Conference on Big Data (BIGDATA). IEEE; 2017.

[98] Vikhorev K, Greenough R, and Brown N. An advanced energy management framework to promote energy awareness. Journal of Cleaner Production. 2013;43:103–112.

[99] Guo Q, and Huang J. A complex event processing based approach of multi-sensor data fusion in IoT sensing systems. In: Computer Science and Network Technology (ICCSNT), 2015 4th International Conference on. vol. 1. IEEE; 2015. pp. 548–551.

[100] Kotenko I, and Saenko I. An approach to aggregation of security events in Internet-of-Things networks based on genetic optimization. In: Ubiquitous Intelligence & Computing, Advanced and Trusted Computing, Scalable Computing and Communications, Cloud and Big Data Computing, Internet of People, and Smart World Congress (UIC/ATC/ScalCom/CBDCom/IoP/SmartWorld), 2016 Intl IEEE Conferences. IEEE; 2016. pp. 657–664.

[101] Akila V, Govindasamy V, and Sandosh S. Complex event processing over uncertain events: Techniques, challenges, and future directions. In: Computation of Power, Energy Information and Communication (ICCPEIC), 2016 International Conference on. IEEE; 2016. pp. 204–221.

[102] Zang C, and Fan Y. Complex event processing in enterprise information systems based on RFID. Enterprise Information Systems. 2007;1(1):3–23.

[103] Higashino WA, Capretz MA, and Bittencourt LF. CEPSim: Modelling and simulation of Complex Event Processing systems in cloud environments. Future Generation Computer Systems. 2016;65:122–139.

[104] Kim YK, and Jeong CS. Risk prediction system based on risk prediction model with complex event processing: Risk prediction in real time on complex event processing engine. In: Big Data and Cloud Computing (BdCloud), 2014 IEEE Fourth International Conference on. IEEE; 2014. pp. 711–715.

[105] Robins D. Complex event processing. In: Second International Workshop on Education Technology and Computer Science. Wuhan. Citeseer; 2010. pp. 1–10.

[106] Akbar A, Carrez F, Moessner K, *et al.* Predicting complex events for pro-active IoT applications. In: Internet of Things (WF-IoT), 2015 IEEE 2nd World Forum on. IEEE; 2015. pp. 327–332.

[107] Hochreiter S, and Schmidhuber J. Long short-term memory. Neural Computation. 1997;9(8):1735–1780.

Chapter 9

Ultra-narrow-band for IoT

Yuqi Mo[1,2], Minh-Tien Do[1] and Claire Goursaud[1]

9.1 Introduction

LPWAN (low power wide area network) is a very recent term (appeared in 2013), referring to a very wide area network (covering up to several tens of kilometers range in rural areas with a single access point). The objective of such network is to provide connectivity to the Internet to a huge number of nodes deployed anywhere, in the Internet of Things (IoT) context. LPWAN gateways are thus needed to settle communication with the devices in their vicinity. To limit the operational cost of the operators, a limited-access infrastructure is suitable. As a consequence, a collecting point should serve nodes deployed in a very wide area. However, this cannot be obtained by tuning up the emission power, because it must be achieved while keeping a low-energy consumption for the nodes to preserve the network lifetime.

In addition, LPWAN are characterized by the fact that industrial, scientific, and medical (ISM) frequency bands are usually used for transmissions as they are license free and thus permit to further reduce the network cost. Furthermore, LPWAN is expected to handle sporadic small data packets, thus targeting new applications such as smart cities, smart metering, logistics, wildlife monitoring and tracking, and home automation, and safety.

As one of the fastest growing technologies in the emerging IoT environment, LPWAN is expected to provide ubiquitous connectivity for smart cities or rural areas. Currently, the available low power wide area (LPWA) communication technologies include a large variety of alternatives such as 3GPP Narrow-Band IoT, long-term evolution for machines, chirp spread spectrum (CSS) (known as LoRaWAN), ultra-narrow-band (UNB) (known as SigFox), and Random Phase Multiple Access (RPMA) (used by Ingenu and Weightless). In this chapter, we introduce one of the mentioned technologies: UNB, which was the first one to be commercially initiated for IoT purpose by SigFox company. All these applications pave the way for new markets and new business operators. Besides, as the infrastructure cost is low, newcomers have

---

[1]Centre for Innovation in Telecommunications and Integration of services (CITI), INSA-Lyon, Villeurbanne, France
[2]SigFox Company, Labège, France

joined the historical telecom operators by launching their proprietary transmission technology. Among them, we can cite SemTech along with LoRa Alliance with the LoRa technology, SigFox with UNB, and Ingenu with RPMA (Figure 9.1).

Aside from the market, LPWAN network has recently fostered many academic works [1–3]. Indeed, this context reveals a new scientific challenge which is moving from the data-rate expansion to the forthcoming number of devices growth and follow the path lead by dense WSN. To sum up, the objective is to define new techniques that verify the following:

- Low-energy consumption: Data have to be sent with the least emission power, and with the smallest time duration.
- Low device and infrastructure costs: Base stations (BSs) number should be the smallest, while devices have low computation capabilities.
- Capability of handling burst transmission of small size packets.
- Scalability and capability to handle a very high number of nodes.
- Extended coverage.

The second requirement is obtained, for the most shared vision, by a star topology with very long range (devices are directly communicating with the BS). To achieve such range, one can do the following:

- Increase the transmission power (but this solution is not acceptable due to the induced power consumption and potential health impact of increased wave exposure).
- Design ultra-sensitive receivers (but they are expensive, so could be deployed at the BS, but not at the node, preventing to deploy a downlink for distant nodes).

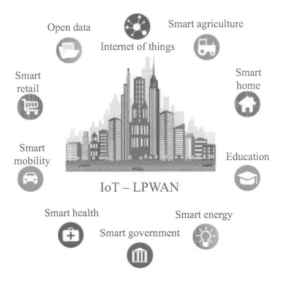

Figure 9.1   Examples of targeted applications for LPWAN

- Design new transmission technologies. This is this last possibility that has been adopted by operators and scientific community. In practice, two main directions (surprisingly in an orthogonal way) have been taken:
  - Spectrum spreading (LoRa with CSS, or Ingenu with RPMA): Data are sent on a much larger band than their baseband occupation. This frequency diversity permits to recover a signal even if its power spectral density is lower than the noise floor, because a specific pattern is searched and provides interesting decoding gains. Besides, different codes, that are verifying good correlation properties, can be affected to simultaneous transmitting devices, for multiple access purpose.
  - Spectrum reducing (SigFox with UNB): Data is sent at a very low rate with a simple modulation scheme, so as to ensure a minimal spectrum occupation. The advantage of such technique is that the perceived noise (after signal filtering) is reduced as it linearly depends on the signal spectrum occupation.

For both techniques, the required received power is significantly reduced. Thus, for the same emission power as in classical systems, a higher transmission range can be reached without degrading the performances capabilities.

The last technology, i.e., UNB, is expected to be more power efficient than spread spectrum, and it permits a longer transmission distance [4,5]. Besides, it can support more simultaneous transmitting nodes. We thus focus on this technology UNB in this chapter.

This chapter is organized as follows: Section 9.2 gives the definition of UNB and the studied network topology. Section 9.3 characterizes the spectral interference which is a specificity of UNB systems. Section 9.4 presents two multiple access schemes based on random frequency selection and their performances. Sections 9.5 and 9.6 provide the performance of UNB network with difference channel conditions: one with perfect power control and another with power attenuation such as pathloss and fading. Then Section 9.7 proposes to use interference cancellation technology to improve the network capacity. Finally, Section 9.8 concludes the chapter.

9.2   UNB system

In this section, SigFox's UNB networks will be presented and analyzed. Although SigFox's network is deployed worldwide and renowned to be efficient for low-throughput point-to-point transmissions, the capacity network based on this technology was not well known. In particular, some recent research [6] has focused on the behavior of a huge amount of non-synchronized operating nodes in a geographically extensive area around a BS.

9.2.1   UNB definition

UNB systems are defined such that each individual node occupies an extremely narrow frequency band to transmit its signal. This frequency band is significantly smaller than the bandwidth of the channel and is usually around a few hundred Hz. In

2004, Walker [7,8] first proposed the use of very minimum shift keying to compress data transmission in the smallest possible band. However, in practice, this modulation technique took a step forward but did not reach the claimed ultra-narrow frequency occupancy [9,10].

In SigFox's network, the UNB occupancy is obtained by transmitting at a very low data rate (100 bps). The transmitted signal thus occupies a band of about $b = 100$ Hz, inside a typical possible band of 192 kHz–2 MHz. A key phenomenon in such system is the oscillator frequency drift which induces an offset between the targeted frequency and the actual one. The currently available technology only permits factoring components with a standard deviation around 2–20 ppm (the state-of-the-art components reaches at best 0.25 ppm [11]). For example, for an operating frequency band of $f = 800$ MHz and a typical oscillator jitter $d_f = 0.25$–2 ppm, the uncertainty of carrier frequency positioning would be around $D_f = 200$–1,600 Hz which is larger than the transmission band occupied by an individual node. In this case, i.e., when the frequency uncertainty is higher than the signal bandwidth, the system is referred to as UNB.

9.2.2   *Topology: single cell design*

The atomic network element of SigFox's network is the star topology, where BSs centered on large cells receive the data from a huge amount of source nodes spread over. From the receiver's point of view, as shown in Figure 9.2, the monitored bandwidth B is filled with a combination of narrow-banded signals randomly located in time and frequency. Their demodulation relies on efficient Software Design Radio algorithms designed to analyze the total band to detect transmitted signals and to retrieve sent data. This is done with a fast Fourier transform (FFT) block applied to the received signal followed by an adaptive detector which aims at identifying the spectral signatures of the transmitted UNB signals. So, any uncontrolled frequency shift at any transmitter is not problematic if this shift is fixed (or slowly varying) during the short message duration. One may note that oscillators also suffer from an additional shift while heating during transmission, but this feature is also managed in SigFox's BS. For each detected transmission, the appropriate frequency band is filtered and demodulated with a standard BPSK demodulator.

9.3   UNB interference characterization

When considering a multiple-access channel, the interference pattern expression can be derived as follows:

For the general case, at the BS side, the received signal is the sum of active nodes' signals and can be expressed as follows:

$$
\begin{aligned}
r(t) = &\sqrt{h_c(r_x, t)} * h_e(f_x, t) * s_x(t) \\
&+ \sum_{y \in \{\mathcal{A}-x\}} \sqrt{h_c(r_y, t)} * h_e(f_y, t) * s_y(t) + w(t)
\end{aligned}
\tag{9.1}
$$

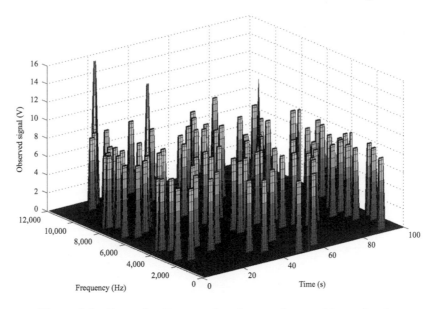

Figure 9.2   Example of temporal and spectral repartitions of nodes

where for any active node $x, y \in \mathcal{A}$, $s(t)$ is the modulated symbol; $h_e(f, t)$ is the transmission FIR filter centered on the randomly chosen carrier frequency f; $*$ denotes the convolution operator; and $w(t)$ is an additive white Gaussian noise with zero mean and variance σ^2, and the pathloss described by $h_c(r, t) = g(t) \cdot h_0 \cdot r^{-\alpha}$, $r \in [r_m, r_M]$, where $\alpha \geq 2$ is the path loss exponent; g is the Rayleigh channel coefficient, which is a random variable following an exponential distribution of unitary mean $g \sim \exp(1)$ considered as constant during the observation instant; and h_0 is the reference gain determined at the reference distance $r_0 = 1$ m.

To recover desired signal, the total signal received at BS is filtered at the carrier frequency of desired node f_x with the matching filter $(h_r(f_x, t) = h_e(f_x, t))$. We can deduce the following:

- The received power corresponding to the signal of the desired node x arriving at the BS: $P_s = h_c(r_x, t) \cdot P_0 = g_x \cdot r_x^{-\alpha} \cdot P_0'$, with $P_0 = \langle |h_e(f, t) * h_e(f, t) * s(t)|^2 \rangle$ which is identical to all signals, and P_0' which stands for $h_0 \cdot P_0$.
- The interference power I_y caused by a single interferer on the desired signal follows: $I_y = h_c(r_y, t) \cdot \beta(|f_x - f_y|) \cdot P_0 = g_y \cdot r_y^{-\alpha} \cdot \beta(|f_x - f_y|) \cdot P_0'$, with:

$$\beta(|f_x - f_y|) = \frac{\langle |h_e(f_y, t) * h_e(f_x, t)|^2 \rangle}{\langle |h_e(f_x, t) * h_e(f_x, t)|^2 \rangle} \tag{9.2}$$

the *rejection coefficient* to characterize the case where the reception filter is centered on a different frequency than the transmission filter. This rejection coefficient quantifies the portion of interfering signal which is kept after filtering. It depends on the frequency spacing between the two carrier frequencies

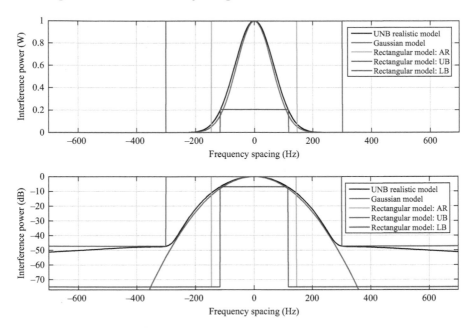

Figure 9.3   Behavior of the interference coefficient vs the frequency difference δ_f between the desired node and the interferer

$\delta_f = |f_x - f_y|$ as presented in Figure 9.3 (black curve) for a realistic filter as used in SigFox's network. One may note that β is a rejection coefficient, thus without unit in linear domain, and expressed in dB in logarithm scale. However, in the following, thanks to normalization with respect to the desired user power, the interference power and the rejection coefficient are the same. Thus, the term "interference" will be used.

This interference can be approximated with two kind of models. First, we can note that the actual interference level can be divided into two main areas. Transition occurs between 200 and 400 Hz, depending on the considered criterion. For high δ_f, the interference level is low, below -50 dB. So a unique interferer in this area will have almost no impact on the performance of the desired node. On the contrary, a unique node will cause a perceptible interference only if δ_f is very small, as the filter is very selective. As the available bandwidth is very large (around 192 kHz in practice) compared to the interference width, the interference level can be approximated by a constant in this area. Thus, the contribution of a single-interferer can be modeled by a rectangular function:

$$\beta(\delta_f) = \begin{cases} I_{\max} & \text{for} \quad \delta_f \leq \Delta/2, \\ I_{\min} & \text{for} \quad \delta_f > \Delta/2. \end{cases} \tag{9.3}$$

where Δ corresponds to the width of δ_f that creates high interference level.

Table 9.1   List of simplified models using rectangular function

Models	I_{max} for $|\delta_f| \leq (\Delta/2)$	I_{min} for $|\delta| > (\Delta/2)$
Upper bound	$I_{max\_up} = 0$ dB and $\Delta_{up} = 440$ Hz	$I_{min\_up}(\Delta_{up})$ dB
Lower bound for BER	$I_{max\_low}(\Delta_{low})$ dB and $\Delta_{low} = 100$ Hz	$I_{min\_low} = -90$ dB
Lower bound for OP	$I_{max\_low}(\Delta_{low})$ dB and $\Delta_{low} = 220$ Hz	$I_{min\_low} = -90$ dB
Optimal model	$I_{max} = -1.77$ dB and $\Delta = 232$ Hz	$I_{min} = -90$ dB

The empirical parameters can be determined for several cases: upper bound, lower bound and optimal model (in red, blue and green, respectively). The values reported in Table 9.1 were obtained by searching for the parameter set that minimizes the simulated bit error rate (BER) (resp. OP (outage probability)) difference with the theoretical BER (resp. OP) ((9.8) and (9.9) that will be presented in few pages).

The interference power can also be approximated by a zero-mean Gaussian function, depending on the frequency difference δ_f (pink curve in Figure 9.3):

$$\beta(\delta_f) = \frac{150}{\sigma\sqrt{2\pi}} \exp\left(-\delta_f^2/2\sigma^2\right) \tag{9.4}$$

with $\sigma = 60$.

When considering several interferers, the AIP (aggregated interference power) is the sum of all interferers' contribution. AIP is plotted in Figure 9.4 and one can refer to [12] for more details. We can observe that for a number of active nodes smaller than 20, AIP remains small. On the other case, AIP gradually converges to the left, near 0 dB (which corresponds to $\delta_f = 0$ for a single interferer case) and more. In fact, when the number of active nodes increases, the probability that at least one node chooses a carrier frequency close to the one of desired node is also increased. This contribution will dominate the other and leads to a high level of interference. Thus, in practice, failure is generally due to a unique interferer. When the intended transmission fails, we say that there is a collision between two packets. This hypothesis has thus been considered throughout the presented work.

9.4   UNB-associated MAC

In SigFox's network, when devices have data to transmit, they choose a carrier frequency within the 192 kHz available band. In theory, such selection can be done in either of the ways:

- In a discrete way: The carrier is elected among a finite set of frequencies. This is called DR-FDMA (discrete random frequency division multiple access). DR-FDMA scheme is characterized by Δ_f the spacing between the possible values of carrier's frequency (CFS: carrier frequency spacing).

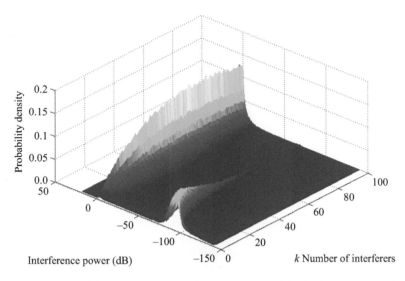

Figure 9.4   PDF of the aggregate interference power (dB), for k = 100 interferers, for BW = 12 kHz

- In continuous way: The carrier is chosen at random in the continuous available frequency band. This is called CR-FDMA (continuous random frequency division multiple access). We can note that the CR-FDMA scheme allows the use of transmitters whose time and frequency are unconstrained (except for being in the transmission total band). In practice, the randomness in frequency domain is easily done, thanks to the frequency jitter. It is reasonable, however, to assume that this frequency remains constant during the transmission of a whole packet. Finally, we can note that CR-FDMA corresponds to DR-FDMA scheme with an infinitely small CFS.

9.4.1   Performance of CR-FDMA and DR-FDMA

In this section, we present the system performance. The OP has been computed for the two previous cases (DR-FDMA and CR-FDMA) [13]. A packet is considered to be lost if the intended packet undergoes an interference level higher than a given threshold.

If the $k + 1$ transmitting nodes are all perceived at the BS with the same power, and no jitter is considered, then the OP is given by the following:

- In the DR-FDMA scheme,

$$OP(k) = 1 - \left(1 - \frac{1 + 2 \times \lfloor \delta_0/\Delta_f \rfloor}{\lfloor BW/\Delta_f \rfloor}\right)^k \tag{9.5}$$

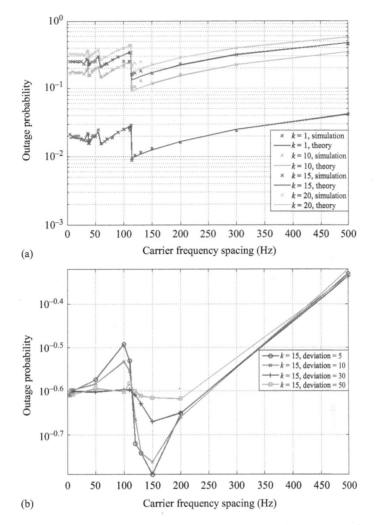

Figure 9.5 R-FDMA OP vs Δ_f for k interferers, $BW = 12$ kHz: (a) validation (no jitter) and (b) with jitter, $K = 10$

- In the CR-FDMA scheme,

$$OP(k) = 1 - \left(1 - \frac{(2 \times \delta_0)}{BW}\right)^k \qquad (9.6)$$

with δ_0 corresponding to the highest frequency difference in the high interference area (Figure 9.3).

We can verify in Figure 9.5(a) that the theoretical model fits with the simulation results. However, one should note that the theoretical model is less pertinent when the number of nodes increases, especially for Δ_f slightly larger than 113 Hz, due to the fact that the aggregated interference was neglected. Besides, we can also observe that the OP curves follow a sawtooth pattern, whose local maximums and minimums do not depend on the number of active interferers, but only on Δ_f, as predicted by the theoretical analysis. Finally, DR-FDMA is optimal for $\Delta_f = 113$ Hz and is more performing than CR-FDMA scheme (as CR-FDMA corresponds to CFS $\rightarrow$ 0).

Such results have been confronted to the jitter impact. To this aim, the frequency jitter has been modeled by an additive random frequency variable, which follows a Gaussian distribution with zero mean and known standard deviation σ. We can observe in Figure 9.5(b), that the DR-FDMA performances are degraded when taking into account jitter. Indeed, the sawtooth pattern is more and more smoothed as the jitter standard deviation increases. Indeed, the statistical distribution of the interferer's carrier around the targeted frequencies tends to reduce the gap between the performances of close Δ_f values, and especially where there was a discontinuity. Without jitter, all the nodes that choose $\delta_f = 112$ Hz (resp. $\delta_f = 113$ Hz) lead (resp. do not lead) to OP. On the contrary, with jitter, in both cases, we get about half carriers under 113 Hz, creating OP, while the second half does not create OP. Thus, there is no discontinuity anymore. As a consequence, the benefit brought by DR-FDMA disappears when jitter is present. In this case, CR-FDMA becomes as efficient as DR-FDMA. Thus, CR-FDMA will be used. Besides, one may note that it allows the use of the cheapest oscillators component without the loss of performance network, as for $\sigma > 50$, the same performances will be obtained.

Finally, there are three main inherent features to UNB systems, that will restraint the available choices for Multiple Access Protocols definition, as illustrated in Figure 9.6:

- Asynchronicity: The data transmission of active node is made in an asynchronous manner, both in time without any scheduling strategies. This feature permits to suppress the traffic overload needed for global synchronization. However, it leads to the packet collision during the transmission of a given packet due to the fact that packets do not simultaneously start and stop.
- Lack of contention-based protocols is considered as a third impact on the data transmission of an active node in the frequency domain. As the contention-based protocol is mitigated for all active nodes, each node is transmitting its packet regardless of carrier frequencies being used by other active nodes in a given bandwidth. As a result, the spectral overlap between their individual transmission bands (i.e., interference) is induced when at least two nodes are transmitting at the same moment. For example, in Figure 9.6, the green node starts transmitting even if the red one is already using the band in common. There is a spectral and temporal overlap between them.
- Randomness in frequency domain as treated previously which concerns the position of carrier frequency of active nodes in the total bandwidth. Active nodes can choose randomly and continuously their carrier frequencies to transmit their data.

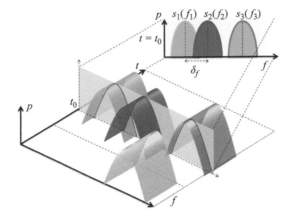

Figure 9.6 Example of temporal and spectral repartition of nodes

9.4.2 Throughput of CR-FTDMA

As the CR-FTDMA is an extension of ALOHA protocol, we have derived the network throughput as a function of the load. We assume that each node transmits a message of duration τ seconds, at a randomly chosen time, every D_p seconds on average. We have shown that the ALOHA success probability, with slotted or unslotted time, and slotted or unslotted frequency, and uniform distribution in time and frequency domain, is given by [14]:

$$P_{2D} = e(-\alpha_t \alpha_f G_{tf}) \tag{9.7}$$

with $G_{tf} = Np_t p_f = (N\tau b/D_p \mathrm{BW})$, and $\alpha_f = 2$ (resp. 1) for frequency-unslotted (FU) (resp. frequency slotted (FS)) ALOHA.

Figure 9.7 presents the throughput as a function of the load G_{tf}. As time and frequency can be independently slotted or unslotted, there are four possible scenarios: frequency-slotted (resp. unslotted) time-slotted: FSTS (resp. FUTS) and frequency-slotted (resp. unslotted) time-unslotted: FSTU (resp. FUTU). We can first note that the FSTS case is the best one as the time-frequency space is divided into orthogonal channels, thus minimizing the probability of collision. On the opposite, FUTU is the worst one as partial overlapping is possible both in time and frequency domain. Finally, FSTU and FUTS coincide due to the time-frequency duality. Thus, there are in fact only three distinct curves, according to the possible values of the product $\alpha_t \cdot \alpha_f$.

One may note that the time-frequency duality brings flexibility. Indeed, if both precise frequency and timing are difficult to handle simultaneously, FSTS cannot be achieved. The duality between FSTU and FUTS allows to decide which constraint to relax, independently of the impact on the performances, but based, for example, on the network-deployment cost.

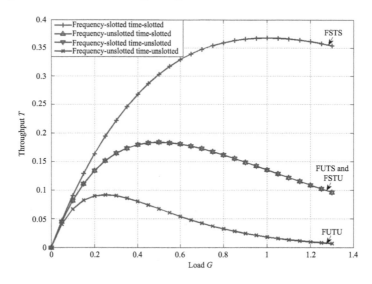

Figure 9.7　Network throughput as a function of the load for all (α_t,α_f)

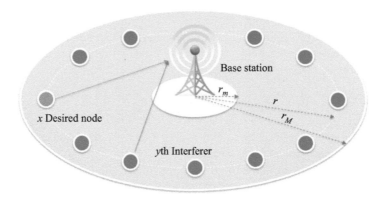

Figure 9.8　Network topology for a unique cell with equal received power

9.5　UNB performances for same received power at the BS

Now that the specific interference model and access method are known, we can focus on the performance analysis. In order to have an insight on the specific interference pattern, the case where nodes are perceived at the BS with the same emission power has to be considered first. This corresponds to the case where all nodes are at the same distance from the BS, and are affected by the same channel conditions, or to the case where power control is performed (Figure 9.8).

Table 9.2   *Maximum nodes numbers for OP = 10^{-1}, non-path-loss*

BW	*N* up	*N* simu	*N* opt	*N* low (BER)	*N* low (OP)
12 kHz	3	6	6	13	6
24 kHz	6	11	11	26	12
48 kHz	12	23	23	51	23
64 kHz	16	30	30	68	31
96 kHz	23	44	45	102	46
1 MHz	124	450	455	1,054	479

The BS is considered to be always in reception mode, and to scan the whole bandwidth for potential transmissions (as done in SigFox network). For each detected transmission (even simultaneous ones), the BS processes the incoming message(s). If the signal to interference and noise ratio (SINR) is higher than a threshold (usually set to 7 dB in the result part), the packet is considered correctly received. In all the following studies, instantaneous metrics will be considered: it is assumed that the transmission conditions remain the same over the packet duration. Thus, the SINR is analyzed at a given moment.

9.5.1   One transmission

It has been shown that, for $k + 1$ total simultaneously active users (i.e., k interferers), the BER and OP can be theoretically obtained with:

$$\text{BER}(k) = \sum_{n_L=0}^{n_L=k} \mathbb{P}(N_L = n_L) \cdot \text{erfc}\left(\sqrt{\frac{P_s}{P_I(k, n_L)}}\right) \tag{9.8}$$

$$\text{OP}(k) = \sum_{n_L/P_I(k,n_L)>\gamma} \mathbb{P}(N_L = n_L) \tag{9.9}$$

with:

$$\mathbb{P}(N_L = n_L) = C_k^{n_L} \cdot p^{n_L} \cdot (1-p)^{(k-n_L)} \tag{9.10}$$

From this, the network capacity, expressed as the maximum number of simultaneously active users while guaranteeing satisfactory OP (Table 9.2), can be derived. We can verify the accuracy of the rectangular model, as well as the parameter set and the theoretical expressions, by observing that the optimal model provides a good estimation of the simulation, while the bounds actually provide lower and higher estimations.

9.5.2   Multiple transmissions

To improve the system capacity, the use of replications during the transmission has been considered. As replications are identical, the message is successfully received if at least one of this replication is correctly received at the BS. The replications are

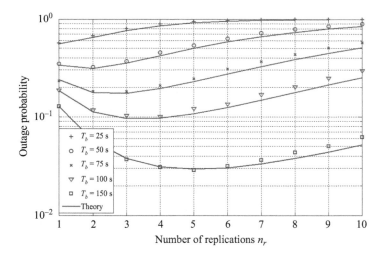

Figure 9.9   OP vs number of replications n_r with different message period T_b,
BW = 12 kHz, N = 1,000

assumed to experience independent transmission conditions, and the success probability of any replication is supposed to be independent of the collision on the previous
ones. The theoretical expression for the OP can be derived as a function of the main
system parameters [15]: the whole transmission band BW; the frequency occupancy
with respect to the carrier $[-b; b]$ Hz; the wake-up duty cycle of nodes T_b; the time
duration of a message d, and the replication number n_r. Accordingly, the OP of one
useful message, transmitted with n_r replication, is:

$$OP = \left(1 - \left(1 - \frac{2b \times d}{BW \times T_b} \times n_r\right)^{N-1}\right)^{n_r} \tag{9.11}$$

We can observe, in Figure 9.9, that there is an optimum number of replications.
This is due to the fact that, at first, when n_r increases, the replications bring redundancy
and a better reliability. However, when n_r is too high, it overloads the network, and
the performances drop due to excessive number of collisions.

As can be seen in (9.11), OP depends on many parameters. However, by derivating
(9.11) and numerically evaluating the optimal n_r, it can be shown that the optimal number of replications depends on a single parameter: the resources occupation parameter
$\Omega = N/(BW \times T_b)$. We can thus plot the optimal number of replications as a function
of this parameter (Figure 9.10). We can observe that $n_{r_{opt}}$ decreases when the node
density gets high (this is due to the fact that the increase of the network load reduces
the available time/frequency resources for the replication process). This result is very
interesting and promising because its urges the potential ability of configuring the
network by relying on a single global parameter: node density over the temporal and
frequency resources Ω.

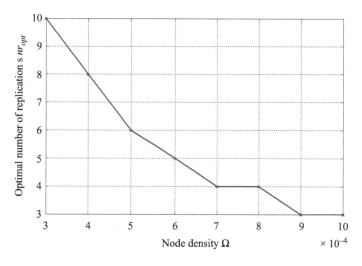

Figure 9.10 Node density Ω vs optimal number of replications $n_{r_{opt}}$

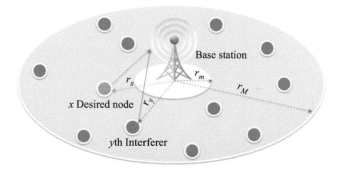

Figure 9.11 Topology network of adopting the spatial node distribution

9.6 UNB performances for diverse received power at the BS

Finally, to derive more realistic performances of the network, the case where the different nodes encounter diverse propagation conditions has been considered. Two complementary approaches can be taken to derive the OP. First, an analytic expression of an UNB-based system performance can be derived, when considering both the attenuation effect and the actual specific behavior of the interference in the spectral domain [16]. Second, the stochastic geometry model can be used to also take into account the Rayleigh fading effect, but with a simplified interference model [17].

Nodes are supposed to be uniformly distributed in a disk-form area, whose range is $[r_m, r_M]$, as shown in Figure 9.11. Nodes are positioned inside the cell, except for the inner disk of the cell (to ensure mathematical tractability by avoiding singularity at the BS location [18]). Nodes are distributed according to a spatial homogeneous

Poisson point process (PPP) of density λ that lies in the Euclidean plan $\mathbb{R}^2$. We assume that nodes emit with the same emission power.

9.6.1   Rectangular interference shape and stochastic geometry

Stochastic geometry is a powerful tool that permits to handle spatial randomness and its implications on metrics observation. In addition to the geometric pathloss, stochastic geometry permits to take into account Rayleigh fading and noise in the interference expression. It is thus perfectly adapted to this study. However, all previous works using this tool were considering channelized transmission. The partial collision in frequency domain $\beta(\delta_f)$ thus needs to be introduced in the stochastic geometry model by considering a marked spatial PPP, where the mark models the residual proportion of interference which is perceived on the desired transmission. However, due to the shape of the rejection coefficient function, according to the very first calculations, such approach leads to intractable expressions. Tractable expressions were obtained by considering the rectangular model as presented in (9.3).

OP can be computed as (one can find more calculation details in [17]):

$$OP = 1 - \exp(-W \cdot s) \cdot \mathcal{L}_{P_I}(s) \tag{9.12}$$

with $\mathcal{L}_{P_I}$ the Laplace transform of the AIP probability density function (PDF), expressed in a general way for any desired node at a distance r_x from the BS, as:

$$\mathcal{L}_{P_I}(s) = \mathbb{E}_{P_I}[\exp(-P_I \cdot s)]. \tag{9.13}$$

$$= \exp\left(-2\pi\lambda\left(\underbrace{\int_{r_m}^{r_M} r_y dr_y}_{A} - \underbrace{\int_{r_m}^{r_M} \frac{p}{1 + s \cdot b \cdot r_y^{-\alpha}} r_y dr_y}_{B(s)}\right.\right.$$

$$\left.\left. - \underbrace{\int_{r_m}^{r_M} \frac{1-p}{1 + s \cdot c \cdot r_y^{-\alpha}} r_y dr_y}_{C(s)}\right)\right) \tag{9.14}$$

For free space $\alpha = 2$, we have:

$$\mathcal{L}_{P_I}(s) = \left(\frac{r_m^2 + sb}{r_M^2 + sb}\right)^{\pi\lambda p s b} \cdot \left(\frac{r_m^2 + sc}{r_M^2 + sc}\right)^{\pi\lambda(1-p)sc} \tag{9.15}$$

For flat earth model $\alpha = 4$, we have:

$$\mathcal{L}_{P_I}(s) = \exp\left(\pi\lambda p \cdot\sqrt{sb} \cdot \arctan\left(\frac{r_m^2\sqrt{sb} - r_M^2\sqrt{sb}}{sb + r_M^2 r_m^2} \right) \right.$$

$$\left. + \pi\lambda(1-p) \cdot\sqrt{sc} \cdot \arctan\left(\frac{r_m^2\sqrt{sc} - r_M^2\sqrt{sc}}{sc + r_M^2 r_m^2} \right) \right) \tag{9.16}$$

9.6.2 Exact interference shape

To take into account the exact interference shape $b(\delta_f)$, the OP has been computed in a more simple case: without fading and noise, and considering free space propagation ($\alpha = 2$). Contrarily to stochastic geometry where aggregated interference was considered, it is assumed here that interference comes from a single interferer. With a free space propagation model, the SIR of the desired node is:

$$SIR_1 = \frac{P_0(r_0/r_x)^2}{P_0(r_0/r_y)^2 b(\delta_f)} = \left(\frac{r_y}{r_x} \right)^2 \frac{1}{b(\delta_f)} \tag{9.17}$$

Consequently, OP can also be expressed as (more details can be found in [16]):

$$OP = P\left(r_y \leq r_x\sqrt{Sb(\delta_f)} \right) \tag{9.18}$$

$$= 0 + \int_{b_1}^{b_2} \left(\frac{r_x^2\gamma^*b(\delta_f) - r_m^2}{k^2} \right) \mathbb{P}(\delta_f)d\delta_f + \int_{b_0}^{b_1} 1 \cdot \mathbb{P}(\delta_f)d\delta_f$$

$$= \left[75a\gamma^* \, \mathrm{erf}\left(\frac{\delta_f}{\sqrt{2\sigma^2}} \right) + \frac{150a\gamma^*\sigma}{B\sqrt{2\pi}}\exp\left(\frac{-\delta f^2}{2\sigma^2} \right) + e\frac{\delta_f^2}{2} - eB\delta_f \right]_{b_1}^{b_2}$$

$$+ \frac{B}{2}\left[\delta_f - \frac{\delta_f^2}{2B} \right]_{b_0}^{b_1} \tag{9.19}$$

with the following constants:

$$d = \frac{2r_x^2}{Bk^2}, \qquad e = \frac{2r_m^2}{B^2k^2}, \qquad b_0 = 0$$

$$b_1 = \min\left(\beta^{-1}\left(\left(\frac{r_M}{r_x} \right)^2 \frac{1}{\gamma^*} \right), B \right), \qquad b_2 = \min\left(\beta^{-1}\left(\left(\frac{r_m}{r_x} \right)^2 \frac{1}{\gamma^*} \right), B \right)$$

Equation (9.18) represents the OP when there are two active nodes. For N active nodes, any of the $N-1$ nodes (i.e., all nodes except the desired node) can be an interfering node. Accordingly, transmission success means that the desired node is not interrupted by any of $N-1$ nodes. Consequently, the OP is given by:

$$OP_{(N)} = 1 - (1 - OP)^{N-1} \tag{9.20}$$

Table 9.3   Simplified models using rectangular function used in this part

Models	Δ (Hz)	$I_{\max}$ (dB)	$I_{\min}$ (dB)
Optimal model (AR)	145	0	−75
Upper bound (UP)	300	0	−47.28
Lower bound for OP (LB)	116	−6.8	−75

9.6.3   Validation and comparison

The previous expressions ((9.12) and (9.20)) have been validated in the realistic SigFox's case ($R_b = 100$ bps, $b = 100$ Hz, $B = 192$ kHz, $\gamma^* = 6.8$ dB). For the rectangular model, new sets of parameters were derived for the optimal model (AR), upper and lower bound. Indeed, it has been identified that higher distance leads to a wider rectangle. Thus, $r_x = r_{\max}$ provides the most pessimistic rectangular model over the cell (Table 9.6.3).

We present in Figure 9.12 the comparison between simulation and theory results. Specific simulations have been run for the fading and no-fading case to validate the theoretical expressions in the corresponding case. Theories validation aside, we can note that OP (no-Rayleigh) is lower than OP (Rayleigh) when r_x is small. But when r_x exceeds a certain distance, these two cases have identical outage probabilities (and close to the real shape simulation results). Rayleigh fading can amplify or attenuate the received signal power. If the received power of the desired node gets attenuated, the area where interfering nodes may lead to error becomes larger. Hence, we have more potential nodes in this case. Meanwhile, if the desired node's received power gets amplified, this area becomes smaller, which leads to less interfering nodes. When r_x is small, the expected area's increase is much bigger than the expected area's decrease. Thus, such a node is sensitive to fading. On the contrary, for high r_x, the area increase is bounded by the cell limit and thus is less important. In addition, for high r_x, the inner interferers are not impacted by fading in average. Hence, such node is barely affected by the fading.

9.6.4   Network spectral efficiency

Finally, the network spectral efficiency defined as the ratio of the maximum node number and the bandwidth $N_{\max}/B$ was evaluated. The spectral efficiency of two cases was compared, without and with a guard band, for different values of α, as shown in Figure 9.13. The *without guard band* corresponds to the ideal case, where targeted frequencies can be obtained, thus allowing the frequency random selection on the whole B. However, in practice, we could obtain such ideal case only if the used bands are placed right next to each other. But, in an UNB network, the oscillator jitter causes imprecise carrier position, which can lead to an overlap between adjacent bands. Therefore, the bands should be separated by a guard interval, which must be taken into account in the spectral efficiency. A 1,736 Hz guard band is considered here,

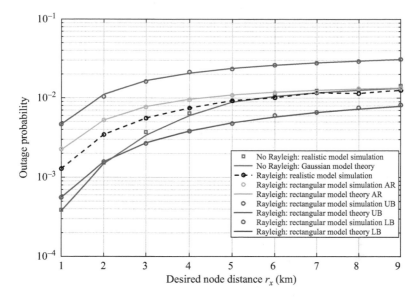

Figure 9.12 OP as a function of the desired node's distance r_x, for $B = 96$ kHz, $N = 6$, $r_M = 10$ km, $r_m = 1$ m, $\gamma^* = 6.8$ dB and path loss $\alpha = 2$

which corresponds to the operating frequency transmission 868 MHz and standard deviation of frequency jitter of 2 ppm. This permits to ensure that no actual carrier frequency would fall outside the intended band.

The rectangular model (with AR set of parameter) is used to study this criteria while varying the path loss exponents. By observing Figure 9.13, we can note that for small bandwidth such as $B = 12$ kHz, the spectral efficiency is highly degraded by the guard band. This is due to the fact that a big portion of the band is wasted for the guard band to counteract the frequency jitter. Meanwhile, the impact of guard band diminishes as B increases. Hence for the large bandwidth length, the spectral efficiency seems the same for both cases. More interestingly, for each B, there exists a highest spectral efficiency obtained with an optimal α. This is because when α increases, the signal power of both the desired node and interfering nodes diminishes. In the first part of the curves, as the desired node is near to the BS, this decrease of power is more important for interfering nodes, which can be anywhere in the cell. Meanwhile, in the second part, when α exceeds a certain value, the power reduction is so severe that the desired node has no more advantage. Thus $N_{\max}$ first increases then decreases. One may note that this behavior is smoothened when r_x is closer to r_M.

Following the previous conclusion, Figure 9.14 presents the optimal bandwidth B (for the guard band case) to achieve the highest ratio $N_{\max}/B$, as a function of the path loss exponent α. This figure provides the optimal choice for B, according to the propagation characteristics. We observe that for urban areas such as $\alpha = 4$, we need a thinner bandwidth than for rural areas to reach the highest spectral efficiency. Hence, it also permits to make effective use of the available bandwidth.

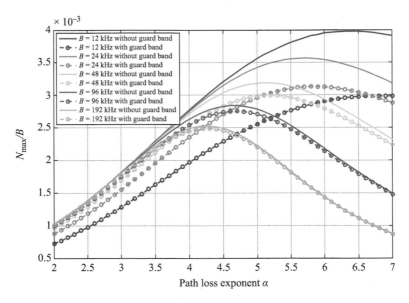

Figure 9.13   Maximum node number to bandwidth ratio N_{max}/B (nodes/Hz) vs exponent path-loss α, for $r_M = 10$ km, $r_x = 2$ km, $r_m = 1$ m, $\gamma^* = 6.8$ dB, with and without guard band

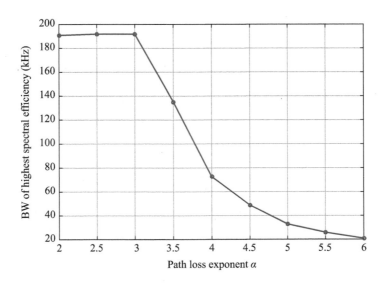

Figure 9.14   Bandwidth for highest spectral efficiency (N_{max}/B) vs exponent path-loss α, for $r_M = 10$ km, $r_x = 2$ km, $r_m = 1$ m, $\gamma^* = 6.8$ dB, with guard band

9.7 Interference cancellation

Finally, to improve the network performances (and thus its capacity), the use of SIC (successive interference cancellation) receiver has been considered [19]. The same methodology as (9.18) was used, by considering the rectangular interference model. However, in this case, the performances were obtained on average in the cell, and not for a fixed r_x. The SIC is supposed to be able to iteratively decode and perfectly remove the highest SINR packet, as long as its SIR is above the required threshold. Thus, a packet is successfully received if its SINR is higher than the threshold or if the colliding packet is itself decodable. Thus, we get:

$$OP_{SIC} = P\left(SIR_x \leq S\right) - P\left(SIR_x \leq S \cap SIR_y > S\right)$$

$$= \int_{b_3}^{b_2} \left(\frac{(d - d_1)}{SIR_{th} b(\delta_f)} + (e - e_1)SIR_{th} b(\delta_f) + (f - f_1) \right) P(\delta_f)\, d\delta_f$$

$$+ \int_{b_4}^{b_3} P(\delta_f)\, d\delta_f \tag{9.21}$$

with the following integral edges: $b_1 = \min\left(\beta^{-1}\left((r_m/r_M)^2\,(1/S)\right), B\right)$, $b_2 = \min\left(\beta^{-1}(1/S), B\right)$ $b_3 = \min\left(\beta^{-1}\left((r_M/r_m)^2\,(1/S)\right), B\right)$, and $b_4 = 0$; and the following constants:

$$d = \frac{r_M^4}{2k^4} - \frac{r_m^2 r_M^2}{k^4} - \frac{r_M^2}{k^2} \qquad\qquad d_1 = \frac{r_M^4}{2k^4},$$

$$e = -\frac{r_m^4}{2k^4} \qquad\qquad\qquad\qquad e_1 = \frac{r_m^4}{2k^4},$$

$$f = \frac{r_m^4}{k^4} + \frac{r_M^2}{k^2} \qquad\qquad\qquad f_1 = -\frac{r_M^2 r_m^2}{k^4} \tag{9.22}$$

where $k^2 = r_M^2 - r_m^2$;

After theoretical expression validation, the SIC benefits can be evaluated by computing the error-reduction percentage ($PER_{noSIC} - PER_{SIC}/PER_{noSIC}$). As seen in Figure 9.15, it can be shown that, no matter how the scale of node number $100N/B$ becomes, as long as the node density is constant, the SIC improvement is identical.

9.8 Conclusion

In this chapter, we have presented a novel radio technology, i.e., UNB, which is designed to enable long-range and low-power transmissions. We aim at providing the knowledge and insight of IoT networks using UNB technique in different aspects. We have started by introducing its specific multiple access behavior, which is both random in time and frequency domain. Then, we have characterized the spectral interference

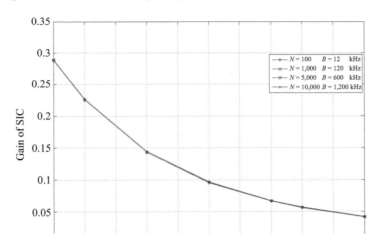

Figure 9.15   *Gain of SIC, for different SIR threshold S (dB), and constant node density 100 N/B, $r_m = 30$ m, $r_M = 1,000$ m*

by two models: one rectangular model and one Gaussian model. We have observed that the failure of one UNB packet is generally due to a unique interferer. We have as well considered the discrete (DR-FDMA) and the continuous (CR-FDMA) random-access schemes. And we have shown that the uncontrolled transmitting carrier frequencies relax the high jitter requirement.

After that, we have analyzed the star-topology UNB networks' performance by considering the spectral interference. We have considered two different channel conditions: an idealized one with perfect power control and a realistic one with pathloss and fading. The first case was evaluated along with the replication mechanism. We have highlighted that there exists an optimum number of replications which permits to attain the best reliability, for a targeted network overloads. And the latter is analyzed by considering aggregated interference and by using stochastic geometry as tools. We have shown that nodes that are far away from the BS are sensible to fading. Moreover, we have also evaluated the spectral efficiency as a function of the path-loss exponent. We highlighted that the bandwidth which achieves the highest spectral efficiency depends on the propagation condition.

Finally, to improve the network capacity, we have completed our studies of UNB network by using SIC technology. We have derived the OP by taking into account only one iteration of SIC. We have shown that the benefits brought by SIC is identical, as long as the node density is constant.

With all these studies, we believe that the UNB network is advantageous in the IoT markets. It can manage the huge amount of devices and maintains their simplicity, without loss of performance.

We note that the performance evaluation was done for a given moment in these studies. However, as transmissions are not slotted, the interference pattern might change during the packet. This degree of freedom should also be considered in future works.

References

[1] Centenaro M, Vangelista L, Zanella A, *et al.* Long-range communications in unlicensed bands: The rising stars in the IoT and smart city scenarios. IEEE Wireless Communications. 2016;23(5):60–67.

[2] Raza U, Kulkarni P, and Sooriyabandara M. Low power wide area networks: An overview. IEEE Communications Surveys & Tutorials. 2017;19(2):855–873.

[3] Boulogeorgos, A-AA, Diamantoulakis, PD and Karagiannidis, GK. Low Power Wide Area Networks (LPWANs) for Internet of Things (IoT) Applications: Research Challenges and Future Trends. arXiv preprint arXiv:1611.07449. 2016.

[4] Reynders B, Meert W, and Pollin S. Range and coexistence analysis of long range unlicensed communication. In: 2016 23rd International Conference on Telecommunications (ICT); 2016. pp. 1–6.

[5] Vejlgaard B, Lauridsen M, Nguyen H, *et al.* Coverage and capacity analysis of SigFox, LoRa, GPRS, and NB-IoT. In: Vehicular Technology Conference. IEEE; 2017.

[6] Goursaud C. Contribution to the uplink PHY/MAC analysis for the IOT and BAN applications. INSA de Lyon (France); 2017.

[7] Walker, HR. Ultra narrow band modulation textbook. 2011. http://www.vmsk.org/, Citeseer, 2010.

[8] Zhang S. Spectrum analyses of UNB modulation formats. In: Consumer Electronics, Communications and Networks (CECNet), 2013 3rd International Conference on. IEEE; 2013. p. 594–597.

[9] Karn P. The VMSK Delusion; last accessed September 2017. Available from: http://www.ka9q.net/vmsk/. 2007.

[10] Xiaocheng CXYQL. The VMSK modulation delusion. Journal of Electronics and Information Technology. 2003;11:018.

[11] Perrott MH, Salvia JC, Lee FS, *et al.* A temperature-to-digital converter for a MEMS-based programmable oscillator with $<\pm0.5$-ppm frequency stability and $<$1-ps integrated jitter. IEEE Journal of Solid-State Circuits. 2013;48(1):276–291.

[12] Do MT, Goursaud C, and Gorce JM. Interference modelling and analysis of random FDMA schemes in ultra narrowband networks. 2014 July; pp. 132–137.

[13] Do MT, Goursaud C, and Gorce JM. On the benefits of random FDMA schemes in ultra narrow band networks. In: Modeling and Optimization in Mobile, Ad Hoc, and Wireless Networks (WiOpt), 2014 12th International Symposium on; 2014. pp. 672–677.

[14]   Goursaud C, and Mo Y. Random unslotted time-frequency ALOHA: Theory and application to IoT UNB networks. In: 2016 23rd International Conference on Telecommunications (ICT); 2016. pp. 1–5.

[15]   Mo Y, Do MT, Goursaud C, *et al.* Optimization of the predefined number of replications in an ultra narrow band based IoT network. In: 2016 Wireless Days (WD); 2016. pp. 1–6.

[16]   Mo Y, Goursaud C, and Gorce JM. Theoretical analysis of UNB-based IoT networks with path loss and random spectrum access. In: 2016 IEEE 27th Annual International Symposium on Personal, Indoor, and Mobile Radio Communications (PIMRC); 2016. pp. 1–6.

[17]   Mo Y, Do MT, Goursaud C, *et al.* Up-link capacity derivation for ultra-narrow-band IoT wireless networks. International Journal of Wireless Information Networks. 2017. Available from: http://dx.doi.org/10.1007/s10776-017-0361-4.

[18]   Baccelli F, Blaszczyszyn B, and Muhlethaler P. Stochastic analysis of spatial and opportunistic ALOHA. IEEE Journal on Selected Areas in Communications. 2009;27(7):1105–1119.

[19]   Mo Y, Goursaud C, and Gorce JM. On the benefits of successive interference cancellation for ultra narrow band networks: Theory and application to IoT. In: 2017 IEEE International Conference on Communications (ICC); 2017. pp. 1–6.

Chapter 10

Fog-computing architecture: survey and challenges

Ranesh Kumar Naha[1], Saurabh Garg[1] and Andrew Chan[2]

Emerging technologies that generate a huge amount of data such as the Internet of Things (IoT) services need latency-aware computing platforms to support time-critical applications. Due to the on-demand services and scalability features of cloud computing, Big Data application processing is done in the cloud infrastructure. Managing Big Data applications exclusively in the cloud is not an efficient solution for latency-sensitive applications related to smart transportation systems, healthcare solutions, emergency response systems and content delivery applications. Thus, the fog-computing paradigm that allows applications to perform computing operations in-between the cloud and the end devices has emerged. In fog architecture, IoT devices and sensors are connected to the fog devices which are located in close proximity to the users, and it is also responsible for intermediate computation and storage. Most computations will be done on the edge by eliminating full dependencies on the cloud resources. In this chapter, we investigate and survey fog-computing architecture which have been proposed over the past few years. Moreover, we study the requirements of IoT applications and platforms, and the limitations faced by cloud systems when executing IoT applications. Finally, we review current research works that particularly focus on Big Data application execution on fog and address several open challenges as well as future-research directions.

10.1 Introduction

IoT is a connected network of things where all connected nodes are constantly communicating together automatically in coordination to produce collective results in order to serve people for a better life and economic advancement. It promises to serve everyone to get access to any service or network related to objects, people, programs and data from anywhere. IoT also enables communication between machines, people

[1]School of Technology, Environments and Design, University of Tasmania, Hobart, Australia
[2]School of Engineering, University of Tasmania, Hobart, Australia

and things to implement an environment for smart living, smart cities, smart transportation systems, smart energy distribution, smart health services, smart industries and smart buildings, and they all work together towards making this planet a smarter planet [1,2].

From the IoT environment, Big Data are generated in each and every moment from sensors, messaging systems, mobile devices and social networks resulting in a new form of network architecture. There are many technical challenges related to the IoT environment arising due to its distributed, complex and dynamic nature. These technical challenges include connectivity, capacity, cost, power, scalability and reliability [1]. Another key issue is the processing of Big Data that is produced from various IoT nodes. Generally, we rely on the cloud to process Big Data, but sometimes it is really not feasible to transfer all generated data to the cloud for processing and storage. The process of sending all generated data to the cloud might occupy a certain amount of network bandwidth, and on the other hand, the cloud is not able to process latency aware applications due to high response times. Hence, fog-computing came into the picture to process Big Data near to user locations.

Processing Big Data from the fog environment is an emerging computing paradigm which brings application services closer to the users with better service quality. Any device that has converged infrastructure can act as a fog node and provide computation, storage and networking services to the users. Fog devices are also connected to the cloud to handle complex processing and long-term storage, and this computing paradigm is also referred to as IoT–fog–cloud framework [3]. Figure 10.1 shows the flow and the processing of Big Data in the IoT environment.

10.2   Fog-computing architecture

Fog computing is designed to be deployed in a distributed manner where edge devices do the processing. In contrast, cloud computing is a more centralized concept. In fog, processing and storage devices are located in close proximity compared to the cloud, and this is the reason why fog is more capable to serve latency-aware services through access points, smart phones, base stations, switches, servers and routers. The services which are referred to as low latency services are mostly emergency services including natural disasters, healthcare and so on. Apart from that, augmented reality, video streaming, gaming and any other smart communication system also require time-sensitive computation. With regards to improving quality of life via technology, fog computing is going to play a major role in the near future. In this section, we discuss several current research studies on fog-computing architecture before presenting a high-level fog-computing architecture.

10.2.1   *Existing research on fog-computing architecture*

As fog computing has emerged recently, no standard architecture is available so far for fog-computing paradigms [4]. Several studies [4–16] have proposed various architecture of fog computing. The first fog-computing architecture was depicted by Bonomi *et al.* [17] where the fog layer was defined as distributed intelligence which resides in between the core network and sensor devices. Bonomi *et al.* [17] also point out several characteristics which makes fog a nontrivial extension of cloud computing. These characteristics are edge location, low latency, massive sensor network, very large number of nodes, mobility support, real-time interaction, dominant wireless connectivity, heterogeneity, interoperability, distributed deployment, on-line analytics and interplay with the cloud. Several types of architecture such as layer-based, hierarchical and network-based are proposed by various researchers for fog computing as described below.

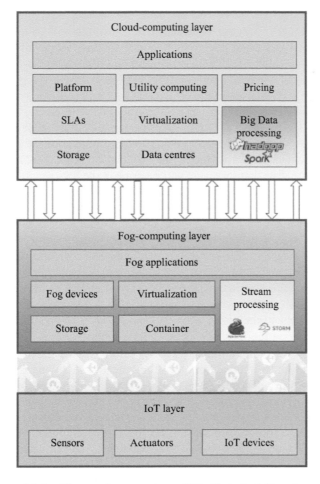

Figure 10.1   Flow and processing of Big Data in IoT environment

10.2.1.1 Fog-layered architecture

Aazam *et al.* [4] presented a layered architecture of fog where six different layers were shown. Physical and virtual nodes as well as sensors were maintained and managed according to their service types and requirements by the lower layer known as the physical and virtualization layer. The next upper layer is the monitoring layer which monitors network and underlying node activities. This layer defines when and what task needs to be performed by which node and also takes care of the subsequent task requirements that need be executed to complete the main task. The same layer also monitors power consumption for energy-constrained devices or nodes. Above the monitoring layer, the preprocessing layer resides which performs data-management-related tasks to get necessary and more meaningful data. After that, data is stored temporarily in the fog resources by the next upper layer known as the temporary storage layer. Once the processed data is uploaded to the cloud, these are removed from the local data storage media. For private data, the security layer provides privacy, encryption and integrity measure-related service. The topmost layer uploads preprocessed and secured data to the cloud. In this way, most processing will be done in the fog environment and allows the cloud to deal with more complex services.

Arkian *et al.* [5] proposed a four-layer fog architecture: (i) data generator layer, (ii) cloud-computing layer, (iii) fog-computing layer and (iv) data consumer layer. A wide range of consumers is considered from individuals to enterprises in the data consumer layer. Consumers can submit their requests to three other layers and get responses for the required services. The data generator layer is where the IoT devices reside and communicate with the cloud-computing layer via the fog-computing layer. In this architecture, data preprocessing will be done in the fog-computing layer. This layer also enables context awareness and low latency. The cloud-computing layer provides centralized control and a wide range of monitoring services. Long-term and complex-behaviour analysis will be performed at this layer to support dynamic decision-making such as relationship modelling, long-term pattern recognition and large-scale event detection. The key difference between this architecture with others above is the direct communication between consumers and all three layers.

The fog layer is presented as an intermediate layer between mobile devices and the cloud in the fog-system architecture by Luan *et al.* [6]. According to this architecture, the main component of the fog layer is the fog server, which should be deployed at a fixed location on the local premises of the mobile users. A fog server could be an existing network component like a base station or Wi-Fi access point. These servers communicate with mobile devices through single-hop wireless connections and provide them with predefined application services in its wireless coverage without seeking assistance from the cloud or other fog servers. This system architecture does not consider many other aspects but discusses the idea of a fog server.

Dastjerdi *et al.* [8] presented a five layer fog-computing reference architecture. The topmost layer is the IoT application layer which provides application facilities to the end users. The next lower layer is the software-defined resource-management layer which deals with monitoring, provisioning, security and management-related issues. The next following layer is responsible for managing cloud services and resources. The next lower layer is the network layer which works to maintain the connectivity between all devices and the cloud. The bottommost layer consists of end devices such as sensors, edge devices and gateways. It includes some apps which belong to this layer, and these apps work by improving the device functionality. In this reference architecture, the fog layer is completely absent, and it also did not testify where the computation is done.

A high-level architecture focusing on the communication in the fog environment is shown by Nadeem *et al.* [11] where communication among devices is shown in three different layers. A similar conceptual architecture was also presented by Taneja *et al.* [12] and Sarkar *et al.* [18] where the devices are located in three different tiers. But Taneja *et al.* [12] and Sarkar *et al.* [18] added gateway devices to connect the fog devices and the cloud. These gateway devices are located in tier 2 which is also denoted as the fog layer.

10.2.1.2   Hierarchical fog architecture

Giang *et al.* [7] presented a hierarchical fog architecture by classifying fog devices into three different types based on their processing resources edge, computing and input/output (IO) nodes. Edge nodes execute actuation messages and generate sensing data. IO nodes have limited computing resources and maintain brokering communications with edge nodes. Compute nodes have some computing resources to offer, and this node is dynamic with a programmable runtime. These three nodes can be implemented separately or with a combination based on system designer preference.

A conceptual hierarchical architecture of fog computing is presented by Hosseinpour *et al.* [13] where the fog-computing layer is divided into three basic levels and can be extended to N numbers of levels. Computation and storage are done at all levels except the lowermost level. Level 0 consists of sensors and actuators, level 1 is named as a gateway fog node and level 2 represents the core fog nodes.

10.2.1.3   OpenFog architecture

The OpenFog architecture explanation is the most comprehensive one in which most fog-computing characteristics were considered [9]. However, OpenFog architecture did not consider lower latency storage facilities near to business deployment and end users. This architecture intends to do computation near to the end user to minimize latency, migration costs and other network-related costs along with bandwidth costs. Without synchronizing and routing all communication to the core network, low-latency communication can take place, and user requests are routed to the location closest to the end-users where computation elements are available. The implementation of management elements, including configuration and control management, and network measurements are deployed near to the endpoint rather than being controlled from the gateway. In addition, the proposed architecture allows collection and processing of data using local analytics, and the results are copied to the cloud in a secure manner for further processing and future use. Although they covered the maximum number of aspects about the fog-computing environment in their fog-computing architecture explanation, there is a lack of proper validation of their described architecture through experimental deployment. However, they intend to collaborate with various related groups, including but not limited to, the Industrial Internet Consortium, ETSI-MEC (mobile edge computing), Open Connectivity Foundation and the Open network function virtualization (NFV) (OpenNFV).

10.2.1.4   Fog network architecture

Intharawijitr *et al.* [10] illustrated the fog network architecture and considered communication latency issues faced by fog devices connected via a 5G cellular network. In their model, the edge router works as a fog server and does the processing for the users as mobile users send packets to the fog server. The fog server does not pass the request to the core network unless the request is for a cloud service. A mathematical model was defined to clarify communication delays and computing delays in the fog network and other related parameters. Three different policies were defined to choose a target fog server for every task. To validate the proposed model, an experimental evaluation was carried out in a simulation environment by employing the proposed policies.

10.2.1.5   Fog architecture for Internet of Energy

An envisioned Fog of Everything (FoE) technology platform was proposed by Baccarelli *et al.* [14]. In the architecture of this platform, all fog devices (IoT sensors, smart car, smartphone or any other station) will be connected to the wireless base station via Fog to Things and Things to Fog two-way connectivity through Transmission Control Protocol/Internet Protocol (TCP/IP) connections functioning onto IEEE802.11/15 single-hop links. All fog devices connected with the same base station are considered to be in the same cluster. All base stations are considered as fog nodes and will be connected via fog-to-fog links by the inter-fog physical wireless backbone. Container-based virtualization is used to make a virtual clone associated with physical things. The virtualization layer supports efficient use of limited resources and generates the virtual clone of physical things. The fog node physical server serves cloned things, and an overlay inter-clone virtual network was established which allows P2P communication among clones by depending on TCP/IP end-to-end transport connections.

10.2.1.6   Fog-computing architecture based on nervous system

Sun and Zhang [15] presented an architecture that was constructed based on the human nervous system. In their proposed architecture, the cloud data centre is considered as the brain nerve centre, the fog-computing data centre is considered as the spinal nerve centre and smart devices are considered as peripheral nerve centres. These three nerve centres spread their connections extensively throughout all of the body of the system. Peripheral nerves scattered in the body and the brain will control all the activities of the spinal cord. The structure of the system is designed based on the neural structure of the human body where the brain is responsible in dealing with all tasks. All the smart devices connected to this system are referred to as the peripheral nerves which are geographically distributed. These devices include tablets, phones, sensors or smart watches. The fog-computing centre would address certain simple and time-sensitive requests, for example, the spinal cord knee jerk reflex can share the resource pressure of the cloud data centre. The spinal cord is the connecting route between the brain and peripheral nerves; this is alike to the location of the fog data centre that joins the IoT with high-level cloud data centres.

10.2.1.7 IFCIoT architecture

Integrated fog cloud IoT (IFCIoT) architecture has been proposed by Munir *et al.* [16]. This architecture enables federated cloud services for IoT devices through an intermediary fog infrastructure. The federated cloud is formed by multiple external and internal cloud servers which match application and business needs. Gateway devices, smart routers, edge servers and base stations are the fog nodes, and much of the

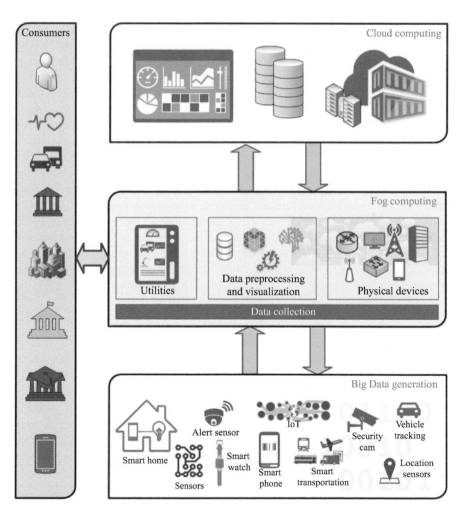

Figure 10.2   Layered architecture of fog computing

processing takes place in these nodes. Fog nodes are autonomous; thus, each node can ensure uninterrupted service by their providers. The entire deployment of the fog-computing environment can be local deployment in the case of automation of single office buildings and can also be distributed in the regional level, including local levels in the case of large commercial companies located in multiple buildings in various places in the IFCIoT architecture. This architecture supports distributed deployment and information from various levels feed to a centralized system. The connectivity of all IoT devices is considered to be wireless connectivity via WLAN, WiMAX and other cellular networks. Fog nodes maintain a connection with IoT devices within its wireless range. The entire fog is connected to the federated cloud service through the core network. For collaborative processing, a fog system could be connected to other fogs wirelessly.

Table 10.1 summarizes the supported features of fog-computing architecture proposed by various researchers in the past few years. According to this table, all proposed architecture represent the concept of data processing at the edge and usage of fog devices for temporary storage, whereas cloud infrastructure will be used for long-term storage. Most of these architecture do not focus on virtualized devices as the fog device but rather represent the fog device as just a physical device. However, fog devices can be virtualized (e.g. Cisco UCS server) and non-virtualized (e.g. smartphones). As reported by [9], scalability is the localized control, command and processing; orchestration and analytics; and avoidance of network taxes. Autonomy represents flexibility, cognition, agility and value of data. Programmability is designated by programmable hardware and software, virtualization, multi-tenant and app fluidity. However, these features were overlooked by most of the reviewed architecture. Some proposed architecture were also not validated by any model or experimental environment [6,9,16]. Alternatively, many of them were validated by theoretical models, simulations or experimental evaluations. Table 10.2.2 summarizes the proposed models, performance metrics and simulation tools used by them.

10.2.2   High-level fog-computing layered architecture

As shown in the layered architecture in Figure 10.2, end users are connected to the fog layer, and this layer is responsible for maintaining communication with the data generation and cloud-computing layer. In fog-computing layered architecture, there are four different layers: consumer layer, cloud-computing layer, fog-computing layer and Big Data generation layer. This architecture is the high-level architecture of fog computing which separates the main actors of the fog-computing environment. The consumer layer represents groups of people and institutes who will use fog-computing services. Actual fog-computation processing will be done by the cloud and the fog-computing layer. Various groups of people or sectors can benefit from the fog-computing services. This includes individuals, healthcare sectors, smart transportation systems, private organizations, government organizations, smart cities, academia and any other smart system that needs time-sensitive processing. The consumer groups mentioned above are connected with various sensors and data-generation devices in various ways.

Table 10.1 Features focused by various architecture

References	Physical fog devices	Virtualized fog devices	Fog server	Monitoring	Energy efficiency	Data preprocessing	Temporary storage	Security and privacy	Cloud storage	Scalability	Autonomy	Programmability	Architecture validation	Reliability
Aazam et al. [4]	✓	✓	✗	✓	✓	✓	✓	✓	✓	✗	✗	✗	✓	✗
Luan et al. [6]	✓	✗	✓	✗	✗	✓	✓	✗	✓	✗	✗	✗	✗	✗
Giang et al. [7]	✓	✗	✗	✗	✗	✓	✓	✗	✓	✓	✗	✓	✓	✗
Dastjerdi et al. [8]	✓	✓	✗	✓	✗	✓	✓	✓	✓	✓	✗	✗	✓	✗
OpenFog [9]	✓	✓	✗	✓	✗	✓	✓	✓	✓	✓	✓	✓	✗	✗
Arkian et al. [5]	✓	✓	✗	✗	✓	✓	✓	✓	✓	✗	✗	✓	✓	✗
Baccarelli et al. [14]	✓	✗	✗	✓	✓	✓	✓	✗	✓	✗	✗	✗	✓	✓
Sun et al. [15]	✓	✗	✗	✗	✗	✓	✓	✗	✓	✗	✗	✗	✓	✗
Munir et al. [16]	✓	✓	✓	✓	✓	✓	✓	✗	✓	✓	✗	✗	✗	✗

Table 10.2 Models for fog-computing architecture evaluation

References	Proposed model	Simulation tools used	Performance metrics
Aazam et al. [4]	Fog-based IoT resource management	CloudSim 3.0.3	Resource prediction, resource allocation and pricing
Giang et al. [7]	Distributed dataflow (DDF) programming	N/A	N/A
Dastjerdi et al. [8]	Dag of query for incident detection	CloudSim	Average tuple delay, core network usage
Arkian et al. [5]	Cost-efficient resource provisioning	Not mentioned	Service latency, power consumption, cost
Baccarelli et al. [14]	V-FoE testbed	iFogSim (extension of CloudSim)	Energy consumption, RTT, connection failure
Sun et al. [15]	Repeated game-based resource-sharing model	Not mentioned	SLA violation, completion time

Based on the necessity of the particular group, they also have strict time and deadline-constraint application requests. Healthcare and transportation systems have the most sensitive applications in these cases. The implementation of fog computing will benefit everyone regardless of group and organization as the cloud has been doing currently. The functionality of three main layers of fog architecture is presented below.

10.2.2.1 Fog-computing layer

The fog-computing layer is the most important layer compared to the others since it maintains communication with all other layers. The consumer layer directly sends processing requests to this layer except communication with data generation and the cloud-computing layer. This layer is responsible for data collection from the end devices. This layer will decide whether or not a processing or storage request needs to be sent to the cloud. Various utilities for various services will be contained by this layer. Small-scale data processing will be done in this layer with virtualization support. The maximum processing is considered as stream processing and needs to be done in an online manner without storing huge amounts of data. However, short-term storage and preprocessing will be done by this layer. All processing and storage-related operations should be executed by any device that has processing power and storage capacity. These devices are generally known as fog devices and fog servers. It could be any type of device including routers, switches, access points, base stations, smartphone, servers and hosts.

Application processing from the consumers can be done without the fog layer with help from the cloud. But, the problem is time-critical applications that cannot rely on the cloud because of the location of the cloud infrastructure. As an example, in a smart transportation system, we assume that if two alternate roads are available from a specific point and one road becomes congested resulting in it taking some time to update the status due to cloud processing, during this processing interval, some vehicles are directed to the congested road. As a consequence, the total travel time to reach the destination is increased by half an hour. It may not affect ordinary people that much, but what if it happens to an ambulance directed to that route? It might even cost a life in some cases. To avoid such kinds of inconvenience, we should not rely on the cloud to process sensor data. Other types of latency critical decisions are also possible in the smarter transportation system, such as dividing traffic into several routes during busy hours, natural disasters (rock falling on the road, extreme fog or rain, etc.), as well as safety of pedestrians, animals and cyclists. The only solution in these kinds of applications is to accomplish processing at the closest location near to the users. This is what the fog layer actually does.

10.2.2.2 Data-generation layer

The data-generation layer contains all devices and sensors from where Big Data can be generated. Big Data are generated in our everyday life. First of all, when we are at home, we are using various smart devices for communication, and many other sensors and actuators belong to lighting systems, music and entertainment systems and alarm sensors are generating data by following certain intervals. Second, our regular activities such as shopping, working out, office work and school work lead us to generate Big Data. Finally, our regular hits to various services also produces data that might have useful insight, for example, we need to know traffic updates, task lists, offers in the various shops, activities and tasks of the school. In this way, data is generated at every moment. We also find many smart devices and sensors everywhere. Security cameras, roadside dash cams, speed cameras, temperature sensors, Global Positioning System (GPS) sensors, alarm sensors and actuators are generating data every jiff as we keep moving. We are also using the smart device for tracking our exercise and other activities or even sleeping activities. Hence, all devices that can generate data belong to this layer and transfer generated data to the fog-computing layer. Any actionable request which is generally done by the actuator will be initiated from the fog-computing layer when necessary. Thus, this layer has two-way communication with the fog-computing layer. Data generated by the Big Data generation layer will be collected and analysed by the fog-computing layer. The fog-computing layer will decide whether storage and processing will be done by its own resources or if there is a need to use cloud resources.

10.2.2.3   Cloud-computing layer

Traditional cloud infrastructure resides in this layer. The main functionality of this layer is to provide long-term storage and complex time-insensitive processing. As this layer cannot communicate directly to the consumers and end devices, it completely depends on the fog-computing layer for communication. From the user's perspective, they are no longer submitting their request to the cloud; instead, they are submitting requests to the fog-computing layer. As a result, processing will be done more quickly when users are depending on fog-computing resources which are located in the close proximity. It is not possible to eliminate the cloud-computing layer because it assumes that the devices located in the fog-computing layer have minimal computing and storage resources. Thus, if we need to store a high volume of data and process the same, we would have no other option but to depend on the cloud.

10.3   Limitation of the cloud to execute Big Data applications

10.3.1   Exploding generation of sensor data

Due to the high pace of IoT technology adoption, Big Data generation is increasing excessively. It is expected that the total number of connected devices worldwide will be about 30 billion by 2020, and it will further increase to 80 billion by 2025 which is nearly triple within a 5-year gap [19]. It is also predicted that by 2025, about 152,000 new devices will be connected to the Internet every minute [19]. According to an International Data Corporation (IDC) report, by 2020, about 40% of data will be processed at the edge [20]. It is hard to send all generated data into the cloud due to communication costs. Hence, it is better to process the generated data near to the users without sending to the cloud. IoT has been crafted to create greater opportunities that can help reshape the modern world via increases in revenue and reductions in operational costs by revealing better insight where collections of huge data alone are not sufficient. To get the real benefit of IoT revolution, organizations need to develop a platform where it is possible to gather, manage and evaluate massive sensor-generated data in an efficient and cost-effective manner [5].

10.3.2 Inefficient use of network bandwidth

The cloud is the best place to process Big Data because it has high computation and processing resources. But sending all generated data to the cloud for processing will significantly increase network traffic. Hence, it is necessary to reduce the volume of data at the edge as well as to mine data to find the pattern at the edge level. Some applications, video-surveillance systems, for example, generate a high volume of video data. There are two critical issues arising from such systems. First, if we send all video data to the cloud, it may occupy the maximum available bandwidth before sending them to the cloud. Second, processing these data at the edge is also challenging because it needs a large amount of processing power. As we mentioned earlier, the cloud is the best for the processing of high volumes of data, but the problem is that we do not have unlimited available bandwidth. The complexity of such systems will be increased day by day, while video data are important for crime control and the implementation of a smart monitoring system in a smart city. So, the cloud is not the convenient way to deal with the applications that need to process video files.

10.3.3 Latency awareness

Applications related to augmented reality, online gaming, smart homes and smart traffic are more latency sensitive. Fog nodes are usually located one or two hop distances from the user. Hence, if the fog concept is used for Big Data processing at the edge, it can easily support latency-aware applications. In contrast, the cloud is located in a multiple hop distance which is quite far from the user where latency is higher than fog. Latency also affects online businesses. As examples, a 100 ms delay may cause a 1% reduction in Amazon sales and a 500 ms delay would cause a 20% drop in Google traffic [21].

10.3.4 Location awareness

Most IoT applications are context aware, meaning that application processing depends on the location and other applications running nearby. Sending all these context-aware application requests to the cloud is not realistic and sometimes not affordable due to bandwidth and delay constraints. Many IoT applications also require minimum processing delays of less than a number of milliseconds [22] such as healthcare applications, vehicular networks, drone control applications and emergency response systems. Such applications also require real-time data processing. These types of application services always depend on the surrounding environmental data rather than information available to other locations.

Location awareness is also used in smart traffic applications to detect the pattern of the traffic such as roadwork, roadblocks, traffic congestion and accidents. These applications share information among connected vehicles to improve vehicle navigation and traffic management [23]. Another example is the smart surveillance application system where a police officer of a local police station can see the video stream of suspicious people around his designated area and is able to track and initialize action to prevent damage to the public [24]. In the above scenarios, processing and running applications on the cloud may not be efficient enough due to the high response times of the cloud.

10.4　Challenges faced when executing Big Data applications on fog

Data preprocessing and post-processing is completely dependent on the cloud while we depend on the cloud for Big Data processing. On the other hand, in fog, Big Data streams are preprocessed locally by using a number of spatially distributed stationary or mobile devices. Then, the processed data are sent to the cloud data centre for further post-processing while necessary. Preprocessing, transformation, and post-processing can be referred to as a three-phase life cycle of data processing in fog. Fog devices can be mobile, and they also have resource-limited properties; therefore, there are many obstacles that exist when executing Big Data applications on fog. This section points out the key issues of Big Data application execution on fog.

10.4.1　Resource limited fog device

Fog devices used for computation have limited resources for processing. Compared to the cloud, the resources of fog devices are very limited. However, Big Data can be executed on these devices by making fog clusters as Google uses commodity machines as the server and also introduced the MapReduce concept to deal with huge data processing using commodity machines. Any device that has computation capabilities can act as a fog device, from user devices to all kinds of network management devices, are considered as fog devices. Generally, these devices have their own operating systems and applications that occupy most of the system resources. Running fog applications on these devices is always the second priority. Thus, efficient and intelligent job allocation policy is required in order to protect a high number of job failures.

10.4.2　Power limitation

First of all, in the fog paradigm, any device that has processing, storage and network capabilities can act as a fog device. Hence, battery-powered mobile devices such as laptops, smartphones and tablets can act as a fog device [25]. The energy of these devices is limited, and due to this, the device may turn off from low battery levels during computation. As a consequence, tasks that were running before power off need to be rescheduled to another device. Thus, the scheduler might be aware of power availability before task allocation to a mobile device. Second, many types of sensor devices are powered by batteries, and these batteries should be recharged frequently. It is a challenging issue in some cases as failure due to the battery may cause serious harm. For example, body sensor networks which are monitoring patients. In such scenarios, we should use energy efficient methods by incorporating primary data analytics which will reduce the volume of data that needs to be stored and transmitted [26].

10.4.3 Selection of master node

In the fog environment, many of the devices might be mobile, and these devices are always moving which may cause a problem to make the cluster of fog devices. Big Data processing using MapReduce where it is necessary to select a master node is mainly responsible for tracking jobs. If the master node moved to another cluster, then it will be necessary to execute the whole job again. To address this issue of master node selection in the fog cluster is challenging. However, selecting a master node among stationary nodes is a good solution.

10.4.4 Connectivity

Most of the fog and IoT devices are connected using wireless connectivity which has problems with interference and fading. These problems cause fluctuations of the access bandwidth. Beside this, in the fog environment, thousands of devices and sensors coexist and communicate with each other repeatedly. Also, the number of connected devices will be increasing over time. To address this issue, it is crucial to develop an efficient model that can estimate the number of connected devices within a fog device and can predict resource incorporation before the failure of the system.

10.5 Recent advances on Big Data application execution on fog

Fog computing is a comparatively recent research trend, and much research work has been done in this area. However, only a few research works have addressed specifically Big Data application execution on the fog paradigm. Most of the work has been focused on the healthcare system and also some work has been done in various areas including smart cities and virtual-learning systems.

Dubey *et al.* [26] proposed a service-oriented architecture for telehealth Big Data in fog computing by adding low powered embedded computers in the fog layer which performs data analytics and data mining on raw data. They considered two use cases, speech motor disorder and cardiovascular detection. Raw data for both use cases were processed in the fog layer. After the processing of raw data from cardiovascular detection sensors or speech motor disorder sensors, all detected patterns are stored and the unique, distinctive pattern is sent to the cloud for further processing. In the first case study, speech data was sent to the fog device by the smartwatch. Then, the fog device does three steps of processing, feature extraction, pattern mining and compression. In this way, it converts speech into average fundamental frequency and loudness features. The compressed speech data is then sent to the cloud. The cloud processes the received average fundamental frequency and loudness to convert it into original speech time-series. For this case study, dynamic time warping (DTW) was used for speech data mining, and clinical speech processing chain (CLIP) algorithm was used for computing relevant clinical parameters such as fundamental frequency and loudness. In the other case study on ECG monitoring, DTW was used for pattern recognition, and after recognizing the pattern, the processed data was sent to the cloud for further processing.

Ahmad *et al.* [27] proposed a framework health monitoring in the fog paradigm where the fog is an intermediate layer between cloud and users. The proposed design feature reduced communication costs compared to other available systems. The work also proposed utilizing the cloud access security broker to deal with security and privacy issues. The sensory data will be generated by a smartphone in 3 s intervals and will be sent to a local machine known as the Health Fog in every minute interval in a batch. Besides activity data, other sensory data from smart homes and hospital activities will be stored in the Health Fog. Then, the intermediate processing will be done on fog and shared with nutritionists or doctors as per user preference. The final processed information on calorie burning and activity detection will be deposited in the cloud and shared according to user preference.

Tang *et al.* [28,29] studied smart pipeline monitoring in smart cities to find threatening events by using a sequential learning algorithm which is based on using fibre optic sensors to analyse Big Data in fog computing. The authors have presented a four-layer architecture for monitoring the pipeline smartly, and it can be used for other infrastructures like smart buildings and smart traffic. The lowest layer of their architecture is the fibre optic sensor network where the cross-correlation method and time-domain filter is used to detect changes in the physical environment such as stress, temperature and strain. The next upper layer consists of small computing nodes working in parallel. Each node is responsible to perform two tasks, the first is to detect potential threat patterns from sensor data using machine-learning algorithms and the second is the feature extraction to do the further processing by the upper layer known as intermediate computing nodes. To reduce communication load, raw data from sensors will not be received by the intermediate computing nodes. This layer coordinates data analysis from various locations to identify hazardous events in a specific region. The most upper layer is the cloud which is basically built by using Hadoop clusters to determine and predict long-term natural disasters. The hidden Markov model is used as a sequential learning method and has been verified successfully in a real environment.

Zhang *et al.* [30] presented a hierarchical model for resource management in inter- and intra-fog environment which considered packet loss and energy efficiency of the intelligent vehicle and fog server. The model comprises two layers: fog layer and edge layer. The fog layer is the association of local fog servers, clouds and coordination servers. On the other hand, vehicular ad-hoc networks, cellular networks and IoT applications are the key elements of the edge layer. The intra-fog resource management manages internal tasks assigned to the virtual machine within the fog server and the task size is ordered by an adaptive load dispatcher where the virtual machine processing rate is adjustable. In inter-fog resource-management operations, all local fog servers update their working states to a server, which coordinates all fog servers and assigns overflow workload to idle fog servers nearby. This inter-fog resource management operation controls the data flow with the help of access control routers without disturbing intra-fog operations.

A distributed resource sharing scheme is proposed by Yin *et al.* [31] where the software-defined networking (SDN) controller dynamically adjusts the quantity of application data that will be preprocessed by the fog nodes for Big Data streaming applications. The problem of application data quantity assignment is formulated as a social welfare maximization problem in their work. Also, the loss of information value occurring in the preprocessing process was contemplated. A hybrid alternating direction method of multipliers (H-ADMM) algorithm was employed to solve computation burdens in a fully distributed environment composed of fog nodes, SDN controllers and cloud. Moreover, an efficient message exchange pattern was integrated to reduce communication costs on the SDN controller when it is dealing with a large number of fog nodes.

Pecori [32] proposed a virtual learning architecture where Big Data streams were processed in a fog-computing environment using Apache Storm and Scalable Advanced Massive Online Analysis (SAMOA) as distributed machine-learning framework. The Storm real-time computation system was chosen for implementation due to its inbuilt master-slave architecture that can be mirrored easily between fog and cloud. The reason behind choosing Storm instead of the spark is that the Storm is event-oriented rather than batching data updates at a routine interval. The SAMOA was selected for the deployment of its finer integration with Storm. In the proposed architecture, cloud infrastructure was used for high volume storage, historical backup operation and mining jobs with high latency. The cloud also provides long-term forecasts and scores of selected features by communicating with intermediate and macro users such as educational institution managers and the policymakers through outer Application Programming Interfaces (APIs). The fog layer is composed of lightweight storage facilities with distributed NoSQL support along with multiple Storm slaves. These slaves can be network gateways, sensors or any other smart devices, and they can perform short-term predictions by using light mining techniques. These predictions provide useful suggestions to all consumers, students, tutors and teachers in an e-learning environment. Using the above proposed technique, the fog-based stream processing virtual learning framework would be beneficial for students and instructors as well as distance-learning institutions.

A summary of the above fog-based Big Data application frameworks and architecture are presented in Tables 10.6.1 and 10.6.1 with their limitations.

10.6 Fog-computing products

10.6.1 *Cisco IOx*

The Cisco IOx application platform enables fog-processing near to the end devices by integrating IoT sensors and the cloud. Cisco IOx is the combination of four

Table 10.3 Research works that focused on both fog and Big Data

References	Address Big Data applications	Fog-computing paradigm	Application type	Layers in architecture	Distributed processing framework for cloud	Distributed processing framework for fog	Devices used as fog
Tang et al. [28,29]	Yes	Yes	Smart cities	4	Hadoop	Not mentioned	Not mentioned
Dubey et al. [26]	Yes	Yes	Telehealth	3	Not mentioned	Not mentioned	Intel Edison
Ahmad et al. [27]	Yes	Yes	Healthcare	3	Not mentioned	Not mentioned	Windows-based machine
Zhang et al. [30]	Yes	Yes	Smart cities	2	NA	NA	NA
Yin et al. [31]	Yes	Yes	Data assignment to each fog node	3	NA	NA	NA
Pecori [32]	Yes	Yes	Visual learning	3	Storm	Storm	Smartphone

Table 10.4 Algorithms, architecture, framework and limitation of various research works on fog computing for Big Data

References	Algorithms used	Proposed architecture or framework	Limitation
Tang et al. [28,29]	Sequential learning algorithms	Big Data analysis architecture in fog computing	Fixed speed of computing nodes and did not consider memory access time
Dubey et al. [26]	Dynamic time warping (DTW) and clinical speech processing chain (CLIP)	Service-oriented architecture for fog computing	Complex speech analysis to recognize more accurate speech disorder
Ahmad et al. [27]	Homomorphic encryption	Framework for health and wellness applications	Distributed fog environment is not present
Zhang et al. [30]	NA	Hierarchical resource management model for intra and inter-fog	Adoption of the model in real environment
Yin et al. [31]	Hybrid alternating direction method of multipliers (H-ADMM) algorithm	Distributed resource sharing scheme with SDN controller	Does not consider incentive mechanism
Pecori [32]	Distributed hash tables (DHT) and machine-learning algorithms	e-learning architecture with the integration of cloud	Fog and Big Data overlooked the security and privacy concern

components: IOS and Linux OS, Fog Director, the Software Development Kit (SDK) and development tools, and fog applications. Cisco IOS is the leading NOS which ensures secure network connectivity and Linux is an open-source customizable platform. However, this platform is designed to execute applications on the Cisco IoT network infrastructure. Fog Director helps to administrate applications over the network running on the Cisco IOx environment. The SDK and development tools provide a collection of tools, command line utility and web-based applications for the developers. Fog applications are readily executable applications that will run on IOx-enabled infrastructure [33]. Cisco 800 series routers support IOx and it can be used as a fog device because it supports two OS on two cores. One core dedicated to IOS and the other core supports Linux-based OS which helps to do the processing in the fog environment [34].

10.6.2   *LocalGrid's fog-computing platform*

This is an embedded software that can be installed on network edge devices. It enables various communication protocols into an open standard by the LocalGrid fog-computing platform. The embedded software can be installed on all sensors, switches, routers, machines and other edge devices which allow secure access for fog processing and also leverage the communication gaps between new and legacy devices. It also forms a P2P communication between multiple edge devices and facilitates real-time coordination and control without a centralized server. The LocalGrid also has a communication infrastructure with the cloud by incorporating intelligence network communication which reduces latency, improves security and reduces usage of bandwidth. On this platform, data processing and decision-making on edge devices can be done on a distributed way [35].

10.6.3   *Fog device and gateways*

Besides proprietary products, there are many other alternatives that can be used for fog devices and gateways commonly known as a computer on modules. These devices include Intel Edison, Raspberry Pi, Arduino, Asus Tinker Board, Odroid-C2, Banana Pi M2 Ultra, and Odroid-XU4. Among them, the Raspberry Pi is the most popular. However, we may find many other vendors whose are producing more powerful devices than the Raspberry Pi at a competitive price. Most of these devices support Android OS and can use other types of OS, including Raspbian, OSMC, OpenELEC, Windows IoT Core, RISC OS and Ubuntu MATE. Many research studies have been done using these computers on modules [26,36–40] in the past couple of years to implement the fog environment for Big Data processing.

10.7   Research issues

There are several research issues currently available that need to be addressed for Big Data application execution on fog. Figure 10.7 represents several research issues in this area.

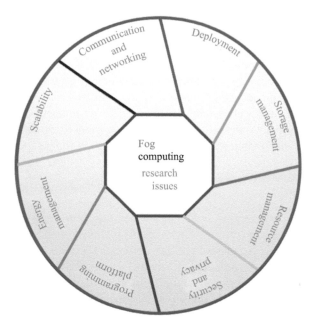

Figure 10.3   Research issues of fog computing for Big Data application execution

To run Big Data IoT applications in fog, stream processing is done in the fog environment, and Big Data processing will be done in the cloud. However, it is possible to implement fog cluster near to users using fog devices and have potential to execute Big Data-related processing to some extent. To do so, one of the key issues is cross-layer communication between the fog to the cloud and the end user to the fog. Besides cross-layer communication, inter-fog communication is also equally important. In inter-fog communication, data transmission is contested by heterogeneous service policies, network topology and device connections [6]. Moreover, integration of emerging technologies such as 5G technologies, SDN and NFV is also necessary to incorporate these technologies with fog.

With regards to the deployment, the main challenges are application placements and scaling. First of all, network operators need to customize the applications based on local demand. Second, due resource-limited properties of fog devices, it is difficult to scale resources as per user demand. Third, since the location is more important in fog environment, placing fog servers in the right place is also challenging [6].

To satisfy low-latency requirements, pre-cache technology needs to be employed and fog nodes should store cache to the Geo-distributed nodes by passively predicting users' demands. In this way, delays when downloading content will be reduced significantly and efficient use of storage resources fulfils fog-application requirements. The storage resource of fog device is limited, so storage expansion technologies are very effective in order to improve overall service quality [41].

Resource management in fog has the utmost priority to maintain the lifespan and performance. Hence, resource scheduling techniques including placement, consolidation, and migration need to be investigated extensively [41]. Application placement to these resources is another research challenge for time-critical computing applications such as emergency response, healthcare, vehicular network, augmented reality, online gaming, brain–machine interface and any other smart environment-related applications. Besides the above challenges, energy management, programming platforms, security, privacy and scalability are also important research issues. Also user's privacy [42] is most important that need to be explore in fog perspective.

10.8   Conclusion

Fog computing is an emerging technology which has flourished in solving Big Data IoT application execution problems by processing continuously generated data at the edge. This computing paradigm is a high-potential computing model that is growing rapidly, but it is not mature enough as many issues still need to be investigated extensively. This chapter reviewed and presented several existing architecture of fog computing in order to identify the research issues related to Big Data application execution using fog paradigm. We presented a high-level fog-computing architecture and discussed many other architecture of fog computing and highlighted the features of numerous proposed architecture. We also discussed key limitations of the cloud to execute Big Data applications, especially in the IoT environment. Following the limitations of cloud, some challenges to execute Big Data application on fog were presented. Also, some recent research works that specifically addressed Big Data application executions on fog were investigated. Consequently, the characteristics of some currently available commercial fog-related platforms and devices were discussed. Finally, several open research issues were presented. Hopefully, these will pave future research directions among industry experts and academia.

References

[1]   Vermesan O, and Friess P. Internet of things-from research and innovation to market deployment. vol. 29. River Publishers Aalborg, Denmark; 2014. pp. 7–112.

[2]   Tammishetty S, Ragunathan T, Battula SK, *et al.* IoT-based traffic signal control technique for helping emergency vehicles. In: Proceedings of the First International Conference on Computational Intelligence and Informatics. Springer; 2017. pp. 433–440.

[3]   Yousefpour A, Ishigaki G, Gour R, *et al.* On reducing IoT service delay via Fog offloading. IEEE Internet of Things Journal. 2018;5(2):1–12.

[4]   Aazam M, and Huh EN. Fog computing micro datacenter based dynamic resource estimation and pricing model for IoT. In: Proceeding of the 29th IEEE International Conference on Advanced Information Networking and Applications (AINA). IEEE; 2015. pp. 687–694.

[5] Arkian HR, Diyanat A, and Pourkhalili A. MIST: Fog-based data analytics scheme with cost-efficient resource provisioning for IoT crowdsensing applications. Journal of Network and Computer Applications. 2017;82:152–165.

[6] Luan TH, Gao L, Li Z, *et al.* Fog computing: Focusing on mobile users at the edge. Networking and Internet Architecture. 2015. Available from: https://arxiv.org/abs/1502.01815.

[7] Giang NK, Blackstock M, Lea R, *et al.* Developing IoT applications in the fog: A distributed dataflow approach. In: Proceeding of the 5th International Conference on the Internet of Things (IoT). IEEE; 2015. pp. 155–162.

[8] Dastjerdi AV, Gupta H, Calheiros RN, *et al.* Fog computing: Principles, architectures, and applications. In: Kaufmann M, editor. Internet of Things: Principle & Paradigms. Elsevier, USA; 2016. pp. 1–26.

[9] Group OCAW, *et al.* OpenFog Architecture Overview. White Paper, February. 2016; pp. 1–35.

[10] Intharawijitr K, Iida K, and Koga H. Analysis of fog model considering computing and communication latency in 5G cellular networks. In: Pervasive Computing and Communication Workshops (PerCom Workshops), 2016 IEEE International Conference on. IEEE; 2016. pp. 1–4.

[11] Nadeem MA, and Saeed MA. Fog computing: An emerging paradigm. In: Proceeding of the 6th International Conference on Innovative Computing Technology (INTECH). IEEE; 2016. pp. 83–86.

[12] Taneja M, and Davy A. Resource aware placement of data analytics platform in Fog computing. Procedia Computer Science. 2016;97:153–156.

[13] Hosseinpour F, Plosila J, and Tenhunen H. An approach for smart management of Big Data in the Fog computing context. In: Proceeding of the IEEE International Conference on Cloud Computing Technology and Science (CloudCom). IEEE; 2016. pp. 468–471.

[14] Baccarelli E, Naranjo PGV, Scarpiniti M, *et al.* Fog of everything: Energy-efficient networked computing architectures, research challenges, and a case study. IEEE Access. 2017;5:9882–9910.

[15] Sun Y, and Zhang N. A resource-sharing model based on a repeated game in fog computing. Saudi Journal of Biological Sciences. 2017;24(3):687–694.

[16] Munir A, Kansakar P, and Khan SU. IFCIoT: Integrated fog cloud IoT: A novel architectural paradigm for the future Internet of Things. IEEE Consumer Electronics Magazine. 2017;6(3):74–82.

[17] Bonomi F, Milito R, Zhu J, *et al.* Fog computing and its role in the internet of things. In: Proceedings of the First Edition of the MCC Workshop on Mobile Cloud Computing. ACM; 2012. pp. 13–16.

[18] Sarkar S, and Misra S. Theoretical modelling of fog computing: A green computing paradigm to support IoT applications. IET Networks. 2016;5(2): 23–29.

[19] Kanellos M. 152,000 smart devices every minute in 2025: IDC outlines the future of smart things. Forbes Magazine; 2016. Available from: https://www.forbes.com/sites/michaelkanellos/2016/03/03/152000-smart-devices-every-minute-in-2025-idc-outlines-the-future-of-smart-things/#3c77fde84b63.

[20]   Connecting the IoT: The Road to Success; 2015. Available from: https://www.idc.com/infographics/IoT.

[21]   Greenberg A. Networking the cloud. In: ICDCS; 2009. p. 264.

[22]   Zhang Y, Ren J, Liu J, *et al.* A survey on emerging computing paradigms for big data. Chinese Journal of Electronics. 2017;26(1):1–12.

[23]   Koldehofe B, Ottenwälder B, Rothermel K, *et al.* Moving range queries in distributed complex event processing. In: Proceedings of the 6th ACM International Conference on Distributed Event-Based Systems. ACM; 2012. pp. 201–212.

[24]   Hong K, Smaldone S, Shin J, *et al.* Target container: A target-centric parallel programming abstraction for video-based surveillance. In: Distributed Smart Cameras (ICDSC), 2011 Fifth ACM/IEEE International Conference on. IEEE; 2011. pp. 1–8.

[25]   Naha RK, Garg S, Georgakopoulos D, *et al.* Fog computing: Survey of trends, architectures, requirements, and research directions. IEEE Access. 2018;6:47980–48009.

[26]   Dubey H, Yang J, Constant N, *et al.* Fog data: Enhancing telehealth big data through fog computing. In: Proceedings of the ASE Big Data & Social Informatics 2015. ACM; 2015. p. 14.

[27]   Ahmad M, Bilal M, Hussain S, *et al.* Health Fog: A novel framework for health and wellness applications. The Journal of Supercomputing. 2016;72(10): 3677–3695.

[28]   Tang B, Chen Z, Hefferman G, *et al.* Incorporating intelligence in fog computing for big data analysis in smart cities. IEEE Transactions on Industrial Informatics. 2017;13(5):2140–2150.

[29]   Tang B, Chen Z, Hefferman G, *et al.* A hierarchical distributed fog computing architecture for big data analysis in smart cities. In: Proceedings of the ASE Big Data & Social Informatics 2015. ACM; 2015. p. 28.

[30]   Zhang W, Zhang Z, and Chao HC. Cooperative fog computing for dealing with big data in the internet of vehicles: Architecture and hierarchical resource management. IEEE Communications Magazine. 2017;55(12):60–67.

[31]   Yin B, Shen W, Cheng Y, Cai LX, and Li Q. Distributed resource sharing in fog-assisted big data streaming. In 2017 IEEE international conference on communications (ICC). IEEE; 2017 May 21. pp. 1–6.

[32]   Pecori R. A virtual learning architecture enhanced by fog computing and big data streams. Future Internet. 2018 Jan;10(1):4.

[33]   Cisco IOx; 2016. Available from: https://www.cisco.com/c/en/us/products/cloud-systems-management/iox/index.html.

[34]   Cisco IOx Local Manager Pages and Options; 2016. Available from: http://www.cisco.com/c/en/us/td/docs/routers/access/800/software/guides/iox/lm/reference-guide/1-0/iox_local_manager_ref_guide/ui_reference.html.

[35]   LocalGrid Fog Computing Platform Datasheet; 2015. Available from: http://www.localgridtech.com/wp-content/uploads/2015/02/LocalGrid-Fog-Computing-Platform-Datasheet.pdf.

[36] Barik R, Dubey H, Sasane S, *et al.* Fog2Fog: Augmenting scalability in fog computing for health GIS systems. In: Connected Health: Applications, Systems and Engineering Technologies (CHASE), 2017 IEEE/ACM International Conference on. IEEE; 2017. pp. 241–242.

[37] Barik RK, Dubey AC, Tripathi A, *et al.* Mist data: Leveraging mist computing for secure and scalable architecture for smart and connected health. Procedia Computer Science. 2018;125:647–653.

[38] Hajji W, and Tso FP. Understanding the performance of low power Raspberry Pi Cloud for big data. Electronics. 2016;5(2):29.

[39] He J, Wei J, Chen K, *et al.* Multi-tier fog computing with large-scale IoT data analytics for smart cities. IEEE Internet of Things Journal. 2017;5(2):1–10.

[40] Giordano A, Spezzano G, and Vinci A. Smart agents and fog computing for smart city applications. In: International Conference on Smart Cities. Springer; 2016. pp. 137–146.

[41] Hu P, Dhelim S, Ning H, *et al.* Survey on fog computing: Architecture, key technologies, applications and open issues. Journal of Network and Computer Applications. 2017;98:27–42.

[42] Aghasian E, Garg S, and Montgomery J. User's Privacy in Recommendation Systems Applying Online Social Network Data: A Survey and Taxonomy. In: Khalid, O, Khan, SU, and Zomaya, AY, editors. Big Data Recommender Systems: Recent Trends and Advances, The Institution of Engineering and Technology, Stevenage, United Kingdom, 2019. pp. 1–26.

Chapter 11

A survey on outlier detection in Internet of Things big data

*Abdullah A. Al-khatib[1], Mohammed Balfaqih[2,3]
and Abdelmajid Khelil[1]*

11.1 Introduction

Over the past 10 years, the overall created and utilized data volume has grown explosively in numerous fields. According to International Data Corporation report, the size of global data that has been generated in 2017 reaches to 20 ZB, where it is expected to be doubled every 2 years till it becomes 160 ZB in 2025 [1]. To perceive, acquire, manage, and process these huge amounts of data within a tolerable time, the term big data has been evolved. Big data is mainly used to analyze unstructured datasets and consequently organize and manage them effectively in order to understand their hidden values.

In the literature, considerable efforts from both the industry and academia [2–4] on the definition of big data have been conducted. One of the widely recognized definitions, because it highlights the meaning and necessity of big data, has been proposed by IBM as a set of five "V-words": volume, velocity, variety, veracity, and value [5,6]. The volume refers to the huge increment in data size over traditional software/hardware systems, while the velocity refers to the data-generation rate that surpasses traditional systems. The variety indicates the forms of diversity of data generated in big data, and the value indicates the potential cost-beneficial addition of a certain dataset for big data to an enterprise's technology portfolio. Moreover, the veracity indicates the reliability and accuracy of the data generated from various data sources.

The chain of data collection consists of four phases; data generation, data acquisition, data storage, and data analysis (Figure 11.2). Data generation is the first step of big data cycle, where the large-scale datasets are generated from multiple data sources. In data-acquisition phase, the data first is inquired from data sources

[1]Faculty of Computer Science, Landshut University of Applied Sciences, Landshut, Germany
[2]Automobile Transportation Department, South Ural State University, Chelyabinsk 454080, Russia
[3]Computer and Networks Engineering Department, Jeddah University, Jeddah 23218, Saudi Arabia

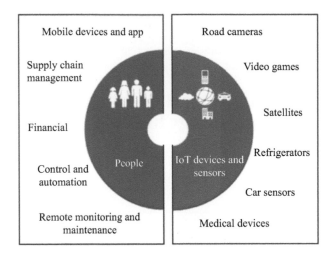

Figure 11.1   IoT data sources

through an appropriate technique and then will be transmitted for storage and pre-processed by cleaning the datasets from useless data. Data storage refers to the phase of storing and managing large-scale datasets with the guarantee of reputability and availability during data access. Lastly, in data-analysis phase, the stored data will be refined to concentrate and extract the beneficial data hidden by using different statistical methods. Analyzing the datasets properly will maximize their value in playing guidance significant role for predicting markets, determining customer needs, and making development plans to name a few.

Internet of Things (IoT) is considered as one of the main data sources, where large data volumes from millions or even billions of connected objects are shared. This generated data is the base of providing smart and new services in IoT. The main sources of IoT data are sensors/devices and people (Figure 11.1). Due to the variety of collected data, IoT data has different features compared to general big data including heterogeneity, variety, noise, and high redundancy. According to the forecast of HP [7], IoT data will be the dominant part of big data by 2030 where the number of deployed connected sensors/devices will reach one trillion. To ensure the highest efficiency and value of the observations based on IoT-collected data, the quality of this data must be high. In other words, the collected IoT data must reflect the actual state of any monitored phenomenon. However, in real world, the collected data from the deployed sensor and people usually contains outliers that degrade observations' quality and reliability based on this data during data-acquisition phase in big data [8].

Generally, outliers, also known as misinformation, anomaly, and deviation, are defined as a dataset that does not confirm well to normal behavior of other data, i.e., there is a significant discrepancy between a few sample data and others. In the literature, several definitions have been introduced based on the data type. For example, the outlier in spatial–temporal data was defined as a spatial–temporal point that has attribute values significantly different from other spatially and temporally referenced points in its spatial or/and temporal neighborhoods [9]. In high-dimensional data, the outlier was defined as a data point that has lower dimensional projection in a local region of abnormal low density [10]. Faulty sensing or lossy communications are the main reasons for outliers, when sensors are the data sources. The former indicates the data loss in IoT-sensing devices which usually occurs due to noisy data, environmental complications, miscalibrations, limited sensing resource, capability, etc. The latter usually is due to communication errors such as signal interference and packet drop. On the other hand, when people are the sensors of data, the outlier refers to inaccurate or wrong information which is intentionally proposed for deceptions. There are many forms of outliers in people-centric sensor networks including incomplete, contradictions, pranks, out-of-date/biased information, unauthorized revisions, improperly translated data, factual errors, software incompatibilities, and scholarly misconduct.

The outliers could be categorized into the following: (i) Fault outlier: It is related to noise during measurement due to sensor's misbehavior, sensor fault, or environment-related issues such as harshness and the difficulties of the deployment areas [11,12]. (ii) Event outlier: It refers to a sudden change in the surrounding environment, for instance, flood, earthquake, rainfall, and others [13,14]. The main characteristics of this type of outlier are that it has smaller probability of occurrence, and removing it causes loss of significant hidden information about the occurred event [15]. (iii) Intrusion outlier: It is related to security issues where the attacker could control sensor nodes and inject false or corrupted data [16].

Fabricated information may result in malfunction of smart devices/machines and degradation of IoT-services. The rise of IoT and crowd-sourced sensing also threatens the proper functioning of IoT-services (in smart cities, etc.). No matter how well we manage our IoT information, it is useless unless it is clean. In the context of IoT and big data, if the collected datasets contain much redundancy or any form of outliers, it is obvious that the analysis will end up with fault findings. Thus, big data system must ensure the deployment of optimal outlier-detection (OD) techniques during data generation and acquisition phases.

Many OD techniques have been proposed in the literature. Several surveys have also been presented for network OD in various domains such as OD in data-generation phase [17–19], event detection [20], and intrusion outliers [21–23]. Figure 11.2 shows big data chain and available surveys of OD techniques in each phase. However, most of these surveys have the major limitation that many new methods are not included in these surveys. To the best of our knowledge, there is no a priori survey that investigated the OD techniques that are sufficient for IoT data over big data (i.e., suitable for big dataset). Motivated by the aforementioned reasons, this chapter contributes a classification framework that categorizes systemically the existing OD techniques for IoT data over big data with completed taxonomy.

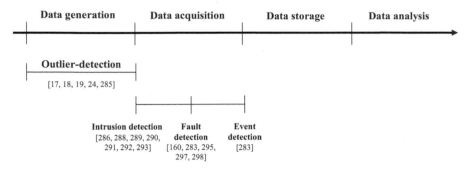

Figure 11.2   Big data chain and available surveys of outlier-detection techniques in each phase

11.2   Outliers-detection techniques

The aim of OD techniques is to find outliers from a large amount of data ensuring data quality by further treatment including data cleaning, network monitoring, and intrusion detection to name a few. The general concept of OD techniques is to create normal data model from training data and use it thereafter to detect outliers in new data. Few works have been conducted specifically for IoT data misinformation detection in big data during data-acquisition phase. In this section, we critically review the previous OD techniques designed over big IoT data. We categorize the techniques based on the following different criteria:

Big data phase: OD techniques are classified based on which phase the technique is designed for. As mentioned before, big data chain consists of four phases. If we think of data as a raw material, the exploitation process will be the phases of data generation and data acquisition, the storage process will be the storage phase, and the production process to produce new value of the raw material will represent the data-analysis phase [4]. Thus, the OD takes place in two phases, where there are techniques specifically designed for data-generation phase from wireless sensor networks point of view [24–27]. On the other hand, other techniques are conducted for OD in data-acquisition phase.

Outlier type: The techniques can also be sorted based on the detected outlier: OD techniques, event OD technique, and intrusion OD techniques.

Detection method: The techniques are categorized based on the method of detecting outliers. Some techniques develop a statistical distribution model that fits a training data and detect outlier by checking if the new incoming data does fit the model or not. These techniques are classified as statistical based. Other techniques adopt machine learning to classify dataset and recognize the outliers, where such techniques are classified as machine learning based. Investigating the distance or density between data point and its neighbors to detect outlier, classify the techniques into distance based and density based, respectively.

Distribution model assumption: Some statistical OD techniques are classified as parametric based because the underlying distribution of the given data is first assumed and then the parameters of the distribution model are estimated. Other techniques have no assumption about distribution characteristics; thus, they are classified as nonparametric based.

User supervision: Machine-learning techniques are categorized as supervised learning if they receive predefined classes from the user. If the techniques automatically classify the data and detect outliers without the user influence, they are classified as unsupervised techniques.

Analyzing approach: Based on conducted analyzing approach in machine learning, the techniques are classified further. Unsupervised learning techniques are classified into partitioning clustering, hierarchical clustering, grid-based clustering, and density-based clustering techniques. On the other hand, supervised learning techniques are classified into support vector machines (SVMs), isolation forest (IForest), and Mahalanobis distance (MD) techniques.

Distance measurement: Distance-based techniques are categorized further based on distance-measurement method between data points. Two measurement concepts are used in the literature; local neighborhood and k-nearest neighbors (NNs) (kNNs).

Density measurement: The method to measure the density of a data point comparing to its surrounding neighbors to detect outliers. Four measurement concepts are used in the literature; connectivity-based outlier factor (COF), local outlier factor (LOF), INFLuenced Outlierness (INFLO), and multi-granularity deviation factor (MEDF).

In this chapter, more than one criteria are combined for better review and characterization of OD techniques. First, we classified the solutions based on big data phase criteria into data-generation and data-acquisition phases. Then, we categorized the techniques that detect outlier in data-acquisition phase on outlier type into fault detection, event detection, and intrusion detection. We classified the fault-detection techniques based on OD method into statistical based, machine learning, distance based, and density based. Thereafter, based on if the techniques assume the underlying distribution model and estimate the parameters of the model or not, are classified into parametric based and nonparametric based, respectively. We classified the machine-learning techniques depending on if the user influences machine-learning technique or not, into supervised and unsupervised techniques, which are classified further based on the analyzing approach. Moreover, we categorized the distance-based and density-based techniques based on distance and density measurements. Figure 11.3 shows the scope of this chapter in the field of OD comparing to other surveys and presents the taxonomy framework to categorize these techniques.

11.3 Requirements and performance metrics

In order for OD techniques to facilitate data reliability and event reporting in IoT, the techniques are required to enhance the quality of measured data and improve robustness of the data analysis even with the existence of noise and faulty sensors. This can be achieved by providing an efficient way to search for values that do not follow the normal data pattern. There are several factors that should be considered in evaluating the efficiency of OD techniques, such as the dataset size and dimensionality, the data

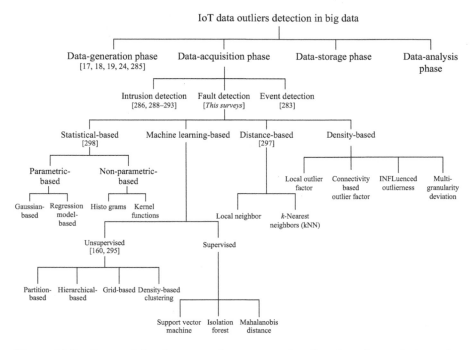

Figure 11.3   Scope of the chapter and taxonomy of outlier-detection techniques for IoT data

structures employed, and other implementation details [28]. Thus, various validation methods have been utilized to estimate the accuracy of OD as efficiency metric [29]. For example, root mean square error (RMSE) and mean prediction error (MPE) metrics have been utilized, where the predication is typically accurate if MPE is 0 and RMSE is the lowest. Another method called bootstrap considers patterns in the data to predict the accuracy of OD techniques [30]. Moreover, other methods consider the detection rate (DR) which calculates how many outliers are correctly identified, and false positive rate (FPR) that represents how many normal data are incorrectly considered as outliers. Here, the OD is accurate if FPR is low and DR is high [31]. On the other hand, other efficiency metrics to evaluate OD techniques such as the computational cost and memory occupation are needed to execute OD process.

11.4   Statistical-based techniques

The idea of statistical-based techniques is to develop a statistical model that fits a training data. Thereafter, the new incoming data will be compared with the model to check if it fits the model or not. In the literature, many statistical-based techniques deployed one of the known mathematical models such as Bayesian and Markov models [32–35] to create a model that fits test training data. Statistical-based techniques include two types: parametric based and nonparametric based. In parametric-based approach, outliers are detected without supervision through presumed corresponding distribution model, while in nonparametric-based approach, there are no distribution assumptions where the model is learned from the input data. On the other hand, the techniques in proximity based are founded based on the calculation of the distances between all data records.

In general, the main limitations of statistical-based techniques can be summarized as follows: (i) Suitable to limited problems only, where a statistical technique will be invalid if outliers disperse uniformly. (ii) Error prone, a statistical technique has high possibility of mistake due to the difficulty of determining the threshold between normal and outliers to spread them. However, statistical-based techniques can be considered good practical method for automatic OD over big IoT data.

11.4.1   Parametric based

The idea of parametric-based approach comes up with the assumption that a given dataset follows certain distribution model(s). The parameters of the distribution model(s) are estimated through training dataset. Parametric-based approach is suitable for large datasets because the new data instances can be evaluated very fast, and the approach only grows with model complexity and not data size. However, parametric models have limited applicability because they employ preselected distribution to fit new data instances. Thus, the accuracy of parametric-based approach depends on if the data fit such a distribution model or not. The main parametric-based techniques proposed in the literature can be categorized further based on assumed distribution type into Gaussian model based and regression model based.

11.4.1.1   Gaussian model based

In the literature, Gaussian distribution models have been extensively employed in OD techniques. The parameter vector θ are estimated during training stage using maximum likelihood estimates. During test stage, the parameters are examined through statistical discordancy tests to ensure that they are optimal or close-to-optima [36–38]. Plenty of outlier tests have been developed to examine different circumstances considering different datasets and distribution parameters [39–43], and expected number of outliers [44,45], where the outliers are data points with slight probability of existence in population.

A Gaussian distribution for normal distributions has been used in the most common outlier tests such as Grubbs, mean–variance, and box-plot tests [46–50]. The population in normal Gaussian distribution is $(\mu, \sigma^2)N$, where μ is the mean and σ is the variance. In the mean–variance test [51], the data points are considered as outliers if they are higher than the mean by 3 or higher standard deviations ($\geq 3\sigma$). The authors in [52] have proposed Grubbs' test which computes a threshold parameter determining the length of the tail that includes the outliers. Usually, three standard deviations from the estimated mean are associated with the tail. The test data points are considered outliers if the distance between them and the estimated sample mean is above the threshold. The box-plot test, on the other hand, has been used in [53] where the data is distributed into five major attributes; the smallest nonoutlier observation (sample minimum), lower quartile ($Q1$), median, upper quartile ($Q3$), and the largest nonoutlier observation (sample maximum). The box-plot test defined *interquartile range (IQR)* as a boundary of normal data, where $IQR = Q3 - Q1$. The data is outlier if it is located outside lower limits (i.e., $Q1 - (1.5 \times IQR)$) and upper limits (i.e., $Q3 + (1.5 \times IQR)$).

More complex data distribution forms may be used for the purpose of data modeling if a single model is not sufficient. Two different models are utilized if the data is labeled; one for the normal data and another for the outliers. The data is considered as outlier if their probability with outlier model is larger than that of the normal data model. If the data is unlabeled, mixture of data-distribution models such as Gaussian mixture models (GMMs) [54,55], the gamma [56,57], the Poisson [58], the Student's [58], the Weibull [59], and Bayesian inference [60,61] distributions are used. Different approaches have been utilized to model the outliers: (i) heavy-tailed distributions [62,63], (ii) generation models based on atypical data in the likelihood function [64,65], and (iii) incorporating number of data points, noise level, and posterior uncertainty [66,67]. The data is considered as outlier if it does not belong to any of the constructed mixture models. However, the limitation of these techniques is assuming that the attributes are independent of each other, where it is not true in practical applications data in reality, especially, for high dimensional [68].

11.4.1.2   Regression model based

The aim of regression models is to predict the value of unknown probabilistic model by finding the conditional probability distribution $Y|X$ between a dependence of random variable(s) Y on another variable(s) X [69]. Regression models have been intensively used in OD techniques especially for time-series data [70–74]. A regression model is constructed to fit a training data, where it can be a linear or nonlinear model. Five basic plots are used in regression models to identify outliers, namely, Graph of predicted residuals, Williams graph, Pregibon graph, McCulloh and Meeter graph, L–R graph [75,76], and others mentioned in chemometrical textbooks [77]. Building a regression model for OD may follow one of the following methods: (i) *reverse search* that builds the regression model based on all data available, where the outliers are the data with the greatest error, and (ii) *direct search* that builds the regression model based on a portion of data, where new data points are added accumulatively upon the construction completion of preliminary model. Subsequently, the most fitting data that have the least deviations from the model constructed so far will be added to the model. Finally, the outliers are the least fitting data that have been added in the last round.

To increase the robustness of regression models, adding weights to different data samples is a common method. In [78], the authors studied the robustness of four different weighting functions, where the results illustrated that Huber and Hampel functions outperform Logistic and Myriad functions in most of the cases [79]. Small weights are proposed to be added to samples with large simulation in [80], while in [81] are added to the sample points with large distance to others. To decrease the effect of different noises, robust loss functions have been proposed in the literature. The authors in [82] identified, from information theoretic learning, a loss function named maximum correntropy criterion. Another loss function called a truncated least squares loss function has been defined in [83]. However, these functions are non-convex; thus, optimization task is difficult. Recently, several other regression models have been proposed [84–87]. Mixture distributions have been used also to model the noise comprehensively and determine a robust linear regression model. The authors in [88,89] proposed nonlinear regression models that applied scale mixtures of skew-normal distributions, with parameters determined by Bayesian inference and expectation-maximization (EM) algorithm, respectively. Heteroscedastic nonlinear regression models have been proposed based on scale mixtures of skew-normal distributions, where the parameters are estimated based on EM algorithm [90].

11.4.2 Nonparametric based

Opposite to parametric approaches, nonparametric approaches have no assumption on the statistical distribution of the data. In addition, the model in nonparametric approaches grows as data size increases and accommodates the complexity of the data. The most common types of nonparametric approaches are histograms and kernel density function. In histograms, the distance between a new test data point and the histogram-based model of normality is measured to detect the outliers [91]. Attribute-wise histograms are used for multivariate data to obtain an overall novelty score for attest data point by accumulating the novelty score of each attribute. On the other hand, kernel density estimation (KDE) function predicts probability density by utilizing large numbers of kernels distributed over the data space [92]. The probability density is estimated at each location in data space that lies within a localized neighborhood of the kernel, where the kernel is placed on each data point and thereafter sums the local contributions of each kernel.

11.4.2.1 Histograms

Such approaches are typically employed for the data with single feature in which its histogram consists of a number of disjoint bins that mapped into single bin. In the histogram graph, the bins are represented with height of the observations number of each bin. The histogram must fulfill the following condition:

$$n = \sum_{i=1}^{k} m_i \tag{11.1}$$

where n represents the total instances, k refers to the total bins, and m_i is the data point number in the ith bin ($1 \le i \le k$).

The outliers are detected based on the measurement between a new test instances and the histogram. The measurement method depends on how the histogram has been constructed. Two ways can be used to build a histogram for IoT data: (i) Constructing the histogram based on normal data only. Consequently, upon evaluating the test instance will be labeled as an outlier if it does not fall in any of the populated bins of the constructed histogram. Such way has been used widely in the literature [93–95].

(ii) Constructing the histogram-based mixture of normal data and outliers. Here, the histogram indicates a rough profile of normal data. The outlier in this way is determined based on the sparsity rate, where a bin is considered outlier if its sparsity rate is lower than a user-predefined threshold. The sparsity rate of a bin in the histogram is calculated by the ratio of its frequency and the average frequency of all the bins. Examples of OD techniques that employed histograms can be found in [96–98].

11.4.2.2   Kernel functions

This approach refers to kernel functions employing for the actual density distribution estimation, in which a new instance is declared as outlier if it lies in the low-probability area. Such an approach is known as Parzen windows estimation [99]. Mathematically, if x_1, x_2, and x_N are independently and identically distributed samples, then, the *probability density function* of kernel density can be calculated as:

$$f_h(x) = \frac{1}{Nh} \sum_{i=1}^{N} K\left(\frac{x - x_i}{h}\right) \tag{11.2}$$

where h refers to the bandwidth and K refers to kernel function which is calculated as a standard Gaussian function with mean $\mu = 0$ and variance $\sigma^2 = 1$:

$$k(x) = \frac{1}{\sqrt{2\pi}} e^{-(1/2)x^2} \tag{11.3}$$

The standard Gaussian kernel is centered on each training point. Kernel function is sensitive to the scaling of the data due to the fixed width of each feature. Outliers detection using kernel function has been used in the literature in several applications [100–103]. A test instance is labeled as outlier if it is placed in low-density area of the learnt density function. Although KDE is applicable for univariate and multivariate data, it is more expensive computationally for multivariate data comparing to univariate data. Thus, KDE methods are inefficient for high-dimensional data. Several OD techniques have been proposed based on kernel functions. Table 11.1 introduces a comparison between statistical-based OD techniques.

11.5   Machine learning

In this section, OD techniques that adopt machine learning to classify dataset and recognize the outlier are discussed. Such techniques are mainly categorized into unsupervised learning and supervised learning.

11.5.1   Unsupervised learning

The concept of unsupervised learning (also known as clustering) techniques is to automatically classify the data without the user influence. It organizes the data into classes or groups based on the similarity between the instances. The main types of unsupervised learning techniques are partitioning clustering, hierarchical clustering, grid-based clustering, and density-based clustering methods.

Table 11.1 Comparison between statistical-based outlier-detection techniques

Reference	Dataset used	Detection method	Method class	Measure
Harrou et al. [104]	UC-Irvine, healthy	PCA-based MCUSUM	Statistics, parametric	MCUSUM statistic
Maciá-Pérez et al. [105]	UC-Irvine	Rough set theory	Statistics, parametric	Theoretical
Akouemo and Povinelli [106]	UC-Irvine, NGTS	Bayesian classifier, linear regression	Statistics, nonparametric, probability	Maximum likelihoods
Zhang et al. [107]	UCSD, subway, UMN	SVDD	Statistics, non-parametric	Optical flow
Kadri et al. [108]	UC-Irvine, healthy	SARMA based, EWMA	Statistics, nonparametric, probability	Meteorological, statistical validation
Bardet and Dimby [109]	UC-Irvine	Tukey, MAD, LOF	Statistics, nonparametric, probability	Lebesgue measure, accuracy
Wang et al. [110]	UC-Irvine, synthetic	LSSVM, WLSSVM, SVM, LR-MOG, SNLR-MOG	Statistics, parametric	Mackey–Glass, RMSE, MAE
Yuen and Ortiz [111]	UC-Irvine	OLS, HE, LTS	Statistics, parametric, probability	PGA prediction, strong-motion records
Ren et al. [112]	UC-Irvine, synthetic	Markov model, LOF	Statistics, parametric	Distance Euclidean

11.5.1.1   Partitioning-clustering methods

The simplest clustering methods are partitioning methods [113]. Partitioning algorithms separate a database into k clusters in which partitioning criteria, such as a dissimilarity function based on distance, are used to match each object with its closest cluster. In these situations, it is critical to identify a priori k. Examples of cluster-based OD algorithms include CBOF [114], CLARA [115], CLARANS [116] FindCBLOF [117], FindOut [118], k-means [119], OFP [120], ORC [121], and PAM [115].

Several researchers have examined different approaches for detecting outliers (Kadam and Pund [122]; Aggarwal [123]). Cluster-based approaches were among the methods studied. Aggarwal [124] studied outlier analysis and Yu *et al.* [125] eliminated outliers from a dataset before using a k-means algorithm when they developed their OEDP k-means algorithm. Aparna and Nair [126] employed a weighted attribute matrix to find outliers in their CHB-k-means algorithm. Jiang *et al.* [127] relied on two initialization methods for the k-modes algorithm to select initial cluster centers that were not outliers. Although the algorithms developed by Kadam and Pund [122], Aggarwal [123], Yu *et al.* [125], Aparna and Nair [126], and Jiang *et al.* [127] have contributed much to the field of outlier analysis, none of these methods used clustering nor did they detect outliers simultaneously.

Other researchers have looked at using clustering to find outliers. For example, Pamula *et al.* [128] relied on a k-means algorithm to trim points from the centers of clusters. They also used the Local Distance-based Outlier Factor (LDOF) measure to detect any outliers in the remaining points. An algorithm known as the OD and clustering (ODC) algorithm was developed by Ahmed and Naser [129]. This algorithm is a type of k-means algorithm. The ODC algorithm classifies any data point that is at least p times the average distance away from its centroid as an outlier. Two parameters (k and l) were used by Chawla and Gionis [130] to create a k-means algorithm. The k parameter sets out the number of clusters and the l parameter provides the number of top outliers. The k-means algorithm is used to simultaneously cluster data and detect outliers. The non-exhaustive overlapping k-means (NEO-k-means) algorithm was the work of Whang *et al.* [131]. NEO-k-means detects outliers during the clustering process. Bansal *et al.* [132] improved the k-mean clustering algorithm so that it can automatically define the number of clusters and assign required clusters to unclustered points. Their improved k-mean clustering algorithm reduced clustering time and improved the accuracy of the algorithm.

To deal with large amounts of data, [133] developed an efficient solution to the k-means problem. These researchers used recursive partitions to divide the entire dataset into small subsets. Each subset was characterized by the mass and weight of its center. This technique reduced computed distances. This algorithm performed better than both the k-means++ and the mini-batch k-means methods. The k-means with outlier removal (KMOR) algorithm in [134] was inspired by [135]. KMOR introduces an additional cluster that is composed of all outliers. During the clustering process, The KMOR algorithm assigns all outliers into this group. Test results have revealed that the KMOR algorithm can simultaneously cluster data and detect outliers. The results have also shown that KMOR is more accurate than other algorithms and that it also performs better than other algorithms in terms of runtime.

Other researchers have worked to create other algorithms that can be used with large datasets including Min *et al.* [136], Jobe *et al.* [137], Capó *et al.* [133], Souza and Amazonas [138], Christy *et al.* [139], and Cui *et al.* [140].

Min *et al.* [136] dealt with large volumes of data by developing an algorithm that used data clustering. Jobe *et al.* [137] focused on multivariate data using a cluster-based OD method. The recursive partition-based k-means (RPKM) algorithm was designed by Capó *et al.* [133]. RPKM partitions a dataset using a series of recursive partitions that are progressively smaller.

To detect outliers, Souza and Amazonas [138] combined a k-means algorithm, big data processing using the Hadoop platform and Mahout implementation, and the architecture of the IoT. This method processed raw data only one time in the middleware layer. The algorithm developed by Souza and Amazonas receives all instances without outliers, thus abolishing the overhead needed to evaluate raw data.

Christy *et al.* [139] created the distance-based OD algorithm and the cluster-based outlier algorithm. Both these algorithms use outlier scores to detect and eliminate outliers. Outliers are removed from the key attribute subset instead of the full-dimensional attributes of a dataset by cleaning the dataset and clustering based on similarities. The algorithm was tested using three built-in health-care datasets from the *R* package. The results of these tests demonstrate that this algorithm developed by Christy *et al.* [139] was more accurate than distance-based-OD algorithms.

The algorithm crafted by Cui *et al.* [140] addressed issues found when processing large-scale data using k-means clustering algorithms. They used MapReduce to eliminate iteration dependence. Overall, their algorithm performed well against other cluster-based OD algorithms, and it was more accurate than distance-based OD algorithms.

11.5.1.2 Hierarchical-clustering methods

Methods that hierarchically decompose entire datasets are known as hierarchical-clustering methods. The categorization of hierarchical-clustering methods depends on if the dendrogram generated a cluster using either agglomerative or divisive methods. In agglomerative methods, each point starts as a distinct cluster. These distinct clusters fuse with the two closest clusters. This process continues till reaching a stopping criterion. By contrast, in divisive methods, points start as single clusters that break down into smaller units in each subsequent step till reaching a stopping criterion. Agglomerative methods are more common than divisive methods. Examples of hierarchical methods include BIRCH [141], CHAMELEON [142], CURE [143], and MST [144] clustering.

In one study [145], a way to improve the clustering performance in large datasets using a hierarchical k-means algorithm was tested. This method simplifies a dataset and then restores it to its original state using a gradual succession of good quality initial centroids. It was tested using an advanced metering infrastructure (AMI) dataset. Benchmarking using common clustering methods was used to assess the performance of this method in terms of common adequacy indices, the detection of outliers, and computational time.

Another hierarchal method for OD is the hierarchical maximum likelihood (HML) clustering algorithm created by Sharma *et al.* [146]. Neither the calculation of triple integrals nor the discovery of the first and second derivatives of the likelihood function are required by the HML algorithm. Furthermore, the HML algorithm can be used with small sample sizes that include greater data dimensionality compared to the number of samples, because during the clustering process, this algorithm takes into account the covariance matrices of the clusters.

According to Aggarwal [288], methods were either sequential ensembles or independent ensembles or model-centered ensembles or data-centered ensembles. Multiple data views were examined studying the issues of surrounding unsupervised clustering in high dimensionality multi-view datasets. In this study, an algorithm was designed that could learn discriminative subspaces unsupervised. This method relied on the theory that reliable clustering will assign the same-class samples to the same cluster in each view. Differently, a spectral-clustering algorithm was proposed in [147] to be used in a multi-view setting with access to multiple views of data. Each view of the data was clustered independently. Dhandapani *et al.* [148] reduced the complexity of time and space and produced an automated hierarchical density shaving (Auto-HDS) cluster hierarchy on a very large (hundreds of millions of data points) dataset by using a Partitioned HDS.

Despite growing interest on the part of researchers in this area, very few studies have found ways to identify outliers in multi-view data. Those researchers who have experience in this area include Das *et al.* [149], Janeja and Palanisamy [150], Müller *et al.* [151], Gao *et al.* [152,153], Alvarez *et al.* [154], and Zhao *et al.* [155]. Das *et al.* [149] drew on multiple kernel learning to create a heterogeneous anomaly detection method. Janeja and Palanisamy [150] found outliers in spatial datasets by looking across multiple domains. Müller *et al.* [151] employed subspace-analysis approaches to build an outlier-ranking method for multi-view data.

Gao *et al.* [152,153] and Alvarez *et al.* [154] both used cluster-based methods. Gao *et al.* [152,153] detected the inconsistent behavior of samples in several sources using a cluster-based method. Alvarez *et al.* [154] also used a cluster-based approach to develop a solution that contained two affinity matrices and four outlier-measurement strategies.

Each type of outlier was classified according to their intrinsic cluster assignment labels and sample-specific errors in the method proposed by Zhao *et al.* [155] in their multi-view OD method that included consensus regularization of the latent representations. In another study, [156] created a multi-view low-rank analysis (MLRA) framework that could show the intrinsic structure of data by conducting a cross-view low-rank analysis. MLRA can also detect outliers by estimating the outlier scores in each sample. The horizontal anomaly detection method developed by Gao *et al.* employed Pareto depth analysis to create a multi-criteria anomaly-detection algorithm [157].

11.5.1.3 Grid-based clustering methods

The foundation of grid-based algorithms [158,159] consists of a multiple-level grid structure, in which all clustering operations are completed. Other clustering algorithms may use grid-based algorithms as an intermediate step [160]. Grid-based techniques perform better than density-based methods. Combining hierarchical and grid-based methods into a hybrid clustering algorithm [161] can be employed to find frequent spatial patterns. In a hybrid clustering algorithm, the data space is partitioned by the grid-based clustering algorithm [162] into a specified number of cells before clustering the cells. One of the advantages of hybrid methods is that they decrease processing times which is impacted by the number of cells in the space and not the amount of data objects.

Finding outliers in ever-growing datasets requires a growing computational investment. Grid structures made using space partitioning that converts space into discrete, smaller intervals improves the detection of outliers and reduces computational overhead because there are less grid cells (in which detection occurs) compared to the number of data instances in the dataset. Consequently, this method can be scaled up to larger datasets [163]. STING [164], WaveCluster [165], DClust [166], BANG [167], SPOT [168], and Grid-DB [169] are all examples of grid-based clustering algorithms.

A grid-growing clustering algorithm was developed in [170]. This algorithm uses a grid structure and a new clustering operation that employs a grid-growing method on the grid structure. The grid structure improves efficiency. This algorithm reduces running times for large geo-spatial datasets, thus making them more competitive. Grid-growing clustering algorithms do not require parameters related to the number of clusters; thus they are recommended when the number of clusters is not known. The clusters detected may have random shapes, and the algorithm regards sparse areas as outliers or noise.

Lee and Cho [171] also developed a grid-based algorithm. Their method decreased the computational time needed by the LOF algorithm to find the kNNs. This algorithm divides the data spaces into a smaller number of grids before calculating the LOF value of each grid. The feature-rich interactive OD (FRIOD) system was designed by Zhu *et al.* [163]. FRIOD employs human interaction to improve and streamline the detection of outliers. FRIOD also employs a technique that optimizes grid-based space partitioning. This technique uses the good outliers detected by integrating human interaction.

Zhang *et al.* [172] identified and eliminated outliers for a training dataset using a multistage method based on Z-test and univariate analysis. They compared the accuracy of the algorithm trained in the presence of outliers against the accuracy of the algorithm trained in the absence of outliers by employing 10-fold cross validation. Their method reduced the variance of the training data.

Zhang *et al.* [173] created the DISTRibuted Outlier Detector (DISTROD) system to detect outliers in multiple large distributed databases. These outliers took the form of unusual instances or observations. DISTROD can find global outliers from distributed databases that are similar to those manufactured by the centralized detection paradigm.

The grid-based outlier detection with pruning searching (GO-PEAS) method designed by [174] is an accurate grid-based OD approach that is scalable. GO-PEAS incorporates techniques that enhance its speed by eliminating or "pruning" unnecessary data spaces, thus making GO-PEAS scalable to large data sources.

Ma *et al.* [175] combined the grid and the DBSCAN algorithm to enhance the efficiency of k-means. They began by finding the distribution of data points through the grid. Then they determined the k values using the DBSCAN algorithm. Finally, they selected the k initial cluster centers using the grid method and removed outliers. Mansoori [176] developed a grid-based hierarchical-clustering algorithm (GACH) to discover clusters in high-dimensional data with no prior knowledge. GACH automatically finds the initial position of a cluster and then it combines clusters hierarchically to create a final cluster.

11.5.1.4　Density-based clustering methods

The clustering algorithms can be classified as either partitioning, hierarchical, grid based, or density-based methods [177]. Data objects are categorized according to their regions of density, connectivity, and boundaries. Data objects resemble point-NNs. A connected dense component is defined as a cluster guided by density, where it can expand in any direction. As a result, density-based algorithms define the arbitrary shapes of clusters and eliminate them from outliers. The total density of a point is evaluated to discover the datasets that can affect a specific data point. Current density-based clustering techniques have several drawbacks. For example, methods, such as CLARANS [178], DBCLASD [179], DBSCAN [180], DENCLUE 1.0 [192], DENCLUE 2.0 [192], and OPTICS [181], rely on multiple critical parameters that the user must provide. Other methods [177,182–187] can only handle certain types of problems or point sets in real coordinate space [188–193].

All density-based clustering algorithms eliminate the outliers and do not include them in clusters. Typically, these algorithms employ the distance to the kNN to uncover outliers. However, in situations where there are different densities, density-based clustering algorithms detect few types of noise only. Outliers are more likely to be an object close to a tight cluster than they are to be an object far away from a weaker cluster [194].

Kim *et al.* have made substantial contributions in this area. They developed a density-based clustering algorithm called DBCURE [195]. This robust algorithm detects clusters with varying densities, and it can be used for parallelizing the algorithm with MapReduce [196]. However, DBCURE is not their only contribution as they also parallelized DBCURE using MapReduce to create DBCURE-MR. Unlike conventional density-based algorithms that detect clusters one at a time, DBCURE-MR can detect several clusters in parallel.

An algorithm called finding density peaks (FDP) was produced by Rodriguez and Laio [197]. This algorithm works very well for finding clusters with different densities and shapes. FDP is a density-based clustering method that employs a two-step process to find clusters. In the first step, cluster centers, or density peaks, are identified using a decision group method. The local density measure is calculated for each data point based on the number of data points in its neighborhood. In the second step, FDP assigns the remaining objects to the same cluster of their NN that has greater density.

Matioli *et al.* [198] develop ClusterKDE, which is an algorithm that clusters data using KDE. The advantages of ClusterKDE include no requirement for a priori number of clusters, and it only requires the original dataset and enough information to calculate the bandwidth value for the KDE as inputs. Fewer input parameters mean that it is easy to use with large databases because additional input parameters can be difficult to supply.

RElative Core MErge (RECOME) clustering algorithm was designed by Geng *et al.* [199]. RECOME makes use of a density measure known as relative kNN kernel Density (RNKD). This algorithm uses RNKD to detect core objects before it partitions noncore objects into atom clusters by successively following the relationships between higher density neighbors and core objects. α-Reachable paths on a kNN graph are used to combine core objects and their corresponding atom clusters.

Aliotta *et al.* [200] developed a software system called DBStrata that combined density-based clustering architecture and several extensions to enhance clustering performance and discover outliers. Cassisi *et al.* [201] created a simple but effective algorithm, called ISDBSCAN, that improved the implementation of density-based clustering to maintain the asymptotic running time of DBSCAN. Another density-based clustering algorithm is reverse NN (RNN)-DBSCAN, and it employs RNN counts to estimate observation density. Bryant and Cios [202] used a DBSCAN-like methodology. In this method, clustering was conducted using a kNN graph traversals through dense observations. In a similar study, [203] produced a framework for density-based clustering, OD, and visualization. Their framework was based on nonparametric density estimates that led to the creation of a hierarchical-clustering algorithm HDBSCAN (Hierarchical DBSCAN).

Mai *et al.* [204] worked to construct an anytime approach to reduce the range query and the label propagation time in DBSCAN. The algorithm developed in this study (AnyDBC) compressed data to produce primitive clusters, which are smaller density-connected subsets, and to label objects based on the components connected to the primitive clusters to decrease label propagation time. Table 11.2 compares between several unsupervised learning OD techniques.

11.5.2   Supervised learning

In supervised learning, the user gives predefined classes, where the instances are organized based on the available classes. The main types of these techniques include SVMs, IForest, and MD methods.

11.5.2.1   Support vector machines (SVMs) methods

The SVM was invented by Vapnik [205,206]. It is a binary classifier and a supervised learning method. It is commonly used for regression and classification, and it is a

Table 11.2 *Comparison between unsupervised learning outlier-detection techniques*

Reference	Detection method	Dataset used	Method class	Measure
Geng et al. [199]	JDD, RECOME, RNKD	UC-Irvine, synthetic	Partitions, density-based clustering	Density measure, RNKD
Zhao et al. [155]	DRMF HOAD, MLRA, DMOD, AP, LRR	UC-Irvine, BUAA	Multi-view clustering	Cosine distance, inconsistent membership
Zhu et al. [163]	FRIOD, k-means, LOF, kNN, DB, SODIT	UC-Irvine, synthetic complex	Grid-based clustering	Effective, efficient
Capó et al. [133]	k-Means++, minibatch k-means, RPKM	UC-Irvine	Partition based, grid based	Euclidean distance
Sharma et al. [146]	Slink, Alink, Mlink, Clink, HML, k-means	UC-Irvine	Hierarchical clustering, distance based	Euclidean distance, similarity
Xu et al. [145]	H-k-means, CK-means, k-means++, fuzzy k-means, WFA-k-means	AMI	Hierarchical clustering	AMI
Jiang et al. [127]	k-Modes	UC-Irvine	Distance based	Euclidean distance
Mai et al. [204]	AnyDBC, DBSCAN	UC-Irvine, synthetic	Grid-based clustering	Euclidean distance
Lee and Cho [171]	LOF, kNN	UC-Irvine	Grid-based clustering, grid-based LOF	Precision, recall
Aparna and Nair [126]	CHB-k-means	NSL-KDD	Partition based	Stability based, mean-square error (MSE)
Yu et al. [126]	OEDP k-means, IDP, DP	DS, Ecoli, UC-Irvine	Partition based	F-Measure
Zhao et al. [170]	DBSCAN, k-means, greedy EM, LSC, PRS	UC-Irvine, synthetic	A grid-growing clustering	Efficiently, validity indexes
Li et al. [156]	MLRA, LRR, HOAD, AP	UC-Irvine, USPS-MNIST	Single view, multi-view clustering	L-2 distance, HSIC
Campello et al. [203]	HDBSCAN, kNN, LOF, LOCI, GLOSH	UC-Irvine, synthetic	Hierarchical density-based clustering	Evaluation, stability measure, dissimilarity
Mansoori [176]	GACH, k-means, AHC, fuzzy ants, FCM, PCM	UC-Irvine, synthetic	Grid based, hierarchical clustering	Histogram, effectiveness, possibility
Kim et al. [195]	DBCURE-MR, DBSCAN-GRID-MR	UC-Irvine, synthetic	Density-based clustering	Euclidean distance, densities, efficiently
Ahmed and Naser [129]	k-Means, ODC, FindCBLOF, ORC	UC-Irvine	Statistical	Accuracy, SSE/SST

well-known classification algorithm in astronomy. The focus of SMV is minimizing structural risk [205]. Early studies found that SVM improves the classification accuracy of other classification algorithms [207–218]. In one study, a one-class SVM (OC-SVM) algorithm was used to watch the health of a system by identifying the start of system irregularities and trend output classification probabilities [219]. The posterior class probability for future test data was modeled using Bayesian linear models. Fu *et al.* [220] improved the reliability of Cloud-computing platforms by developing a self-evolving framework to detect anomalies by combining an OC-SVM and a two-class SVM. Anomalies in the Wide-field Infrared Survey Explorer data were detected by Solarz *et al.* [221] to improve the early all-sky classification results of [222] by looking for abnormal objects with unanticipated properties. An *et al.* [223] developed an OC-SVM classifier for detecting outliers. OC-SVM took advantage of the inner class structure of the training set by minimizing the within-class scatter of the training data. As a result, the hyperplane for OD performed better. Amer *et al.* [224] made two modifications when they designed their robust one class and eta OC-SVMs that were better for unsupervised anomaly detection. Both of their modifications meant that outliers contributed less than normal instances to the decision boundary.

Ngan *et al.* [225] compared OD techniques of large-scale traffic data. Traffic data is continuously collected in every city, and it is massive. In their study, dynamic data related to the flow of traffic was gathered from a very busy intersection in Hong Kong over a 31-day period and included 764,027 vehicles. A correlation study was conducted to evaluate the data points. Three variant coefficients, an OC-SVM, and a KDE were used in the correlation study. Lam *et al.* [226] also examined large-scale traffic data. In their study, naïve bayes (NB) and gaussian mixture model (GMM) classifiers were examined. Their results revealed that NB methods scored a 93.78% detection success rate, and the GMM methods obtained a 94.50% detection success rate. These results are comparable to the results achieved by similar OD studies [225,227] including studies that looked as the success of GMMs (80.86%), OC-SVMs (59.27%), S-estimators (76.20%), and KDE (95.20%). Peng *et al.* [228] developed an OD method that analyzed practical copper-matte converting production data. Their results demonstrated that their method effectively and accurately found high-dimensional nonlinear outliers indicating that this method has a high practical value. Sotiris *et al.* [229] looked at the application of an OC-SVM algorithm for identifying the beginning of system anomalies and trend output classification probabilities to watch over a system's health. When "unhealthy" or negative information is not available, marginal kernel density can be used to estimate a "healthy" or positive distribution and to estimate a negative class. The results from a one-class support vector classifier are calibrated to posterior probabilities by fitting a logistic distribution to the support vector predictor model to oversee false alarms.

Jiang and Yasakethu [230] examined automated anomaly detection in central supervisory control and data acquisition (SCADA) systems and related commands and measurements in SCADA-field equipment communications. Their study used OC-SVMs that could adaptively control decision parameters to find atypical input patterns and warn on-site engineers.

11.5.2.2   Isolation-forest methods

The complexity of linear time and low memory usage can be analyzed using a machine-learning technique called the IForest developed by Liu *et al.* [231,232]. IForest detects anomalies using isolation without using distance or density measure. IForest uses recursive axis-parallel subdivisions to isolate each instance. Anomalous instances are often easy to isolate. One of the greatest advantages of IForest is its linear execution time, which makes it very efficient and a good option for large datasets.

Emmott *et al.* [233] introduced a way to convert classified datasets into ground-truthed benchmark datasets to detect anomalies. This method was used to generate datasets to benchmark anomaly detection algorithms such as Ensemble GMM (EGMM), IForest, LOF, Split-selection Criterion IForest (SCIF), and SVM, under many different conditions.

Bandaragoda *et al.* [234] designed an alternative isolation mechanism using Nearest Neighbor Ensemble (iNNE) method. iNNE method is faster than other, similar methods for datasets containing several instances or dimensions even though iNNE depends on its NNs. Chen *et al.* [235] created IForest OD and Subset selection (IOS) to simultaneously find outliers and select representative subsets. Unlike conventional methods for selecting subsets, IOS is cluster based and has a uniform design.

Inspired by IForest, Liu *et al.* [236] created a similar method called SCIF. SCIF performs better in terms of clustered anomaly detection. The partitioning process in SCIF employs a random hyperplane rather than relying on axis-parallel subdivisions. A q-dimensional attribute space is selected at random from the feature space in the dataset to construct a random hyperplane Ting *et al.* [237,238] created mass estimation, which is a generalized type of isolation method. This method is employed for a broad range of data-mining applications including anomaly detection. Mass estimation uses half-space trees that are different from isolation trees in terms of their split-selection criteria, to conduct axis-parallel subdivisions. Space is divided into two equal areas as the half-space tree finds the mid-point of the selected attribute at each node. Consequently, selection is not as randomized as the selection process conducted by isolation trees. The results of the study conducted by Ting *et al.* [238] demonstrated that in tested benchmark datasets, the mass-estimation method performed as well as IForest.

The greatest advantage of isolation methods is their efficiency. Unlike the quadratic efficiency of conventional methods, the efficiency of isolation methods is linear with dataset size n. Despite this advantage, isolation methods do have their drawbacks. The greatest weakness exhibited by isolation-based methods is that they cannot detect local anomalies because their isolation measures are global measures and can only measure isolation susceptibility in a global perspective.

11.5.2.3   Mahalanobis-distance methods

The MD forms the backbone of a method designed by Jayakumar and Thomas to expose outliers. In one study [239], the MD was used in the iterative procedure of a clustering method for multivariate OD. At each iteration, the mean was tested to determine the degree of discrimination between outlier and inlier clusters.

The iterations and outlier clustering processes were graphically represented using multivariate control charts.

Mohammadi and Sarmad [240] graphically represented their data by employing the MD using the re-weighted minimum covariance determinant estimator. The resulting "outlier map" is commonly used in multivariate robust statistics. In another study [241], the MD was used to find anomalies in analog filters. The first step in this study was to discover how often the circuit responded to a sweep signal. The next step was to calculate the distance between each healthy and each whole health frequency using the MD. The healthy samples were converted to one-dimensional MD datasets.

In another study that used MD [242], Kumar *et al.* diagnosed a health condition using a diagnostic tactic based on MD that used a probabilistic approach to establish thresholds. Fan *et al.* [243] focused on finding chromaticity shift abnormalities in high-powered white LEDs using MD and a distribution estimation method. They developed a fault indicator that used an MD to reveal irregularities in analog circuits. However, the detection threshold was determined using an experimental method that was recommended by Vasan *et al.* [244] but was not rational. Table 11.3 presents a comparison between supervised learning OD techniques.

11.6 Distance-based techniques

The distance-based OD approach concept is identifying local outliers by investigating the distance between data point and its neighbors. Several OD techniques were defined in the literature based on distance-related metrics. These techniques are mostly based on the following concepts; local neighborhood and kNN. Different than statistical-based methods, distance-based methods generalize many concepts from distribution-based methods without assuming any data distribution. The computation in distance-based methods is more efficient due to its scalability with multidimensional space. To compute the distance between a pair of data points, any Lp metrics can be used such as Manhattan distance or Euclidean-distance metrics. In some other application domains, nonmetric distance functions are used which make the definition of outliers very general.

11.6.1 Local neighborhood

The first notion of outliers based on local neighbor has been defined in [245]. The notion DB (k, λ)-outlier refers to distance-based outlier (detected using parameters k and λ). Based on the notion, a data point p will be labeled as an outlier if at least fraction k of the data point in T lies greater than distance λ. The main drawback of distance-based approach is its sensitivity to the parameter λ that is difficult to be determined a prior. Once the data dimension increases, specifying a suitable circular local neighborhood, which is determined by λ, becomes more difficult. In other word, it becomes difficult to evaluate the outlier of each data point because most of the points lie in a thin shell about any point [246]. All data points will be labeled as outliers if λ value is assumed too small, while no data point will be labeled as outlier upon

Table 11.3 Comparison between supervised learning outlier-detection techniques

Reference	Type of phases	Dataset used	Detection method	Method class	Measure
Lam et al. [226]	Testing + training	UC-Irvine	NB, GMM, S-estimator, kernel density	SVM, NB	Accuracy, PPV, NPV, sensitivity, FPR
Solarz et al. [221]	–	SDSS, WISE	OC-SVM	Standard classification, semi-supervised OC-SVM	Similarity, distance, WISE
Kurcz et al. [222]	Testing	SDSS, WISE	SVM	Statistical, supervised	Accuracy, w1mpro, WISE
Mohammadi and Sarmad [240]	Testing	UC-Irvine	RMCD-SVM	Mahalanobis distance, statistics	Robust Mahalanobis distance
Hu et al. [241]	Testing + training	Health dataset, health MD	OCSVM	Mahalanobis distance (MD)	Frequency features, Mahalanobis distance, probability density
Chen et al. [235]	Testing	UC-Irvine, NIR, QSAR	IOS, KS, SPXY, RS, IForest OC-SVM, OC-WCSSVM, GDD, NNDD, PCA	Partitioning based, isolation forest	Distance, density
An et al. [223]	–	UC-Irvine, synthetic		One-class classification	Sensitivity, recall
Emmott et al. [233]	Testing	UC-Irvine	LOF, SCIF, SVDD, IForest, OCSVM, EGMM	Isolation forest	Euclidean distance, semantic variation
Ting et al. [238]	Testing+training	COREL, GDD	IForest, ORCA, LOF, OC-SVM, MassAD	Density based, distance based	Euclidean distance

specifying large λ value. Hence, it is important to specify suitable λ to detect outliers with a very high degree of accuracy.

As an extension to the first notion, DB (*pct*; *dmin*)-outlier has been proposed to facilitate determining the parameters' values. A data point is labeled as an outlier if at least *pct*% of data points in the datasets have distance larger than *dmin* from this data point [247,248]. Here, the local neighborhood of data points is calculated based on the percentage instead of the absolute number as in DB (k; λ)-outlier. According to [249,250], the definition of outliers in the existing statistical detection methods can be unified by DB (*pct*; *dmin*) using discordancy tests. For instance, the definition of outliers in a normal distribution based has been unified by DB (*pct*; *dmin*) with $pct = 0{:}9988$ and $dmin = 0{:}13$. Although specifying *pct* value is more easier than k value in DB (k; λ)-outliers, it has the problem of finding the suitable value of the local neighborhood parameter *dmin* [247].

Three main types of algorithms have been introduced in the literature to calculate the percentage or the number of data points placed within the local neighborhood of each point. These algorithms are nested loop, index loop, and cell-based algorithms. Here, calculating the number of data point in DB (k; λ)-outlier in each algorithm is discussed. In nested-loop algorithm, two nested loops are used to calculate DB (k; λ)-outlier; outer and inner loops. Each point in the dataset is considered first in the outer loop, and then the inner loop calculates the number of data points placed within the specified λ-neighborhood. Although the algorithm does not require the construction of indexing structure, its complexity is a quadratic in respect of data point number in the dataset. In index-based algorithm, a preconstructed multidimensional index structure is used to compute the number of points falling into the λ-neighborhood of each data to facilitate kNN search [251]. Here, the complexity is logarithmic in respect of data points' number in the dataset.

On the other hand, the cell-based algorithm divides the data space into cells and then maps the data points into cells. Heuristics method is developed to accomplish rapid OD by estimating the pair-wise distance of data points in cell with known size a priori. The data with d-dimensional space is split into cells with side length of $\lambda/(2\sqrt{d})$. Consequently, the distance between data points from two neighboring cells will be not more than λ. Hence, none of the data points in a cell will be outlier if the total number of points in that cell and its neighbors is larger than k. In addition, the distance between data points that belong to cells that are more than three cells apart is at least λ. Hence, all data points in a cell will be labeled as outlier if the total number of data points in that cell and a cell that is at most three cells away from it is less than k. However, the complexity in this algorithm is linear with dataset size and exponential with the number of dimensions d. Thus, cell-based algorithm performance degrades significantly when the number of cells grows exponentially as a result of increasing the number of dimensions. The nested loop algorithm performs better in the case of four dimensions or higher dataset.

Another algorithm of OD using distance-based approach has been introduced in [252]. The algorithm computes the number of data points within w-radius and considers points that have low neighborhood density as outliers. To estimate the local density of data points, a clustering method for an efficient estimation has been introduced. The concept of the clustering method uses fix-width clustering to estimate the local density of all data points in a cluster by its size. Another outlier definition has been proposed in [253], where the data point is labeled as outlier if the probability that there are enough neighbor points surrounded within a specified distance is very low.

11.6.2 k-Nearest neighbors

Several distance-based OD methods have been introduced based on kNN. The methods defined various distance notion to calculate the distance between every data point and its kth NNs [254,255]. The first proposal denoted D^k to rank data points and detect outliers efficiently [255]. The outlier was defined as Dn^k-outlier, where a data point is labeled as an outlier if the distance to its kth NN is less than the corresponding value of $(n-1)$ other data points. Obviously, the top n data points that have the highest D^k values in the dataset are labeled as outliers. Three different algorithms have been introduced to calculate D^k for each data point efficiently including the nested-loop, index-based, and partition-based algorithms.

In nested-loop algorithm, the distance D^k between each input point p and its kth NN is computed first by scanning the database. The data points are sorted and the top n points with the maximum D^k values are selected. In order to compute D^k for a data point p for instance, the distance between p and each point q from the database is measured.

In index-based algorithm, an index structure such as the R*-tree is used to speed up the computation process. The algorithm takes advantage of storing all data points in a spatial index to decrease the number of distance computations by applying the following pruning optimization. Let us assume that a portion of the input points has already been processed to compute for data point p.

On the other hand, the partition-based algorithm first divides the data space into partitions and thereafter prunes any partition that cannot include outliers. During preprocessing phase, the data space is divided into partitions, generating the minimum bounding rectangles of them. Instead of performing preprocessing phase at points, it is performed at the granularity of partitions to reduce significantly the computations number, where n is typically very small.

As an extension of the Dn^k-outlier, the authors in [256] proposed to consider the sum of kNNs of each data point. The definition of D^k considers only the distance between an object with its kth NN without considering the distances between this object and its another $k-1$ NNs. Thus, D^k does not measure the outliers accurately in most of the cases. Although the extension requires more computational effort in summing up the distances, it increases the outlier measurement accuracy of data points in some cases. Another extension of kNN-based distance metric is proposed to take into account the k-nearest dense regions too, such as in the largest cluster [257,258] and grid-ODF (outlying degree factor) [259] methods. The first method was proposed for labeling wireless network traffic records. The outlier was defined as any instance that has a distance larger than αd ($\alpha \geq 1$), where d refers to the biggest distance of an instance to the centroid of the biggest cluster. In the second method, each data points are ranked based on the sum of the distances between them and their k-nearest dense regions. Consequently, the algorithm can measure the outlier of data points from a global perspective in which both global and local outliers can be detected. In [260], the authors proposed angle-based OD (ABOD) technique to detect outliers in high-dimensional data. The algorithm considers the variances of measurement over angles between the difference vectors of data objects. ABOD is less sensitive to the increase of dataset dimension as it takes into account the properties of the variances. A comparison between distance-based OD techniques is presented in Table 11.4.

11.7   Density-based techniques

The concept of density-based OD techniques is to sense the density of data. Data objects are considered as outlier if they are different from their surrounding neighborhood, and in regions of very low density [267]. Such techniques estimate first the density of the neighborhood for each data object; thereafter, they compare the estimated density with the densities of the data object's neighbors. The data object is declared as an outlier if the density is greatly different from its neighbors. The main types of density-based techniques include LOF [268], COF [269], INFLO [270], and MEDF [271]. In general, the main limitation of density-based techniques that they are sensitive to parameters is used to determine the size of the neighborhood to be examined and show poor performance when the observations have a variety of densities.

11.7.1   Local outlier factor

LOF is the first major density-based method that formulates the outlier density degree of a data point. It reflects the density contrast of an object with its neighborhood that is determined by the distance to the *MinPts*th NN. For a given parameter *MinPts*, *LOF* of data point p is denoted as follows [268]:

$$LOF_{MinPts}(p) = \frac{\sum_{0 \in MinPts(p)} (lrd_{MinPts}(o)/lrd_{MinPts}(p))}{|N_{MinPts}(p)|} \tag{11.4}$$

where $|N_{MinPts}(p)|$ is the number of objects belonging to *MinPts*-neighborhood of p, while $lrd_{MinPts}(p)$ is the local reachability density of data point p which is defined [268] as inverse of the average reachability distance based on the *MinPts* NNs of p,

$$lrd_{MinPts}(p) = \frac{1}{\left(\sum_{0 \in MinPts(p)} reach_{dist_{MinPts}}(p, o)\right)/|N_{MinPts}(p)|} \tag{11.5}$$

where $reach_{dist_{MinPts}}(p, o)$ refers to the reachability distance of point p, and it is calculated as [268]:

$$reach_{dist_{MinPts}}(p, o) = \max\left(MinPts_{distance(o)}, dist(p, o)\right) \tag{11.6}$$

As shown in equations, LOF represents the mean value of the ratio of the estimated density distribution of an object to the distribution densities of that object's neighbors.

Table 11.4 Comparison between distance-based outlier-detection techniques

Reference	Type of phase	Dataset used	Detection method	Method class	Measure
Liu and Deng [261]	Testing	UC-Irvine	ULOF, LOF, BULOF	Distance based, local neighbors	Probability density, deviation, precision, recall
Shaikh and Kitagawa [262]	Testing	UC-Irvine, synthetic	Cell based, naive approach	Distance based, local neighbors	Precision, recall
Schubert et al. [263]	Training	UC-Irvine, ALOI	PINN, LSH, LOF, SFC, PINN	Distance based, k-nearest neighbors	Recall, LOF, distance measure
Wang et al. [264]	Testing	UC-Irvine, synthetic	ZH-tree, DBOZ, ZHkNN, PRE, DSS	Distance based, k-nearest neighbor	Distance measure
Mohseni and Fakharzade [265]	Testing+ training	Fuzzy data	LODF	Distance based, local neighbors, top-n	Precision LDOF
Xu et al. [266]	Testing	UC-Irvine	HOD, iHOD, ORCA, iORCA, LOF	Distance based, k-nearest neighbors, nonparametric	Statistical

Accordingly, the value of $LOF(p)$ will be high indicating that p has high degree of being an outlier, if the density of p is low and/or the densities of p's neighbors are high. Similar to LOF, OPTICS-OF has been presented as an outlier metric [272].

LOF computation is required for all objects in the dataset and consequently requires a large number of kNN search. Thus, the computation effort is significantly high to detect outliers. In [273], an efficient micro-cluster-based local OD method was introduced to limit the search to the top n outliers instead of computing LOF for each object in the database. However, the main limitation of LOF is that the neighborhood density of the points is only considered for ranking; hence, the potential outliers could be missed if their densities are close to the densities of their corresponding neighbors. In addition, LOF is influenced to the choice of *MinPts* that specifies the local neighborhood.

11.7.2   Connectivity-based outlier factor

To address the aforementioned issue in LOF method, COF has been presented in [269]. It increases OD efficiency of LOF method in the scenario when data and outlier have similar neighborhood density. In COF, the connectivity of a data point with respect to a group of its neighbors is modeled using a set-based nearest path (SBN-path) and further an SBN-trail. The pattern of a data point starts from the neighbors of SBN-trail starting point. The COF outlier metric of a point p with respect to its k-neighborhood is computed as [269]:

$$COF_k(p) = \frac{|N_k(p)| \times ac_{dist_{N_k(p)}}(p)}{\sum_{o \in N_k(p)} ac_{dist_{N_k(p)}}(o)} \tag{11.7}$$

where $ac_{dist_{N_k(p)}}(p)$ represents the average chaining distance from point p to the rest of its kNNs, while $\sum_{o \in N_k(p)} ac_{dist_{N_k(p)}}(o)$ is the weighted sum of the cost of all SBN-trail constituting edges representing that the cost of SBN-trail is calculated. The results have shown that COF outperforms LOF, however, it has more expensive computations and more time complexity.

11.7.3   INFLuenced outlierness

LOF may fail to estimate outliers in some cases, for instance, when the outlier is located in a neighborhood having significantly different density distributions. This issue has been studied in [270], where the authors found that this occurs due to the fact that LOF is applied in a space with an inaccurate specification. The authors proposed an enhanced method of LOF called INFLO that improves the neighborhood's density distribution. The concept of INFLO is considering for density distribution both NNs and RNNs of a data point. For a data point p, the term RNNs refers to data points that p is one of their kNNs. Applying both NNs and RNNs determined k-influence space of a data point which is defined as the space of an object influenced by other objects. The INFLO of a data point p is calculated as follows [270]:

$$INFLO_k(p) = \frac{den_{avg}(IS_k(p))}{den(p)} \tag{11.8}$$

Table 11.5 *Comparison between density-based outlier-detection techniques*

Reference	Type of phase	Dataset used	Detection method	Method class	Measure
Bhattacharya et al. [274]	Training	UC-Irvine, synthetic	LOF, COF, INFLO, RBDA, RDOS	Density based, rank based	Recall, rank-power
Ha et al. [275]	Testing + training	UC-Irvine, synthetic	agg-kNN, kNN, LDOF, LOF, INFLO, LDF, LoOP, OF	Density based, rank based	Observability factor
Van Hieu and Meesad [276]	Testing + training	UC-Irvine, TDriveTrajectory, Simulation2D1, NASA	Cell-DROS, RDOS, LOF, COF, INFLO, RBDA, ORMRD	Density based, rank based	Influential measure
Zheng et al. [277]	Testing	UC-Irvine, synthetic	KDE, KDEDisStrOut, LOCI, Knorr	Density based, kernelized depth based	Recall, precision
Liu and Wang [278]	Testing	Synthetic	LMDOF, OF, LOF, kNN	Density based, local outlier detection	LMDOF
Zhang et al. [279]	Testing + training	UC-Irvine, synthetic	Adaptive-KD, SVDD, LOF, KPCA	Density based, kernelized depth based	Outlierness measure, hyper-sphere, similarity measure
Tang and He [280]	Testing + training	UC-Irvine, synthetic	KDE, RDOS, RNN, SNN, LKDE, ODIN, MNN, INFLO	Density based, kernelized depth based	Local outlierness measure
Kirner et al. [281]	Testing + training	ALOI	LOF	Density based, local outlier detection	Recall, LOF ROC
Zhang and Wan [282]	Testing	UC-Irvine	Weight based, LOF	Density based, kernelized depth based	LOD

Since the INFLO considers data points in its k-influence space only for density ratio calculation, the densities of neighborhood points will be well estimated and defined outliers will be more meaningful.

11.7.4   Multi-granularity deviation factor

Another concept of density-based outlier definition called MEDF has been proposed in [271]. For a data point P_i at radius r, the MEDF is defined as the relative deviation of P_i local neighborhood density from the average local neighborhood density in its r-neighborhood. The MEDF is calculated as follows [271]:

$$MDEF(P_i, r, \propto) = 1 - \frac{n(P_i, \alpha r)}{\hat{n}(P_i, r, \alpha)} \tag{11.9}$$

where $n(P_i, \alpha r)$ refers to the number of objects in the αr-neighborhood of P_i, while $\hat{n}(P_i, r, \alpha)$ refers to the average, over all objects p in the r-neighborhood of P_i, of $n(P_i, \alpha r)$, and $\alpha = 1/2$. A data point is labeled as an outlier if its MDEF is large for any $r \in [r\_min; r\_max]$. The r_min and r_max represent the minimum and the maximum values of different values that are set for the sampling radius r. Table 11.5 compares between density-based OD techniques.

11.8   Conclusion

This survey introduced a taxonomy framework categorizing OD techniques that are intended for IoT data. The key characteristics of each category are illustrated with a brief explanation of its OD techniques. Furthermore, we introduced a comparison table for each category that compares the techniques in terms of the nature of IoT data, characteristics of outlier, and OD method. Several promising research directions can be considered in OD. One direction is unifying the assumptions of different techniques based on the outlier behavior into a statistical or machine-learning framework. Another direction is to develop contextual and collective OD techniques that minimize false-positive detection. The techniques must include alerting platforms that can be tuned to appropriately balance noise and information. In addition, due to the fact that the data is not always normally distributed, an outlier technique must be robust to work on not normally distributed data.

References

[1]   D. Reinsel, J. Gantz, and J. Rydning. Data age 2025: The evolution of data to life-critical, in: *International Data Corporation (IDC)*, April 2017, pp. 1–25, Sponsored by Seagate, white paper.

[2]   EMC. Big Data-as-a-Service: A Market and Technology Perspective, July 2012. http://www.emc.com/collateral/software/white-papers/h10839-big-data-as-a-service-perspt.pdf (Accessed January 2017).

[3] D. E. O'Leary. Big data, the Internet of Things and the internet of signs. *Intelligent Systems in Accounting, Finance and Management*, 20(1):53–65, 2013.

[4] M. Chen, S. Mao, and Y. Liu. Big data: A survey. *Mobile Networks and Applications*, 19(2):171–209, 2014.

[5] P. Zikopoulos and C. Eaton. *Understanding Big Data: Analytics for Enterprise Class Hadoop and Streaming Data*. McGraw-Hill Osborne Media, IBM, 2011.

[6] P. Zikopoulos, D. DeRoos, K. Parasuraman, T. Deutsch, J. Giles, and D. Corrigan. *Harness the Power of Big Data – The IBM Big Data Platform*. McGraw-Hill, 2013. ISBN: 9780071808187.

[7] M. Chen, S. Mao, Y. Zhang, and V. C. M. Leung. *Big Data: Related Technologies, Challenges and Future Prospects*. Springer, Heidelberg, 2014.

[8] J. Han and M. Kamber. *Data Mining: Concepts and Techniques*. Morgan Kaufmann, San Francisco, CA, USA, 2006.

[9] T. Cheng and Z. Li. A multiscale approach for spatio-temporal outlier detection. *Transactions in GIS*, 10(2), 253–263, 2006.

[10] C. C. Aggarwal and S. P. Yu. An effective and efficient algorithm for high dimensional outlier detection. *VLDB Journal*, 14, 211–221, 2005.

[11] V. Chandola, A. Banerjee, and V. Kumar. Outlier detection: A survey. Anomaly detection: A survey. *ACM Comput. Surv.*, 41(3), Article 15, July 2009, pp. 1–58.

[12] L. A. Bettencourt, A. Hagberg, and L. Larkey. Separating the wheat from the chaff: Practical anomaly detection schemes in ecological applications of distributed sensor networks, in: *Proc. IEEE International Conference on Distributed Computing in Sensor Systems*, 2007.

[13] S. Rajasegarar, C. Leckie, M. Palaniswami, and J. C. Bezdek. Distributed anomaly detection in wireless sensor networks, in: *Proceedings of IEEE International Conference on Communications*, vol. 30, IEEE Computer Society, Singapore, October–1 November 2006, pp. 1–5.

[14] K. X. Thuc and K. Insoo. A collaborative event detection scheme using fuzzy logic in clustered wireless sensor networks. *AEÜ – International Journal of Electronics and Communications*, 65, 485–488, 2011.

[15] D. Mingtao, T. Zheng, and X. Haixia. Adaptive kernel principal component analysis, in: *Signal Process*, 2010, pp. 1542–1553.

[16] Z. A. Baig. Pattern recognition for detecting distributed node exhaustion attacks in wireless sensor networks. *Computer and Communications*, 34, 468–484, 2011.

[17] D. McDonald, S. Sanchez, S. Madria, and F. Ercal. A survey of methods for finding outliers in wireless sensor networks. *Journal of Network and Systems Management*, 23(1), 163–182, 2015.

[18] P. Oluwasanya. Anomaly detection in wireless sensor networks, signal processing and communications: project & thesis-pgee11110, 2017.

[19] I. Esnaola-Gonzalez, J. Bermúdez, I. Fernández, S. Fernández, and A. Arnaiz. Towards a semantic outlier detection framework in wireless sensor networks,

in: *Proceedings of the 13th International Conference on Semantic Systems*, ACM, September 2017, pp. 152–159.

[20]   W. Cho and E. Choi. Big data pre-processing methods with vehicle driving data using MapReduce techniques. *The Journal of Supercomputing*, 73.7, 3179–3195, 2017.

[21]   C. Modi, D. Patel, B. Borisaniya, H. Patel, A. Patel, and M. Rajarajan. A survey of intrusion detection techniques in cloud. *Journal of Network and Computer Applications*, 36(1), 42–57, 2013.

[22]   I. Butun, S. D. Morgera, and R. Sankar. A survey of intrusion detection systems in wireless sensor networks. *IEEE Communications Surveys & Tutorials*, 16(1), 266–282, 2014.

[23]   A. L. Buczak and E. Guven. A survey of data mining and machine learning methods for cyber security intrusion detection. *IEEE Communications Surveys & Tutorials*, 18(2), 1153–1176, 2016.

[24]   Y. Zhang, N. Meratnia, and P. Havinga. Outlier detection techniques for wireless sensor networks: A survey. *IEEE Communications Surveys & Tutorials*, 12(2), 159–170, 2010.

[25]   C. C. Aggarwal, Data Mining: The Textbook, Springer International Publishing, Switzerland, 2015. DOI: 10.1007/978-3-319-14142-8 695.

[26]   M. Ahmed, A. N. Mahmood, and J. Hu. A survey of network anomaly detection techniques. *Journal of Network and Computer Applications*, 60, 19–31, 2016.

[27]   A. Ayadi, O. Ghorbel, A. M. Obeid, and Abid, M. Outlier detection approaches for wireless sensor networks: A survey. *Computer Networks*, 129, 319–333, 2017.

[28]   H.-P. Kriegel, E. Schubert, and A. Zimek. The (black) art of runtime evaluation: Are we comparing algorithms or implementations? *Knowledge and Information Systems*, 52.2, 341–378, 2017.

[29]   R. Webster and M. A. Oliver. *Geostatistics for Environmental Scientists*. Springer, Chichester, 2007.

[30]   B. Efron. Bootstrap methods: Another look at the jackknife. *Annals of Statistics*, 7(1), 1–26, 1979.

[31]   A. R. Ganguly, J. Gama, O. A. Omitaomu, M. Gaber, and R. R. Vatsavai (Eds.). *Knowledge Discovery from Sensor Data*. Boca Raton: CRC Press, 2008. Available from: https://doi.org/10.1201/9781420082333.

[32]   Z. Liu, J. Yu, L. Chen, and D. Wu. Detection of shape anomalies: A probabilistic approach using hidden Markov models, in: *Proc. IEEE Intl Conf. Data Engineering*, 2008, pp. 1325–1327.

[33]   M. Markou and S. Singh. Novelty detection: A review part 2: Neural network based approaches. *Signal Process*, 83(12), 2499–2521, 2003.

[34]   U. Rebbapragada, P. Protopapas, C. Brodley, and C. Alcock. Finding anomalous periodic time series. *Machine Learning*, 74(3), 281–313, 2009.

[35]   I. I. N. Azha, N. E. A. Khalid, A. Ismail, N. Sakamat, and R. A. Latif. Pattern recognition using Pearson correlation on neuron values, in: *Proc. IEEE Intl Conf. Control and System Graduate Research Colloquium*, 2016, pp. 24–30.

[36]   V. Barnett and T. Lewis. *Outliers in Statistical Data*. John Wiley, 3rd edition, John Wiley & Sons, Chichester,UK, 1994, 584 pp., ISBN 0-471-93094-6.

[37]   V. Barnett. The ordering of multivariate data (with discussion). *Journal of the Royal Statistical Society. Series A*, 139, 318–354, 1976.

[38]   R. J. Beckman and R. D. Cook. Outliers. *Technometrics*, 25(2), 119–149, 1983.

[39]   C. Bishop. *Pattern Recognition and Machine Learning*, vol. 4. Springer, New York, NY, USA, 2006.

[40]   G. J. Mc Lachlan and K. E. Basford. *Mixture Models: Inference and Applications to Clustering*, vol. 1. Marcel Dekker, New York, NY, USA, 1988.

[41]   Y. Agusta and D. Dowe. Unsupervised learning of gamma mixture models using minimum message length, in: M. H. Hamza (Ed.), *Proceedings of the 3rd IASTED Conference on Artificial Intelligence and Applications*, 2003, pp. 457–462.

[42]   I. Mayrose, N. Friedman, and T. Pupko. A gamma mixture model better accounts for among site rate heterogeneity. *Bioinformatics*, 21(2), 151–158, 2005.

[43]   A. Carvalho and M. Tanner. Modelling nonlinear count time series with local mixtures of Poisson auto regressions. *Computational Statistics & Data Analysis*, 51(11), 5266–5294, 2007.

[44]   J. Han, Kamber, M. *Data Mining, Concepts and Techniques*. Morgan Kaufmann, San Francisco, 2001.

[45]   E. M. Knorr and R. T. Ng. Algorithms for mining distance-based outliers in large dataset, in: *Proc. Of 24th International Conference on Very Large Data Bases (VLDB'98)*, New York, NY, USA, 1998, pp. 392–403.

[46]   F. E. Grubbs. Procedures for detecting outlying observations in samples. *Technometrics*, 11(1), 1–21, 1969.

[47]   S. E. Guttormsson, R. J. Marks, M. A. El-Sharkawi, and I. Kerszenbaum. Elliptical novelty grouping for on-line short-turn detection of excited running rotors. *IEEE Transactions on Energy Conversion*, 14, 1, 1999, pp. 16–22.

[48]   P. S. Horn, L. Feng, Y. Li, and A. J. Pesce. Effect of outliers and nonhealthy individuals on reference interval estimation. *Clinical Chemistry*, 47(12), 2137–2145, 2001.

[49]   J. Laurikkala, M. Juhola1, and E. Kentala. Informal identification of outliers in medical data, in: *Fifth International Workshop on Intelligent Data Analysis in Medicine and Pharmacology*, 2000, pp. 20–24.

[50]   H. E. Solberg and A. Lahti. Detection of outliers in reference distributions: Performance of Horn's algorithm. *Clinical Chemistry*, 51(12), 2326–2332, 2005.

[51]   D. Freedman, R. Pisani, and R. Purves. *Statistics*. W. W. Norton, New York, NY, USA, 1978.

[52]   C. Aggarwal and P. Yu. Outlier detection with uncertain data, in: *Proceedings of the SIAM International Conference on Data Mining*, 2008, pp. 483–493.

[53] H. Solberg and A. Lahti. Detection of outliers in reference distributions: Performance of Horn's algorithm. *Clinical Chemistry*, 51(12), 2326–2332, 2005.

[54] C. Bishop. *Pattern Recognition and Machine Learning*, vol. 4. Springer, New York, NY, USA, 2006.

[55] G. J. McLachlan and K. E. Basford. *Mixture Models: Inference and Applications to Clustering*, vol. 1. Marcel Dekker, New York, NY, USA, 1988.

[56] Y. Agusta and D. Dowe. Unsupervised learning of gamma mixture models using minimum message length, in: M. H. Hamza (Ed.), *Proceedings of the 3rd IASTED Conference on Artificial Intelligence and Applications*, 2003, pp. 457–462.

[57] I. Mayrose, N. Friedman, and T. Pupko. A gamma mixture model better accounts for among site rate heterogeneity. *Bioinformatics*, 21(2), 151–158, 2005.

[58] M. Svensén and C. Bishop. Robust Bayesian mixture modelling. *Neurocomputing*, 64, 235–252, 2005.

[59] A. Stranjak, P. Dutta, M. Ebden, A. Rogers, and P. Vytelingum. A multi-agent simulation system for prediction and scheduling of aero engine overhaul, in: *Proceedings of the 7th International Joint Conference on Autonomous Agents and Multi agent Systems: Industrial Track*, International Foundation for Autonomous Agents and Multiagent Systems, 2008, pp. 81–88.

[60] K. Chaloner and R. Brant. A Bayesian approach to outlier detection and residual analysis. *Biometrika*, 75(4), 651–659, 1988.

[61] A. Zellner. Bayesian analysis of regression error terms. *Journal of the American Statistical Association*, 70(349), 138–144, 1975.

[62] M. West. Outlier models and prior distributions in Bayesian linear regression. *Journal of the Royal Statistical Society. Series B, Statistical Methodology*, 46(3), 431–439, 1984.

[63] H. Zhu, H. Leung, and Z. He. A variational Bayesian approach to robust sensor fusion based on Student-*t* distribution. *Information Sciences*, 221, 201–214, 2013.

[64] E. T. Jaynes. *Probability Theory: The Logic of Science*. Cambridge University Press, Cambridge, UK, 2003.

[65] M. Woolrich. Robust group analysis using outlier inference. NeuroImage, 41(2), 286–301, 2008.

[66] K. V. Yuen and H. Q. Mu. A novel probabilistic method for robust parametric identification and outlier detection. *Probabilistic Engineering Mechanics*, 30, 48–59, 2012.

[67] K.-V. Yuen and A. O. Gilberto. Outlier detection and robust regression for correlated data. *Computer Methods in Applied Mechanics and Engineering*, 313, 632–646, 2017.

[68] Z. Liu, J. Yu, L. Chen, and D. Wu. Detection of shape anomalies: A probabilistic approach using hidden Markov models, in: *Proc. IEEE Intl Conf. Data Engineering*, 2008, pp. 1325–1327.

[69]   Y. Anzai. *Pattern Recognition and Machine Learning.* Academic Press, Inc., New York, NY, USA, 1989.

[70]   C. C. Aggarwal. On Abnormality Detection in Spuriously Populated Data Streams, in: *SIAM International Conference on Data Mining (SDM'05)*, Newport Beach, CA, USA, 2005.

[71]   B. Abraham and G. E. P. Box. Bayesian analysis of some outlier problems in time series. *Biometrika*, 66(2), 229–236, 1979.

[72]   B. Abraham and A. Chuang. Outlier detection and time series modeling. *Technometrics*, 31(2), 241–248, 1989.

[73]   A. J. Fox. Outliers in time series. *Journal of the Royal Statistical Society, Series B (Methodological)*, 34(3), 350–363, 1972.

[74]   X. Li and J. Han. Mining approximate top-k subspace anomalies in multi-dimensional time-series data. In: *Proceedings of the 33rd international conference on Very large data bases.* VLDB Endowment, pp. 447–458, 2007, September.

[75]   M. Meloun, J. Militký, M. Hill, and R. G. Brereton. Crucial problems in regression modelling and their solutions. *Analyst*, 127, 433–450, 2002.

[76]   M. Meloun and J. Militký. Detection of single influential points in OLS regression model building. *Analytica Chimica Acta*, 439, 169–191, 2001.

[77]   M. Meloun, J. Militky. *Statistical Data Analysis: A Practical Guide.* Woodhead Publishing, Limited, 2011.

[78]   K. De Brabanter, K. Pelckmans, J. De Brabanter, M. Debruyne, J. A. Suykens, M. Hubert, and B. De Moor. Robustness of kernel based regression: a comparison of iterative weighting schemes, in: *International Conference on Artificial Neural Networks*, Springer, Berlin, Heidelberg, 2009, September, pp. 100–110.

[79]   C. F. Chen, C. Q. Yan, and Y. Y. Li. A robust weighted least squares support vector regression based on least trimmed squares. *Neurocomputing*, 168, 941–946, 2015.

[80]   J. A. K. Suykens, J. De Brabanter, L. Lukas, and J. Vandewalle. Weighted least squares support vector machines: Robustness and sparse approximation. *Neurocomputing*, 48, 85–105, 2002.

[81]   W. Wen, Z. Hao, and X. Yang. A heuristic weight-setting strategy and iteratively updating algorithm for weighted least-squares support vector regression. *Neurocomputing*, 71, 3096–3103, 2008.

[82]   X. Chen, J. Yang, J. Liang, and Q. Ye. Recursive robust least squares support vector regression based on maximum correntropy criterion. *Neurocomputing*, 97, 63–73, 2012.

[83]   X. Yang, L. Tan, and L. He. A robust least squares support vector machine for regression and classification with noise. *Neurocomputing*, 140, 41–52, 2014.

[84]   K. N. Wang and P. Zhong. Robust non-convex least squares loss function for regression with outliers. *Knowledge-Based Systems*, 71, 290–302, 2014.

[85]   Y. L. He and Q. X. Zhu. A novel robust regression model based on functional link least square (FLLS) and its application to modeling complex chemical processes. *Chemical Engineering Science*, 153, 117–128, 2016.

[86] Y. F. Ye, L. Bai, X. Y. Hua, Y. H. Shao, Z. Wang, and N. Y. Deng. Weighted Lagrange ε-twin support vector regression. *Neurocomputing*, 197, 53–68, 2016.

[87] J. Hu and K. Zheng. A novel support vector regression for data set with outliers. *Applied Soft Computing*, 31, 405–411, 2015.

[88] V. G. Cancho, D. K. Dey, V. H. Lachos, and M. G. Andrade. Bayesian non-linear regression models with scale mixtures of skew-normal distributions: Estimation and case influence diagnostics. *Computational Statistics & Data Analysis*, 55, 588–602, 2011.

[89] A. M. Garay, V. H. Lachos, and C. A. A. Valle. Nonlinear regression models based on scale mixtures of skew-normal distributions. *Journal of the Korean Statistical Society*, 40, 115–124, 2011.

[90] V. H. Lachos, D. Bandyopadhyay, and A. M. Garay. Heteroscedastic nonlinear regression models based on scale mixtures of skew-normal distributions. *Statistics & Probability Letters*, 81, 1208–1217, 2011.

[91] V. Chandola, A. Banerjee, and V. Kumar. Outlier detection: A survey. *Technical Report 07-017*. University of Minnesota, 2007.

[92] E. Eskin. Anomaly detection over noisy data using learned probability distributions, in: *Proceedings of the Seventeenth International Conference on Machine Learning (ICML)*, Morgan Kaufmann Publishers Inc., 2000.

[93] D. Anderson, T. Frivold, A. Tamaru, and A. Valdes. Next generation intrusion detection expert system (NIDES), software users manual, beta-update release. *Technical Report*. Computer Science Laboratory, SRI International, 1994.

[94] H. S. Javitz and A. Valdes. The SRI IDES statistical anomaly detector, in: *Proceedings of the 1991 IEEE Symposium on Research in Security and Privacy*, 1991.

[95] P. Helman and J. Bhangoo. A statistically based system for prioritizing information exploration under uncertainty. *IEEE International Conference on Systems, Man, and Cybernetics*, 27, 449–466, 1997.

[96] M. J. Desforges, P. J. Jacob, and J. E. Cooper. Applications of probability density estimation to the detection of abnormal conditions in engineering. *Proceedings of the Institution of Mechanical Engineers, Part C: Journal of Mechanical Engineering Science*, 212.8, 687–703, 1998.

[97] F. Kadri, F. Harrou, S. Chaabane, Y. Sun, and C. Tahon. Seasonal ARMA-based SPC charts for anomaly detection: Application to emergency department systems. *Neurocomputing*, 173, 2016, 2102–2114.

[98] A. Appice, P. Guccione, D. Malerba, and A. Ciampi. Dealing with temporal and spatial correlations to classify outliers in geophysical data streams. *Information Sciences*, 285, 162–180, 2014.

[99] C. Bishop. *Pattern Recognition and Machine Learning*, vol. 4. Springer, New York, NY, USA, 2006.

[100] C. Bishop. Novelty detection and neural network validation. *Proceedings of IEEE Vision, Image and Signal Processing*, 141, 217–222, 1994.

[101] C. Chow and D. Y. Yeung. Parzen-window network intrusion detectors, in: *Proceedings of the 16th International Conference on Pattern Recognition*, vol. 4, Washington, DC, USA, 2002, p. 40385.

[102]   M. Desforges, P. Jacob, and J. Cooper. Applications of probability density estimation to the detection of abnormal conditions in engineering, in: *Proceedings of Institute of Mechanical Engineers*, vol. 212, 1998, pp. 687–703.

[103]   L. Tarassenko. Novelty detection for the identification of masses in mammograms, in: *Proceedings of the 4th IEEE International Conference on Artificial Neural Networks*, vol. 4, Cambridge, UK, 1995, pp. 442–447.

[104]   F. Harrou, F. Kadri, S. Chaabane, C. Tahon, and Y. Sun. Improved principal component analysis for anomaly detection: Application to an emergency department. *Computers & Industrial Engineering*, 88, 63–77, 2015.

[105]   F. Maciá-Pérez, J. V. Berna-Martinez, A. F. Oliva, and M. A. A. Ortega. Algorithm for the detection of outliers based on the theory of rough sets. *Decision Support Systems*, 75, 63–75, 2015.

[106]   H. N. Akouemo and R. J. Povinelli. Probabilistic anomaly detection in natural gas time series data. *International Journal of Forecasting*, 32(3), 948–956, 2016.

[107]   Y. Zhang, H. Lu, L. Zhang, and X. Ruan. Combining motion and appearance cues for anomaly detection. *Pattern Recognition*, 51, 443–452, 2016.

[108]   F. Kadri, F. Harrou, S. Chaabane, Y. Sun, and C. Tahon. Seasonal ARMA-based SPC charts for anomaly detection: Application to emergency department systems. *Neurocomputing*, 173, 2102–2114, 2016.

[109]   J. M. Bardet and S. F. Dimby. A new nonparametric detector of univariate outliers for distributions with unbounded support. *Extremes*, 20(4), 751–775, 2017.

[110]   H. Wang, Y. Wang, and Q. Hu. Self-adaptive robust nonlinear regression for unknown noise via mixture of Gaussians. *Neurocomputing*, 235, 274–286, 2017.

[111]   K. V. Yuen and G. A. Ortiz. Outlier detection and robust regression for correlated data. *Computer Methods in Applied Mechanics and Engineering*, 313, 632–646, 2017.

[112]   H. Ren, Z. Ye, and Z. Li. Anomaly detection based on a dynamic Markov model. *Information Sciences*, 411, 52–65, 2017.

[113]   M. S. Ahuja and J. S. Bal. Exploring cluster analysis. *International Journal of Computer and Information Technology*, 3, 594–597, 2014.

[114]   L. Duan, L. Xu, Y. Liu, and J. Lee. Cluster-based outlier detection. *Annals of Operations Research*, 168(1), 151–168, 2009.

[115]   L. Kaufman and P. J. Rousseeuw. *Finding Groups in Data: An Introduction to Cluster Analysis*. John Wiley & Sons, UK, 1990.

[116]   R. Ng and J. Han. Efficient and effective clustering methods for spatial data mining, in: *Proceedings of the 20th VLDB Conference*, 1994, pp. 144–155.

[117]   Z. He, X. Xu, and S. Deng. Discovering cluster-based local outliers. *Pattern Recognition Letters*, 24(9), 1641–1650, 2003.

[118]   D. Yu, G. Sheikholeslami, and A. Zhang. FindOut: Finding outliers in very large datasets. *Knowledge and Information Systems*, 4(4), 387–412, 2002.

[119]   J. MacQueen. Some methods for classification and analysis of multivariate observations, in: *Proc. of 5th Berkeley Symp. Math. Statist, Prob.*, vol. 1, 1967, pp. 281–297.

[120] M.-F. Jiang, S.-S. Tseng, and C.-M. Su. Two-phase clustering process for outliers detection. *Pattern Recognition Letters*, Elsevier, 22(6), 691–700, 2001.

[121] V. Hautamäki, S. Cherednichenko, I. Kärkkäinen, T. Kinnunen, and P. Fränti. Improving *k*-means by outlier removal, in: *Scandinavian Conference on Image Analysis*, Springer, Berlin, Heidelberg, June 2005, pp. 978–987.

[122] N. V. Kadam, and M. A. Pund. Cluster Based and Distance Based Approach for Outlier Detection. *International Journal of Advanced Research in Computer Science*, 4(1), 256–258, 2013.

[123] C. C. Aggarwal. Outlier analysis, in: *Data Mining*, Springer, Cham, 2015, pp. 237–263.

[124] C. C. Aggarwal and C. K. Reddy. Data Clustering: Algorithms and Applications. 1st edition, Chapman & Hall/CRC, 2013, pp. 652.

[125] Q. Yu, Y. Luo, C. Chen, and X. Ding. Outlier-eliminated k-means clustering algorithm based on differential privacy preservation. *Applied Intelligence*, 45(4), 1179–1191, 2016.

[126] K. Aparna and M. K. Nair. Effect of outlier detection on clustering accuracy and computation time of CHB K-means algorithm, in: *Computational Intelligence in Data Mining*, vol. 2, Springer, New Delhi, 2016, pp. 25–35.

[127] F. Jiang, G. Liu, J. Du, and Y. Sui. Initialization of K-modes clustering using outlier detection techniques. *Information Sciences*, 332, 167–183, 2016.

[128] R. Pamula, J. Deka, and S. Nandi. An outlier detection method based on clustering, in: *Second International Conference on Emerging Applications of Information Technology*, 2011, pp. 253–256.

[129] Ahmed, M. and Naser, A. A novel approach for outlier detection and clustering improvement. In: Proceedings of the 8th IEEE Conference on Industrial Electronics and Applications (ICIEA), 2013, pp. 577–582.

[130] S. Chawla and A. Gionis. k-means: A unified approach to clustering and outlier detection. in: *Proceedings of the 2013 SIAM International Conference on Data Mining*, Society for Industrial and Applied Mathematics, 2013, May, pp. 189–197.

[131] J. Whang, I. S. Dhillon, and D. Gleich. Non-exhaustive, overlapping *k*-means, in: *SIAM International Conference on Data Mining (SDM)*, 2015.

[132] A. Bansal, M. Sharma, and S. Goel. Improved k-mean clustering algorithm for prediction analysis using classification technique in data mining. *International Journal of Computer Applications (0975–8887)*, 157, 33–40, 2017.

[133] M. Capó, A. Pérez, and J. A. Lozano. An efficient approximation to the *k*-means clustering for massive data. *Knowledge-Based Systems*, 117, 56–69, 2017.

[134] G. Gan and M. Ng. *k*-Means clustering with outlier removal. *Pattern Recognition Letters*, 90, 8–14, 2017.

[135] R. Dave and R. Krishnapuram. Robust clustering methods: A unified view. *IEEE Transactions on Fuzzy Systems*, 5(2), 270–293, 1997.

[136] H. Kim and J. K. Min. An Efficient Outlier Detection Technique in Wireless Sensor Networks, in: *Ubiquitous Information Technologies and Applications*, Springer, Berlin, Heidelberg, 2014, pp. 345–353.

[137]   J. M. Jobe and M. Pokojovy. A cluster-based outlier detection scheme for multivariate data. *Journal of the American Statistical Association*, 110(512), 1543–1551, 2015.

[138]   A. M. C. Souza and J. R. A. Amazonas. An outlier detect algorithm using big data processing and internet of things architecture. *Procedia Computer Science*, 52, 1010–1015, 2015.

[139]   A. Christy, G. M. Gandhi, and S. Vaithyasubramanian. Cluster based outlier detection algorithm for healthcare data. *Procedia Computer Science*, 50, 209–215, 2015.

[140]   X. Cui, P. Zhu, X. Yang, K. Li, and C. Ji. Optimized big data K-means clustering using MapReduce. *The Journal of Supercomputing*, 70(3), 1249–1259, 2014.

[141]   C. T. Zahn. Graph-theoretical methods for detecting and describing gestalt clusters. *IEEE Transaction on Computing*, C-20, 68–86, 1971.

[142]   S. Guha, R. Rastogi, and K. Shim. CURE: An efficient clustering algorithm for large databases, in: *Proceedings of the 1998 ACM SIGMOD International Conference on Management of Data (SIGMOD'98)*, Seattle, WA, USA, 1998.

[143]   G. Karypis, E.-H. Han, and V. Kumar. CHAMELEON: A hierarchical clustering algorithm using dynamic modeling. *IEEE Computer*, 32, 68–75, 1999.

[144]   T. Zhang, R. Ramakrishnan, and M. Livny. BIRCH: An efficient data clustering method for very large databases. *ACM SIGMOD Record*, 25(2), 103–114, 1996.

[145]   T. S. Xu, H. D. Chiang, G. Y. Liu, and C. W. Tan. Hierarchical k-means method for clustering large-scale advanced metering infrastructure data. *IEEE Transactions on Power Delivery*, 32(2), 609–616, 2017.

[146]   A. Sharma, K. A. Boroevich, D. Shigemizu, Y. Kamatani, M. Kubo, and T. Tsunoda. Hierarchical maximum likelihood clustering approach. *IEEE Transactions on Biomedical Engineering*, 64(1), 112–122, 2017.

[147]   A. Kumar and H. Daumé. A co-training approach for multi-view spectral clustering, in: *Proceedings of the 28th International Conference on Machine Learning (ICML-11)*, 2011, pp. 393–400.

[148]   S. Dhandapani, G. Gupta, and J. Ghosh. Design and implementation of scalable hierarchical density based clustering (Doctoral dissertation, University of Texas), 2010.

[149]   S. Das, B. L. Matthews, A. N. Srivastava, and N. C. Oza, Multiple kernel learning for heterogeneous anomaly detection: Algorithm and aviation safety case study, in: *Proc. ACM SIGKDD Int. Conf. Knowl. Discovery Data Mining (KDD)*, 2010, pp. 47–56.

[150]   V. P. Janeja and R. Palanisamy. Multi-domain anomaly detection in spatial datasets. *Knowledge and Information Systems*, 36(3), 749–788, 2013.

[151]   E. Müller, I. Assent, P. I. Sanchez, Y. Müller, and K. Böhm. Outlier ranking via subspace analysis in multiple views of the data, in: *Proc. IEEE Int. Conf. Data Mining (ICDM)*, December 2012, pp. 529–538.

[152]   J. Gao, W. Fan, D. S. Turaga, S. Parthasarathy, and J. Han, A spectral framework for detecting inconsistency across multi-source object relationships, in: *Proc. IEEE Int. Conf. Data Mining (ICDM)*, December 2011, pp. 1050–1055.

[153]   J. Gao, N. Du, W. Fan, D. Turaga, S. Parthasarathy, and J. Han. A multi-graph spectral framework for mining multi-source anomalies, in: *Graph Embedding for Pattern Analysis*, Springer, New York, NY, USA, 2013, pp. 205–228.

[154]   A. M. Alvarez, M. Yamada, A. Kimura, and T. Iwata. Clustering-based anomaly detection in multi-view data, in: *Proc. ACM Int. Conf. Conf. Inf. Knowl. Manage. (CIKM)*, 2013, pp. 1545–1548.

[155]   H. Zhao, H. Liu, Z. Ding, and Y. Fu. Consensus regularized multi-view outlier detection. *IEEE Transactions on Image Processing*, 27(1), 236–248, 2018.

[156]   S. Li, M. Shao, and Y. Fu. Multi-view low-rank analysis for outlier detection, in: *Proceedings of the 2015 SIAM International Conference on Data Mining*. Society for Industrial and Applied Mathematics, June 2015, pp. 748–756.

[157]   J. Gao, W. Fan, D. S. Turaga, S. Parthasarathy, and J. Han. A spectral framework for detecting inconsistency across multi-source object relationships, in: *ICDM*, 2011, pp. 1050–1055.

[158]   G. Sheikholeslami, S. Chatterjee, and A. Zhang. Wavecluster: A multiresolution clustering approach for very large spatial databases, in: *Proceedings of the International Conference on Very Large Data Bases*, New York, NY, USA, 1998, pp. 428–439.

[159]   W. Wang, J. Yang, and R. Muntz. Sting: A statistical information grid approach to spatial data mining, in: *Proceedings of the 23th International Conference on Very Large Data Bases*, Athens, Greece, 1997, pp. 186–195.

[160]   P. Berkin. A survey of clustering data mining techniques, in: J. Kogan, C. Nicholas and M. Teboulle (Eds.), *Grouping Multidimensional Data: Recent Advances in Clustering*, 2006, pp. 25–71.

[161]   C. C. Aggarwal and P. Yu. Finding generalized projected clusters in high dimensional spaces, in: *Proc. of 2000 ACM SIGMOD International Conference on Management of Data (SIGMOD'00)*, 2000, pp. 70–81.

[162]   K. Beyer, J. Goldstein, R. Ramakrishnan, and U. Shaft. When is nearest neighbors meaningful? in: *Proc. of 7th International Conference on Database Theory (ICDT'99)*, Jerusalem, Israel, 1999, pp. 217–235.

[163]   X. Zhu, J. Zhang, H. Li, P. Fournier-Viger, J. C. W. Lin, and L. Chang. FRIOD: A deeply integrated feature-rich interactive system for effective and efficient outlier detection. *IEEE Access*, 5, 25682–25695, 2017.

[164]   W. Wang, J. Yang, and R. Muntz. STING: A statistical information grid approach to spatial data mining, in: *Proceedings of 23rd VLDB Conference*, Athens, Green, 1997, pp. 186–195.

[165]   G. Sheikholeslami, S. Chatterjee, and A. Zhang. WaveCluster: A wavelet based clustering approach for spatial data in very large database. *VLDB Journal*, 8(3–4), 289–304, 1999.

[166]   J. Zhang, W. Hsu, and M. L. Lee. Clustering in dynamic spatial databases. *Journal of Intelligent Information Systems (JIIS)*, 24(1), 5–27, 2005.

[167]   E. Schikuta and M. Erhart. The BANG-clustering system: Grid-based data analysis, in: *International Symposium on Intelligent Data Analysis*, Springer, Berlin, Heidelberg, August 1997, pp. 513–524.

[168]   J. Zhang, Q. Gao, H. H. Wang, Q. Liu, and K. Xu. Detecting projected outliers in high-dimensional data streams, in: *Proc. DEXA*, 2009, pp. 629–644.

[169]   M. Elahi, X. Lv, M. W. Nisar, and H. Wang. Distance based outlier for data streams using grid structure. *Information Technology Journal*, 8(2), 128–137, 2009.

[170]   Q. Zhao, Y. Shi, Q. Liu, and P. Fränti. A grid-growing clustering algorithm for geo-spatial data. *Pattern Recognition Letters*, 53, 77–84, 2015.

[171]   J. Lee and N. W. Cho. Fast outlier detection using a grid-based algorithm. *PLoS One*, 11(11), e0165972, 2016.

[172]   J. Zhang, X. Tao, and H. Wang. Outlier detection from large distributed databases. *World Wide Web*, 17(4), 539–568, Springer, 2014.

[173]   J. Zhang, Q. Gao, H. H. Wang, Q. Liu, and K. Xu. Detecting projected outliers in high-dimensional data streams, in: *Proc. DEXA*, 2009, pp. 629–644.

[174]   H. Li, J. Zhang, Y. Luo, F. Chen, and L. Chang. GO-PEAS: A scalable yet accurate grid-based outlier detection method using novel pruning searching techniques, in: *Australasian Conference on Artificial Life and Computational Intelligence*, Springer, Cham, February 2016, pp. 125–133.

[175]   L. Ma, L. Gu, B. Li, L. Zhou, and J. Wang. An improved grid-based k-means clustering algorithm. *Advanced Science and Technology Letters*, 73, 1–6, 2014.

[176]   E. G. Mansoori. GACH: A grid-based algorithm for hierarchical clustering of high-dimensional data. *Soft Computing*, 18(5), 905–922, 2014.

[177]   D. Pascual, F. Pla, and J. S. Sanchez. Nonparametric local density-based clustering for multimodal overlapping distributions, in: *Proceedings of the 7th International Conference on Intelligent Data Engineering and Automated Learning (IDEAL)*, Burgos, Spain, 2006, 671–678.

[178]   R. T. Ng and J. Han. CLARANS: A method for clustering objects for spatial data mining. *IEEE Transactions on Knowledge and Data Engineering*, 14(5), 1003–1016, 2002.

[179]   X. Xu, M. Ester, H.-P. Kriegel, and J. Sander, A distribution-based clustering algorithm for mining in large spatial databases, in: *Proc. 14th Int. Conf. on Data Engineering (ICDE'98)*, Orlando, FL, 1998, pp. 324–331.

[180]   M. Ester, H. P. Kriegel, J. Sander, and X. Xu. A density-based algorithm for discovering clusters in large spatial databases with noise, in: *Proc. 2nd Int. Conf. on Knowledge Discovery and Data Mining (KDD'96)*, Portland, OR, 1996, 291–316.

[181]   M. Ankerst, M. M. Breunig, H.-P. Kriegel, and J. Sander. OPTICS: Ordering points to identify the clustering structure, in: *Proc. of Int'l Conf. on Management of Data, ACM SIGMOD*, Philadelphia, PA, USA, June 1999, pp. 49–60.

[182]   D. Coomans, D. L. Massart, I. Broeckaert, and A. Tassin. Potential methods in pattern recognition: Part 1. Classification aspects of the supervised method ALLOC. *Analytica Chimica Acta*, 1;133(3):215–24, 1981 September.

[183]   D. Comaniciu and P. Meer. Distribution free decomposition of multivariate data. *Pattern analysis and applications*, 2(1), 22–30, 1999.

[184]   L. Ertoz, M. Steinbach, and V. Kumar. A new shared nearest neighbor clustering algorithm and its applications, in: *Workshop on clustering high dimensional data and its applications at 2nd SIAM international conference on data mining*, pp. 105–115, 2002, April.

[185]   W. Stuetzle. Estimating the cluster tree of a density by analyzing the minimal spanning tree of a sample. *Journal of Classification*, 20(1), 25–47, 2003.

[186]   L. Sander, X. Qin, Z. Lu, N. Niu, and A. Kovarsky. Automatic extraction of clusters from hierarchical clustering representations, in: *Proceedings of the 7th Pacific-Asia Conference on Knowledge Discovery and Data Mining (PAKDD)*, Seoul, Korea, 2003, pp. 75–87. DOI: http://dx.doi.org/10.1007/3-540-36175-8_8.

[187]   S. Brecheisen, H.-P. Kriegel, P. Kroger, and M. Pfeifle. Visually mining through cluster hierarchies, in: *Proceedings of the 4th SIAM International Conference on Data Mining (SDM)*, Lake Buena Vista, FL, 2004, pp. 400–412.

[188]   M. Daszykowski, B. Walczak, and D. L. Massart. Looking for natural patterns in data: Part 1. Density-based approach. *Chemometrics and Intelligent Laboratory Systems*, 56(2), 83–92, 2001.

[189]   A. Foss and O. R. Zaïane. A parameterless method for efficiently discovering clusters of arbitrary shape in large datasets, in: *Proceedings of the 2nd IEEE International Conference on Data Mining (ICDM)*, Maebashi City, Japan, 2002, pp. 179–186.

[190]   T. Pei, A. Jasra, D. J. Hand, A.-X. Zhu, and C. Zhou. DECODE: A new method for discovering clusters of different densities in spatial data. *Data Mining and Knowledge Discovery*, 18(3), 337–369, 2009. DOI: http://dx.doi.org/10.1007/s10618-008-0120-3.

[191]   T. Pei, A.-X. Zhu, C. Zhou, B. Li, and C. Qin. A new approach to the nearest-neighbour method to discover cluster features in overlaid spatial point processes. *International Journal of Geographical Information Science*, 20(2), 153–168, 2006.

[192]   A. Hinneburg and H. H. Gabriel. DENCLUE 2.0: Fast clustering based on kernel density estimation, in: *Proceedings of the 7th International Symposium on Intelligent Data Analysis (IDA)*, Ljubljana, Slovenia, 2007, pp. 70–80. DOI:http://dx.doi.org/10.1007/978-3-540-74825-0_7.

[193]   A. Foss and O. R. Zaïane. A parameterless method for efficiently discovering clusters of arbitrary shape in large datasets, in: *Proceedings of the 2nd IEEE International Conference on Data Mining (ICDM)*, Maebashi City, Japan, 2002, pp. 179–186.

[194]   C. Cassisi, A. Ferro, R. Giugno, G. Pigola, and A. Pulvirenti. Enhancing density-based clustering: Parameter reduction and outlier detection. *Information Systems*, 38(3), 317–330, 2013.

[195]   Y. Kim, K. Shim, M. S. Kim, and J. S. Lee. DBCURE-MR: An efficient density-based clustering algorithm for large data using MapReduce. *Information Systems*, 42, 15–35, 2014.

[196]   J. Dean and S. Ghemawat. MapReduce: Simplified data processing on large clusters, in: *OSDI*, 2004, pp. 137–150.

[197]   A. Rodriguez and A. Laio. Clustering by fast search and find of density peaks. *Science*, 344(6191), 1492–1496, 2014.

[198]   L. C. Matioli, S. R. Santos, M. Kleina, and E. A. Leite. A new algorithm for clustering based on kernel density estimation. *Journal of Applied Statistics*, 45(2), 347–366, 2018.

[199]   Y. A. Geng, Q. Li, R. Zheng, F. Zhuang, R. He, and N. Xiong. RECOME: A new density-based clustering algorithm using relative KNN kernel density. *Information Sciences*, 436, 13–30, 2018.

[200]   M. Aliotta, A. Cannata, C. Cassisi, R. Giugno, P. Montalto, and A. Pulvirenti. DBStrata: A system for density-based clustering and outlier detection based on stratification, in: *Proceedings of the Fourth International Conference on SImilarity Search and APplications*, ACM, June 2011, pp. 107–108.

[201]   C. Cassisi, A. Ferro, R. Giugno, G. Pigola, and A. Pulvirenti. Enhancing density-based clustering: Parameter reduction and outlier detection. *Information Systems*, 38(3), 317–330, 2013.

[202]   A. Bryant and K. Cios. RNN-DBSCAN: A density-based clustering algorithm using reverse nearest neighbor density estimates. *IEEE Transactions on Knowledge and Data Engineering*, 30(6), 1109–1121, 2018.

[203]   R. J. Campello, D. Moulavi, A. Zimek, and J. Sander. Hierarchical density estimates for data clustering, visualization, and outlier detection. *ACM Transactions on Knowledge Discovery from Data (TKDD)*, 10(1), 5, 2015.

[204]   S. T. Mai, I. Assent, and M. Storgaard. AnyDBC: An efficient anytime density-based clustering algorithm for very large complex datasets, in: *Proceedings of the 22nd ACM SIGKDD International Conference on Knowledge Discovery and Data Mining*, ACM, August 2016, pp. 1025–1034.

[205]   V. Vapnik. *The Nature of Statistical Learning Theory*. Springer Science & Business Media, New York, USA, 2013.

[206]   V. N. Vapnik. An overview of statistical learning theory. *IEEE Transactions on Neural Networks*, 10(5), 988–999, 1999.

[207]   B. Schölkopf, R. C. Williamson, A. J. Smola, J. Shawe-Taylor, and J. C. Platt. Support vector method for novelty detection, in: *Advances in Neural Information Processing Systems*, 2000, pp. 582–588.

[208]   G. Valentini. Gene expression data analysis of human lymphoma using support vector machines and output coding ensembles. *Artificial Intelligence in Medicine*, 26, 281–304, 2002.

[209]   L. Shutao, J. T. Kwok, H. Zhua, and Y. Wang. Texture classification using the support vector machines. *Pattern Recognition*, 36, 2883–2893, 2003.

[210]   Y. Zhan and D. Shen. Design efficient support vector machine for fast classification. *Pattern Recognition*, 38, 157–161, 2005.

[211]   A. Chaudhuri and K. De. Fuzzy support vector machine for bankruptcy prediction. *Applied Soft Computing*, 11, 2472–2486, 2011.

[212]   J. Qu and M. J. Zuo. Support vector machine-based data processing algorithm for wear degree classification of slurry pump systems. *Measurement*, 43, 781–791, 2010.

[213]   S. Dutta, A. Chatterjee, and S. Munshi. Correlation technique and least square support vector machine combine for frequency domain-based ECG beat classification. *Medical Engineering & Physics*, 32, 1161–1169, 2010.

[214]   H. Cevikalp. New clustering algorithms for the support vector machine based hierarchical classification. *Pattern Recognition Letters*, 31, 1285–1291, 2010.

[215]   D. Li, W. Yang, and S. Wang. Classification of foreign fibers in cotton lint using machine vision and multi-class support vector machine. *Computers and Electronics in Agriculture*, 74, 274–279, 2010.

[216]   E. A. Zanaty. Support vector machines (SVMs) versus multilayer perception (MLP) in data classification. *Egyptian Informatics Journal*, 13, 177–183, 2012.

[217]   Z. Wu, H. Zhang, and J. Liu. A fuzzy support vector machine algorithm for classification based on a novel PIM fuzzy clustering method. *Neurocomputing*, 125, 119–124, 2014.

[218]   Z. Qi, Y. Tian, and Y. Shi. Structural twin support vector machine for classification. *Knowledge-Based Systems*, 43, 74–81, 2013.

[219]   V. A. Sotiris, W. T. Peter, and M. G. Pecht. Anomaly detection through a Bayesian support vector machine. *IEEE Transactions on Reliability*, 59(2), 277–286, 2010.

[220]   S. Fu, J. Liu, and H. Pannu, A hybrid anomaly detection framework in cloud computing using one-class and two-class support vector machines, in: *Advanced Data Mining and Applications*, Springer, Berlin, Heidelberg, 2012, pp. 726–738.

[221]   A. Solarz, M. Bilicki, M. Gromadzki, A. Pollo, A. Durkalec, and M. Wypych. Automated novelty detection in the WISE survey with one-class support vector machines. *Astronomy & Astrophysics*, 606, A39, 2017.

[222]   A. Kurcz, M. Bilicki, A. Solarz, M. Krupa, A. Pollo, and K. Małek. Towards automatic classification of all WISE sources. *Astronomy & Astrophysics*, 592, A25, 2016.

[223]   W. An, M. Liang, and H. Liu. An improved one-class support vector machine classifier for outlier detection. *Proceedings of the Institution of Mechanical Engineers, Part C: Journal of Mechanical Engineering Science*, 229(3), 580–588, 2015.

[224]   M. Amer, M. Goldstein, and S. Abdennadher. Enhancing one-class support vector machines for unsupervised anomaly detection, in: *Proceedings of the ACM SIGKDD Workshop on Outlier Detection and Description*, ACM, August 2013, pp. 8–15.

[225]   H. Y. Ngan, N. H. Yung, and A. G. Yeh. A comparative study of outlier detection for large-scale traffic data by one-class SVM and kernel density estimation, in: *Image Processing: Machine Vision Applications VIII*, vol. 9405, International Society for Optics and Photonics, February 2015, p. 94050I.

[226]   P. Lam, L. Wang, H. Y. Ngan, N. H. Yung, and A. G. Yeh. Outlier detection in large-scale traffic data by Naïve Bayes method and Gaussian mixture model method. *Electronic Imaging*, 2017(9), 73–78, 2017.

[227]   H. Y. T. Ngan, N. H. C. Yung, and A. G. O. Yeh. Detection of outliers in traffic data based on Dirichlet process mixture model. *IET Intelligent Transportation Systems*, 9(7), 773–781, 2015.

[228]   X. Peng, J. Chen, and H. Shen. Outlier detection method based on SVM and its application in copper-matte converting, in: *Control and Decision Conference (CCDC)*, 2010 Chinese, *IEEE*, May 2010, pp. 628–631.

[229]   V. A. Sotiris, W. T. Peter, and M. G. Pecht. Anomaly detection through a Bayesian support vector machine. *IEEE Transactions on Reliability*, 59(2), 277–286, 2010.

[230]   J. Jiang and L. Yasakethu. Anomaly detection via one class SVM for protection of SCADA systems, in: *Cyber-Enabled Distributed Computing and Knowledge Discovery (CyberC), 2013 International Conference on*, IEEE, October 2013, pp. 82–88.

[231]   F. T. Liu, K. M. Ting, and Z. H. Zhou. Isolation forest, in: *Proceedings of the 8th IEEE International Conference on Data Mining, IEEE Computer Society*, Pisa, Italy, 2008.

[232]   F. T. Liu, K. M. Ting, and Z. H. Zhou. Isolation-based anomaly detection. *ACM Transactions on Knowledge Discovery from Data (TKDD)*, 6(1), 3, 2012.

[233]   A. F. Emmott, S. Das, T. Dietterich, A. Fern, and W. K. Wong. Systematic construction of anomaly detection benchmarks from real data, in: *Proceedings of the ACM SIGKDD Workshop on Outlier Detection and Description*, ACM, August 2013, pp. 16–21.

[234]   T. R. Bandaragoda, K. M. Ting, D. Albrecht, F. T. Liu, Y. Zhu, and J. R. Wells. Isolation-based anomaly detection using nearest-neighbor ensembles. *Computational Intelligence*, 2018, 34(4), 968–998.

[235]   W. R. Chen, Y. H. Yun, M. Wen, H. M. Lu, Z. M. Zhang, and Y. Z. Liang. Representative subset selection and outlier detection via isolation forest. *Analytical Methods*, 8(39), 7225–7231, 2016.

[236]   F. T. Liu, Ting, K. M., and Zhou, Z. H. On detecting clustered anomalies using SCiForest. In: *Joint European Conference on Machine Learning and Knowledge Discovery in Databases*. Springer, Berlin, Heidelberg, 2010, September, pp. 274–290.

[237]   K. M. Ting, G.-T. Zhou, F. T. Liu, and J. S. C. Tan. Mass estimation and its applications, in: *Proceedings of the 16th ACM SIGKDD International Conference on Knowledge Discovery and Data Mining, KDD '10*, ACM, New York, NY, USA, 2010, pp. 989–998.

[238]   K. Ting, G.-T. Zhou, F. Liu, and S. Tan. Mass estimation. *Machine Learning*, 90(1), 127–160, 2013.

[239]   G. S. D. S. Jayakumar and B. J. Thomas. A new procedure of clustering based on multivariate outlier detection. *Journal of Data Science*, 11(1), 69–84, 2013.

[240]   M. Mohammadi and M. Sarmad. An outlier pruning prepr ocessing approach for support vector machine. In 13th Iranian Conference on Statistics, Shahid Bahonar Uvi. of Kerman, 2016, August, pp. 402–410.

[241] Z. Hu, M. Xiao, L. Zhang, S. Liu, and Y. Ge. Mahalanobis distance based approach for anomaly detection of analog filters using frequency features and Parzen window density estimation. *Journal of Electronic Testing*, 32(6), 681–693, 2016.

[242] S. Kumar, W. Tommy, and M. Pecht. Approach to fault identification for electronic products using Mahalanobis distance. *IEEE Transactions on Instrumentation and Measurement*, 59(8), 2055–2064, 2010.

[243] J. Fan, K. C. Yung, and M. Pecht. Anomaly detection for chromaticity shift of high power white LED with Mahalanobis distance approach, in: *Electronic Materials and Packaging (EMAP), 2012 14th International Conference on,* IEEE, December 2012, pp. 1–5.

[244] A. S. S. Vasan, B. Long, and M. Pecht. Diagnostics and prognostics method for analog electronic circuits. *IEEE Transactions on Industrial Electronics*, 2012. DOI:10.1109/TIE2012.2224074.

[245] E. M. Knorr and R. T. Ng. Algorithms for mining distance-based outliers in large dataset, in: *Proc. Of 24th International Conference on Very Large Data Bases (VLDB'98)*, New York, NY, USA, 1998, pp. 392–403.

[246] K. Beyer, J. Goldstein, R. Ramakrishnan, and U. Shaft. When is nearest neighbors meaningful? in: *Proc. of 7th International Conference on Database Theory (ICDT'99)*, Jerusalem, Israel, 1999, pp. 217–235.

[247] E. M. Knorr and R. T. Ng. Finding intentional knowledge of distance-based outliers, in: *Proc. Of 25th International Conference on Very Large Data Bases (VLDB'99)*, Edinburgh, Scotland, 1999, pp. 211–222.

[248] E. M. Knorr, R. T. Ng, and V. Tucakov. Distance-based outliers: Algorithms and applications. *VLDB Journal*, 8(3–4), 237–253, 2000.

[249] E. M. Knorr and R. T. Ng. A unified approach for mining outliers, in: *CASCON'97*, vol. 11, 1997.

[250] E. M. Knorr and R. T. Ng. A unified notion of outliers: Properties and computation, in: *KDD'97*, 1997, pp. 219–222.

[251] N. Beckmann, H.-P. Kriegel, R. Schneider, and B. Seeger. The $R*$-tree: An efficient and robust access method for points and rectangles, in: *Proc. of 1990 ACM SIGMOD International Conference on Management of Data (SIGMOD'90)*, Atlantic City, NJ, 1990, pp. 322–331.

[252] E. Eskin, A. Arnold, M. Prerau, L. Portnoy, and S. Stolfo. A geometric framework for unsupervised anomaly detection: Detecting intrusions in unlabeled data, in: *Applications of Data Mining in Computer Security*, Springer, Boston, MA, 2002, pp. 77–101.

[253] B. Wang, G. Xiao, H. Yu, and X. Yang. Distance-based outlier detection on uncertain data, in: *CIT (1), IEEE Computer Society*, 2009, pp. 293–298.

[254] E. M. Knox and R. T. Ng. Algorithms for mining distancebased outliers in large datasets. In: *Proceedings of the international conference on very large data bases*. Citeseer, pp. 392–403, 1998, August.

[255] S. Ramaswamy, R. Rastogi, and S. Kyuseok. Efficient algorithms for mining outliers from large data sets, in: *Proc. of 2000 ACM SIGMOD International*

Conference on Management of Data (SIGMOD'00), Dallas, Texas, 2000, pp. 427–438.

[256] F. Angiulli and C. Pizzuti. Fast outlier detection in high dimensional spaces, in: *Proc. of 6th European Conference on Principles and Practice of Knowledge Discovery in Databases (PKDD'02)*, Helsinki, Finland, 2002, pp. 15–26.

[257] T. M. Khoshgoftaar, S. V. Nath, and S. Zhong. Intrusion detection in wireless networks using clusterings techniques with expert analysis, in: *Proceedings of the Fourth International Conference on Machine Leaning and Applications (ICMLA'05)*, Los Angeles, CA, USA, 2005.

[258] S. Zhong, T. M. Khoshgoftaar, and S. V. Nath. A clustering approach to wireless network intrusion detection, in: *ICTAI*, 2005, pp. 190–196.

[259] W. Wang, J. Zhang, and H. Wang. Grid-ODF: Detecting outliers effectively and efficiently in large multidimensional databases, in: *Proc. of 2005 International Conference on Computational Intelligence and Security (CIS'05)*, Xi'an, China, 2005, pp. 765–770.

[260] H.-P. Kriegel, M. Schubert, and A. Zimek. Angle-based outlier detection in high-dimensional data, in: *Proc 14th ACM SIGKDD Int Conf on Knowledge Discovery and Data Mining (KDD)*, 2008, pp. 444–452.

[261] J. Liu and H. Deng. Outlier detection on uncertain data based on local information. *Knowledge-Based Systems*, 51, 60–71, 2013.

[262] S. A. Shaikh and H. Kitagawa. Efficient distance-based outlier detection on uncertain datasets of Gaussian distribution. *World Wide Web*, 17(4), 511–538, 2014.

[263] E. Schubert, A. Zimek, and H. P. Kriegel. Fast and scalable outlier detection with approximate nearest neighbor ensembles, in: *International Conference on Database Systems for Advanced Applications*, Springer, Cham, April 2015, pp. 19–36.

[264] X. T. Wang, D. R. Shen, M. Bai, T. Z. Nie, Y. Kou, and G. Yu. An efficient algorithm for distributed outlier detection in large multidimensional datasets. *Journal of Computer Science and Technology*, 30(6), 1233–1248, 2015.

[265] S. Mohseni and A. Fakharzade. A new local distance-based outlier detection approach for fuzzy data by vertex metric, in: *Knowledge-Based Engineering and Innovation (KBEI), 2015 2nd International Conference on*, IEEE, November 2015, pp. 551–554.

[266] H. Xu, R. Mao, H. Liao, H. Zhang, M. Lu, and G. Chen. Index based hidden outlier detection in metric space. *Scientific Programming*, 2016, 11, 2016.

[267] C. Cassisi, A. Ferro, R. Giugno, *et al.* Enhancing density based clustering: Parameter reduction and outlier detection. *Information Systems*, 38(3), 317–330, 2013.

[268] M. M. Breunig, H. P. Kriegel, R. T. Ng, and J. Sander. LOF: Identifying density-based local outliers. *ACM SIGMOD Record*, 29(2), 93–104, 2000.

[269] J. Tang, Z. Chen, A. W.-C. Fu, and D. W.-L. Cheung. Enhancing effectiveness of outlier detections for low density patterns, in: *Proc. 6th Pac.-Asia Conf. Knowl. Disc. Data Min. (PAKDD)*, 2002, pp. 535–548.

[270] W. Jin, A. K. H. Tung, J. Han, and W. Wang. Ranking outliers using symmetric neighborhood relationship, in: *Proc. 10th Pac.-Asia Conf. Knowl. Disc. Data Min. (PAKDD)*, 2006, pp. 577–593.

[271] S. Papadimitriou, H. Kitagawa, P. B. Gibbons, and C. Faloutsos. LOCI: Fast outlier detection using the local correlation integral, in: *ICDE'03*, vol. 315, 2003.

[272] M. M. Breunig, H.-P. Kriegel, R. T. Ng, and J. Sander. OPTICS-OF: Identifying local outliers, in: *PKDD'99*, 1999, pp. 262–270.

[273] W. Jin, A. K. H. Tung, and J. Han. Finding top n local outliers in large database, in: *Proc. of 7th ACM International Conference on Knowledge Discovery and Data Mining (SIGKDD'01)*, San Francisco, CA, USA, 2001, pp. 293–298.

[274] G. Bhattacharya, K. Ghosh, and A. S. Chowdhury. Outlier detection using neighborhood rank difference. *Pattern Recognition Letters*, 60, 24–31, 2015.

[275] J. Ha, S. Seok, and J. S. Lee. A precise ranking method for outlier detection. *Information Sciences*, 324, 88–107, 2015.

[276] D. Van Hieu and P. Meesad. Cell-DROS: A fast outlier detection method for big datasets. *International Journal of Advances in Soft Computing and its Applications*, 8(3), 2016, 1–17.

[277] Z. Zheng, H. Y. Jeong, T. Huang, and J. Shu. KDE based outlier detection on distributed data streams in multimedia network. *Multimedia Tools and Applications*, 76(17), 18027–18045, 2017.

[278] J. Liu and G. Wang. Outlier detection based on local minima density, in: *Information Technology, Networking, Electronic and Automation Control Conference*, IEEE, May 2016, pp. 718–723.

[279] L. Zhang, J. Lin, and R. Karim. Adaptive kernel density-based anomaly detection for nonlinear systems. *Knowledge-Based Systems*, 139, 50–63, 2018.

[280] B. Tang and H. He. A local density-based approach for outlier detection. *Neurocomputing*, 241, 171–180, 2017.

[281] E. Kirner, E. Schubert, and A. Zimek. Good and bad neighborhood approximations for outlier detection ensembles, in: *International Conference on Similarity Search and Applications*, Springer, Cham, October 2017, pp. 173–187.

[282] S. Zhang and J. Wan. Weight-based method for inside outlier detection. *Optik—International Journal for Light and Electron Optics*, 154, 145–156, 2018.

[283] M. Gupta, J. Gao, C. C. Aggarwal, and J. Han. Outlier detection for temporal data: A survey. *IEEE Transactions on Knowledge and Data Engineering*, 26(9), 2250–2267, 2014.

[284] C. C. Aggarwal. Outlier ensembles [position paper]. *ACM SIGKDD Explorations*, 14(2), 49–58, 2012.

[285] S. Rajasegarar, C. Leckie, and M. Palaniswami. Anomaly detection in wireless sensor networks. *IEEE Wireless Communications*, 15(4), pp. 34–40, 2008.

[286] O. Can and O. K. Sahingoz. A survey of intrusion detection systems in wireless sensor networks, in: *Modeling, Simulation, and Applied Optimization (ICMSAO), 2015 6th International Conference on*, IEEE, May 2015, pp. 1–6.

[287]   C. Modi, D. Patel, B. Borisaniya, H. Patel, A. Patel, and M. Rajarajan. A survey of intrusion detection techniques in cloud. *Journal of Network and Computer Applications*, 36(1), 42–57, 2013.

[288]   T. Anantvalee and J. Wu. A survey on intrusion detection in mobile ad hoc networks, in: *Wireless Network Security*, Springer, Boston, MA, USA, 2007, pp. 159–180.

[289]   T. F. Lunt. A survey of intrusion detection techniques. *Computers & Security*, 12(4), 405–418, 1993.

[290]   S. Axelsson. Intrusion detection systems: A survey and taxonomy. *Technical Report*, vol. 99, 2000.

[291]   P. Kabiri and A. A. Ghorbani. Research on intrusion detection and response: A survey. *International Journal of Network Security*, 1(2), 84–102, 2005.

[292]   F. Sabahi and A. Movaghar. Intrusion detection: A survey, in: *Systems and Networks Communications, 2008. ICSNC'08. 3rd International Conference on*, IEEE, October 2008, pp. 23–26.

[293]   A. Lazarevic, V. Kumar, and J. Srivastava. Intrusion detection: A survey, in: *Managing Cyber Threats*, Springer, Boston, MA, USA, 2005, pp. 19–78.

[294]   V. Hodge and J. Austin. A survey of outlier detection methodologies. *Artificial Intelligence Review*, 22(2), 85–126, 2004.

[295]   A. Zimek, E. Schubert, and H. P. Kriegel. A survey on unsupervised outlier detection in high-dimensional numerical data. *Statistical Analysis and Data Mining: The ASA Data Science Journal*, 5(5), 363–387, 2012.

[296]   V. Chandola, A. Banerjee and V. Kumar. Anomaly detection: A survey. Tech. rep. 07-017, Computer Science Department, University of Minnesota, pp. 83.

[297]   Tang, J., Chen, Z., Fu, A. W., & Cheung, D. W. (2007). Capabilities of outlier detection schemes in large datasets, framework and methodologies. Knowledge and Information Systems, 11(1), 45–84.

[298]   Youcef Djenouri and Arthur Zimek. 2018. Outlier Detection in Urban Traffic Data. In Proceedings of the 8th International Conference on Web Intelligence, Mining and Semantics (WIMS '18), ACM, New York, NY, USA, Article 3, 12 pages. DOI: https://doi.org/10.1145/3227609.3227692.

Chapter 12

Supporting Big Data at the vehicular edge

Lloyd Decker[1] and Stephan Olariu[1]

12.1 Introduction and motivation

Internet of Things (IoT) is a broad term encompassing any devices connected to the Internet. The first such devices that come to mind are smartphones, smart watches, smart glasses, tablet computers, smart meters, connected vehicles, etc. The number of these smart-device users is expected to exceed 4 billion by 2019, and Cisco predicts that the number of connected IoT devices will reach 50 billion by 2020 [1–4].

These devices form the periphery of the Internet and are referred to as *edge devices*. It was also predicted that, by 2019, the amount of data generated each month at the edge of the Internet by edge devices will surpass 24.3 EB [5]. Being rich in contextual information, the data generated at the edge may be extremely valuable. As contexts change frequently, the contextual data is inherently ephemeral and its value may decay rapidly over time. Due to the gap between available bandwidth and the volume of data generated at the edge, much of the data collected at the edge will have to be processed at the edge or it will be lost. Furthermore, the transient nature of this data will require it to be processed in near real time. Due to the latency costs in moving data between the edge and a datacenter or cloud, cloud-based real-time processing may neither be feasible nor economical. Hence, there is a need to process data at the edge.

It is interesting to note that edge devices offer computing and storage resources that, generally, remain underutilized. Indeed, it is estimated that the collective computing and storage capacity of smartphones has exceeded than that of worldwide servers at the end of 2017 [6]. These devices have the potential to take on the role of servers. For example, StoreDot (http://www.store-dot.com) and uBeam (http://ubeam.com) have demonstrated game-changing battery technologies. Implementations of LTE Direct [7], Wi-Fi Direct [8], and WiGig [9] standards will increase peer-to-peer connectivity among edge devices. Finally, container approaches such as Docker [10] on android will make application portable by addressing security and heterogeneity concerns for edge devices. This is similar to what virtualization has done for servers.

[1]Department of Computer Science, Old Dominion University, Norfolk, VA, USA

A particular edge device that is of unmistakable interest is the *smart car*. A smart car is a vehicle that not only has enough processing power and storage to handle the basics of running the vehicle but it has additional capacity to handle services for the operator of the vehicle. These could be situational awareness, entertainment, and communications. Many studies are underway to use the computing resources and sensor resources of the smart vehicles to create dynamic sensor networks. While the smartphone is currently the driving force in IoT, smart vehicles are quickly coming to prominence.

To any computer engineer or computer scientist, one of the greatest "disasters" is to have a processor sitting idle. A great deal of effort has been devoted to optimizing the flow of instructions through a processor to minimize wasted clock cycles. As with processors, any computing resource that is left idle is a waste of that resource. Vehicle networks are commonplace and many applications have been developed to utilize their sensor and computing resources. This is a great utilization of these resources as long as they are mobile. When the vehicles are parked, these resources are sitting idle. The question to ask is whether these resources could be put to use when the vehicles are not mobile. If the vehicles have connections to a larger computing infrastructure, they can put their resources toward that infrastructure. With enough vehicles interconnected, there exists a datacenter-computing environment that could handle many cloud-based application services. One such service is that of Big Data processing. This thesis will investigate the use of parked vehicles to form a datacenter infrastructure for supporting Big Data processing. This discussion will provide a baseline for this computing infrastructure, and the basis for further investigation on the use of these untapped resources.

The discussion of supporting Big Data at the vehicular edge will focus on a simple case of parked vehicles. A model will be created to evaluate processing Big Data using a datacenter comprising these parked vehicles. The model will simulate a datacenter implemented on the vehicles in the parking lot of a business that operates 24 h a day, 7 days a week. The employees of the business work in staggered 8-h shifts. This provides a pool of vehicles that can serve as the basis for a datacenter for the business. The vehicles in the parking lot are provided a standard power outlet for charging their vehicles in return for the use of their computing resources. The challenge of facing the implementation of the datacenter is to maintain high availability and reliability.

12.2   The Internet of Things

The expansion of broadband service and the ease at which to connect devices to broadband has created a surge in the number of devices connected to the Internet. No longer are computers the sole devices connecting to the Internet. Smartphones, coffee makers, washing machines, headphones, lamps, wearable devices, and almost anything else that you can think are being connected. The analyst firm Gartner says that by 2020 there will be over 26 billion connected devices [11]. Some think that this number is low. Cisco predicted that the number of connected IoT devices will reach 50 billion by 2020 [3,4]. Every day it seems that more and more devices are connecting to the Internet.

What is the purpose of all these connected devices? Does IoT constitute an end goal or a just means to an end? Being connected allows for a greater efficient use of our time. With greater connectivity comes the ability to efficiently use every waking moment of our day. No longer do you need to make a grocery list. Your refrigerator will keep track and order the groceries for you. No longer do you have down time while driving to work. Your smart vehicle will drive you to work allowing you to start your workday on the road. This seems to be something that makes our lives easier and less stressful. IoT is a tool that will provide the means to an end goal.

On a broader scale, the IoT can be applied to things like transportation networks: "smart cities" which can help us reduce waste and improve efficiency for things such as energy use [11]. At the heart of transportation networks is the smart vehicle. The sensor resources and computing resources of smart vehicles will combine to enable the smart cities of the future. The aggregate computing power of these vehicles will be tremendous and allow for the processing of the enormous volume of data from a variety of sensors.

While not addressed in this discussion, an important issue with IoT is security. There are many stories of smart houses that have been hacked. Hackers yelling at children through baby monitors, constantly changing the temperature on the thermostat, or unlocking the front door are all examples of the concerns in security [12]. Houses are not the only targets. Vehicles have become popular targets the more their onboard processors control more and more of the vehicles system. Hackers have demonstrated the ability to completely take over a vehicle from the driver. This included environmental, entertainment, steering, and engine control [13]. As the IoT grows, so must our vigilance in protecting the multitude of connected devices.

12.3   Big data processing

Our modern lives involve the collection of large quantities of data. The volume of this data is fueled by the IoT. If one were to doubt this, simply look at social media. It is not uncommon for a single person to create numerous high-definition photographs and video on a daily basis. Smartphones have enabled this and they are becoming an integral part of our lives. Smartphones are not the only means of collecting data. IoT includes numerous forms of data collection such as appliances, watches, smart cars, and sensor networks [14]. The volume of data being collected and subsequently analyzed is growing exponentially [15]. There is currently estimated over 15 billion devices, and it is estimated that this will increase to 30 billion devises by 2020 and increase to 75 billion devices by 2025 [16]. Furthermore, it is estimated that by 2019, monthly data generated by devices such as smartphones, wearable devices of all sorts, and vehicles will surpass 24.3 EB [5]. With these devices, comes the requirement to process the large data sets that are created.

An example of large data sets that need to be processed are those associated with e-commerce applications. In this context, the user's experience is of the utmost importance. Managing searches and shopping carts created by a prospective customer require the ability to efficiently store and recover a customer's information in the form of preferences, purchase histories, and returns. Any delays in presenting requested information to the customer could result in an unhappy customer who likely will not return [17].

Another example is associated with customer searches involving composite services. For example, a customer may need directions to a location along with hotels or restaurants near that location. The searching algorithms need to traverse all available paths and determine the most efficient route based upon current conditions. This requires near real-time processing of current sensor data for traffic conditions and processed data for hotels and restaurants. Furthermore, the sensor data and processed data may be located in various locations and must be processed and delivered to the customer in a timely fashion irrespective of how many servers may be down at any moment [18].

Big Data processing involves the processing of terabytes or petabytes of data. The size of the data involved obsoletes the traditional method of processing data where one application on one computer processes one set of data. With this method, the processing time of Big Data becomes so vast that the results are no longer worthwhile when the processing is done. Data processing at "near real" time is required. Latency is the biggest hurdle to the processing of Big Data. Hardware upgrades in the devices performing the processing are simply not capable of keeping pace with the exponential increase in the volume of data. Different strategies for the processing of data are required.

The idea is not to necessarily change upon what the processing is done. The method of processing the data is the key. As it turns out, emerging Big Data applications involve sophisticated multiphase data processing [19]. Google's MapReduce [20,21] and Apache's Hadoop [22–24] are the options that enable the processing of Big Data. The processing performed by MapReduce has two sequential stages, Map and Reduce. In the map phase, a user-defined function is applied to every logical input record to produce an intermediate result of key-value pairs. The reduce stage collects all the key-value pairs produced by the map stage and collapses them using yet another user-supplied function [21]. This method utilizes the idea of distributed computing. By using multiple nodes to process both the map and reduce phases, a large increase of performance can be expected [25].

12.4 Cloud computing and the datacenter

Cloud computing has become a driving force in computing and application deployment. Cloud computing is a method of consolidating computing resources into large facilities [26]. This allows the cost to be minimized in infrastructure costs. It also allows for the ease of administration. Virtualization of computing resources allows for an abstraction from physical servers. This in turn allows for efficient use of resources. It also allows for maintenance and reliability. Virtualized computing resources are simply migrated to physical servers that need maintenance or repair.

Cloud computing allows businesses to provide computing resources to customers. This could range for resources for a single application or for large-scale database and search engines. Simply put, cloud computing is the delivery of computing services such as servers, storage, databases, networking, software, and analytics [27]. Customers only pay for what they need. This allows for lower costs for the customers since they do not incur overhead costs of physical resources, facilities, and personnel [27]. In general, there are three types of cloud services offered to customers. These are Infrastructure as a Service (IaaS), Platform as a Service (PaaS), and Software as a Service (SaaS) [28].

IaaS offers its customers full computing resources such as computing and storage. The customer specifies how many processors, how much random-access memory, and how much storage is needed. The cloud-computing company provides virtual servers to the customer. An example is Amazon Web Services. Amazon provides its customers' computing resources through the Elastic Compute Cloud and storage both Simple Storage Services and Elastic Book Store [29].

PaaS offers its customers a platform on which to develop applications. This frees the customer from maintaining infrastructure needed to develop their applications. A good example of this type of service would be web hosting. Customers design and implement their web sites with nothing more than a web browser. Google AppEngine [30] and Microsoft Azure [31] are examples of this type of cloud service.

SaaS is a "pay-as-you-go" application subscription service. Customers can simply purchase software that they require. This is a benefit to customers who cannot afford the cost of expensive software and the resources required. Google AppEngine [30] is an example of this type of service.

At the heart of the cloud computing is the datacenter [26]. The datacenter is a collection of hardware components such as servers, routers, network switches, and disk libraries [28]. These datacenters can range in size from a single room to that of a large warehouse.

12.5 A survey of recent work on vehicular clouds

A review of previous work with vehicular clouds is in order. The first papers to introduce the idea of vehicular clouds were of Eltoweissy *et al.* [32] and Olariu *et al.* [33–36]. These papers introduced a cluster of vehicles as a means for creating a cloud-computing environment. They presented various possibilities and configurations of vehicle clouds. Research has also offered the viability of vehicle clouds with current technology [33,34].

Arif *et al.* [37] investigated datacenters created from the vehicles parked in a parking lot of a major airport. They presented a stochastic model for predicting the occupancy of the parking lot based upon given time-varying arrival and departure times. They derived a probability distribution for the occupancy of the parking lot as a function of time. They confirmed their model with empirical results.

Vignesh *et al.* [38] investigated services that could be provided by a vehicular cloud. They detailed a master-provider model in which certain vehicles act as controllers (master) and others act as workers (provider). In a Computation as a Service role, the master receives requests for computation from user clients. The master then determines the best available vehicle participant to handle the computational request. In a SaaS role, the master receives storage requests form user clients. The master then determines the optimal vehicle participant to handle the storage. All user clients request and associate data flow through the vehicle masters.

Hussain *et al.* [39] proposed a network consisting of both a vehicular network and a conventional cloud-computing environment. Roadside gateway terminals provided connectivity between the vehicular network and the ground-based cloud-computing environment.

He *et al.* [40] proposed services that could be provided by new IoT-based vehicular data clouds. These services include predicting road safety, reducing road congestion, and recommending vehicle maintenance. One useful service that any frustrated driver attempting to find a parking spot would appreciate is that of a service that would direct the driver to the most appropriate parking spot for their needs. They stressed that IoT-based vehicular data clouds need to be efficient, scalable, secure, and reliable. They concluded that existing algorithms and mechanisms are unsatisfactory to meet all these needs simultaneously.

Florin *et al.* [41] investigated a vehicular cloud based on vehicles in parking lot of a medium-sized business. They determined that current wireless technology could not efficiently support Big Data applications on a vehicular cloud. They investigated migration techniques to increase the reliability of Big Data processing on vehicular clouds.

12.6　Our contributions

The concept of cloud computing based upon vehicle networks is an interesting subject. It has been proposed in many papers. The majority have discussed forming clouds upon nonstationary vehicles utilizing wireless communications. Our work has concluded that wireless communications in its current incarnation will not support Big Data processing on a vehicle network. It is yet to be determined if wireless communications can progress to the point in the near future where Big Data processing will be practical.

One of the biggest concerns for vehicular clouds is that of vehicular residency. Arif *et al.* [37] presented a stochastic model for predicting the occupancy of a vehicle in an airport parking lot. While this is of great help to vehicular clouds with longer residency times and a modicum of knowledge of arrival and departure statistics, this does not help for vehicular clouds with completely random arrival, departure, and residency times. This is more akin to what one might find in a general vehicular cloud. Furthermore, this would be more in line with other IoT devices such as smartphones. It is the goal to use the research on vehicular clouds as a basis to study the use of other IoT devices to form clouds such as using smartphones. Our goal is to investigate the feasibility of a vehicular cloud that operates with no knowledge of arrival, departure, and residency. While we will investigate a model that has well-defined arrival, departure, and residency times, this information is not "given" to the simulation.

As with all research endeavors, finding incarnations of theoretical models that are practical is the challenge. Since we assume that the residency is neither known nor predictable, migration techniques used by Florin *et al.* [41] are not used. Furthermore, scalability is a cause for much concern as discovered by He *et al.* [40]. Our approach is that simple mechanisms scale easier than more complex mechanisms.

While this model has been previously examined, we take a unique look at a practical model that cannot forecast the residency of a vehicle in the vehicular cloud. This removes the idea of migration of processing as a means of redundancy. Our model is similar to flow control in the Transmission Control Protocol. If a piece of a job does not complete, it is simply restarted. This is predicated on finding a way to segment a job into smaller pieces that prevent the restart from being a major impact on the overall performance. This segmentation is currently the center of a great deal research. It is the idea that job segmentation will become a common element of Big Data processing.

12.7 The vehicle datacenter model

A datacenter utilizing a vehicular cloud would be similar to any existing datacenter that supports cloud computing. The major difference is that the physical servers for the cloud architecture are no longer located within server racks in a large building. The physical servers themselves are distributed within a large parking lot. The vehicles are the servers. This discussion does not deal with small parking lots with few vehicles resident. The topic of this discussion deals with large parking lots with many vehicles that are resident for a long period of time. This is the case for airports and medium-to-large businesses that operate 24 h a day and 365 days a year. The latter will be the focus of discussions.

The model will simulate a datacenter implemented on the vehicles in the parking lot of a business that operates 24 h a day and 365 days a year. The employees of the business work on staggered 8-h shifts. This provides a pool of vehicles that can serve as the basis for a datacenter for the business. The vehicles in the parking lot are provided a standard power outlet for charging their vehicles in return for the use of their computing resources. Wireless connections to local access points (APs) are provided for all vehicles. The challenge facing the implementation of the datacenter is to maintain high availability and reliability.

The business is a medium-size establishment that employs 7,680 people and operates around the clock, 7 days a week. Each employee drives their own vehicle to work. To avoid bottlenecks in the parking lot, the business implements staggered 8-h shifts. In the beginning of each shift, 320 employees end their workday and leave the plant, only to be replaced by 320 fresh employees that start their 8-h workday. The parking lot has a capacity to park 2,560 vehicles. The 320 vehicles belonging to departing employees leave the parking lot before the 320 new vehicles pull in. There are no reserved slots and an employee picks a random slot when arriving. In this manner, the parking lot remains full during the entire day excluding the change of vehicles at the top of each hour. For the sake of simplicity, there is no time between the departing and arriving vehicles.

The vehicle datacenter offers its users a virtualized instance of their desired hardware platform and operating system bundled as a virtual machine (VM). This VM with associated operating system is hosted by a vehicle in the parking lot. The vehicles are assumed to have been preloaded with a suitable VM monitor that maps between the VM and the vehicle's resources. Each vehicle can host multiple VMs and has ample disk space to accommodate VMs and any data being processed. The size of the VMs is uniformly 1 GB.

The customers of the vehicle datacenter run MapReduce jobs whose durations are uniformly distributed between 2 and 24 h. The duration of a job is taken to be the amount of time it takes the job to execute in the absence of any overhead. Each customer's job takes an input of 2 GB of raw data and generates final data uniformly distributed between 0.5 and 2 GB in size. Specifically, the MapReduce job generates the same amount of intermediate data (at the end of the map stage) and final data (at the end of the reduce stage).

The network that interconnects the vehicles in the parking lot is organized in a tree architecture. The root of the tree is a switch called the datacenter controller (DC). DC has four children, termed region controllers (RCs). Each RC is a switch and has four children, termed group controllers (GCs). Finally, each GC is a switch and has four children, termed AP. Each AP is a switch in connecting a cluster of 40 parking spots (vehicles). The vehicles in a cluster communicate solely through their designated AP. The links between DC and RCs are 40 Gbps. The links between the RCs and GCs and the links between the GCs and the APs are 10 Gbps. Finally, the links between the APs and the vehicles are 1 Gbps.

12.8   The vehicle datacenter simulation

The goal of this simulation is to create a vehicle cloud upon the vehicles in a parking lot of a medium-sized business. The parking lot is assumed to be constantly full. When a vehicle leaves, there is another to take its place. The emphasis on the simulation is the effect of random residency times, not that of capacity. The simulation consists of a DC, a resource manager, a job manager, log manager, a network, and vehicles in the parking lot. The binary code for this simulation is available upon request.

12.8.1   Datacenter controller

The DC is assumed to be ground based. This means that it is not a vehicle but is a resource that is provided to the vehicular cloud. This model is similar to the model presented by Hussain *et al.* [39]. It comprises a resource manager, job manager, and log manager (see Figure 12.1).

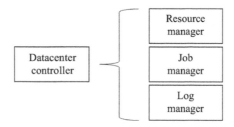

Figure 12.1   Components of the datacenter controller

12.8.2   Resource manager

The resource manager handles the acceptance of user's jobs for processing. It handles the injection of jobs into the system via the job manager. The resource manager keeps track of the number of current jobs being processed. It compares the number of current jobs being processed to the maximum number of simultaneous jobs allowed. If this maximum has not been reached, new jobs are sent to the job manager until the maximum number of simultaneous jobs is reached.

The resource manager is responsible for polling the parking spaces to determine the occupancy of a space. It is further responsible for polling the vehicles to determine if the vehicle is available for task assignment. In other words, it maintains information on the status of the parking spaces and vehicles. The resource manager is responsible for selecting available vehicles for job assignment. These assignments can be for job processing or for backups for intermediate data backups. Furthermore, it handles all downloads and uploads of data. This could be VM images, raw data, or final processed data.

12.8.3   Job manager

The job manager controls each job that is submitted by the user for processing. This entails many tasks. The job manager divides the job into sub-jobs for processing. This is the core idea for this simulation, divide the job into smaller pieces and perform parallel processing. The job manager requests resources from the resource manager to perform the job processing. It requests the allocation following vehicles for the user's job: one vehicle for each sub-job processing and two vehicles for each sub-job to act as backups for intermediate data. The job manager identifies the VM that is required for the user's job. It directs the resource manager to download the VM to all allocated vehicles. It further directs the resource manager to download the respective sub-job raw data to the allocated vehicles for processing.

The job object keeps track of the progress of the overall job and all sub-jobs by the means of seven designated levels (see Figure 12.2). Before the overall job progresses from one level to the next, all the sub-jobs need to have completed the current level. Level 0 is the assignment of vehicles to handle the processing of the job. Level 1 is the downloading of the VM and raw data to allocated vehicles. Level 2 is the map phase of the data processing. Level 3 is the collection and backing up of intermediate

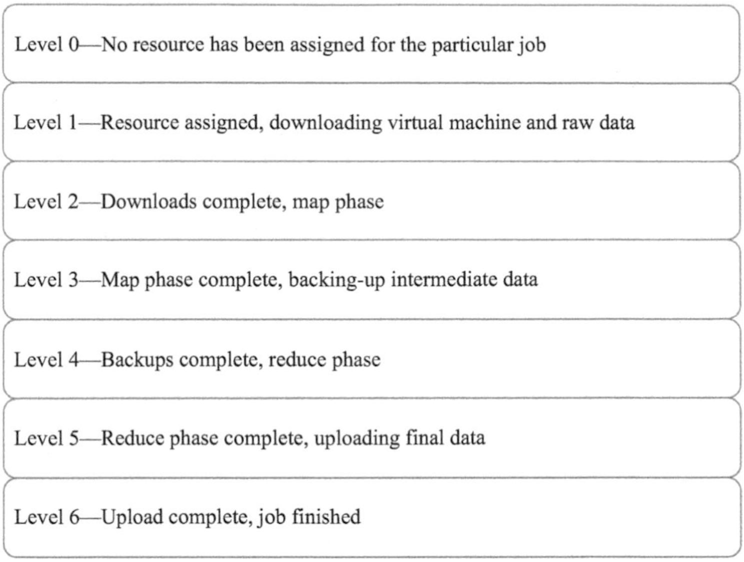

| Level 0—No resource has been assigned for the particular job |

| Level 1—Resource assigned, downloading virtual machine and raw data |

| Level 2—Downloads complete, map phase |

| Level 3—Map phase complete, backing-up intermediate data |

| Level 4—Backups complete, reduce phase |

| Level 5—Reduce phase complete, uploading final data |

| Level 6—Upload complete, job finished |

Figure 12.2   Levels of job completion

data vehicles allocated to handle the backups. Level 4 is the reduce phase. Level 5 is the uploading of the final processed data to the datacenter. Level 6 designated the job as being complete.

12.8.4   Log manager

The log manager is responsible for logging the statistics of the user's jobs for the entire simulation. Once a simulation has reached its prescribed number of time intervals, all statistics for evaluation are logged by the DC. These are recorded to a file for the specifics of the completed simulation. A separate running file is used to record the statistics for all the simulations being run.

12.8.5   Network

The parking lot consists of a set number of parking spaces. Each of these parking spaces keeps track of the occupancy of a vehicle. Furthermore, the vehicle maintains information on whether it is currently running a job. It also keeps track of when it arrives and leaves the parking lot. It is assumed that the vehicles in the parking lot are resident for eight consecutive hours. While this knowledge would facilitate the migration of working jobs in a preemptive manner, the intent of this thesis is to investigate the viability of the vehicle datacenter to perform with no knowledge of residency and therefore not perform any preemptive migrations. The vehicles will form a network node on the network. This will be done via the network interface associated with each parking space.

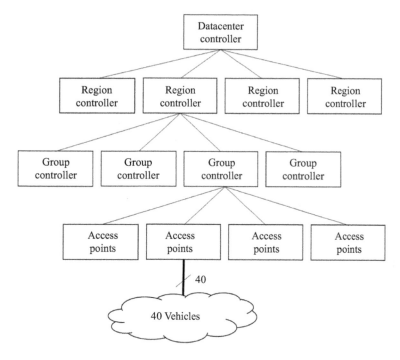

Figure 12.3   Network tree hierarchy

The network consists of a tree structure with the vehicles in the parking spaces being the leaf nodes (see Figure 12.3). The root of the network tree is a network switch that comprises the core layer of the network. The datacenter attaches directly to the core and forms the DC. There exist two levels of network switches comprising the distribution layer of the network. These are the RC and the GC. There are four RCs directly connected under the datacenter switch. Under each RC, there are four GCs. The access layer of the network comprises the access controllers. They are either wireless APs in the wireless model or network switches in the wired model. There are four access controllers connected to each GC. Each access controller can support 40 vehicles.

The network switches are those that may be found in a current high-performance network. All connections are wired. The throughput of the connections between the DCs and the RCs are 40 Gbps. The throughput of the connections between the RCs, GCs, and APs are 10 Gbps. The last-mile connections between the APs and the vehicles are 1 Gbps.

The simulation of the complexity of a packet network is accomplished by using average throughput over a time interval. Since greater time intervals create a larger error in throughput simulation, smaller time intervals are utilized. In the case of this simulation, 1 s time interval is used. The simulation of network traffic is a two-part process. The first counts the number of connections across each link between nodes.

The second calculates the bandwidth for an entire communication path between two nodes.

The first part involves calculating all traffic paths for all communications that will occur in the next time interval. Every link is marked with the number of communication paths that will traverse it. If the link is a full duplex link, as in the case of most wired links, just one communication path is added to the link for communications between two nodes. This is done since transmitting and receiving can be accomplished simultaneously on a full duplex link. If the link is half duplex, as is the case for most wireless links, two communication paths are added to the link for communications between two nodes. For this simulation, multicast traffic is not simulated. All traffic is unicast traffic. Furthermore, the 80% threshold of half duplex connections is ignored. This means that 100% of a link's bandwidth is assumed to be used.

The second part involves calculating the bandwidth for each link that will be available in the next time increment. This is accomplished by dividing the link's bandwidth by the number of connections utilizing that link in the next time increment. This implies that there is no priority of service and every communication is allocated an equal bandwidth on all links. Then each communication path is evaluated to determine the bandwidth for the entire path. This is done by finding the link with the lowest bandwidth along the communication path for each communication path. This negates any possibility of buffer overruns on network devices and the associated retransmits that occur due to the buffer overrun.

12.8.6   Vehicles

The vehicles are assumed to have a VM manager preinstalled prior to parking in the parking lot. This will allow them to host a VM with the user-preferred operating system that will be used as a node in the vehicle cloud. This node will be used in the processing of a user's Big Data job. In essence, these components can be seen as stacking upon one another. As Figure 12.4 shows, the VM manager is installed on the vehicle hardware. The VM with the user's operating system is installed on the VM manager. The VM is then able to handle user jobs. The jobs are assigned by the DC.

12.9   Empirical performance evaluation

In accordance with design of experiment techniques, the variables for this simulation are grouped into two categories: factors and response variables. Factors are those variables that are considered to be the independent variables that are changed in order to test the performance of the system. Response variables are the dependent variables that are recorded to investigate the performance of the system. The purpose of this simulation is to determine if a vehicular datacenter is a viable mechanism for the processing of Big Data. The important aspect of this model is that no migrations of jobs are allowed. This simple model serves to baseline a model for further study. It is necessary to find a configuration that proves the viability of processing Big Data at the vehicular edge. Only if this is the case would further study be practical. Furthermore,

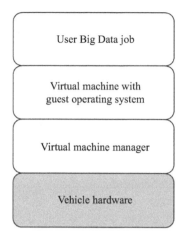

Figure 12.4   Virtual machine hierarchy

Table 12.1   Simulation factors

Simulation factors	Method	Values
Size of parking lot	Static	2,560 vehicles
Residency time of vehicles	Static	8 h
Network configuration	Static	Tree
Network throughput	Static	40–10–1 Gbps
Percentage of vehicles tasked	Static	100%
Number of worker objects	Static	5 workers
Number of simultaneous jobs	Varied	100, 200, 300, 400, 500, 600, 700, 800, 900, 1,000
Size of jobs	Varied	3,600, 7,200, 10,800, 14,400, 18,000, 21,600, 25,200, 28,800, 32,400, 36,000, 39,600, 43,200

future innovations to the model can then be compared with the baseline to form a tradeoff analysis between cost and performance of the innovation.

12.9.1   Simulation factors

Many factors will affect the viability of the simulation results. Factors were prioritized based upon their impact on the simulation. These factors with associated priorities are listed in Table 12.1. A process was then employed to evaluate the factors to determine the most viable simulation.

12.9.1.1   Size of parking lot

As previously described, the simulation will model a medium-sized business with a 2,560 space parking lot. Many different settings were possible. Airport parking lots, large shopping-center parking lots, and arena parking lots were all viable solutions. It was decided that a scenario with a set size parking lot with a guaranteed full occupancy would be the ideal model. This is the model that is reflected with the medium-sized business.

12.9.1.2   Residency time of vehicles

Many different models could be used for the residency of vehicles in the parking lot. Stochastic models have been developed to model the residency time of vehicles in airport parking lots. These same models could be used to predict arena or shopping-mall parking lot residency. While migration is not considered to be an option for this particular model, static residency times are used to create a simplified model for a baseline case. In this thesis, we assume that the residency time for each vehicle is 8 h. This being said, the simulation does not allow any prediction to time remaining for each vehicle. When the vehicles leave the parking lot, it is as though they randomly left the parking lot. Truly random residency will be left for further investigation.

12.9.1.3   Network configuration

The network configuration chosen for this simulation is that of a tree. This model creates a simplified network approach that also helps to distribute the network traffic across network components. It also helps to simplify the network simulation.

12.9.1.4   Network throughput

A completely wired model was used for this simulation. Current network technologies were used as the basis for the network throughput model. The throughput of the connections between the DCs and the RCs is 40 Gbps. The throughput of the connections between the RCs, GCs, and APs is 10 Gbps. The last-mile connections between the APs and the vehicles are 1 Gbps. For purposes of simplicity, multicast traffic was not allowed.

12.9.1.5   Percentage of vehicles tasked

Since migration is not allowed for this model, it is assumed that all available vehicles will be tasked. This enables the full utilization of the parking lot. In other words, 100% of vehicles are available for tasking. If a job requires a vehicle and none are available, the job must wait until vehicles become available.

12.9.1.6   Number of worker objects

The simulation will be run with a range of different number of workers. The number of workers corresponds to the number of sub-jobs that will be created from each job. For this simulation, a value of five workers per job is used.

12.9.1.7   Number of simultaneous jobs

A simple job-injection model is used for this simulation. It simply creates new jobs until a specified number of jobs are reached. This is considered to be the number of simultaneous jobs. These values range from 100 to 1,000 in increments of 100 simultaneous jobs.

12.9.1.8 Size of jobs

The simulation will be run having random job sizes ranging from 2 to 24 h in length. To better understand the impact of job sizes on the efficacy of the system, the simulation will also be run with set job sizes ranging between 2 and 24 h in length.

12.9.2 Response variables

There are two response variables for this simulation. They are the number of jobs completed during a simulation run and the average time to complete a job. These will be used to evaluate the viability of the vehicle datacenter.

12.10 Simulation results

To understand the impact of factors on the response variables, some factors are held constant while others are evaluated to find a viable model. This becomes the baseline for future research. Toward this end, a step-by-step refinement process is used. The first step is to evaluate the correlation of job completion times for set job sizes. Then a performance comparison is conducted between job completion times for models with set job sizes compared to that of the job completion times of models with random job sizes.

12.10.1 Correlation of job completion times

A series of simulations are run for set job sizes and number of simultaneous jobs. The goal of this is to determine if for each combination of job size and number of simultaneous jobs, the average completion time will become consistent over time. In other words, the system will become stable over time and not become unstable and average completion times increase without bounds. If the completion times do not stabilize then that case of job size and number of simultaneous jobs would have to be considered not viable. To this end, it is desired that the job completion times will approach a static state correlation. For the 12 different job sizes and 10 different number of simultaneous jobs, there are 120 combinations tested. With these, there were discovered to be three levels of correlation: strong, weak, and none.

Figure 12.5 represents a case of strong correlation. The figure shows the completion times of each job in the order in which they were completed. As the simulation starts, there is a ramp-up of completion times. The important thing to note is that the completion times settle into a consistent and stable average. This is evident in the horizontal swath of completion times. This case of strong correlation would represent a viable vehicle datacenter model for the given job size and number of simultaneous jobs.

Figure 12.6 represents a case of weak correlation. As with the previous figure, the figure shows the completion times of each job in the order in which they were completed. As the simulation starts, there is a ramp-up of completion times. After the ramp-up, the completion times appear to settle into an average, but it is not definitive. This is evident in the loose group of completion times. This case of weak correlation

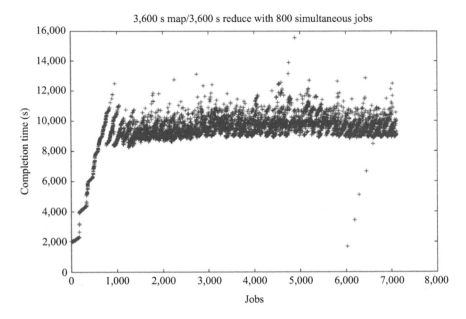

Figure 12.5   Example of strong correlation

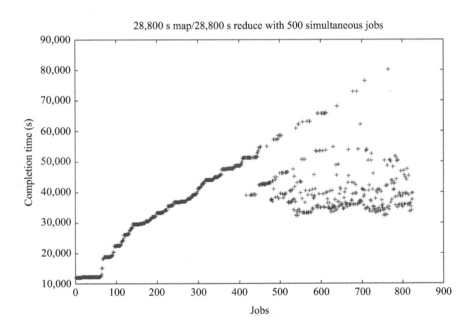

Figure 12.6   Example of weak correlation

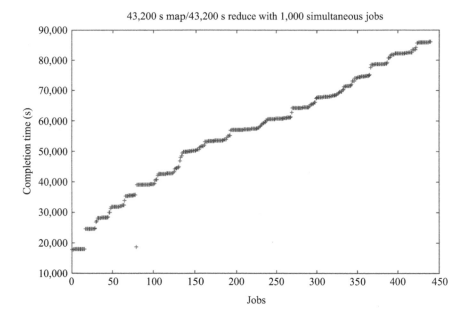

Figure 12.7   Example of no correlation

implies that a viable vehicle datacenter is possible for the given job size and number of simultaneous jobs.

Figure 12.7 represents a case of no correlation. As with the previous figure, the figure shows the completion times of each job in the order in which they were completed. As the simulation starts, there is a ramp-up of completion times. The important issue is that the ramp-up does not stop for the duration of the simulation. This case of no correlation represents that a vehicle datacenter is not viable for the given job size and number of simultaneous jobs.

Table 12.2 summarizes the correlations for each of the 120 combinations. The results reveal that the vehicle datacenter is viable for job sizes of 3,600–14,400 s across all numbers of simultaneous job sizes. The vehicle datacenter is possible for all other job sizes except in the cases of large job sizes and large numbers of simultaneous jobs. As the number of simultaneous jobs increases, the available resources are overwhelmed. This causes a great deal of contention for resources and results in the model not being viable for large job sizes with large numbers of simultaneous jobs.

12.10.2   Performance between random and set job sizes

Now that a baseline of simulations has identified the behavior of set job sizes, simulations are run to identify the behavior with random job sizes. The series of simulations that are run for set job sizes are compared to the simulations run for random job sizes. The intention is to see if each job size within the random job sizes will follow the average completion time as for the set job size simulation runs. In other words,

Table 12.2   Summarization of correlations

Job size (s)	Number of simultaneous jobs									
	100	200	300	400	500	600	700	800	900	1,000
3,600	Strong	Strong	Strong	Strong	Strong	Strong	Strong	Strong	Strong	Strong
7,200	Strong	Strong	Strong	Strong	Strong	Strong	Strong	Strong	Strong	Strong
10,800	Strong	Strong	Strong	Strong	Strong	Strong	Strong	Strong	Strong	Strong
14,400	Strong	Strong	Strong	Strong	Strong	Strong	Strong	Strong	Strong	Strong
18,000	Weak	Weak	Weak	Weak	Weak	Weak	Weak	Weak	Weak	Weak
21,600	Weak	Weak	Weak	Weak	Weak	Weak	Weak	Weak	Weak	Weak
25,200	Weak	Weak	Weak	Weak	Weak	Weak	Weak	Weak	Weak	No
28,800	Weak	Weak	Weak	Weak	Weak	Weak	Weak	Weak	No	No
32,400	Weak	Weak	Weak	Weak	Weak	Weak	Weak	No	No	No
36,000	Weak	Weak	Weak	Weak	Weak	No	No	No	No	No
39,600	Weak	Weak	Weak	Weak	Weak	No	No	No	No	No
43,200	Weak	Weak	Weak	Weak	Weak	No	No	No	No	No

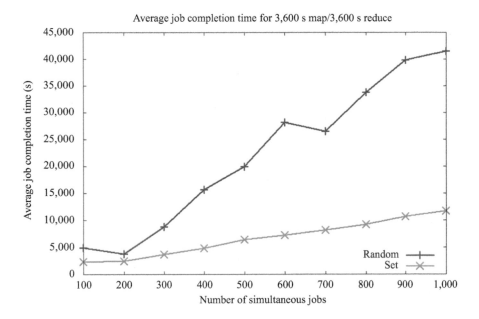

Figure 12.8   Small job size comparison

determine if vehicle datacenter will be able to process numerous different size jobs simultaneously with the same performance as handling only set sized jobs.

Figure 12.8 demonstrates that for the 3,600 s job sizes, the randomizing of job sizes has a significant effect on job completion time. The average completion times for the jobs in the randomized job-size simulations are considerably higher than that for

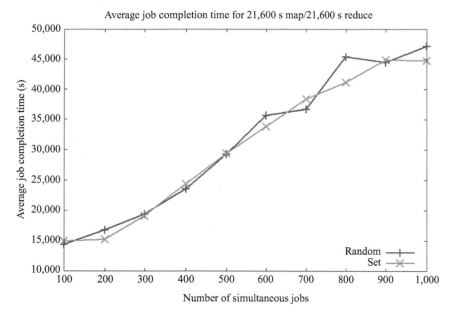

Figure 12.9   Medium job size comparison

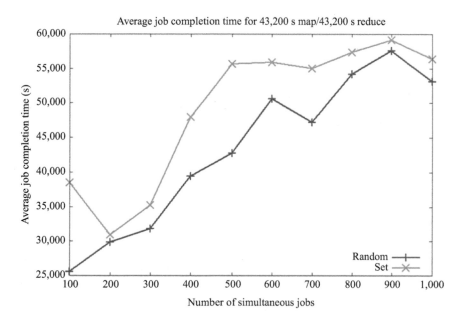

Figure 12.10   Large job size comparison

the set job size simulations. Figure 12.9 demonstrates that for the 21,600 s job sizes, the randomizing of job sizes does not affect the job-completion time. An interesting result is found for the 43,200 s job sizes. Figure 12.10 demonstrates that for the 43,200 s job sizes, the randomizing of job sizes has an effect on the job-completion time. The average completion times for the jobs in the randomized job-size simulations are lower than that for the set job-size simulations. This cannot be taken as ground truth since the previous section determined that large job sizes have a weak to no correlation on average job completion times.

12.11   Concluding remarks

This model took a simplistic approach to handling Big Data by utilizing a simple divide and conquer approach. Large jobs are divided into smaller subtasks that can be processed in parallel. This division helps to reduce the time requirement for any one node in the datacenter thereby reducing the need for long residency times. The model does not predict residency times. Even with this limitation, it has been shown that a vehicular datacenter could be effectively implemented under certain conditions. It must be noted that with five workers per job, the total vehicle allocation for each job is 15 vehicles. This results from every one of the workers having two vehicle backups. With this allocation, the 2,560 vehicles in the vehicle datacenter become fully allocated around 170 simultaneous jobs. Unsurprisingly, analysis revealed that large job sizes with large number of simultaneous jobs were not viable. However, with the proper throttling of simultaneous jobs, the vehicle datacenter is viable.

12.12   Looking into the crystal ball

A baseline has now been conducted and shown that a viable datacenter can be created from collection of vehicles in a parking lot. This opens the door to a wide variety of interesting research. At the very least, the vehicle datacenter model can now be refined. Scheduling managers could be used to inject job sizes based upon utilization or prioritization. Migration techniques could be employed to reduce job restarts. With the baseline that has been produced, the cost of implementation of performance improvements can be weighted with the actual performance improvements to determine that viability of these improvements.

The vehicle datacenter could be expanded to dynamic datacenters. This vehicle datacenter has been constructed here in a parking lot that guarantees a specific capacity. However, there are many other occurrences of vehicles coming together. For example, shopping malls and athletic events. What if these vehicles could be organized into dynamic datacenters to serve needed services? In shopping malls, the vehicle datacenters could run applications supporting the customers' needs. These could deliver advertisements offered dynamically for the stores in the shopping mall. They could notify of the lengths of checkout lines at stores so that customers could adjust their shopping patterns. It must be noted that the need for these applications would be proportional to the number of customers. In other words, the dynamic datacenter would be a good fit for the dynamic need of the applications.

This dynamic need would be even more appropriate for athletic events. As parking lots fill with vehicles and "tail gate parties," finding an available parking space and route to that parking space becomes a daunting task. An application to alleviate this would be greatly needed. Furthermore, finding one's seat can be difficult enough without adding numerous other people trying to find their seat causing pedestrian congestion. What if an application existed to guide one efficiently to their seat? This would then reduce the number of seating attendants needed. Finally, the most important aspects of all athletic events are that of food and restrooms. No one wants to wait long periods for either. An application displaying the lines at all concessions and restrooms could limit the time away from the event increasing the enjoyment of the attendees.

One of the most exciting technologies on the horizon is that of the smart city. Smart vehicles will play an important role in the creation of smart cities. Smart vehicles will fully utilize their abilities. Smart vehicles will be processing nodes, sensor nodes, data-aggregator nodes, and consuming nodes. The datacenter has been shown to utilize the smart vehicle as a processing node. With just this, a smart city with total communication coverage could make every vehicle a processing node. With constant communications, residency is not an issue. With an easy gathering of hundreds of thousands of people with similar numbers of smart vehicles, the datacenter becomes enormous. Think of the computing power of 200,000 processing nodes.

The smart vehicle also has sensor capabilities. Add to this, the data aggregation capability of smart vehicles and there now exists a powerful tool for the smart city. In the case of traffic patterns, the smart vehicle could aggregate data from other vehicles to provide recommendations to the smart city to alter traffic lights. For example, someone is sitting at a red light and seeing the next light in their path show green while no traffic approaches only to have that further light turn red when their light turns green is a great annoyance and a cause of congestion. Smart vehicles could help the smart city optimize the use of signals so that traffic is nearly always flowing through traffic signals.

Of course, the smart vehicle would be a consumer of data. Self-driving cars are becoming more and more a reality. Smart cars in smart cities would be self-driving. Route selection, traffic avoidance, and parking are all consuming data that a vehicle would require.

A very promising variation of the vehicle datacenter is that of hybrid storage. If there existed a central storage facility that allowed all vehicles to mount external storage, then virtualization becomes a viable option for all vehicles regardless of their transient nature. A vehicle mounts the external storage and executes a VM image that is stored on that external storage. This reduces the "spin-up" time of the VM since the entire operating system does not have to be downloaded. Furthermore, any data that needs to be processed is accessed and saved on the external storage. This prevents the necessity of downloading a large data set before processing the data. The most important aspect of this is that a memory file of the working VM is kept on the external storage. This allows a vehicle to in theory pick up a terminated VM from another vehicle quickly and efficiently.

This idea holds great potential when working in conjunction with small footprint-operating systems. These small VMs can be created to support individual applications making them extremely small. This would allow a smart city processing manager to assign these VMs to vehicles with no concern of loss of data or functionality. If a vehicle is suddenly removed from the network, the VM, memory file, and data are assigned to another vehicle. This vehicle would then launch the VM and memory file and continue processing data with little time interruption and not loss of data.

This would also be a great benefit to smart vehicles that are acting as data aggregators. Vehicles will collect a large amount of data. The vehicle will need to decide which data is worth keeping and which is not. This sometimes requires applications to process both local and external data to find the relevance of the local data. These applications could be small VMs that the vehicle "spins-up" to perform the analysis of the data. Finally, any processed data is then stored on the external storage thereby saving space on the vehicle and assuring that the processed data is persistent and available to others.

References

[1]   eMarketer, "Tablet users to surpass 1 billion worldwide in 2015," January 2015. [Online]. Available: http://www.emarketer.com/Article/Tablet-Users-Surpass-1-Billion-Worldwide-2015/1011806.

[2]   eMarketer, "Worldwide smartphone usage grow 25% in 2014," June 2014. [Online]. Available: http://www.emarketer.com/Article/Worldwide-Smartphone-Usage-Grow-25-2014/1010920.

[3]   Directive Outsource IT, C. Chase, "The internet of things as the next big thing," June 2013. [Online]. Available: http://www.directive.com/blog/item/the-internet-of-things-as-the-next-big-thing.html.

[4]   WIRED, S. Amyx, "Why the internet of things will disrupt everything," July 2014. [Online]. Available: http://innovationinsights.wired.com/insights/2014/07/internet-things-will-disrupt-everything.

[5]   Advanced Network Systems, "Global mobile data traffic forecast update, 2014–2019," March 2015. [Online]. Available: http://www.fastdas.com/uploads/3/4/7/6/34761169/cisco_white_paper_c11-520862.pdf.

[6]   IBM Research Zurich, A. P. Haig, "Data at the edge, IBM global technology outlook," 2015. [Online]. Available: http://www-935.ibm.com/services/multimedia/Vortrag_IBM_Peter-Krick.pdf.

[7]   Qualcomm, "LTE direct proximity services," 2015. [Online]. Available: https://www.qualcomm.com/invention/technologies/lte/direct.

[8]   WiFi Alliance, "Discover Wi-Fi – Wi-Fi direct," 2015. [Online]. Available: http://www.wi-fi.org/discover-wi-fi/wi-fi-direct.

[9]   WiFi Alliance, "Discover Wi-Fi – Wi-Gig certified," 2016. [Online]. Available: http://www.wi-fi.org/discover-wi-fi/wigig-certified.

[10] opensource.com, "What is Docker?," [Online]. Available: http://open source.com/resources/what-docker.

[11] J. Morgan, "A Simple Explanation of 'The Internet Of Things'," Forbes, May 2014. [Online]. Available: https://www.forbes.com/sites/jacobmorgan/2014/05/13/simple-explanation-internet-things-that-anyone-can-understand/#5721 53f71d09. [Accessed 18 December 2017].

[12] L. S. a. R. H. Erica Fink, "Your Hackable House," CNN, 2017. [Online]. Available: http://money.cnn.com/interactive/technology/hackable-house/. [Accessed 18 December 2017].

[13] Greenberg, "Hackers Remotely Kill a Jeep on the Highway—With Me in It," WIRED, July 2015. [Online]. Available: https://www.wired.com/2015/07/hackers-remotely-kill-jeep-highway/. [Accessed 18 December 2017].

[14] F. Mohammed, V. T. Humbe and S. S. Chowhan, "A review of Big Data environment and its related technologies," in *International Conference on Information Communication and Embedded Systems (ICICES),* Chennai, India, 2016.

[15] M. Hilbert and P. Lpez, "The world's technological capacity to store, communicate, and compute information," *Science,* vol. 332, no. 6025, pp. 60–65, 2011.

[16] L. Columbus, "Roundup of Internet of Things forecasts and market estimates, 2016," Forbes, November 2016. [Online]. Available: https://www.forbes.com/sites/louiscolumbus/2016/11/27/roundup-of-internet-of-things-forecasts-and-market-estimates-2016/#50251a66292d. [Accessed 16 January 2018].

[17] G. DeCandia, D. Hastorun, M. Jampani, *et al.,* "Dynamo: Amazons highly available key-value store," in *23th ACM Symposium on Operating Systems Principles, (SOSP07),* Stevenson, Washington, 2007.

[18] L. A. Barroso, J. Clidaras and U. Holzle, The Datacenter as a Computer: An Introduction to the Design of Warehouse-Scale Machines, 2nd ed., San Rafael, California, Morgan & Claypool, 2013.

[19] D. C. Marinescu, Complex Systems and Clouds: A Self-Organization and Self-Management Perspective, Elsevier, Morgan Kaufmann, Cambridge, MA, USA, 2016.

[20] J. Dean and S. Ghemawat, "MapReduce: Simplified data processing on large clusters," *Communications of the ACM,* vol. 51, no. 1, pp. 107–113, 2008.

[21] J. L. Hennessy and D. A. Patterson, Computer Architecture a Quantitative Approach, Elsevier, Morgan Kaufman, Cambridge, MA, USA, 2012.

[22] C. J. Shafer, S. Rixner and A. L. Cox, "The Hadoop distributed file system," in *IEEE Symposium on Mass Storage Systems and Technologies, (MSST10),* Lake Tahoe, Nevada, 2010.

[23] B. K. Shvachko, H. Kuang, S. Radia and R. Chansler, "The Hadoop distributed file system: Balancing portability and performance," in *IEEE International Symposium on Performance Analysis of Systems and Software, (ISPASS10),* White Plains, NY, 2010.

[24] T. White, Hadoop: The Definitive Guide, O'Reilly Media, Inc., Sebastopol, CA, USA, 2009.

[25]   X. Liu, "Understanding Big Data Processing and Analytics," September 2013. [Online]. Available: https://www.developer.com/db/understanding-big-data-processing-and-analytics.html.

[26]   K. Hwang, G. Fox and J. Dongarra, "Cloud architecture and datacenter design," May 2010. [Online]. Available: https://edisciplinas.usp.br/pluginfile. php/98907/mod_resource/content/1/Chapter7-Cloud-Architecture-May2-201 0.pdf.

[27]   Microsoft Inc., "What is cloud computing?," Microsoft Inc., 2018. [Online]. Available: https://azure.microsoft.com/en-us/overview/what-is-cloud-computing/.

[28]   Z. Kerravala, "How a data center works, today and tomorrow," Network World, September 2017. [Online]. Available: https://www.networkworld.com/ article/3223692/data-center/what-is-a-data-center-architecture-components-standards-infrastructure-cloud.html.

[29]   Amazon Inc, "Amazon web services," Amazon Inc, 2010. [Online]. Available: http://aws.amazon.com.

[30]   Google, Inc, "Google app engine," Google, Inc, 2010. [Online]. Available: http://code.google.com/appengine/, 2010.

[31]   Microsoft Corporation, "Windows azure," Microsoft Corporation, 2010. [Online]. Available: http://www.microsoft.com/windowazure/.

[32]   M. Eltoweissy, S. Olariu and M. Younis, "Towards autonomous vehicular clouds," in *Proceedings of AdHocNets'2010*, Victoria, BC, Canada, August 2010.

[33]   S. Olariu, I. Khalil and M. Abuelela, "Taking VANET to the clouds," *International Journal of Pervasive Computing and Communications*, vol. 7, no. 1, pp. 7–21, 2011.

[34]   S. Olariu, T. Hristov and G. Yan, "The next paradigm shift: From vehicular networks to vehicular clouds," in *Mobile Ad Hoc Networking Cutting Edge Directions*, 2nd ed., New York, Wiley and Sons, 2013, pp. 645–700.

[35]   S. Olariu and R. Florin, "Vehicular cloud research: What is missing?," in *7th ACM International Symposium on Design and Analysis of Intelligent Vehicular Networks and Applications, (DiVANET'2017)*, Miami, Florida, November 2017.

[36]   A. G. Zadeh and S. Olariu, "Vehicular clouds: A survey and future directions," in *Cloud Computing for Optimization: Foundations, Applications and Challenges*, Springer International Publishing, Cham, Switzerland, 2018, pp. 435–463.

[37]   S. Arif, J. W. Olariu, G. Yan, W. Yang and I. Khalil, "Datacenter at the airport: Reasoning about time-dependent parking lot occupancy," *IEEE Transactions on Parallel and Distributed Systems*, vol. 23, no. 11, pp. 2067–2080, 2012.

[38]   N. Vignesh, S. Shankar, S. Sathyamoorthy and V. M. Rajam, "Value added services on stationary vehicular cloud," *Distributed Computing and Internet Technology*, vol. 8337, pp. 92–97, 2014.

[39]   R. Hussain, F. Abbas, J. Son and H. Oh, "TIaaS: Secure cloud-assisted traffic information dissemination in vehicular ad hoc networks," in *Cluster, Cloud and*

Grid Computing (CCGrid), 2013 13th IEEE/ACM International Symposium, pp. 178–179, May 2013.

[40]   W. He, G. Yan and L. D. Xu, "Developing vehicular data cloud services in the IoT environment," *IEEE Transactions on Industrial Informatics,* vol. 10, no. 2, pp. 1587–1595, 2014.

[41]   R. Florin, S. Abolghasemi, A. G. Zadeh and S. Olariu, "Big Data in the Parking Lot," in *Big Data: Management, Architecture, and Processing,* New York, Taylor and Francis, 2017.

Chapter 13

Big data-oriented unit and ubiquitous Internet of Things (BD-U2IoT) security

Ata Ullah[1,2], Xuanxia Yao[2], Qingjuan Li[2] and Huansheng Ning[2]

13.1 Introduction

With the abrupt increase in the number of online devices, Internet of Things (IoT) has evolved as a promising solution that comprises a large set of enabling technologies to support interconnectivity among the smart devices. A huge amount of sensing, computation, communication and storage resources involve the unit and ubiquitous things that cannot be handled by just increasing the resources. It needs a new architecture that can manage the sensing bottlenecks from physical space and appropriately grows the cyber space to meet the challenging requirements. In future IoT, social impact should also be considered in designing new architecture so as to support big data. To address huge storage and computation requirements, a cloud is considered to be the promising solution along with a set of services. Third party cloud-service providers are also managing the big data repositories for users, organization and applications. The role of unit and ubiquitous IoT (U2IoT) is essential for providing sensed data from a large number of devices to local, industrial and national-level management and data centers that are linked with cloud servers for central storage and analysis of big data. We have presented a security architecture that comprises physical security, information security and management security in the prospective of big data-oriented U2IoT.

13.2 Unit and ubiquitous Internet of Things

Unit IoT comprises certain application scenarios at organization levels that utilize sensors and actuators as persistent or intermittent data producers. A unit-level management and data center (M&DC) (uM&DC) is maintained for processing the data

[1]Department of Computer Science, National University of Modern Languages, Islamabad, Pakistan
[2]School of Computer and Communication Engineering, University of Science and Technology, Beijing, China

at the edge and then transmits the valuable information at upper layers for storage, intelligent decisions, data processing and systemic management. Different heterogeneous networks with various technology enablers also interact within unit IoT. Multiple unit IoT connected across different organizations using various technologies in countrywide or worldwide scenarios constitute the ubiquitous IoT [1].

13.2.1   Storage and resource management in U2IoT

In U2IoT, a large amount of data is stored at uM&DC for one unit of an organization like health unit of a hospital, postal unit, transportation unit and banking unit in one city. Different units of various organizations in one region or city constitute a local M&DC (lM&DC). For the multiple branches of the same organization in different cities, a centralized industrial M&DC (iM&DC) is maintained. For example, a bank can have multiple units in different cities to constitute an iM&DC by deploying local schema at branches and global schema at headquarter in existing relational database-management systems. But current requirements of big data have driven the path for NoSQL or SQL-free oriented data access policies instead of relational database management systems (DBMSs) for big data scenarios. Moreover, by combining all the M&DCs, a national-level M&DC is constituted as nM&DC that is further linked with other nM&DCs [2] in a global setup.

In U2IoT, the resources are usually context sensitive [3] where different context providers adopt a specific model for context reasoning and context delivering. It can be either static or dynamic, the former follows the same formats and the latter is changeable. Both can be aggregated by the devices to provide a high-level context for developing new context-aware services. In U2IoT, the context can be categorized mainly into four aspects, including physical, cyber, social and thinking. Moreover, it can be further subcategorized as cyber-enabled physical, cyber-enabled social and cyber-enabled thinking aspects for identifying the inter-context classification of data and information exchange [4]. In the meantime, additional service selection and adaptation management are applied to support the resource management for sensor and actuator resources [5].

13.2.1.1   Resource management in unit IoT

Unit IoT includes sensors, actuators and servers that utilize the unit-level storage at uM&DCs. The unit resources provide a set of services for low-power devices and can also communicate with upper layers in ubiquitous IoT. A service directory is maintained for matching the requested resources with the available services. In the case of data access by the sensors, a service request is initiated for availing internal resources and uM&DC. If the matching service is available, it can be bound with resources; otherwise, the request is gradually forwarded to upper layers. The services availed by a sensor can be concurrently used by other sensors and application because of its self-organized resource-management approach. Due to self-adaptive mode, the service's specifications can be autonomously configured to support connectivity and data exchange in different networks [2].

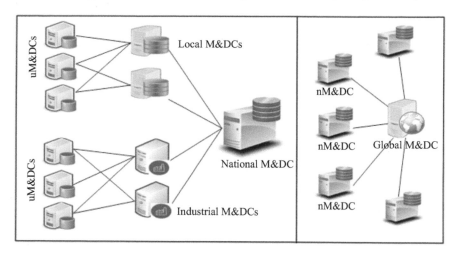

Figure 13.1   Resource management in ubiquitous IoT

13.2.1.2   Resource management in ubiquitous IoT

Ubiquitous resources comprise connecting layer for the unit resources where the physical and cyber resources are managed at local, industrial and national IoT level by using iM&DC, lM&DC and nM&DC, respectively, as illustrated in Figure 13.1. Additionally, the global IoT-level resource is also mandatory to manage the multiple national-level resources and connectivity with international resources as well. The local and industrial resources can also communicate with each other for sharing the resources and services.

Current cloud computing and big data support have enabled the applicability of innovative application scenarios along with the availability of huge storage. Cloud management in U2IoT provides anything as a service (XaaS), where X represents a set of sub-services including software, platform and infrastructure represented as software as a service (SaaS), platform as a service (PaaS) and infrastructure as a service (IaaS), respectively [6,7]. These services enable the applicability of processing and storage at the big data in dense IoT deployments where a large number of linkages can be setup with applications. With the increase in IoT devices up to many billions in recent years and still growing rapidly, an enormous demand is created to manage the huge amount of data generated by these devices. It is quite challenging to store the valuable and demandable data in central repositories by eliminating redundancy. Meanwhile, the monitoring data services need to timely extract and analyze the desired data and generate timely alerts for emergency medical conditions, road-accidents prevention, structural health criticality and alarming weather conditions [8].

13.2.2   Security in big data-oriented U2IoT

The growth of IoT and big data depend on each other, which means increasing billions of devices will raise the need for storage. On the other side, the increase in storage

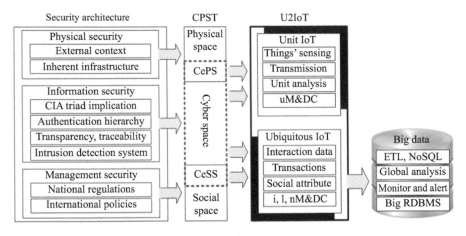

Figure 13.2   Security architecture for big data-oriented U2IoT

capacity increases the scalability of IoT and also improves the data storage and accessibility capabilities. In 2017, there were 28.4 billion devices connected in the IoT, and it can grow up to 50 billion in 2020. Meanwhile, the need of data storage can grow up to 44 ZB which is equal to 44 trillion gigabytes by 2020 [9]. The rapid growth in IoT and big data arises the need for a scalable, dependable and secure framework that can also handle the impact of social behaviors over cyber and physical spaces. Due to the rapid enhancements in sensing capabilities at physical space, a need is created to appropriately enhance the cyber space by considering the future social behaviors and interaction patterns with the IoT.

The devices from the physical space transmit the confidential data to central repositories for storage, analysis, monitoring and alerting the data owners about emergency situations. The exchange of data should be performed in a secure manner to ensure the reliability of the systems and achieve the users' satisfaction. Due to massive increase in the number of online devices, the chances of security attacks are increased for fraudulent activities to illegally get the passwords of bank cards, anonymous transaction. Moreover, intruders also grab more precious information than money including personal health details, family and official activities, relationships, social contacts, business deals and confidential legal details [10]. It arises the need for dependable security solutions for securing the information exchange over enormous number of connections available in U2IoT. The unit-level secure storage capabilities lead to the national and global-level secure transmission and storage at central repositories for big data storage. Security requirements are amplified when big data guarantees for velocity, volume and variety to provide rapid data in big volumes with a large variety of data formats and sources as well at U2IoT.

The security architecture for the big data-oriented U2IoT is presented in Figure 13.2, where ubiquitous IoT is mainly linked with the big data where the extract transform and load operations are performed to compliance with existing data sources.

A global-level analysis is performed on the big data stored at big relational database-management system to take critical decisions for maintaining the history or analytical report generation. The monitoring systems also continuously analyze the records to alert about the alarming situations when different threshold values are bypassed. All these records should be kept confidential from illegal access at big data repositories and during the transit from servers to the intended users. In this regard, we have explored the layers of security discussed in the following subsections.

13.2.2.1 Physical security

The devices at physical space need the security for the inherent structure to guard against the denial of service attack, jamming attack, physical capturing attack and physical damage. The devices or things in the cyber-enabled physical space exchange the sensed data with the cyber entities in cyberspace that can further communicate within unit IoT scenario along with uM&DC. The devices should be guarded against the external context for providing dependable and continuous availability of sensing and related services. Intruders can monitor the environment to perform motion detection and passive traffic capturing to analyze the communication model and current topology of the network. Intruders can also identify the number of nodes in the network and then identify the central nodes where most of the communication are transmitted. Moreover, the consuming energy can be predicted and then an active attack can be launched after acquiring the previously mentioned parameters. Safe environments at physical space are mandatory to ensure that correct, authentic and useful data is saved at distant big data repositories. A large amount of energy consumed due to data transit is wasted when the initiator of the data is compromised. The intrusion-detection algorithm is mandatory for monitoring and analyzing the sensor's behavior, sensor or collector node capturing and other misbehaviors from routine tasks.

13.2.2.2 Information security

The raw data and the contextualized data that is processed by cyber entities in cyber space for ubiquitous IoT scenario need to be secured. In this scenario, the transactions are also handled along with dynamic session establishment and freshness as well. It also ensures the ubiquitous delinking among pre, post and instantaneous data exchanges to guard against information accessibility out of the context. It eliminates the chances that a lost node that rejoins as a compromised node to get the prior information exchanged between the cyber entities. It can also attempt to grab the privileged information accessed by other entities from the big data.

1. *Confidentiality integrity availability (CIA) triad:* It involves (a) confidentiality where data is not exposed to intermediaries and protected using encryption before it reaches big data servers; (b) integrity involves the lossless transmission of data to the big data repositories by taking checksum using hash functions and message authentication codes; and (c) availability ensures the continuous accessibility to the service without any denial of service attacks.
2. *Authentication hierarchy:* It includes the heterogeneous sources for providing authentication where the semantic-based access control is mandatory to acquire the information from the big data in ubiquitous IoT scenario.

3. *Transparency and traceability:* It depends on the nature of the data being exchanged. For tracking scenarios in ubiquitous IoT, the user should be privileged to access the entity that contains the required data when it was forwarded to next entities for traceability. In the case of privacy assurance for some confidential data, the communicating entities should be transparent to the user and internally processed.

4. *Intrusion-detection system:* It ensures the timely identification of an intruder and getting it busy with honey pots to deviate from critical cyber entities and big data repositories as well. Meanwhile, the source of attacker is tracked to mitigate the interrupts and the illegal access to ensure privacy preservation is saved.

13.2.2.3 Management security

Technological security solutions in future need to involve the social attributes as well to design a foolproof and reliable security mechanisms. It necessitates the conjunction of management with the physical and information security [11] by sharing social attributes from cyber-enabled social space with the cyber entities at cyber space. Cyber entity can utilize physical and social attributes during the encryption process to strengthen the security solutions. In this regard, attribute-based encryption using policy trees in mobile cloud computing and mobile crowd sensing scenarios has boost up the big data security models. Attribute-based encryptions [12] also support the outsourced policy-based encryption where smart devices from physical space can outsource the extensive encryption operations to high-power devices in U2IoT to transmit the cipher text to big data repositories. The management-security solutions also consider the assurance of national regulations and international policies to utilize the resources in a controlled manner.

References

[1] Ning, H. *Unit and Ubiquitous Internet of Things*, New York, NY, USA: CRC Press; 2013. p. 13.

[2] Ning, H., and Wang, Z. 'Future Internet of Things Architecture: Like Mankind Neural System or Social Organization Framework?'. *IEEE Communication Letters*. 2011;15(4):461–463.

[3] Liu, J., and Tong, W. 'Dynamic Service Model Based on Context Resources in the Internet of Things'. *Proceedings of 6th International Conference on Wireless Communications Networking and Mobile Computing*, Chengdu, China, Sep 2010, pp. 1–4.

[4] Ning, H., and Liu, H. 'Cyber-Physical-Social-Thinking Space Based Science and Technology Framework for the Internet of Things'. *Science China Information Sciences*. 2015;58(3):1–19.

[5] Cid, P. J., Matthys, N., Hughes, D., Michiels, S., and Joosen, W. 'Resource Management Middleware to Support Self-managing Wireless Sensor Networks'. *Proceedings of 4th IEEE International Conference on Self-Adaptive and Self-Organizing Systems Workshop*, Budapest, Hungary, 2010, pp. 251–255.

[6] Hendryx, A. *Cloudy Concepts: IaaS, PaaS, SaaS, MaaS, CaaS and XaaS*. [Online]. 2011. Available from https://www.zdnet.com/article/cloudy-concepts-iaas-paas-saas-maas-caas-xaas/ [Accessed 14 April, 2018].

[7] Shi, Y., Sheng, M., and He, F. 'A Resource Management and Control Model Supporting Applications in the Internet of Things'. *Proceedings of International Conference on Cyber, Physical and Social Computing*, Dalian, China, Oct 2011, pp. 721–725.

[8] Riggins, F. J., and Wamba, S. F. 'Research Direction on the Adoption, Usage and Impact of the Internet of Things Through the Use of Big Data Analytics'. *Proceedings of 48th Hawaii International Conference on System Sciences*, Kauai, HI, USA, Jan 2015, pp. 1531–1540.

[9] Charles, M. *The Internet of Things and Big Data: Unlocking the Power*. [Online]. 2015. Available from https://www.zdnet.com/article/the-internet-of-things-and-big-data- unlocking-the-power/ [Accessed 15 April, 2018].

[10] Hyun-Woo, K., Jong, H. P., and Young-Sik, J. 'Efficient Resource Management Scheme for Storage Processing in Cloud Infrastructure with Internet of Things'. *Wireless Personal Communications*. 2016;91(4):1635–1651.

[11] Ning, H., and Liu, H. 'Cyber-Physical-Social Based Security Architecture for Future Internet of Things'. *Advances in Internet of Things*. 2012;2(1):1–7.

[12] Zhiyuan, Z., and Wang, J. 'Verifiable Outsourced Ciphertext-Policy Attribute-Based Encryption for Mobile Cloud Computing'. *KSII Transactions on Internet and Information Systems (TIIS)*. 2017;11(6):3254–3272.

Chapter 14

Confluence of Big Data and Internet of Things—relationship, synergization, and convergence

Tony Shan[1]

As Big Data and Internet of Things (IoT) keep evolving and play an increasingly important role in the digitization, it is crucial to crystalize how these two are related to each other. This article investigates the correlation between Big Data and IoT systematically and introduces a comprehensive relationship model to synergize IoT and Big Data. The overarching model is broken down into pillars to manage the complexity: independent, interconnecting, interacting, and intertwined (i4). The independent pillar is concerned with stand-alone operations and distinct functionalities, composed of four components: difference, implementation, similarity, and capability (DISC). The interconnecting pillar deals with the structural connections with four units: composition, realization, atomicity, and multiplicity (CRAM). The interacting pillar covers four behavioral styles with four modules: control, association, range, and dependency (CARD). Lastly, the intertwined pillar is in regard to the intermesh of working together cohesively, consisting of four parts: touchpoints, integration, mapping, and enablement (TIME). We delve into each individual element in greater detail, followed by the guidelines and best practices on how to effectively apply the i4 model in real-life initiatives.

14.1 Introduction

Data continues to grow exponentially at an unprecedented pace today. It is estimated that the world will reach 44 ZB by 2020 [1], and machine data is increasing at $50\times$ growth rate [2]. The number of connected devices is expected to grow to 50 billion by 2020 [3]. Big Data keeps changing the world, while IoT further accelerates transforming to Industry 4.0. Obviously, Big Data and IoT are the two key drivers in this new paradigm. How Big Data and IoT are related to each other? Are they separate driving forces? Do they play together? Does one overlap with the other?

[1]CTS Inc., Charlotte, USA

There have been a variety of discussions and interpretations on this topic, such as what is presented in [4–16]. IoT is treated as the major sources of Big Data, which offers data storage and processing services [4]. A sensor integration framework on cloud architecture is proposed to integrate massive data points in electronic health record [5]. Mobile Big Data from billions of smartphones and wireless sensors is characterized by multidimensionality, personalization, and multisensoriality [6]. IoT devices can be smarter with the implementation of machine-learning algorithms [7]. To make the IoT useful, we need an Analytics of Things [8]. IoT and Big Data must shake hands with each other for Big Data to fit in the shoes of IoT [9].

The views on the IoT-Big Data relationship vary dramatically from different authors and organizations. Some people say that IoT and Big Data are exactly the same. Some think that Big Data and IoT are similar, working hand in hand. Some suggest that IoT is an extension of Big Data. Some claim that these two are much more alike than they are different. Some propose that Big Data is a subset of IoT, or vice versa. Some insist that Big Data and IoT complement each other. Others argue that Big Data has nothing to do with IoT, as they evolved from different areas.

The industry lacks clarity and convincing explanation on the connection, in spite of efforts like [4] attempting to lay out a thematic taxonomy of Big Data and analytics solutions designed for IoT systems. The ambiguity has caused confusion and misunderstanding in the market, resulting in misuse and waste of time and resources in the innovation journey for an organization. There is a desperate need to understand the correlation between Big Data and IoT more systematically.

The rest of the chapter is structured as follows: Section 14.2 outlines the anatomy of Big Data and IoT separately in the dimensions of 6W+2H. Then Section 14.3 introduces a holistic relationship model. Subsequently, Section 14.4 drills down to the components of relationship model pillars. Afterward, Section 14.5 discusses how to apply the relationship model in real-world projects, followed by the conclusion drawn in Section 14.6.

14.2   Anatomy of Big Data and IoT

First of all, we must obtain a clear understanding of what Big Data and IoT mean individually. We level-set the context by anatomizing Big Data and IoT, respectively, in terms of what, which, why, where, when, who, how, and how much.

14.2.1   Big Data

Big Data is a term for large or complex data sets that exceed the capability of traditional data-processing approaches and tools to handle such quantity and diversity at the desired speed.

Big Data is characterized by volume, velocity, and variety—amount of data in petabyte (PB) order, real-time speed, and structured/semi-structured/unstructured types.

The key drivers of Big Data include more efficient processes, better customer experience, lower cost, and reduced risks.

Selected use cases of Big Data are fraud detection, predictive maintenance, demand forecasting, disease analysis, text mining, surveillance, and sentiment analysis.

John Mashey was arguably the first person who used the term "Big Data" in his public speech in 1998 [17]. Francis X. Diebold published a paper in a conference in 2000 [18], which was the first academic reference found to Big Data.

There are hundreds of companies in the Big Data space, including traditional powerhouses like IBM, and startups like Hortonworks. They cover a wide range of areas such as data sources, applications, analytics, infrastructure, platforms, and open-source projects.

Big Data needs a pragmatic approach for efficient solutioning and development end to end. Big Data Engineering is an effective way to manage a variety of tasks and tame ambiguities in a lifecycle manner.

Some large Big Data projects reveal that the total cost of ownership for a Hadoop solution is about a third of a traditional data warehouse appliance in a 5-year span, including the costs of application development and system/data administration for a 500 TB data repository.

14.2.2 Internet of Things

IoT is a system of interrelated objects, devices, sensors, mechanical equipment, analog machines, digital apparatus, and computing servers with unique identifiers to exchange data over a network with no need of human-to-human or human-to-computer interactions.

IoT is characterized by devices, sensing, connectivity, scale, and informatics.

The major benefits of IoT are improved quality, enhanced productivity, increasing reliability, reduced cost, better customer satisfaction, faster time to market, fewer risks, and product insights.

IoT is used in the consumer market, industrial domains, and enterprise environments, such as connected energy, smart cities, connected cars, and Internet of medical things. Asset tracking, fleet management, health monitoring, and smart metering are sample use cases.

Kevin Ashton coined the term "IoT" in a presentation at Procter & Gamble in 1999 [19].

We have even more vendors in IoT than Big Data. There are about 500 IoT platforms in the market today. This space is overwhelmingly crowded with solutions on personal products, home applications, vehicles, enterprise, industrial IoT (IIoT), platforms, interfaces, hardware, software, connectivity, and partners.

IoT requires a blend of top-down and bottom-up methods to cope with the complication. A cross-disciplinary discipline is a mandate for adoption, strategization, operationalization, and mobilization.

In terms of return on investment (ROI), 89% of IoT projects have a ROI within 2 years. The cost is recovered by 66% within 1 year, and 31% get payback within 6 months [20].

14.3 Relationship model

It is important to clarify how Big Data is pertinent to IoT. As discussed in the previous section, both are complex subjects comprising various aspects and factors. An approach of multiple viewpoints is a necessity to defog the interlink. We now introduce a comprehensive relationship model to synergize IoT and Big Data. The relationship model describes interrelated nuance of interest in a specific extent of Big Data and IoT.

The overarching model is broken down into pillars to manage the complexity: independent, interconnecting, interacting, and intertwined (i4), as illustrated in Figure 14.1.

- *Independent:* Big Data and IoT operate separately in a stand-alone mode.
- *Interconnecting:* Big Data and IoT are linked together for sequential activities.
- *Interacting:* Big Data and IoT work in tandem reciprocally in a collaborative manner.
- *Intertwined:* Big Data and IoT are mixed jointly to reinforce each other or converge in unison.

These four pillars represent the closeness levels of Big Data and IoT in a progressive fashion, ranging from autonomous, attached, coupled to united. We will take a look at some real-world solutions for these four types.

14.3.1 Independent

In the Big Data scenario, a large amount of data from diverse sources is acquired and aggregated in a batch mode to generate various reports scheduled to run in a preset timetable. An enterprise data warehouse or appliance is a typical example to pump transactional data into a central place.

In the IoT situation, sensors accumulate signals or events of interest and then process them locally or remotely. A real-world case is that an outdoor thermostat gathers data like temperature and humidity and then sends the info to the indoor display station wirelessly.

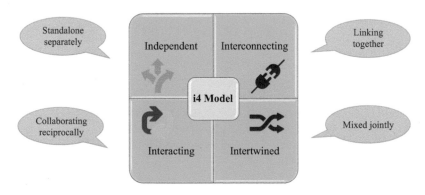

Figure 14.1 Relationship model of Big Data and IoT

14.3.2 Interconnecting

A sensor collects data in the field and then feeds to the Big Data pipeline for subsequent analysis. For example, a wearable device uses a three-dimensional accelerometer to sense user movement. The tracker on the device measures the activity duration, intensity, speed, location, steps taken, distance walked, floors climbed, calories burned, and other parameters. After these measurements are collected on the wearable, they are subsequently sent to a backend Big Data system intermittently for persistent storage. Diagnostic analytics are also conducted at the Big Data side.

14.3.3 Interacting

As an example, a natural gas firm acquires a terabyte of operational data from 1,700 wellheads and separator tanks, including temperatures, pressures, tank levels, and flow rates via IoT. The collected data is large, diverse, noisy, often erroneous, and incomplete. At the Big Data side, many munging rules are developed and applied to clean the data and impute estimated values when data feeds are down or unreliable. A predictive maintenance model is developed and trained to forecast the well freezing, the need for plunger pump installation, and the impact of interventions on the gas-production volume. This data science model is tuned via live data in operations to predict preventive maintenance. As a result, the timing of plunger pump installation is optimized with production deferrals reduced by 15%–20%.

14.3.4 Intertwined

For instance, a delivery company uses sensors to capture more than 200 data points for each vehicle in a fleet of more than 80,000 every day. The firm also subscribes the feeds of weather information for hundreds of millions of address data points on demand. In addition, the traffic data and road conditions are acquired in real time based on events and triggers. These data are mixed with other data on the deliveries like service-level agreement (SLA) and nearby vehicle/driver availability, for prescriptive analysis with deep learning and artificial intelligence (AI). The situational outcome is displayed to truck drivers and end users to optimize delivery routes, sequence, pickup, timing and reprioritization for efficiency, and effective dispatching on the fly.

14.4 Model pillars

Furthermore, each pillar comprises various components that represent various aspects of the relationship. The independent pillar is concerned with stand-alone operations and distinct functionalities, composed of four constituents: difference, implementation, similarity, and capability (DISC). The interconnecting pillar deals with the structural connections with four units: composition, realization, atomicity, and multiplicity (CRAM). The interacting pillar covers four behavioral styles with four modules: control, association, range, and dependency (CARD). Lastly, the intertwined pillar is in regard to the intermesh of working together cohesively, consisting of four parts: touchpoints, integration, mapping, and enablement (TIME).

Next, we will drill down to each individual component of these four pillars in greater detail and further dive deep to the elements in the components.

14.4.1 Difference, implementation, similarity, and capability

As shown in Figure 14.2, the independent pillar has the following components:

- *Difference:* Distinction in the operating model.
- *Implementation:* Suitability for the appropriate usage.
- *Similarity:* Commonalities in the build-out and execution.
- *Capability:* Key features and functions.

14.4.1.1 Difference

IoT and Big Data behave differently in various facets:

1. *Execution:* IoT usually runs on the edge, while Big Data commonly executes in a central place of a data center or public cloud.
2. *Mode:* IoT is more event driven, but Big Data is used to batch jobs, though data streaming is becoming popular.
3. *Physicality:* IoT ties closely with physical devices, and Big Data tends to be digital and virtual.
4. *Processing:* IoT typically has simple processing and transmission of the data collected, whereas Big Data is more complex with data integration and machine learning (ML) analytics.

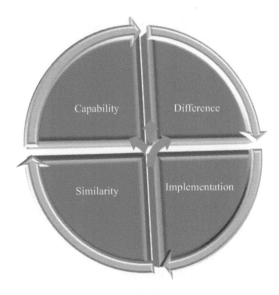

Figure 14.2 Independent pillar

14.4.1.2 Implementation

Not all industries are equally suitable for either Big Data or IoT, from an implementation perspective. A heatmap provides the relative applicabilities on different categories in a comparative way. As charted in Figure 14.3 [21], Big Data is the most suitable for the government, communications, media and services, manufacturing and natural resources, and banking and securities sectors.

On the contrary, Figure 14.4 [22] is the heatmap for IoT, indicating that the most applicable verticals are transportation and logistics, government and education/social services, high-tech and industrial production, and retail and wholesale industries.

14.4.1.3 Similarities

In common terms, Big Data and IoT share some resemblances:

1. *Data-intensive:* Both handle large amount of data in various types.
2. *Quality:* Both deal with the data management and SLA for user experience.
3. *Governance:* Both need new disciplines to supplement the existing IT and corporate governance practices.
4. *Risks:* Both technologies are relatively young and evolving, which makes the maturity-driven adoption and journey a risky undertaking inside an organization.

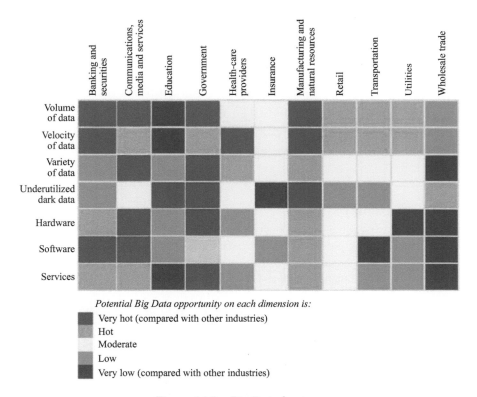

Figure 14.3 Big Data heatmap

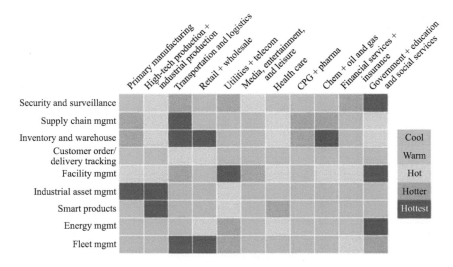

Figure 14.4   IoT heatmap

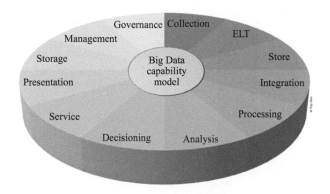

Figure 14.5   Big Data capability model

14.4.1.4   Capability

From a capability standpoint, Big Data is more focused on data transformation, store, analysis, and reporting/presentation, as schemed in Figure 14.5.

In contrast, IoT primarily deals with sensing, capturing, and connectivity and triggers for operations management and decision support, as plotted in Figure 14.6.

14.4.2   Composition, realization, atomicity, and multiplicity

As revealed in Figure 14.7, the interconnecting pillar is made of the following components:

- *Composition:* Big Data is IT based, and IoT is OT oriented.
- *Realization:* Big Data takes care of the cyber side, and IoT handles the physical world.

Figure 14.6   IoT capability model

- *Atomicity:* Distributed long running vs localized short duration.
- *Multiplicity:* Diverse representation of the counterpart.

14.4.2.1   Composition

IoT and Big Data partner in the front and at the back to compose a data-intensive application, as designated in Figure 14.8.

The front-facing IoT uses heterogeneous devices or embedded sensing capabilities on equipment to capture events or signals in the physical processes. The back-side Big Data processes the data collected from IoT for analytics. Typically, the Big Data machines are largely homogenous, providing network-computing resources and persistence storage as the system of records.

14.4.2.2   Realization

Big Data and IoT play complementary roles in the realization of data-driven systems, as marked in Figure 14.9. Big Data is software intensive with data science algorithms

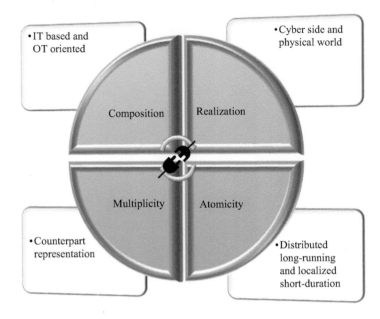

Figure 14.7   Interconnecting pillar

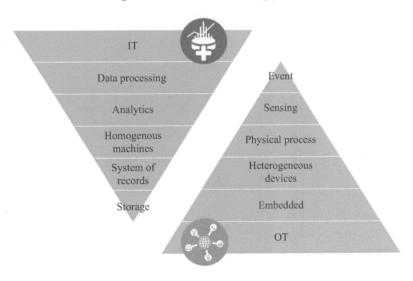

Figure 14.8   Composition

for the cyber side. The digital data center is well protected with more secured measures applied like firewalls and demilitarized zone (DMZ). Conversely, IoT is hardware intensive with infrastructural gears for the physical side. The nondigital environment in the field tends to be less safe with more vulnerabilities exploited by malicious attacks.

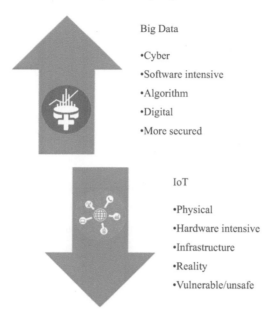

Big Data

•Cyber
•Software intensive
•Algorithm
•Digital
•More secured

IoT

•Physical
•Hardware intensive
•Infrastructure
•Reality
•Vulnerable/unsafe

Figure 14.9   Realization

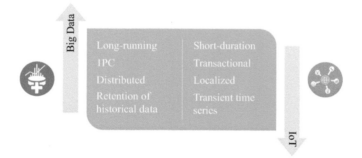

Figure 14.10   Atomicity

14.4.2.3   Atomicity

As labeled in Figure 14.10, IoT data capture on a single device is regularly localized in short-duration transactions. IoT mostly generates time-series data in a periodical collection or continuous stream, in a transient mode with constrained storage capacity.

By contrast, Big Data processing is long-running in a pipeline with multiple sources ingested concurrently. One-phase commit is more applicable in Big Data with compensational actions for undo. Big Data also stores the historical data for a long-term retention, with archiving and backup. In the NoSQL setting, the Big Data workloads are distributed to run on different nodes in a cluster for parallel processing.

14.4.2.4 Multiplicity

As characterized in Figure 14.11, the twins on the Big Data side are the replicas of physical systems, processes, and assets that can be used for various purposes, such as device twin, process twin, and digital twin. At the IoT side, the virtual twin refers to the physical model of digital objects like a schedule. The twin representation signifies both the structure and behaviors of how an IoT-empowered Big Data solution operates and improves throughout its lifecycle. The pairing of the digital and physical worlds allows the data analysis and system monitoring to decouple elements, simulate scenarios, predict potential issues prior to occurring, minimize downtime, conduct preventive maintenance, and develop new opportunities.

14.4.3 Control, association, range, and dependency

As presented in Figure 14.12, the interacting pillar owns the following components:

- *Control:* Distinct control types, mechanisms, and entities.
- *Association:* Bimodal styles of management and operations.
- *Range:* Varied speed and span in processing.
- *Dependency:* Source–target assembly.

14.4.3.1 Control

As pinpointed in Figure 14.13, IoT deals with controllers like programmable logic controller (PLC), whereas Big Data handles computing servers and nodes in a cluster.

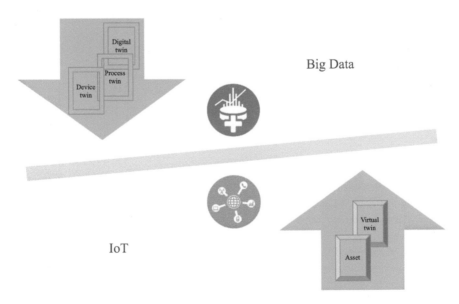

Figure 14.11 Multiplicity

Figure 14.12   Interacting pillar

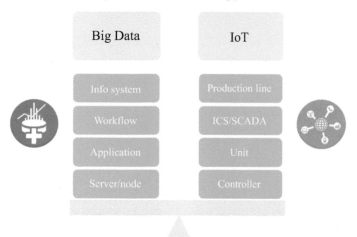

Figure 14.13   Control

There are usually many deployed units of the same function on the IoT end point, but a single application instance is typically deployed on the Big Data side. IoT uses industrial control systems for industrial processes, while Big Data leverages workflows for task processing. IoT manages the production lines like mining or oil/gas, though Big Data copes with information systems like databases.

14.4.3.2   Association

We employ the practice of managing two separate but coherent styles of work in operations: one focused on predictability for Big Data, and the other on exploration for IoT. Applying IoT to Big Data is explorative with experiments for rapid innovation and fail-fast turnaround. On the other hand, applying Big Data to IoT is more predictive

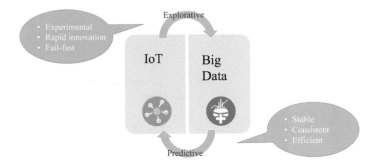

Figure 14.14　Association

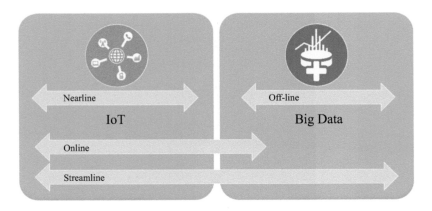

Figure 14.15　Range

in an orderly fashion with stable, consistent, and efficient action dispatched to the IoT side for process and operations management, as indicated in Figure 14.14.

14.4.3.3　Range

There are four modes of operations, which cover different ranges of band in IoT and Big Data, as plotted in Figure 14.15: streamline, off-line, online, and nearline.

1. *Off-line:* Data at rest—completely in a batch mode as scheduled jobs for data mining, machine learning, deep learning, and statistical modeling.
2. *Streamline:* Data in motion—event driven in microbatches or sliding windows for long-running signal or data streaming with out-of-order data arrivals.
3. *Nearline:* Data in haste—near real time with small latency, for localized in-memory on-device or on-gateway processing in edge/fog computing.
4. *Online:* Data at speed—real-time interaction in request–response, transactional, and short-span processing.

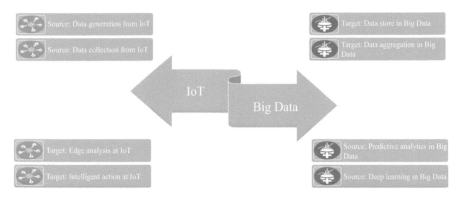

Figure 14.16   Dependency of Big Data and IoT

14.4.3.4 Dependency

Big Data can be a source to IoT as the target, and vice versa, as described in Figure 14.16.

When IoT is a source, there are a couple of scenarios:

1. Data is generated at the IoT side, like a user making a payment in a purchase at a location via a mobile device. This transaction is transmitted to the target and stored at the Big Data side.
2. Data is collected at the IoT device, such as the glucose readings by a blood glucose meter in a diabetes management system. The logbook data is transferred via a mobile phone to the Big Data side and further aggregated to display color-coded charts and graphs. The data is also tracked to monitor treatment progress and outcome.

Likewise, when Big Data is a source, there are two scenarios:

1. A data science model is developed and trained for predictive analytics at the Big Data side. The model is executed for the edge analytics at the IoT side.
2. Deep learning is employed in Big Data to create course correction and adjustment. Correspondingly, the intelligent action is taken at the IoT side to execute the recommendations sent by Big Data.

14.4.4 Touchpoints, integration, mapping, and enablement

As demonstrated in Figure 14.17, the interconnecting pillar encompasses the following components:

- *Touchpoints:* Different points of contact in the data-aggregation spectrum.
- *Interplay:* Dynamic execution of intermingled data workloads at edge, fog, cloud, or on-premise.
- *Mapping:* Interlock matrix of key characteristics.
- *Enablement:* Groups of shared enablers and tailored enabling technologies.

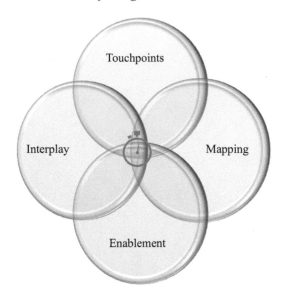

Figure 14.17   Intertwined pillar

14.4.4.1   Touchpoints

The data value chain is explained in Figure 14.18, including *data, information, knowledge, hindsight, foresight, insight, decision,* and *action*.

Big Data is related to the first part of stages in the chain, i.e., *data, information, knowledge, hindsight, foresight,* and *insight*. Big Data is responsible for the intake of source data and information and then turns them into knowledge. The subsequent analysis helps develop hindsights, foresights, and insights. On the contrary, IoT is more concerned with the two extreme ends on the spectrum, namely, *data, information, foresight, insight, decision,* and *action*. IoT is the main source of raw data and information. It also harvests the foresights and insights for decision-making, and the consequent actions taken.

14.4.4.2   Interplay

Big Data and IoT join forces to provide business values and impacts in commercial solutions. As highlighted in Figure 14.19, raw data is generated from things at the edge. One stream of data is from consumer products and the other comes from IIoT like manufacturing. Other steam of data is originated from enterprise applications. Additional stream of data is generated by the users on the web, such as social networks and online forums. Extra stream of data results from user interactions on mobile devices or wearables.

All these source data are ingested, processed, combined, mingled, and analyzed to generate intelligence and judgments of the business processes and workflows in operations. The forethoughts help make sound and informed decisions in a timely manner. The computation workloads are dynamically executed and autoprovisioned on demand in the data center, cloud, regional sites, or fields, to obtain the best results

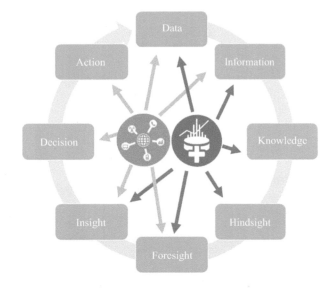

Figure 14.18   Touchpoints

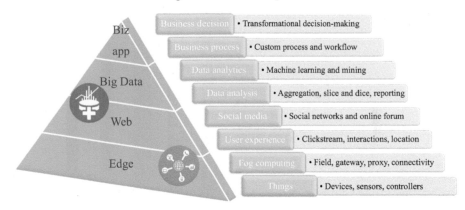

Figure 14.19   Interplay

and event-driven adjustments in real time. The combinatory output is rationalized with lively scenarios and constraints to identify the best course of action, which takes place on the same or other IoT devices and equipment.

14.4.4.3   Mapping

Big Data is characterized by volume, velocity, variety, and veracity. IoT is attributed to connectivity, collection, context, and cognition. As diagramed in Figure 14.20, the representative traits pinpoint the characters of Big Data and IoT in the mapping.

The characteristics of Big Data and IoT are mapped one-to-one in a matrix, as laid out in Figure 14.21. The cells intersect the individual attributes in the row and column, supplementing and/or reinforcing each other. Taking the first cell as

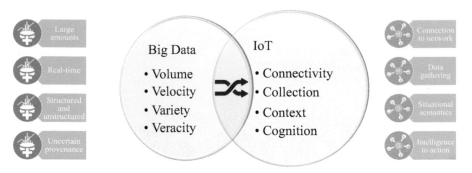

Figure 14.20   *Mapping of Big Data and IoT*

⤬	Connectivity	Collection	Context	Cognition
Volume	Bandwidth to handle the data pipeline, embedded capacity, edge, fog computing	Sheer amount of data generated and collected in sensors, mobile devices, wearables, etc.	Data deluge—sort out data, cleansing, ingest, extract, transform, load	Descriptive, diagnostic, predictive and prescriptive analysis
Velocity	Network latency, high speed Wi-Fi, LPWAN connection, HaLow, field/edge gateway	Fast requests/responses or one-way traffic between devices and backend systems	Timely processing, streaming, near real time, seamless scale-out	Just-in-time analytics, on-demand intelligence, hybrid, fog computing
Variety	Flexibility on protocols, e.g., Http, CoAP, MQTT, WebSocket	Different formats of data, diverse devices, proprietary apps	Location data, time-series, clickstream, user behaviors, motion	Sift through all data for a 360° view and conduct persuasive analytics
Veracity	Shut down devices or disconnect the network as needed	Shield the noise or bad data, data wrangling of cleaning dirty data	Filter false data and unify/ correlate applicable data for semantics	Smart recommendations with engaging, relevant, and trustworthy sources

Figure 14.21   *Matrix of 4Vs meet 4Cs*

an example for volume connectivity, sufficient bandwidth is required for connecting devices that transfer a large amount of data. The communications must be lightweight and scalable for the data pipeline, by means of representational state transfer (REST) and message queuing telemetry transport (MQTT) from different data locations—on a device, at the edge, in the fog, or on a moving vehicle.

14.4.4.4   Enablement

We group the key enablers for Big Data and IoT in the enablement element in three categories: foundational, common, and unique, as depicted in the "house" model in Figure 14.22.

1. *Foundational:* Baseline enablers for the project execution and solution development from a lifecycle perspective, including process, engineering, integration, DevOps, project management office (PMO), governance, risk, competence, and total cost of ownership (TCO)/ROI.
2. *Common:* Horizontal enabling technologies and tools usable across the board, like cloud, microservices, end point, containerization, security, and identity and access management (IAM).

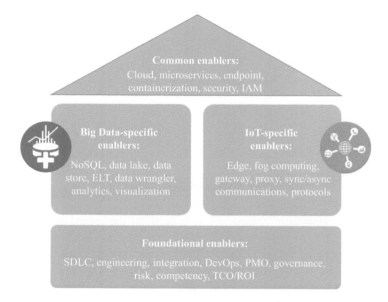

Figure 14.22   Enablement

3. *Unique:* Domain-specific enablers that are tailored to particular disciplines, such as NoSQL, data lake, data store, extract, transform, load (ETL), data wrangler, analytics, and visualization for Big Data, as well as edge, fog computing, gateway, proxy, sync/async communications, and protocols for IoT.

14.5   Application of relationship model

Moreover, how can we use i4 relationship model in real life? We will look into the guidelines and best practices of how to apply the i4 relationship model effectively in real-world projects.

14.5.1   Independent pillar

*   Use the "capability" component to understand individual abilities and usage scenarios.
*   Leverage the "similarities" component to find what is sharable and reusable.
*   Take advantage of the "difference" component to identify uniqueness and individuality.
*   Apply the "implementation" component to discover the sweat spots and long-hanging fruits.

14.5.2   Interconnecting pillar

*   Make use of the "composition" component to link IT and OT together seamlessly.
*   Employ the "realization" component to differentiate the cyber and physical sides.

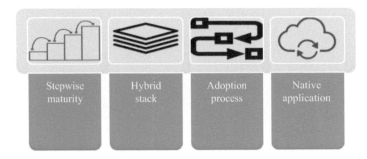

Figure 14.23   Best practices

- Utilize the "atomicity" component to understand the nature of processing and unit of work.
- Exploit the "multiplicity" component to design right duplicates and pairing.

14.5.3   Interacting pillar

- Take the "control" component to recognize communication flavors.
- Adopt the "association" component to run bimodal styles.
- Embrace the "range" component to handle various latencies and responsiveness.
- Follow the "dependency" component to hash out producer and consumption.

14.5.4   Intertwined pillar

- Tap the "touchpoints" component to separate duties and overlapping.
- Exercise the "mapping" component to synergize the linkage.
- Exert the "enablement" component to design the best-of-breed combination for arriving at a solution.
- Deploy the "interplay" component to rebalance workload execution dynamically in optimal distribution on the edge, fog, cloud, and on-premise.

14.5.5   Putting it all together

To facilitate implementations, additional artifacts are developed based on the i4 model: stepwise maturity, hybrid stack, adoption process, and native application, as painted in Figure 14.23.

14.5.5.1   Stepwise maturity

We define the maturity models on top of the "capability" component. Figure 14.24 is the capability maturity model for IoT. Five levels of maturity are specified: primitive, tentative, advanced, dynamic, and optimized. The representative indicators and relevant technologies are detailed at each level correspondingly, as a stepwise journey for transformation. The model is used to gauge where an organization is at the current state and subsequently defines what level is the reasonable next step as the target state. The model helps assess the gaps and design a roadmap for transformation.

IoT Maturity Model (IoTMM)

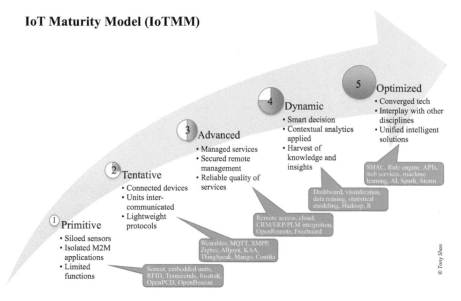

Figure 14.24   Capability maturity model for IoT

14.5.5.2   Hybrid stack

The hybrid stack is a stack of stacks: protocol, engineering, DevOps, ambience, location, and standards, as stacked in Figure 14.25.

1. *Protocol:* Communication protocols on the layers in a stack similar to the open systems interconnection (OSI) model—App, transport, network, data link, and physical.
2. *Engineering:* Patterns and techniques for technology, platform, and physical world.
3. *DevOps:* Toolchain from construct, build, quality assurance (QA) to deploy—software configuration management (SCM), code, build, package, provision, etc.
4. *Ambience:* Aspects covering market, business, and user experience—industry sectors, business model, context, interface, and device.
5. *Location:* Workload execution place—device, field, edge, region, cloud, and on-premise.
6. *Standards:* Specifications for application, network, and physical functionality IEEE, IETF, IEC, RFC.

14.5.5.3   Adoption process

To reduce the barriers to entry, a process model for IoT is fabricated by means of the rudiments constructed in the i4 model, as portrayed in Figure 14.26. IoTification contains several modules for transformation and migration: anatomy, ramp-up, use case, business case, architecture, technology selection, implementation, and platform.

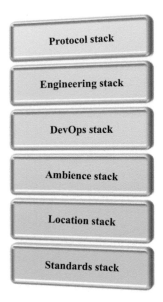

Figure 14.25   Hybrid stack

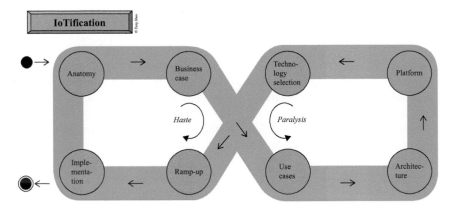

Figure 14.26   IoTification process

It includes two antipatterns for classic missteps taken by inexperienced teams—haste (too fast in lightweight approaches) and paralysis (too slow in heavyweight undertakings).

14.5.5.4   Native application

Big Data and IoT systems tend to be native applications, which are solutions developed on a particular platform or device. A native cloud application is specifically

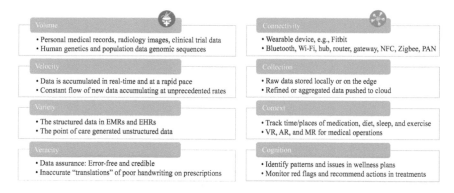

Figure 14.27   Health-care example

designed for a cloud-computing architecture, leveraging platform as a service (PaaS), microservices, containerization, and function as a service (FaaS) in the practice of 12-factor app.

A good starting point is a thorough examination of data, structure, format, flow, processing, and interpretation in a domain. In the health-care vertical, for example, we map out the medial data along the characteristics of Big Data and IoT by way of the i4 model, as itemized in Figure 14.27, which are further used to link with the "mapping" matrix in the intertwined pillar.

As a rule of thumb, the i4 model should be applied incrementally in the journey. It is not meant to be waterfall, though there is sequential usage in different parts. The model must also be employed iteratively. As an organization matures on Big Data and IoT, various features and capabilities can be tapped to harness the wisdom and acumen of the disciplines. The model also helps to converge the practices in a complex environment, smoothing the path of adoption, enablement, implementation, and operations. Coupled with other knowledge and fields of specialty like software development life cycle (SDLC), engineering, project management, and agile approaches, the i4 model accelerates the efficient execution of Big Data and IoT strategization and operationalization.

14.6   Conclusion

We are in need of an in-depth understanding of the relationship of Big Data and IoT. This chapter investigates the correlation between Big Data and IoT systematically. First, we level-set the context by anatomizing Big Data and IoT, respectively, in terms of what, which, why, where, when, who, how, and how much. We then introduce a comprehensive relationship model to synergize IoT and Big Data. The overarching model is broken down into pillars to manage the complexity: independent, interconnecting, interacting, and intertwined (i4).

Table 14.1 Summary of i4 model pillars

Pillar	Component	Description	Annotation	Usage guidelines
Independent	Difference	Distinction in the operating model	• *Execution:* IoT usually runs on the edge, while Big Data usually runs in a central place of a data center or public cloud • *Mode:* IoT is more event driven, but Big Data is used to batch jobs, though streaming data is becoming popular • *Physicality:* IoT ties closely with physical devices, and Big Data tends to be virtual • *Processing:* IoT typically has simple processing and transmission of data collected, whereas Big Data is more complex with data integration and ML analytics	Identify uniqueness and individuality
	Implementation	Suitability for the appropriate usage	• Not all industries are equally suitable for either Big Data or IoT • A heatmap shows the applicability of the technology in different industry sectors	Discover the sweat spots and long-hanging fruits
	Similarity	Commonalities in build-out and execution	• *Data intensive:* Both handle large amount of data in various types • *Quality:* Both deal with the data management and SLA for user experience • *Governance:* Both need new disciplines to supplement the existing IT and corporate governance practices • *Risks:* Both technologies are relatively young and evolving, which makes the maturity-driven adoption and journey a risky undertaking inside an organization	Find what is sharable and reusable
	Capability	Key features and functions in individual discipline	• Big Data is more focused on data transformation, store, analysis, and reporting/presentation • IoT primarily deals with sensing, capturing, connectivity, and events for operations management and decision support	Understand individual abilities and usage scenarios

Interconnecting	Composition	Big Data is IT based, and IoT is OT oriented	• Big Data is concentrated on data processing with analytics and storage as system of records • IoT is more about embedded connectivity capability in physical devices for sensing and events	Link IT and OT together seamlessly
	Realization	Big Data takes care of the cyber side, and IoT handles the physical world	• Big Data is software intensive to process digital info with algorithms in a well-secured environment • IoT is hardware intensive to cope with the objects in reality with more vulnerabilities	Differentiate the cyber and physical sides
	Atomicity	Distributed long-running vs localized short duration	• The IoT processing tends to be localized transactions in short duration • Big Data takes the input data in a long-running pipeline with distributed sources and working nodes in a cluster	Understand the nature of processing and unit of work
	Multiplicity	Diverse representation of the counterpart	• Big Data has IoT twins like digital twin, process twin, and device twin • IoT has virtual twin in an asset as representation of digital objects on Big Data side	Design duplicates and pairing
Interacting	Control	Distinct control types, mechanisms, and entities	• IoT deals with controllers like PLC • Big Data handles computing servers and nodes in a cluster	Recognize communication flavors
	Association	Bimodal styles of management and operations	• Applying IoT to Big Data is explorative with experiments for rapid innovation and fail-fast turnaround • Applying Big Data to IoT is more predictive in a controlled fashion with stable, consistent, and efficient action	Run bimodal styles

(Continues)

Table 14.1 (Continued)

Pillar	Component	Description	Annotation	Usage guidelines
	Range	Varied speed and span in processing	• *Off-line:* Data at rest—completely in a batch mode as scheduled jobs for data mining, machine learning, deep learning, and statistical modeling • *Streamline:* Data in motion—event driven in microbatches or sliding windows for long-running signal or data streaming with out-of-order data arrivals • *Nearline:* Data in haste—near real time with small latency, for localized in-memory on-device or on-gateway processing in edge/fog computing • *Online:* Data at speed—real-time interaction in request–response, transactional, and short-span processing	Handle various latencies and responsiveness
	Dependency	Source–target assembly	• Data is generated at the IoT, like a user making a payment in a purchase at a location via a mobile device. This data is transmitted to the target and stored at the Big Data side • Data is collected at the IoT, such as the speed, distance traveled, calories burned, and heart beat rate by a wearable when a user is in exercise. The data is aggregated at the Big Data side • The data science model is developed and trained for predictive analytics at the Big Data side. The model is executed for the edge analytics at the IoT side • Deep learning is employed in Big Data to create course correction and adjustment. Correspondingly, the intelligent action is taken at the IoT side to execute the recommendations sent by Big Data	Hash out producer and consumption
Intertwined	Touchpoints	Different points of contact in the data aggregation spectrum	• Big Data is related to the first half of the stages—raw/refined data and Xsights • IoT is more concerned with the two extreme ends on the spectrum	Separate duties and overlapping

Interplay	Dynamic execution of intermingled data workloads at edge, fog, cloud, or on-premise	• All these source data are ingested, processed, combined, mingled, and analyzed to generate insights and foresights • The processing and analysis workloads are executed at the optimal location in dynamic adjustment, depending on the events, criticality, available resources, bandwidth, cost, and constraints	Rebalance workload execution dynamically in optimal distribution
Mapping	Interlock matrix of key characteristics	• 4Vs meet 4Cs • Volume, velocity, variety, and veracity for Big Data • Connectivity, collection, context, and cognition for IoT	Synergize the linkage
Enablement	Groups of shared enablers and tailored enabling technologies	• *Foundational enablers*: SDLC, engineering, integration, DevOps, PMO, governance, risk, competency, and TCO/ROI • *Common enablers*: cloud, microservices, end point, containerization, security, and IAM • *Individual enablers—Big Data*: NoSQL, data lake, data store, ELT, data wrangler, analytics, and visualization • *Individual enablers—IoT*: Edge, fog computing, gateway, proxy, sync/async communications, and protocols	Design the best-of-breed combination for arriving at a solution

The independent pillar is concerned with stand-alone operations and distinct functionalities, composed of four components: difference, implementation, similarity, and capability (DISC). The interconnecting pillar deals with the structural connections with four units: composition, realization, atomicity, and multiplicity (CRAM). The interacting pillar covers four behavioral styles with four modules: control, association, range, and dependency (CARD). Lastly, the intertwined pillar is in regard to the intermesh of working together cohesively, consisting of four parts: touchpoints, integration, mapping, and enablement (TIME). We delve into each individual element in greater detail.

Further, we examine how the i4 relationship model can be effectively used in real-life projects. We itemize the guidelines for each element in the i4 model, summarized in Table 14.1. We also present the best practices of applying the relationship model: stepwise maturity, hybrid stack, adoption process, and native application.

The i4 model is evolving to keep pace with the latest advancements and growing practices in the field. We continue to refine the basic constructs, expand the model features, and converge with additional disciplines like cognitive computing in the future.

References

[1] A. Adshead. Data Set to Grow 10-Fold by 2020 as Internet of Things Takes Off IDC Annual Digital Universe Study, April 2014. http://www.computerweekly.com/news/2240217788/Data-set-to-grow-10-fold-by-2020-as-internet-of-things-takes-off

[2] InsideBigData. The Exponential Growth of Data, February 2017. https://insidebigdata.com/2017/02/16/the-exponential-growth-of-data

[3] D. Evans. The Internet of Things – How the Next Evolution of the Internet Is Changing Everything Cisco Whitepaper, April 2011. https://www.cisco.com/c/dam/en_us/about/ac79/docs/innov/IoT_IBSG_0411FINAL.pdf

[4] E. Ahmed, I. Yaqoob, I. Hashem, *et al.* (2017). The Role of Big Data Analytics in Internet of Things Computer Networks. http://doi.org/10.1016/j.comnet.2017.06.013

[5] C. Vuppalapati, A. Ilapakurti, and S. Kedari. The role of big data in creating sense EHR, an integrated approach to create next generation mobile sensor and wearable data driven electronic health record (EHR). 2016 IEEE Second International Conference on Big Data Computing Service and Applications (BigDataService), Oxford, 2016, pp. 293–296. http://doi.org/10.1109/BigDataService.2016.18

[6] E. Ahmed, I. Yaqoob, I. Hashem, *et al.* (2018). Recent Advances and Challenges in Mobile Big Data. IEEE Communications Magazine, Vol. 56 (Issue 2), pp. 102–108. http://doi.org/10.1109/MCOM.2018.1700294

[7] A. Onal, O. Berat Sezer, M. Ozbayoglu, and E. Dogdu. Weather data analysis and sensor fault detection using an extended IoT framework with semantics, big data, and machine learning. Proc. of 2017 IEEE International Conference on Big Data, 2018. http://doi.org/10.1109/BigData.2017.8258150

[8]   T. Davenport, Internet of Things (IoT): What It Is and Why It Matters. https://www.sas.com/en_us/insights/big-data/internet-of-things.html

[9]   G. Ravi (2017). Big Data-Fitting in the Shoes of Internet of Things. International Journal of Computer Science Trends and Technology (IJCST), Vol. 5 (Issue 1), pp. 84–87. ISSN: 2347-8578. http://www.ijcstjournal.org/volume-5/issue-1/IJCST-V5I1P15.pdf

[10]   A. Al-Fuqaha, M. Guizani, M. Mohammadi, M. Aledhari, and M. Ayyash (2015). Internet of Things: A Survey on Enabling Technologies, Protocols, and Applications. IEEE Communications Surveys & Tutorials, Vol. 17 (Issue 4), pp. 2347–2376. http://doi.org/10.1109/COMST.2015.2444095

[11]   S. Verma, Y. Kawamoto, Z. Fadlullah, H. Nishiyama, and N. Kato (2017). A Survey on Network Methodologies for Real-Time Analytics of Massive IoT Data and Open Research Issues. IEEE Communications Surveys & Tutorials, Vol. 19 (Issue 3), pp. 1457–1477. https://doi.org/10.1109/COMST.2017.2694469

[12]   O. Berat Sezer, E. Dogdu, M. Ozbayoglu, and A. Onal. An extended IoT framework with semantics, big data, and analytics. Proc. of 2016 IEEE International Conference on Big Data, 2016. http://doi.org/10.1109/BigData.2016.7840803

[13]   F. Chovatiya, P. Prajapati, J. Vasa, and J. Patel (2018). A Research Direction on Data Mining with IOT. In: Satapathy S., Joshi A. (eds) Information and Communication Technology for Intelligent Systems – Volume 1. ICTIS 2017. Smart Innovation, Systems and Technologies, vol 83. Springer, Cham. http://doi.org/10.1007/978-3-319-63673-3_22.

[14]   O. Berat Sezer, E. Dogdu, and A. Ozbayoglu (2018). Context-Aware Computing, Learning, and Big Data in Internet of Things: A Survey. IEEE Internet of Things Journal, Vol. 5 (Issue 1). http://doi.org/10.1109/JIOT.2017.2773600.

[15]   J. Kaivo-oja, P. Virtanen, H. Jalonen, and J. Stenvall (2015). The Effects of the Internet of Things and Big Data to Organizations and Their Knowledge Management Practices. In: Uden L., Herièko M., Ting I. H. (eds) Knowledge Management in Organizations. KMO 2015. Lecture Notes in Business Information Processing, vol 224. Springer, Cham. https://doi.org/10.1007/978-3-319-21009-4_38.

[16]   S. Yerpude and T. Singhal (2017). Internet of Things and Its Impact on Business Analytics. Indian Journal of Science and Technology, Vol. 10 (Issue 5). http://doi.org/10.17485/ijst/2017/v10i5/109348.

[17]   J. Mashey. Big data and the next wave of InfraStress problems, solutions, opportunities. USENIX Conference, 1999. http://static.usenix.org/event/usenix99/invited_talks/mashey.pdf.

[18]   F. Diebold. 'Big Data' Dynamic Factor Models for Macroeconomic Measurement and Forecasting. Eighth World Congress of the Econometric Society. Cambridge: Cambridge University Press, 2000, pp. 115–122. https://doi.org/10.1017/CBO9780511610264.005.

[19]   K. Ashton (2009). That 'Internet of Things' Thing. RFID Journal. http://www.rfidjournal.com/articles/view?4986.

[20]   P. Tyreholt. 89% of M2M/IoT Projects Have a ROI Within Two Years!. Vodafone IoT – Barometer Report, 2014. https://www.cybercom.com/About-Cybercom/Blogs/Business-and-technology-in-the-connected-world/89-of-M 2MIoT-projects-have-a-ROI-within-two-years.

[21]   J. Cha, J. Shin, and C. Yeom. A Review on Applicability of Big Data Technology in Nuclear Power Plant. Transactions of the Korean Nuclear Society Spring Meeting, May 2015. https://inis.iaea.org/search/search.aspx?orig_q=RN:47023518.

[22]   M. Pelino, F. Gillett, C. Voce, C. Mines, P. Matzke, and M. Mai. The Internet of Things Heat Map. Forrester Report, 2016. https://www.forrester.com/report/The+Internet+Of+Things+Heat+Map+2016/-/E-RES122661.

Chapter 15

Application of Internet of Things and big data for sustainability in water

Olakunle Elijah[1], Tharek Abdul Rahman[1] and Chee Yen Leow[1]

The increasing world population and rapid industrial development is driving the need for sustainable management solutions and preservation of the natural resources and the ecosystem. The Internet of Things (IoT) and big data (BD) analytics are expected to play key role toward sustainability in areas such as water, agriculture, energy, transportation and smart city. In this chapter, the focus is sustainability in water. To address the issues of sustainability of clean accessible water for human use and other living things, a water ecosystem is presented. The water ecosystem consists of five major elements which are water source, treatment, reservoir, consumption and wastage. There are several issues faced in sustainable water supply such as decreasing fresh water resources, loss of revenue due to water loss, complexity in managing the increasing demands. Existing water-management models are not efficient in addressing these issues. In addition, due to seasonal variations, changes in environmental laws, varying plant-operating conditions and other factors, there is a need for effective and efficient monitoring. The application of IoT and BD analytics technology is promising and can provide sustainable management solution in water. The practical deployment of IoT and BD analytics consists of four major components which are IoT devices, communication technology, internet and BD. The emerging low power wide area (LPWA) communication technology is expected to enhance massive connectivity required for water monitoring, data acquisition and promote sustainability in water. Hence, in this chapter, the features of the water ecosystem, the system architecture of IoT and BD and the application in water sustainability, challenges such as cyber security, policy and regulations, accuracy of the data and technology interoperability are discussed.

15.1 Introduction

Water connects every aspect of our lives, and the scarcity of it amounts to economic, health, and work crisis. There is a need to sustain the supply and the availability of unpolluted water such that it exceeds demand. Sustainability in water can be defined

[1]Wireless Communication Center (WCC), Universiti Teknologi Malaysia (UTM), Johor, Malaysia

as the continual supply of clean water for human uses and for other living things. Certain factors have contributed to the precipitous changes in the availability of water quality (WQ) and water quantity all over the world. Such factors are population growth, climate change, land use change, increased human demand and overuse of water, and global poverty. The shortage of water is expected to have negative impact on agriculture, municipal water supply and increase in water stress level.

To address the issues of sustainability of clean accessible water for human use and other living things, a water ecosystem is presented. The water ecosystem consists of five major elements which are water source, treatment, reservoir, consumption and wastage. These five elements need to be effectively managed using smart techniques in order to ensure the continuous availability of WQ and the quantity needed for consumption. There are different source of water which include storm water, rain water harvesting, river, atmosphere and wastewater. The water gotten from the source needs to be treated before they are stored in reservoirs. The reserved water are distributed to consumers via water-distribution networks. The consumers is classified into domestic, agriculture, commercial and industrial. The consumed water is later converted into wastewater which needs to be properly managed or reclaimed for human use.

As a result of rapid population growth and industrial development, there are several issues related to current water supply management. These issues range from inability to forecast demands, increased pollution threat to source of water, mismanagement and over use of clean water, non-real-time monitoring process, deteriorating supply infrastructure, delays in leakage detection and untraceable nonrevenue water use. The use of IoT and BD are promising technologies that can sustain our water from source, processing, distribution, end user consumption and waste management [1]. Furthermore, as a result of dynamic nature of water treatment systems, and the need to maintain reliability and quality, a higher resolution and degree of precision in the monitoring and control of water treatment processes are needed. Parameters such as conductivity, pH, dissolved oxygen, corrosion rate, temperature, biological activities, halogens, turbidity, fouling, heavy metals can be continuously monitored in real-time using IoT.

The use of BD collection using IoT for water management and sustainability has been discussed in the literature [1–3]. While these articles have discussed the benefits of IoT and BD analytics in water sustainability, the discussion did not cover the water ecosystem. Also, the communication technology for IoT mentioned is not suitable for massive IoT needed for water sustainability. To address this gap, this chapter takes a look at the different aspect of the water ecosystem and how IoT and BD can be applied to enhance the water sustainability. In addition, the use of LPWA communication technology in enhancing the use of IoT and BD toward sustainability in water is discussed. The challenges of IoT and BD are also presented.

15.2   Sustainability in water

The sustainability in water is described under the five elements in the water ecosystem as shown in Figure 15.1. The details of each element are discussed in the following subsections.

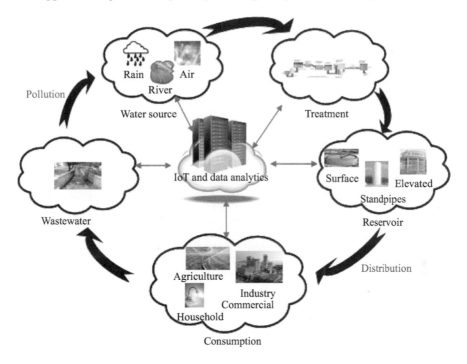

Figure 15.1   Water ecosystem

15.2.1   Source

There are different sources of freshwater supply, some of which are storm water [4], rain water harvesting [5], river [6], and atmosphere [7]. Others sources of water are ocean and reclaimed wastewater. The river is a major source of fresh water in many countries and of which pollution is considered a major threat. The sources of pollution include effluent discharges from industries and sewage treatment plant, sullage and surface runoff [8].

15.2.2   Treatment

The water collected from river, storm water, rain water harvesting, ocean and atmosphere contains dissolved gases, minerals, natural organic matters and inorganic substances. To ensure WQ, untreated water collected goes through processes such as screening, aeration, coagulation, flocculation, sedimentation, filtration and disinfection. There are different technologies that are currently been used to treat the collected water. Examples are nanotechnology [9], membrane technology [10], ultraviolet irradiation, advanced oxidation, ion exchange and biological filtration. Some of the challenges faced in treatment plants are energy consumption, cost of man power in operating the plants especially during seasonal changes, cost of maintenance and capital cost of building centralized treatment plants. The cost of man power can be reduced using IoT and BD for remote and real-time monitoring and automation.

Table 15.1 Summary of treatment processes and parameters

Technology	Types of process	Important variables
Nanotechnology [11]	Adsorption, enabled membranes, photocatalysts, microbial control	Permeability, size, temperature, pH, water quality, light intensity
Membrane [10]	Microfiltration, ultrafiltration nano filtration, reverse osmosis electrodialysis, membrane distillation	Pressure, temperature
Ultraviolet irradiation [12]	Low pressure, low intensity; low pressure, medium intensity; medium pressure, high intensity; pulsed-UV	Flow rate, turbidity, iron, suspended solids
Advanced oxidation [13]	Fenton's reagent, peroxonation photolysis of H_2O_2, photolysis of O_3, heterogeneous photocatalysis, photo-Fenton, sonochemical	Ultrasonic frequency iron type, pH, ultraviolet radiations, turbidity
Ion exchange [12]	Strong acid cationic resin, weak acid anionic resin, strong base anionic resin, weak base anionic resin	pH
Biological filtration [14,15]	Biologically activated carbon, sand filtration, riverbank filtration, managed aquifer recharge	Temperature, hydraulic loading rate, empty bed contact time, media type

Decentralized treatment plants are expected to reduce the investment cost per capital in building centralized plants [10] and this can be effectively managed using IoT and BD. Furthermore, important variables needs to be checked during treatment process in order to successfully disinfect water. For instance in ultraviolet irradiation, the flow rate and level of suspended particles needs to be within the acceptable limit for ultraviolet (UV) to be effective. Some of the process and important variables that needs to be monitored are summarized in Table 15.1. The use of IoT will allow the processes to be monitored from anywhere and anytime.

15.2.3 Reservoirs

Reservoirs are built for storage purposes in order to increase water supply reliability. Reservoir managers are faced with the challenge of forcing operators to enforce water supply restrictions due to occurrence of severe or sustained droughts or water contamination. Hence, reservoir operators need to forecast when droughts may occur, how long it will last and how severe it will be. In addition, reservoir managers need to be able to manage the depletion in the reservoir and find optimal number of reservoirs that can meet the demand of the increasing population. To address this, several models which considers the inflow from external sources such as rivers and rain and the amount of water to be released during the period. Examples of such models that have been developed for optimization of water-reserve networks are stochastic dynamic programming [16], tree-based reinforcement learning [17], data mining based on historical inflows [18], neural networks, wavelet analysis and fuzzy methodology [19,20]. Some of the models have limitations in the sense that the resulting operating policies are inefficient and of scarce relevance in practice due to current trends. Other issues related with reservoirs are the need for continuous sampling and test for contaminants (pharmaceuticals and personal care products) to ensure they remain within the permissible limit of human consumption [21,22]. It is interesting to note that the use of data analysis and real-time monitoring using wireless sensor has proven to increase efficiency in the reservoir process [22,23].

15.2.4 Consumption

There are various demands for fresh water consumption. This can be classified into agriculture, domestic, commercial and industrial. Agriculture is said to consume more water than any other human activity [24]. The excessive consumption of water and the misuse has resulted to the disappearance of rivers. The water consumed are classified into billed authorized consumption and unbilled authorized consumption. Large amounts of treated water are considered as loss due to customer metering inaccuracies, leakage and overflows at utility's storage tanks, and leakage on service connections up to the point of customer metering. To address these problems, IoT smart meters are currently been used to eliminate metering inaccuracies, help consumers and utility provider proactively manage water usage and also auto detect leakages. Leakages and breakdown in infrastructure can be detected early by using IoT real-time monitoring devices.

15.2.5 Wastewater

Wastewater is generally categorized by properties like total dissolved solids, turbidity, chemical oxygen demand, biological oxygen demand, dissolved oxygen, hardness, pH and color. Reclaimed water sources also known as biologically treated secondary effluents from wastewater treatment plants helps to offset the shortage in clean water resources [25] and represent a stable nonseasonal source [26]. The treatment of wastewater can be done either by physical, chemical, or biological processes, or in some cases, a combination of these operations. There are several wastewater-treatment technologies which include adsorption, sedimentation, filtration, chemical and membrane technology, chlorination and advanced oxidation processes (AOP) [25]. The AOP has increasingly attained great attention because it can effectively eliminate organic compounds in aqueous phase rather than collecting or transferring pollutants into another phase when compared to other conventional methods. However, AOP requires advance technology to monitor several operational parameters such as concentration of semiconductor catalysts (e.g., titanium dioxide), pH, temperature, dissolved oxygen, contaminants, light wavelength and light intensity. These operational parameters and AOP process can be effectively and efficiently monitored using IoT.

15.3 IoT and BD system architecture

The IoT enables humans and computers to interact via billions of things such as sensors, actuators, services and internet-connected objects [27]. On the hand, BD involves capturing of high volume, high velocity or high-variety data from sensors, devices, networks and other sources. The use of advanced analytics techniques such as machine learning, predictive analytics, and data mining helps to make better and faster decisions. The practical deployment of IoT and BD analytics consists of four major components which are IoT devices, communication technology, internet and BD processing. The IoT involves the use of IoT devices, gateway, network connectivity, IoT cloud server for remote access to data at anywhere and anytime. The communication technology plays an important role and one of the promising communication technology for IoT deployment is the LPWA technology. The LPWA offers low-device power consumption, ultra-low device cost, simpler to implement, support of a massive number of low throughput devices, and long-distance coverage. The internet forms the core network layer where paths are provided to carry and exchange data and network information between multiple subnetworks. The connection of IoT devices to the internet enables data to be available anywhere and anytime. The BD involves collection of captured data from IoT devices for descriptive, diagnostic, predictive and prescriptive analyses.

15.3.1 IoT device

The IoT devices consist of embedded systems interfaced with sensors and actuators and requires wireless connectivity. The architecture of a typical IoT device is shown in Figure 15.2. There are several types of IoT devices that are available in the market. Examples are Pycom which supports several communication modes such as Wi-Fi, LoRa, Sigfox, Bluetooth and NB-IoT. The choice of IoT device depends on mode of communication supported, power consumption, cost, memory, processor and input/output pins among many others.

15.3.2 Communication technology

The communication technology plays an important role in the deployment of IoT. The conventional technologies which include Zigbee, Wi-Fi, Bluetooth, Z-Wave, and passive and active radio frequency identification systems, 2G and 3G cellular are being replaced with LPWA communication technologies. This is a result of the short-distance communication range and high-power consumption which makes them unsuitable for massive IoT connectivity. The use of LPWA is advocated for massive IoT connectivity due to their promising features such as low long-range communication, low-power consumption, low cost and support for increased number of connected devices. The LPWA communication technologies can provide wider

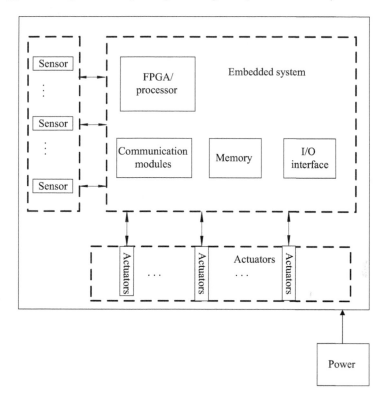

Figure 15.2   Architecture of IoT device [28]

coverage for monitoring of WQ in rivers, reservoirs and treatment plants. It can also provide better signal penetration for smart water meters installed in indoor or underground placements compared to conventional technologies like Wi-Fi, Zigbee and Bluetooth. Some of the LPWA technologies include LoRA and LoRaWAN, Sigfox, Weightless (SIG), Ingenu, Narrow Band IoT (NB-IOT), LTE-M and extended GSM for IoT (EC-GSM-IoT). There are several features that makes the NB-IoT technology attractive compared to the other LPWA communication technologies. First it uses licensed spectrum which makes it prone to less interference, thereby providing high reliability. Furthermore, it requires no network BS infrastructures and maintenance fee which allows water vendors water utilities to save considerable amount of time and money. The drawback to the use of NB-IoT is that it requires Telcos to upgrade their existing networks to support 5G NB-IoT network.

15.3.3   Internet

The internet over the years has enabled global collection of computer networks to link together. This has evolved to global connection of device-to-device, device-to-cloud, device-to-gateway and back-end data-sharing. The connection of IoT devices to the internet enables data to be available anywhere and anytime. However, the transfer of data via the internet requires adequate security, support of real-time data and ease of accessibility. The use of common set of connectivity protocol and IoT middle-ware enables IoT devices to connect over the internet [28]. The internet supports different layer of abstractions which include sensing, accessing, networking, middle-ware, and application layer for IoT devices [29].

15.3.4   Big data processing

Data collection and analysis plays an important role in the water ecosystem. The internet has paved way for cloud computing where large data are gathered for storage and processing. Cloud computing involves the management of user interface, services, organizing and coordinating of network nodes, computing and processing data [30]. The BD involves data source, data structure, data storage, data processing, data visualization and data analytics [31]. The BD can be applied in different areas of the water ecosystem. For instance, in assessment of WQ, data collected helps to know WQ status and the suitability for different uses [32]. It can be used in pipe-condition assessment [1], provide water-consumption patterns, optimize water production and distributions, as well as efficient wastewater management. The use of BD analytics will enable operators to understand the dynamics in diurnal variations, weekly trends, seasonal shifts, peak and average demands and supply of water. Furthermore, BD analytics can lead to improved algorithms for solving problems such as deterioration modeling, pressure and flow modeling, and leak and loss detection modeling [1]. It is important to note that the quality of the data depends largely on the accuracy of the sensors.

15.4   Application of IoT and BD in water sustainability

Water management is defined as the activity of planning, developing, distributing and managing the optimum use of water resources [33]. There are different aspects of the water management such as sourcing, treatment, storage and distribution in the water ecosystem. In addition, factors to be considered in water management are cost of billing and monitoring of water consumption, operations and maintenance. The use of IoT and data analytics in the water management is attracting more research interest because of the many benefits it provides. Figure 15.3 shows the application of IoT in water sustainability. This involves IoT devices used as sensor nodes for collection and transmission of data either via the gateway to the IoT cloud server or directly from the sensor nodes to the IoT cloud server. Sensor nodes which use the unlicensed spectrums such as LoRaWAN need a gateway, while licensed spectrum like NB-IoT can directly transfer data to the IoT cloud server via the base station. The data collected in the IoT cloud server are saved and analyzed in application or analysis server. The mobile and web platform allows for users to monitor or control water-related operations from anywhere and at any time using the internet. The areas of application of IoT and data analytics in water management include the following.

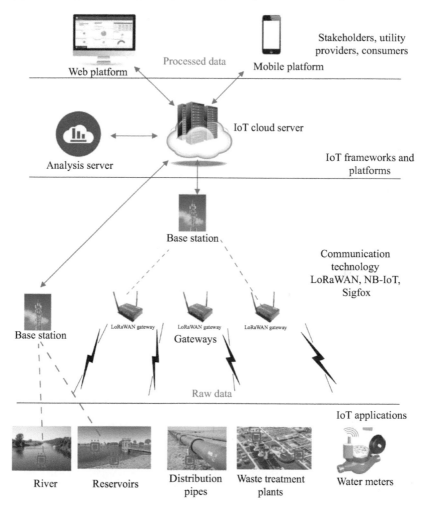

Figure 15.3 Application of IoT

15.4.1 Smart metering

The use of smart metering allows for real-time monitoring of hydrological-related data (quality, pressure and temperature), elimination of inaccurate meter reading and user complaints [34], determine individual end-user's consumption patterns [35]. It enables the average day, peak day and mean day maximum month demand curve of individual end-use levels to be known and the hourly demand patterns can be generated from the smart meters.

15.4.2 Leakage detection

Leakage detection and localization in large-scale water distribution system is of paramount importance in water-resource management. Some of the methods include use of leakage detection techniques such as signal processing, statistical methods, balancing methods, and negative pressure wave. Other methods include the use of acoustic systems, ground penetration radar, magnetic induction and gas-injection method. The efficiency of this methods depends largely on operational cost, response time, ability to locate leakages, usage and false alarms [36]. It is a challenging task which requires the use of smart technologies. Recent technology advancements have seen the use of UAV for leakage monitoring [37], wireless sensor network [36], online sensor monitoring [38] and IoT for monitoring and burst detection [39].

15.4.3 Water pollution

Pollution is a major threat to river and river a major source of fresh water. Conventional monitoring schemes such as manual WQ monitoring (MWQM) and continuous WQ monitoring (CWQM) are considered inefficient. The MWQM involves taking of water samples from rivers for *in-situ* and laboratory measurement, while the CWQM involves the use of fixed stations at strategic locations. These methods are costly and less efficient in identifying the pollutants, pollution level and the source of the pollutants. The use of IoT and BD analytics enables the use of innovative methods such as UAV [37,40] for real-time monitoring and *in-situ* measurement of water pollution [40].

15.4.4 Prediction and forecasting

The data collected from environmental conditions and hydrological information can help to streamflow forecasts, reservoir inflow forecasts, reservoir operation planning and scheduling [41]. The study in [41] demonstrates the use of artificial intelligence and data-mining methods such as random forest artificial neural network and support vector regression for predicting 1 month-ahead reservoir inflow to two headwater reservoirs in USA and China. Other studies carried out in [42] shows the use of BD platform with heterogeneity of data coming from different sources to model and manage water resources such as floods and droughts. The combination of IoT and cloud computing increases the efficiency and the time in collecting, analyzing and providing useful information in real-time to all stakeholders in the water-management system. The data collected using IoT and BD with machine learning and artificial intelligence can be used to implement predictive maintenance for water infrastructures, machines, operating and treatment processes.

15.5 Challenges

The implementation of IoT and BD in water sustainability is faced with several challenges such as cyber security, policy and regulations, accuracy of the data and technology interoperability.

15.5.1 Cyber security

Cyber threat remains a major challenge to the implementation of IoT and BD in water sustainability. This is because several stakeholders, including utilities, regulators, residential and commercial customers if connected to IoT infrastructure can be a target of cyberattack [43]. The diversity of IoT devices and the different level of IoT architecture poses enormous challenge. For example, vulnerabilities in IoT device firmware due to lack of complicated encryption and authentication algorithms owing to lack of memory and power consumption constraints [44]. Another security issue is privacy concerns. The release of personal information from consumers over the internet makes them prone to privacy leak as information can be shared with authorized service providers.

15.5.2 Data accuracy

The accuracy of the sensors used in gathering data in water ecosystem requires periodic cleaning or auto-cleaning, frequent calibration and validation. This can be a major challenge because of the continuous exposure of these sensors chemicals, pollutants or unsuitable environmental conditions. To address this, routine calibration and validation of the sensors are required.

15.5.3 Policy and regulations

The integration of IoT and BD with business process coordination requires a good policy and regulation practices. There are varieties of functions and process involved in management of the water ecosystem. Hence international standards are needed for effective inter-working of water-management infrastructures and components [33]. The standard will cover remote management of physical elements and operations, interoperability among applications related to weather forecast, environment water-related activities, integration of different systems related to IoT water devices, and integration to legacy system. To address this, [33] proposed a high-level architecture for effective water management.

15.5.4 Technology interoperability

Several heterogeneous IoT devices developed by different companies operate with propriety frameworks. In most cases, these IoT devices are interdependent, use different communication protocols, authentication and IoT platforms. This opens up so many challenges which include security treats and difficulty in coordination for the different aspects of water management.

15.6 Conclusion

In this chapter, the different elements that constitute a water ecosystem has been discussed. The role each element plays in sustainability of water, the challenges and how IoT and BD can be applied has been discussed. The use of IoT and BD can help in improving the global water availability and scarcity reduction by enhancing real-time analysis of WQ, availability, water consumption, water stress and projection of future water needs. The emergency of IoT and BD will allow for the funneling of disparate data into a single and meaningful pool of information within the water ecosystem. IoT and BD technology can be implemented in the source of water supply, treatment, reservoirs, distribution and consumption management and also in waste control. This will be to address the increasing demands and challenges of water supply. The key enabler for the IoT and BD in water sustainability is the LPWA communication technology which has been discussed in this chapter. The various application of the IoT and BD and the challenges of implementing IoT and BD have been presented. However, there are more opportunities that can be harnessed in ensuring water sustainability by using IoT and BD analytics.

References

[1]   Koo D, Piratla K, and Matthews CJ. Towards sustainable water supply: Schematic development of big data collection using internet of things (IoT). Procedia Engineering. 2015;118:489–497.

[2]   Narendran S, Pradeep P, and Ramesh MV. An Internet of Things (IoT) based sustainable water management. In: 2017 IEEE Global Humanitarian Technology Conference (GHTC); 2017. pp. 1–6.

[3]   Anjana S, Sahana MN, Ankith S, *et al.* An IoT based 6LoWPAN enabled experiment forwater management. In: 2015 IEEE International Conference on Advanced Networks and Telecommuncations Systems (ANTS); 2015. pp. 1–6.

[4]   Hutchinson A, Woodside G, and Ralph F. Increasing storm water capture for water supply using forecast informed reservoir operations (FIRO) in Orange County, California. In: AGU Fall Meeting Abstracts; 2017.

[5]   Sample DJ, and Liu J. Optimizing rainwater harvesting systems for the dual purposes of water supply and runoff capture. Journal of Cleaner Production. 2014;75:174–194.

[6]   Chin CM, and Ng YJ. A perspective study on the urban river pollution in Malaysia. Chemical Engineering. 2015;45:745–750.

[7]   Wang J, Wang R, Wang L, *et al.* A high efficient semi-open system for fresh water production from atmosphere. Energy. 2017;138:542–551.

[8]   Zhang Y, Collins A, Murdoch N, *et al.* Cross sector contributions to river pollution in England and Wales: Updating waterbody scale information to support policy delivery for the Water Framework Directive. Environmental Science & Policy. 2014;42:16–32.

[9]   Brame J, Li Q, and Alvarez PJ. Nanotechnology-enabled water treatment and reuse: Emerging opportunities and challenges for developing countries. Trends in Food Science & Technology. 2011;22(11):618–624.

[10]   Schäfer AI, Hughes G, and Richards BS. Renewable energy powered membrane technology: A leapfrog approach to rural water treatment in developing countries? Renewable and Sustainable Energy Reviews. 2014;40:542–556.

[11]   Mahadik S. Applications of nanotechnology in water and waste water treatment. AADYA—Journal of Management and Technology (JMT). 2017;7: 187–191.

[12] National Research Council & Others. Identifying future drinking water contaminants. National Academies Press, Washington, D.C; 1999.

[13] Oturan MA, and Aaron JJ. Advanced oxidation processes in water/wastewater treatment: Principles and applications. A review. Critical Reviews in Environmental Science and Technology. 2014;44(23):2577–2641.

[14] Reungoat J, Escher B, Macova M, *et al.* Biofiltration for advanced treatment of wastewater. Urban Water Security Research Alliance, Australia; 2012.

[15] Basu OD, Dhawan S, and Black K. Applications of biofiltration in drinking water treatment—A review. Journal of Chemical Technology & Biotechnology. 2016;91(3):585–595.

[16] Cervellera C, Chen VC, and Wen A. Optimization of a large-scale water reservoir network by stochastic dynamic programming with efficient state space discretization. European Journal of Operational Research. 2006;171(3): 1139–1151.

[17] Castelletti A, Galelli S, Restelli M, *et al.* Tree-based reinforcement learning for optimal water reservoir operation. Water Resources Research. 2010;46(9): 1–19.

[18] Bessler FT, Savic DA, and Walters GA. Water reservoir control with data mining. Journal of Water Resources Planning and Management. 2003;129(1): 26–34.

[19] Pourshahabi S, Nikoo MR, Raei E, *et al.* An entropy-based approach to fuzzy multi-objective optimization of reservoir water quality monitoring networks considering uncertainties. Water Resources Management. 2018;32(13):4425–4443.

[20] Kumar S, Tiwari MK, Chatterjee C, *et al.* Reservoir inflow forecasting using ensemble models based on neural networks, wavelet analysis and bootstrap method. Water Resources Management. 2015;29(13):4863–4883.

[21] Aristizabal-Ciro C, Botero-Coy AM, López FJ, *et al.* Monitoring pharmaceuticals and personal care products in reservoir water used for drinking water supply. Environmental Science and Pollution Research. 2017;24(8): 7335–7347.

[22] Hansen CH, Williams GP, Adjei Z, *et al.* Reservoir water quality monitoring using remote sensing with seasonal models: Case study of five central-Utah reservoirs. Lake and Reservoir Management. 2015;31(3):225–240.

[23] Yang L, Yu J, Ju M, *et al.* Intelligent monitoring and controlling technology of water injection in ultra-low permeability reservoir of Ordos Basin. In: Proceedings of the International Field Exploration and Development Conference 2017. Springer; 2019. pp. 1353–1362.

[24] Brauman KA, Siebert S, and Foley JA. Improvements in crop water productivity increase water sustainability and food security—A global analysis. Environmental Research Letters. 2013;8(2):024030.

[25] Chong MN, Jin B, Chow CW, *et al.* Recent developments in photocatalytic water treatment technology: A review. Water Research. 2010;44(10): 2997–3027.

[26]   Deng Y, and Zhao R. Advanced oxidation processes (AOPs) in wastewater treatment. Current Pollution Reports. 2015;1(3):167–176.

[27]   Ngu AH, Gutierrez M, Metsis V, *et al.* IoT middleware: A survey on issues and enabling technologies. IEEE Internet of Things Journal. 2017;4(1):1–20.

[28]   Elijah O, Rahman TA, Orikumhi I, *et al.* An overview of internet of things (IoT) and data analytics in agriculture: Benefits and challenges. IEEE Internet of Things Journal. 2018:5(5):3758–3773.

[29]   Abbasi AZ, Islam N, Shaikh ZA, *et al.* A review of wireless sensors and networks' applications in agriculture. Computer Standards & Interfaces. 2014;36(2):263–270.

[30]   TongKe F. Smart agriculture based on cloud computing and IOT. Journal of Convergence Information Technology. 2013;8(2):1–7.

[31]   Hashem IAT, Yaqoob I, Anuar NB, *et al.* The rise of "big data" on cloud computing: Review and open research issues. Information Systems. 2015;47:98–115.

[32]   Rahmanian N, Ali SHB, Homayoonfard M, *et al.* Analysis of physiochemical parameters to evaluate the drinking water quality in the State of Perak, Malaysia. Journal of Chemistry. 2015;2015:1–10.

[33]   Robles T, Alcarria R, de Andrés DM, *et al.* An IoT based reference architecture for smart water management processes. Journal of Wireless Mobile Networks, Ubiquitous Computing, and Dependable Applications. 2015;6(1):4–23.

[34]   Mudumbe MJ, and Abu-Mahfouz AM. Smart water meter system for user-centric consumption measurement. In: 2015 IEEE 13th International Conference on Industrial Informatics (INDIN); 2015. pp. 993–998.

[35]   Gurung TR, Stewart RA, Sharma AK, *et al.* Smart meters for enhanced water supply network modelling and infrastructure planning. Resources, Conservation and Recycling. 2014;90:34–50.

[36]   Adedeji KB, Hamam Y, Abe BT, *et al.* Towards achieving a reliable leakage detection and localization algorithm for application in water piping networks: An overview. IEEE Access. 2017;5:20272–20285.

[37]   DeBell L, Anderson K, Brazier RE, *et al.* Water resource management at catchment scales using lightweight UAVs: Current capabilities and future perspectives. Journal of Unmanned Vehicle Systems. 2015;4(1):7–30.

[38]   Yu HW, Anumol T, Park M, *et al.* On-line sensor monitoring for chemical contaminant attenuation during UV/H_2O_2 advanced oxidation process. Water Research. 2015;81:250–260.

[39]   Afifi M, Abdelkader MF, and Ghoneim A. An IoT system for continuous monitoring and burst detection in intermittent water distribution networks. In: 2018 International Conference on Innovative Trends in Computer Engineering (ITCE); 2018. pp. 240–247.

[40]   Koparan C, Koc AB, Privette CV, *et al.* In situ water quality measurements using an unmanned aerial vehicle (UAV) system. Water. 2018;10(3):264.

[41]   Yang T, Asanjan AA, Welles E, *et al.* Developing reservoir monthly inflow forecasts using artificial intelligence and climate phenomenon information. Water Resources Research. 2017;53(4):2786–2812.

[42] Chalh R, Bakkoury Z, Ouazar D, *et al.* Big data open platform for water resources management. In: 2015 International Conference on Cloud Technologies and Applications (CloudTech); 2015. pp. 1–8.

[43] Cleveland FM. Cyber security issues for advanced metering infrastructure (AMI). In: 2008 IEEE Power and Energy Society General Meeting – Conversion and Delivery of Electrical Energy in the 21st Century; 2008. pp. 1–5.

[44] Zhou W, Jia Y, Peng A, *et al.* The effect of IoT new features on security and privacy: New threats, existing solutions, and challenges yet to be solved. IEEE Internet of Things Journal. 2018;6(2):1606–1616.

Chapter 16

IoT-based smart transportation system under real-time environment

Sanjukta Bhattacharya[1], Sourav Banerjee[2]
and Chinmay Chakraborty[3]

This book chapter represents an overall idea of the Internet of Things (IoT)-based smart transportation system under real-time environment. IoT technology is growing very fast in recent years in the industry and business areas with lots of opportunities. IoT is used to connect between different objects or things in the real world to the internet. IoT is a new concept area, which is also known as a riskless, powerful and precise architectural infrastructure which is very much related to our daily life. IoT is continuously reducing cost and also power consumption. IoT is known as an emerging technological world where anyone or anything can be connected, interacted and communicated with each other anytime and anywhere in a perceptive way through different types of gadgets like smartphones and computers. In IoT, physical objects like actuators and sensors are wirelessly or physically connected to the internet. An enormous amount of data is produced by the network to the analytical devices to scrutinize it. IoT is known as an infrastructural environment where communication and computing system consistently embedded to achieve some specified targets. In the IoT, multiple physical objects of the real world associated with each other to collect and interchange the data. The application areas of IoT spread out at various segments, including transportation, health-care environments, home automation, agriculture, smart appliances and smart city. The IoT technology along with the Big Data framework is created a huge change in the transportation sector, especially in motorways. Nowadays, traffic congestion is a very serious problem throughout the world. Moreover, day by day the number of vehicles is also increased in a terrible way to create an inescapable traffic condition. After that, this disorganized and chaotic traffic situation is also responsible to increase the pollution level and wastage of natural resources because most of the vehicles keep their engine active at any traffic congestion. Apart from this, it is also seen that using the same lane for heavy and light vehicles, the number of accidents is also increased day by day. So those aforesaid issues are very much responsible to create terrible congestion on the road, which is the prime suspect for several crashes

[1]Department of Information Technology, Techno International Newtown, Kolkata, India
[2]Department of Computer Science & Engineering, Kalyani Govt. Engg. College, Kalyani, India
[3]Department of Electronics & Communication Engineering, Birla Institute of Technology, Ranchi, India

of vehicles and the violation of safety environment on road. The performance of most of the existing techniques is not good enough to provide the solution of the aforesaid problem because those techniques are itself very costly and always face various maintenance issues. So to overcome the aforesaid problems and to give more safety on the road, intelligent transportation system (ITS) or smart transportation system performs an active role to increase the efficiency of the transportation system on road. This smart transportation system is developed with the help of lots of sensors such as pressure sensors, proximity sensors, light sensors, humidity sensors, temperature sensors and wireless sensor network (WSN) such as Zigbee, Xbee and Wi-Fi. This book chapter presents an overview of the data acquisition (DAQ), data-processing and data-analysis technique, various work, existing trends, challenges and future scope of this smart transportation system.

16.1   Introduction

IoT that is nowadays known as an emerging technology empowers human life in such a way which drastically changes the lifestyle of every individual. IoT authorizes each and every individual object in such a way that at any instance of time, the object can communicate, see and hear the surrounded world. IoT is recognized as an open-network paradigm, which made with the ability of smart things or objects of the real world with the capabilities of information sharing, properly organized data, resource and storage handling, automatic organizing facility and reacting in the case of environmental changes. The environment must be distributed for any type of IoT application areas. Many different origins and devices, which are used to gather data from different entities and different vendors, are used to collaborate to achieve the desired objective. Devices from other manufacturers are used to share data in a way, which maintain the interoperability from different protocols and systems. Each and every object should be a part of the network, which maintains scalability. IoT has given a wide range of application area in each and every segment of daily life. IoT application has the advantages, which are very much related to the internet to share data, proper connectivity, etc. Embedded devices are used to collect data and always connected to the global and local networks. IoT provides a huge amount of data, which belongs to the object, human; space and time always combine with the internet to gain cost-effective communication techniques. IoT technology provides a lot of application areas, which are commonly known as a cyber-physical system, including the smart concept in the areas of city, transportation, medical facility and home. Each and every individual thing is identified uniquely with the help of emerging embedded system along with incorporating within the existing infrastructure with the help of internet technology. The objective of IoT is to generate a new technological era to raise the real-world objects or things by enabling communication, storage, application and computing abilities. IoT not only plays an important role but also improves human life in an efficient way in different domains such as transportation, health care and natural disasters [1]. Nowadays, transportation is an area, which absorbs various types of application of IoT. The load of the traffic system is mostly dependent on real-time environmental parameters, which include weather constraint, temperature fluctuation, seasonal restriction, the turbulence of water or air and also any uncertain or incalculable situations due to construction-based activities and accident.

Different types of transportation system that is emerged through IoT consists of a lot of IoT-supported devices and networks such as radio frequency identification (RFID), various actuators, Zigbee or Xbee also responsible to generate a massive amount of same or various data, which is defined as Big Data [2]. This Big Data plays an important role to make any type of decision-making movements at different types of transportation system with various analytical techniques. An enormous amount of devices are involved to form different IoT-based systems such as real-time transportation system where these devices sense their surrounding different activities to transmit an enormous volume of raw data to nearest base stations where these data are used for processing, analyzing and prediction purpose [3].

In the recent decade's transportation system faces a lot of problems due to the poor infrastructure and unscientific distribution of traffic-signaling system. Moreover, day by day the number of vehicles is also increased in a terrible way to create an inescapable traffic condition. After that, this disorganized and chaotic traffic situation is also responsible to increase the pollution level and wastage of natural resources because most of the vehicles keep their engine active at any traffic congestion. Apart from this, it is also seen that using the same lane for heavy and light vehicles, the number of accidents is also increased day by day [4]. Therefore, to reduce or to overcome traffic congestion problems, the IoT infrastructure along with Big Data has taken an important and massive role. IoT framework is an enough response to build an ITS with the help of several sensor devices and sensing network system, but using this ITS, an enormous volume of real-time data is continuously generated. Analysis of these generated data is excessively required for taking any type of crucial decision in the real-time transportation system. The transportation system does not have enough capacity to deal with the data that are growing or generating too quickly. Generally, different types of real-time data, which are always generated in the transportation system or traffic system, are enough rich in nature. These real-time data are generated from different sources such as customer-related data, which are generally generated from public transportation or railway reservation system or airline reservation system, operation-related data from different companies such as courier, data that are dynamic in nature and are also dynamically generated from different sensors such as microwave detector, laser detector, infrared detector, video detector and ultrasonic detector and the data that are achieved from the Global Positioning System. A large storage area or space and modern equipment are needed to handle this massive volume of real-time data. There are several traditional data processing techniques which are not able to handle fast-growing data smoothly and efficiently and that is the reason why the existing data-processing methods collapsed and various failures have taken place. Moreover, the traditional traffic system consists of inefficient integration, underdeveloped and unsophisticated technology and nonuniform DAQ techniques, which actually make the transportation system more stagnant and unsynchronized. The application of Big Data within the transportation system is enough capable to solve most of the aforesaid problematic situation in an efficient way.

In the transportation system, Big Data is used to solve the storage issue of real-time data, the database-management issue and the accurate analysis of data. Big Data is able to introduce a system named Hadoop to efficiently handle large scale of real-time data or to efficiently complete a large and complicated task with the help of Hadoop's Map Reduce technique to maintain the fault tolerance and stability at the same time. Big Data is also used to properly and accurately improve the efficiency and accuracy of the transportation system by reducing the incorrect alarm probability or upgrading all the traffic information in time, providing proper traffic instruction to the travelers through which the travelers can take the right decision by choosing the right path in a heavy traffic zone. Big Data is also capable to identify the accident zone very quickly and also responsible for providing quick emergency services to save a valuable life [5]. The IoT infrastructure along with Big Data makes the transportation system more information oriented, well organized, well planned, methodical, extensive and systematic. Big Data also has some prime characteristics to properly handle the massive volume of real-time data where the speed of processing data is very high. Moreover, Big Data is also responsible to operate traffic-related operation, synchronize different networks related to traffic road and control efficiently the traffic-related demand. Big Data is also used to minimize the congestion of traffic and also reduce the bad effects of the transportation system on surrounding environments by using a different type of congestion system and various emission-related forecasting and monitoring models [6].

16.1.1   Challenges

Today the whole world needs to live in a smart way. That is why each and every domain of our socioeconomic system is changed to improve the citizen's lifestyle in a smarter way. The information and communication technology (ICT) [7] helps to provide the framework through which the daily life of the citizens would be safer, smoother and time convenient. IoT is one of the main areas in this case, and the transportation system on road is one of the fundamental areas, which is rising with the help of IoT. There are many challenges and constraints are taken place while developing the transportation system based on IoT both in hardware and software region. In the case of software segment data storage, data retrieval and data collection in an effective way, the proper infrastructure of the resources of the network, privacy and security issues, Big Data infrastructure, platforms, efficient interoperability criteria, valuable context, reliability, diversity and scalability factor, smart applications are the major challenging issues. In the hardware segment, the total number of devices that are connected with internet, the overall cost, the ideal specification of the devices and longevity of all the hardware devices are the prime challenge factors in the case of smart transportation environment.

16.1.2   Objective

IoT, in this case, used to enhance the efficiency and effectiveness of real-time parameters. Here, traffic-management system for a smart city deals all real-time data-monitoring components. So, we consider all issues and our data space enhances in a large order day by day. In IoT, we have taken all parameters from the environment through sensors. So as per the World Health Organization, our futuristic approach and used components must be eco-friendly and gradually updated for each environmental issue like pollutions [8]. Initially, the ITS is developed on the transportation system based on urban automotive vehicles, but nowadays the ITS-based research includes different levels or types of transportation where one of the well-known transportation is defined as freight transportation in which a lot of research work can be done in near future [9]. Apart from this, ITS that consists of two subparts known as advanced fleet management systems and commercial vehicle operations will also acquire different emerging technologies as a future scope. Different types of decision-making system and various data-processing methodologies will also explore in the case of ITS. The freight based it will be deployed, which includes the integration and exchange of addresses and also will maintain the security issues especially in ports and border areas as a future scope.

16.2 Recent trends in IoT application for the real-time transportation system

IoT that is defined by the ICT is considered a dynamic global network infrastructure with self-configuring capabilities based on standard and interoperable communication protocols where physical and virtual things have identities, physical attributes and virtual personalities use intelligent interface and seamlessly integrated into the information network. IoT is the internetworking of physical devices, vehicles, buildings and other items embedded with electronics, software, sensors, actuators and network connectivity that enable these objects to collect and exchange data. Urban population is one of the most serious problems, which is rising up each and every day, and the whole world is terrified through the problems to depend on the urban population. Another major problem, which is nowadays increasing depending on the urban population, is the transportation system where traffic management is an important factor. The major portion of the population is dependent on the automobile, and road congestion is an unavoidable matter nowadays. Apart from the aforesaid matter, there are several issues that occurred depending on constantly increasing automobile numbers, and that is why an efficient and effective traffic-management system is always required. Nowadays, IoT plays an important role to resolve the traffic-related problems and makes the traffic management smarter with the help of lots of sensing devices, so that the smart traffic management should be modeled in such a way, which requires better infrastructure in the case of traffic lights, street lights, division on highways, emergency base station in the case of any accidents, identify the stolen vehicles, provide the proper parking area, reduce the pollution a level (in case sound and emission) and utilize the natural resources properly. IoT-based traffic-management system, which deals with real-time information related to traffic system, provides more renewable options for other traffic activities by properly utilizing the traffic flow and providing road safety as much as possible. These smarter traffic systems are also capable of the analysis of data based on real-time information.

The latest trend that is based on automated and intelligent traffic-control management is controlling the traffic on the road based on the density of vehicles. In this dynamic and automated traffic-signaling system, the signal is automatically changed depending upon the density of the vehicles at the congested roads with the help of some kind of sensors [8]. In this system, the proximity sensors are used to detect the number of vehicles present in a congested road and convey this message to the Arduino microcontroller where the decision is made whether extra time duration of the signaling light is required or not to clear the congestion of any road [9].

Another latest trend is to organize the parking area in an efficient and systematic way, which is defined as intelligent parking assistance (IPA), to solve the massive parking zone problem with the help of IoT framework in which proper utilization of parking space is a prime factor. At the same time, searching for the suitable parking space in a minimum amount of time is also considered a primary constraint.

The next trend is reducing the waiting time of the vehicles at any toll booth with the help of mobile technology and sensor technology. This new trend not only decreases the waiting time of the vehicles, but also using this technology the congestion of traffic, which is mainly occurred near any toll plaza, can be reduced at a high volume, which clears the traffic throughout that entire road. The next trend is scheduling the emergency vehicles in such a way so that they can reach their destination in proper time. Actually in the present days, maximum traffic signals hold the characteristics of fixed mode, which is not changed dynamically, even if there are any type of emergency situation occurring in a congested traffic, such as long waiting time is not accepted for the vehicles such as fire engines, ambulance or police cars because late arrival of these emergency vehicles can lose several valuable properties and precious lives. The new system is introduced to amalgamate the distance measured between that emergency vehicle and one particular intersection with the help of counting the number of vehicles, visual methods, which are based on different sensors, sensitive and sensor alert sound transmission within a WSN, to smoothly schedule the emergency vehicles so that several lives and properties sustain in a proper way. The next trend depends upon the vehicle ad-hoc network (VANET), which is a subclass of mobile ad-hoc network (MANET). The VANET scheme combines the automobile infrastructure and wireless technology to develop the congestion-less road and to improve the road much safer. The VANET consists of the vehicle-to-infrastructure (V2I) and vehicle-to-vehicle (V2V) wireless communication with the help of different wireless technologies such as IEEE 802.11. In this VANET, the nodes are the vehicles, which are allowed to exchange data within this VANET to develop an ITS to achieve safe and congestion-free motorways.

Figure 16.1 describes an ITS or smart transportation system with the help of IoT infrastructure where all the vehicles are communicated with each other through the V2V communication; and at the same time, these vehicles are also communicated with the base station through the V2I communication. These base stations can be a local server or remote server, which is the prime considered a prime data exchanging center. The automobiles can exchange information with other vehicles and base stations, which are eventually stored and process in cloud framework with the help of Big Data concept. Here Big Data is mainly used to properly and systematically store the massive

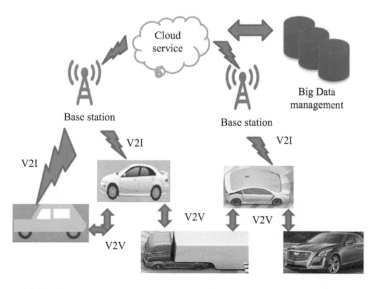

Figure 16.1   Smart transportation system based on IoT and Big Data concept

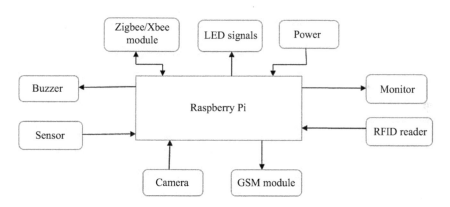

Figure 16.2   Block diagram of automatic traffic control system

volume of data and then analyze the data with efficient algorithms. The analyzed result is used to solve a lot of traffic-related problems such as traffic-signaling issue, parking problem, the single path for heavy vehicle and emergency vehicle, accident-zone-identification issue and the heavy congestion in high roads, which are increasing in a horrified way in recent days.

Figure 16.2 describes the block diagram of an automatic traffic control system with the help of IoT-based real-time environment which is very useful to solve mainly the heavy congestion problem on road where the Raspberry Pi which is defined as a microcontroller is considered a central component which is connected to other components such as sensors, buzzer, Zigbee/Xbee module, LED signals, power supply

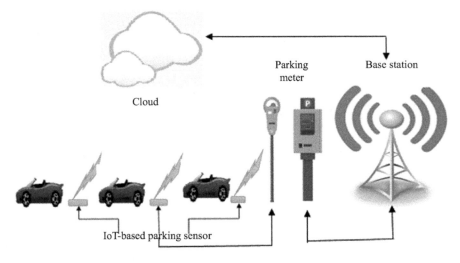

Figure 16.3　Intelligent parking assistance

module, monitor or display screen, RFID reader, GSM module and camera. Apart from these, many other devices also can be associated with this system. Different types of sensors, such as proximity sensor, temperature sensor and pressure sensor, are attached to this system to efficiently transfer the real-time traffic data. The Buzzer device is generally used to create an alarm in an emergency or crucial situation. Zigbee/Xbee/GSM module is used in WSN segment to provide the continuous network connection. The RFID reader is used for any object-identification purpose, e.g., to identify the stolen cars. Monitor unit is used as a display unit to observe the various surrounding activities. LED lights are used to provide the traffic condition and the time that is generally spent on the traffic movement on road. The camera unit is used to catch or to record all the activities that are happened on road throughout the day. Each and every component of this automatic-traffic-control system is taking an active part to develop congestion-free road with other advantages.

Figure 16.3 describes an IPA framework with the help of IoT infrastructure to provide the solution of recent day's huge parking problem. Here the system is developed with lots of sensor especially parking sensor, which is actually used to provide the information on free parking space with the help of a parking meter device very quickly and efficiently. The acquired information is captured and analyzed in the base station and cloud infrastructure by distributing the information to the cars that are eligible for that parking area.

16.3　Data acquisition

DAQ serves an important position in the different sectors such as industrial field, different research activities, health-care field, transportation area and different utilities of public requirements. The data, which are collected, stored and distributed properly through DAQ, are used to ensure safety, reliability, efficiency and any decision-making to smoothen and provide safety to the daily life of human beings [10]. A process or a system through which data or information are acquired from various region depend on different conditions with the help of some specialized hardware and software is defined as DAQ. This process is also used to measure a physical or electrical phenomenon with the help of a specialized computer such as temperature, sound, voltage, pressure and current. DAQ is made with the help of DAQ-supported hardware devices, efficient programmable computer and a collection of various sensors (combination of sensors, actuators are also important to efficiently develop DAQ procedure). In the DAQ environment, the data or information, which are generally collected through several sensors, are passed to the computer for digitization and after that, for analysis purpose to make any prime decision. There are three important segments, which are very crucial in any DAQ, are defined as sensor devices, signal conditioning criteria and analog-to-digital converter (ADC). The sensors that are also known as transducers are used to convert the real-time phenomenon into current or voltage signals. These analog signals are converted into a digital signal with the help of ADC, and the process is defined as digitization [11]. Sometimes extra circuitry is needed to make a bridge between the sensor device and ADC for the accurate measurements of quality issue. This extra circuitry is known as a signal conditioning, which includes the completion of Wheatstone bridge, calibration, attenuation/amplification, linearization, filtering and calibration. The data or information, which are related to the transportation system or traffic system, are also acquired through DAQ. This traffic-related information is very essential information, which is used to serve different ways in our socioeconomic system. The traffic-related information is very useful for the passengers, vehicles and traffic surgeon or traffic controller to develop congestion-free and safe transportation system [12]. These real-time transportation/traffic-related data, such as accident-related data, weather-related data, data related to one or more vehicles, and any identification data of objects are acquired from several sensors such as pressure sensors, image sensors, humidity sensors, gas RFID sensors, proximity sensors, light sensors and temperature sensors. The main objective of DAQ is to gather all the real-world traffic-related information from various sensors devices, monitor them properly and then transfer them to the next level for further processing purpose. DAQ supports wireless sensors, which are used to gather the real-world traffic-related information, such as a number of automobiles, speed limit and road condition. The wireless sensors are very effective in DAQ environment for their specific features such as minimum power consumption, cost-effectiveness, self-organization capability and distributed processing feature. Basically, this DAQ is used to acquire and serve all kind of data/information such as the flow of traffic and identification of object based on mainly different types of sensor devices and sensor networks such as Zigbee and Xbee to develop an intelligent or smart transportation system [13]. Data collection procedure has also faced some challenges, such as errors or anomalies, which come in a natural way or the insufficient collection of data. The sensors that are used to collect data are sometimes facing inadequate battery problem through which those sensors are unable for the collection or transmission of data for a long duration. Different methods and algorithms are used to solve these problems, so that the acquired data through the sensors always efficiently enlarge the database to efficiently predict or solve any critical situation in the real world [14].

16.4   Data processing

The data-processing technique is defined as a conversion method/process which is used to convert the data that are acquired from different sensor devices into valid and relevant information. Data processing, which is recognized as a complex procedure, is controlled by several constraints such as sensor type and the condition of environment. Whether this process is executed either in server machine globally or client machine locally depends on the influence of several application types. The transmission of data, which is achieved from various sensors, is very expensive due to the bandwidth limitation and the high rate of streaming data [15]. The data that are acquired from various sensors are so large in volume that sometimes it is very difficult to accumulate that huge volume of data. So that is why it is very necessary to extract the desired segment of data or to discard some segment from these huge data or to compress the huge data. The different types of fusion and aggregation techniques are used to accurately compress or filter that large amount of acquired data, so that it can be transmitted in an effective way. In any IoT-based environments, the data are generally acquired from various wireless sensor devices, and these acquired data are in different structure and format. The acquired data are required to preprocess so that different anomalies such as missing data, noisy data, redundancy constraints or integration problem due to several sources are eliminated accurately, and a proper uniform schema is produced, defined as data cleaning [16]. Nowadays, different types of processing are used, which involve the practical implementation of the real world such as real-time processing where the sensors are designed in such a way so that these can be suitable for real-world application in which the algorithms are executed in a single data pass. The stream processing is mostly used in Big Data concept in the case of any analytical problems [17]. Another data processing, which is defined as in-network processing, is also important where the processing method is not done in any centralized server rather performed in a specific network that requires an efficient framework of various distributed algorithms. In the case of in-network processing, the permanent storing process of data is not required because the storage and processing of data are performed within the specific network [18]. The data-processing technique is also facing a problematic situation due to query processing and indexing areas where processing of the event is itself a big challenge. The data-processing technique is actually performed to clean and filter the ambiguous and spurious data to achieve the meaningful data that provide the solution of different IoT applications.

16.4.1   Data analysis

Nowadays, the data that are collecting or acquiring from the real-world environment are mostly coming from different types of sensor and also defined as sensor data or sensor-based data. These data are gathered from different sources such as health-care-related data, transportation-associated data, environmental data, water-treatment-related data, intelligent-metering-system-related data, security-based data, retail-related data, logistics-based data, agriculture-based data, different industry-related data and animal farming data. The sensor-based data, which are also described as spatiotemporal, contain numerical data, locational data and temporal data, and it is achieved from different signals [19].

These sensor-based data, which are growing very fast with different structure/format and different diversion, also are the core component of any IoT framework. These various structure-based large volumes of data are actually the introducer of the concept named Big Data where data-analysis procedure is truly needed. The data-analysis procedure is not only used to quantify the data at any instance of time but also to keep the data in the context with a certain period and also examine the correlation of the acquired sensor data. The data-analysis process is mainly performed in any base station, servers or cloud environment, but it is also accomplished within a particular hub of the sensor where many sensors are transmitted their collected data [20]. This local data-analysis process, which is actually first done in any sensor-based hub, is used to decrease the volume of the large scale of data when any efficiency is sincerely needed. There are generally two divisions in the data-analysis procedure, which are defined as online data analysis and offline data analysis. The offline data-analysis procedure is responsible for extracting the data in a particular time gap and then builds the required model for a specific application. The online data-analysis procedure is mainly responsible for constant monitoring and creates the report by analyzing the genuine state of each component continuously. The conventional data mining method is not pretty much developed for the processing of real-time, complex and large volume of data, so that is why different new algorithms are used to perform the analysis process in an efficient and cost-effective way [21]. Various types of algorithm, method and procedure are used to properly perform the data-analysis procedure where depend on the application machine-learning concept also can be used. Apart from machine-learning concept, different data mining methods/process, such as frequent pattern mining, clustering, outline detector, classification, sequential pattern, association rule, are also used to accurately analyze the sensor-based data. The analysis of sensor-based data is not only applicable to decrease the volume of data but is also essential in different application levels, such as the prediction of maintenance of any equipment, any diagnostics cases, accurate error detection and human behavior prediction can be easily done using data-analysis process. The particular platform, which is developed for data analysis, is planned in a well-mannered way so that the data are shared in various distributions. Data analysis is categorized into different levels and types. There are two most important categorizations in the data-analysis process that depend on historical data and real-time data. In the case of historical data analysis, an additional analysis process and the extraction of knowledge are also available based on the classification of the event [22]. In the case of real time, data analysis recognizing the real-time events and then labeling those levels are the prime factors where these levels are responsible for the knowledge sharing to the architectural framework. This framework after that performs the real-time event classification with the help of the previously obtained levels. Most accurate data analysis is performed based on the increasingly gathered level of events.

16.5   Existing works on IoT in the real-time transportation system

Barone *et al.* [23] proposed a framework for managing car-parking procedure in hi-tech cities. In this study, the proposed system solved the public car- parking problems that generally occur due to excessive traffic on the roads. Yan *et al.* [24] discussed the architecture of a parking arrangement, which is defined as the intelligent system as well as security that is used to solve the limited parking problem in different metro cities. Mathur *et al.* [25] implemented an intelligent mobile-based parking process where the vehicle finds out its own parking space when it is moving on the road. In this chapter, the proposed system solved the parking problem very efficiently as well as it is used to save the time that is used for searching the parking space. Giuffrè *et al.* [26] discussed a novel architecture of smart parking system, which is also defined by IPA that is used to solve the current parking problem of different smart cities due to excessive traffic congestion. Giuffrè *et al.* [27] reported an experimental analysis result, which showed that in a specific condition, the pollution emissions of vehicle can be estimated from different factors of emissions, which are related to various vehicle's different types of modal activity. Terziyan *et al.* [28] proposed an intelligent and fully dynamic environment based on different roads where a middleware Belvedere has been customized with the help of an agent-based mechanism that is defined as UbiRoad, in such a manner where each and every device, agent and service will create an efficient coordination to ensure the compatibility between them. Kaiwartya *et al.* [29] introduced an exhaustive framework that is related to the Internet of Vehicles (IoV) consists of the protocol stack, architecture, network-related model, future scopes and different challenges to provide the safety and efficiency of road traffic.

Fangchun *et al.* [30] proposed an abstract model of a network of the IoV and also provided an abstract classification, which consists of IoV maintenance, IoV application and activation for the traffic safety purposes. Hasan *et al.* [31] discussed the usability of the network simulator to analyze the handovers that are used in the various vehicular territories. In this chapter, it can also be shown that the network simulator also needs improvement when it is used in the vehicular territory to analyze different handovers. Toutouh *et al.* [32] analyzed the various use of laptops, smartphones and tablets in the case of a V2V environment where two different specifications were included such as IEEE 802.11a and IEEE 802.11g. These IEEE 802.11a and IEEE 802.11g are used to generate the strength of the wireless signal and the Quality of Service (QoS) of the V2V territory. Hasan *et al.* [33] suggested some models that measure the disruption of the traffic pattern, which can be occurred in various patterns of traffic. In this chapter, the disruption quantifies, and quantitative measurement was determined in an effective way. Bitam *et al.* [34] proposed a cloud-based model for the VANET, which consists of three layers and two submodels. This cloud-based VANET model that is also defined as VANET-Cloud is used to improve the road traffic more protective and safe. Kwak *et al.* [35] proposed cloud-based service in vehicles, which is used for planning an appropriate route with the help of the cameras attached to each vehicle. This chapter also represented a proper architectural framework to share all traffic-related information, which actually helps to provide the situation of the road as well as the approximated arrival time, etc. Zheng *et al.* [36] discussed the wireless network that is widely used nowadays in any type of communication environment. In this chapter, non-safety and safety services were also compared as well as different network layer and MAC layer protocols and various wireless networking techniques were discussed too. Bujari [37] proposed a message propagation technique in context of the network which is linear by nature where the fast broadcast is taken place incidentally than intentionally which helps to achieve effective network coverage. Bujari *et al.* [38] implemented a modeling framework that is used to capture the efficiency of forwarding multi-hop protocols with the help of duration and the number of tentative hops. This framework provided to improve the alert system in a vehicular networking environment. Coppola *et al.* [39] discussed the technical problems and issues which are related when the functionality of multiple cars are connected along with software and hardware features and their solutions. Zhao *et al.* [40] implemented a sensor-based application in VANET, which is used to gather the data, analyze those data, and then the decision-making process is taken place. In this chapter, an approach defined as 3GDD (3G-assisted data delivery) was also introduced in VANET. Benslimane *et al.* [41] introduced an architectural framework where the VANET network and 3G/UMTS network are integrated to provide mobility-based features, proper signaling strength of different vehicles and stable route specifications, etc. Li *et al.* [42] proposed a unique solution known as VehicleView, which is used to monitor the performance of the different vehicle and to analyze different application in the vehicle VANET. In this chapter, the proposed system has characteristics such as flexibility, cost-effectiveness, secure analysis and monitoring capabilities. Al-Sultan *et al.* [43] recommended a detection framework in the VANET based on the behavior of the driver. This system consists of five-layer architecture, an algorithm dynamic bayesian network (DBN) and the different behaviors of the vehicle's driver. Sou *et al.* [44] analyzed the improvement when the deployment can be done with the help of a fixed number of the roadside units in the VANET and routing efficiency can also be investigated to achieve the safe environments on road. Kumar *et al.* [45] proposed a routing technique that is based on collaborative learning automata, which is helpful in any urban areas for the rescue purpose with the help of vehicular sensor networks. Yu *et al.* [46] introduced a hierarchical framework that combines the vehicular network and cloud infrastructure together so that the vehicles can be able to share the different types of resources such as bandwidth, computation and storage for facilitating the resources very efficiently. Rahim *et al.* [47] discussed the comparison about the VANET and MANET. In this chapter, it is defined that the VANET that is a subclass of MANET provides higher mobility and better battery life compare to MANET. The broadcasting technique is used in unicast and multicast protocols for both VANET and MANET to handle the traffic system by providing the weather, road and safety information. Wen [48] proposed an expert system to solve the traffic congestion, which is a serious problem nowadays. This expert system that consists of a combination of six submodels to form a large simulation model controls the traffic light automatically and dynamically in such a way which receives the inter-departure time and inter-arrival time to calculate the number of vehicles on highways or roads. Hussian *et al.* [49] implemented an intelligent and automated traffic system, which is developed with the sensor technology and also used as an application of the WSN. In this system, the WSN is used to get the idea about the density of traffic at any junction or circle on road. This intelligent and automated traffic system is very inexpensive and implemented within a shorter time period. Krause *et al.* [50] compared the outcome between the previous and newly recommended approach. This new perspective or approach used fuzzy logic to properly detect the congestion at any remote road and also used the fuzzy model to control the traffic movements safely on road. Koller *et al.* [51] introduced a surveillance technique prototype, which is a combination of reasoner-based high-level and vision-based low-level techniques. This system is used to obtain the traffic information such as the number of vehicles, stolen vehicles, the flow of traffic in a busy interval, the quick decision in an accident case and quick lane changing procedures which are used to develop the congestion-free road in near future. Figueiredo *et al.* [52] discussed the ITS and its various application areas for the improvement of traffic congestion on the road where different techniques or modeling are used to improve the real-time transmission based on traffic system, navigation approach and to introduce different new concepts based on vehicular approach. Wang [53] proposed an intelligent and automated system for urban areas where artificial transportation systems, hierarchical intelligent control systems and agent-based control systems are integrated. This system is used to develop a network-supported traffic system, which has the ability to control a different type of traffic movements such as to control the intersection signal on street or to control the traffic network accurately. Ou *et al.* [54] implemented a smart transportation system with the help of a field programmable gate array approach. The supported technologies such as WSN and RFID are used in this system, and the simulation of this smart system is done a through software invented by Milanés *et al.* [55] who introduced an intelligent and smart traffic system based on AUTOPIA technique through the V2I approach, which is used to control the traffic movements properly. This system uses the control algorithms, which are a fuzzy-based approach to achieve a safe distance between the vehicles and to adjust the speed of vehicles. Baskar *et al.* [56] proposed a framework of automated and integrated traffic-management system for highway-based system. This system is developed with the help of hierarchical architecture, which is used for traffic control and also the road-based network in a combined manner, to detect the allocation of lanes and speed limits dynamically. Horowitz *et al.* [57] discussed the architectural design of a highway, which is defined as a lager, complex and automated system. This discussion proved that, in this automated system advancement in actuators and sensors, technologies along with analysis, testing, design and simulation are highly required. Jaisinghani *et al.* [58] implemented a real-time-based automated and intelligent traffic-control and monitoring system, which is used to improve the congestion of traffic on road. A lot of sensors, such as infrared sensors, gas sensors, light sensors, temperature sensors and some technologies, such as WSN, iterative dichotomiser 3 data mining technique, are used to strengthen the system much more so that this system is able to calculate the flow of traffic on road, to measure various scenarios of climate and to detect the congestion of traffic accurately. Xiao *et al.* [59] recommended an IoT-based framework of an inexpensive, feasible and smart traffic-management system where the electronic product code, RFID, General Packet Radio Service are used to find out vehicles' unique identification, positioning accuracy, etc. in any adverse condition of weather. Eze *et al.* [60] discussed the potentials, research scope and challenges of VANET and its several applications in the area of smart transportation. This chapter also described that the VANET supports two types of communications such as V2I and V2V for the smoother and efficient traffic movement on road. Nellore *et al.* [61] suggested an approach where the vehicles that are defined as emergency vehicles are scheduled as a high-priority basis. The scheduling feature is achieved by using a different type of method and measurement where Canberra distance, Euclidean distance, Manhattan distance technique are highly required. Wang [62] discussed a current mechanism that is used for parallel management and control in the transportation management system. This mechanism is a combination of different methods and concept such as computation intelligence, artificial intelligence, complexity theory, cloud programming and social programming to improve the transportation system. Zhang *et al.* [63] described the automated and intelligent transportation management system based on data-driven technology, which is used to improve the transportation system for the safety purpose and other various activities such as congestion-free road or quick action in any accident cases. Sourav *et al.* [64] discussed the different issues and solution for smart transportation.

16.6 Conclusion

Smart transportation system, which is developed on the real-time environment with the help of sensor technology and Big Data concept, is very useful in a recent day's traffic scenario and is applicable very easily in any real-time environment. The era is not very far away when most of the traffic roads would be equipped with this smart transportation system, which will assist to solve several unpredictable and critical situations of several road-traffic territories such as automatic change of signal light which depend upon the density of traffic on road will help to clear the road congestion very quickly in an efficient way, the vehicles which are standing in front of toll booth for a long period of time will reduce their waiting time through the quick response from toll tax system, decrease the pollution level using different emission control techniques, detection of incidents automatically, forecasting the situation of traffic conditions, dynamic guidance of proper route, fast movements of the emergency vehicles such as fire engines, ambulance will save precious lives and properties by reaching their destinations in time, V2V communication and V2I communication will reach in a remarkable position which will help to obtain the optimum safety conditions on road.

16.7 Future scope

Nowadays, people can solve their problem by using innovations of science by reducing their effort and time. IoT infrastructure may have several practical benefits, but until now, the literature of e-commerce has given the IoT infrastructure very little attention. IoT is considered a practical framework where real-life objects are associated with other objects and the internet for communication and identification purpose. These associated devices are used to produce a large volume of sensor data. These acquired data are then processed and analyzed to serve better advantage, comfort and security issue in any real-life applications. The smoother traffic route is always preferable which is generally dependent on the traffic system, and this traffic system is going to be smarter with the help of IoT. IoT provides the facility to the traffic system to dynamically operate the traffic lights depending on the traffic condition of the road such as if the number of vehicles is increased in one lane at a particular time stamp compared to the other lanes, the traffic light should turn green for that particular lane. The lights that are generally mounted on pavements of the road also have facilitated with the help of IoT to work depend on the condition of weather. The urban areas are also facing a major problem in parking availability especially in the case of the parallel and shortage of spaces, which can also be resolved with the help of different sensing devices based on IoT. Highways can also be organized in such a way with the help WSN based on IoT, so that different lanes are available to categorize the heavy and light vehicles and that is why reducing the accident rate. IoT also provides the service to identify any accidental area very quickly and to communicate with the emergency situation that is most closely located to the accident spot. This smart transportation system can also be upgraded using more good quality sensors especially the infrared sensors for the huge detection range and also the satellite system [65].

References

[1] Ahmad, A., Paul, A., MazharRathore, M., and Chang, H. (2016). Smart cyber society: Integration of capillary devices with high usability based on cyber-physical system. *Future Generation Computing Systems*, *56*, 493–503.

[2] Zhang, D., Zhou, J., Guo, M., Cao, J., and Li, T. (2011). TASA: Tag-free activity sensing using RFID tag arrays. *IEEE Transactions on Parallel and Distributed Systems*, *22*(4), 558–570.

[3] Rathore, M. M., Awais, A., Anand, P., and Seungmin, R. (2016). Urban planning and building smart cities based on the internet of things using big data analytics. *Computer Networks*, *101*, 63–80.

[4] Gowri, A., and Gugulothu, S., (2017). Overtaking behaviour of vehicles on undivided roads in non-lane based mixed traffic conditions. Journal of Traffic and Transportation Engineering (English Edition), 4(3), 252–261. Available from https://www.sciencedirect.com/science/journal/20957564.

[5] Zeng, G. (2015). Application of big data in intelligent traffic system. *IOSR Journal of Computer Engineering*, *17*(1), 01–04.

[6] Hu, S. (2017). Research on the application of big data in intelligent transportation system. *Revista de la Facultad de Ingeniería*, *32*(5), 517–524.

[7] Bawany, N. Z., and Shamsi, J. A. (2015). Smart city architecture: Vision and challenges. *International Journal of Advanced Computer Science and Applications*, *6*(11), 246–255.

[8] Faruk, B. P., Amit, K. B., Durga, M., Iman., A., Arghya, S., and Awanish, P. R. (2016). Density based traffic control. *International Journal of Advanced Engineering, Management and Science, 2*(8), 1379–1384.

[9] Teodor, G. C., Michel, G., and Jean, Y. P. (2009). Intelligent freight-transportation systems: Assessment and the contribution of operations research. *Transportation Research Part C: Emerging Technologies, 17*(6), 541–557.

[10] Gaur, A., Scotney, B., Parr, G., and McClean, S. (2015). Smart city architecture and its applications based on IoT. *Procedia Computer Science, 52,* 1089–1094.

[11] Talari, S., Shafie-khah, M., Siano, P., Loia, V., Tommasetti, A., and Catalão, J. P. (2017). A review of smart cities based on the internet of things concept. *Energies, 10*(4), 421.

[12] Al-Sakran, H. O. (2015). Intelligent traffic information system based on integration of Internet of Things and Agent technology. *International Journal of Advanced Computer Science and Applications (IJACSA), 6*(2), 37–43.

[13] Bandyopadhyay, D., and Sen, J. (2011). Internet of things: Applications and challenges in technology and standardization. *Wireless Personal Communications, 58*(1), 49–69.

[14] Jin, J., Gubbi, J., Marusic, S., and Palaniswami, M. (2014). An information framework for creating a smart city through internet of things. *IEEE Internet of Things Journal, 1*(2), 112–121.

[15] Jayavardhana, G., Rajkumar, B., Slaven, M., and Marimuthu, P. (2013). Internet of Things (IoT): A vision, architectural elements, and future directions. *Future Generation Computer Systems, 29*(7), 1645–1660.

[16] Pires, I. M., Garcia, N. M., Pombo, N., and Flórez-Revuelta, F. (2016). From data acquisition to data fusion: A comprehensive review and a roadmap for the identification of activities of daily living using mobile devices. *Sensors, 16*(2), 184.

[17] Abu-Elkheir, M., Hayajneh, M., and Ali, N. A. (2013). Data management for the internet of things: Design primitives and solution. *Sensors, 13*(11), 15582–15612.

[18] Vongsingthong, S., and Smanchat, S. (2015). A review of data management in internet of things. *Asia-Pacific Journal of Science and Technology, 20*(2), 215–240.

[19] Aggarwal, C. C. (2013). An introduction to sensor data analytics. In *Managing and Mining Sensor Data* (pp. 1–8). Springer, Boston, MA.

[20] Kameswari, U. S., and Babu, I. R. (2015). Sensor data analysis and anomaly detection using predictive analytics for process industries. In *Computational Intelligence: Theories, Applications and Future Directions (WCI), 2015 IEEE Workshop on* (pp. 1–8). IEEE.

[21] L'Heureux, A., Grolinger, K., Higashino, W. A., and Capretz, M. A. (2017). A gamification framework for sensor data analytics. In *Internet of Things (ICIOT), 2017 IEEE International Congress on* (pp. 74–81). IEEE.

[22]   Mukherjee, A., Pal, A., and Misra, P. (2012). Data analytics in ubiquitous sensor-based health information systems. In *Next Generation Mobile Applications, Services and Technologies (NGMAST), 2012 6th International Conference on* (pp. 193–198). IEEE.

[23]   Barone, R. E., Giuffrè, T., Siniscalchi, S. M., Morgano, M. A., and Tesoriere, G. (2013). Architecture for parking management in smart cities. *IET Intelligent Transport Systems*, *8*(5), 445–452.

[24]   Yan, G., Yang, W., Rawat, D. B., and Olariu, S. (2011). SmartParking: A secure and intelligent parking system. *IEEE Intelligent Transportation Systems Magazine*, *3*(1), 18–30.

[25]   Mathur, S., Jin, T., Kasturirangan, N., *et al.* (2010, June). ParkNet: Drive-by sensing of road-side parking statistics. In *Proceedings of the 8th International Conference on Mobile Systems, Applications, and Services* (pp. 123–136).

[26]   Giuffrè, T., Siniscalchi, S. M., and Tesoriere, G. (2012). A novel architecture of parking management for smart cities. *Procedia-Social and Behavioral Sciences*, *53*, 16–28.

[27]   Giuffrè, O., Granà, A., Giuffrè, T., and Marino, R. (2011). Emission factors related to vehicle modal activity. *International Journal of Sustainable Development and Planning*, *6*(4), 447–458.

[28]   Terziyan, V., Kaykova, O., and Zhovtobryukh, D. (2010, May). UbiRoad: Semantic middleware for context-aware smart road environments. In *Internet and Web Applications and Services (ICIW), 2010 Fifth International Conference on* (pp. 295–302).

[29]   Kaiwartya, O., Abdullah, A. H., Cao, Y., *et al.* (2016). Internet of vehicles: Motivation, layered architecture, network model, challenges, and future aspects. *IEEE Access*, *4*, 5356–5373.

[30]   Fangchun, Y., Shangguang, W., Jinglin, L., Zhihan, L., and Qibo, S. (2014). An overview of internet of vehicles. *China Communications*, *11*(10), 1–15.

[31]   Hasan, S. F., and Siddique, N. H. (2012, August). Analyzing handovers in vehicular communication using Network Simulator. In *Cybernetic Intelligent Systems (CIS), 2012 IEEE 11th International Conference on* (pp. 129–132). IEEE.

[32]   Toutouh, J., and Alba, E. (2016). Light commodity devices for building vehicular ad hoc networks: An experimental study. *Ad Hoc Networks*, *37*, 499–511.

[33]   Hasan, S. F., Siddique, N. H., and Chakraborty, S. S. (2013, February). Traffic patterns affecting disruption in vehicular communication. In *National Conference on Communications (NCC)* (pp. 1–4).

[34]   Bitam, S., Mellouk, A., and Zeadally, S. (2015). VANET-cloud: A generic cloud computing model for vehicular Ad Hoc networks. *IEEE Wireless Communications*, *22*(1), 96–102.

[35]   Kwak, D., Liu, R., Kim, D., Nath, B., and Iftode, L. (2016). Seeing is believing: Sharing real-time visual traffic information via vehicular clouds. *IEEE Access*, *4*(1), 3617–3631.

[36]   Zheng, K., Zheng, Q., Chatzimisios, P., Xiang, W., and Zhou, Y. (2015). Heterogeneous vehicular networking: A survey on architecture, challenges,

and solutions. *IEEE Communications Surveys and Tutorials*, *17*(4), 2377–2396.

[37] Bujari, A. (2016). A network coverage algorithm for message broadcast in vehicular networks. *Mobile Networks and Applications*, *21*(4), 668–676.

[38] Bujari, A., Conti, M., De Francesco, C., and Palazzi, C. E. (2019). Fast multi-hop broadcast of alert messages in VANETs: An analytical model. Ad Hoc Networks, 82, 126–133.

[39] Coppola, R., and Morisio, M. (2016). Connected car: Technologies, issues, future trends. *ACM Computing Surveys (CSUR)*, *49*(3), 46.

[40] Zhao, Q., Zhu, Y., Chen, C., Zhu, H., and Li, B. (2013). When 3G meets VANET: 3G-assisted data delivery in VANETs. *IEEE Sensors Journal*, *13*(10), 3575–3584.

[41] Benslimane, A., Taleb, T., and Sivaraj, R. (2011). Dynamic clustering-based adaptive mobile gateway management in integrated VANET-3G heterogeneous wireless networks. *IEEE Journal on Selected Areas in Communications*, *29*(3), 559–570.

[42] Li, Z., Liu, C., and Chigan, C. (2012). VehicleView: A universal system for vehicle performance monitoring and analysis based on VANETs. *IEEE Wireless Communications*, *19*(5), 90–96.

[43] Al-Sultan, S., Al-Bayatti, A. H., and Zedan, H. (2013). Context-aware driver behavior detection system in intelligent transportation systems. *IEEE Transactions on Vehicular Technology*, *62*(9), 4264–4275.

[44] Sou, S. I., and Tonguz, O. K. (2011). Enhancing VANET connectivity through roadside units on highways. *IEEE Transactions on Vehicular Technology*, *60*(8), 3586–3602.

[45] Kumar, N., Misra, S., and Obaidat, M. S. (2015). Collaborative learning automata-based routing for rescue operations in dense urban regions using vehicular sensor networks. *IEEE Systems Journal*, *9*(3), 1081–1090.

[46] Yu, R., Zhang, Y., Gjessing, S., Xia, W., and Yang, K. (2013). Toward cloud-based vehicular networks with efficient resource management. *IEEE Network*, *27*(5), 48–55.

[47] Rahim, A., Ahmad, I., Khan, Z. S., *et al.* (2009). A comparative study of mobile and vehicular ad-hoc networks. *International Journal of Recent Trends in Engineering*, *2*(4), 195.

[48] Wen, W. (2008). A dynamic and automatic traffic light control expert system for solving the road congestion problem. *Expert Systems with Applications*, *34*(2008), 2370–2381.

[49] Hussian, R., Sharma, S., Sharma, V., and Sharma, S. (2013). WSN applications: Automated intelligent traffic control system using sensors. *International Journal of Soft Computing and Engineering*, *3*(3), 77–81.

[50] Krause, B., von Altrock, C., and Pozybill, M. (1996, September). Intelligent highway by fuzzy logic: Congestion detection and traffic control on multi-lane roads with variable road signs. In *Fuzzy Systems, 1996. Proceedings of the Fifth IEEE International Conference on* (Vol. 3, pp. 1832–1837). IEEE.

[51] Koller, D., Weber, J., Huang, T., *et al.* (1994, October). Towards robust automatic traffic scene analysis in real-time. In *Pattern Recognition, 1994.*

Vol. 1 – Conference A: Computer Vision and Image Processing, Proceedings of the 12th IAPR International Conference on (Vol. 1, pp. 126–131). IEEE.

[52]   Figueiredo, L., Jesus, I., Machado, J. T., Ferreira, J. R., and De Carvalho, J. M. (2001). Towards the development of intelligent transportation systems. In *Intelligent Transportation Systems, 2001. Proceedings. 2001 IEEE* (pp. 1206–1211).

[53]   Wang, F. Y. (2003, October). Integrated intelligent control and management for urban traffic systems. In *Intelligent Transportation Systems, 2003. Proceedings. 2003 IEEE* (Vol. 2, pp. 1313–1317). IEEE.

[54]   Ou, H., Zhang, J., and Wang, Y. (2016). Development of intelligent traffic control system based on internet of things and FPGA technology in Proteus. *Traffic, 20*, 2.

[55]   Milanés, V., Villagra, J., Godoy, J., Simo, J., Rastelli, J. P., and Onieva, E. (2012). An intelligent V2I-based traffic management system. *IEEE Transactions on Intelligent Transportation Systems, 13*(1), 49–58.

[56]   Baskar, L. D., De Schutter, B., and Hellendoorn, H. (2012). Traffic management for automated highway systems using model-based predictive control. *IEEE Transactions on Intelligent Transportation Systems, 13*(2), 838–847.

[57]   Horowitz, R., and Varaiya, P. (2000). Control design of an automated highway system. *Proceedings of the IEEE, 88*(7), 913–925.

[58]   Jaisinghani, D., and Bongale, A. M. (2015). Real-Time Intelligent Traffic Light Monitoring and Control System to Predict Traffic Congestion Using Data Mining and WSN. International Journal of Engineering Research and Technology (IJERT), 4(2), 33–38.

[59]   Xiao, L., and Wang, Z. (2011). Internet of things: A new application for intelligent traffic monitoring system. *Journal of Networks, 6*(6), 887.

[60]   Eze, E. C., Zhang, S. J., Liu, E. J., and Eze, J. C. (2016). Advances in vehicular ad-hoc networks (VANETs): Challenges and road-map for future development. *International Journal of Automation and Computing, 13*(1), 1–18.

[61]   Nellore, K., and Hancke, G. (2016). Traffic management for emergency vehicle priority based on visual sensing. *Sensors, 16*(11), 1892.

[62]   Wang, F. Y. (2010). Parallel control and management for intelligent transportation systems: Concepts, architectures, and applications. *IEEE Transactions on Intelligent Transportation Systems, 11*(3), 630–638.

[63]   Zhang, J., Wang, F. Y., Wang, K., Lin, W. H., Xu, X., and Chen, C. (2011). Data-driven intelligent transportation systems: A survey. *IEEE Transactions on Intelligent Transportation Systems, 12*(4), 1624–1639.

[64]   Sourav, B., Chinmay, C., and Sumit, C. (2018). A survey on IoT based traffic control and prediction mechanism. In Intelligent Systems Reference Library, Internet of Things and Big dataAnalytics for Smart Generation, Ch. 4 (Vol. 154, pp. 53–75). Springer Nature Switzerland AG.

[65]   Arthi, S., and Sabyasachi, R. (2017). Intelligent traffic control system. *International Journal of Electrical, Electronics and Data Communication, 5*(5), 43–45.

Chapter 17

Edge computing: a future trend for IoT and big data processing

Zhongyi Fu[1] and Young Choon Lee[1]

Centralised clouds and data centres have been used by many organisations to support big data processing from disparate Internet of Things (IoT) devices [1–3]. While the amount of IoT devices with their data is increasing rapidly, the efficiency of processing these data in a pure centralised location has become a challenge. Edge computing, as an emerging distributed computing technology, is one of the solutions to address this problem. It can be used to provide underlying service environment for IoT and big data processing by leveraging available computing resources in the network edge. However, this technology is only recently emerging lacking identification and realisation of its potential.

The emergence of IoT has significantly changed our world in many ways. By analysing the data collected from IoT devices, people's lives have become more efficient and safer [4]. In recent years, there has been a tremendous growth in the number of IoT devices with their data. It is predicted that 50 billion IoT devices will be connected to the Internet by 2020, and 507.5 ZB data will be produced each year by 2019 [5]. Shi and Dustdar [6] also predict that 180 PB of data will be produced each day by 1 million people in a city. Consequently, it is increasingly difficult to manage the massive amount of data and produce meaningful insights [4].

Traditionally, big data is transmitted to the cloud for further processing. While centralised data centre has virtually unlimited computing capacity to process these data, it is under pressure due to the growth of IoT devices with their data and increasing requirements from applications and IoT devices. Cloud computing is insufficient to support applications and IoT devices demanding low-latency, real-time processing, location-awareness and high quality of service (QoS) [7]. This is caused by several architectural and practical reasons. First, the round-trip transmission between the data source and data centre will consume huge amount of bandwidth, energy and time [5]. Second, the bandwidth of the current network infrastructure and its growth cannot keep up with the growth of data-processing speed [5]. In addition, even though the current network infrastructure can be reconstructed to increase the bandwidth, it may be an uneconomic and non-universal solution. Third, the intermittently unpredictable

[1]Department of Computing, Macquarie University, Sydney, Australia

network latency, especially in wireless local area network (WLAN), can significantly affect the functionality and user experience of delay-sensitive applications and IoT devices [8]. Lastly, Sharma *et al.* [7] claim that the complexity of big data depends on the computational cost instead of the size itself, and thus it is inefficient to transmit all raw data generated from IoT devices for processing.

To address these problems, researchers proposed the concept of edge computing. The basic idea of this concept is to process data at the network edge. The implementation of edge computing is of great practical importance because cloud computing is insufficient to meet the increasing requirements from IoT devices and big data processing.

While cloud computing can bring computational cost and administrative benefits to subscribers, the high delay caused by round-trip transmission between the data source and the data centre cannot be overlooked. The problem of delay significantly limits the development and implementation of applications, IoT devices and big data processing. Several studies [9] claim that it is more efficient to process data at the network edge due to the proximity to the data source and the reduced bandwidth consumption towards the core network. Edge computing can leverage the available computing resources in the edge networks and thus address some of the drawbacks of cloud computing [7]. Examples scenarios include autonomous vehicles, fleet management and building energy management systems.

The effective adoption of edge computing needs to address several security issues [10] particularly when exchanging data between end devices and edge nodes. Data can be intercepted by attackers; thus, this violates the confidentiality, integrity and authenticity. In addition, although data can be encrypted in the IoT devices before transmission, this process can significantly affect the application performance and cause extra delay.

This chapter aims to provide a comprehensive view of edge computing in the aspect of IoT and big data processing in order to demonstrate the potential of edge computing. It is primarily focused on the description of the definition, deployment scenarios, service scenarios, business values and challenges of edge computing. In addition, the differences between edge computing and cloud computing, the role of edge computing, driving forces behind edge computing, and the current state are discussed.

17.1   Definition of edge computing

The term 'edge computing' has emerged in recent years. It can be simply defined as a distributed computing paradigm which leverages available computing and storage resources at the edge of network to enable data processing close to the data source [11]. Since data can be processed at the network edge, it reduces the bandwidth and time consumption during the transmission between the network edge and cloud data centre.

As can be seen in Figure 17.1, the architecture of edge computing can be generally divided into three layers. The lower layer consists of various end devices, such as wearable devices, smartphones, sensors, traffic lights, and automated cars, that are

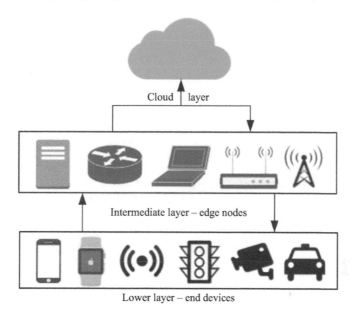

Cloud layer

Intermediate layer – edge nodes

Lower layer – end devices

Figure 17.1   Architecture for edge computing

data sources. The intermediate layer consists of a large number of IoT devices at the network edge which receive data from end devices and provide data processing and storage services. These IoT devices are called edge devices including, but not limited to, routers, switches, access points, servers and smartphones. Data generated from end devices are sent to edge devices for initial processing; subsequently, edge devices can independently decide how to process these data based on specific implementations without the intervention from the cloud. For example, edge devices can either forward the data to the cloud data centre for further processing or deal with the data themselves and respond to end devices. Edge devices are resource-constrained, thus edge computing cannot replace the role of cloud computing.

17.2   Deployment scenarios

Due to various implementations in the intermediate layer of edge computing, deployment scenarios can be divided into three types: mobile edge computing (MEC) [12], fog computing (FC) [3] and cloudlet computing [11].

   MEC: According to Dolui and Datta [11], MEC can be defined as a form of edge computing implementation where it is deployed within the radio-access network to reduce latency and improve context awareness. Hu *et al.* [13] further explain that MEC can be deployed at multiple locations, such as Long-Term Evolution (LTE) macro-base station sites and 3G radio-network controller sites. Figure 17.2 shows MEC architecture. MEC nodes are usually co-located with radio-network controller and controlled

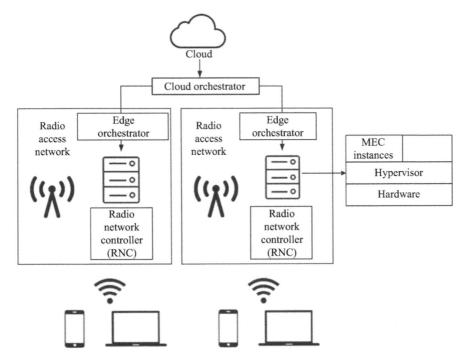

Figure 17.2   Mobile edge computing architecture

and managed by an edge orchestrator. Each node runs multiple MEC instances to support data processing and storage services. The development and deployment of MEC-based applications in the MEC platform is similar to that in the cloud platform. Since MEC is enabled by virtualisation, the MEC platform provides flexibility and on demand self-service for customers who have different service requirements.

FC: The concept of FC is first proposed by Cisco. Cisco turns its IOx-framework-based network devices, such as routers and switches, into minicomputers by adding a Linux operating system which runs Internetwork Operating System in parallel [14]. However, FC is not limited to Cisco devices. According to Stojmenovic *et al.* [15] and Dolui *et al.* [11], FC services can also be hosted at other IoT devices such as smartphones, IP video cameras, set-top boxes, access points and IoT gateways. Due to the open-source nature of Linux operating system, developers can easily develop third-party applications and deploy them in IoT devices enabling data processing at the network edge. Consequently, FC is able to provide low latency, location awareness and real-time processing with end devices. FC nodes can be deployed in two models: independent model and interconnected model; nodes in the first model support direct interaction with the cloud data centre, whereas nodes in the latter model are deployed to interact with each other.

Cloudlet computing: Cloudlet computing can be defined as computing requirements of IoT devices can be satisfied with the support of intermediate and moderately

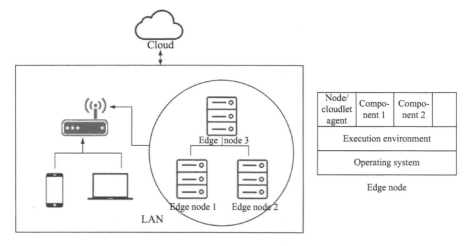

Figure 17.3　Cloudlet architecture

powerful computing servers close to those devices. Satyanarayanan *et al.* [16] propose a cloudlet model which utilises a group of trusted and resource-rich computers – each of which running a virtual machine – provide services for nearby mobile devices, e.g., Google Glasses. Verbelen *et al.* [17] claim that this model has two drawbacks because it is dependent on the service provider to deploy the infrastructure and the coarse granularity of virtual machines (VMs) as unit of distribution. They propose a three-layer cloudlet deployment architecture which utilises a group of IoT devices or VMs to deliver services for mobile devices. As can be seen in Figure 17.3, nodes within each cloudlet and cloudlets can interact with each other through node agent and cloudlet agent. Nodes with cloudlet agent can be considered as super nodes; it controls edge nodes and communicates with the super nodes in another LAN. Each node runs an execution environment which manages multiple components, and each component provides services to upper layer through interfaces. It can be deployed in two models, ad hoc cloudlet model and elastic cloudlet model [17]. Nodes in the first model are more flexible as any IoT devices can join or leave the cloudlet at anytime, whereas in the elastic cloudlet model, nodes are virtual machines running in one or multiple deployed servers.

17.3　Service scenarios

Through the implementation of edge computing, data can be cached and processed at the network edge; thus, this brings a variety of benefits to various applications and IoT devices. For example, Taleb *et al.* [18] propose two-service scenarios utilising MEC to support video streaming services and augmented reality (AR) services. They deploy an intelligent video acceleration scheme in MEC nodes, where each node can cache videos recorded vicinity of its location and display these videos to people visiting this location if the uploader is willing to share. In addition, introductory videos of a specific location can be streamed in real time to visitors who wear location-aware interactive glasses from each node instead of remote data centres.

Shi *et al.* [9] propose a service scenario in which an application in the edge computing node is deployed to accelerate video uploading speed. Since many people use social networking applications such as Facebook and Instagram, uploading large videos to a remote data centre or downloading these videos requires high bandwidth and large-time consumption. However, the size of videos can be reduced in the network edge before uploading to the cloud through the reduction of video clips resolution. This scheme can also be used in automated cars, where they require real-time processing of the huge amount of videos captured by the cameras for driving decision-making [6].

Chen *et al.* [8] propose an FC-based smart urban surveillance system which is supported by real-time video processing in FC nodes. The architecture can be seen in Figure 17.4. In this scheme, drones are used to capture videos of vehicles and upload the raw videos to the ground remote controller in real time. When a target is found, the drone will extract the video frames which contain the suspicious vehicle and send them to FC nodes for tracking and speed calculation. The calculation is based on the pixel position of the suspicious vehicle in each frame. Subsequently, the FC nodes respond to the remote controller with the calculation results.

Sharma *et al.* [7] propose a collaborative edge-cloud processing scheme for high-performance data aggregation and processing at the network edge. This scheme utilises edge-computing nodes as IoT gateway to cache, aggregate and analyse data and perform delay-sensitive tasks while offloading computation-intensive tasks and meaningful information to the cloud. In addition, the cloud acts as an orchestrator to effectively manage and guide the operation and processing of edge-computing

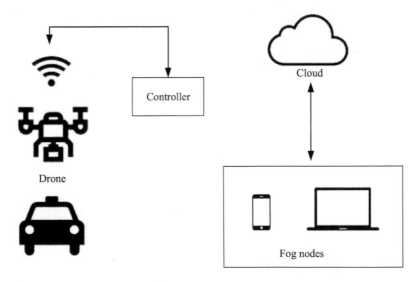

Figure 17.4   Architecture of an FC-based smart urban surveillance system

nodes. Edge computing nodes are able to extract, process and utilise useful features from raw data collected from IoT devices before sending them to the data centre. Shi *et al.* [9] also propose that sensitive data collected from IoT devices can be processed or encrypted at the network edge to protect privacy since unencrypted data can be intercepted by attackers.

17.4 Case studies

Varghese *et al.* [19] deploy iPokeMon game based on the FC deployment model to experiment how much latency and bandwidth consumption it can reduce. iPokeMon game is an open source and VR-based Pokemon-like mobile game. It requires GPS, low-latency and high-compute capacity. There are two types of game server: a cloud-side server and an FC-node server. The cloud-side server maintains a global view of the game, which hosts in Amazon EC2 Dublin data centre. The FC-node server runs in a Linux container of a server located in Queen's University Belfast in Northern Ireland. It is assumed that iPokeMon users are located within 1 km of the FC node. The test shows that the average response time is increased by 20%, and the bandwidth towards the cloud server is reduced by over 90% when comparing with a pure cloud-only model [19]. Similarly, another iPokeMon-based test, conducted by Varghese *et al.* [20] and implemented in their proposed edge-as-a-service platform, shows higher performance, where 6% of overhead, 95% of traffic towards the cloud and 40%–60% of latency are reduced.

Femminella *et al.* [21] conduct the performance evaluation of big data processing on resource-constrained devices, which represent edge-computing nodes. In their experiment, they compare the performance of running a benchmark suit using Hadoop in three different configurations (Table 17.1). These configurations simulate the possible configurations of edge-computing nodes. In the native configuration, Hadoop directly run on the physical machine, while the cloud configurations are based on an Openstack cloud implemented to simulate the execution of Hadoop in the cloud environment. They execute three different dataset sizes for the test, which are 100, 200 and 300 GB. The experimental results show that although there is performance loss when Hadoop is running in a resource-constrained cloud environment, edge-computing nodes can still provide relatively adequate capacity to enable data processing at the network edge before sending to the cloud.

17.5 Business values

The implementation of edge computing can create a new value chain as well as an ecosystem; thus, edge computing benefits all participators, including customers, application vendors, service providers and network equipment vendors [13].

Ahmed *et al.* [22] explain that application vendors can translate the advantages of edge computing into value through the development of innovative applications and

Table 17.1   Performance evaluation for big data processing

Configuration	PC0	PC1-5
Role	NameNode	DataNode
Native configuration	Processor: i7-3770 CPU (4 cores, 8 threads) RAM: 16 GB DDR3 Storage: 1*1 TB HDD (Operating system), 1*8 TB HDD (backups and test results) Network: 2 * Gigabit Ethernet controller	Processor: i7-3770 CPU (4 cores, 8 threads) RAM: 24 GB DDR3 Storage: 1*1 TB HDD (Operating system), 1*8 TB HDD (backups and test results) Network: 2 * Gigabit Ethernet controller
Cloud configuration 1	1 VM • 4 Virtual CPUs • 8 GB RAM	1 VM • 8 Virtual CPUs • 20 GB RAM
Cloud configuration 2	1 VM • 4 Virtual CPUs • 8 GB RAM	2 VM • 4 Virtual CPUs • 10 GB RAM

IoT devices utilising low latency and location awareness. Service providers can benefit from edge computing due to the reduction of bandwidth consumption between the network edge and the core network. In addition, both Satyanarayanan [23] and Ahmed *et al.* [22] state that this reduction can decrease management and operational cost of the centralised infrastructure. Furthermore, Bittman [24] claims that service providers can become more competitive through the implementation of edge computing since they can provide customers with lower costs, higher performance and better QoS. Since the deployment of edge computing may require new types of network equipment, network equipment vendors can benefit. Finally, the quality of life, user experience and productivity of customers and enterprises can be improved through the use of the edge-computing-based applications and devices.

17.6 Challenges

Although processing data at the network edge can bring benefits, the deployment of edge computing also faces a variety of challenges, such as security and resource allocation and the development of edge layer applications.

Ahmed *et al.* [22] highlight the security concern in implementing MEC. They explain that the data can be intercepted by malicious attackers when traversing through the wireless network. Although data can be encrypted in IoT devices before transmission, such encryption can significantly affect application performance and cause extra delay. Garcia Lopez *et al.* [25] underline the potential risks of using edge computing platform. They claim that excluding the necessary security techniques, such as encryption and access control, more secure techniques are required to secure the platform. Furthermore, since the MEC platform shares resources among multiple users, it could also pose similar security issues in the public cloud platform.

Another challenge in edge computing is how to effectively allocate constrained computing and storage resources for data processing [22]. Unlike cloud data centres which have virtually unlimited resources, the computing and storage resources in the network edge are constrained. However, the huge amount of data produced by IoT devices can overhead the edge-computing nodes at the network edge. Thus, efficient resource allocation mechanisms are needed to gain better performance and provide higher QoS.

17.7 Discussion

In this section, we first discuss similarities and differences of edge computing in comparison with cloud computing. We then describe the driving forces and current state of edge computing.

17.7.1 The difference between cloud computing and edge computing

Although edge computing is similar to cloud computing in many ways, there are still many disparate features including resource capacity and capability and network latency. Table 17.2 summarises key differences between cloud computing and edge computing.

17.7.2 The role of edge computing

Although edge computing can provide low latency and context awareness, it cannot replace cloud computing. This is because it is insufficient to individually provide computing and storage services to customers due to its restrained capacity. Similarly, cloud computing is not best suited to provide services for delay-sensitive applications. The collaborative edge-cloud processing scheme described in the service scenario best represents the role of edge computing in the current IT environment. The collaboration of edge computing and cloud computing can address limitations of both computing paradigms; thus, it brings benefits to all participants.

With the respect to challenges when implementing edge computing, service providers should learn from experiences with cloud computing. For example, the security responsibilities of edge computing should not rest with the service providers. Similar to cloud computing, edge computing should design its own service models and implement the shared security model [25] to reduce the security risks. Therefore, all participants in the edge-computing value chain should collaborate with each other to secure the product, platform and infrastructure.

Table 17.2 Comparison of cloud computing and edge computing

Features	Cloud computing	Edge computing
Architecture	Centralised	Distributed
Geographic coverage	Global	Local or wider
Computational and storage capacity	High	Medium to low
Node devices	Node devices	Various IoT devices, such as servers, routers, switches, access points, gateways, smartphones
Internode communication	Supported	Supported or partial based on different deployment scenario
Deployment	Complicated deployment planning	No or minimal planning
Access mechanisms	Leased line	Wireless
Proximity	Multiple hops	One hop
Fronthaul/backhaul communication overhead	Low	High
Latencies	Maximum	Minimum
Context awareness	Low	High
Application	Suitable for delay-tolerant and computationally intensive applications	Suitable for delay-sensitive, real-time operation and high QoS required applications
How long data is stored	Months or years	Transient or short duration

17.7.3 Driving force

In the 2G era, due to the limitation of bandwidth and hardware performance, the major behaviours of mobile device users were browsing websites or listening to music. In the 3G era, mobile device users were enabled to watch online videos and play a variety of online games. Nowadays, in the 4G era, although the bandwidth and the performance of mobile devices have significantly increased compared with before, a large number of mobile device users still desire low-latency and better QoS due to several reasons, such as the emergence of innovative applications and IoT devices.

The advantages provided by edge computing, especially low-latency and context-awareness, can be an incentive for application and IoT vendors to develop more innovative applications and services resulting in more revenue. The emergence and popularity of Pokemon Go game has attracted a lot of attention on AR. Although it quickly fades away due to several reasons, such as high-power consumption and delay, Pokemon Go leaves mobile device users with an unforgettable impression and experience. This can demonstrate the popularity of the innovative products as well as the potential market needs of edge computing.

Recently, as the new feature introduced by Apple with the release of iPhone X, mobile device users' attention has been further drawn towards AR. Consequently, application vendors have been increasingly developing new AR-based applications and games. Other mobile phone vendors have also been developing AR-supported devices and applications to compete with Apple. Furthermore, the increasing requirements from delay-sensitive and compute-intensive IoT devices, such as Google Glass, automated cars and smart surveillance cameras, have been making the issue of delay especially in mobile-network environment more noticeable. The rapid growth in the number of IoT devices with their data has imposed the burden on the core network significantly. As a result, service providers must find a way to reduce delay and improve the QoS to stay competitive as well as create more revenue.

Imagine a city where there is only one bank located in the city centre. Everyone has to drive to the city centre to make transactions or withdraw money. This would cause the roads to the city centre overcrowded and waste a lot of time of the customers. Simply making the bank in the city centre bigger or hire more bank clerks to accelerate the processing speed may be easy to achieve but is not the best solution. Neither broadening the roads nor making people drive faster are good solutions. However, deploying more branches in different locations within the city can share the burden of the centre bank and thus improve the efficiency and QoS.

In the digital world, data centres are in the similar situation to the case with only bank in a city. Although the computing and storage resources in centralised cloud data centres are highly scalable, the bandwidth and response time which are supported by the underlying infrastructures between the data source and the data centre, such as routers, networking cables, and the number of hops, cannot be easily upgraded. Utilising the network edge to process data close to the data source seems to be the most reasonable, practically feasible and economical solution. As stated by Bittman [24], 'The edge will need some serious muscle'. In summary, all the reasons described above and many others can be the driving forces behind the evolution towards edge computing.

17.7.4   Current state of edge computing

Many service providers and network-equipment vendors have realised the potential of edge computing. For example, AWS Greengrass is a software developed by Amazon to extend AWS cloud capabilities to the network edge. Devices running the Greengrass Core software are enabled to collect and analyse data at the network edge, provide computing and storage resources to Lambda-based applications and ensure the communication security between devices and the AWS cloud.

Dell EMC introduced micro modular data centres (MDCs), each of which is a small data centre designed specifically for the deployment of edge computing. A MDC (Figure 17.5) contains compute, storage, cooling and power modules and supports up to 75 kW of IT workload to support data processing at the network edge. It can be easily deployed due to its small size and simplicity, while it can be a single point of failure.

17.8   Conclusion

The huge amount of data generated by IoT devices at the edge of network has been imposing significant burden on cloud computing in terms of network latency and bandwidth in particular. Edge computing provides a way to address several

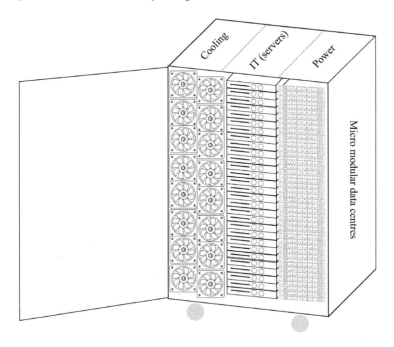

Figure 17.5   Micro modular data centres (MDCs)

latency-related limitations of cloud computing. Nevertheless, edge computing does not aim to replace cloud computing; instead, it can be implemented to cooperate with the data centre to address several limitations of cloud computing, including, but not limit to, reduce latency and bandwidth consumption, provide location-awareness service and improve computing performance and QoS. Although the implementation of edge computing can face a variety of issues, especially in the security and resource-allocation aspects, edge computing can create a new value chain and thus benefits all participants, including customers, service providers, and application and network equipment vendors. The driving forces behind the development of edge computing may include the demand for the applications and IoT devices which require low-latency and real-time processing. Currently, many organisations have realised the potential of edge computing, including Amazon and Dell, and thus they have been developing corresponding products and services. Edge computing can be the next era after cloud computing which brings benefits to all participants as well as changes the world.

References

[1]   Huang G, Liu Z, Ma Y, *et al.* Programming Situational Mobile Web Applications With Cloud-Mobile Convergence: An Internetware-Oriented Approach. IEEE Transactions on Services Computing. 2016;12(1):6–19.

[2]   Zhou Y, Yu FR, Chen J, *et al.* Resource Allocation for Information-Centric Virtualized Heterogeneous Networks With In-Network Caching and Mobile Edge Computing. IEEE Transactions on Vehicular Technology. 2017;66(12): 11339–11351.

[3]   Beraldi R, Alnuweiri H, and Mtibaa A. A Power-of-Two Choices Based Algorithm for Fog Computing. IEEE Transactions on Cloud Computing. 2018 (in press).

[4]   Kirsch D. The value of bringing analytics to the edge. Hurwitz and Associates; 2015.

[5]   Sun X, and Ansari N. EdgeIoT: Mobile Edge Computing for the Internet of Things. IEEE Communications Magazine. 2016;54(12):22–29.

[6]   Shi W, and Dustdar S. The Promise of Edge Computing. Computer. 2016;49(5): 78–81.

[7]   Sharma SK, and Wang X. Live Data Analytics With Collaborative Edge and Cloud Processing in Wireless IoT Networks. IEEE Access. 2017;5:4621–4635.

[8]   Chen S, Zhang T, and Shi W. Fog Computing. IEEE Internet Computing. 2017;21(2):4–6.

[9]   Shi W, Cao J, Zhang Q, *et al.* Edge Computing: Vision and Challenges. IEEE Internet of Things Journal. 2016;3(5):637–646.

[10]   Stojmenovic I, Wen S, Huang X, *et al.* An Overview of Fog Computing and Its Security Issues. Concurrency and Computation: Practice & Experience. 2016;28(10):2991–3005.

[11]   Dolui K, and Datta SK. Comparison of edge computing implementations: Fog computing, cloudlet and mobile edge computing. In: Global Internet of Things Summit (GIoTS), 2017. IEEE; 2017. pp. 1–6.

[12]   Abbas N, Zhang Y, Taherkordi A, *et al.* Mobile Edge Computing: A Survey. IEEE Internet of Things Journal. 2018;5(1):450–465.

[13]   Hu YC, Patel M, Sabella D, *et al.* Mobile edge computing – A key technology towards 5G. ETSI white paper no. 11; 2015. pp. 1–16.

[14]   Jain A, and Singhal P. Fog computing: Driving force behind the emergence of edge computing. In: System Modeling & Advancement in Research Trends (SMART), International Conference. IEEE; 2016. pp. 294–297.

[15]   Stojmenovic I. An Overview of Fog Computing and Its Security Issues. Concurrency and Computation: Practice and Experience. 2016;28(10):2991–3005.

[16]   Satyanarayanan M, Bahl P, Caceres R, *et al.* The Case for VM-Based Cloudlets in Mobile Computing. IEEE Pervasive Computing. 2009;8(4):14–23.

[17]   Verbelen T, Simoens P, De Turck F, *et al.* Cloudlets: Bringing the cloud to the mobile user. In: Proceedings of the Third ACM Workshop on Mobile Cloud Computing and Services. ACM; 2012. pp. 29–36.

[18]   Taleb T. Mobile Edge Computing Potential in Making Cities Smarter. IEEE Communications Magazine. 2017;55(3):38–43.

[19]   Varghese B, *et al.* Feasibility of fog computing. CoRR abs/1701.05451. 2017.

[20]   Varghese B, and Buyya R. Next Generation Cloud Computing: New Trends and Research Directions. Future Generation Computer Systems. 2018;79: 849–861.

[21]   Femminella M, Pergolesi M, and Reali G. Performance evaluation of edge cloud computing system for big data applications. In: Cloud Networking (Cloudnet), 2016 5th IEEE International Conference on. IEEE; 2016. pp. 170–175.

[22]   Ahmed E, and Rehmani MH. Mobile Edge Computing: Opportunities, Solutions, and Challenges. Future Generation Computer Systems. 2017;70:59–63.

[23]   Satyanarayanan M. The Emergence of Edge Computing. Computer. 2017;50(1):30–39.

[24]   Bittman T. The Edge Will Eat The Cloud [Blog]. Gartner Blog Network; 2017. Available from: https://blogs.gartner.com/thomas_bittman/2017/03/06/the-edge-will-eat-the-cloud/.

[25]   Garcia Lopez P, Montresor A, Epema D, *et al*. Edge-Centric Computing: Vision and Challenges. Computer Communication Review. 2015;45(5):37–42.

Chapter 18

Edge computing-based architectures for big data-enabled IoT

Ziad Nayyer[1,2], Imran Raza[1] and Syed Asad Hussain[1]

Internet of Things (IoT) is the internetworking of different electronic devices and a building block of future information and communication technology (ICT). The data produced by IoT devices and sensors is classified as big data due to its extensive volume, velocity, variety and variability. The IoT devices and sensors do not possess the requisite computation power to manage and process such a huge amount of data. This requirement of additional computational power poses resource-scarcity challenges. Solutions to address these challenges are provided by cloud computing (CC), mobile CC (MCC) and edge computing (EC). These solutions provide resource-rich environment to IoT devices and sensors to offload their data and compute intensive tasks. In the case of CC and MCC, the rich computational environment is available in the form of distant remote server. However, EC follows the principle of closer proximity of the user. Furthermore, there are different architectural layouts followed by CC, MCC and EC solutions categorized as distributed, centralized, peer-2-peer (P2P) and hybrid. Every layout has its own advantages and disadvantages. In this chapter, we will first discuss the resource requirements, challenges and available solutions offered by CC, MCC and EC for big data-enabled IoT. Furthermore, the critical analysis of existing solutions detailing their limitations, different architectural layouts and offered features with advantages and disadvantages will be presented. Our detailed analysis and discussion will conclude and highlight the best possible solution for big data-enabled IoT.

18.1 Introduction

Big data refers to the huge volume of data that is challenging to handle due to its volume, velocity, variety, variability and veracity. The frequency of data generation has increased massively in the last decade demanding more computing resources to handle operations of data capture, storage, analysis and visualization [1]. More computing resources mean more power utilization and complexity in terms of distributed algorithms and applications necessary to handle big data. Provisioning and handling of

[1]Department of Computer Science, COMSATS University Islamabad, Lahore, Pakistan
[2]Department of Computer Science, GIFT University, Gujranwala, Pakistan

such resources at organizational level is costly and difficult. Therefore, organizations seek third-party services.

CC provides a viable solution for infrastructure and resources by offering different service-oriented models such as infrastructure as a service (IaaS), platform as a service and software as a service. CC makes use of virtualization technology to maximize resource utilization with minimum cost. International Data Corporation indicates that the revenue generated by CC will reach $554 billion by 2021 [2].

18.1.1   Cloud-computing architecture

18.1.1.1   Mobile cloud computing

MCC architecture shown in Figure 18.1 is also called two-tier architecture. The mobile devices are directly connected with access point that is further connected to the remote cloud via Internet [3]. The remote cloud provides computational facility for mobile devices.

18.1.1.2   Edge computing

EC architecture is also called three-tier architecture, in which the computation facility is in the closer proximity of the user as shown in Figure 18.2. An edge server is connected with the access point one hop away from the mobile devices to provide computational facility [4].

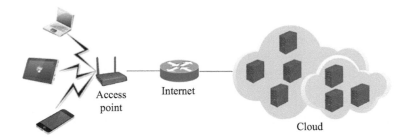

Figure 18.1   Two-tier architecture

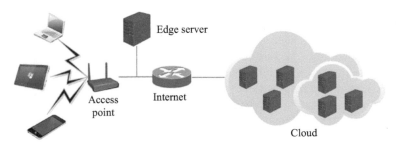

Figure 18.2   Three-tier architecture

18.1.2   Mobile cloud computing applications

MCC is a combination of mobile, cloud and wireless infrastructure to provide rich computational resources to mobile users [5,6]. The word 'mobile' refers to any device such as mobile phone, laptop and tablet that can be moved. Cloud services are hired by organizations with limited resources. Cloud is a concept of interconnected virtualized computers or servers that are dynamically provisioned to work in a unified manner based on service-level agreements [6]. Resource-rich environment and parallel execution of tasks make it possible to execute millions of instructions in a very short time. A shared pool of resources is used to make it cost effective [7]. The last element is wireless communication medium that is most suitable for mobile devices. There are various short- and long-range wireless communication technologies available to connect a mobile device with the fixed infrastructure such as access point or mobile tower. These include 3G/4G/long term evolution (LTE), Wi-Fi, Bluetooth, infrared, near-field communication (NFC) and satellites [8].

The goal of MCC is to provide a resource-extensive platform for running compute-intensive applications. Mobile devices with less computation and energy resources can offload their tasks, demanding more resources from a resource-rich cloud. All computations are executed on the cloud, and the result is sent back to the mobile device. Mobile applications such as image online gaming, image processing and social networks can get advantage from the resource-rich environment of MCC [9–13]. MCC enables cloud and mobile-network operators to expand their business opportunities. The customers are charged according to 'pay-per-use' rule. Hence, MCC addresses the resource-scarcity challenges of limited power, low computational resources and wireless connectivity challenges [14] by offloading task or data on the cloud. This concept is also known as cloud-based augmentation of mobile devices [15] or cyber foraging [16].

18.1.3   Edge-computing applications

18.1.3.1   Cloudlet computing

A cloudlet is a resource-rich fixed or mobile device in the closer proximity of a wireless access point with stable Internet connection providing services to the mobile device in the vicinity [17–20]. Cloudlets can also be formed dynamically over the Wi-Fi network as per need. The key advantage of cloudlet over a cloud is closer proximity and local-area network (LAN). For example, Amazon's EC2 infrastructure is located only in 21 cities worldwide, so when a customer accesses one of these sites over wide-area network (WAN), its end-to-end path includes many network segments causing communication delay. This direct contact to remote cloud is inadequate and highly dependent upon Internet availability. Hence, cloudlets are necessary to provide resource-rich environment in closer proximity [21].

18.1.3.2   Fog computing

Fog-computing solutions are based on fog-computing nodes (FCN) that can be placed anywhere near the end device. FCNs are heterogeneous in nature and provide support for multiple protocols. These FCNs even provide support for non-Internet Protocol-based devices and play a role of an intermediator between an end device and the cloud. On the other hand, integration of IoT and smart cities gives an equal opportunity to cloud service providers (CSPs) for expanding their business. The cloud must adapt and provide diversified services required by different IoT devices and the smart city ICT, thus expanding its scope [22]. The three-layered taxonomy of an application, IoT devices and cloud in the middle, serves the purpose of hiding all the complexities from the user. This also helps in achieving abstraction, isolation and portability at each layer [23].

18.1.3.3   Mobile edge computing

The term 'EC' is generally used for user proximity-based solutions to provide an offloading facility at the edge of the network [24]. Mobile EC (MEC) nodes are located in the macro base station and are managed by a mobile edge orchestrator (MEO). MEO is responsible for handling services and resources offered by these MEC nodes. MEO is also responsible for the management of network topology and MEC applications [25]. A summary of the advantages and disadvantages of EC-based applications has been presented in Table 18.1.

The use of IoT devices and sensors is increasing every day producing a huge amount of data that needs to be stored and processed to extract meaningful information. The task of storing and processing such voluminous amount of data requires extensive computational resources, thus posing resource-scarcity challenges for IoT devices. CC solutions provide adequate resources for the compute-intensive jobs locally using fixed infrastructure of LAN or remotely over the Internet using wired Internet. MCC offers a similar solution for the low computational mobile and IoT devices for offloading their data and computational tasks to the distant remote cloud using wireless infrastructure. However, both CC and MCC solutions have certain limitations of delay and bandwidth. On the other hand, EC solutions work on the principle of closer proximity addressing the limitations of cloud and MCC solutions. The EC nodes are present in closer proximity of the user or at the edge of the core network to avoid delay and Internet bandwidth dependency problems rendering them

Table 18.1   Advantages and disadvantages of edge computing applications

Advantages	• *No dependency over Internet:* Since most of the communication is on local-area network (LAN)
	• *Closer proximity:* Being one hop away from mobile device make it faster and easier to access
	• *Stable connectivity:* Wi-Fi and LAN are used that provide stable connectivity
Disadvantages	• *Less features:* As compared to the remote cloud, edge devices support less number of features
	• *Number of user limitation:* Edge devices also suffer from user limitation as compared to a public cloud

suitable for big data-enabled IoT devices. The contributions of this chapter are as follows:

- This study provides a detailed analysis of the requirements and challenges faced by big data-enabled IoT.
- To the best of our knowledge, EC-based architecture for big data-enabled IoT have not been discussed in the literature.
- A detailed comparison of different architectural layouts of EC-based solutions has been presented highlighting the desirable features for big data-enabled IoT.

The remaining sections of this chapter are presented as follows: challenges faced by EC have been presented in Section 18.2. Big data-enabled IoT requirements and challenges have been presented in Section 18.3. Cloud and EC-based architecture for big data-enabled IoT have been discussed in Section 18.4, and comparative analysis of the EC-based solutions is presented in Section 18.5.

18.2 Challenges faced by edge computing

Challenges faced by MCC include frequent disconnections, mobility and resource scarcity [26]. MCC architecture suffers from delay and bandwidth challenges due to latency induced by WAN and bandwidth requirement. The remote cloud in MCC architecture is a distant one, and offloading time is dependent upon available bandwidth and link condition [27]. In EC architecture, the latency and bandwidth challenges have been eliminated by bringing the computational facility in the closer proximity of the user [28–30]. However, the EC solutions face other challenges that can be divided into four categories discussed in the following subsections.

18.2.1 *Offloading decision challenges*

Challenges related to offloading decisions include selection of offloading mode and fragmentation. The parameter of mode may refer to task, application or code, while fragmentation refers to their proportion that is to be offloaded. These decisions are dependent upon the application developer since partitioning of application or code can only be performed at the time of development. Application partitioning means splitting the executions into local and remote parts. The local part is executed on mobile device and remote part is offloaded to the cloud for execution [31]. However, an optimal partitioning is required to obtain maximum benefit from computation offloading. Two types of application partitioning schemes are used, namely static partitioning (SP) and dynamic partitioning (DP). SP solutions are not suitable for mobile networks due to instability of the wireless network and service nodes, as SP requires fixed bandwidth and system speed.

Instability of resources refers to bandwidth fluctuations, network latency, different CPU speeds and memory sizes of mobile devices and cloud servers. On the other hand, DP automatically determines the location of execution (mobile or cloud) for each part of the application to improve performance by minimizing energy consumption, latency and response time [32]. The other aspects are time and placement decisions such as time for offloading and optimal destination [33]. These decisions are dependent upon the resource availability and selection algorithm.

18.2.2   Interoperability challenges

The interoperability challenges have been extensively discussed in [34]. These include variations of software, hardware and applications among different service providers. Interoperability challenges have increased due to the popularity and rapid growth of mobile industry, the variations of brand, operating system (OS), communication medium and hardware and software features.

18.2.3   Safety and security challenges

With the rapid growth of cloud services, there is an increased trend of data placement on cloud by individuals and companies [35]. On the other hand, due to the concerns about the safety of cloud environment, customers are still hesitant to shift their business to the cloud [36]. Security has always been a challenge for CC paradigm as user's personal data is offloaded to a public cloud [37]. Concerns about safety, privacy, security and trust have created a bottleneck to the growth of CC. The challenges include data accessibility, integrity, tampering, verification, and loss and theft [38].

18.2.4   Performance optimization challenges

The performance-related challenges as mentioned earlier have been extensively discussed in the literature [39]. Various solutions for optimal cloudlet (OC) selection, load balancing and placement focusing on different challenges of energy, available resources, job queue, etc. have been proposed [26,40–43]. Virtual machine (VM) migration is one of the popular techniques used for load management and performance improvement [44].

18.3   Big data-enabled IoT requirements and challenges for IoT and smart cities

With the introduction of IoT, the devices and the data generated by these devices have grown massively [45–48]. The IoT nodes need to transfer this data to someplace, where ample computational and storage resources are available to execute analytics. These computational resources are provided by CC. However, to offload the data in cloud environment, additional resources of energy and Internet bandwidth are required. Even if these resources are managed, the performance of CC and MCC-based solutions suffer with latency and limited bandwidth issues, hence making these solutions undesirable for big data-enabled IoT.

EC solutions on the other hand provide closer proximity-based solutions, minimizing the additional energy requirement and dependency over the Internet. The problem of latency is also minimized in the LAN environment. However, there are various challenges associated with EC solutions, which are related to performance, security and interoperability. The performance-related challenges include offloading decision, mobility, optimization and cost. Security-related challenges are related to privacy, spoofing and denial of service. Interoperability challenge is linked to communication reliability among devices with diversified features and standards.

18.3.1 Edge computing requirements

IoT is an internetworking of different electronic devices [45,47,48], as shown in Figure 18.3. Smart city is a concept of integrating different ICTs [49–51] as shown in Figure 18.4. These two paradigms are building blocks of information technology and are integrated with EC to obtain maximum benefits [52–54].

The data produced by IoT devices and services requires more computing resources rendering resource handling and management more challenging. IoT can take advantage of the resources offered by EC in the closer proximity. The solutions offered by EC must adapt and provide diversified services required by different IoT devices and smart city ICT, expanding its scope [22].

Increasing digitization of records and services requires more resourceful infrastructure to satisfy customers' need. Integration of ICTs is necessary to formulate a complete view of the information requiring additional resources that generate more load on the edge devices. Hence, integration of IoT and smart cities with EC has amplified the potential challenge of resource scarcity at edge devices [55].

Figure 18.3   Internet of Things paradigm

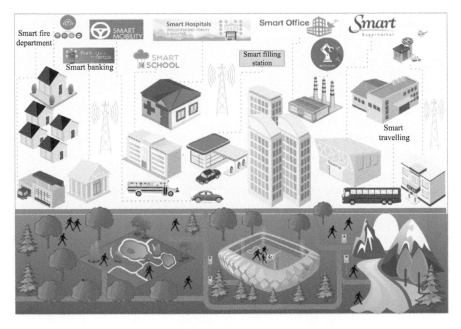

Figure 18.4   Smart city paradigm

18.3.2   Edge computing challenges

The challenge of resource scarcity has now appeared at edge level due to the limitation of resources. The resources offered by edge devices are limited as compared to the resources offered by remote cloud. Hence, available resources at edge level are not enough to address the collective need of mobile devices, IoT devices and smart city ICTs. This challenge can be addressed by further offloading the task to the remote cloud but suffers due to delay and bandwidth challenges. Hence, a more optimal resolution is required at edge level.

The challenges at edge level include the following:

- Performance challenges due to increased devices, mobility and workload:
  - Load balancing: Transfer of task from one edge device to another requires parameters such as transfer size, transfer time and downtime to be considered [26].
  - Efficient and stable resource allocation: Parameters such as resource contention, scarcity, overprovisioning, under provisioning and quality of service (QoS) are considered for this task [40,41].
  - User mobility and seamless services: To maintain seamless services for a mobile device, parameters such as closer proximity, stable connection and handoff services must be deliberated [42].
  - OC selection: This task is performed on the basis of parameters such as job queue time, offloading time, execution time and hop count [43].

- Support for more features such as code or application partitioning and migration.
- Cost-effectiveness.

It is now clear from the previous discussion that resource-scarcity challenge is elevated at edge devices due to the integration of IoT and smart cities. On the other hand, increased use of compute-intensive applications has posed many challenges in terms of performance, efficiency and resource allocation at edge level.

18.4   Edge computing-based architecture for big data-enabled IoT

This section provides a classification of EC-based architecture for big data-enabled IoT. The big data-enabled IoT architecture can be categorized as distributed, centralized, P2P and hybrid, as shown in Figure 18.5.

The common objective shared by these architecture is resource sharing and collaboration for big data handling and management. A detailed overview of the ongoing research for each model is presented in the following subsections.

18.4.1   Distributed EC-based approaches

The purpose of distributed EC approaches is to provide an edge-based computational facility in a distributed fashion as shown in Figure 18.6, where there is no central entity managing the operations of placement, allocation, offloading, execution and migration.

Any device belonging to network A, B or C can target a cloudlet in any other network for acquiring some resources to fulfil the need generated by big data applications and vice versa. A device behaves as a cloudlet when it has some free resources to share. This type of scheme is less prone to failures as there is no central point of failure, but it is complex in design and dependent upon Internet. The distributed EC approaches are designed with the objectives to share resources, minimize delay, network traffic, cost and energy consumption.

18.4.2   Centralized EC-based approaches

The objective of providing an offloading facility in the closer proximity is also shared by centralized EC-based approaches, as shown in Figure 18.7. However, the presence

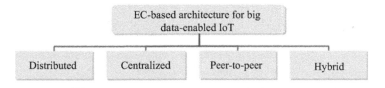

Figure 18.5   EC architecture for big data-enabled IoT

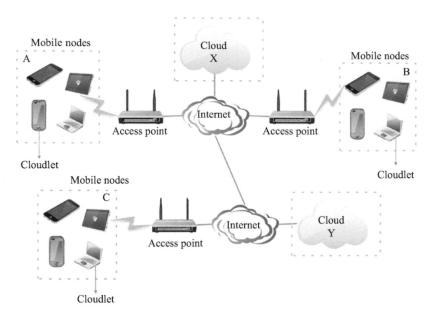

Figure 18.6　Distributed edge computing architecture

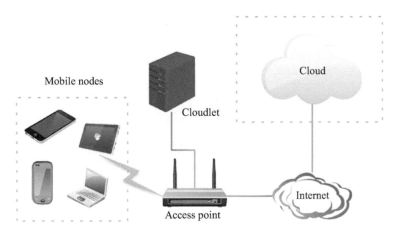

Figure 18.7　Centralized edge computing architecture

of a central server or device available to manage resource allocation, task placement, offloading and execution operations minimizes the complexity of the model as compared to distributed approaches.

The central edge device is available in the closer proximity of the user preferably one hop away in the same LAN avoiding Internet dependency. However, like any other central system, there is a single point of failure making it more prone to failures. On the other hand, centralized model is less scalable as compared to distributed architecture,

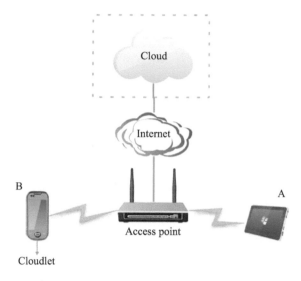

Figure 18.8   Peer-to-peer edge computing model

since adding more nodes to the model generates more load on the central offloading facility causing resource scarcity at edge level.

18.4.3   Peer-to-peer EC-based approaches

In P2P mobile augmentation model shown in Figure 18.8, there is neither any central entity managing the operations nor this architecture is dependent upon the Internet. This architecture is the simplest one among the others. Any communication medium such as infrared, Bluetooth, NFC or Wi-Fi can be used to connect two devices.

However, this architecture neither provides scalability nor ensures the long-term availability of the cloudlet device. An extra effort is required at peer level to maintain logs and data for the smooth execution of placement, offloading, resource allocation and execution operations. This architecture is more prone to failures as it is highly dependent upon the availability of the cloudlet device in the range of the shared communication medium.

18.4.4   Hybrid EC-based approaches

This approach is a combination of distributed, centralized and P2P architecture as shown in Figure 18.9; hence, it carries pros of all categories with very less weakness.

However, this approach is highly complex due to the use of different communication technologies and protocols. The operational management mechanism for one approach is not valid for the other, so the hybrid architecture must either follow a standard mechanism for all or there must be some translation mechanisms available for the working of all architecture together. These constraints are hard to realize but

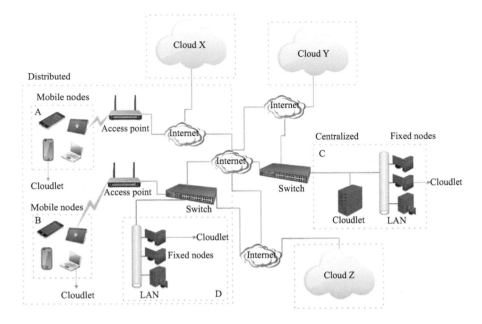

Figure 18.9   Hybrid edge computing architecture

Table 18.2   Advantages and disadvantages of edge-based computing architecture

Architecture	Scalability	Robustness	Complexity	Internet dependency
Distributed	High	High	High	Very high
Centralized	Low	No	Low	No
Peer-to-peer	No	No	No	No
Hybrid	Very high	Very high	Very high	Low

work very well for big data-enabled IoT as there are multiple options available to offload the task, thus making it robust and highly available.

If a peer device is out of range, then the mobile device can get the offload facility provided by the central cloudlet in the closer proximity. Even if the central edge device is not available, it can find any cloudlet device in another network. A comparative analysis of all architectural layouts according to scalability, robustness, complexity and Internet dependency has been presented in Table 18.2.

18.5   Comparative analysis of edge computing-based approaches

This section discusses the state-of-the-art EC-based approaches. The related work is reviewed from the perspective of its applicability to big data-enabled IoT.

An interactive MCC application based on IaaS using three-tier MCC architecture has been proposed in [56]. The edge device is connected with the remote cloud using high-bandwidth wireless communication medium. This technique provides the best results in improving delay for request transfer and throughput. The proposed scheme assumes that nodes are static, and edge device is at maximum two hops away from user. However, if the assumptions are not fulfilled, the edge-based scheme performs poorly than the cloud-based one. An adaptive combination of both schemes (edge based and cloud based) is recommended in this scenario. The scope of this scheme is limited as it covers only performance impact of interactive mobile applications in a specific scenario. The overall performance impact considering big data applications has been ignored.

An adaptive VM-handoff technique has been proposed to keep the VM in the closer proximity of the user by moving it along user's movement [42]. The design considerations of this scheme are as follows: (1) total handoff time optimization rather than downtime, (2) dynamically adaptable to WAN bandwidth and cloudlet load and (3) leverage-existing VM state at cloudlets. Existing VM state at the destination is compared with the updated state at source. The difference is evaluated and encoded with delta approach to de-duplicate and compress before transfer. The parameters used in the whole process are dynamically re-optimized according to available resources and bandwidth. The focus of this scheme is to keep the medium latency minimum by moving the user VM in closer proximity. This scheme lacks scalability and collaboration features required for big data-enabled IoT. In the case of big data, the focus of keeping the VM in the closer proximity of the users is not a priority task but to place the VM at such a location where the computation needs is fulfilled.

An integrated mobile-network solution (MobiScud) based on software-defined networks (SDNs) and cloud has been proposed in [57]. The cloud has been established in the closer proximity of radio access network (RAN), where customer's VMs are instantiated. The compute-intensive applications are then offloaded to these newly created customized VMs. Control messages between mobile devices and SDNs are monitored by MobiScud, which are used to move the VM with user to keep it in the closer proximity. Live VM-migration technique is used by MobiScud to transfer a VM from source to destination. MobiScud also updates flow rules of SDNs according to user mobility and VM movement to ensure that during migration, running connections are not disrupted. However, it has been observed that users often switch to Wi-Fi networks when in range and prefer to use it instead of mobile networks due to cost, speed and reliability challenges. Thus, RANs and Wi-Fi networks are required to be bridged for providing continuous connectivity between user and VM. Moreover, VM migration between these two networks is also vital to cope with the resource requirements generated by big data-enabled IoT. These two aspects have not been addressed in this scheme.

A P2P model using short-range radio communication technologies to form a P2P network of mobile devices has been proposed in [58]. A mobile device in this P2P network can either offer resources to another mobile device or take resources from another mobile device. There are three modes of services to offload computations: (1) remote cloud service, where a mobile device is using remote cloud as offloading site, (2) connected ad hoc cloudlet service, where a mobile device is using a cloudlet as offloading site and (3) opportunistic ad hoc cloudlet service, where a mobile device is using another mobile device as offloading site. P2P schemes are not desirable for big data-enabled IoT as this model is highly unreliable due to the dependency on the availability of another mobile device.

A cloudlet-assisted ad hoc MCC scheme has been proposed in [59] to allocate task and offload data from device-to-device (D2D) directly rather than using a centralized cloud. A device having computational task is called a master device, and it can access other devices in a closer proximity for resources such as slave devices or cloudlets. This reduces the computational cost and energy consumption. This cooperative scheme of workload sharing also provides better results in terms of reducing bandwidth consumption and offload latency as compared to traditional CC. However, this model assumes that the task is completely offloaded, and there is no interruption in-between which is hard to realize in the case of big data due to the increased frequency and volume of data.

A context-aware code offloading scheme using nearby edge devices, mobile devices and remote clouds as offloading sites has been presented in [60]. The objective of this scheme is to provide seamless offloading service by sensing the changes in the context and adjusting accordingly. A novel algorithm has been devised to calculate optimal offloading site considering the changes in the context of mobile device and cloud. This scheme has shown to improve performance and reduce energy consumption. This hybrid scheme provides maximum support for big data-enabled IoT due to increased possibility of offloading sites and more computational power. However, a complex control mechanism is required for this model to work smoothly and error free.

VM-based cloudlets using temporary customization of edge infrastructure adopting hardware VM technology have been discussed in [61]. Customization is performed in advance to use, and a clean-up process is instantiated after use to ensure that the infrastructure changes are reverted to its original state. The whole process is carried out automatically without any manual intervention. The use of VM is to ensure that the temporary guest software environment has been separated from the infrastructure's permanent host software environment. The interface between the guest and host environments is narrow, steady and pervasive. It increases the chances of finding more compatible edge devices for a mobile user. The customizable software interface of mobile application is encapsulated by the guest environment. These are re-created during customization of cloudlet infrastructure in advance before use. This model provides diversified features that are in favour of big data-enabled IoT but lacks in providing support for workload sharing and load balancing that is desired for big data-enabled IoT.

A middleware platform has been deliberated in [62], which provides guarantee of smooth collaboration among edge devices with minimized average CPU load. It has the capability to deploy, remove and move different software components on runtime. Thus, only required components are employed reducing the load on the CPU. Application concepts such as augmented reality (AR) perform poorly due to limited resources on mobile devices. The concept of cyber foraging or cloud-based mobile augmentation has proven to be the best solution to offload resource-intensive applications on a resource-rich cloud. The same solution is also valid for collaborative scenarios, in which massive amount of data and processing is shared between multiple mobile devices offering offloading facility. However, the scope of this scheme is limited to AR-based applications only.

A super-peer-based scheme using community role and awareness has been discussed in [63], which integrates remote cloud, edge devices and mobile devices for resource sharing. D2D communication is also supported by this model to exploit resources from a peer mobile device. A point system is used to quantify incentive based on credit and reputation. Points are given to a device when its resources are being utilized by other devices. A device may lose points when using community resources. A community is formed with a group of devices that can be trusted for offloading tasks and data. HyMobi is more effective to deal with the selfishness of the peers. The concept of credit and reputation is more successful in a static environment where participating nodes often remain the same and maximum availability is ensured. Since mobile networks are highly volatile, the benefit of such credit and reputations system is hard to realize for big data-enabled IoT that demands more stability.

A new edge-based scheme has been introduced using a central enterprise cloud that stores all the information of mobile devices connected with any edge device in the enterprise [64]. If a mobile device moves from one edge device to another, it may resume offloading job since the enterprise cloud has the information about the previous job, thus saving energy. A mobile device only needs to communicate with enterprise cloud if a service or file is not available on the edge device. In the case of big data-enabled IoT, keeping tags for such a huge amount of data is hard to realize. This scheme lacks in providing the details of the model including joining and leaving of an enterprise cloud by edge devices, handing over the task to next edge device, resuming offloading of the task and tracking mobile node, it is hard to conclude that this scheme is ready for big data-enabled IoT.

A green cloudlet network architecture has been proposed in [65]. A software clone preferably a VM of the mobile device is established and maintained in the nearby edge device to provide workloads offloading. SDN has been used for efficient communication between mobile device and its clone. A mobile device and its clone may not be in the same vicinity, hence result in VM migration from a host cloud to another mobile device. This decreases the delay but produces huge amount of traffic between edge devices. SDNs play an important role in improving the performance in terms of saving energy, delay time and throughput. Network paths are dynamically configured between edge devices, and different QoS criteria can be used for different data flows. However, this scheme requires some fundamental changes in the core cellular network to integrate with the SDNs and incorporate support for big data-enabled IoT. Hence, currently it is not compatible with the existing cellular architecture.

MeshCloud [66] integrates wireless mesh networks (WMNs) and edge devices to provide seamless localized services. WMNs are highly robust as various paths are available to reach a certain edge device. More edge devices can be added to the mesh network at any time to enhance the coverage and resource demand of the proposed model. This provides an opportunity for the edge devices to further offload any task to another edge device in the mesh network for load sharing making it suitable for big data-enabled IoT. Mesh clients are also not dependent upon LAN performance as in conventional Internet-based cloud. However, this technique is dependent upon wireless links that are inherently unreliable and with the increase of each hop the challenge of unreliability increases thus limiting its scope for big data-enabled IoT.

A novel scheme has been proposed in [67] using a root server that works as a directory having information about linked edge devices. Every edge device has to be registered with the root server. The connection status (connected/disconnected) and services offered by edge devices are stored and managed by the root server. A user may request the root server for an offloading task and can be directed to a suitable edge device. An edge device may make use of another edge device's resources or break the task in smaller proportions and work collaboratively with other edge devices. A LAN environment has been used to interconnect different edge devices. Every edge device is connected to the root server. This model exerts suitable functionality for big data-enabled IoT but does not support scalability.

PacketCloud [68] is a cloudlet-based approach that offers to host in-network services using shared commodity servers. Customized set of services can be used to manage the network traffic and achieve elasticity. The desired services can be scaled up and down as per traffic demand. This provides suitable means to deploy more resources in peak hours and release unnecessary resources in off-peak hours. This also helps application and Internet-service providers to deploy their services on suitable locations as per service and resource availability. However, to shift on commodity hardware solution, a lot of work such as acquiring the hardware, software and expertise is required. This solution has many challenges, for example, lower performance, poor onsite hardware support, difficult patching, security and compatibility. These are all desired features for big data-enabled IoT.

An edge-based distributed multilateral resource exchange technique has been described in [19]. Flexible pricing strategies have been introduced using a virtual currency concept like bitcoin. A user may earn credit by providing services to another user and hence can purchase services from the other edge devices. However, a trusted party is required to mediate the exchange and maintain the credit system. A P2P crypto-currency system is used to handle the transaction. A brief transaction history is maintained on both peers to avoid duplicate payments. Digital signatures are used to prove the ownership and legitimacy of the currency. Just like a P2P system, a tracker can help an individual edge device to find another edge device to form a P2P overlay for the distributed trading mechanism. The two main drawbacks of this system are as follows: (1) a user has to wait for his services to be lent, in order to gain some money to buy further services and (2) there is no financial institution to back up the system in case a party is bankrupted. The first drawback is highly undesirable for big data-enabled IoT as big data applications cannot afford delay or wait time.

A decentralized public resourced cloudlet for Ad-hoc networks called DRAP has been proposed in [69] that serves as a middleware to provide means for communication between mobile devices to form a cloudlet. It also serves as a middleware between application and OS. This cloudlet developed by a group of volunteer devices serves

Table 18.3   Comparative analysis of EC-based architecture for big data-enabled IoT

Technique	Architecture	Objectives	Performance parameters		
			ET	E	R
[56]	Distributed	Minimize execution time	✓	–	–
[42]		Minimize execution time by placing VM on optimal edge device	✓	–	✓
[57]		Migrate VMs to edge devices with ample resources	–	–	✓
[65]		Minimize energy consumption and execution time	✓	✓	–
[19]		Resource collaboration	–	–	✓
[69]		Edge device management to reduce energy and optimize resources	–	✓	✓
[72]		Offloading the task to another edge device to reduce execution time	✓	✓	–
[59]	Centralized	Load balancing to minimize energy consumption and resource sharing	–	✓	✓
[60]		Offloading optimization to reduce execution time, energy consumption and resource wastage	✓	✓	✓
[61]		Minimize energy consumption	–	✓	–
[67]		Resource sharing between edge devices	–	–	✓
[68]		In-network services to minimize energy consumption and resource wastage	–	✓	✓
[58]	P2P	Load balancing to improve execution time	✓	–	–
[62]		Performance improvement by minimizing energy consumption and execution time	✓	✓	–
[63]	Hybrid	Offloading optimization to minimize energy consumption, execution time and resource wastage	✓	✓	✓
[64]		Minimize energy consumption	–	✓	–
[66]		Minimize cost as per available resources at edge device	–	–	✓

ET, execution time; E, energy; R, resources.

as a resourceful unit in the closer proximity to provide services to other devices. The jobs of the DRAP are to (1) detect unused resources and offer the same to cloudlet, (2) initiate the device discovery to find neighbouring nodes and (3) control the role of the cloudlet, such as client or service provider. The system is highly robust as it restructures the cloudlet topology dynamically upon joining and leaving of a cloudlet node. However, to log each event some buddy nodes are introduced to provide continued services in the case of a failure. A trust and incentive mechanism has been used to attract more participating nodes. However, highly distributed and volatile nature of the system makes it unsuitable for big data-enabled IoT.

A profit-maximization scheme for cloudlets has been proposed in [70]. This technique uses a stochastic-control algorithm based on stochastic Lyapunov optimization technique [71]. The algorithm handles all requests and unpredictable resource requirements from mobile devices. The requests are assigned to cloudlets based on purchased resources keeping the operating profit maximum. It also handles the purchasable computing resources on the cloudlet. The control operations are determined on the basis of following computations: (1) request admittance and forwarding and (2) resource allocation and service purchasing. This technique does not require offline statistical knowledge as is the case with traditional approaches. However, it is not always desirable to keep only profit perspective in view. Some priority requests may be delayed due to the profit being a decision parameter which is undesirable for big data-enabled IoT. An overview of all previously cited literature for EC techniques in CC for big data-enabled IoT has been summarized in Table 18.3 with respect to their architecture, objectives and performance parameters.

We can observe from the previous comparative study that major focus of these techniques is on the optimization of offloading time, execution time, energy consumption and cost. The techniques based on distributed and hybrid architecture are more suitable for big data-enabled IoT and smart cities due to the desired features. These features include resource sharing, collaboration, load balancing, optimal placement, minimized energy consumption, resource wastage and cost. Centralized and P2P architecture also offer some of the aforementioned features, but they are unable to provide scalability and reliability.

18.6   Conclusion

This chapter presents the detailed discussion on EC-based architecture for big data-enabled IoT with their advantages and disadvantages. The EC-based architecture provide closer proximity-based solutions avoiding latency and limited bandwidth issues. However, to support big data handling and management of IoT sensors and smart city infrastructure, load balancing and resource sharing features are required. We can conclude from the earlier discussion that increased number of devices and data generated by them have posed resource-scarcity challenges at edge devices. In the worst case, the edge device is forced to forward the request to a distant remote cloud eliminating the beneficial features of reduced latency and Internet dependency offered by EC architecture.

Hence, the resource collaboration must have the feature to address resource-scarcity challenge at edge level. The state-of-the-art techniques offering resource sharing, load balancing, minimized energy consumption and cost must consider the attributes of scalability and robustness that are desired for big data-enabled IoT solutions. The analysis of existing technique shows that the parameters of energy, execution time and available resources have been considered by majority of them for performance enhancement and load balancing. However, these techniques lack the features of scalability and robustness. The distributed and hybrid architecture do offer scalability and robustness, but their application in real-life scenarios is very complex and costly. On the other hand, centralized and P2P models do not offer these features. The future work in the domain of EC architecture for big data-enabled IoT must focus on distributed and hybrid models to reduce their complexity and cost. The aggregation of different resource allocation and load balancing mechanisms and translation of protocols in hybrid scheme is also an open research area.

References

[1]   C. P. Chen, and C.-Y. Zhang, "Data-intensive applications, challenges, techniques and technologies: A survey on Big Data," *Information Sciences,* vol. 275, pp. 314–347, 2014.

[2]   "International Data Corporation," 2018: Accessed URL (December, 2018): https://www.idc.com/getdoc.jsp?containerId=prUS43696418

[3]   Z. Pang, L. Sun, Z. Wang, E. Tian, and S. Yang, "A Survey of Cloudlet Based Mobile Computing," in *International Conference on Cloud Computing and Big Data (CCBD)*, pp. 268–275, 2015.

[4]   K. Gai, M. Qiu, H. Zhao, L. Tao, and Z. Zong, "Dynamic energy-aware cloudlet-based mobile cloud computing model for green computing," *Journal of Network and Computer Applications,* vol. 59, pp. 46–54, 2016.

[5]   S. Abolfazli, Z. Sanaei, E. Ahmed, A. Gani, and R. Buyya, "Cloud-based augmentation for mobile devices: Motivation, taxonomies, and open challenges," *IEEE Communications Surveys & Tutorials,* vol. 16, no. 1, pp. 337–368, 2014.

[6]   M. Satyanarayanan, "A brief history of cloud offload: A personal journey from odyssey through cyber foraging to cloudlets," *GetMobile: Mobile Computing and Communications,* vol. 18, no. 4, pp. 19–23, 2015.

[7]   M. T. Desai, R. Patel, P. Patel, T. Desai, R. Patel, and P. Patel, "Cloud computing in education sector," *International Journal,* vol. 2, pp. 191–194, 2016.

[8]   P. P. Parikh, M. G. Kanabar, and T. S. Sidhu, "Opportunities and challenges of wireless communication technologies for smart grid applications," *in Power and Energy Society General Meeting, 2010 IEEE*, pp. 1–7, 2010.

[9]   E. Ahmed, A. Gani, M. K. Khan, R. Buyya, and S. U. Khan, "Seamless application execution in mobile cloud computing: Motivation, taxonomy, and open challenges," *Journal of Network and Computer Applications,* vol. 52, pp. 154–172, 2015.

[10]   N. Aminzadeh, Z. Sanaei, and S. H. Ab Hamid, "Mobile storage augmentation in mobile cloud computing: Taxonomy, approaches, and open issues," *Simulation Modelling Practice and Theory,* vol. 50, pp. 96–108, 2015.

[11]   S. Distefano, F. Longo, and M. Scarpa, "QoS assessment of mobile crowdsensing services," *Journal of Grid Computing,* vol. 13, no. 4, pp. 629–650, 2015.

[12]   M. Othman, S. A. Madani, and S. U. Khan, "A survey of mobile cloud computing application models," *IEEE Communications Surveys & Tutorials,* vol. 16, no. 1, pp. 393–413, 2014.

[13]   M. Othman, A. N. Khan, S. A. Abid, and S. A. Madani, "MobiByte: An application development model for mobile cloud computing," *Journal of Grid Computing,* vol. 13, no. 4, pp. 605–628, 2015.

[14]   H. Qi and A. Gani, "Research on mobile cloud computing: Review, trend and perspectives," in *Digital Information and Communication Technology and it's Applications (DICTAP), 2012 Second International Conference on,* pp. 195–202, 2012.

[15]   A. Mohammad, and L. Chunlin, "Cloud-based mobile augmentation in mobile cloud computing," *International Journal of Future Generation Communication and Networking,* vol. 9, no. 8, pp. 65–76, 2016.

[16]   P. Patil, A. Hakiri, and A. Gokhale, "Cyber Foraging and Offloading Framework for Internet of Things," in *Computer Software and Applications Conference (COMPSAC), 2016 IEEE 40th Annual,* pp. 359–368, 2016.

[17]   K. Ha, P. Pillai, W. Richter, Y. Abe, and M. Satyanarayanan, "Just-in-time provisioning for cyber foraging," in *Proceeding of the 11th annual international conference on Mobile systems, applications, and services,* pp. 153–166, 2013.

[18]   S. Simanta, K. Ha, G. Lewis, E. Morris, and M. Satyanarayanan, "A reference architecture for mobile code offload in hostile environments," in *International Conference on Mobile Computing, Applications, and Services,* pp. 274–293, 2012.

[19]   Y. Wu and L. Ying, "A cloudlet-based multi-lateral resource exchange framework for mobile users," in *Computer Communications (INFOCOM), 2015 IEEE Conference on,* pp. 927–935, 2015.

[20]   Y. Zhang, D. Niyato, and P. Wang, "Offloading in mobile cloudlet systems with intermittent connectivity," *IEEE Transactions on Mobile Computing,* vol. 14, no. 12, pp. 2516–2529, 2015.

[21]   Y. Gao, W. Hu, K. Ha, B. Amos, P. Pillai, and M. Satyanarayanan, *Are Cloudlets Necessary?,* School of Computer Science, Carnegie Mellon University, Pittsburgh, PA, 2015.

[22]   K. Lee, D. Murray, D. Hughes, and W. Joosen, "Extending sensor networks into the cloud using amazon web services." pp. 1–7.

[23]   S. Aguzzi, D. Bradshaw, M. Canning, *et al.,* "Definition of a Research and Innovation Policy Leveraging Cloud Computing and IoT Combination," *Final Report,* European Commission, SMART, vol. 37, 2013.

[24]   M. Satyanarayanan, "The emergence of edge computing," *Computer,* vol. 50, no. 1, pp. 30–39, 2017.

[25]   P. Mach, and Z. Becvar, "Mobile edge computing: A survey on architecture and computation offloading," *IEEE Communications Surveys & Tutorials,* vol. 19, no. 3, pp. 1628–1656, 2017.

[26]   N. Fernando, S. W. Loke, and W. Rahayu, "Mobile cloud computing: A survey," *Future Generation Computer Systems,* vol. 29, no. 1, pp. 84–106, 2013.

[27]   Raei, Hassan, and Nasser Yazdani. "Analytical performance models for resource allocation schemes of cloudlet in mobile cloud computing." *The Journal of Supercomputing* vol. 73, no. 3, 1274–1305, 2017.

[28] M. R. Rahimi, J. Ren, C. H. Liu, A. V. Vasilakos, and N. Venkatasubramanian, "Mobile cloud computing: A survey, state of art and future directions," *Mobile Networks and Applications,* vol. 19, no. 2, pp. 133–143, 2014.

[29] H. T. Dinh, C. Lee, D. Niyato, and P. Wang, "A survey of mobile cloud computing: Architecture, applications, and approaches," *Wireless Communications and Mobile Computing,* vol. 13, no. 18, pp. 1587–1611, 2013.

[30] Y. Jararweh, L. Tawalbeh, F. Ababneh, and F. Dosari, "Resource efficient mobile computing using cloudlet infrastructure," in *Mobile Ad-hoc and Sensor Networks (MSN), 2013 IEEE Ninth International Conference on,* pp. 373–377, 2013.

[31] H. Wu, W. Knottenbelt, K. Wolter, and Y. Sun, "An optimal offloading partitioning algorithm in mobile cloud computing." In *International Conference on Quantitative Evaluation of Systems,* pp. 311–328. Springer, Cham, 2016.

[32] H. Wu and K. Wolter, "Software aging in mobile devices: Partial computation offloading as a solution," in *Software Reliability Engineering Workshops (ISSREW), 2015 IEEE International Symposium on,* pp. 125–131, 2015.

[33] K. Kumar, J. Liu, Y.-H. Lu, and B. Bhargava, "A survey of computation offloading for mobile systems," *Mobile Networks and Applications,* vol. 18, no. 1, pp. 129–140, 2013.

[34] Z. Sanaei, S. Abolfazli, A. Gani, and R. Buyya, "Heterogeneity in mobile cloud computing: Taxonomy and open challenges," *IEEE Communications Surveys & Tutorials,* vol. 16, no. 1, pp. 369–392, 2014.

[35] N. Leavitt, "Is cloud computing really ready for prime time," *Growth,* vol. 27, no. 5, pp. 15–20, 2009.

[36] M. Armbrust, A. Fox, R. Griffith, *et al.,* "A view of cloud computing," *Communications of the ACM,* vol. 53, no. 4, pp. 50–58, 2010.

[37] K. So, "Cloud computing security issues and challenges," *International Journal of Computer Networks,* vol. 3, no. 5, pp. 247–255, 2011.

[38] S. Subashini, and V. Kavitha, "A survey on security issues in service delivery models of cloud computing," *Journal of Network and Computer Applications,* vol. 34, no. 1, pp. 1–11, 2011.

[39] A. Beloglazov, J. Abawajy, and R. Buyya, "Energy-aware resource allocation heuristics for efficient management of data centers for cloud computing," *Future Generation Computer Systems,* vol. 28, no. 5, pp. 755–768, 2012.

[40] S. Bohez, T. Verbelen, P. Simoens, and B. Dhoedt, "Discrete-event simulation for efficient and stable resource allocation in collaborative mobile cloudlets," *Simulation Modelling Practice and Theory,* vol. 50, pp. 109–129, 2015.

[41] M. Jia, J. Cao, and W. Liang, "Optimal Cloudlet Placement and User to Cloudlet Allocation in Wireless Metropolitan Area Networks." *IEEE Transactions on Cloud Computing,* vol. 5, no. 4, 725–737, 2017.

[42] K. Ha, Y. Abe, Z. Chen, *et al.,* "Adaptive VM Handoff Across Cloudlets," *Technical Report CMU-CS-15-113,* CMU School of Computer Science, 2015.

[43] G. Lewis, S. Echeverría, S. Simanta, B. Bradshaw, and J. Root, "Tactical cloudlets: Moving cloud computing to the edge," in *Military Communications Conference (MILCOM), 2014 IEEE,* pp. 1440–1446, 2014.

[44] J. Hu, J. Gu, G. Sun, and T. Zhao, "A scheduling strategy on load balancing of virtual machine resources in cloud computing environment," in *Parallel Architectures, Algorithms and Programming (PAAP), 2010 Third International Symposium on*, pp. 89–96, 2010.

[45] F. Xia, L. T. Yang, L. Wang, and A. Vinel, "Internet of things," *International Journal of Communication Systems*, vol. 25, no. 9, p. 1101, 2012.

[46] H. Kopetz, *Real-Time Systems: Design Principles for Distributed Embedded Applications*: New York, pp. 307–322: Springer Science & Business Media, 2011.

[47] L. Atzori, A. Iera, and G. Morabito, "The internet of things: A survey," *Computer Networks,* vol. 54, no. 15, pp. 2787–2805, 2010.

[48] J. Gubbi, R. Buyya, S. Marusic, and M. Palaniswami, "Internet of Things (IoT): A vision, architectural elements, and future directions," *Future Generation Computer Systems,* vol. 29, no. 7, pp. 1645–1660, 2013.

[49] T. Nam and T. A. Pardo, "Conceptualizing smart city with dimensions of technology, people, and institutions," in *Proceedings of the 12th annual international digital government research conference: digital government innovation in challenging times*, pp. 282–291, 2011.

[50] A. Cocchia, "Smart and digital city: A systematic literature review," *Smart city,* pp. 13–43: Springer, Cham, 2014.

[51] K. Su, J. Li, and H. Fu, "Smart city and the applications," in *Electronics, Communications and Control (ICECC), 2011 International Conference on*, pp. 1028–1031, 2011.

[52] N. Alhakbani, M. M. Hassan, M. A. Hossain, and M. Alnuem, "A framework of adaptive interaction support in cloud-based internet of things (iot) environment," in *International Conference on Internet and Distributed Computing Systems*, pp. 136–146, 2014.

[53] R. Aitken, V. Chandra, J. Myers, B. Sandhu, L. Shifren, and G. Yeric, "Device and technology implications of the internet of things," in *VLSI Technology (VLSI-Technology): Digest of Technical Papers, 2014 Symposium on*, pp. 1–4, 2014.

[54] M. M. Gomes, R. da Rosa Righi, and C. A. da Costa, "Future directions for providing better IoT infrastructure." pp. 51–54.

[55] A. Botta, W. De Donato, V. Persico, and A. Pescapé, "Integration of cloud computing and internet of things: A survey," *Future Generation Computer Systems,* vol. 56, pp. 684–700, 2016.

[56] D. Fesehaye, Y. Gao, K. Nahrstedt, and G. Wang, "Impact of cloudlets on interactive mobile cloud applications," in *Enterprise Distributed Object Computing Conference (EDOC), 2012 IEEE 16th International*, pp. 123–132, 2012.

[57] K. Wang, M. Shen, J. Cho, A. Banerjee, J. Van der Merwe, and K. Webb, "Mobiscud: A fast moving personal cloud in the mobile network," in *Proceedings of the 5th Workshop on All Things Cellular: Operations, Applications and Challenges*, pp. 19–24, 2015.

[58] M. Chen, Y. Hao, Y. Li, C.-F. Lai, and D. Wu, "On the computation offloading at ad hoc cloudlet: Architecture and service modes," *IEEE Communications Magazine,* vol. 53, no. 6, pp. 18–24, 2015.

[59] X. Guo, L. Liu, Z. Chang, and T. Ristaniemi, "Data offloading and task allocation for cloudlet-assisted ad hoc mobile clouds," *Wireless Networks,* vol. 24, no. 1, pp. 1–10, 2018.

[60] B. Zhou, A. V. Dastjerdi, R. N. Calheiros, S. N. Srirama, and R. Buyya, "A context sensitive offloading scheme for mobile cloud computing service," in *Cloud Computing (CLOUD), 2015 IEEE 8th International Conference onx,* pp. 869–876, 2015.

[61] M. Satyanarayanan, P. Bahl, R. Caceres, and N. Davies, "The case for VM-based cloudlets in mobile computing," *IEEE Pervasive Computing,* vol. 8, no. 4, 14–23, 2009.

[62] S. Bohez, J. De Turck, T. Verbelen, P. Simoens, and B. Dhoedt, "Mobile, collaborative augmented reality using cloudlets," in *MOBILe Wireless Middle-WARE, Operating Systems and Applications (Mobilware), 2013 International Conference on,* pp. 45–54, 2013.

[63] H. Flores, R. Sharma, D. Ferreira, *et al.,* "Social-aware hybrid mobile offloading," *Pervasive and Mobile Computing,* vol. 36, pp. 25–43, 2017.

[64] Y. Jararweh, F. Ababneh, A. Khreishah, and F. Dosari, "Scalable cloudlet-based mobile computing model," *Procedia Computer Science,* vol. 34, pp. 434–441, 2014.

[65] X. Sun, and N. Ansari, "Green cloudlet network: A distributed green mobile cloud network," *IEEE Network,* vol. 31, no. 1, pp. 64–70, 2017.

[66] K. A. Khan, Q. Wang, C. Grecos, C. Luo, and X. Wang, "MeshCloud: Integrated cloudlet and wireless mesh network for real-time applications," in *Electronics, Circuits, and Systems (ICECS), 2013 IEEE 20th International Conference on,* pp. 317–320, 2013.

[67] J. Rawadi, H. Artail, and H. Safa, "Providing local cloud services to mobile devices with inter-cloudlet communication," in *Mediterranean Electrotechnical Conference (MELECON), 2014 17th IEEE,* pp. 134–138, 2014.

[68] Y. Chen, Y. Chen, Q. Cao, and X. Yang, "PacketCloud: A cloudlet-based open platform for in-network services," *IEEE Transactions on Parallel and Distributed Systems,* vol. 27, no. 4, pp. 1146–1159, 2016.

[69] R. Agarwal and A. Nayak, "DRAP: A decentralized public resourced cloudlet for ad-hoc networks," in *Cloud Networking (CloudNet), 2015 IEEE 4th International Conference on,* pp. 309–314, 2015.

[70] W. Fang, X. Yao, X. Zhao, J. Yin, and N. Xiong, "A stochastic control approach to maximize profit on service provisioning for mobile cloudlet platforms," *IEEE Transactions on Systems, Man, and Cybernetics: Systems,* vol. 48, no. 4, pp. 522–534, 2016.

[71] M. J. Neely, "Stochastic network optimization with application to communication and queueing systems," *Synthesis Lectures on Communication Networks,* vol. 3, no. 1, pp. 1–211, 2010.

[72] L. Tang, X. Chen, and S. He, "When social network meets mobile cloud: A social group utility approach for optimizing computation offloading in cloudlet," *IEEE Access,* vol. 4, pp. 5868–5879, 2016.

Chapter 19

Information-centric trust management for big data-enabled IoT

Usama Ahmed[1,2], Imran Raza[1] and Syed Asad Hussain[1]

Trust management (TM) plays a significant role in big data-enabled Internet of Things (IoT) for trustworthy data mining and fusion operations. It helps to deal with uncertainty and risk when users engage in an increased consumption of IoT services and applications. However, big data-enabled IoT has introduced newer challenges for TM. These challenges are due to the information-centric nature of the IoT rather than the trivial device-centric nature of legacy networks. Given the heterogeneous nature of IoT systems, this has initiated a new debate on ways to manage trust for big data-enabled IoT in a holistic context-dependent way with greater interoperability. From a user's perspective, a fully acceptable IoT-based analytics must be a trustworthy system that offers a range of competent context-aware services, along with effective security and privacy for its personalized data. Focused on this discussion, this chapter first tends to offer the reader with a general understanding of definitions, objectives and necessity of trust. Then it aims to identify the trust requirements of big data-enabled IoT systems such as interoperability, security, privacy, identity and policy requirements. Afterwards, along with an overview of information-centric trusted systems, it discusses the state-of-the-art frameworks, models and methods for information-centric TM in big data-enabled IoT systems and also tries to identify the future trends and open challenges in these areas.

19.1 Introduction

In recent years, users have become more conscious about the significance of safe guarding their private and sensitive information. Along with that, companies have also started realizing that inappropriate security planning can lead to huge loss of economic value and reputation. The advantages of IoT could be extremely compromised if users, organizations and administrations feel that IoT systems cannot be trusted [1]. Currently, trust and reputation establishment is a widely studied topic in different fields. Although the importance of trust is widely recognized, it is a multifaceted concept about which no definitive consensus exists in the scientific literature [2]. In

[1]Department of Computer Science, COMSATS University Islamabad, Lahore, Pakistan
[2]Department of Software Engineering, G.C. University, Faisalabad, Pakistan

computing science, trust is a complex phenomenon with respect to expectation of an entity on the reliability and dependability of another entity. This expectation may be based on various parameters like performance, integrity, and security and privacy.

Big data-enabled IoT has introduced numerous unique challenges in terms of trust evaluation. In a general perspective, an IoT system consists of a physical perception layer, a network layer and an application layer. All layers are interconnected with each other via cyber-physical social characteristics [3]. A dependable and trusted IoT system depends both on reliable coordination among different layers and on the performance of the entire system regarding security, privacy and other properties of trust. Trust assurance at one layer of IoT (e.g. physical) should not determine the trustworthiness of entire system [4].

Recently, many TM mechanisms for IoT systems have been defined. However, current research on IoT is unable to comprehensively investigate how to manage trust in a holistic manner [4]. Along with the foremost issue of interoperability, many other issues, such as trust in big data gathering, processing and mining along with usage [5]; stakeholders' relationship-based trust evaluation [6], its enhancement and evolution [7]; and user-device trust interaction [8] and user-privacy preservation [9] have not been comprehensively resolved. IoT systems present newer challenges when offering pervasive services, especially when trust and privacy are to be stringently considered and supported in dynamic and heterogeneous environments.

The most common method of assessing trust in legacy applications is to estimate trust level of the end entities (entity-centric) relative to the trustor. In these systems, trust level of the data is assumed to be the same as that of the data source. However, there is a fundamental mismatch of such entity-centric trust and information-centric nature of IoT [10]. Most of the IoT-based systems are data centric and operate in dynamic environments, which need immediate actions without waiting for a trust report from end entities. Trust models for a given 'thing' are not only based on its behaviour but also on context in which that thing is present. Therefore, the dynamic nature of a trust model could only be ensured if we are able to define the factors that impact trust in that given context. In the case of heterogeneous IoT devices, there can be a large number of contexts even if we are considering a single use case [11].

Consolidating this discussion, the trustworthy data fusion and mining in big data-enabled IoT is essential; however, it is difficult to achieve. A great amount of accuracy, efficiency, security, privacy and reliability is required along with a holistic view of entire data process and analysis [4]. Design and deployment of suitable TM solutions independent from the exploited platform to ensure that a unified vision of the system is required. This vision should be based on confidentiality, privacy and access control for users and things. Moreover, trust among users and devices, security and privacy policy compliance must be considered.

Research efforts are also needed to focus on developing a secure middleware for integration of IoT and communication technologies so that it can cope with the defined protection constraints. One of the many challenges requiring immediate attention in IoT-TM is the context awareness. Other open issues include but are not limited to the defining of a distinct trust arbitration language that should be able to support the interoperability of IoT context. Moreover, an effective identity-management system and trust-negotiation mechanisms to handle access control for data stream are also the need of the day.

19.2 Overview of trust management

This section aims to deliver an overview of TM in a general context. It discusses the concept of trust as perceived in various disciplines mainly social psychology and philosophy before moving to technical discussion. The basic aim of this discussion is to ensure that the reader has enough basic knowledge of trust before starting with technical details.

19.2.1 Definitions of trust

Trust is a complex social phenomenon and is a critical factor of everyday life. We all make trust decisions every day and many times a day in our lives. These decisions are established on evidence to believe or have confidence in good intentions of someone or something towards us. Most of such decisions we make in the world relate others, although occasionally they concern ourselves or the environment in which we exist [12]. Trust has been extensively studied in social science and psychological literature. However, detailed explanation and semantics of trust have always been investigated in the context of its application domain [13,14]. Therefore, in this chapter, the concept of trust is first being reviewed from the viewpoint of social psychology and philosophy as the most significant definitions of trust mainly come from these disciplines.

19.2.1.1 Trust in social psychology

Social psychology views the trusting behaviour as being in a potentially vulnerable position relative to others; however, having some knowledge of their good intentions inspires trust [12]. Therefore, risk and some information regarding the potentially trusted person or situation are seen as mandatory conditions for trust. Trust has been seen as a function of insufficient information by most of the researchers [15]. They consider that there is no trust but only rational assumptions under perfect information. In [16], trust is defined as a dominant variable responsible for collaboration of the processes in a system and the usefulness of the system resulting from that collaboration.

Trust is typically viewed to be situation dependent, and if one relies on an entity without considering its trust, this dependence is then to be highly considered as a function of influence and control other than trust [17].

19.2.1.2 Trust in philosophy

In philosophical literature, trust is considered as a good gesture, and the lack of known trust always has a negative impact [18]. Few philosophers have implied trust as a function of cooperation, friendship and the qualities of the human being [18,19]. Whenever a context is specified for a trust judgement, a person or an entity is considered to be relied upon only in those certain aspects that are covered in the context. Thus, trust is always implicit and is never taken as a rational option. Trust is also considered an accepted vulnerability to another person's possible but not expected ill will towards the others [18].

19.2.2   Semantics of trust

There are many prevailing concepts in the current literature, which are commonly used interchangeably in the place of trust [12]. Although they convey similar meanings as that of trust, a more precise deliberation on their meanings in relation to big data-enabled IoT is required to differentiate their use cases. A few of these concepts are described as follows:

- *Credibility:* The word credibility is the most commonly used synonym of trust-worthiness meaning, for instance, that a system can actually perform according to its claimed ability. This means that it has the necessary means to take action on a request. It also means that all entities involved in a system can be believed under respective circumstances.
- *Competence:* Competence is a closely matching concept with credibility. This means that an entity is supposed to have ability to accomplish some tasks. The only difference between competence and credibility is the understanding that it is much impassive and independent from the declaration of a subject entity.
- *Confidence:* When no alternative actions in a situation are considered, an entity is considered to be in a situation of confidence. If a certain action is considered in preference to other actions, this case is considered as trust. A concise difference between confidence and trust is that confidence is a belief in oneself (self-confidence), while trust is belief in others.
- *Reliance:* Reliance can be viewed as a prerogative of an entity to depend only on certain features or characteristics of another entity. Another case may be to depend on the entire system but for a given context. Moreover, relation between reliance and trust can be a narrower concept than trust, meaning that a trusting entity relies on all aspects of the system after individual judgement.

19.2.3   Elements of trust

Trust between two entities can be viewed as a bridge between their historical experiences and expected future. Importance of past interactions and the future predictions to enable trust usually changes over time. A case might be that in the relationship-establishment phase, there is not much historical knowledge to go on with. As the relationship advances, there are more interactions giving further experiences and insights. The entities thus become more competent to form a well-informed trust assessment of each other. Trust is typically perceived as a consequence of interactions between entities such that the relationships between them mature steadily. However, reputation and initial impression are equally significant. There are many situations in which an entity might never get a second chance to demonstrate their trustworthiness.

In many cases, trust is specific to a particular environment forming a context. Such a trust is known as situational trust due to the fact that a particular entity might be behaving in an appropriate manner under the influence of some elements external to it. Moreover, extending this concept of trust, there is a difference between trusting an entity and the system. A system is said to be in a trustworthy state when trust is placed in the functioning of that system as a whole instead of the entities involved in its composition. The latter is considered more of a reliance as discussed previously.

Concluding this discussion, different disciplines have different basic rules for trust. Social psychologists emphasize the steadfastness of the words, keeping of the promises and the fulfilment of obligations. However, philosophers emphasize the individual and interpersonal characteristics of participants. Such varying and fragile conceptualization of trust somewhat owes to the fact that trust is always situation specific, i.e. the context always matters [13,14].

Keeping in view the entire discussion, it seems that no absolute definition of trust seems to be conceivable. In order to define trust usefully, the theory should by and large be applicable to the given context but should be definitive in its scope. This leads us to the point where the advent of IoT and big data-enabled information systems demands newer theoretical foundation to be established for enabling trust within these systems. In the following sections, this discussion is augmented by presenting the prevailing methods of enabling trust, followed by challenges and requirements of trust within IoT systems and the recent advancements therein.

19.3   Trust-management systems

This section highlights the prominence of TM with technical perspective, before going into further details regarding the trust for IoT. Starting with the idea of trust representation as a formal concept to its implementation in the form of TM system (TMS), this section provides the reader with the knowledge of basic components involved in a complete TM cycle.

19.3.1   Overview

In the context of distributed and multi-agent systems, the concept of trust is mostly bound to 'performance', 'security' and 'privacy'. These factors are represented in the form of trust models focusing on the formal definitions, semantics and modelling of trust. Trust modelling in distributed systems has its roots in the seminal works by Zadeh [20], Dampster and Shafer [21], Marsh [22] and Jøsang [23].

The most significant of these works for trust modelling has been done by Marsh [22]. He proposed a formal treatment of trust evaluation by integrating different trust concepts from sociology, social psychology and philosophy. Recently, with the advent of decision support systems, context-dependent implementation of these models is observed in different types of distributed systems leading its way to the emergence of TMS. In general, a TMS seeks to deliver a trust assessment as a representative view of the overall confidence in the ability of a system. Figure 19.1 shows a block representation of a TMS functionality involving entities like cloud consumer, cloud service provider and TM authority responsible for governing the overall system environment.

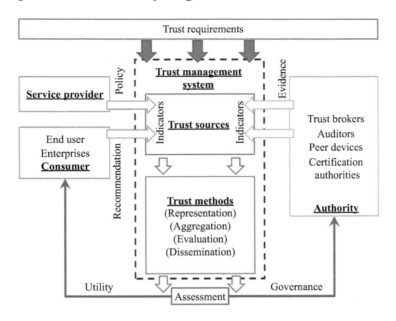

Figure 19.1   A block representation of trust-management system functionality

Figure 19.1 represents a generic TMS and its basic components. A TMS is basically built on two fundamental components, namely trust sources and trust methods. Trust sources include but may not be limited to certified assessments, policy matters, service level agreements (SLAs), recommendations, audit reports and third-party monitoring. Trust indicators from these sources are passed to the second component referred in Figure 19.1 as trust methods. Trust indicators are collected, aggregated and evaluated based on formal models of trust assessment within the trust method component. Afterwards, the evaluated trust result indicative of the overall assessment of the entity is disseminated for use, comparison and update within the infrastructure [24,25]. The overall functionality of the TMS and its underlying components should be governed by a set of requirements and is discussed in the following sections.

19.3.2   Trust sources

Sources of trust are the origins of trust values based on human behaviour, perception and interaction experiences with the system. In this section, we classify trust sources into three categories based on their type of trust indications. From the following deliberation, we see that trust decision based on individual source may address one aspect of the trust but not others. We argue that a viable solution is to implement all kinds of trust sources into the TMS to facilitate better trust decisions.

- *Recommendation:* Recommendation is the most widely used source of trust in various environments [26,27]. Recommendations are of two types, namely (i) *explicit recommendation* and (ii) *transitive recommendation*. Explicit recommendation is the one that is provided to a cloud consumer by a close and trusted relation (e.g. friends). It is also known as first-hand recommendation. On the other hand, transitive recommendation is the one that is received by a cloud consumer from its trusted relationship, which in turn has received the same recommendation from another trusted source.

- *Policy:* Policy as a trust indicator is another way for trust establishment among various parties. Mostly it has been used in grid computing [28], peer-to-peer (P2P) systems [29] and web-based applications [30] to name a few. The service provider offers services on the basis of these policies, which can be regarded as a commitment to their performance and hence as trust in their system.

- *Evidence:* The terms and conditions as mentioned in the service contract serve the basis to measure the performance and security strength of a cloud service provider (CSP) and estimate the level of variation from the defined thresholds. These performance evidences may be used as a source of trust within the TMS [31,32]. However, a major issue with utilizing evidence as a trust source is the lack of cloud users' capability to monitor quality of service (QoS) parameters and verify SLA in a fine-grained manner [32]. Therefore, a trusted third party (TTP) offering these services is mandatory for the cloud users to collect evidence.

19.3.3   Trust methods

Trust methods are a collection of different operations and functions that are performed within a TMS to generate a comprehensive representation of the system's trust. As shown in Figure 19.1, the basic function of any TMS is to collect raw input in the form of trust indications from different sources and convert them into a representable form. Afterwards, information from all sources is aggregated before making them available to the trust-evaluation function. This trust-evaluation function is responsible to evaluate the resultant trustworthiness of the system based on formal trust models. This evaluation operation can be from one of two categories, i.e. static or dynamic. Static approach is a simple mathematical operation that does not cater for the evolving nature of the underlying system. However, the dynamic or adaptive operation involves a trust update function that allows the trust decisions to evolve with the nature of system. In the case of highly dynamic nature of big data-enabled IoT applications, adaptive approaches are highly recommended as the devices may join or leave at random intervals.

The output of the trust-evaluation function is often a numerical representation showing confidence in the provider. This result or trust assessment is then distributed or disseminated to the trust requester or the entire system. This assessment of a provider serves as a utility to the consumer and mode of governance to the authority within the system. A consumer can utilize this assessment for making decision regarding service selection. After service contracts, a consumer acts as a source of trust of indicator by providing recommendation for the contracted service. This recommendation is again an input to the trust-evaluation function, which may further be utilized to update the trust decisions regarding the same provider.

This trust assessment may serve as an input to the governance domain of any authority regulating the entire system. This authority may be a consumer itself or any TTP like brokers, accreditors, auditors or certification authorities. The objective of such authority is to monitor and audit the providers for compliance with the policy requirements established with the consumer. This monitoring or audit reports serve as a source of evidence to report the overall performance of the service provider to the TMS.

19.4   Trust management for big data-enabled IoT

This section enables a reader to understand why and how trust can be achieved and enforced within a big data-enabled IoT system. First, it highlights the necessity of trust in an IoT environment. Second, it elaborates the motives for having an information-centric TM instead of entity centric. Afterwards, it explains the requirements of information-centric trust in IoT environments.

19.4.1   *Information-centric trust-management systems*

Trust is a complex notion in relation to the assurance, certainty and expectancy of the dependability, honesty, security, soundness, capability and various other characteristics of an entity. As big data originates from a variety of sources in huge amounts, and usually in real time, the role of TM cannot be neglected. With all the devices, sensors or other data-collecting mechanisms linked to a private individual, trusted and reliable mechanism for fusion and mining of data is the need of the day. It is only then that these mechanisms can ensure provisioning of competent services with intelligent context awareness, information security and improved privacy of user data. TM in IoT will help people overcome perception of risk and uncertainty in IoT applications. Moreover, it helps to create a better user approval and usage of personalized application and services. However, the architecture and recent trends in big data-enabled IoT pose several novel concerns when it comes to the enabled trust therein.

Consider a generic IoT-enabled system containing three layers, namely (i) a physical perception layer for perceiving physical environment, (ii) a network layer for transforming and processing raw perceived data and (iii) an application layer for intelligent ubiquitous context-aware services. These layers are inherently connected with each other using cyber-physical social features [3]. For an IoT system to be trustworthy, it should rely not only on dependable collaboration between layers but also on the entire system's performance with respect to privacy, security and other trust-related information. Assuring trust at one IoT layer (for instance, at network) is not an indication for the whole system to be trustworthy.

In traditional TMSs, the evaluation of trust is based on the relationship between end objects and their interactions in various transactions [33,34]. Moreover, these systems use certain set of metrics like honesty, reputation, cooperativeness and duration of interaction, to evaluate the trustworthiness of participants. However, in IoT scenario, behaviour of end entities or devices is only obvious and dependant on the data of various types that they generate. For example, consider a case when reliable, up-to-date and location-based weather, traffic and safety warnings information is required from a smart city application. The consistency and reliability of information is more important than the facts about trustworthiness of entities who are actually generating them.

The other common misinterpretation is that the assumption of having entity trust would guarantee data trust. This assumption is in fact different in various aspects like validity of data, timeliness and other properties unique to data which are often ignored in calculating trust for end entities.

Further, information is the governing factor for any IoT system and is generated from the data by combining it with the context. Hence, if there is a data quality problem, it would eventually lead to information-quality problem [35]. In other words, information quality can only be guaranteed once the right data item is delivered to a desired entity at the precise time in a clear, useable and meaningful manner. Therefore, it is important to address the challenges of establishing an information-centric trust while preserving the traditional form of trust computation.

19.4.2 Challenges of information-centric trust

Information-centric TM poses numerous challenges that must be addressed for quality and assurance of information. Once identified, these challenges are a key factor to define requirement for an information-centric TMS for big data-enabled IoT. These challenges can be divided into three major categories related to (i) *data processing*, (ii) *security and privacy* and (iii) *interoperability.*

19.4.2.1 Data processing

The entire mechanism of data processing starting from data perception (sensing and collection) to data handling (data fusion and mining) and afterwards data transition (transmission and communication to the interested parties) offers the most crucial challenges for trust awareness. First, trust in data perception or data gathering in big data-enabled IoT is a critical concern. If the massive amount of collected data cannot be trusted enough due to, for instance, detection of loss or malign participation of some sensing devices, the QoS for IoT shall be considerably effected. Such poor-quality service can be hardly accepted by users, although the trust at other two layers, i.e. the application and network, might be fully acceptable.

Second, data handling trust must be guaranteed. Trusted fusion of data and mining process necessitates secure, privacy preserved, efficient and dependable processing and analysis of data in a comprehensive way. Realizing all trust objectives in data-handling process is really a challenging job. Provisioning of personalized IoT services is greatly dependant on mining and analysis of users' private data. This fact greatly results in the intrusion of user privacy, and hence there is always a trade-off between the customization of services and the limit of privacy invasion.

Third, providing reliance and preserving user privacy to an acceptable level in information communicated to different platforms for the context dependant and per-sonalized service provisioning introduce many new challenges. More specifically, provisioning of trustworthy services connected to the social networking offers unique and significant challenges related to reliability, responsiveness and privacy of user data.

19.4.2.2   Security and privacy

This concept of privacy in big data-enabled IoT is strongly linked to the user identity and the term personal identifiable information (PII) and its sensitivity rather than the devices connected to the network. The term PII is used to describe information that could potentially relate to a person. A prevailing trend for research in trust for IoT considers privacy of the user information as the primary indicator of trust. Trust is considered as a combination of 'honesty, cooperativeness, and community interests' [6]. According to the recommendation by Poore in [36], trust follows the definition of privacy and is 'the assurance that PII will be only used as agreed and will be protected against unauthorized access'. Leister and Schulz follow the same notion of trust but as a scalar metric [37].

19.4.2.3   Interoperability

One of the core features of IoT-enabled system is the diversity of things that are connected with each other. This might result in interaction of different trust models and their necessity to recognize and understand each other's syntax and semantics of deriving trust. This can be achieved by creating a mapping among these models as different mathematical functions. For instance, different models should use the same scale of measuring trust with the same resulting trust values and might be able to negotiate this before their interaction. Such interoperability support should be able to define the specific definition of these mappings. Expressing such definition is arduous and is difficult to generalize as it depends on numerous scenarios with varied modelling requirements.

19.4.3   *Requirements for trust in big data-enabled IoT*

In context of the discussed unique challenges that are posed by big data-enabled IoT, specific requirements are observed that need to be thoroughly examined and resolved. In this section, we provide a categorization of these requirements that are posed on the TM in IoT.

- *Data-processing requirements:* Data-processing requirements, within big data-enabled systems for trust, can be categorized into (i) *data sensing and collection*, (ii) *data fusion and mining* and (iii) *data communication* requirements and are described as follows:
  - *Data sensing and collection:* The main focus for trust in data sensing and collection should be on achieving trust in terms of physical-layer attributes. These attributes include receptivity, precision, security, dependability, persistence and data collection efficiency for sensors.
  - *Data fusion and mining:* The massive volumes of data gathered in big data-enabled IoT need to be treated in a trusted manner to achieve privacy preservation, reliability and precision for a comprehensive data process. This

requirement is also related to social computing for analysis of users' social activities and connections in order to mine their demands in a trustworthy manner.

- *Data transmission and communication:* Private data related to a certain user should be transferred securely in the IoT system. Private information of communicating parties should not be accessible to unauthorized entities during data transition. Secure key management and trusted routing within IoT networks are two significant concerns to be addressed [38].

• *Security and privacy requirements:* Security and privacy requirements can be categorized into (i) *system security and reliability*, (ii) *privacy protection* and (iii) *identity management* requirements.

- *System security and reliability:* A trusted IoT system should be able to successfully defend against attacks to increase assurance of users in IoT system. All layers of IoT system are equally affected by this requirement, resulting in system security, reliability and availability in entirety.

- *Privacy protection:* Personal data and information privacy must be preserved as per policy and users' expectation from the IoT system. This requirement is generally related to IoT system in entirety.

- *Identity management:* The identifiers of entities within the IoT system should be effectively managed for achieving trustworthiness of these entities. Highly scalable and efficient identity-management methods are required at all IoT layers. Moreover, an effective interlayer coordination for system wide identity management is also required along with identity privacy and context awareness. For instance, an effective identity-management system should be able to assign context-dependent identities to each entity. For example, in the case of a smart watch that is used by a person in context C_0, its identity should be different from the one that is issued when the same person uses the same watch in context C_1. An obvious reason for this requirement is that the watch may be gathering different information for different moments in time.

• *Interoperability requirements:* TM should be generic for different IoT systems and services and must be widely applicable. Devices from multiple manufacturers offering diverse capabilities according to different standards must be able to communicate with each other. This heterogeneity is elevated when IoT devices communicate with each other in context-dependant environments. Different things will have their own ways of exchanging information with others, and thus different types of information and contexts may coexist. To deal with this situation, there are two types of requirements; one that deals with device interoperability and the other that deals with human interaction and context interoperability.

19.5 Recent advancements in information-centric trust management in big data-enabled IoT

This section outlines the issues of TM in big data-enabled IoT that are covered in literature with possible solutions. Moreover, an effort has been made to highlight the shortcomings of these mechanisms in the available literature that need further research.

19.5.1   Trusted data processing

19.5.1.1   Data sensing and collection

Data sensing and collection trust is undeniably fundamental in IoT system. It plays a crucial part in facilitating service trust as almost all customized IoT services are dependent on data mining and analysis. An IoT-system architecture has been proposed by Ning *et al.* [3], which presents resolution to different challenges in trusted IoT service delivery. The proposed work considers system, network and application security from the view point of data confidentiality, integrity and availability along with authorization, non-repudiation and privacy.

Sicari *et al.* [39] proposed an architecture named 'Data Accuracy using node REputation' (DARE) for secure data aggregation and node reputation in wireless sensor networks (WSNs). The proposed approach is a hybrid combination of WSNs with wireless mesh networking using a secure 'multilateration' technique. This technique allows the network to retain the trustworthiness of aggregated data even when there are malicious nodes in the network. The proposed approach efficiently minimizes the data exchanged in the network and improves battery life for wireless sensors. However, this work has not considered privacy preservation of user data.

A trusted architecture is suggested by Quan *et al.* [40] containing different logical layers. These layers are identified as perception, mark recognition, decision control and trusted interface layer on top of all. This trusted interface layer comprises inter-layer protocols for trusted communication between these layers. However, the major focus of the proposed work is on the data perception layer discussing involvement of sensor network. Moreover, TM for data in transit is also discussed.

Validation of information collected from multiple sensors governed by separate entities is one of the key issues of data-sensing trust. Javed and Wolf [41] proposed a solution to this problem using outlier detection. They developed a method for representing the physical phenomenon measured by the sensors as a model. Afterwards, sensor readings are mapped to this model by spatial and temporal interpolation to identify outliers. The proposed research has been evaluated for a weather forecast system. However, the same is valid for other applications that have continuous underlying phenomenon of data perception.

Ukil *et al.* [42] used the concept of trusted computing to introduce temper resistance for embedded devices in IoT. The proposed work has addressed not only the concern of security for data but also for hardware platform. Moreover, it also supports data processing as well as data transmission trust. Khoo [43] has reviewed the security and privacy concerns raised by radio-frequency identification (RFID) technology and analysed risk and impact of several threats within the RFID system. They have identified blocking and jamming of end devices, relay and replay attacks, and eavesdropping and tag cloning. Moreover, personal and location privacy intrusion attacks are also discussed. The details of these attacks are followed by methods to resolve these issues and mitigation of risks introduced by them.

Huang *et al.* [44] suggested security protocols based on 'human–system' inter-actions to protect collection of sensitive personal information. These protocols allow dynamic dissemination of keys and IDs within the system without any prior distri-bution of secrets. This ensures an easy mechanism for replacement of compromised or expired keys. The proposed work perceives users as ad-hoc TTPs, to disseminate secure IoT system updates.

19.5.1.2 Data fusion and mining

Trust in data fusion and mining is explicitly achieved by utilizing mechanisms for privacy-preserving data mining and computations within the system. Therefore, the available literature has been divided into two major categories, namely (i) *privacy-preserving computation* and (ii) *privacy-preserving mining*.

- *Privacy-preserving computation:* Research in this domain includes numerical and statistical computation, vectors' scalar product, quadratic functions, secure mul-tiparty computation, and steganography and computational geometry. However, the basic theoretical research in this field is still in its infancy. Mostly, this research is always targeted towards a unique discipline focused on its respective computing scenario and problems therein. Therefore, practical implementation of this work into IoT applications and big data-enabled services is still an open question and the biggest challenge to overcome. It is recommended to consider the usability of such research in practical IoT applications based on actual requirements and constraints of IoT system.
- *Privacy-preserving data mining:* This is another significant problem in providing trusted IoT services due to the computational complexity and communication cost for data mining. A novel architecture proposed by Mishra and Chandwani [45] enables privacy-preserving data mining by hiding the identities of all parties contributing in business process outsourcing. This architecture consists of a range of functions that provide additional capability to a party to split its large volume data before sending it to computation process. This process of splitting the data makes it infeasible for other parties to know the actual source of the data, thus providing data mining that is secure and privacy preserved.

Zhu *et al.* [46] proposed a scheme for secure extraction of knowledge from private data of more than one parties. They focused on privacy-preserving 'add and multiply exchanging technology' and proposed three distinct approaches to it. Another privacy-preserving protocol named 'shared dot product' is studied by Wang and Luo [47]. This protocol acts as a building block for numerous privacy-preserving data-mining algorithms. The proposed two-party shared dot-product protocol is based on basic cryptographic methods, which are provably secure in malicious and semi-honest threat model. A Horizontal Distribution of the Privacy Protection DK-Means algorithm is proposed by Shen, Han and Shan [48]. The proposed protocol is based on horizontal partitioned database and DK-Means idea to achieve distributed clustering. They also utilized a secure multiparty computation protocol to realize privacy protection.

Statistical hypothesis test is a significant technique used in data analytics. Liu and Zhang [49] explored nonparametric sign test theory for a scenario of two parties, each having their own private dataset. Authors consider a case when both parties want to conduct a sign test on their combined dataset. However, none of them is ready to disclose its dataset to other. The proposed approach does not use any cryptographic primitives and can be considered a lightweight solution.

Association rule mining is another popular research area in which previously unknown rules or patterns are extracted from huge volumes of data. A secure protocol to perform this kind of mining is suggested by Zhan *et al.* [50]. The proposed protocol works for multiple parties in a distributed manner use the concept of homomorphic encryption. Hence, all participants can exchange their private data using this technique while preserving its privacy. In another work for privacy-preserving association rule mining [51], Kantarcioglu and Clifton proposed two protocols for horizontally parti-tioned data. This work was further revised by Zhang and Zhao for its security resilience [52]. Wang [53] critically surveyed the concept of privacy-preserving association rule-mining approach with respect to its basic concepts, principles and methods. According to this survey, existing approaches are not practically implementable. Moreover, these approaches prove to be ineffective, less accurate and merely flexible.

Keeping in view the above literature, there have been a lot of efforts to support privacy-preserving data mining operations. However, current solutions are still not practical as they hardly satisfy all critical requirements of real-world usage. These requirements include flexibility, accuracy, security, efficiency and trustworthiness. Mainly, the existing research has not investigated the entire range of data mining-related operations in a holistic way.

19.5.1.3   Data transmission and communication

Trust for data in transition process has always been critical for realizing overall system-level trust. Ongoing research in networks and communications can be utilized for achieving such trust in IoT systems. Essentially, the trustworthy IoT data transmission and communication protocols should upkeep with the diverse IoT-networking context. Such an effort has been done by Isa *et al.* [54] by proposing a security protocol for massive data transfer within IoT network. The proposed security framework offers enhanced security, privacy and trust for embedded system infrastructures. They have proposed to utilize lightweight mechanisms for data encryption and key exchange in Trivial File Transfer Protocol to make it applicable for big data-enabled IoT context.

Granjal *et al.* [55] performed an experimental study to recognize suitable secure communication protocols. They have proposed mechanisms to ensure security at the network and application layer. Moreover, they have identified the data trans-mission constraints of current platforms to support end-to-end secure data delivery within IoT system. SVELTE [56] is an intrusion detection system for IoT to defend against general routing attacks. These attacks include spoofed or altered information, selective-forwarding and sinkhole. Evaluated overhead for the proposed approach is sufficiently small, and therefore it can be deployed on resource constrained IoT nodes.

Keeping in view the pivotal role of data transmission within the IoT system, the recent advancements in this field have truly focused on suggesting security protocols suitable for IoT scenarios. However, examining the interoperability of various TM mechanisms in different environments is still an open research area.

19.5.2   Security and privacy-enabled trust management

Enhancing identity trust and privacy preservation has been a major focus of research in IoT. A scalable and lightweight framework [57] for authentication and integrity protection within IoT has been proposed by Fongen. Similarly, identity management for preserving privacy related to user location has been studied by Hu *et al.* [58]. They have considered the adaptability of their approach in context of various contexts, mainly differentiating them as emergency and non-emergency situations.

The threat of unauthorized tracking by a compromised discovery service within an RFID-enabled infrastructure has been analysed by Yan *et al.* [59]. They proposed an architecture for secure discovery service that provides privacy protection against unauthorized tracking. The suggested architecture also protects against a semi-trusted discovery service attack and supports efficient key management and access control for database reading attack.

Huang *et al.* [44] proposed a privacy-protection solution containing a user-controlled access-control protocol. This protocol is accompanied by a context-aware 'k-anonymity' privacy policy. The proposed mechanism controls the nature of personal data that is being accessed and accumulated by a service. Moreover, the proposed method keeps track of timing and authority of the entity collecting and accessing private data.

Zhang and Tian [60] proposed an extended role-based access-control model for protecting context information. The proposed model can efficiently increase the security and access control for web-enabled IoT services. Gusmeroli *et al.* [61] have proposed a capability-based access control system that can help enterprises and individuals to manage their access control for various IoT services. The proposed mechanism supports delegation of rights and customization of access control in even more complex scenarios.

Most of these approaches successfully address the requirements of identity trust and/or privacy preservation. However, interoperability with other TM mechanisms in order to achieve similar goals in different contexts must be explored in future research.

19.5.3   Trust frameworks for interoperability

The research progress of IoT has been briefly reviewed by Suo *et al.* [62] in context of security. This research discusses the security requirements in each layer of IoT by analysing the security architecture and features of IoT. These requirements emphasize cryptographic algorithms and protocols to be lightweight. Moreover, the need for authenticity and integrity of sensed data, scalable identity management and privacy-enhanced key-establishment agreements between entities is also highlighted. In addition, they have also briefly outlined challenges of security structure, key management, legal and regulatory challenges for big data-enabled IoT services.

A considerably elaborative survey of trust in IoT is presented by Køien [63]. This survey presents a multidimensional perspective for trust in devices and services of IoT environment. Moreover, psychological aspects of risk, reputation and its association with human mind are also explained. It is highlighted that none of the IoT system components can be fully trusted. Regardless of this fact, however, humans should trust IoT services in entirety. It is argued that human instincts of handling threats and opportunities can often fail, but use of trusted intermediary objects or devices can enable trust in IoT services without too much reluctance.

Li *et al.* [64] proposed a general architecture of trusted security system for IoT. This architecture mainly includes a number of trusted modules including perception, network, terminal, user and an agent module. This architecture also supports requirements of data perception trust as well. It is suggested that there is still a considerable void in resolving security problems of IoT. This mostly owes to the openness and the immature development of IoT and therefore requires further study. However, the proposed architecture has not been evaluated in any scenario and hence lacks any verdict on its practicality.

19.6   Discussion and future research

This section summarizes the entire discussion with an indication on the known issues, anticipated challenges and trends in research that may shape the upcoming landscape of trust for big data-enabled IoT.

19.6.1   Anticipated challenges and research trends

Considering the challenges and the recent literature available to address these challenges, the foremost concern involves contextualization and user-dependent trust evaluation. Trust evaluation should be contextualized to intelligently provide personalized IoT services. The success of IoT-enabled services is going to be determined largely by holistic TM with good user experience.

Second, the literature is lacking a comprehensive framework for TM to overcome all defined challenges for trust establishment. Currently, most of the research is focused on security and privacy issues and that too for supporting perception and communication of user data. Moreover, identity management is substantially addressed with all other remaining challenges rarely considered for investigation. Recent advances in privacy-preserving computation have not yet been applied in practice and are recommended to be used in real IoT systems. Also, research for privacy preservation is not enough and lacks methods to ensure comprehensive privacy protection at all layers of the IoT system. Moreover, interoperability of various TM techniques from various contexts and vendors should be explored in the future research. In addition to this all, autonomic TM is another anticipated challenge. However, extensive research is required for its realization because of scalability of the IoT infrastructure, mobility and low-computation capacity of nodes.

Third, current privacy-preserving computation and mining techniques are still in their initial stages. Almost none of these solutions are practical with respect to complexity and cost of computation. Moreover, their high communication cost, lack of flexibility and generality make them hard to be practically applied. It is really challenging to observe the practical applicability of these schemes to IoT applications and big data-enabled services. For this purpose, requirements and restrictions of practical IoT systems must be taken into consideration.

In addition to the previously mentioned challenges, one of the biggest challenges for IoT-based trustworthy personalized services is energy efficiency to support miniature devices. TM algorithms and mechanisms are supposed to be faster but with less energy consumption. Present research has not yet fully focused on this issue but an anticipated way out could be to enable lightweight trust mechanisms that may avoid cryptographic algorithms.

At last, but by no means least, some legal issues continue to remain blurry and need explanation, e.g. what is going to be the impact of location on privacy regulations and how data ownership could be managed in the networks of cloud of 'things'. Big data-enabled IoT requires a legal framework that constitutes heterogeneous and differentiated policies considering the scalability, ubiquity and interoperability of the IoT systems.

It is anticipated that future research for TM in the IoT is going to be focused on resolving many existing open issues. The focus of such research should be to overcome challenges for gaining user acceptance and adoption of technology in practice. More importantly, research should be concerned with and driven by practical requirements and user demands, e.g. lightweight and energy efficient solutions, and IoT user contextual trust. Thus, TM for big data-enabled IoT services should be designed for easy user acceptance.

19.7 Conclusion

Big data-enabled IoT has to be a trustworthy system offering security and privacy for its personalized data while maintaining the usability and flexibility of the system. This chapter has gathered the requirements imposed by trustworthy analytics and has highlighted the key challenges required to be overcome for a holistic TMS. A review of literature also emphasizes the currently available research in the subject domain and highlights the anticipated complications and future trends that are evident from the context-specific requirements of big data-enabled IoT. Among the various challenges, user-based contextualization of trust, holistic TM, privacy preservation and energy efficient trust algorithms are few areas that need to be addressed.

References

[1] F. J. Riggins and S. F. Wamba, "Research directions on the adoption, usage, and impact of the internet of things through the use of big data analytics," in *48th Hawaii International Conference on System Sciences (HICSS '15)*, 2015, pp. 1531–1540.

[2] S. Sicari, A. Rizzardi, L. A. Grieco, and A. Coen-Porisini, "Security, privacy and trust in internet of things: The road ahead," *Computer Networks*, vol. 76, pp. 146–164, 2015.

[3] H. Ning, H. Liu, and L. T. Yang, "Cyberentity security in the internet of things," *Computer*, 2013 Mar 7;46(4):46–53.

[4]   Z. Yan, P. Zhang, and A. V. Vasilakos, "A survey on trust management for internet of things," *Journal of Network and Computer Applications,* vol. 42, pp. 120–134, 2014.

[5]   C. C. Aggarwal, N. Ashish, and A. Sheth, "The internet of things: A survey from the data-centric perspective," in *Managing and Mining Sensor Data*: Springer, Boston, MA, 2013, pp. 383–428.

[6]   F. Bao and R. Chen, "Trust management for the internet of things and its application to service composition," in *IEEE International Symposium on a World of Wireless, Mobile and Multimedia Networks (WoWMoM),* 2012, pp. 1–6.

[7]   F. J. Riggins and T. Mukhopadhyay, "Interdependent benefits from interorganizational systems: opportunities for business partner reengineering," *Journal of Management Information Systems,* vol. 11, pp. 37–57, 1994.

[8]   A. R. Sfar, E. Natalizio, Y. Challal, and Z. Chtourou, "A roadmap for security challenges in the internet of things," *Digital Communications and Networks,* vol. 4, pp. 118–137, 2018.

[9]   S. Yu, "Big privacy: Challenges and opportunities of privacy study in the age of big data," *IEEE Access,* vol. 4, pp. 2751–2763, 2016.

[10] Y. Zhang, D. Raychadhuri, L. Grieco, *et al.*, "Design considerations for applying ICN to IoT," *draft-zhang-icnrg-icniot-01.txt, IRTF/ICNRG,* 2017.

[11] C. Fernandez-Gago, F. Moyano, and J. Lopez, "Modelling trust dynamics in the internet of things," *Information Sciences,* vol. 396, pp. 72–82, 2017.

[12] N. Luhmann, *Trust and power*: John Wiley & Sons, Chichester, 1979.

[13] I. Marková and A. Gillespie, *Trust and distrust: Sociocultural perspectives*: IAP, Charlotte, NC, 2007.

[14] D. E. Denning, "A new paradigm for trusted systems," in *Workshop on New Security Paradigms,* 1993, pp. 36–41.

[15] J. D. Lewis and A. Weigert, "Trust as a social reality," *Social Forces,* vol. 63, pp. 967–985, 1985.

[16] J. R. Gibb, *Trust: A new view of personal and organizational development*: Guild of Tutors Press, Los Angeles, 1978.

[17] R. H. Frank, *Passions within reason: The strategic role of the emotions*: WW Norton & Co, New York City, 1988.

[18] A. Baier, "Trust and antitrust," *Ethics,* vol. 96, pp. 231–260, 1986.

[19] L. T. Hosmer, "Trust: The connecting link between organizational theory and philosophical ethics," *Academy of management Review,* vol. 20, pp. 379–403, 1995.

[20] L. A. Zadeh, "The role of fuzzy logic in the management of uncertainty in expert systems," *Fuzzy Sets and Systems,* vol. 11, pp. 199–227, 1983.

[21] G. Shafer, *A mathematical theory of evidence* vol. 42: Princeton University Press, Princeton, NJ, 1976.

[22] S. P. Marsh, "Formalising trust as a computational concept," 1994.

[23] A. Jøsang, "The right type of trust for distributed systems," in *Workshop on New Security Paradigms,* 1996, pp. 119–131.

[24] T. H. Noor, Q. Z. Sheng, Z. Maamar, and S. Zeadally, "Managing trust in the cloud: State of the art and research challenges," *Computer,* vol. 49, pp. 34–45, 2016.

[25] S. M. Habib, S. Ries, and M. Muhlhauser, "Towards a trust management system for cloud computing," in *10th International Conference on Trust, Security and Privacy in Computing and Communications (TrustCom '11),* 2011, pp. 933–939.

[26] F. Skopik, D. Schall, and S. Dustdar, "Start trusting strangers? bootstrapping and prediction of trust," in *International Conference on Web Information Systems Engineering,* 2009, pp. 275–289.

[27] S. Park, L. Liu, C. Pu, M. Srivatsa, and J. Zhang, "Resilient trust management for web service integration," in *IEEE International Conference on Web Services (ICWS '05),* 2005.

[28] S. Song, K. Hwang, and Y.-K. Kwok, "Trusted grid computing with security binding and trust integration," *Journal of Grid Computing,* vol. 3, pp. 53–73, 2005.

[29] S. Song, K. Hwang, R. Zhou, and Y.-K. Kwok, "Trusted P2P transactions with fuzzy reputation aggregation," *IEEE Internet Computing,* vol. 9, pp. 24–34, 2005.

[30] S. D. C. D. Vimercati, S. Foresti, S. Jajodia, S. Paraboschi, G. Psaila, and P. Samarati, "Integrating trust management and access control in data-intensive web applications," *ACM Transactions on the Web (TWEB),* vol. 6, p. 6, 2012.

[31] S. A. De Chaves, R. B. Uriarte, and C. B. Westphall, "Toward an architecture for monitoring private clouds," *IEEE Communications Magazine,* vol. 49, pp. 130–137, 2011.

[32] J. Spring, "Monitoring cloud computing by layer, part 1," *IEEE Security & Privacy,* vol. 9, pp. 66–68, 2011.

[33] U. Jayasinghe, H.-W. Lee, and G. M. Lee, "A computational model to evaluate honesty in social internet of things," in *Proceedings of the Symposium on Applied Computing,* 2017, pp. 1830–1835.

[34] U. Jayasinghe, N. B. Truong, G. M. Lee, and T.-W. Um, "RpR: A trust computation model for social internet of things," in *Ubiquitous Intelligence & Computing, Advanced and Trusted Computing, Scalable Computing and Communications, Cloud and Big Data Computing, Internet of People, and Smart World Congress (UIC/ATC/ScalCom/CBDCom/IoP/SmartWorld), 2016 Intl IEEE Conferences,* 2016, pp. 930–937.

[35] Y. W. Lee, D. M. Strong, B. K. Kahn, and R. Y. Wang, "AIMQ: a methodology for information quality assessment," *Information & Management,* vol. 40, pp. 133–146, 2002.

[36] R. S. Poore, "Anonymity, privacy, and trust," *Information Systems Security,* vol. 8, pp. 16–20, 1999.

[37] W. Leister and T. Schulz, "Ideas for a trust indicator in the internet of things," in *The First International Conference on Smart Systems, Devices and Technologies, SMART,* 2012, pp. 31–34.

[38]   Y. Liu and K. Wang, "Trust control in heterogeneous networks for internet of things," in *Computer Application and System Modeling (ICCASM), 2010 International Conference on,* 2010, pp. V1-632–V1-636.

[39]   S. Sicari, A. Coen-Porisini, and R. Riggio, "Dare: Evaluating data accuracy using node reputation," *Computer Networks,* vol. 57, pp. 3098–3111, 2013.

[40]   Z. Quan, F. Gui, D. Xiao, and Y. Tang, "Trusted architecture for farmland wireless sensor networks," in *Cloud Computing Technology and Science (CloudCom), 2012 IEEE 4th International Conference on,* 2012, pp. 782–787.

[41]   N. Javed and T. Wolf, "Automated sensor verification using outlier detection in the internet of things," in *Distributed Computing Systems Workshops (ICDCSW), 2012 32nd International Conference on,* 2012, pp. 291–296.

[42]   A. Ukil, J. Sen, and S. Koilakonda, "Embedded security for Internet of Things," in *Emerging Trends and Applications in Computer Science (NCETACS), 2011 2nd National Conference on,* 2011, pp. 1–6.

[43]   B. Khoo, "RFID as an enabler of the internet of things: Issues of security and privacy," in *Internet of Things (iThings/CPSCom), 2011 International Conference on and 4th International Conference on Cyber, Physical and Social Computing,* 2011, pp. 709–712.

[44]   M. Huang, B. Lin, and Y. Yang, "Privacy-preserving path-inclusion protocol through oblivious automata," in *Intelligent Control, Automatic Detection and High-End Equipment (ICADE), 2012 IEEE International Conference on,* 2012, pp. 128–132.

[45]   D. Mishra and M. Chandwani, "Anonymity enabled secure multi-party computation for Indian BPO," in *TENCON 2007 – 2007 IEEE Region 10 Conference,* 2007, pp. 1–4.

[46]   Y. Zhu, L. Huang, W. Yang, *et al.,* "Privacy-preserving approximate convex hulls protocol," in *Education Technology and Computer Science, 2009. ETCS'09. First International Workshop on,* 2009, pp. 208–214.

[47]   T. Wang and W. Luo, "Design and analysis of private-preserving dot product protocol," in *2009 International Conference on Electronic Computer Technology,* 2009, pp. 531–535.

[48]   Y. Shen, J. Han, and H. Shan, "The research of privacy-preserving clustering algorithm," in *Third International Symposium on Intelligent Information Technology and Security Informatics,* 2010, pp. 324–327.

[49]   M.-c. Liu and N. Zhang, "A solution to privacy-preserving two-party sign test on vertically partitioned data (P 2 2NST v) using data disguising techniques," in *Networking and Information Technology (ICNIT), 2010 International Conference on,* 2010, pp. 526–534.

[50]   J. Zhan, S. Matwin, and L. Chang, "Privacy-preserving collaborative association rule mining," in *IFIP Annual Conference on Data and Applications Security and Privacy,* 2005, pp. 153–165.

[51]   M. Kantarcioglu and C. Clifton, "Privacy-preserving distributed mining of association rules on horizontally partitioned data," *IEEE Transactions on Knowledge and Data Engineering,* vol. 16, pp. 1026–1037, 2004.

[52]   F. Zhang and G. Zhao, "A more well-founded security proof of the privacy-preserving distributed mining of association rules protocols," in *Proceedings of the First International Workshop on Model Driven Service Engineering and Data Quality and Security,* 2009, pp. 25–28.

[53]   P. Wang, "Research on privacy preserving association rule mining a survey," in *Information Management and Engineering (ICIME), 2010 The 2nd IEEE International Conference on,* 2010, pp. 194–198.

[54]   M. A. M. Isa, N. N. Mohamed, H. Hashim, S. F. S. Adnan, J. Manan, and R. Mahmod, "A lightweight and secure TFTP protocol for smart environment," in *Computer Applications and Industrial Electronics (ISCAIE), 2012 IEEE Symposium on,* 2012, pp. 302–306.

[55]   J. Granjal, E. Monteiro, and J. S. Silva, "On the effectiveness of end-to-end security for internet-integrated sensing applications," in *Green Computing and Communications (GreenCom), 2012 IEEE International Conference on,* 2012, pp. 87–93.

[56]   S. Raza, L. Wallgren, and T. Voigt, "SVELTE: Real-time intrusion detection in the Internet of Things," *Ad Hoc Networks,* vol. 11, pp. 2661–2674, 2013.

[57]   A. Fongen, "Identity management and integrity protection in the internet of things," in *2012 Third International Conference on Emerging Security Technologies,* 2012, pp. 111–114.

[58]   C. Hu, J. Zhang, and Q. Wen, "An identity-based personal location system with protected privacy in IoT," in *Broadband Network and Multimedia Technology (IC-BNMT), 2011 4th IEEE International Conference on,* 2011, pp. 192–195.

[59]   Q. Yan, R. H. Deng, Z. Yan, Y. Li, and T. Li, "Pseudonym-based RFID discovery service to mitigate unauthorized tracking in supply chain management," in *Data, Privacy and E-Commerce (ISDPE), 2010 Second International Symposium on,* 2010, pp. 21–26.

[60]   G. Zhang and J. Tian, "An extended role based access control model for the internet of things," in *Information Networking and Automation (ICINA), 2010 International Conference on,* 2010, pp. V1-319–V1-323.

[61]   S. Gusmeroli, S. Piccione, and D. Rotondi, "A capability-based security approach to manage access control in the internet of things," *Mathematical and Computer Modelling,* vol. 58, pp. 1189–1205, 2013.

[62]   H. Suo, J. Wan, C. Zou, and J. Liu, "Security in the internet of things: A review," in *Computer Science and Electronics Engineering (ICCSEE), 2012 International Conference on,* 2012, pp. 648–651.

[63]   G. M. Køien, "Reflections on trust in devices: An informal survey of human trust in an internet-of-things context," *Wireless Personal Communications,* vol. 61, pp. 495–510, 2011.

[64]   X. Li, Z. Xuan, and L. Wen, "Research on the architecture of trusted security system based on the internet of things," in *Intelligent Computation Technology and Automation (ICICTA), 2011 International Conference on,* 2011, pp. 1172–1175.

Chapter 20

Dependability analysis of IoT systems using dynamic fault trees analysis

Ernest Edifor[1] and Raheel Nawaz[1]

The Internet of Things (IoT) is proving to be an essential part of the fourth industrial revolution (4IR). In highly critical environments, IoT systems are required to be secure, reliable and available. Although there are many investigations on the security and privacy of IoT systems, there are relatively far fewer efforts expended on their dependability. The individual 'things' of an IoT system may be unfailing, but that does not make the complete IoT system – from sensor to server – dependable. In this chapter, a technique is proposed to evaluate the dependability of a complete IoT ecosystem by using a modified version of the classical fault tree analysis (FTA) and Monte Carlo simulation techniques. The propose technique is applied to a hypothetical case study, and the results are promising.

20.1 Introduction

In the twenty-first century, digital technology has become ubiquitous; it has permeated almost every facet of life. The IoT is undoubtedly a technology that is playing a crucial role in the 4IR that is currently unfolding [1]. Just as with new technologies, IoT has many uncharted fields that need exploration. One of such fields is the dependability analysis associated with the implementation of IoT architecture. Implementation of any system (as part of a new setup or legacy system upgrade) possesses challenges that must be addressed. Nowhere are these challenges of more concern than in high-consequence systems where an implementation failure can have high financial impact, reputational damage and/or catastrophic consequences relating to health and the environment. For this reason, investigators and designers who are involved in constructing an implementation architecture for an IoT system need to invest time and resources into the dependability analysis of these systems.

FTA [2] is a risk-assessment technique that is useful for determining how combinations of basic component failures can lead to an overall system failure using the traditional AND and OR Boolean logic gates. These Boolean gates are unable to capture some of the dynamic behaviours exhibited by real-world systems [3]. For example, if an output event occurs only when its input events occur in a

---

[1]Operations, Technology Events and Hospitality Management (OTEHM), Manchester Metropolitan University, Manchester, United Kingdom

sequence – strictly one after another – neither the AND nor the OR would be able to capture the behaviour [4]. To this end, FTA has seen various modifications to enable it capture dynamic behaviours inherent in real-world environments. Unfortunately, though, most of these improvements focus on dynamic logic gates and are themselves unable to capture peculiar attributes of systems such as time of operation and inflow/outflow rate of materials.

IoT may be at the forefront of modern technology, but the techniques for analysing the dependability of IoT system are decades behind. Extant literature on IoT implementation usually focus on security and privacy – only few research efforts focus on useful dependability metrics such as reliability and availability. The best-known dependability technique [5] uses classical FTA gates and is unable to capture dynamic behaviours or attributes of a system or repair/maintenance data. Thus, there is a need for a framework or technique that would enable the complete evaluation of IoT system dependability. To be at par with the speed and complexity of modern systems, a novel technique is required to accurately capture, model and analyse IoT systems featuring dynamic behaviours. The technique would need to possess the following characteristics: consider heterogeneous failure data with different failure distributions, capture dynamic relationships between components and model and analyse different system configurations.

The authors are unaware of a proposed technique in extant literature that possesses all the characteristics mentioned above. The aim of this chapter, thus, is to present an FTA-based Monte Carlo simulation framework for analysing the dependability of an IoT system that meets all the characteristics above. This will be done by proposing a modified FTA that captures the sequential dependencies and peculiar attributes in modern systems. The FTA will then be analysed using the temporal truth table [6] to reduce it to its most efficient configuration. The model will then be constructed in and analysed with the GoldSim software [7] and simulated using Monte Carlo simulation.

The remaining sections of this chapter are arranged as follows: Section 20.2 reviews extant literature on IoT dependability analysis and IoT security. The proposed solution is described in Section 20.3; a modified FTA technique is presented, some dynamic gates are explained and a clear guidance on how to perform logical analysis is discussed. In Section 20.4, a hypothetical case study is presented. The proposed techniques discussed in Section 20.3 are applied to the case study, and the results are discussed. Conclusions are made in Section 20.5.

20.2   Background

The dawn of the 4IR has launched an era that marries digital, physical and biological systems to produce powerful and economical solutions to industrial and domestic problems [1]. The IoT [8], also known as 'connected devices' or 'smart devices', is a global network of interconnected objects (or things) that are uniquely identifiable and share data based on an established communication protocol [9]. IoT is a key player in the creation of this new revolution [1]. With an estimation of over 20 billion units to be installed worldwide by 2020, it is no news that IoT has come to stay [10,11].

IoT is a promising technology with a plethora of benefits in many fields. In healthcare, it can enhance the monitoring of diseases [12]. In cities, it can be used in the development of smart parking [13], potentially reduce traffic congestions [14], monitor and control pollution [15], monitor and manage waste [16] and many more [17]. It has seen implementation in agriculture [18] and aquaculture [19] to enable productive, efficient and profitable farming. Other areas that are benefiting from IoT include smart grids [20], homes [21], supply chain [22], manufacturing [23] and many more [24].

Although IoT presents myriads of benefits in many fields, it has some serious limitations such as privacy, security, data storage, trust and reliability [25–29]. These limitations have been the focus of many researcher, and various solutions have been proposed to various degrees [29]. By far, security and privacy are the most researched areas [30–33] of IoT challenges. Although privacy and security are of great concern, in highly critical systems with major failure consequences, dependability is of utmost importance. For example, in the health, automotive, nuclear or chemical industries, failure of IoT setups that are critical to human life and the environment would be considered most important. Some authors agree with the fact that studies on IoT dependability are vastly limited [28] – a green field that needs further exploration.

According to [34], dependability 'is the ability to avoid service failures that are more frequent and more severe than is acceptable' and has the following attributes: availability, reliability, safety, integrity, confidentiality and maintainability. Avizienis and Laprie [34] define the security of a system as the ability of the system to protect itself from accidental or deliberate external attack; security encompasses availability, confidentiality and integrity. In some cases, security is seen as a being fully part of dependability [35]. Dependability in this chapter will refer to the definition by [34,36] and will consider only the reliability and availability characteristics. The reliability of a system is the 'probability that the system will perform its intended function under specified design limits' and availability is 'the probability that the system is successful at time *t*' [36]. Sections 20.2.1 and 20.2.2 provide a brief review of dependability and security in IoT systems, while Section 20.2.3 will describe classical FTA.

20.2.1 *IoT security*

Security is one of the most researched areas in IoT systems [30–33]. In [37], the authors use Bayesian networks (BNs) and the decision-making trial and evaluation laboratory (DEMATEL) to access the privacy security of IoT. They use BN 'to structure risk propagation network and to generate risk probability by using evidence inference' and DEMATEL to 'calculate influence weights of propagation path that supports decision-making for risk management effectively'. Based on the results of their proposed technique, decision-makers can develop countermeasures or mitigating circumstances for high-risk aspects of an IoT system. Another DEMATEL-based solution [33] uses the fuzzy analytical network-processing (ANP) technique to create a security-assessment framework for an IoT setup. In this solution, the authors define and categorise security requirements into logical components. A hybrid Fuzzy

DEMATEL and fuzzy ANP technique is then used to analyse the system to provide information on how security assets and resources should be allocated.

The authors in [32] provide a framework for modelling and assessing the security of IoT and provide a formal definition for the framework that has five phases: data processing, security model generation, security visualisation, security analysis and model updates. The framework allows investigators to identify potential attack scenarios in IoT, analyse the security risks using predefined metrics and to assess the effectiveness of different mitigation strategies or countermeasures. In [38], the authors use FTA to analyse the security risks associated with IoT in a smart home. First, they generate a fault tree based on a generalised architecture for a smart home. Second, they use classical FTA techniques [2] to probabilistically analyse security vulnerabilities that could be exploited by an attacker. The results of the analysis allow investigators to know the risks associated with an IoT implementation architecture.

A review of extant literature, as discussed above, reveals that most research efforts geared towards the security of IoT systems focus primarily on the confidentiality and integrity characteristics and usually ignore the availability characteristic as defined in [34]. Even if a technique considers all three characteristics but misses out on reliability, it would be missing out a key component of dependability analysis. For a technique to pass a dependability-analysis technique, it must be able to evaluate at least the probability of a system to provide continuity of correct service (reliability) and readiness for correct service (availability) [34] in addition to safety, integrity and maintainability.

Security and dependability are critical measures in safety-critical environments. However, this chapter stresses on the importance of dependability (availability, reliability, safety, integrity, confidentiality and maintainability) in IoT system architecture/implementation. Dependability should have matching research effort.

20.2.2   *IoT dependability*

Dependability analysis in IoT systems is relatively scarce. In [5], the authors propose a tool for the evaluation of the reliability of IoT systems using FTA. In the proposed tool, various components of an IoT setup/network are modelled into a fault tree, and the relationships between these components are represented using the Boolean gates AND and OR. The resulting information is fed into a software tool that uses some algorithms to create and analyse the fault tree. From the result of the analysis, a reporting tool would compute the reliability, unreliability, availability, unavailability, mean time-to-failure (MTTF) and component importance of the fault tree. However, assumptions are made: event failures are permanent and exponentially distributed.

Another FTA-based solution used fuzzy neural networks and FTA for fault diagnosis in aquaculture [39]. The case study was an outdoor pond where the elements of the weather in the environment could be harsh and monitoring and controlling equipment would fail more frequently. The proposed solution provides investigators information regarding faults so that they can make decision on maintenance and allocation of resources. However, the solution does not consider the dynamic relationships between events or the peculiar attributes the systems possess. In [40], other authors propose a novel conceptual framework to model and estimate the cost of implementing new architectures for legacy systems. They do so using what they refer to as the Cost Assessment Model for Smart Manufacturing Implementation in Legacy Systems. The solution considers the impact of costs of different IoT architectures. However, the system has a major limitation – it is not practical.

All the techniques discussed above are either conceptual, impractical or are unable to

1. capture the dynamic behaviours (such as sequential dependencies),
2. capture peculiar attributes of systems (such as times of operation, inflow and withdrawal rates),
3. perform a logical analysis of dynamic systems to produce the most efficient system architecture,
4. model various system data (such as failure, repair and maintenance and replacement data),
5. model and analyse components with different failure distributions (such as lognormal, exponential or Weibull distributions),
6. model and analyse various system configurations (such as new systems or upgrades), and
7. produce useful quantitative results (such as reliability, availability, MTTF and mean time-to-repair (MTTR)).

20.2.3 Fault tree analysis

FTA is a failure analysis tool developed by Bell Laboratories in the early 1960s. It is a very simple top-down, deductive approach of determining how the occurrence of basic component faults can propagate to cause an entire system failure. The first step in the analysis is to construct the tree, which is a top-down graphical representation of how a system failure is related to basic component failures. The relationships between the failure events are described with Boolean gates – typically AND and OR.

The AND gate represents the situation where all input events occur to trigger an output event. Figure 20.1(a) is a representation of the AND gate with two input events X and Y and an output event Z. Figure 20.1(b)–(d) shows the timing diagrams for the AND gate. In Figure 20.1(b), X occurs before Y and Z occurs when Y occurs. In Figure 20.1(c), Y occurs before X and Z occurs when X occurs. In Figure 20.1(d), both X and Y occur at the same time and Z occurs when both X and Y occur.

Given that $t(\alpha)$ is the lifetime of an event α, Figure 20.1(b), (c) and (d) can be represented using the expressions in (20.1), (20.2) and (20.3), respectively.

$$t(X) < t(Y) \rightarrow t(Z) = t(Y) \tag{20.1}$$

$$t(X) > t(Y) \rightarrow t(Z) = t(Y) \tag{20.2}$$

$$t(X) = t(Y) \rightarrow t(Z) = t(Y) \tag{20.3}$$

The OR gate represents the situation where at least one input event must occur to trigger the occurrence of an output event. Figure 20.2(a) is a representation of the OR gate with two input events X and Y and an output event Z. Figure 20.2(b), (c)

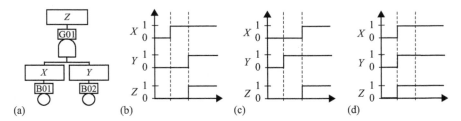

Figure 20.1   (a) AND Gate with X and Y input events, (b) X before Y timeline, (c) Y before X timeline, (d) X and Y timeline

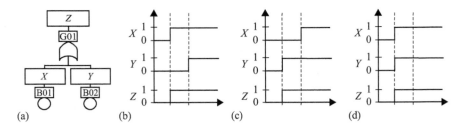

Figure 20.2   (a) OR Gate with X and Y input events, (b) X before Y timeline, (c) Y before X timeline, (d) X and Y timeline

and (d) are the timing diagrams for the OR gate. In Figure 20.2(b), X occurs before Y and Z occurs when X occurs. In Figure 20.2(c), Y occurs before X and Z occurs when Y occurs. In Figure 20.2(d), both X and Y occur at the same time and Z occurs when both X and Y occur.

Given that $t(\alpha)$ is the lifetime of an event α, Figure 20.2(b), (c) and (d) can be represented using the expressions in (20.4), (20.5) and (20.6), respectively.

$$t(X) < t(Y) \rightarrow t(Z) = t(X) \tag{20.4}$$

$$t(X) > t(Y) \rightarrow t(Z) = t(Y) \tag{20.5}$$

$$t(X) = t(Y) \rightarrow t(Z) = t(X) \tag{20.6}$$

Once a fault tree has been created and relationships between events have been established, the tree can be translated into an expression called cut sets (CSs). CSs are all the possible combination of basic events that can lead to the occurrence of the system failure. Using Boolean logic, the CSs are reduced to what is called the minimal CSs (MCSs). The MCS is a combination of events that are necessary and sufficient to cause the system failure. Meaning, no term in the MCS can be logically reduced by another term and no sub-term of a MCS can, on its own, lead to the system failure. For example, where '·' and '+' represent AND and OR, respectively, the CS $X + X \cdot Y + Y \cdot Z$ will have the MCS $X + Y \cdot Z$. The evaluation of the MCS from the CS using Boolean logic is termed the qualitative or logical analysis.

Probabilistic or quantitative analysis involves the calculation of the probability of a total system failure or the contributions of each term in the MCS or the basic events towards the occurrence of the system failure. Quantitative analysis can be performed using analytical techniques [2], binary decision diagram [41,42] or simulation [43,44]. Basic event or MCS contributions to the system failure can be evaluated using the Fussell–Vesely or Birnbaum's importance [2]. For statistically independent events, the formulas for evaluating the AND and OR gates are (20.7) and (20.8), respectively.

The probability of an output event Q with OR gates occurring at a particular time, t, is:

$$P(Q)\{t\} = \sum_{i=1}^{n} P(MCS_i)\{t\} \qquad (20.7)$$

Each MCSs in (20.7) is usually a product term with m independent events, X.

$$P(MCS_i)\{t\} = \prod_{k=1}^{m} P(X_k)\{t\} \qquad (20.8)$$

Using the Esary–Proschan formula [45], the probability of a system failure (Q) of n MCSs with each CS having a combination of m basic events is:

$$P(Q)\{t\} = 1 - \prod_{j=i}^{n} \left(1 - \prod_{i=1}^{mj} P(MCS_{i,j})\{t\} \right) \qquad (20.9)$$

As mentioned earlier in Section 20.1, classical FTA is unable to capture dynamic features inherent in modern system [3]. As an example, consider an IoT system that has two critical sensors A and B. A is a primary sensor and B is the standby or secondary sensor. The system is configured such that when A fails, a controller C detects the failure of A and activates the B to provide the service that A has failed to provide. Considering the failures of A, B and C only, classical fault tree will evaluate the failure of the sensors, Q, to be expressed as follows:

$$Q = A \cdot B + A \cdot C \qquad (20.10)$$

Unfortunately, (20.10) is not very accurate if the order in which A and C fail is to be considered [4]. This is not new; many research efforts have been made to extend FTA in modelling dynamic behaviour [3,46,47]. If A fails before C: immediately A fails but C has not failed, C activates B to provide the service A has failed to provide – the system does not fail. Conversely, if C fails before A: when A fails, C has already failed, so it is unable to activate B to provide the service A has failed to provide – the system fails. A more accurate expression to capture the above scenario, where the system fails when C fails before A is (20.11), given that $C < A$ means C fails before A.

$$Q = A \cdot B + C < A \qquad (20.11)$$

This is the priority-AND (PAND) scenario and is represented by '$<$'. $C < A$ or C PAND A means C occurs strictly before A. In a system configuration where C could be repaired, the system fails when A fails and C has already failed but has not yet been repaired. A detailed description of the PAND gate will be provided in Section 20.3.

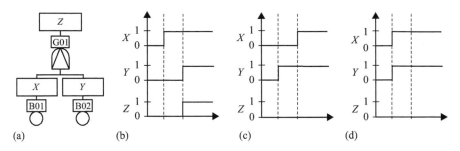

Figure 20.3   (a) PAND Gate with X and Y input events, (b) X before Y timeline, (c) Y before X timeline, (d) X and Y timeline

20.3   Methodology

Classical FTA uses the AND and OR Boolean logic gates in its analysis. However, as discussed earlier in Section 20.2.3, these gates are unable to capture dynamic behaviour in most systems. Another limitation of the traditional FTA is that it is unable to include other system attributes (such as fuel level, pump flow rate, time of operation) in its models and analyses. This section discusses the use of an existing FTA extension and presents the probabilistic evaluation of the fault tree by using temporal fault tree logic for qualitative analysis and the GoldSim software for quantitative analysis.

In order to capture dynamic behaviours of systems, many dynamic gates have been added to the classic AND and OR gates. An earlier extension of FTA is the dynamic fault tree (DFT) analysis [3]. In this chapter, the term 'DFT' is used to refer to a fault tree that is able to capture dynamic behaviours in systems and not as described in [3]. A detailed review of other extensions to classical FTA has been discussed in [6]. In [6], the author proposes two new dynamic gates – priority-OR (POR) and simultaneous-AND (SAND) – and a new logic (temporal logic) for analysing the PAND, POR and SAND gates.

The SAND gate represents scenarios where all input events occur at exactly the same time. Statistically, it is improbable for the SAND to occur [48], so an extension, called the pSAND, has been described in [49]. The POR gate is used to model the situation where an event occurs before its subsequent events for an output event to occur, but the occurrence of the preceding event is also sufficient to trigger the output event. Only the PAND gate will be described in details and used in the case study in Section 20.4; the reader is referred to [49–51] for descriptions and practical applications of the POR and pSAND gates.

The PAND gate represents the situation where all input events occur in a strict sequence – one after the other. Figure 20.3(a) is a graphical representation of the PAND gate with two input events X and Y and an output event Z. Figure 20.3(b)–(d) are the timing diagrams for the PAND gate. Consider the events X PAND Y, Figure 20.3(b) represents X occurs before Y and Z occurs when Y occurs. In Figure 20.3(c), Y occurs before X and Z does not occur. In Figure 20.3(d), both X and Y occur at the same time and Z does not occur.

Given that $t(\alpha)$ is the lifetime of an event α, Figure 20.3(b), (c) and (d) can be represented using the expressions in (20.12), (20.13) and (20.14), respectively.

$$t(X) < t(Y) \rightarrow t(Z) = t(Y) \tag{20.12}$$

$$t(X) > t(Y) \rightarrow t(Z) = \emptyset \tag{20.13}$$

$$t(X) = t(Y) \rightarrow t(Z) = \emptyset \tag{20.14}$$

A detailed step-by-step procedure for creating fault trees is described in [2]. Although pertinent information about events can be written in classical fault trees, this information is usually not used in logical or probabilistic analysis. The event names are used in logical analysis and failure data in probabilistic analysis.

The GoldSim software [7] allows the modelling and simulation of discrete and continuous events. It has prebuilt logical gates for modelling the Boolean AND and OR gates, but it is very flexible for the modelling of custom dynamic gates. It is built with the ability to model and perform dependability analysis using Monte Carlo simulation [52]. Using Monte Carlo simulation, GoldSim is able to model and analyse different failure distributions, system configuration and dynamic behaviours inherent in complex systems. It has algorithms to use some important sampling techniques for analysing rare events and is able to evaluate the reliability, availability, MTTF, MTTR and causal analysis. Unlike most dependability techniques proposed in extant literature, GoldSim is able to include repair, replacement and preventive maintenance in its analysis. GoldSim is a probabilistic tool; it is unable to perform logical analysis of DFTs. The recommendation is to use temporal logic [6] for logical analysis and GoldSim for probabilistic analysis – dynamic gates would need to be modelled in GoldSim.

The rate at which data is produced globally has increased exponentially within the past two decades [53,54]. With the proliferation of mobile devices, cloud computing and IoT, this trend is set to continue [55] with IoT being a big contributor [56]. Big data (BD) refers to the vast amount of heterogeneous data created by various entities at an unprecedented speed and across many platforms. BD has many benefits if collected and analysed properly [53]; however, to fully harness all the benefits of BD, there are many hurdles to overcome [57]. There are ongoing efforts to explore how BD could be used to improve dependability analysis [58,59]. Components' independent failure data alone is insufficient to determine the failure behaviour of an IoT system; the system's operating and/or environment (SOE) [58] data are required. IoT coupled with BD have the ability to provide real-time SOE for the dependability analysis of IoT systems. This chapter proposes that original equipment manufacturers producing components for IoT systems collaborate with the owners of IoT system to provide a data warehouse of SOEs which can be used for real-time dependability analysis of IoT systems.

20.4 Case study

To validate the proposed method, a case study is adapted from [40,60]. The system under consideration is a hospital IoT system that consists of heart rate monitor

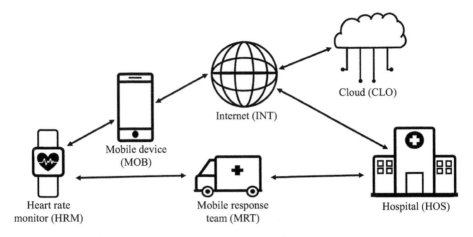

Figure 20.4   Top-level view of case study

(HRM), mobile device (MOB), the Internet (INT), digital cloud solution (CLO), the hospital's medical system (HOS) and the medical response team (MRT). An HRM and instructions on how to set it up will be given to a patient to take home. The HMR will read vital bio data such as heart rate and blood pressure and send the data via Bluetooth to the patient's mobile device. The mobile device, connected to the internet using the long-term evolution (LTE) or the wireless connection (WIR), will transmit the information through the Internet (INT) to a cloud platform (CLO).

The operation of the LTE and WIR is such that whichever is operational at the time of demand is used. A cloud-based software analyses the data and triggers an administrator (ADM) in the hospital when there are irregularities in the data. If the irregularities are life threatening, a mobile response team is dispatched to the patient's location immediately; otherwise, no action is taken. An administrator works between 06.00 and 20.00 every day. In the absence of an administrator or if he/she is not available during his/her regular time, a medical professional (MED) will be alerted to undertake the administration. The hospital relies heavily on the operation of its power system (POW) which is mainly powered by a primary source of power (PRI). In the event that the primary power fails, a switch (SWI) activates a secondary source of power (SEC), such as a standby generator, to provide the needed power.

An abstract view of the scenario is depicted in Figure 20.4. The double-headed arrows are used to indicate the flow of data and/or information. For example, the MRT may need to communicate with the patient while they are en route to the patient's location. In this case study, the entire system failure is represented by IoT and each aspect of the system are known as entities and represented by the abbreviations used in the earlier paragraph. For example, ADM stands for administrator and MRT stands for medical response team. The top-event or system failure under consideration is an entire failure in the system. The question being asked is 'what can cause the system to fail to deliver its intended function in operational conditions?'.

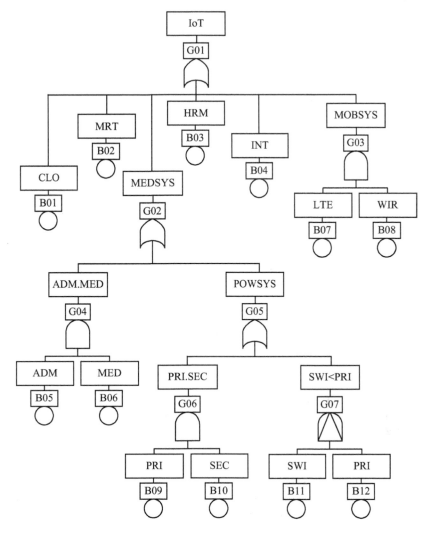

Figure 20.5   Resulting fault tree from logical analysis

A DFT was constructed from the description above and logically analysed using the temporal logic presented in [6] to produce the most efficient configuration. The resulting fault tree is Figure 20.5. MOBSYS is the mobile subsystem, POWSYS is the power subsystem and MEDSYS is the hospital subsystem.

Failure and repair data (or SOE) are necessary for any analysis to commence. In this study, some failure data will be assumed. Realistically, the data could be extracted from historical records or from live analysis of BD as presented in Section 20.3. For example, if the medical research council in the United Kingdom had live data on medical operations such as hospital operations, it could provide an estimated failure

Table 20.1   Failure and repair (SOE) data

Entity	Failure type	λ(F)	α(F)	β(F)	λ(R)	μ(R)	δ(R)
HRM	Power failure	1/4 y	–	–	–	2 d	5 h
HRM	Internal failure	1/2 y	–	–	–	2 d	1 d
HRM	Network failure	–	500 d	2	–	5 d	2 d
HRM	Setup failure	–	280 d	1.5	–	1 h	10 m
MOB	Internal failure	1/5 y	–	–	–	–	–
MOB	Power failure	1/200 d	–	–	–	1 h	30 m
MOB	Replacement	–	–	–	3 d	–	–
LTE	Con. failure	–	600 d	2	–	1 h	30 m
LTE	ISP failure	1/2 y	–	–	1 d	–	–
WIR	Con. failure	–	500 d	3	12 h	–	–
WIR	ISP failure	1/1 y	–	–	1 d	–	–
WIR	Internal failure	1/3 y	–	–	–	–	–
INT	Internal failure	1/20 y	–	–	2 d	–	–
CLO	Internal failure	1/2 y	–	–	2 d	–	–
CLO	Cyber attack	–	580 d	3	3 d	–	–
ADM	Unavailable	–	400 d	2	–	1 d	12 h
ADM	Human error	2/1 y	–	–	2 d	–	–
PRI	Internal failure	1/4 y	–	–	–	2 d	12 h
SEC	Internal failure	1/3 y	–	–	–	1 d	12 h
SWI	Internal failure	–	1,000 d	2	–	2 d	1 d
POW	Internal failure	1/4 y	–	–	12 h	–	–
MED	Unavailable	–	300 d	2	–	3 h	1 h
MRT	Strike action	–	450 d	3	–	2 d	12 h
MRT	Com. failure	1/1 y	–	–	–	2 h	20 m

and repair data for the HOS and MRT entities. Since such data is currently not available for this study, the assumed data in Table 20.1 would be used.

In the table λ is the hazard rate (exponential distribution), α, β are the scale and shape parameters, respectively (Weibull distribution) and μ, δ are the mean and standard deviation, respectively (lognormal distribution). (F) and (R) are the failure and repair data, respectively; m, h, d, y represent minutes, hours, days and years, respectively. It must be noted that 'X/Y y' means 'X occurrences in Y years'. Similarly, 'X/Y d' is 'X occurrences in Y days'. 'Con.' and 'Com.' stand for connection and communication, respectively, while ISP is Internet Service Provider. Therefore, 'LTE Con. Failure' for the MOB means the failure of the mobile device due to LTE communication failure, which has a Weibull failure distribution with scale and shape parameters 600 days and 2 respectively and a Lognormal repair distribution with a mean of 1 h and standard deviation 30 min.

Given the failure data in Table 20.1, the system was modelled and simulated in the GoldSim software for a system lifetime of 6 months using 10,000 trials with the time step of 1 day. It emerged that at the end of the simulation period, the mean reliability of the entire system is 0.032 with 0.029 as the 5 per cent confidence bound and 0.035 as the 95 per cent confidence bound. This means that the probability that

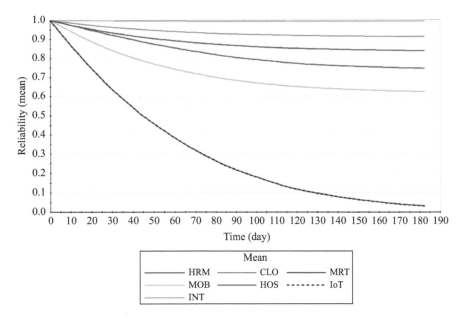

Figure 20.6   System/entities mean reliability over time

the entire system will perform its intended function over a period of 6 months is approximately 3 per cent. Such a system is unreliable. Given that the entire system is a high-consequence system, such a result would be concerning in a real-world scenario. The MTTF is 58.729 days with 57.872 days as the 5 per cent confidence bound and 59.587 days as the 95 per cent confidence bound. Meaning, the duration between when the system starts operating and when it fails is around 58 days. The MTTR is 0.468 days with 0.093 days as the 5 per cent confidence bound and 0.843 days as the 95 per cent confidence bound. Meaning, the duration between when the system fails and when it is repaired to start operating again is less than a day.

Figure 20.6 and Table 20.2 compare the mean reliability of each entity in Figure 20.4. It is clear that the entire system's mean reliability deteriorates faster than all the individual entities except the HOS subsystem, which has a very similar failure pattern. As expected, all entities are fully reliable from day 1 but as time progresses, their mean reliabilities differ. The Internet is the most reliable entity in the system with a mean reliability of over 99 per cent. The hospital system is the least reliable entity in the system; it has a mean reliability of 3.2 per cent. It is also the least available entity with an availability of 31 per cent; it has the least MTTF and MTTR. The medical system is the biggest contributor to the system failing. It has the most combination of components and bigger probabilities of failure. In complex scenarios, this failure pattern will not be easy to detect without such techniques. The next least reliable entity is the mobile device, which has a mean reliability of 62 per cent.

From the data in Table 20.2 and the criticality analysis in Figure 20.7, it is clear that the power system contributes about 46 per cent to the system failure. To know

Table 20.2   System/individual entity, reliability, availability, MTTF and MTTR

Entity	Reliability	Availability	MTTF (days)	MTTR (days)
IoT	0.032	0.314	58.729	0.468
HRM	0.745	0.998	762.448	1.351
MOB	0.624	0.787	414.443	1.71
INT	0.992	1.000	18,011.126	1.848
CLO	0.911	0.999	2,330.049	2.033
HOS	0.032	0.316	59.108	0.363
MRT	0.837	1.000	1,169.792	0.18

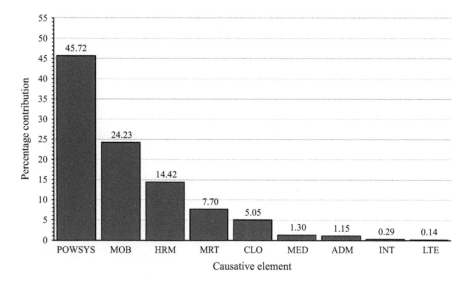

Figure 20.7   General percentage contributions

exactly why the hospital subsystem has a very low reliability, further investigations are required; each aspect of it must be comparatively evaluated. ADM, MED, POW, PRI, SEC and SWI have independent mean reliabilities of 0.03, 0.032, 0.032, 0.965, 1.000 and 0.995, respectively. The hospital system as a whole has a reliability of 0.321. It is clear that the ADM, MED and POW must be improved to improve the entire system.

The mobile device is not too far behind; it contributes about 24 per cent to the entire system failure. It is not expedient to suggest that a more reliable mobile device should be used to improve the system's reliability without further investigations to establish that should be the case. The individual reliabilities of the LTE and WIR are 0.906 and 0.803, respectively. Comparing the power failure of the mobile device (MOBPWR), LTE, WIR and internal failure of the mobile device (MOBINT), the MOBPWR contributes 95 per cent to the system failure. This means that there is no

Table 20.3   Failure and repair data

Entity	Failure type	λ(F)	α(F)	β(F)	λ(R)	μ(R)	δ(R)
MOB	Power failure	1/3 y	–	–	–	1 h	30 m
LTE	ISP failure	1/2 y	–	–	12 h	–	–
WIR	ISP failure	1/3 y	–	–	12 h	–	–

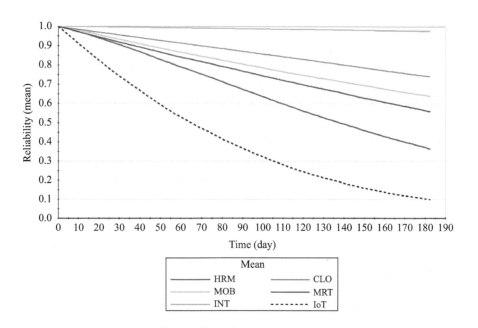

Figure 20.8   Improved system

need to change the mobile device but rather to ensure there is constant power supply to the device either through a backup power system of or a longer lasting battery.

Given the reasons above, the failure data has been updated so that the power fails once in 2 years. The WIR_ISP has also been given the same hazard rate. Both repair rates for WIR_ISP and LTE_ISP have been halved. The recommendation is also made to send the data straight to the MRT – bypassing the HOS subsystem. If it were possible to send the data straight to the MRT but the ADM and MED are kept informed, the entire HOS subsystem would not be required in the analysis. Table 20.3 shows these updates.

The system has been rerun with the changes in Table 20.3 and the HOS system has been removed from the model. Figure 20.8 shows the system has improved but not significantly. The reliability of MOB has increased, and it is not the most contributing entity to the entire system failure.

20.5 Conclusion

The IoT has permeated almost every facet of life and has greatly improved the way resources and assets are monitored, controlled and managed remotely. This has provided enormous benefits to individuals and industries. However, just like any new technology, it has limitations and challenges. Clearly, security and privacy are the main challenges it faces. In very critical scenarios such as health-related or environment-related circumstances, the reliability of IoT systems becomes paramount. Unfortunately, not much is done in this field.

FTA is a technique used in evaluating the probability of an undesired state of a system occurring and how basic component failures lead to the system failure. In extant literature, FTA has been used to analyse various aspects of IoT implementation architectures. However, none of these techniques is able to capture the dynamic behaviours exhibited by real-world events. Most of the techniques assume all component failures to have exponential distribution. All the techniques proposed consider only failure data of the components; they are unable to include attributes of the components (such as times of operation) to the model. Finally, these techniques also assume that all failures are permanent, that is, all failures are non-repairable. All these limitations make most of the proposed solutions in extant literature unpractical in the real world.

In this chapter, an FTA simulation model is presented using the GoldSim tool. First, an upgrade of FTA presented, where classical FTA is given further annotations and descriptions to capture some real-world scenarios. Finally, using the GoldSim software, a model is created and simulated using the Monte Carlo simulation technique. Discussions on how BD can be used as a source of failure data have been presented. Using a social pool, data can be captured, structured and analysed to be used as failure data for IoT components in an IoT implementation. The proposed methods in this chapter have been applied to a hypothetical case study in the health industry where the consequences of failure can be critical. The results are illuminating. Investigators using the proposed technique are able to identify critical/risky aspects of the system implementation. They can evaluate the probability of a system failure and determine the contribution of component failures towards the system failure. With this information, they are able to implement mitigation measures or redesign the system for a more reliable design.

The proposed technique has many benefits – it is able to (1) capture sequential dependencies featured in events, (2) model and analyse repairable and non-repairable events, (3) consider preventive maintenance of components, (4) analyse component failures with many failure distributions, (5) include special attributes of events that classical FTA is unable to capture and (6) model and analyse different system configurations. System availability and reliability are of utmost importance in many industries. These metrics can potentially save lives and/or the environment, enable users to implement reliable systems that lead to realising bigger profit margins, gaining consumer confidence, and building reputation and competitiveness. The solution proposed is generic and can be easily used to model and analyse other IoT implementation designs that are not within the health industry. Future research efforts would be focused on developing a more robust framework for extracting failure data from BD.

It may also prove useful to include a cost variable into the model so that investigators can evaluate the cost of implementing IoT devices or the cost of failures if they should occur.

References

[1] Schwab K. The Fourth Industrial Revolution. Cologny: World Economic Forum; 2016. pp. 1–50, ISBN 1944835008.

[2] Vesely WE, Stamatelatos M, Dugan JB, Fragola J, Minarick J, and Railsback J. Fault Tree Handbook with Aerospace Applications. Washington, DC: NASA Office of Safety and Mission Assurance; 2002.

[3] Dugan JB, Bavuso SJ, and Boyd MA. Dynamic fault-tree models for fault-tolerant computer systems. IEEE Trans Reliab [Internet]. 1992;41(3):363–77. Available from: http://ieeexplore.ieee.org/lpdocs/epic03/wrapper.htm?arnumber=159800.

[4] Walker M, and Papadopoulos Y. Synthesis and analysis of temporal fault trees with PANDORA: The time of priority AND gates. Nonlinear Anal Hybrid Syst [Internet]. 2008 [cited 2012 Dec 10];2(2):368–82. Available from: http://linkinghub.elsevier.com/retrieve/pii/S1751570X06000574.

[5] Silva I, Leandro R, Macedo D, and Guedes LA. A dependability evaluation tool for the Internet of Things. Comput Electr Eng [Internet]. 2013;39(7):2005–18. Available from: http://dx.doi.org/10.1016/j.compeleceng.2013.04.021.

[6] Walker M. Pandora: A Logic for the Qualitative Analysis of Temporal Fault Trees [Internet]. University of Hull; 2009 [cited 2012 Nov 11]. Available from: http://ethos.bl.uk/OrderDetails.do?uin=uk.bl.ethos.518653.

[7] GoldSim. GoldSim [Internet]. 2018 [cited 2018 Dec 15]. Available from: https://www.goldsim.com/web/home/.

[8] Ashton K. That "Internet of Things" thing. RFID J [Internet]. 2009 [cited 2018 Feb 13]. Available from: https://www.rfidjournal.com/articles/view?4986.

[9] Ray PP. A survey on Internet of Things architectures. J King Saud Univ – Comput Inf Sci [Internet]. 2018;30(3):291–319. Available from: https://doi.org/10.1016/j.jksuci.2016.10.003.

[10] AIG. The Internet of Things: Evolution or Revolution? Part 1 in a Series [Internet]. The Internet Society (ISOC). 2015 [cited 2018 Dec 14]. pp. 1–28. Available from: https://www-160.aig.com/content/dam/aig-mktg/america-canada/us/documents/landing-pages/disruptive-tech/iot/aigiot-english-report.pdf.

[11] Gartner Inc. Gartner Says 8.4 Billion Connected "Things" Will Be in Use in 2017, Up 31 Percent From 2016 [Internet]. Press Release. 2017 [cited 2018 Dec 13]. Available from: https://www.gartner.com/en/newsroom/press-releases/2017-02-07-gartner-says-8-billion-connected-things-will-be-in-use-in-2017-up-31-percent-from-2016.

[12] Gómez J, Oviedo B, and Zhuma E. Patient Monitoring System Based on Internet of Things. In: Procedia Computer Science [Internet]. Elsevier Masson SAS; 2016. pp. 90–7. Available from: http://dx.doi.org/10.1016/j.procs.2016.04.103.

[13]   Ji Z, Ganchev I, O'Droma M, Zhao L, and Zhang X. A cloud-based car parking middleware for IoT-based smart cities: Design and implementation. Sensors (Switzerland). 2014;14(12):22372–93.

[14]   Li X, Shu W, Li M, Huang HY, Luo PE, and Wu MY. Performance evaluation of vehicle-based mobile sensor networks for traffic monitoring. IEEE Trans Veh Technol. 2009;58(4):1647–53.

[15]   Al-Ali A, Zualkernan I, and Aloul F. A mobile GPRS-sensors array for air pollution monitoring. IEEE Sens J [Internet]. 2010;10(10):1666–71. Available from: http://ieeexplore.ieee.org/document/5483217/.

[16]   Anagnostopoulos T, Zaslavsky A, Sosunova I, *et al.* A stochastic multi-agent system for Internet of Things-enabled waste management in smart cities. Waste Manage Res. 2018;36(11):1113–21.

[17]   Zanella A, Bui N, Castellani A, Vangelista L, and Zorzi M. Internet of things for smart cities. IEEE Internet Things J. 2014;1(1):22–32.

[18]   Jayaraman PP, Yavari A, Georgakopoulos D, Morshed A, and Zaslavsky A. Internet of things platform for smart farming: Experiences and lessons learnt. Sensors (Switzerland). 2016;16(11):1–17.

[19]   Chen Y, Zhen Z, Yu H, Xu J. Application of fault tree analysis and fuzzy neural networks to fault diagnosis in the internet of things (IoT) for aquaculture. Sensors (Switzerland). 2017;17(1): 1–15.

[20]   Tan S, De D, Song WZ, Yang J, and Das SK. Survey of security advances in smart grid: A data driven approach. IEEE Commun Surv Tutor. 2017;19(1):397–422.

[21]   Darby SJ. Smart technology in the home: Time for more clarity. Build Res Inf [Internet]. 2018;46(1):140–7. Available from: https://doi.org/10.1080/09613218.2017.1301707.

[22]   Cortés B, Boza A, Pérez D, and Cuenca L. Internet of Things applications on supply chain management. Int J Comput Inf Eng [Internet]. 2015;19(2):2493–8. Available from: https://waset.org/publications/10003163/internet-of-things-applications-on-supply-chain-management.

[23]   Xu Y, and Chen M. An Internet of Things based framework to enhance just-in-time manufacturing. Proc Inst Mech Eng Part B J Eng Manuf. 2018;232(13):2353–63.

[24]   AIG. IoT Case Studies: Companies Leading the Connected Economy Part 2 in a Series [Internet]. American International Group. 2016 [cited 2018 Dec 14]. pp. 1–16. Available from: https://www.aig.co.uk/content/dam/aig/emea/united-kingdom/documents/Insights/iot-case-studies-companies-leading-the-connected-economy-digital.pdf.

[25]   Juels A. RFID security and privacy: A research survey. IEEE J Sel Areas Commun [Internet]. 2006;24(2):381–94. Available from: https://ieeexplore.ieee.org/document/1589116.

[26]   Atzori L, Iera A, and Morabito G. The Internet of Things: A survey. Comput Networks [Internet]. 2010;54(15):2787–805. Available from: http://dx.doi.org/10.1016/j.comnet.2010.05.010.

[27]   Roman R, Zhou J, and Lopez J. On the features and challenges of security and privacy in distributed internet of things. Comput Networks [Internet].

2013;57(10):2266–79. Available from: http://dx.doi.org/10.1016/j.comnet. 2012.12.018.

[28] Riahi Sfar A, Natalizio E, Challal Y, and Chtourou Z. A roadmap for security challenges in the Internet of Things. Digit Commun Networks [Internet]. 2018;4(2):118–37. Available from: https://doi.org/10.1016/j.dcan. 2017.04.003.

[29] Komal M, and Amandeep V. Internet of Things (IoT) architecture, challenges, applications: A review. Int J Adv Res Comput Sci. 2018;9(1): 389–393.

[30] Sha K, Wei W, Andrew Yang T, Wang Z, and Shi W. On security challenges and open issues in Internet of Things. Future Gener Comput Syst [Internet]. 2018;83:326–37. Available from: https://doi.org/10.1016/j.future. 2018.01.059.

[31] Kraijak S, and Tuwanut P. A Survey on IoT Architectures, Protocols, Applications, Security, Privacy, Real-World Implementation and Future Trends. In: 11th International Conference on Wireless Communications, Networking and Mobile Computing (WiCOM 2015) [Internet]. Shanghai: IET; 2015. pp. 1–6. Available from: https://ieeexplore.ieee.org/document/7446846.

[32] Ge M, Hong JB, Guttmann W, and Kim DS. A framework for automating security analysis of the internet of things. J Netw Comput Appl [Internet]. 2017;83:12–27. Available from: http://dx.doi.org/10.1016/j.jnca.2017. 01.033.

[33] Park KC, and Shin DH. Security assessment framework for IoT service. Telecommun Syst. 2017;64(1):193–209.

[34] Avizienis A, and Laprie J. Basic concepts and taxonomy of dependable and secure computing. IEEE Trans Dependable Secur Comput [Internet]. 2004 [cited 2014 Jan 8];1(1):11–33. Available from: http://ieeexplore. ieee.org/xpls/abs_all.jsp?arnumber=1335465.

[35] International Electrotechnical Commission. Dependability/Basic Concepts [Internet]. 2015 [cited 2018 Dec 20]. Available from: http://www.electropedia. org/iev/iev.nsf/display?openform&ievref=192-01-22.

[36] Pham H. System Reliability Concepts. In: System Software Reliability. London: Springer-Verlag; 2006. pp. 9–75.

[37] Wu T, and Zhao G. A novel risk assessment model for privacy security in Internet of Things. Wuhan Univ J Nat Sci. 2014;19(5):398–404.

[38] Wongvises C, Khurat A, Fall D, and Kashihara S. Fault tree analysis-based risk quantification of smart homes. In: Proceeding of 2017 2nd International Conference on Information Technology, INCIT 2017. 2018. pp. 1–6.

[39] Seungjun Y, and Hyojung J. Issues and implementation strategies of the IoT (internet of things) industry. In: 2016 10th International Conference on Innovative Mobile and Internet Services in Ubiquitous Computing (IMIS) [Internet]. Fukuoka: IEEE; 2016. pp. 503–8. Available from: https://ieeexplore. ieee.org/stamp/stamp.jsp?tp=&arnumber=7794519.

[40] Tedeschi S, Rodrigues D, Emmanouilidis C, Erkoyuncu J, Roy R, and Starr A. A cost estimation approach for IoT modular architectures implementation in legacy systems. Procedia Manuf [Internet]. 2018;19:103–10. Available from: https://doi.org/10.1016/j.promfg.2018.01.015.

[41]   Rauzy A. New algorithms for fault trees analysis. Reliab Eng Syst Saf. 1993;40(3):203–11.

[42]   Sinnamon R. Binary Decision Diagrams for Fault Tree Analysis [Internet]. 1996 [cited 2012 Dec 17]. Available from: https://dspace.lboro.ac.uk/dspace-jspui/handle/2134/7424.

[43]   Durga Rao K, Gopika V, Sanyasi Rao VVS, Kushwaha HS, Verma AK, and Srividya A. Dynamic fault tree analysis using Monte Carlo simulation in probabilistic safety assessment. Reliab Eng Syst Saf [Internet]. 2009 [cited 2012 Nov 17];94(4):872–83. Available from: http://linkinghub.elsevier.com/retrieve/pii/S0951832008002354.

[44]   Yevkin O. An Improved Monte Carlo Method in Fault Tree Analysis. In: Reliability and Maintainability Symposium (RAMS) [Internet]. 2010 [cited 2013 Aug 27]. pp. 1–5. Available from: http://ieeexplore.ieee.org/xpls/abs_all.jsp?arnumber=5447989.

[45]   Esary D, and Proschan F. Coherent structures with non-identical components. Technometrics. 1963;5(2):191–209.

[46]   Palshikar GK. Temporal fault trees. Inf Softw Technol [Internet]. 2002;44(3):137–50. Available from: http://linkinghub.elsevier.com/retrieve/pii/S0950584901002233.

[47]   Walker M, and Papadopoulos Y. Pandora: The Time of Priority-AND Gates. In: 12th IFAC International Symposium on Information Control Problems in Manufacturing [Internet]. 2006 [cited 2013 Sep 27]. Available from: http://citeseerx.ist.psu.edu/viewdoc/summary?doi=10.1.1.108.5165.

[48]   Edifor EE. Quantitative Analysis of Dynamic Safety-Critical Systems Using Temporal Fault Trees [Internet]. University of Hull; 2014. Available from: https://hydra.hull.ac.uk/resources/hull:10592.

[49]   Edifor E, Walker M, and Gordon N. Quantification of Simultaneous-AND Gates in Temporal Fault Trees. Adv Intell Syst Comput [Internet]. 2013 [cited 2013 Nov 8];224:141–51. Available from: http://link.springer.com/chapter/10.1007/978-3-319-00945-2_13.

[50]   Edifor E, Walker M, and Gordon N. Quantification of priority-OR gates in temporal fault trees. Comput Saf Reliab Secur [Internet]. 2012 [cited 2012 Nov 12]. Available from: http://www.springerlink.com/index/D2212861Q6068646.pdf.

[51]   Edifor EE, Lascelles D, and Dixon G. Analyzing Supply Chain Resilience Using Temporal Fault Tree Analysis. In: The 23rd Annual Conference of The Chartered Institute of Logistics and Transport. 2018.

[52]   Kossik R, Knopf S, and Miller I. GoldSim Reliability Module: User Guide Version 12.1. London: GoldSim Technology Group; 2018.

[53]   Jin X, Wah BW, Cheng X, and Wang Y. Significance and Challenges of Big Data Research. Big Data Res [Internet]. 2015;2(2):59–64. Available from: http://dx.doi.org/10.1016/j.bdr.2015.01.006.

[54]   Sivarajah U, Kamal MM, Irani Z, and Weerakkody V. Critical analysis of Big Data challenges and analytical methods. J Bus Res [Internet]. 2017;70:263–86. Available from: http://dx.doi.org/10.1016/j.jbusres.2016.08.001.

[55] Botta A, De Donato W, Persico V, and Pescapé A. Integration of cloud computing and Internet of Things: A survey. Future Gener Comput Syst [Internet]. 2016;56:684–700. Available from: http://dx.doi.org/10.1016/j.future.2015.09.021.

[56] Chen M, Mao S, Zhang Y, and Leung V. Related Technologies. In: Big Data: Related Technologies, Challenges and Future Prospects [Internet]. New York, Cham: Springer; 2014. pp. 11–18. Available from: https://doi.org/10.1007/s40558-015-0027-y.

[57] Oussous A, Benjelloun FZ, Ait Lahcen A, and Belfkih S. Big data technologies: A survey. J King Saud Univ – Comput Inf Sci [Internet]. 2018;30(4):431–48. Available from: https://doi.org/10.1016/j.jksuci.2017.06.001.

[58] Hong Y, Zhang M, and Meeker WQ. Big data and reliability applications: The complexity dimension. J Qual Technol. 2018;50(2):135–49.

[59] Dunn S. Big Data, Predictive Analytics and Maintenance [Internet]. 2018 [cited 2018 Dec 19]. Available from: https://www.assetivity.com.au/article/maintenance-management/big-data-predictive-analytics-and-maintenance.html.

[60] Yang SH, Dai C, and Knott RP. Remote maintenance of control system performance over the Internet. Control Eng Pract. 2007;15(5):533–44.

Index